K. Haines
1973

W9-BNF-495

REVOLUTIONARY LEADERS
OF MODERN CHINA

GARY LIBRARY
VERMONT COLLEGE
36 COLLEGE STREET
MONTPELIER, VT 05602

WITHDRAWN

Please remember that this is a library book,
and that it belongs only temporarily to each
person who uses it. Be considerate. Do
not write in this, or any, library book.

Revolutionary Leaders
of Modern China

Edited by CHÜN-TU HSÜEH

NEW YORK
OXFORD UNIVERSITY PRESS
LONDON 1971 TORONTO

951.04
X8
1971

Copyright © 1971 by Oxford University Press, Inc.
Library of Congress Catalogue Card Number: 73–83002
Printed in the United States of America

TO THOSE GRACIOUS WOMEN WHO HAVE
BEEN ESPECIALLY IMPORTANT IN MY LIFE

Preface

This book contains a number of original articles and reprints concerning top leaders of the three revolutions of modern China: the Taiping Rebellion, the Republican Revolution, and the Communist movement. Of the twenty articles including the Introduction, eight were written especially for the volume, four are reprints with extensive revisions by the authors, one is a reprint with minor revisions, and only seven are reprints without any textual changes. About one-third of the volume was written by the editor.

The introductions to each part are intended to set the scene for the articles that follow. The articles are generally arranged in chronological order in each section. Overlapping is unavoidable, and it is not necessarily undesirable. Variations of romanizations and geographical names have been kept to a minimum.

The authors of both the original pieces and the reprints are recognized authorities on their subjects and are, of course, solely responsible for their own essays. Needless to say, they do not always agree on the interpretation of any given event. The selection of the leaders in this volume is unfortunately limited by the availability of suitable writings.

Throughout the book, family names for Chinese and Japanese persons are given first, followed by their given names, as is customary in China and Japan. However, several Chinese authors who live in the West follow the Western practice of giving their own family names last, while retaining the Chinese and Japanese form within their articles. With the exception of some of the reprints where the *sui* is used, ages are given in Western reckoning rather than in the Chinese way, in which a man is considered one year old (*sui*) on the day he is born.

Hsüeh chün-tu
Visiting Professor of Chinese Politics

Otto Suhr Institute
The Free University of Berlin
May 1970

Acknowledgments

As a New York State Faculty Scholar in Oriental Studies at Columbia University for 1964–65, and Associate of the Columbia University Seminar on Modern China since 1966, I have had the privilege of meeting periodically with other specialists in the field. The University Seminar has not only offered me an opportunity to *"hsüeh-hsi,"* it has also enabled me to use the fine Chinese library at Columbia University and do research work frequently in New York.

I wish to thank Dr. Wallace S. Sayre, Eaton Professor of Public Administration and former Chairman of the Department of Political Science at Columbia University, for inviting me to teach at Columbia in the summer of 1969. My sojourn on Morningside Heights greatly facilitated the final preparations of the book for publication. For encouragement and support given to me in recent years, I am grateful to Mr. Albert Hamilton Gordon, Board Chairman of the Kidder, Peabody & Company and a member of the Board of Overseers of Harvard University; Dean Philip E. Mosely, Professors John N. Hazard and C. Martin Wilbur of Columbia University; and Professor Theodore H. McNelly and other colleagues of the University of Maryland.

My special thanks go to Professor Howard L. Boorman, not only for his introduction to the book, but also for his advice and enthusiasm for the project. I should like to thank all the contributors as well as the authors and publishers of the reprints. Without their co-operation, this book would not have been published. Two summer research grants awarded by the General Research Board of the

ix

Graduate School of the University of Maryland enabled me to complete some of my writings included in this volume.

I wish to thank the late Dr. F. T. Cheng (1884–1970), former Chinese Ambassador to the Court of St. James's, and Dr. Frank W. Price for their translations of Huang Hsing's poems. I also wish to express my appreciation to Mr. James J. Anderson of Oxford University Press, Mr. Chien Yu-wen of Hong Kong, Professor James P. Harrison of Hunter College of the City University of New York, Professor Ho Ping-ti of the University of Chicago, Professor Lin Han-sheng, formerly of the University of British Columbia, Miss Marcia Reed, formerly of the Library of Congress, Professor Teng Ssu-yü of Indiana University, Professor Y. C. Wang of Queens College of the City University of New York, and Miss Dodo Tai for their helpful comments and suggestions; to Chang Kuo-t'ao for permission to quote his articles published in the *New York Times*; to Miss Ho Min-kwan of Hong Kong for her preliminary translations of Chou Fo-hai's reminiscences; to Dr. Lee Ngok of the University of Hong Kong for showing me his works on Chang Kuo-t'ao; to Dr. Odoric Y. K. Wou, formerly of Hong Kong, for his preliminary translation of an article on Huang Hsing; to Miss Kathryn M. Lawrence and Miss Ann Li for their editorial assistance; to Mrs. Marjorie Kossmann, Miss Cynthia Walker, Miss Judith Butler, and Miss Julie Alenick for typing part of the manuscript; to Mr. Karl Li, who prepared the index, and my former assistants Messrs. Clair Blong, Cho Byung Chan, Lee Chongsoo, and Yiu Myung Kun at Maryland.

The Chinese title of the book is the calligraphy of my wife, Huang Te-hua.

C.T.H.

Contents

xi

❈ Introduction ❈

Chinese Leaders and Chinese Politics

BY HOWARD L. BOORMAN

The modern Chinese revolution from mid-nineteenth century to the present has embraced a dual quest: for self-generated domestic modernization and for self-sustained international status. The record of the search, so far as the West is concerned, still consists largely of gaps, lacunae in understanding compounded of imperfect documentation and the ambiguities of competing realities inherent in the Central Kingdom. Yet such difficulties should not impede an attempt to throw light, from whatever source, across a confused scene. Even as for any society in process of change, so for China one clue to political transition is the manner in which strategic elites committed to the varieties of structural innovation which permit and impel modernization supplant leadership groups wedded to traditional institutions and values.

In his introduction to a recent volume on *Modern Japanese Leadership,* Professor Harry D. Harootunian suggests that one problem with the scholarly conference (or academic symposium) is that the participants tend to agree on the answer but rarely discover the question.[1] No one dealing with revolutionary leadership in modern China will debate the importance of systematic compilation of

[1] Bernard S. Silberman and Harry D. Harootunian (eds.), *Modern Japanese Leadership: Transition and Change* (Tucson: University of Arizona Press, 1966).

biographical data, fragmentary though much of it may be, regarding the men who have prodded, shaped, and occasionally led China in her slow progress from tradition to modernity. Few specialists, however, will as yet hazard theoretical generalizations regarding the essential question: how did personalities and politics interact to produce by mid-twentieth century the distinctive amalgam that is Communist China? Nevertheless, it is the hope that this book, by adopting a chronological approach to Chinese revolutionary leadership over the decades, will serve in its way as bridge between the question and possible answers.

Revolution depends upon two ingredients simultaneously present: a society that, for reasons domestic or external, is in a state of disorientation or upheaval, and a body of revolutionaries motivated to seek major political power in order to effect radical institutional changes in the society. Modern China has lacked neither chaos nor conspirators. After 1850, the stability which had characterized the Ming and early Ch'ing dynasties was gone. In the ensuing years a succession of revolutionaries appeared, with varying motivations, programs, obstacles, and successes. Certain of these leaders are the subject of this book. All were born in the nineteenth century: some early, some late. Each reflects the historical context in which he operated, and each has in some manner left his mark, for better or for worse, upon modern China.

A first round in the extended series of changes labeled the modern Chinese revolution was dominated by leaders of the Taiping Rebellion (1850–64), one of the great mass movements of the nineteenth century and one of the most destructive wars in modern Chinese history. These leaders had come to maturity in a period marked by erosive economic and social pressures and complicated by modern China's initial contacts with the West. These contacts introduced a tincture of Christianity to clash with traditional Chinese cultural patterns. The resultant brew, blended with and distorted by indigenous secret society motifs, sparked a massive, peasant-related revolt in the south China countryside that came to embrace both antidynastic and social reform objectives. Moving from their areas of origin and early success in south China, the Taiping leaders came to dominate, for a decade after 1853, the major part of the Yangtze valley in central China.

While many aspects of the Taiping upheaval remain controversial, the lack of cohesion within its leadership group is known. Internal dissension led to coups, counter-coups, and power struggles which contributed directly to the disintegration of Taiping authority and power. Despite eventual defeat by the imperial authorities, the Taiping leaders did, however, succeed in launching a major attack on the traditional social fabric to effect modern China's first significant break with its inherited past. Whereas earlier rebellions had primarily aimed at removal of those in power, the Taipings presented a program, based partly on ideas from the West, which directly challenged China's social and political institutions. Although its leaders were all killed, executed, or committed suicide in the early 1860's, the Taiping Rebellion signaled the beginning of the end of traditional China and projected a model of popular revolt that greatly influenced later Chinese revolutionary leaders.

A second round in China's struggle for modernization and status began in the last decade of the nineteenth century and projected well into the twentieth. The major leaders of the Republican Revolution, all born in the 1865–85 period after the demise of the Taiping Rebellion, held as their dominant objective the overthrow of the reigning Ch'ing (Manchu) dynasty and the consolidation of a new, republican political apparatus as replacement for the imperial structure. The dominant figures of the early period of the Republican Revolution—men such as Sun Yat-sen, Huang Hsing, and their associates—found fuel for frustration in the incompetence of the central imperial government and in the decisive and humiliating defeat of China at the hands of Japan in the war of 1894–95. For years, however, the patriotic groups through which they sought the overthrow of the Ch'ing dynasty were riven by factionalism, hampered by lack of secure territorial and financial bases, unable to develop formulae for action beyond the traditional secret societies historically used by opposition groups to gain political goals.

The Republican revolutionary leaders stumbled into authority in

China in 1911–12 after a political coup at Wuchang finally toppled the imperial dynasty. Yet the decline and fall of the Chinese empire, the most enduring political-military structure in history, was perhaps more the result of its inherent inadequacies than of the effectiveness of the revolutionary movement. Post-1912 China came to be dominated not by an effective Republican form of government but by Yüan Shih-k'ai and the structures of regional militarism. Only a dozen years later did the still uncertain forces of modern Chinese republicanism and nationalism come to an ambiguous rendezvous with revolutionary communism.

That rendezvous led in January 1924 to reorganization of the Nationalist Party (Kuomintang) on Leninist lines and to a drastic transformation in both structure and ideology accompanied by an unprecedented blending of modern Western forms (institutionalization of party leadership and discipline) with those of traditional China (personal loyalty). When the first party leader, Sun Yat-sen, died in 1925, a succession crisis ensued. In the competition for top position Chiang Kai-shek, largely because of his military position, outdistanced more experienced political leaders such as Hu Hanmin and Wang Ching-wei. After 1928 Chiang became, and remained, the leader and dominant symbol of Nationalist China.

The positive accomplishments of the leaders of the Republican Revolution between 1900 and 1950 have been blurred by time and polemics. Their aspirations exceeded their power; their political vision was rarely broad enough to distinguish between national and personal goals; their drive toward the creation of a modern national state was ultimately blocked both by domestic opposition and, after 1937, by the crippling foreign invasion by Japan.

A third, still uncompleted, round of development in modern China's revolutionary century overlapped the republican phase and shared with it common stimuli during the second decade of the twentieth century. Most important among these stimuli were the Bolshevik Revolution of 1917 in Russia and the patriotic May Fourth outburst of 1919 in China. The leaders of the Communist phase had many characteristics in common with the republican revolutionaries, notably militant nationalism laced with anti-imperialism, but differed in laying major emphasis on the necessity of restructuring the economic and social bases of the society. Its early leaders, men like Ch'en Tu-hsiu and Li Ta-chao who were dominant figures in the May Fourth upsurge, committed themselves to wholesale attack on many deeply rooted Chinese values which, they felt, constituted obstacles to self-generating modernization. Later leaders, of the generation of Mao Tse-tung, were born shortly before the turn of the century and first experienced revolutionary activity as the young patriots and radical nationalists of the 1919 period. Frustrated by the constraints of their environment, impatient with republican China's impotence in coping with domestic problems and external pressures, they turned to Marxism-Leninism (or at least to what gradually evolved as the Chinese Communist version of Marxism-Leninism) as the key to creation of a new apparatus to spur revolutionary change in agrarian China.

The historian or social scientist may deal in generalizations; the biographer must concern himself with specifics. Nearly a half century ago, when Lytton Strachey and his imitators were revolutionizing biographical writing in the West, André Maurois published a short volume in which he defined the major traits of modern biography as the search for historical accuracy and concern for the complexity of personality: the first a matter of scholarship; the second, of art. Only one who has toiled to piece together jigsaw puzzles of available documentation can appreciate the problems inherent in the task of constructing biographical portraits of modern Chinese leaders, either revolutionary or conservative. The number of variables involved in casting a paragraph is normally forbidding; the number involved in writing a meaningful profile often appears to approach infinity. Both as chronicler and as historian, the biographer writing on a modern Chinese subject must regularly attempt critical interpretation at the same time that he does elementary spadework; and often it is only at the end of the study that he has learned enough to know what questions should have been posed at the beginning.

In part, the problems of biographical writing on modern Chinese subjects are created by the paucity of data. The biographer of a major modern Western figure such as Winston Churchill or Franklin Roosevelt confronts such a superabundance of information that comprehensive assessment of potentially relevant evidence is impossible. Even for lesser or more remote figures in the West, the biographer, depending upon the constraints of family and/or personal discretion, is often able to draw upon materials of the more intimate sort—diaries or letters, for example—to support, expand, or inform research in manuscript sources or printed materials. In the case of modern Chinese subjects, however, the biographer normally confronts frustrating difficulties even in locating and assembling basic printed documentation. Sources are scattered, often difficult of access, usually unindexed. Even with documentation under reasonable control, the biographer remains trapped by the nature of the Chinese materials with which he must work: sources that are often sketchy, inadequate, or unreliable representations of reality; sources that are shaped by conventionalized cliché or ritualized formulae; sources that are designed to project symbolic images for reasons that may be obscure to, or only partly comprehended by, a non-Chinese author writing outside China.

Given the elusiveness of the materials with which he deals, it is hardly surprising that the biographer of a modern Chinese revolutionary leader generally ends by presenting not a man but a reproduction of the public image of a man. The reader, even farther removed from the modern Chinese environment, is left with the sense of viewing the Chinese subject from without and from a considerable distance: a feeling not dissimilar to that of the translator attempting to decode the ideographs used to describe individuals recorded in the biographical sections of the Chinese dynastic histories. These dilemmas are well known to the authors of the papers included in this volume, and it would be invidious to criticize for failure to achieve what could not realistically be attempted. Yet because of these inherent dilemmas, it is perhaps more accurate to consider these profiles as "approaches to revolutionary leadership in modern China" rather than as examples of conventional biographical writing.

The group of modern Chinese leaders dealt with here is statistically insignificant, for it is limited in greater part to individuals who functioned politically either as members of the top leadership or as revolutionary propagandists or polemicists. Nor does it focus attention on the significant group of female leaders, from Ch'iu Chin (1879–1907) through Ch'en Pi-chün (1891–1959) to Ts'ai Ch'ang (1900–   ), who, either directly or through their husbands, have also played major roles in the course of the modern Chinese revolution.

Given the limitations and inevitable unevenness of the sample of modern Chinese leaders included in this book, it is nevertheless pertinent to note the unusual continuity in their basic political goals. While the long-range visions of the Taiping leaders remain problematical, all major leaders of the twentieth-century period looked ultimately toward creation of a strong, unified, and modernized China free of external restraints and intrusions. Nationalism, though cloaked in different uniforms at different periods, has unquestionably been the major vehicle of modern China's revolution. Yet individual Chinese leaders shaped their nationalism in varying ways. The record of their revolutionary careers, the manner in which they were influenced by the expectations of their contemporaries, and the degree of success or failure in attaining their goals may be informed by consideration of the variables affecting both political performance and historical significance.

One element often ignored in assessing modern Chinese political leadership is the geographical factor. While a notable feature of the Chinese political tradition has been the conviction on the part of its people that "China" constitutes a single entity, the Chinese have long been acutely, often proudly, aware of regional differences and of local traditions within the Chinese culture area. The geographical origins of modern Chinese revolutionary leaders thus provide important data for the historian and the social scientist. The major Taiping leaders were predominantly southerners, natives of the provinces of Kwangtung and Kwangsi farthest removed from the capital at Peking and closest to Hong Kong. Republican leadership was more complex in origins. In its early phase, the T'ung Meng Hui established at Tokyo in 1905 constituted an alliance of preexisting revolutionary societies and radical student groups, each having strong ties to a particular

Chinese province (notably Kwangtung, Hunan, and Chekiang). Because Sun Yat-sen was a native of Kwangtung, it was hardly accidental that many of his closest associates were also natives or adopted sons of that province. The importance of Fukienese in the early republican movement may, in turn, be partly ascribed to financial support provided by overseas Chinese communities in Southeast Asia (many of whom had blood ties with the maritime provinces of Fukien and Kwangtung). In a later period, the position of Chiang Kai-shek as a native of Chekiang province in east China did much to affect the composition of the post-1928 Kuomintang elite; while the influence of the Soong family (related by marriage to Chiang) in the politics of the republican period was not unrelated to the fact that it possessed family connections in both Chekiang and Kwangtung. The province of Hunan, particularly after the deaths of Huang Hsing (1916) and other early republican worthies such as Sung Chiao-jen (1913) and Ts'ai O (1916), tended to be excluded from the dominant power structure of the Kuomintang. This omission was not unnoted by the Communists, and a notable facet of the Communist conquest of power in China lies in the unusual concentration in its pre-1949 party elite of a major group of Hunanese, with a significant admixture of natives from the adjoining interior provinces of Hupeh and Szechwan.

The social backgrounds of modern Chinese revolutionary leaders are as significant a variable as geographical origin. Innovative political leadership in quest of modernization may emerge from several sources: dissident elements in the traditional political leadership itself; members of new professions or new armies where rank is dependent upon performance; displaced intellectuals from various walks of life. In the case of modern China, revolutionary leaders came from a notable spectrum of backgrounds ranging from scholar-official families to socially marginal or dispossessed groups. The Taiping leaders (of the era before the rise of modern Chinese nationalism) were mostly from impoverished or obscure backgrounds: Hung Hsiu-ch'üan, Hung Ta-ch'üan, and Hung Jen-kan all failed in efforts to gain the initial *hsiu-ts'ai* degree through the imperial examination system. The Republican revolutionaries tended to come from modest backgrounds, often from families whose economic position had become straitened by the late nineteenth century. All received their early educations in the conventional Chinese curriculum, and a high proportion were exposed to modern schools in China or in Meiji Japan. Sun Yat-sen, who came after his death to be projected as the unchallengeable symbol of modern Chinese nationalism, was an atypical political figure: born of humble peasant origins in the Canton delta area, he spent most of his adult life in an ambiguous world blended of strong Western and Japanese stimuli. Data regarding the social origins of the leaders of the pre-1949 Chinese Communist Party are more uneven, though research to date suggests that, aside from the relatively small group that emerged from obscure poor peasant antecedents, the backgrounds of many Communist leaders were not greatly dissimilar to those of many Republican revolutionary leaders.

Another variable affecting analysis of modern Chinese political leadership is the role played by organization in the revolutionary process. To gain its objectives, a serious revolutionary effort in modern China required, at minimum, a comprehensive doctrinal base (to replace the embracing social ethic formerly provided by Confucianism) and a durable organizational apparatus. The Taiping Rebellion, even on a favorable estimate, demonstrated a relatively confused ideology and a relatively inchoate organization. The Republican leaders, at least after 1924, did offer a Leninist-type party apparatus and the Three Principles of the People articulated by Sun Yat-sen. Yet the post-1924 Kuomintang apparatus was never well constructed for mass mobilization, and Kuomintang political formulae tended to become stereotyped and irrelevant to young Chinese during the critical decade of the 1940's. The Communist leaders, at least during the years from 1938 to 1958, were able to develop realistic linkage of ideology and organization capable of powering a major thrust toward political unification and economic and social modernization. Even during the confused years since the Great Leap Forward effort, organizational controls on the mainland have remained sufficiently strong to prevent widespread civil conflict, mass starvation, or currency inflation. And the Thought of Mao Tse-tung has clearly owed much of its success with young Chinese to the fact that its blend of nationalism and anti-imperialism has been more virulent than the mixture provided earlier by Sun Yat-sen, Chiang Kai-shek, or any other Republican political leader.

Behind efforts at periodization and social analysis lie, finally, the human beings who generate and energize the drama. Politics—as General Morris "Two-Gun" Cohen, bodyguard of Sun Yat-sen at Canton in the 1920's, once observed—"is personalities." Cohen's summation was excessively simplistic. But its very concision suggests the importance for Western observers of attempting to gain increased sensitivity to the interaction of politics and personalities during the extended process of revolution in modern China from the Taiping explosion of the 1850's to the Cultural Revolution of the 1960's. The gaining of this knowledge will not be easy, for the Western observer is blocked by the relative remoteness of the Chinese stage, by the uneven nature of available evidence, and by the perverse imperviousness of the Chinese personality.

In assessing a complex revolutionary process, understanding of its leadership is both fundamental and inadequate. As Professor Dankwart A. Rustow has aptly suggested, it is never sufficient to ask who the leader is. A more meaningful question is: Who is leading whom from where to where? [2] The materials on Chinese leaders contained in this volume are not designed to provide detailed answers to this fourfold question. Rather, they indicate that the road from traditionalism to modernization in China is long, and suggest that ardor and ideology are not in themselves sufficient unless the dreams of the few become the aspirations of the many.

If the future of the Chinese revolution is unpredictable, it is clear at least that meaningful appraisal of that future must be partly based on knowledge of past accomplishments and failures of leaders

[2] Dankwart A. Rustow, Introduction, "Philosophers and Kings: Studies in Leadership," *Daedalus*, Summer 1968, pp. 683–84.

such as those documented in this book. *Revolutionary Leaders of Modern China* represents a notable contribution not only to the conventional field which is the study of modern Chinese political history but also to the evolving, still inchoate, field which is the comparative study of revolutions and revolutionary elites.

REVOLUTIONARY LEADERS
OF MODERN CHINA

✸ I ✸

THE TAIPING REBELLION

EDITOR'S INTRODUCTION

The Taiping Rebellion (1850–64) began the revolutionary process in modern China. It was caused primarily by the deterioration of domestic conditions and in part by the impact of foreign aggressions. When the rebellion broke out, the alien rulers of the Ch'ing dynasty, established by the Manchus in 1644, had long before lost their vigor. During the Opium War (1840–42), China had already proved herself to be a "paper dragon" against the British invaders who were determined to forcefully "open" agricultural China for her raw materials and for use as a market for industrial products.

The political goal of the Taiping uprising, eight years after the Opium War, was the overthrow of the Manchu dynasty. The ideology of the Taiping movement was based on a fanatical religious faith derived from Christianity. An "organized" superstition manipulated by the leaders to rally the support of the masses and to control them, it alienated the scholar-gentry class, thereby making it impossible to recruit the talented among the elite. Characterized by dynastic decline and violent social revolution against the existing order, the Taiping Rebellion differed from previous peasant uprisings: it attacked not only the ruling dynasty, but also the tradi-

3

tional social order. It established a political system that included and combined military discipline, primitive equality, land reform, the church and state. Its leaders exercised absolute power over the people and controlled their economic, social, and intellectual life. It was characterized by both the equality of men and women among the followers and the possession of large harems by the leaders.

The revolt began in Chintien village, Kwangsi province, in 1850. On January 11, 1851 Hung Hsiu-ch'üan (1814–64), the 38-year-old leader of the rebellion, proclaimed the formation of a new dynasty, the Heavenly Kingdom of Great Peace (T'ai-p'ing t'ien-kuo). From Chintien the Taipings moved on to other areas. In the fall they captured Yungan, a city in Kwangsi, where they stayed until April 1852 when they broke through the government siege into Hunan province. Although they failed to take the provincial capital of Changsha, they did succeed in capturing Wuchang, the provincial capital of Hupeh, also the seat of the Governor-General of Hunan and Hupeh. From there they moved down the Yangtze River and in March 1853 took Nanking, which they renamed the "Heavenly Capital." By this time their followers reportedly numbered over a million men.

A northern expedition was initiated in Nanking to take Peking while a simultaneous force was dispatched up the Yangtze River to conquer western China. Both offensives failed, the northern forces reaching the suburbs of Tientsin before their defeat. The campaign eventually came to an end in March 1855.

Hung Ta-ch'üan, a co-leader of the Taiping Rebellion, had been killed during an early stage, and a violent power struggle soon developed within the top leadership of the Taipings in Nanking. The chain of command among the five leaders that formed around Hung Hsiu-ch'üan had been made clear at Yungan. Yang Hsiu-ch'ing, from Kwangsi province, emerged as the most powerful commanding general in this original group of five, two of whom (Feng Yün-shan and Hsiao Ch'ao-kuei) were killed in battles during the march from Yungan to Nanking.

While the position of Hung Hsiu-ch'üan as leader of the movement could not be challenged in view of his part in starting it and of his claim as God's younger son, Yang, as God's Holy Ghost and actual government leader, gradually gained power over Hung and established himself as the dominant figure in Nanking. In September 1856 Yang was assassinated by Wei Ch'ang-hui, one of the five kings who was, in turn, assassinated. Another king, Shih Ta-k'ai, had to leave the capital with his troops for his own safety. Hung became more distrustful of his ministers and retained confidence only in his own brothers and other relatives. Thus the power struggle left only incompetent men in charge of state affairs. Among the second generation of leaders, only Ch'en Yü-ch'eng and Li Hsiu-ch'eng showed any ability for command. In 1859 Hung's cousin, Hung Jen-kan, arrived at Nanking from Hong Kong to take over the premiership, but he failed to revitalize the regime. In June 1864 Hung Hsiu-ch'üan, the Heavenly King, died at the age of fifty. Contrary to the beliefs of historians of the last hundred years, he did not commit suicide. The original testimony of Li Hsiu-ch'eng, published for the first time in 1962, revealed that Hung had refused to take medicine and had died of a lingering illness.

The Taiping uprising raged in China for over fifteen years, involving at one time or another sixteen out of eighteen provinces south of the Great Wall. It ended with the fall of Nanking in July 1864. As Professor Franz Michael noted:

> The Taiping Rebellion and its extraordinary attempt to destroy the whole social and political fabric of China and replace it with a fantastic totalitarian order of its own ended thus in complete defeat, leaving no trace of its early victories nor of its faith once imposed upon its million followers. The traditional order reasserted itself for a time, and the prolonged and deadly battle fought between the Taipings and the defenders of the existing order contributed to the eventual collapse of this order itself. . . . The Ch'ing dynasty truly never recovered. There was no real T'ung-chih restoration.[1]

One result of the Taiping uprising was the shift of power in the government from the Manchu to the Chinese, an indirect factor of the downfall of the Manchu dynasty after the outbreak of the

[1] Franz Michael, *The Taiping Rebellion: History and Documents*, Vol. I (Seattle: University of Washington Press, 1966), p. 198.

Wuchang Revolution in 1911. The emergence of regional power from the gentry leadership during the Taiping Rebellion saved the dynasty but gravely undermined the central authority and eventually contributed to its collapse.

While there were no direct organizational links between the Taipings and the subsequent revolutionaries, many of the early followers of Huang Hsing in the Republican Revolution were secret society members who could claim remote connections with the rebels or the subsequently disbanded Hunan Army. At one time Sun Yat-sen reportedly considered himself a Hung Hsiu-ch'üan. The Taiping movement served as a spiritual inspiration for the Republican revolutionary movement in that it fostered anti-Manchu sentiment.

The man most responsible for the defeat of the Taiping was a Hunanese Confucian scholar-official, Tseng Kuo-fan (1811–72), who began to organize the Hunan Army in 1853. Being Chinese, he could not oppose the Taipings on the grounds of their anti-Manchu stand. Instead, he opposed them in the name of the defense of "the Chinese way of life." However, the behavior of the soldiers under his younger brother after the capture of Nanking turned the slogan "defending the Chinese traditional culture" into a mockery.

Tseng Kuo-fan reported to the throne that when Nanking was taken, not one of the 100,000 rebels in the city surrendered but in many cases gathered together and burned themselves and passed away without repentance. Evidence shows that the report was false. From the private accounts of important government official eye-witnesses and the confession of Li Hsiu-ch'eng, it is now known that the final campaign to retake Nanking lasted for more than two years and that at the last stage of the siege Tseng and his brother mobilized some 50,000 men against less than 10,000 rebels in the city. In order to conceal this ineffectual performance in spite of superior arms and numbers, Tseng deliberately exaggerated the enemy's strength by adding civilian deaths to the rebels' total loss.

Among the many factors that might account for the failure of the Taiping Rebellion were the shortcomings of those in leadership and the power struggle of its ruling group. Indeed, from what we know of Hung Hsiu-ch'üan, it is difficult to understand how such a charismatic leader, who was capable of leading a gigantic rebellion, could believe in the 1860's that the "Heavenly soldiers" would come to his aid during the siege at Nanking. It is just as difficult to understand how the Empress Dowager (1835–1908), the real ruler of the Manchu dynasty for almost forty years, could declare war against the world in 1900, with the belief that the Boxers could not be killed by bullets; and capable as they were, how the Communist leaders could think it possible, in 1958, that steel could be produced in one's own backyard.

Speaking of the power struggle, Professor Franz Michael explains it in terms of a "special relationship" of the ruling group:

> From the beginning, the group of secondary leaders that formed around Hung Hsiu-ch'üan, consisting of men of different origins, shared the authority. These men were set apart from the rest of the followers and were "more equal than others." Together with their prophet, Hung Hsiu-ch'üan himself, they formed among themselves a special brotherhood, the group of seven "brothers" mentioned in several of the Taiping proclamations of this time [at Chintien, 1851] and later. Though all the Taipings were children of God, these seven "brothers" by implications were in a different category. . . . The list of brothers mentioned in the proclamations begins with Jesus and Hung and then lists the Taiping leaders, Yang, Hsiao, Feng, Wei, and Shih, who share in this way in the highest authority over their followers. It is easy to see that this special relationship of the collective brothers could lead to a grim and bitter power struggle.[2]

Hung Hsiu-ch'üan, leader of the rebellion, was born in Kwangtung province. With regard to the geographical origins of the revolutionary leaders of modern China, it should be noted that Sun Yat-sen also came from Kwangtung. Because of the significant roles of Hunanese in the Republican Revolution (Huang Hsing) and in the Communist movement (Mao Tse-tung), it is interesting to observe that another Hunanese, Hung Ta-ch'üan, had held a position during the early part of the Taiping Rebellion that was equal to that of Hung Hsiu-ch'üan.

[2] *Ibid.,* p. 48.

Hung Ta-ch'üan adopted his name after he had become a "sworn brother" of Hung Hsiu-ch'üan. When the rebel forces in Yungan broke through Manchu government lines in April 1852, Hung Ta-ch'üan, then aged thirty and eight years younger than Hung Hsiu-ch'üan, was captured by the government troops and subsequently executed.

According to his own testimony, Hung Ta-ch'üan came from the Hungshan district of Hunan province. An ambitious man with a humble background, he met repeated failure in the civil examinations. (Indeed, most of the Taiping leaders failed the civil examinations, which was the most important avenue for advancement in China's traditional society.) Traveling as a Buddhist monk through Kwangtung, he met Hung Hsiu-ch'üan in the latter's native district. Then in 1851 he joined forces with Hung Hsiu-ch'üan, who conferred upon him the title "King of Heavenly Virtue," which put him above all other leaders who followed Hung Hsiu-ch'üan in the Kwangtung and Kwangsi provinces. However, the significance of the Hunan faction in the movement diminished with his death. His death early in the history of the movement led some historians to doubt his importance and even his existence. Available evidence and characteristic leadership patterns of the revolutions in modern China suggest that he did in fact exist and that he was the co-leader of the Taiping Rebellion in its early stage.[3]

This section contains two selections on Hung Hsiu-ch'üan. The first selection, by Professor Franz Michael, gives an excellent account of the origins of the Taiping movement and its rise in Kwangsi province. Although the second selection is a psychological study made by Dr. Yap ninety years after the death of Hung Hsiu-ch'üan, the

---

[3] *Ibid.*, p. 66. A corrected version of the English translation of Hung's confession appears in the same work, Vol. II, Document No. 37. For a discussion of the "Problem of Hung Ta-ch'üan," see Ssu-yü Teng, *New Light on the History of the Taiping Rebellion* (Harvard University Press, 1950), pp. 20–24; and William James Hail, *Tseng Kuo-fan and the Taiping Rebellion* (Yale University Press, 1927; reprint, Paragon, 1964), Chap. III, "The Suppressed Leader."

author probably had more data on his subject than a psychiatrist today could get on Mao Tse-tung. Dr. Yap did have access to accounts written by people who were very close to his subject. It should be noted that Dr. Yap's article is one of the very few, and neglected, pioneering works of Chinese studies in the direction of psychological interpretation.

As a result of the power struggle in 1856, Hung the Heavenly King made a new attempt at leadership by bringing his cousin Hung Jen-kan (1822–64) to Nanking in 1859 to take over the premiership. Until then Hung Jen-kan worked as a catechist for the missionaries in Hong Kong, playing no part in the movement.

The new prime minister sought in vain to bring about an improvement in relations between the Taipings and the foreigners, especially the foreign missionaries. He failed to see that foreign relations were dictated not by religious affiliation but by political realities. His attempt at political reorganization failed to rejuvenate the regime. The article on Hung Jen-kan by Professors So Kwan-wai and Eugene P. Boardman included in this section is the best available study in English on the career of Hung Jen-kan.

Among the second generation of Taiping leaders Li Hsiu-ch'eng (c. 1824–64), the subject of Professor Stephen Uhalley's article in this section, was the most remarkable figure. He is considered the main hero of the last years of the Taiping period, partly because of the Chinese admiration for a man who would take the responsibility for state affairs when the ruler was no longer capable of governing, and partly because of the legacy of his "confession" after his capture. The handwritten text of his testimony, which had been kept by Tseng Kuo-fan's descendants for nearly a century, was published in Taiwan in photographic reproduction in 1962. Although it is identical in substance to the versions heretofore used by historians, the original document does reveal several crucial points that differ from the earlier accepted version of the movement.

After he had written down the record, Li Hsiu-ch'eng was executed on Tseng's order. Tseng did not wait for an order from the Throne indicating whether Li should be sent to Peking. This "bureaucratic maneuver" made it possible for Tseng to alter the "confession" and to prevent Li from revealing information to the court that might have been derogatory to the Tseng brothers.

The evaluation of Li's role by Communist writers, which was favorable at one time, has become a controversial matter. In the early stage of the Proletarian Cultural Revolution in 1966, when Peking mayor P'eng Chen and a number of other leaders who had once been arrested by the Kuomintang were purged, Li Hsiu-ch'eng and Ch'ü Ch'iu-pai were taken as case studies concerning the correct behavior of a revolutionary after capture. Li was now criticized for capitulating to the enemy. Although debates will continue concerning Li's reasons for writing the testimony, it is likely that his image as a hero will survive.

❊ 1 ❊

Hung Hsiu-ch'üan and
the Taiping Uprising

FRANZ MICHAEL

The Organization of the God Worshippers

The prophet and head of the Taiping Rebellion was Hung Hsiu-ch'üan, a man of simple origin. Hung was born on January 1, 1814, in the village of Fu-yüan-shui in Hua-hsien, Kwangtung province. He came from a Hakka family which, four generations before Hung was born, had moved to Hua-hsien from Chia-ying-chou, a Hakka district in eastern Kwangtung at the border of Fukien province. Hung's father, Hung Ching-yang, was a small farmer who worked his own fields, first in Fu-yüan-shui and later in Kuan-lu-pu in the same district, a Hakka village of some four hundred people to which the family moved during Hung Hsiu-ch'üan's childhood. Hung had two elder brothers, Hung Jen-fa and Hung Jen-ta, who helped their father with the work on the farm.

Hung Hsiu-ch'üan was said to have been a very intelligent child, and his family had great hopes that the youngest son would be able to acquire the learning and the academic degrees that alone opened the way to a better life in traditional China, not only for the scholar himself but also for his family and relatives. The privileges and opportunities enjoyed by members of the scholar-

Reprinted with footnotes deleted from Franz Michael (in collaboration with Chung-li Chang), *The Taiping Rebellion: History and Documents,* Vol. I (Seattle: University of Washington Press, 1966), pp. 21–42. By permission of University of Washington Press. All rights reserved.

gentry and especially by those who succeeded in entering upon an
official career enabled them to advance and support their relatives
and friends, who were therefore willing to make great sacrifices to
help a promising child acquire the learning that was the source of
all this fortune. Hung Hsiu-ch'üan was sent to school at the age
of seven and was said to have made rapid progress. In 1827, at
the age of fifteen *sui,* he began to participate in the official examinations. But though he passed the preliminary examinations, he failed
in the main examination in Canton, the examination for the *sheng-
yüan* degree that would have admitted him to the privileged status of
the gentry.

In view of the difficulty of the examination, the large number of
candidates—sometimes over a thousand—and the small quota of
about a dozen who were permitted to pass in these examinations,
the failure was not surprising. But with so much at stake it can
easily be understood that the candidates labored under great nervous
strain. Those who failed tried again whenever the examination was
held, and Hung Hsiu-ch'üan tried several times to pass the examination, the last time in 1843, but he never succeeded. During all this
time when he was preparing for the examination, he, like many
other student candidates, supported himself by teaching school in
his village. He was, then, one of the unsuccessful scholars who were
disappointed and frustrated—the marginal group from which in
periods of crisis the leaders or supporters of rebellious movements often
came. Men who had not succeeded under the existing system could
easily become hostile to it; in their futile attempts to obtain a degree
they had gained enough education to organize or direct a political
uprising.

When Hung failed in another attempt in 1837, he became
critically ill. The humiliation of his failure and the realization of the
disappointment he had become to his family and neighbors must
have been hard to take, and this experience, together with the
nervous strain of the examination itself, brought on a serious breakdown. He was carried home from Canton and remained delirious
for several days, during which time his family regarded him as mad

and feared for his life. At times he was unable to recognize others. He talked irrationally and had fits of rage during which he could be restrained only with difficulty. When Hung recovered from his illness, those who knew him felt that his personality as well as his appearance had changed. "He was careful in his conduct, friendly and open in his demeanor, his body increased in height and size, his pace became firm and imposing, his views enlarged and liberal." Hung also started to take an active interest in political affairs, both local and national, and obviously regarded himself as a man with a mission. He began to assume authority in his native district, deposed on his own authority an "Inspector of the Ground" named Moo, used a whip of nine rods for lashing evildoers, and became generally feared. He claimed later that his knowledge of the problem of opium import and of the Opium War made him even then a confirmed enemy of opium-smoking and of the government for its policy of permitting the trade. In his words:

> Each year they [the Manchus] transform tens of millions of China's silver and gold into opium and extract several millions from the fat and marrow of the Chinese people and turn it into rouge and powder. . . . How could the rich not become poor? How could the poor abide by the law?

Several odes that he composed in these years immediately after this illness show Hung's expansive mind and new notions of grandeur and express his vague ambitions to conquer the land and become a ruler. These odes, though, do not yet contain the elements of Christian teaching that were soon to give Hung's restless mind a new focus. Hung, even in his new condition, made a last attempt to pass the examination in 1843 and failed again. And shortly afterwards there came to his attention a Christian tract which seemed to him to provide an explanation of his own experiences and which gave a new direction to his thinking, affected as it was by his illness.

This tract had actually come into his hands seven years earlier, in 1836, while he was in Canton for the examination. It was given to him on the street by a Chinese Christian convert, named Liang A-fa, and the title of the tract, which was in Chinese, was "Good

Words to Admonish the Age." The tract admonished the reader to believe in God and Jesus Christ, to obey the Ten Commandments and never to worship demons.

Hung took the pamphlet, but at the time paid little attention to it. Now, in 1843, shortly after he had failed again in what was his last attempt at the examination, a cousin of his, Li Ching-fang, while looking through Hung's bookcase found the Christian pamphlet, read it, and immediately told Hung about its extraordinary content. Hung, who now read the pamphlet carefully, found in it not only a doctrine that he was willing to accept but also what he believed to be an explanation of his own experience. His illness, which must have been embarrassing to him in spite of his new self-assurance, based on his delusions, could now be ascribed to a religious experience.

Hung had the fantastic notion that he had been chosen by the Christian God, of whom he now learned, for a special mission to defeat evil, which was represented by devils and demons, and to bring about God's rule on earth. His illness now became for him the turning point in his life, the time he had met God and been given his new task. When he had been ill and delirious, he had simply left this world and had been up in heaven where he had met God and Jesus Christ, who taught him the doctrine and gave him his assignment. On God's command, he had battled the demons, and his wild behavior during the delirious seizures viewed by his family and friends had been simply the signs of the battle he had carried on in that mysterious other world, of which he could now give glorious accounts. His behavior during his illness could therefore be readily explained through this fantastic story of his ascent to the heaven about which he had read in the pamphlet and which he now embellished by the fantasy of his story. And the mission which he now believed to have received, to return to earth, fight the demons, and bring man back to the worship of the true God gave a purpose to his new ambitions. Hung had thus found the basic elements of a system of teachings into which he could pour his own vague ideas of his mission and which provided the framework for the delusions of grandeur created by his illness. Hung's interpretation of these Christian teachings formed the basis of what became the ideology of the Taiping Rebellion.

Hung immediately accepted the religious doctrine as given in the pamphlet and embellished it with his own story. He and his cousin baptized each other in the way prescribed in the pamphlet. Hung then wrote another poem that dealt with these newly found ideas of God, Christ, atonement, heaven and hell, repentance, and the worship of God, and began to preach these concepts to his family, his friends, and the villagers.

The ideas Hung received from the tract itself were later enlarged by his reading of the Bible and a few months' instruction with a Protestant missionary, the Reverend Issachar T. Roberts in Canton. Hung went to Canton in March of 1847 to study with the Reverend Roberts, an American Southern Baptist, but left again when he was unable to find means of support, possibly because two other students of Roberts intrigued against him. Hung left without having received formal baptism. Hung's original limited understanding of Christianity cannot have been greatly affected by this exposure to Christian teaching, as can be seen from the writings in which he put down his beliefs and which were made public later as official proclamations of his Taiping movement.

Since Hung believed that he himself had been in heaven, he could be his own witness to prove the fancies of his imagination. Hung believed in a God as the creator of all things, a God whom man must worship and serve; but it was a very personified God, with whom Hung had a very personal relationship. This God was an imposing figure with a golden beard who sat in heaven like an emperor in a dignified posture, in a black dragon robe, with a high brimmed hat, hands on knees, and who was surrounded by his heavenly family and court. It was a God who expressed his problems in personal conversation and who had feelings of great sadness about the state of the world. In spite of God's wrath and the flood, in spite of Christ's sacrifice, men continued to serve the demons. In the fight against these demons, who looked very much like the demons of Chinese folk tales, God now enlisted Hung's services.

It is only natural that Hung's views of God and heaven were also colored by his Chinese ideas on the family. God had a heavenly wife, and Jesus Christ, who as God's son played his part in the family, had also his own heavenly wife. When Hung was in Heaven, Jesus' wife, a kindhearted woman, was like a mother to Hung, and exerted her modifying influence on Christ when He was angry with Hung for not learning his biblical lessons well. Altogether heaven was a beautiful place with beautiful maidens and angels, with heavenly music and a heavenly wife for Hung, who was understandably reluctant to follow God's command and go back to earth for his mission, though he had eventually to obey.

This personified image of the Christian God and of heaven had its counterpart in Hung's personification of evil. The reason for God's sadness was the success of the demons in taking over the earth and misguiding the people. Even heaven had been penetrated by these demons, of whom the serpent god was the worst and most powerful.

Christianity to Hung was a battle between God and the devil, and this battle was in Hung's mind a very personal one. It was his mission to fight for God and to kill the demons or send them to hell. God had been exasperated before when he sent the flood and when his Son, Christ, had descended to earth to redeem the sins of man. When he was received in heaven, Hung learned that he was God's son too, a younger brother of Jesus Christ, and therefore charged to take his role in the battle. His raving during his illness was now interpreted by Hung as his battle with the demons in heaven so dramatically described by him for his followers. And now on earth it was his task to bring the people back to the worship of God and to slay the demons. The demons were all those who refused to accept God's will as now interpreted and represented by Hung—especially the Manchus. This simplified righteousness was a very suitable ideology for a rebellious movement.

Essentially Hung's preaching was an appeal to believers to worship God the creator, on whose favor and grace all things depended, and thus to receive God's care in this world and go to heaven afterwards— and to fight the demons that stood in the way of the fulfillment of God's kingdom. In addition to this basic appeal to all to worship God the creator and to attack the demons, Hung's writings contained, however, a complex mixture of ideas taken from Chinese tradition. Hung had indeed little understanding of Christian teaching or theology, of such problems as original sin and redemption, or of the teachings of Christ in the New Testament. Hung stressed the story of the Old Testament, of the creation, the flood, and of God's anger with man, a story which he interpreted literally and which he related to Chinese history. Up to the time of the Three Dynasties, the people had worshipped God, but then they had been led astray. Buddhism and Taoism, which he must have hated as competitive ideologies for rebellion, were false teachings of the devil, and Confucianism itself, though not without value, had misled the people. Though he used Confucian references at first to support his teaching, Hung eliminated some of these later. And psychologically most interesting is his later embellishment of the story of his experience in heaven where Confucius was taken to task by God for having misled the people and was given a beating, obviously a great satisfaction to Hung, the luckless candidate in the Confucian examination. To the mixture of the Bible and Chinese history was added Hung's story of his ascent to Heaven and of his mission to establish God's kingdom. The promise he gave was that behind him was the supernatural power of God that would bring success in a miraculous way.

Among Hung's first converts were his cousin Hung Jen-kan, who was later to play an important role in the Taiping movement, and Hung Hsiu-ch'üan's close friend and fellow teacher, Feng Yün-shan, who came from a nearby village, Ho-lo-ti, in the same district. To demonstrate his faith, Hung Hsiu-ch'üan removed the idols from his and his colleagues' schoolrooms and together with Hung Jen-kan composed a poem to recognize the occasion. When asked by the elders of their village to compose the customary poems in praise of the local gods at the occasion of the lantern festival early in 1844, the two Hungs refused and when criticized for this disrespectful attitude, wrote instead a verse to confess their new faith.

This attack against tradition cost Hung his position as school-teacher, and with it his income. This may have been the primary reason that he and his friend Feng Yün-shan left their home villages and started on a career as traveling preachers. The two (with two other friends who soon turned back) set out on April 2, 1844, and traveled through several regions of Kwangtung province on the border of Kwangsi, regions that were known to have many branches of the Triad Society. They also covered the border areas inhabited by Yao tribal people and then moved into Kwangsi, where they settled down in the village of Kuei-hsien with some relatives of Hung's. They preached and seemed to have gained some followers; but when the son of his host was arrested, possibly because of suspicions aroused by Hung Hsiu-ch'üan's activities, the feelings toward Hung changed. Hung decided to leave but was implored to stay until the arrested man had been released, while Feng and two other relatives went on their way back. Feng remained, however, in a place called Hsün-chou, while Hung Hsiu-ch'üan eventually returned to his home village in Kuangtung in September, 1844.

It was Feng Yün-shan who succeeded in setting up a new society that made an organized group of the adherents of the preaching of Hung Hsiu-ch'üan and of Feng himself, and the core of the later rebellious movement. Feng continued his preaching in several villages in the neighborhood, and established himself in Tzu-ching-shan (Thistle Mountain), a strategic mountain area in southern Kwangsi. There Feng founded the *Pai-Shang-ti-hui,* or God Worshippers Society, a formal organization of the followers of the new faith with branches in many villages.

The God Worshippers Society had some of the characteristics of traditional Chinese secret societies. Its members were held together by a bond of loyalty in the defense of their interests against outsiders and by the general spirit of brotherhood that prevailed among the members of all Chinese secret societies. But the belief that united the members of the new society differed fundamentally from the vague Buddhist, Taoist, and Confucian concepts used by the traditional societies. The members of the God Worshippers Society accepted a new religious faith, a faith quite contrary to all tradition of Chinese imperial society, a faith in a personal God and his guidance for one's personal salvation as well as in all matters of daily life and in the larger problems of economic, social, and political affairs. It was this faith that enabled the God Worshippers to accept some of the most revolutionary changes in their personal lives and in their social and political order.

This religious organization was established by Feng Yün-shan in the absence of Hung Hsiu-ch'üan whose alleged religious experiences could all the more effectively be referred to by Feng, the preacher of the new faith. However Christian the new faith may have been, there can be little doubt of the sincerity of the God Worshippers. In the record preserved of their simple prayers to be offered on ordinary and special occasions can be found genuine religious feeling and great trust in God, whose blessing is sought at the beginning and end of each day, at birth, marriage, and death, and in the ordinary affairs of life. There was as yet very little of the political doctrine in which religious teachings were later to be used by the Taiping leaders to give their authority and power divine sanction. To help the inarticulate and uneducated members of the group, special forms of prayers for each occasion were written down, so that the faithful had only to have their names included on the form and then the paper was burned as in Buddhist practice.

But from the outset the political reality of the intervillage fighting gave the branches of the God Worshippers Society their militant character. In most cases, conversions were not of individuals alone but of whole families and clans or of whole occupational groups, such as charcoal burners and miners. The various local groups of the God Worshippers founded regular congregations within the villages, large enough to form local military units which could defend themselves against other such local forces. Often a whole village or occupational group would form such a congregation, and these local groups sometimes numbered several hundred.

What gave this God Worshippers Society its special militant character was the fact that it was formed among Hakka by Hakka leaders. Once the society was established and its many branches were functioning, the Hakka found in it an organizational protection in their fight against the Punti. Large groups of Hakka, already in conflict with their non-Hakka neighbors, joined the rapidly growing society. In the villages where they predominated, the Hakka congregations took over local control and forced others to join. The conflict

between Hakka and non-Hakka was thus transformed into one between the God Worshippers Society and opposing militant organizations. In the words of one of the later Taiping leaders:

> For several years after the members began worshipping God, no
> apparent move was made. In the twenty-seventh and twenty-eighth
> years of Tao-kuang (1847–48), however, bandits in Kwangsi were
> ravaging the country everywhere, disturbing cities and towns, and
> the various inhabitants organized themselves into local corps [*t'uan-
> lien*]. The local-corps members and the God-worshippers were dis-
> tinguished from one another. The God-worshippers would form
> themselves into one group, and the local-corps men would form
> themselves into another group. Each party pursued its own course
> and endeavored to surpass the other, and the pressure finally led to
> the uprising. At the outset of the uprising, there would be both
> local-corps men and God-worshippers in one and the same village,
> and there were also attacks by one village on another. Therefore
> the members gathered themselves together.

Branches (*fen-hui*) of the God Worshippers Society were established wherever there were enough members, and were therefore
scattered widely. They were more numerous in Kuei-hsien, where
some of Hung Hsiu-ch'üan's relatives lived and where Hung and
Feng had visited in 1844, and in the district of Kuei-p'ing, where
Feng had centered his efforts around his headquarters at Tzu-ching-
shan.

Tzu-ching-shan was a mountain area that could easily be defended. It could only be approached from two sides, the west and
the south, and had a small number of villages connected by goat
trails. This area could not easily be penetrated by official authority
and military forces, and had been pretty much on its own. Each of
the small villages had formed its own organization, a *pao*, under the
authority of a local *pao* chief. The isolation of this area had, however, its own disadvantages, since it could be easily blockaded, and
the leaders trapped. An ideal gathering point to assemble the
members of the various groups for an open outbreak was in the
small town of Chin-t'ien at the foot of the mountain area.

In August, 1847, Hung Hsiu-ch'üan went to Thistle Mountain
and joined Feng Yün-shan in the leadership of the God Wor-

shippers Society, which Feng had established and which by this time had grown to a following of over two thousand converts, mostly peasants and miners. Together the two expanded the organization and its program. In the preceding years Feng had used Hung's poems, odes, and essays, together with his own understanding of the biblical story, as the basis for the God Worshippers' religious creed. Now Hung wrote a record of his preaching activities, and his writings at this time clearly indicate that in his mind the preaching of his religious experiences and ideas was to be used to realize his political aspirations. The demons that had to be fought were not only the evil spirits of the supernatural world but were now also the Manchus and their supporters who had misled the people, and the movement thus took on a rebellious character.

While traveling in nearby tribal territory, Hung increased his reputation by smashing some of the statues of the local deities. Since descriptions of the local beliefs indicate that the myths and customs attacked by Hung were derived from tribal tradition and were anathema to the Chinese, Hung's attack upon the demon worshippers must have been quite acceptable to the Chinese population and to the Chinese magistrates, who were not aware of the more dangerous content of Hung's preaching.

At that time, Hung was already using the term T'ai-p'ing, which was later to be bestowed on his rebellious movement, and called himself the *Chün Wang*, or Noble King, indicating the political character of his group and the role he himself assumed. He also stated that he and his followers "wrote a memorial asking the Heavenly Father, the Supreme Lord and Great God, to select for them a firm stronghold where they could settle themselves."

Hung's writings of this time are full of allusions to the heroes of Chinese history. This appeal to history is another indication that he himself planned to play a historical role, in fact a greater one than the role played by the figures alluded to. These historical allusions are used as examples to demonstrate how failure and success had depended in the past upon whether or not God's precepts had been followed.

The religious doctrine which Hung preached was therefore now taking on more of its political character. The strange mixture of concepts that formed Hung's religious teachings lent itself easily to such political application. In the direct and simple interpretation of the biblical story and its miracles, which he embellished with his own fantasies, Hung saw proof of God's political interest in the state of mankind and in the establishment of his rule on earth. The battle against evil that had started with the flood and had been continued by Jesus Christ was now in the hands of Hung, who carried out God's command. He had to organize the faithful, to establish on earth the Heavenly Kingdom of Great Peace, the T'ai-p'ing T'ien-kuo.

There was no grasp of the deeper theological meaning of Christian teachings, of the problems of original sin and redemption, or of the Holy Ghost and of the Trinity. The Holy Ghost became simply God's voice and was later to be used by the most powerful of Hung's lieutenants to assume command through trances in which he claimed that God's voice spoke through him. And in analogy to Christ's role of redeemer of sin, this man claimed to be the redeemer of illness for mankind, after having suffered a prolonged illness himself.

This literal interpretation of the Christian doctrine provided the authority of command for the Taiping leaders. The rules of the Ten Commandments which were set by Hung into poems were used as a system of discipline for the God Worshippers community and enforced like a code. But the real basis of the political system that was established was the concept of the Christian community as one great family whose members were all children of God. This concept fitted into the Chinese tradition as well, and provided a justification for the new order that was to be organized. Since Hung had found in heaven a replica of the Chinese family system, complete with wives and sisters-in-law for everyone, it was not difficult for him to fit himself into this system as the younger brother of Jesus Christ and to lead the large family of the faithful on earth. This family concept may help to explain the principle of the common treasury—the family property—which the Taipings were to establish, and the Taiping idea of the followers as equal children of God, brothers and sisters all, who were to live in complete chastity until God's purpose was accomplished, when they could live happily together as husbands and wives ever after.

Hung's preaching thus provided the framework of an ideology for a rebellious movement and as such was a most suitable and extraordinary basis for the Taiping Rebellion, but beyond that his fantasies and the interpretation given to them by his lieutenants cannot be formulated into a logical or coherent system, and his own story indicates that the symptoms of insanity which began with his illness in 1837 increased during the following years. Yet under the conditions of chaos and local crisis his claim of divine guidance carried conviction with his followers. The new family system of the kingdom of God that he proclaimed seemed to them to promise a better world, and instilled in them a religious fervor that lifted their organization above the level of a troop banded together for local fighting to that of a disciplined army, ready for a rebellious movement.

At first, however, the God Worshippers had to deal with the opposition of rival local organizations. The gazetteer of the area recounts some of the clashes between the gentry-led local corps and the God Worshippers that occurred before the Taiping uprising in which the local bandits had connections with a member of the gentry who covered up their raids and disposed of the stolen goods. In 1847, when in the district of the early Taiping concentration in Kuei-hsien a local corps was first started, the leader of this local corps, a member of the gentry, had connections with bandits. The magistrate therefore considered this local corps quite unreliable, and the more respectable people of the community remained aloof. After the death of its first leader, the local corps did fight against pirates and bandits who were becoming more numerous. But no clear line was drawn between legitimate defense and illegal activities.

When Feng Yün-shan organized the God Worshipper units and was accused by a local gentry before the magistrate, the latter therefore did not act. This unwillingness of an official to take sides in clashes between the Punti and Hakka, or between the local corps and the God Worshippers, favored the leadership of the God Worshippers in their preparations for local uprisings.

The officials, obviously regarding the God Worshippers as another force for local self-defense, were very slow in taking any action. When Feng Yün-shan first organized the local groups of followers in the districts of Kuei-p'ing and Kuei-hsien, he was twice taken prisoner by the leader of the local corps. On the first occasion, in December, 1847, his own group of God Worshippers freed him by force. In January, 1848, the leader of the local corps petitioned the local magistrate to arrest Feng, but the magistrate, following his policy of neutrality, declined to act. The local-corps leader then took Feng prisoner again with the help of his troops and sent him this time to the magistrate, accusing him of planning a rebellion.

The repeated capture of Feng indicates that he was regarded as the true organizer of the God Worshippers Society and that Hung, its religious leader, was of less interest to the local military leader. When Feng was taken and detained by the magistrate, together with another Taiping leader, Lu Liu, Hung Hsiu-ch'üan left for Canton to petition the governor-general for Feng's release. Hung hoped to use the imperial promise of tolerance toward Christianity for this purpose. However, the governor-general, Ch'i-ying, had left for Peking, and Hung started back to Kwangsi. In the meantime, Lu Liu died in prison, but Feng was released by the magistrate in exchange for a monetary payment, which was collected by the God Worshippers to buy him off. The only limitation placed on his freedom by the magistrate was that Feng should return to his home province, Kwangtung.

When Hung returned to Kwangsi and found that Feng Yün-shan had been sent back to Hua-hsien in Kwangtung, he himself left for Kwangtung to meet his friend there again. The arrest and banishment of Feng and the temporary absence of Hung Hsiu-ch'üan created a problem of leadership for the God Worshippers in the districts of Kuei-p'ing and Kuei-hsien. The absence of the main organizer and the spiritual leader of the movement provided an opportunity for new leaders to emerge, men who did not derive their authority from a close allegiance to Hung Hsiu-ch'üan.

There must have been a strange atmosphere in the camp of the God Worshippers while their regular leaders were gone. At prayer sessions people came forth and began to speak with tongues. Most of the people who thus spoke up were incoherent, and arguments seemed to have arisen whether it was God or the devil who spoke through the persons who were thus possessed. But this method of speaking in tongues was used by two men to assert their authority.

The man who took over the leadership in this way was Yang Hsiu-ch'ing, from Hsin-ts'un village near Chin-t'ien. Yang came from a family of farmers who had originally emigrated from Kwangtung province. From the descriptions of his colleagues, his biography in an imperial intelligence report, and from the history of the rebellion itself, Yang emerges as a shrewd and ruthless man, who eventually used every means to concentrate all power in his hands. He had lost his parents at an early age and had become a charcoal burner and seems to have established himself as a leader of a group of charcoal burners and miners who joined the God Worshippers. He must have had some education, since it is reported that he was at one time a clerk in a government office. It was also said that he had been a servant and that he later organized convoys for transporting merchandise through the area. If this is true, he had control over a group of men and enough power to guarantee the secure passage of goods through a bandit-infested area. The government intelligence report that gives this information also claims that Yang was supposed to have shared the profits of this convoy system with Hung Hsiu-ch'üan. All these statements may be true, but cannot be verified. From the Taiping records, we know that Yang was the maternal uncle of a local patron of Hung and Feng.

Yang is mentioned in these records for the first time in April, 1848, as assuming a position of authority during the absence of Hung and Feng from the headquarters area. According to his own account, he had been taken ill and had been deaf and mute for about two months. Then suddenly he spoke up in the meetings. He had trances, simulated or perhaps genuine seizures, in which he claimed to be possessed by the Holy Ghost, representing the person of God the Father, who through Yang instructed the God Worshippers as to what they should do. Since neither Hung nor Yang nor the group of God Worshippers had a clear understanding of the concept of the Holy Ghost, Yang's performances were fully accepted and gave him the divine sanction of his leadership which was effective in this group of religious fanatics. But while Hung must have been genuinely convinced of his own ascent to Heaven and of his divine mission, Yang's actions seem to indicate that he was playing a part.

Together with Yang, another leader came into prominence. This was Hsiao Ch'ao-kuei from Wu-hsüan in Kwangsi, who had been a farmer in the area of Thistle Mountain. Hsiao seems to have cooperated closely with Yang Hsiu-ch'ing and may have been a relative of his. Hsiao established himself as a leader in the same way as Yang had done—by having trances. He claimed to represent Jesus Christ, whose spirit spoke through him to the God Worshippers. In October, 1848, he was reported to have had his first seizure. In April, 1849, Yang had another trance or, in the Taiping parlance, "The Heavenly Father again descended to the world." This occurred at Kuei-hsien, where Yang also asserted his authority in this role.

Between the two of them, Yang and Hsiao thus took command of the God Worshippers and tried to impress them with the necessity of obeying their divine leaders. They took the precaution always to include Hung in their story, referring to him as the "sovereign" who had ascended to heaven and received his mission from God, but their own authority was directly derived from God and Jesus Christ and therefore obviously potentially above that of Hung, "the younger brother" of Jesus Christ. When Hung and Feng returned to the area of Kuei-p'ing in the summer of 1849, they had to take note of this new type of leadership based on trances. According to a report, they investigated the trances and repudiated those that they declared to have been the inspirations of the devil, but recognized Yang's and Hsiao's performances as true manifestations of God's and Jesus' appearances on earth and in this way sanctioned the leading role of these two ambitious men.

The Rising at Chin-t'ien

When Hung and Feng rejoined the God Worshippers in the districts of Kuei-hsien and Kuei-p'ing, the organization had grown strong enough to prepare for the open rebellious uprising that the leaders had contemplated for some time. Now clashes with the local corps grew more intense. In February of 1850, the local corps fought, defeated, and captured a bandit leader of the Kuei-p'ing district named Ch'en A-kuei. On the way home from this campaign, the victorious local-corps troops passed through villages of God Worshippers in the area of Chin-t'ien, manhandled the villagers, and threatened to kill them because they were God Worshippers. This threat was used by Feng Yün-shan in what seems, according to local history, to have been the first open summons to rebellion addressed to the God Worshippers by one of their leaders. Feng argued that there was no choice but to rebel, for otherwise the God Worshippers would be suppressed and killed by their enemies. It was a small group of some 130 people who gathered at the home of one of their leaders, Wei Ch'ang-hui, a rich owner of a pawnshop and land, and a man of some education. Wei belonged to a large clan, which joined the God Worshippers Society and strengthened Wei's prominent role in the group. From the outset, therefore, Wei was one of the prominent leaders of the God Worshippers Society, though his authority was not derived from any supernatural sanction, as was that of Yang and Hsiao, and of Hung himself.

The gathering at Wei's home was reported by the local corps to the district magistrate, who ordered the God Worshippers to disperse. The group seems to have obeyed temporarily, but gathered again when some of the local-corps men kidnapped a concubine from a Hakka family. This time the gathering grew to include some 300 people who would not by themselves have been a sufficient threat to the authorities had they been dealt with immediately. But the officials were slow in attributing to the God Worshippers a more serious role than that of trouble-makers and rivals of other local defense units, and thus the God Worshippers had time to bring up their forces by calling in groups from other communities of the area.

When they began to gather their followers, the God Worshippers' movement and organization were seriously threatened by a strange division of their forces which can only be understood as a conflict and power struggle in the leadership. In May, 1850, Yang Hsiu-ch'ing, who before the return of Hung and Feng had through his trances asserted himself as the highest authority, fell ill and withdrew from all activity. According to the account by the leaders of the rebels, Yang's illness lasted until November, a period of six months. As had happened once before, he became deaf and dumb and "pus came out of his ears and water from his eyes." Yang thus became incapacitated and had been given up, as he complains in his later description of his ordeal. Later on, he claimed that he had undergone this illness and the earlier one for the sake of others; God, in his anger that Hung Hsiu-ch'üan had not yet been heeded in his mission to establish God's kingdom on earth, was ready to punish man with illness and disease. Yang had suffered his illness to redeem all others and thus had become the "redeemer from illness," a title which begins to appear about two years later among the titles describing Yang's role and status.

In 1850, however, this illness became of immediate political importance; whether Yang actually had a disease or whether he faked an illness to cover up his wish to withdraw from co-operation is impossible to tell. We can only speculate about the reasons for Yang's action, which was followed by the departure of Hung and Feng, who left Chin-t'ien for Hua-chou in the neighboring district of P'ing-nan and stayed away from this primary center of the God Worshippers all during the critical time of the latter half of the year 1850. It is possible that Yang's withdrawal resulted in the refusal of some of Yang's adherents to participate in action for the common cause and that a tense situation at Chin-t'ien was the reason for Hung and Feng's departure.

Although they stayed away from Chin-t'ien, Hung and Feng proceeded with their plans for an uprising. That they had decided to go ahead can be seen from the fact that in June, 1850, Hung sent for the members of his family in Hua-hsien, Kwangtung, to join him in Kwangsi, where they would be safe from reprisals by government officials. In July the leaders of the God Worshippers called for a concentration of the forces of all branches at Chin-t'ien. The original group there had already been joined by a larger group of Hakka, more than 3,000 strong, who had been driven from their homes by a local conflict with Punti and had joined the God Worshippers at Po-pai. When this group crossed the river at Kuei-p'ing and joined the God Worshippers' camp, the group at Chin-t'ien became formidable. It was then joined by other groups from P'ing-nan, Kuei-hsien, Wu-hsüan, and Lu-ch'uan and became in a short time a force estimated at 10,000 to 30,000 people. This concentration was obviously too large to be dealt with by the local corps or by a local official without the help of regular army units. The uprising thus became a problem for the provincial administration and the regular military forces, and soon for the central government.

The various groups that assembled at Chin-t'ien were very uneven in strength and were brought together by a number of local leaders. One group came from Kuei-p'ing under the leadership of a man called Su Shih-chiu. Another local leader, Lai Chiu, brought the God Worshippers from all the localities of Yü-lin prefecture. Another group from Kuei-hsien had been well organized before they marched to Chin-t'ien and had already on the way increased their number from the original 1,000 to more than 4,000 people and had brought their own cannon. They were led by Shih Ta-k'ai, a Hakka from Kuei-hsien who had studied for the examination but had failed. Like Hung, Shih was therefore a man with some education who was frustrated by his failure in his attempt at a regular career. Shih was to become one of the chief leaders of the movement.

The groups that gathered at Chin-t'ien consisted mostly of Hakka who had joined the God Worshippers in part as a protection in their conflict with the Punti. The movement seems, however, to have included also some followers who were Punti, and there may well have been a conflict between the Hakka and the Punti to be overcome as the movement became broader in its purpose. Since all of the major leaders and most of the followers must have been Hakka, it was necessary to reassure the Punti that there would be no discrimination against them in the rebellious movement. This problem is still reflected in an account which was written in 1860 at Nanking on the orders of Hung Hsiu-ch'üan. Hung, trying to reassert the original principles of the movement, referred to this problem in the words: "Whether Hakka or Punti, they are all treated alike."

The movement was also joined by several bandit units, the most important of which was a gang of several thousand pirates under a well-known leader, Lo Ta-kang. In contrast to other bandit and pirate chiefs who soon left the movement because they were unwilling to accept the strict moral code and discipline of the God Worshippers, Lo Ta-kang became a faithful follower and one of the leading figures in the movement. Among the groups who joined were also people of the Miao tribes and other local tribal groups. Their motive in joining the rebellion must have been their bitterness over official extortion and over their economic troubles. They had been the very targets of Hung Hsiu-ch'üan's idol-smashing campaign, and those who joined must have been fully converted to Hung's teaching. It was a considerable force that gathered at Chin-t'ien to form a military camp (*t'uan-ying*).

It was all the more remarkable that the two primary leaders of the movement, Hung and Feng, remained absent from the main theater of operations. Whether Yang's illness and his withdrawal from all action with the effect it had on Yang's own following was so embarrassing to Hung and Feng in their attempt to centralize and organize the uprising that they left, or whether they wanted to broaden the movement, the two stayed away from Chin-t'ien at the time of the formation of the camp there. They remained in Hua-chou in the neighboring district of P'ing-man, where they stayed in the house of Hu I-kuang, a member of a wealthy family who held the academic degree of military *sheng-yüan* and was therefore a member of the lesser gentry. Hu was a friend of Hung and especially of Feng, who formerly had been a teacher in Hu's home. At this place, Hung and Feng gathered another, obviously smaller, military force.

At the outset, there were thus two military concentrations. The main one at the headquarters in Chin-t'ien was during Yang's illness under the control of Wei Ch'ang-hui, Hsiao Ch'ao-kuei, Shih Ta-k'ai, and Ch'in Jih-kang, also a native of Hua-hsien, who was "an ordinary laborer by trade." Of these, Hsiao was the only one whose authority was based on what he claimed to be divine revelation. But there was also Yang, who was inactive but whose presence had to be taken account of by the others. The other concentration was at Hua-chou, directly under Hung and Feng and their host, Hu I-kuang.

Both these concentrations were now attacked by local government troops. At the end of September, 1850, forces under the prefect of Hsün-chou and a district magistrate of Kuei-p'ing attacked the concentration at Chin-t'ien but were repulsed. At the beginning of November, government troops in P'ing-nan district surrounded the concentration under Hung and Feng at Hua-chou. The situation became critical, and the God Worshippers at this place and their leaders seem to have been in great danger. At this moment Yang Hsiu-ch'ing suddenly recovered from his illness and claimed to have been informed of Hung's trouble by the Heavenly Father. He led the forces from Chin-t'ien in an attack against the government troops at P'ing-nan, broke the encirclement, and saved Hung and Feng. Yang thus saved the leader of the movement and demonstrated his quality as a military leader. At the same time he claimed that his action had been the result of his own divine guidance. He had thus become the main military commander of the concentration at Chin-t'ien; but the lack of clarification of his role vis-à-vis Hung and Feng may have been the reason that even after this military cooperation the two units did not join.

Though the forces remained separate, Yang had obviously succeeded in assuring his supremacy in the management of the Chin-t'ien concentration. It must have been necessary to yield this position to him as a price for his cooperation and possibly also for that of the groups of charcoal burners and miners who were under his authority and whose special skills—such as the miners' knowledge of explosives and their experience as sappers—were essential for military success. When, in January, 1851, the two groups finally combined their forces at the village of Ts'ai-ts'un in Kuei-p'ing district, Yang became the commander of the central corps and the chief of staff and therefore the most powerful military leader of the movement.

The united force won a decisive victory over government troops and then returned to Chin-t'ien, where on January 11, 1851, Hung Hsiu-ch'üan, on his thirty-eighth birthday, declared the formation of a new dynasty, the T'ai-p'ing T'ien-kuo, The Heavenly Kingdom of Great Peace. Hung himself assumed the title of T'ien Wang, or Heavenly King, and now issued orders from Chin-t'ien under this name.

❧ 2 ❧

The Mental Illness
of Hung Hsiu-ch'üan, Leader
of the Taiping Rebellion

P. M. YAP

The evolution of China into a modern nation-state has seen few episodes more meaningful than the Taiping Rebellion occurring in the
latter half of the last century. In the leader of this rebellion, Hung
Hsiu-ch'üan, there is much that is of special interest to the sociologist
and the psychiatrist. In the origin of this vast movement can be seen
the great importance of individual psychological factors which elevate
a leader and help to precipitate a revolutionary social transformation
—for Hung is known to have suffered an acute mental disturbance
which undoubtedly moulded his destiny.

The rebellion has been interpreted variously as a peasant uprising
against official corruption, a protest against intolerable economic distress, or simply a nationalistic revolt against the Manchu dynasty.[1]
Be that as it may, there is general agreement that it was a movement
unique in Chinese history because it instituted a radical change in
the political system which had existed for more than two thousand

Reprinted with permission from *The Far Eastern Quarterly,* Vol. XIII, No. 3
(May 1954), pp. 287–304.

The author is indebted to Mr. Chien Yu-wen, formerly of Yenching University, for his encouragement, help and criticism in the preparation of this
essay; to Professor Eugene P. Boardman for assistance in editing it; and to
Dr. K. C. Yeo, Director of Medical and Health Services, Hong Kong, for permission to publish it.

[1] Vincent Yu-chung Shih, "Interpretations of the Taiping T'ien-kuo by non-
Communist Chinese Writers," FEQ, 10.3 (May 1951), 248–57.

years, and brought about economic, social, cultural, and religious reforms over the greater part of Central and South China between 1851 and 1864.

The reasons for the failure of the rebellion are complex, but it is probable that two of the factors responsible were the religious element in the rebels' ideology and the religious nature of Taiping society.[2] Perhaps the most remarkable features of the rebellion lay in its Christian inspiration and its use of Christian ideas and rituals as an important means of social control, within its military organization as well as outside it. The Taiping faith had special elaborations, and was sufficiently unorthodox to be called "Taiping Christianity." To this faith the rebels brought much asperity and fanaticism, qualities which prevented the gaining of either native or foreign allies.

By rejecting Confucianism for a foreign religion, Hung antagonised the whole class of scholar-officials who since Han times had been the mainstay of the state, and without whose support rebellions had always failed. On the other hand, because he believed that he had had a revelation and a commandment from God, more recent and therefore more authoritative than any knowledge or instruction that missionaries might bring, the latter were put in an impossible position vis-à-vis Hung and his subjects. As C. P. Fitzgerald puts it: "It might have been supposed that so vast an upheaval, which promised, if successful, to result in the complete conversion of the whole Chinese people to Taiping Christianity, entitled the leader to be considered a prophet, indeed to be the most outstanding Christian prophet known to history. The English missionaries, however, would have none of him. Christianity, if it came to China, must come through their direct teaching. Direct inspiration to a Chinese was unthinkable."[3] But the problem was more complex than Fitzgerald sur-

[2] This is emphasized in Ch'en Hsün-tzu, "T'ai-p'ing t'ien-kuo chih tsung-chiao cheng-chih" (The Religion and Government of the T'ai-p'ing t'ien-kuo), *Shih-hsüeh tsa-chih* (Magazine of History), I:6 (1929), 4. Also see Eugene P. Boardman, "Christian Influence upon the Ideology of the Taiping Rebellion," *Far Eastern Quarterly*, 10:2 (Feb. 1951), 115–24 and, for fuller reference, Eugene Powers Boardman, *Christian Influence upon the Ideology of the Taiping Rebellion, 1851–1864* (Madison: University of Wisconsin Press, 1952).

[3] Charles Patrick Fitzgerald, *China, A Short Cultural History* (London: Cresset Press, 1950), 581.

mised, for Hung completely secularized the "Kingdom of God" and substituted for this goal of Christian endeavor a state of blessedness not yet realized: his own Heavenly Kingdom of Great Peace, which was in fact his own theocratic dynasty.

It is possible to explain the failure of the rebellion not only by using social, economic, political, or cultural terms, but also by finding Hung weak as a leader. Boardman sums up the matter by saying that he was no Chinese Lenin, and was unable to formulate an ideology to suit his times and his circumstances. The problem then becomes essentially a psychological one. It is clear, moreover, that Hung's freedom of choice in matters of ideology was circumscribed by a peculiar cast of mind, and that he was the victim of a certain psychic compulsion and of fixed ideas, which, along with a change of personality, resulted from his early mental disturbance. It is to be noted that the qualities of mind and character which contributed to his failure were also the very ones which brought him such portentous success to begin with. His weakness as well as his strength as a leader were both determined in an intimate manner by his illness.

Early Life and Mental Illness

Ssu-yü Teng has pointed out that Hung's visions are mentioned in five primary sources which differ from one another only in detail, though the later accounts have been somewhat elaborated and embellished. There can be no doubt whatever that Hung did undergo such an experience.[4]

The most reliable and informative account of Hung's mental illness is to be found in a slim volume by the Rev. Theodore Hamberg published in Hong Kong in 1854.[5] This book consists of recollections of Hung Hsiu-ch'üan's early life, as told to Hamberg by Hung Jen-kan, a cousin of Hung's. It is one of the earliest reports of Hung's

---

[4] Ssu-yü Teng, *New Light on the History of the Taiping Rebellion* (Cambridge: Harvard University Press, 1950), 53.

[5] Theodore Hamberg, *The Visions of Hung-Siu-Tshuen and Origin of the Kwangsi Insurrection* (Hongkong, 1854). Reprinted Peiping: Yenching University Library, 1935 with Chinese translation by Chien Yu-wen under the title *T'ai-p'ing t'ien-kuo ch'i-i chi.*

visions, which occurred in 1837. While it is possible that this early account may have been guilty of certain elaborations or omissions in the sections dealing with the acute mental disturbance, it is improbable that any striking or impressive features were missed. Hung Jen-kan was an educated person who lived with Hung Hsiu-ch'üan during the period of the illness and afterwards; he was in sympathy with the rebellion, but his account shows that he regarded his cousin as insane. Hamberg's report of what was told him appears to be singularly free from political or religious bias, unlike the writing of later authors, after the uprising had aroused the inevitable political passions. Certain information concerning the behavior and conduct of Hung after he had installed himself in Nanking (1853) is available from the autobiography of one of his lieutenants, Li Hsiu-ch'eng, the *Chung Wang*.[6] This autobiography was ordered by Tseng Kuo-fan while the *Chung Wang* was awaiting his fate to be decided, and it contains bitter remarks about Hung; there is reason to believe that they were made by the *Chung Wang* not only with an eye to his immediate future, but also as an expression of long-continued resentment. Indeed, it is generally agreed that Hung's exalted and unbending conception of his own status and destiny in the end alienated many of his followers. In attempting a psychiatric assessment of Hung's illness and its sequels, I shall adhere strictly to what is found in Hamberg's account, and not go beyond the data given there. I shall use the *Chung Wang's* autobiography for one or two points concerning his later life. It is necessary to emphasize once again that, however inadequate from the scientific point of view available data concerning Hung's illness may be adjudged, a psychiatric study of it may still be of interest. It must be remembered that during his illness Hung was never regarded by the immediate circle of his relatives and friends as anything but insane.

Hung came from a poor peasant family living in a depressed village about thirty miles from Canton. They were Hakkas, that is to say, settlers in the province who were always regarded by the natives as somehow foreign. His father, the village headman, married twice; he had four children by his first wife, who died early. Hung, the third

[6] *Vide* the English translation by W. T. Lay, Shanghai, 1865.

son was born in 1813.* He was able to attend school from the age of seven and in his studies he showed such keenness that his relatives shared clothing with him and brought him provisions from afar so that he did not have to work. He was the hope of the family; and even his teachers were reluctant to receive fees from him. He was regarded as a future scholar-official certain to repay all those who made sacrifices to help him attain office. Despite this assistance, at the age of sixteen Hung had to leave his studies to help in the fields and earn his keep. However, two years later he obtained the post of a teacher in his own village, it being recognized that his talents should not be wasted in manual labor.

Hung's youth was thus characterized by a consuming passion to attain through scholarship the dignities, affluence, and power of officialdom. In the Empire, with its restricted social mobility, this was the only accepted way for a poor boy to improve his social status and gain great respect. So, at as early an age as sixteen, he presented himself for the civil service examinations in Canton. Hung always placed high in the district qualifying examinations, but never managed to pass the examinations for the designation *hsiu-ts'ai*. In 1833 or 1834 while in Canton for the circuit examinations, on two successive days he happened to meet on the streets a foreign missionary whose interpreter gave him a number of tracts entitled *Good Words to Admonish the Age*. After a cursory glance, he brought them home with him and apparently forgot them until he was taken ill.

Hung's illness occurred in 1837, after he had for the third time failed to pass the examinations. He was plunged into grief and depression, and had to be carried back to his village where he arrived in an enfeebled state and had to be put to bed. He was to remain mentally disturbed for forty days. (The *Chung Wang* said in his autobiography that he was in a trance or stupor for a week, but although he recovered consciousness he remained for some time incoherent.) His mood was at first melancholic; he told his parents that he would soon die and expressed grievous regret that he had not

* It has been verified since the publication of this article that Hung Hsiu-ch'üan was born on January 1, 1814.—Ed.

been able to make a name for himself and his family to compensate his parents for the love they had shown him. He appeared then to have gone into a flaccid, stuporous condition, and for about a month or more had a succession of dream-like, hallucinatory experiences. He saw a multitude of people welcoming him, as he thought, in hell. He saw, with his eyes closed, a dragon, a tiger, and a cock entering the room; and then he was carried in a chair, accompanied by many musicians, to a beautiful palace, where he was received with great joy. An old woman next took him down to a river, reprimanded him for having associated with people who had defiled him, and proceeded to wash him clean. Then, accompanied by many of the sages of China, he was brought to another gorgeous palace, where his heart and other organs were changed for new, red ones; and the wounds closed instantaneously, leaving not a single scar. On the walls of the room were numerous tablets, with exhortations to virtue. In another hall, the most splendid of all, he was brought before an old man in black with a golden beard, and tears in his eyes. The latter spoke to him: "All human beings are produced and sustained by me; they eat my food, and wear my clothing; but not a single one among them remembers and venerates me. What is still worse, they take my gifts and worship demons. They purposely rebel against me and arouse my anger. Do not thou imitate them." [7] He then gave Hung a sword with which he was to exterminate demons, but spare his brothers and sisters; a seal, with which to overcome evil spirits; some insignia of royalty; and golden fruit, sweet to the taste, for him to eat. Hung then addressed the company and exhorted them to venerate the old man, admonishing them the while with tears. Then with words of encouragement, they led him out and revealed to him the depravity of the people on earth. "Behold," said the old man, "a hundredfold is the perverseness of their hearts. Do thy work: I shall assist thee in every difficulty." It was reported that Hung thereupon woke from his trance and in great anger and excitement dragged himself before

[7] These and the following excerpts of Hung's speech and writing during his illness are reported in Hamberg: *The Visions of Hung Siu-Tshuen and the Origin of the Kwangsi Insurrection* (Peking, 1935) 10–12.

his parents and told them: "The Venerable Old Man above has commanded that all men shall turn to me, and all treasure shall flow to me."

On several occasions in the course of his illness he saw a middle-aged man whom he called his elder brother, who gave him constant advice, accompanied him to the farthest regions of the earth in search of demons, and assisted him in slaying them. At other times he heard the old man reproaching Confucius for not having preached the true doctrine and making the latter guilty and discomfited. He used to leap, run, fight, and attack enemies not visible to others, shouting out over and over again, "Slay them, slay the demons." In great excitement he would say, "There is one, and there another— many, many cannot withstand a single blow of my sword!" And as he fought them the demons appeared to him to undergo transformation into birds, lions, etc. He had only to hold out his seal for them to flee in terror, whereupon he pursued them to the ends of the Universe. He would at times shout and sing in exultation, and at others cry out in tears, "You have no heart to venerate the old Father, but you are on good terms with the fiends; indeed, you have no heart, nor conscience any more!" He told his visitors that he had been made Emperor of China and was pleased if people addressed him as such. He had no insight into his own condition whatsoever, and when others told him he was mad he flung their words back at them. Sometimes he would identify his visitors as demons. He had to be constantly watched. In apparently more lucid intervals he scribbled mediocre poetry on bits of paper, as scholars of that time were wont to do. These compositions are of interest because they reveal his trend of thought, his mood, and enable us to assess the degree of mental disorganization he showed. The following translations are based partly on Hamberg's:

My hands hold in Heaven and Earth the power to punish and to kill,
To slay the wicked, spare the virtuous, and relieve men's
    distress.
From North to South beyond the rivers and mountains my eyes
    behold,
From East to West to the reaches of Sun and Moon my voice
    resounds.

The Dragon unsheaths his claws to break from cloud-enveloped
    paths,
And ascending why need he fear the bend of the Milky Way!
Like drums will roll Thunder and Tempest, and the waves will
    foam:
In Heaven assuredly dwells the Flying Dragon of the Classics.

The Birds in their flight all seek the light
And thus resemble me:
For now am I King and everything
At will to do I'm free.
As the Sun to the sight my body shines bright,
And from all affliction we are free.
The Dragon and the Tiger rampant
Are each assisting me.

One day a piece of paper was discovered on which he had written
in red, the following cryptic motto: "The Noble Principles of the
Heavenly King, the Sovereign King Ch'üan." In Chinese this sounds
grandiloquent and has an arresting cadence, but does not convey any
clear meaning. Hung gradually recovered his balance of mind after
about forty days, and appeared to have retained afterward a fair
memory of the trance experiences he had gone through.

Religious Conversion and Later Life

After having recovered from his illness Hung kept to himself and
a few intimates his memory of the odd experiences he had gone
through. Only occasionally did his speech and feelings reveal that
the memory was still there; this remained for the most part quiescent,
and the full force of it was not to strike him until six years later.
However, the illness had wrought a definite change in his personality.
It is not sufficiently clear from the records what his personality was
like before, although Hamberg recorded that in early youth he was
witty, frank, straightforward, and authoritative in demeanour. He
now became, it was noticed, careful in manner and dignified in
bearing, sitting himself down squarely and solemnly, and walking
about with a measured tread. Although friendly in manner, and
sometimes gay, he was often severe in scolding others for what he

considered to be moral lapses. His remarks were occasionally regarded as peculiar and eccentric and he was made fun of by some, though many accepted him as superior. In later life he was described as a tall man, with large, bright eyes, a piercing look, a sonorous voice, and possessed of considerable strength both of body and mind. Although we may doubt the details, there is no reason to suppose that a change of personality following the psychotic illness could not have occurred.

For the next few years Hung continued teaching. In 1843 he sat for the examinations again, and failed for the fourth time. In the same year his attention happened to be directed again to the books entitled *Good Words to Admonish the Age* which had been given him six years previously before his illness. For the first time he seriously studied the contents, which consisted of translations of portions of the Bible and odd sermons on various texts therein. He then discovered, with a sudden flood of exaltation and a certain degree of surprise, what he thought to be the key to the meaning of his past visions. He now understood that the old man he saw was God the Heavenly Father and the middle-aged man who helped him in exterminating demons none other than Jesus Christ. The demons were idols, and his brothers and sisters the populace of the world. This episode, the final step in his conversion to Christianity, Hung himself related to I. J. Roberts, an American missionary in Canton in 1847; it appeared that he was convinced that his visions confirmed the contents of the books.[8]

Convinced of everlasting life in Heaven, Hung passed into a phase of great exhilaration and joy. He was so full of his new knowledge and faith, and talked so excitedly and at such length about them that it was feared that he might have suffered a relapse. He and his cousin, who had also become converted by the books, baptized each other; they broke the temple idols, removed the tablet in honour of Confucius from the school, and started to preach their new-found faith. Hung was, moreover, certain that he had been chosen by God to restore all China to the true worship. "Those books," he wrote,

[8] I. J. Roberts, untitled article in *The Chinese and Missionary Gleaner,* Oct. 1852.

"are certainly sent on purpose by Heaven to me to confirm the truth of my former experiences; if I had received the books without having gone through the sickness, I should not have dared to believe in them and on my own account to oppose the customs of the whole world; if I had merely been sick but not received also the books, I should have had no other evidence as to the truth of my visions, which might also have been considered the productions of a diseased imagination." [9] He boldly proclaimed: "I have received the immediate command from God in his presence: the will of Heaven rests with me. Although thereby I should meet with calamity, difficulties and suffering, yet I am resolved to act." [10]

It is clear that the insight into the abnormal nature of his illness he had gained with recovery had now been transformed. That it was in fact madness he had never fully convinced himself; and now, after the whole complex of ideas generated by his visions had been crystallized by the catalytic touch of the Christian tracts and had erupted into full consciousness, he was sure that the visions constituted a divine revelation. It was not a personal faith or religion that he had evolved for himself; he was converted to a limited form of Christianity. But his conversion brought with it certain bizarre qualities that cannot be ascribed to an understandable failure to comprehend fully the new ideology or grasp adequately the new *mystique* simply because he had never received formal instruction in the religion. Thus, in the books he found meanings which were not obvious to anyone else. When he came across the pronouns "you" or "he," he would understand them as pointing to himself. When he encountered the word "Ch'üan" (meaning "whole," "all" or "complete," and also the same ideograph as was contained in Hung's own name), he felt that it referred to him.[11] For example, in the 19th Psalm, when he read the words "Their voice is gone out to the whole (*ch'üan*) world," he understood it as "gone out to the world of Ch'üan," i.e., Hung Hsiu-ch'üan; when the text read "The judgements of the Lord are true, and altogether (*ch'üan*) righteous," he read "The

[9] Hamberg, 21.
[10] *Ibid.*, 22.
[11] *Vide* Hamberg, 22f.

judgements of the Lord are true, and Ch'üan is righteous"; and when it read "who can understand all (*ch'üan*) his errors," he took it to mean "who can, like Ch'üan, understand his errors." These are very much like the ideas of reference in insanity. Many passages he took to be a direct call to himself in particular. Similarly, he believed that the Heavenly Kingdom and God's chosen race were China and the Chinese, and he later appropriated the former term for the name of his own revolutionary state. He prepared for the struggle by ordering two swords to be made with the words "Demon-exterminating Sword" inscribed on them. When his ideas found no acceptance among the village elders, and later aroused hostility, he took to heart the literal meaning of the words: "A prophet is not without honor, save in his own country, and in his own house," and with a few friends he departed from his native village in order to spread his creed.

In the course of his rise to power, Hung was not lacking in political sagacity, but he often conducted himself in a manner which seemed to show the continued influence of his illness. Great caution is needed in judging whether or not any particular aspect of his behaviour was abnormal. When, before Changsha, he told his troops that he had received from Heaven a seal of state, he was probably trying to strengthen morale. Again, when he later proclaimed that he was the first younger brother of Jesus (the others being his lieutenants), he may only have been guilty of making propaganda. It is true that he believed in dream prophecy and is reported to have moved his family at one time from their village because a coming disaster had been revealed to him. Such incidents are difficult to evaluate even if they are true. However, he clearly showed towards the end of his career an inflexibility of mind and a submission to dominating ideas so marked that he must in this respect at least be regarded as abnormal. According to the *Chung Wang*, during the siege of Nanking he would do nothing to help; he did not answer memorials but only issued decrees saying that Heaven could do anything and men nothing. He refused to listen to anyone. After Nanking was relieved he did not interest himself in matters of administration, but merely instructed his ministers to follow the precepts of Heaven and indicated to them that the surrounding aspects showed signs of great peace. When it was suggested that preparations should be made to forestall a seventh siege, he asked unperturbedly, "Are you afraid of death? I, the truly appointed Lord, can, without the aid of troops, command great peace to spread its sway over the whole region." [12] When he was later besought to escape from Nanking, he was sarcastic, and still grandiloquent: "I have received the commands of God and of Jesus to come down upon earth and rule the Empire. I am sole Lord of the thousand nations, and what should I fear? You are not asked your opinion on anything and the fort does not require your supervision. You can please yourself whether you wish to leave the capital or remain. I hold the Empire, hills, and streams with an iron grasp, and if you do not support me there are those who will." And again: "Heaven will settle everything without occasion on your part to speculate or predict. You go and obey. . . ."

For a long time he had secluded himself from his ministers in the sanctum of his Palace, and the only persons who had ready access to him were his brothers and Hung Jen-kan, his Prime Minister and cousin. To his subordinates he left much freedom, so long as they obeyed or professed obedience for his decrees. He was, however, most particular where any reference to his ruling delusion was concerned; he threatened to draw asunder anyone who failed to use in official documents the adjective "Heavenly" to describe his brothers, the King, the army and so forth. If any of his officers spoke of "his" army, etc., without using the adjective "Heavenly," he would accuse them of plotting treason. According to the second memorial to the Throne by Tseng Kuo-fan appended to the *Chung Wang's* autobiography, he had not seen any of his ministers for a year before he committed suicide shortly before the fall of Nanking.* Before that he had actually fed himself on herbs and grass for several days, as an

---

[12] *Vide* Lay, *op. cit.*, Chap. 7.

* The handwritten testimony of Li Hsiu-ch'eng, which was kept by Tseng Kuo-fan's descendants for nearly a century until it was published in photographic reproduction in 1962, reveals that Hung actually died of illness for believing in "Heavenly treatment." For personal reasons and to please the Court, Tseng in his memorial to the Throne falsified a number of crucial points of Li's testimony, including Hung's suicide.—Ed.

example to the populace, whom he had ordered previously to store these unusual comestibles. He called these "sweet-dew," this being the translation of manna ("Manna from Heaven"). It is as impossible not to indict him for incapable leadership as it is not to admire him for such staunch faith; nor is it possible not to regard him as suffering from delusional ideas of psychotic intensity.

A Psychiatric Interpretation

It would be superficial to speak of madness without reference to the social and cultural background of the subject. Madness is not solely a medical problem; it is also a social one. The madman is essentially one who is socially helpless and incapable, and indeed E. Bleuler has in his classic *Textbook* defined insanity as social incapacity. From this point of view, any attempts to assess the sanity of Hung Hsiu-ch'üan must take into account not only his creative, original, and revolutionary qualities, his success in imposing on the people his unusual ideas and in persuading them to accept him and what he stood for, but also the fact that the complex of ideas he took over from his most unusual visionary experiences can be regarded as merely a derivative (if not a part) of the Christian religion. The whole episode might then be an example of the relatively commonplace phenomenon known as religious conversion (a psychological process perhaps better called in these days of fiercely held ideologies which are sometimes suddenly transmuted in the mind of the subjects into their exclusive opposite, ideological conversion). To this point we shall later return, but it is clear that from the rather narrow standpoint of psychological medicine Hung had definitely passed through an acute psychotic illness.

The account that has been left us of this part of his life is sufficiently detailed for an examination of it to be fruitful. He was under the greatest psychological stress. Once again he had failed the uniquely important examination and thus lost the sole chance open to him of attaining power and wealth. He had to return home to his people in disgrace. The strain of the examination itself must have been considerable. We might also surmise that he was aware, perhaps acutely so, of the times. The rulers of China were alien Manchus, and there was much anti-dynastic sentiment among the people. Not only was he Chinese, but a Hakka, not fully accepted by the natives of Kwangtung Province as one of themselves. He is said to have felt that his repeated failures were due to prejudice against him on this score, but this was probably only imagination on his part. In his family tradition too were records of illustrious ancestors who had attained high rank. This might not have been true, but the belief in such a tradition must have made his failure seem more ignominious. Thus with his regard for his family, as well as his consciousness of race, he must have been sorely wounded in his sense of personal worth. He was then only twenty-four years old, and probably still somewhat immature, like so many bookish youths.

He arrived home weak and ill. There is nothing to suggest that he was febrile,[13] or that he suffered from any toxic-infective or exhaustive illness due to bodily causes. At first he was depressed, full of guilt and of ideas of unworthiness, and sought his parents' indulgence and forgiveness. Then he passed into what must have been undoubtedly a "twilight-state," undergoing a series of dream-like, wish-fulfilling experiences as only a person in this condition could. He first found himself in hell, as might have been expected from his deep melancholy. A Tiger, symbol of courage and ferocity, first appeared to him. Then came a Dragon, which ever since the first royal dynasty had been an emblem of sovereignty, and unlike the western conception of it, a symbol of greatness and virtue. Finally appeared a Cock, the symbolic meaning of which may be the heralding of a new day, a call to new tasks. These signs set the tone for the apocalyptic events to follow. He was then taken to a river, where he was washed of all defilement; no longer would he have earthly taint or guilt. (Chinese mythology regards the Milky Way as the River of Heaven; and there are legends of immortals—e.g., Chi-kung Lao-fo P'u-sa— entering Nirvana or reaching the Western Paradise after cleansing

[13] Mr. Chien Yu-wen's interpretation is possibly mistaken in this respect, but his treatment of the illness as a delirium shows great psychological insight. Chien Yu-wen, *T'ai-p'ing chün kuang-hsi shou-i shih* (History of the Uprising of the Taiping Army in Kwangsi) (Chungking: Commercial Press, 1944), 78–9.

baths.) Then his heart was exchanged for another one, so that he obtained an inner purification and a new spirit. At last he was brought to the old man, who revealed to him in one cosmic glance (as one might expect in a dream) the evils of the world, and gave him the commandments. This old man had a "golden beard"—impossible for a Chinese. Could he be the dream representation of the foreign missionary Hung saw in Canton one year previously? Mr. Chien Yu-wen makes this interpretation, and also suggests that the middle-aged man who assisted Hung in exterminating demons might well have been a representation of the missionary's assistant. It is certain that the *leit-motif* of the twilight experience—redemption, renewal, and the reception of divine command—must have been determined by the meeting with the missionary and by contact with his ideas as expounded in the books he gave Hung, just as the illness itself was precipitated by the various frustrations he had encountered. He found in a purely psychogenic "twilight-state" or "delirium-fable" the satisfactions which life denied him, and in this he differed little from many psychotics.

This "delirium fable" or "twilight-state" was of the typically ecstatic kind. Its content was supplied by a combination of Chinese and Christian ideas, and its meaning was complete wish-fulfilment, with the overcoming of all personal frustrations. He created a whole world of his own as in a day-dream, but he also acted the dream out in the real world. Ideas and perceptions he could not tell apart, for his world of phantasy was projected into his real surroundings. He thus had hallucinations of demons in the room and fought them furiously; sometimes he perceived his friends, and scolded them for saying he was unbalanced; at other times he thought they were also demons. He dragged himself to his parents to report to them his Heavenly commission, just as he had at first besought them for forgiveness. He was also deluded that he was Emperor and liked his visitors to address him as such. He expressed his exaltation and his convictions in poetry. The external world was excluded in varying degree at different times, beginning with a marked stupor, which apparently lightened later. When autism (or withdrawal from reality) was almost complete, he acted much like a normal person who is dreaming.

With a lesser degree of autism, he showed "double orientation," i.e., perceiving his visitors as friends but regarding them simultaneously as demons (or disguised demons). When he was in a more or less lucid state, he could even compose poetry. But at all times he lacked insight into his own abnormal state.

The twilight-state is an acute psychotic condition in which the patient behaves as though in a waking dream. It differs from a febrile delirium in that there is no fever or other sign of bodily disease; moreover, it is usually less chaotic and disconnected than the latter, and is accompanied by elation rather than anxiety. Twilight-states mostly arise from purely psychogenic causes and are precipitated by strong emotions. Less commonly, they may be epileptic in origin, when the illness will be recurrent and perhaps associated with fits. Psychogenic cases are frequently hysterical in basis, when the twilight experiences will be more or less understandably related to the patient's immediate needs and difficulties—for example, as wish-fulfilment or as repetition of some disturbing episode in his past history. Hysterical twilight-states are not always inimical to the future well-being of the patient. However, this cannot be said of many psychogenic cases which are schizophrenic in basis arising from "splitting" of the personality (*intra-psychic ataxia*) due to obscure causes less clearly related to the immediate frustrations or traumatic experiences of the patient. There is, it might be added, no reason to suppose that such psychic processes in the Chinese insane differ essentially from those studied in the West.

On balance, it appears likely that Hung's illness was hysterical rather than schizophrenic in basis. The question of an epileptic origin clearly need not be considered. Given Hung's personal difficulties, his cultural background, and the influence upon him of the Christian tracts, his abnormal reaction is easily understandable. There was nothing really bizarre in his symptoms, and no evidence in the record of "splitting" expressing itself in sudden blocking, transitions, perseveration, or other oddities in the clinical picture. In analysing his illness one meets with very little difficulty. The predominance of complex visual hallucinations (in contrast to those of hearing and touch) points to hysteria. The almost direct relationship to psychic trauma as well as the comparatively short course of the illness also support this view. (According to Bleuler,[14] schizophrenic twilight-states last rather longer than hysterical ones, often as long as six months.) We are of course on very uncertain grounds in attempting so detailed an interpretation of the illness, for the available accounts are probably too inaccurate for such a purpose. Nevertheless, we need to have a correct understanding of the nature of the illness in order to evaluate or appreciate the curious qualities of character that Hung showed in his later life.

The fact that Hung's personality and character underwent change following the illness has already been pointed out. This would be unusual following a hysterical illness, but not unknown, especially in cases where religious sentiments and ideas are involved. In schizophrenia, a change of personality is not uncommon and usually the change is for the worse in the sense of becoming less spontaneous and adaptable, although intelligence as such may remain unimpaired for a long time. Sometimes, however, a patient's personality may show improvement, and Bleuler[15] quoted six cases of this kind described by C. Wille. Bleuler also mentioned the case of a schizophrenic woman who said she felt better after the illness inasmuch as the world appeared to have taken on a different aspect for her and she could at will go into religious (and sexual) ecstasy.[16] The diagnosis of schizophrenia does not exclude that of hysteria, and indeed a given case may show features of both diseases, especially in the acute twi-light-states. In schizophrenia, characterized by twilight-states, the course is usually benign. Deterioration of the personality need not follow the illness, nor need the rigid, suspicious, megalomanic para-noid character develop until one or more "prodromal hallucinatory states of God-communication." Such delusions as appear during the acute illness may be in varying degree forgotten only to appear again in a relapse, or be suddenly revived in the memory by a passing im-pression, as is the case with the memory for normal dreams. Bleuler

[14] Eugen Bleuler, *Dementia Praecox*, English transl. by Joseph Zinkin (New York: International Universities Press, 1950), 218.
[15] *Ibid.*, 257.
[16] *Ibid.*, 68.

affirmed that seldom if ever did a schizophrenic recover full insight into the nature and content of his illness: "As yet I have seen no schizophrenic who after his 'cure' was completely objective about his delusions. Either the patient discusses them lightly without real associations, or they are still emotionally charged; sometimes the patients even produce thoughts which are only understandable if it is assumed that the delusions maintain some reality for these patients even though consciously they may reject them." [17]

If then we take into consideration the facts of the latter part of Hung's life, we see that his megalomanic convictions and unswerving rigidity of mind and character raise some suspicion of a schizophrenic-paranoiac element in his illness. However, it must be admitted that we do not really possess sufficient data to decide conclusively this diagnostic point. His seclusiveness should not be over-emphasized in this respect, for this was the manner in which Chinese emperors often conducted themselves. However, paranoia-like psychopathic character developments are not impossible following cases of religious conversion essentially hysterical in basis,[18] and certainly there is little evidence to suggest that Hung, apart from conversion to an over-powering belief in his divine destiny following a single abnormal episode in his life, displayed any traits which might be expected to accompany personality deterioration of an essentially schizophrenic kind.

It is interesting to speculate on the reason why Hung unconsciously seized upon essentially Christian ideas in the course of his illness, so that he in fact experienced a conversion to Taiping Christianity.

The idea of salvation is not exclusively a Christian one. In Confucianism (which is a religion in the sense that E. Spranger and E. Eichele have defined the term) the idea is weakly presented without any reference to the supernatural, by presenting the precept and example of the complete and ideal "Princely Man," which is to be faithfully followed. In Taoism, there is a saviour in the person

---

[17] *Ibid.*, 137f, 229, 246.

[18] *Vide* H. I. Schou, *Religion and Morbid Mental States,* Engl. transl. (London, 1926), *passim.*

of Lü Ch'un Yang, a being with supernatural powers of combating demons, who had been raised to immortality by having survived much temptation: and also, at the head of the Taoist pantheon, Yü-huang Shang-ti; but there is little moral content and no clear recognition either of sin or of human sorrow. Of all the Chinese faiths, Buddhism provides an ideology of salvation which in its appeal to the weak and sorrowing is comparable to that found in Christianity. Chinese (Mahayana) Buddhism, in contrast to the Hinayana Buddhism of southern lands with its intellectual striving for *Nirvana*, is not atheistic; it recognizes divine beings who can bring salvation to men oppressed by worldly pain, distress, and sorrow by promising them life in a heaven of pure souls. Such salvation can be obtained by "merit" through religious exercise as well as by good deeds like the repair of roads or the giving of alms. Like Jesus Christ, who is both God and Saviour responding to human prayer, Kuan Shih Yin, the Goddess of Mercy and Compassion, listens to the suffering of the world and brings the souls of men across the Sea of Life and Death to the Pure Land. Buddhist ideas of salvation are focused both on her and on the Buddha, apparently one of the best ways of obtaining salvation being to meditate on the Buddha.

Hung, like many educated Chinese, no doubt possessed the humanistic Confucian temper, and probably in the normal course of events paid little attention to Buddhist salvation and even less to the Taoist equivalent, with its degenerated background of superstition. Sinitic religion (to use a term of Hu Shih's), against the background of a culture in decay, did not possess the vitality and force of Christianity as the symbol and expression of a powerful and expanding civilization destined to dominate the age. Moreover, there was nothing in the native religion to compare with the democratic, revolutionary, and challenging tone of much of Christian teaching. More than any notion of salvation or potency of symbol this aspect of the new faith must have made, in Hung's personal predicament, a powerful, if not wholly conscious appeal. When Christianity is first brought to ardent and sensitive individuals, troubled by the need for change, it has not infrequently created in them a "Messiah complex." It is recognized that Christianity, when introduced to cultures already breaking down under the impact of modern commercial industrialism, may produce in them certain messianic movements.[19] In 1850 a prophet arose in the Rio Negro region of South America under precisely this set of circumstances; in 1888, another, called Wovoka, proclaimed a similar messianic destiny among the Plains Indians of North America; and such movements have also arisen in South Africa. In Moslem lands such social phenomena have been called *Mahdism*. The Taiping revolt is also to be regarded as a social movement of this kind, although occurring in a much more complicated context. The idea of Jesus as both God and man, the Saviour of the world, appears to have a unique appeal for disturbed and sensitive natures by making possible their own identification with the Saviour.[20] In the case of Hung, the new religion not only appeared to him to be the secret source of Western power, so successful at that time in overcoming the resistance of the Manchus, but the concept of a Man-God must have exerted upon him an over-powering, hypnotic appeal. He was not only converted, but converted in such a way as to see in himself a Christ-like pre-ordination to save his world.

Religion conversion consists in the achievement of a new pattern of stability after a period of doubt and uncertainty. Most cases are characterised initially by suffering and sorrow, the result of social pressure acting on unusually sensitive minds. It is hardly ever merely a matter of intellectual conflict, but usually involves an acute emotional disturbance which often presents pathological features, the more so if it occurs in adult persons. The initial depression can be seen in the cases of John Bunyan, George Fox, and St. Augustine more clearly than in others; and Hung too was at first full of guilt and sorrow. The occurrence of visions during mystical, revelatory

[19] Wilson Dallam Wallis, *Messiahs: Their Role in Civilization* (Washington: American Council on Public Affairs, 1943).

[20] Such identification occurs even within the Christian tradition; cf. the case of James Naylor, a fervent supporter of Fox, who later thought he was the Messiah.

experiences is common; witness the well-known cases of St. Paul, George Fox, and Emanuel Swedenborg, the last of whom, like Hung, gave accounts of his sojourn in Heaven. Acceptance of, or conversion to a new religion is always preceded by a period of incubation. Apollonius of Tyana meditated for five years before he proclaimed acceptance of the Pythagorean philosophy. Saul had no doubt undergone sub-conscious preparation for his final momentous conversion for a long time before he underment that acute disturbance when he was blind for three days and had hallucinations. On the other hand, Hung passed through the acute phase of his conversion at the beginning, and the process was not completed until five years later, the intervening period being apparently quiescent, in contrast with the stormy onset.

Psychologically, there is probably little essential difference between the mystical experience and the experience of conversion. The former, however, does not involve the rejection and acceptance of traditional or formally verbalized religious systems, but only results, like the latter, in a re-ordering of the ultimate values of an individual, and may be experienced in the progressive acceptance of any ideology built around the ultimate valuation of a transcendental object. During mystic states, as William James[21] pointed out, the subject experiences the perception of new truths, a passive, yielding ecstasy, a liberation of energy, and often a sense of objective change in the world. These experiences are characteristically ineffable. If the subject, agnostic to begin with, attempts to understand and describe them at all, he must use such recognized religious terms and concepts as he himself has already taken over from his culture, and thus the mystic experience becomes one of religious conversion, either partial or complete. Either condition is, at the psychological level, amenable to interpretation by "psychopathological" (better *psychodynamic*) concepts. T. K. Osterreich[22] thought that revelatory experiences associated with "possession" were due to hysterical auto-suggestion which was sometimes based on obsessions and compul-

[21] William James, *The Varieties of Religious Experience* (London, 1902) Modern Library ed. 1925 242, 371f.

[22] Trangott Konstantin Osterreich, *Possession Demoniacal and other Among Primitive Races,* Engl. transl. (London, 1922), 84.

sions. T. W. Mitchell [23] regarded the process as involving hysterical splitting of the personality, much in the same way as James and Delacroix[24] had before him. The particular case of Saul's conversion was interpreted by the theologian and psychoanalyst Pfister as a simple "reaction-formation," one set of ideas having changed into another opposed to it, without the introduction of anything new;[25] the blindness which afflicted him for three days, only to be cured by a mere touch from Ananias telling him that he had been sent to him in order to restore his sight, can be understood by the medical man only as a hysterical symptom.[26] We have already seen that Hung's conversion also could have been essentially hysterical in basis, taking the form of a twilight-state during the acute initial stage.

Conclusion

There is apparent doubt in some quarters[27] whether Hung actually saw visions and was really ill, and it is suggseted that he merely "professed" visions as well as communication with God in order to buttress his own leadership. This is clearly an untenable position for historians to take. The recorded facts are themselves clear, and to a psychiatrist they are in no way beyond explanation or understanding. The same applies to the reported occurrence of convulsive, ecstatic experiences among the early group of rebels, for nothing is more common in the atmosphere of religious revivalism that usually surrounds such groups than hysterical phenomena of this kind. These are not necessarily simulated, although the group's interpretation of such experiences may be mistaken. There is no need to con-

[23] Thomas Walker Mitchell, *Medical Psychology and Psychical Research* (London, 1930), 161.
[24] Henri Joachim Delacroix, *Etudes d'histoire et de psychologie du mysticisme* (Paris: F. Alcan, 1908), *passim*.
[25] Oskar Robert Pfister, *The Psycho-analytic Method,* Engl. transl. (London: Kegan Paul, 1917), 462.
[26] This view has been expressed in W. A. Brend, *Sacrifice to Attis,* quoted by G. Godwin, *The great mystics* (London, 1945), 23.
[27] E.g., Ssu-yü Teng, *op. cit.,* 53–4; also Teng in his article on Hung in Arthur W. Hummel, ed., *Eminent Chinese of the Ch'ing Period* (Washington: U. S. Govt. Printing Office, 1943–4).

demn reports of these incidents as spurious fabrications. Psychiatry can often be a handmaid to both history and sociology.

The life and career of Hung Hsiu-ch'üan provides one of the clearest examples in history of the process by which vast social, economic and political forces inpinge on the mind of an unusually perceptive and possibly unstable person, and having worked in him a transformation of mind and character, are through him gathered together and given meaning, and then released as an indomitable psychic drive to bring about social change. It is only in this light that Hung's place in history can be understood. Chinese authors have as a rule overlooked his mental illness, while many foreign authors have regarded him as a madman, although others also speak of him as a genius. The principle of cultural relativity applies to insanity as to other aspects of human behaviour.[28] In the case of Hung an evaluation of his conduct and thinking is a rather delicate task not only because of his own special cultural background, but also because he lived in a period when the whole of Chinese culture was in violent transformation. But such an evaluation is really not important. The manner in which he arrived at his renovating ideas might have been grossly abnormal judged by ordinary standards, but it should be remembered that, while his religion ended in rejection, and his revolution in failure, yet, in the light of history, many of the aims he cherished were also those sought by later Chinese leaders in the gradual process of the adaptation of China to the modern world. That is the measure of his genius, and the meaning of his madness.

[28] I have discussed inter-cultural norms in mental disease, but without reference to social change, in P. M. Yap, "Mental Diseases Peculiar to Certain Cultures, A Survey of Comparative Psychiatry," *Journal of Mental Science* (1951), 97, 313–27.

❈ 3 ❈

Hung Jen-kan, Taiping Prime Minister, 1859–1864

KWAN-WAI SO AND EUGENE P. BOARDMAN
with the assistance of CH'IU P'ING

Reasons for the Study

The Taiping[1] Rebellion is of interest to students of modern China because of its reforming zeal, which under other circumstances might have developed a program of modernization for China. "Even in the midst of constant warfare, the rebels tried or intended to secure an equal distribution of land, to simplify the Chinese language, to enforce monogamy . . . , and to prohibit prostitution, footbinding, the sale of slaves, opium smoking, adultery, witchcraft, and gambling." [2] The thinking of some Taiping leaders appears to have been, if not more advanced, at least more imaginative than that of contemporary Ch'ing dynasty officials.

In the forefront of Taiping leaders interested in reform was Hung Jen-kan, a cousin of the head of the rebel movement and the Taiping prime minister from 1859 to 1864. Through almost a decade of association with Westerners in Hongkong and Shanghai prior to 1859 he had learned more than any Taiping of Western political

Reprinted with permission from *Harvard Journal of Asiatic Studies,* Vol. XX, Nos. 1–2 (June 1957), pp. 262–81. All but two footnotes have been deleted.

[1] Except for the transliteration of Chinese titles, the simpler form *Taiping* is used throughout the article in place of *T'ai-p'ing,* the correctly romanized term.

[2] Cf. Ssu-yü Teng, and John K. Fairbank, *China's Response to the West* (Cambridge: Harvard University Press, 1954), p. 56.

ideas and science. The nature of his knowledge is revealed in his booklet *Tzu-cheng hsin-p'ien* [*A New Work for Aid in Administration*], printed in 1859. In this work Hung had in mind, apparently, a program of economic change and industrial development.

Hung was also familiar with Christian theology and was the personal friend of a number of Western Protestant missionaries. Absent from the Taiping military campaigns of 1851–1859 as a refugee, he received more Christian training from Western missionaries than any other Taiping leader. For three years he was employed in the London Mission in Hongkong by James Legge, a pioneer translator of the Classics into English. When he left Hongkong for Nanking in 1859, he had the good will and respect of the mission communities in Hongkong and in Shanghai. In the post of Prime Minister he was ideally fitted to establish friendly relations with Christians in the treaty ports and with the representatives of the British and French governments. It is conceivable that British and French intervention in the Rebellion could have been prevented through the efforts of a man of his background and position. Help given the imperial forces by the Western powers after 1860 was, of course, one of the reasons for the Taiping failure to drive out the Manchus and establish a kind of communistic and theocratic state.

It has long been our conviction that an important reason for the Taiping failure was lack of competent leadership. Granted such a dearth of talent, why was Hung Jen-kan, with such a background and with a favorable family relationship, so ineffectual? Did the nature of the Taiping system necessarily involve the neglect of Hung's talents? Did Hung have the character to match his talents and education? Was the lack of congenial supporters a factor? By the time Hung reached Nanking was it too late for any Taiping, even Hung, to have influenced decisively either the state of foreign attitudes or the external military situation? The discovery of answers to these questions has appealed to us.

*Early Connection with Hung Hsiu-ch'üan
and the Taiping Rebellion*

Hung Jen-kan (known in contemporary Western sources as "Hung Jin," Feb. 18 or 20, 1822—Nov. 23, 1864) was a paternal third cousin of Hung Hsiu-ch'üan, styled the *T'ien Wang* of the *T'aip'ing t'ien-kuo* or "Heavenly King of the Heavenly Kingdom of Great Peace." Both were descended from the same great-great-grandfather, but Jen-kan was nine years (*sui*) junior to Hsiu-ch'üan. The relationship of cousin between the two was rendered more intimate by the fact that both of them lived in the same village, Kuan-lu-p'u of Hua-hsien, Kwangtung. The ancestors of the Hung family had originally settled in Ch'ao-chou fu and then, later, migrated to Chiaying chou before they finally came to Hua-hsien. In Kuan-lu-p'u settled the four family branches (fang) which were descended from Jen-kan's great-great-grandfather. Thus did Jen-kan come to know the leader of the Rebellion, his cousin Hsiu-ch'üan.

Besides the relationship of cousin to cousin there were experiences in common that led to a close association between Jen-kan and Hsiu-ch'üan before the start of the Taiping movement. Both belonged to the scholar class, Chinese who when successful in the civil service examinations became career officials in the government. From his youth on Jen-kan was interested in the study of history and astronomy. But, like his relative, he failed in the official examinations. Though there is no record of how Jen-kan reacted toward his failure, it is safe for us to conclude from what Jen-kan did later that he could have conceived the same hatred and opposition toward the Manchu government as Hung Hsiu-ch'üan did; otherwise Hsiuch'üan would not have disclosed to him his secret plans to overthrow Ch'ing rule. In these times, as a rule, scholars who failed in the official examinations turned to teaching for their livelihood if they lacked private means. As matters turned out, Jen-kan and Hsiu-ch'üan shared the same experience—failure followed by teaching. So, until 1851 Jen-kan taught school in Ch'ing-yüan, a *hsien* near Hua-hsien.

Hsiu-ch'üan seems to have had an early influence upon Jen-kan. In 1843, when Hsiu-ch'üan said he came to the realization of the meaning of Liang A-fa's tract *Ch'üan-shih liang yen* [*Good Words to Admonish the Age*], he also converted Jen-kan to his new religion and even baptized him. Together with Feng Yün-shan, another cousin and an intimate friend of Hsiu-ch'üan, they studied Liang's tract in detail and then began to carry out its injunctions by destroying images of deities in their schools. Their interest in the new faith is reflected in the fact that in 1847 Hsiu-ch'üan and Jen-kan went together to Canton to study Christian doctrine with an American missionary whom they had heard about, the Reverend Issachar J. Roberts. Jen-kan stayed with Roberts a month and then returned to his teaching post, leaving his cousin in Canton for another month of study. Whatever the reason for his early departure, it is plain to see that Jen-kan was from the beginning under Hsiu-ch'üan's influence and often followed the latter's lead.

Part of the explanation for Jen-kan's inclination to follow his cousin's lead can be found in his possession of a disposition to give way to a strong personality or give in to adverse circumstances. If we may judge from what he told Theodore Hamberg, Jen-kan believed himself to be a man of a very pliable nature. A few instances will show the basis for his belief. In 1843, after his conversion to the new religion, Jen-kan was beaten and driven from home by his older brother with his clothes torn and ragged because his removal of the shrine of Confucius had caused all the students to leave his school. No one but an obedient and pliable individual would have allowed himself, in the position of village teacher, a post that commanded some respect, to be treated in this fashion at the age of 22. When Hsiu-ch'üan, who had lost his teaching position through acts of iconoclasm, wanted to have Jen-kan go along with him to a distant area where they could preach the new faith, Jen-kan was not allowed by his family to go, and apparently did not oppose his family, at least to the extent of running away. Later Jen-kan, taking the advice of his friends, made the concession of allowing his students to pay reverence to Confucius, though he himself abstained. It is worthy of note that Jen-kan, even though he knew Hsiu-ch'üan's ambitious plan of starting a revolution at an early date, did not join in the planning and postponed joining the revolutionary group in Kwangsi until unable to escape the attention of rebel-hunting, Ch'ing officials. It seems clear that he became involved in the maelstrom of the Rebellion more because of his family connection and early association with Hsiu-ch'üan than because of the strength of any pro-rebel convictions he may have held. In sum, Jen-kan in his early life was by no means as strong or commanding a character as his older cousin.

A further point should be taken into account in apprasing both the early and later relationship between Jen-kan and Hsiu-ch'üan. To start with, the older cousin's seniority and assured and patronizing attitude, particularly after his "visions," placed Jen-kan in an inferior position both socially and psychologically. Even had Jen-kan had the strong personality which he lacked and which would have made him more influential later in his life, Hsiu-ch'üan had the advantage of beginning their relationship in a position to influence rather than to be influenced by Jen-kan. This advantage he never relinquished. Despite the aberrations and increasing mysticism that marked the last years of Hsiu-ch'üan's life, the relative position of the two personalities did not change.

The Years 1851–1859

Unlike other associates of Hung Hsiu-ch'üan, Jen-kan failed to take an active part in the Rebellion until nine years after it began. According to his own account he did not participate in the planning phases at all. He managed somehow to finance the last trip of the two leaders, Hsiu-ch'üan and Feng Yün-shan, to Kwangsi, but this was the extent of his participation. When the Rebellion began in 1851, Hsiu-ch'üan sent messengers back to Kwangtung to summon to Kwangsi the relatives of the Hung and Feng families and God-Worshippers of the area generally, so that on the one hand they might strengthen the revolutionary forces and on the other hand avoid falling into the hands of government officials bent on retaliation because of the revolt in Kwangsi. At this invitation Jen-kan and fifty others went westward to a local headquarters where they learned that the God-Worshippers of the area had already left and that the Manchu government officials were vigilant and ready to seize all people suspected of connection with the revolt. As a result of the watchfulness of the government officials, Jen-kan and his friends failed to overtake the main body of the rebels, by this time on the march, and had to return to Kwangtung. From then on Jen-kan could not live peacefully at home and had to play a game of hide-and-seek with the government officials, for news of the insurrection had reached the authorities of Kwangtung province also.

The following year, 1852, the *T'ien Wang*, as Hsiu-ch'üan was called by the rebels, again sent a messenger back home to summon his relatives and friends. Fired by the successes which the Taiping host had had in Kwangsi, the messenger and a few others planned an uprising in Kwangtung using a following of about two hundred people. Due to his reckless, careless leadership, the uprising was easily crushed. A late arrival on the scene, Jen-kan was captured by natives, but fortunately managed to escape and with the help of a friend fled to Hongkong.

So, in April 1852, through the assistance of a Christian friend, Jen-kan came to Hongkong, there to see the Reverend Theodore Hamberg and to study Christian doctrine under him. Hamberg (1819–1854) was the first Swedish missionary to China. Sent out by a missionary society of Basle, he had reached China in 1847. For a time he was in the work of the China Union, an organization for the dissemination of Christian materials founded by Gützlaff. Hamberg listened to Jen-kan's surprising account of the Taiping uprising and was responsible for asking him to put it down on paper. Later, when Hamberg wrote in English "The Visions of Hung-Siu-Tshuen and Origin of the Kwangsi Insurrection," he relied largely on Jen-kan's oral and written accounts. To protect his informant Hamberg concealed Jen-kan's identity and gave him the name "Hung Jin" instead.

Presently Jen-kan felt he could leave Hongkong and return to the mainland where he became a teacher in a village school in Tungkuan, Kwangtung province. But he was not satisfied to teach school quietly; now he longed to join the revolution—which by now had displaced the Manchu government from control of the Yangtze River. In November 1853 Jen-kan went to see Hamberg in Hongkong again and this time stayed there till sometime before May 1854 when, financed by Hamberg, he took ocean passage with two friends for Shanghai with the plan of reaching Nanking, which had become the Taiping capital. During his second stay in Hongkong Jen-kan studied Christian doctrine and was baptized by Hamberg. On his arrival in Shanghai he found that the city had fallen into the hands of a band of rebels separate from the Taipings called the *Small Sword Society*. There was no response from Nanking to his efforts at communication, much less, acknowledgment of his claim to be the *T'ien Wang's* cousin. Nor could he obtain help in Shanghai from his Western friends. Meanwhile, waiting and planning, he studied in a Shanghai missionary school. In the winter of the same year he returned to Hongkong. There he resided until 1859 when he finally succeeded in reaching Nanking, capital of the Taipings.

During the years 1855–1858 in Hongkong, Jen-kan was employed as a catechist and preacher by members of the London Missionary Society. He also studied theology, as well as secular subjects such as geography and world history. He made, besides, many acquaintances among the foreigners. He seems to have produced a very good impression upon his foreign friends; he was described by James Legge of the Society in the *Missionary Magazine* in the following terms.

> . . . He soon established himself in the confidence and esteem of the members of the mission, and the Chinese Christians connected with it. His literary attainments were respectable; his temper amiable and genial; his mind was characterized by a versatility unusual in a Chinese. His knowledge of Christian doctrine was largely increased, and of the sincerity of his attachment to it there could be no doubt.

In short, we have here a man of supple disposition and loyalty, with certain literary attainments and a keen mind for knowledge. Jen-kan's later years could testify to this also. He was known, as we have seen, to have been "under Dr. Legge in Hongkong for a time." He was also a student in Hongkong of the Reverend J. Chalmers, Legge's associate in the London Missionary Society. The latter spoke highly of him, saying, "Whenever you see anyone having long and frequent intercourse with Hung-jin, you may be sure there is something good going on in him."

The four years in Hongkong may have been a period of anxiety and longing for Jen-kan at the time, though later he told Griffith John in retrospect that they had been very happy ones. It is certain that he profited from residence in Hongkong, particularly by an enlarged understanding of Western customs. His work as a native assistant of Westerners and his circle of acquaintances directed his eyes to foreign things and Western learning. He came to know much more about the world as a whole than the average Chinese scholar of the time, content with ignorance of areas outside China. While studying foreign administrative methods, Jen-kan came to appreciate the merits of Western political institutions and later advocated the adoption of many of them ardently. Jen-kan was in Hongkong intermittently between 1852 and 1854 and continuously from 1855 through 1858; this was a time when certain measures of democratization were being put into effect. His recommendations to the Taipings may have been influenced by the course which a movement to democratize was taking when he first arrived.

Due to agitation on the part of British residents while John Davis was governor (1844–1848), British subjects there, at odds with Davis, had asked for a municipal body to be given the power of determining the appropriation of income raised for local purposes. Their plea was noticed in 1847 by a Select Committee of Parliament and resulted in the recommendation that a share in the administration of the local affairs of the Island be given to the British residents. In accordance with the tenor of the Select Committee's report, Davis' successor Bonham began a plan of unofficial consultation with a committee of fifteen or sixteen unpaid Justices of the Peace. These were then asked to nominate two members of the Legislative Council. Following their appointment in 1850 the Legislative Council was composed of three officials and two representatives who were not officials. Bonham's successor Bowring went farther. In 1855 he proposed to the Secretary of State that the Council include five non-official members to be elected every third year by registered holders of land under a Crown lease returning a yearly rental of ten pounds. The Secretary of State decided against the elective principle but posed no objection to an increase in the number of non-official members. In the end the agitation resulted in the addition of one non-official and also one official member with Bowring continuing Bonham's practice of asking advice of the Justices of the Peace. The type of government which he observed taking form in Hongkong may have influenced Jen-kan against advocating for China the kind of popular government which existed in the United States of America, though he spoke highly of the latter in *A New Work for Aid in Administration.* His other suggestions about the separation of the judicial and executive branches of government and the establishment of a patent office, railroads, steamship companies, shipyards, a banking system, a post office, a police force, information collecting agencies, and a limited bill of rights, and his willingness to give profit inducement to private enterprise may very well have been inspired by the success of what he observed in Hongkong. It is hard to avoid the conclusion that the Hongkong experience provided him with considerable preparation for his later task as Taiping premier.

Probably the ablest estimate of Jen-kan as he was several years later than the Hongkong experience is contained in the report of R. J. Forrest, an English consul and interpreter who was in Nanking in 1861. Forrest's report reads that Jen-kan was "rather fat than otherwise and has an open and very pleasing countenance. . . . I must confess that he is the most enlightened Chinaman I ever saw. He is perfectly acquainted with geography, moderately so with mechanics, acknowledges the superiority of Western civilization, has books of reference with plates on all imaginable subjects, is generous, and very desirous of doing good." It is also very interesting to read Forrest's description of Jen-kan's study. Forrest describes the disposition of the man in the following terms. "His ambition is counteracted by his indolence. Pride and innate Chinese love of concealment and trickery but too often develop themselves in the man, and are made evident almost immediately by his openness and candour." In another place, Jen-kan was said to be "indolent and consequently takes but little trouble to see his theories put into practice." We have a picture here of a clever person but not a strong-minded one.

Career as a Taiping Leader, 1859–1864

After an arduous and devious journey at long last Jen-kan arrived in Nanking on April 22, 1859. He had taken the land route this time. Sometime in the middle part of 1858 (probably June), with the financial help of his foreign friends, he left Hongkong for Kwangtung and then went by a circuitous route through Kiangsi, Hupei, and Anhwei to reach Nanking, the "Heavenly Capital."

To Jen-kan the warm welcome which was accorded him by his cousin the *T'ien Wang* more than compensated for the past years of anxiety and hardship. Before leaving Hongkong Jen-kan had told James Legge that his journey to Nanking had two objects, the correction of certain religious errors and the prosecution of a line conciliatory to foreigners. Jen-kan the following year told several missionaries that his sole object in leaving Hongkong for Nanking was to preach the gospel to the Taipings, an aim for which his Hongkong experience had well fitted him. Hsiu-ch'üan, however, had his own plans for his cousin and insisted on promoting him at once to high political rank in the regime, possibly because he considered himself the sole fount of religious truth, but more likely because educated Taipings with family connections that prom-ised loyalty to him were at a premium. Jen-kan had hardly settled down when Hung Hsiu-ch'üan conferred upon him the title of *Kan T'ien Fu.* [On] May 8, 1859 he was given a higher title, *Kan T'ien I* with the additional rank of Generalissimo. Three days later, on May 11, he was promoted to the position of Premier with the title of *Kan Wang* ("Shield Prince"), or, given in full, *K'ai-ch'ao ching-chung chün-shih ting-t'ien fu-ch'ao-kang Kan Wang.* These quick promotions were really unusual and doubtless reflect

Taiping scarcity of able personnel. It is likely that the *T'ien Wang* was glad to see his intimate companion of early days again and was, moreover, eager to have someone of reliable loyalty who had the training to be capable of administering court affairs. Ever since the elimination of the Eastern and Western Kings, who had plotted against him, and the flight of the Assistant King in 1857, the Heavenly King had chosen the top leaders where possible from members of his own family or relatives.

As the Taiping premier, Jen-kan was presumed to be the most influential person in the government next to the *T'ien Wang* himself. His actual position, however, was not as powerful a one as it should have been and it certainly was not an enviable one. Jen-kan's sudden rise incurred for him the jealousy of the fighting generals, none of whom had at that time been given the top title of *Wang*. For example, the brilliant Li Hsiu-ch'eng, soon to be awarded the title of *Chung Wang* or "Loyal Prince," reacted to Jen-kan's rapid rise by the statement that after receiving his title of *Kan Wang* Hung Jen-kan contributed nothing to the welfare of the Taiping state. Ch'en Yü-ch'eng, a Cantonese who won the official title of *Ying Wang,* was possibly the only supporter that Jen-kan had among the top Taiping leaders. At the time, Nanking was in difficulties owing to a long and menacing siege so that the military situation called for the *Kan Wang*'s attention too. The Taiping situation became worse as the generals seemed to care only for their own selfish ends. What was more distressing, the *T'ien Wang* became increasingly abstracted and obsessed with his own imaginary world. In the words of Forrest, an able observer, "At dinner, he (the *Kan Wang*) will tell you what difficulties he has to encounter in introducing reforms; how the Tien Wang's 'head is in the skies, while his feet are on the earth,' and how little the other Wangs care for his authority."

Jen-kan does not seem to have gone to Nanking for a chance at power and wealth. In contrast to an earlier lack of enthusiasm, he now appeared to profess fervent zeal and enthusiasm for the Taiping cause. During his stay in Hongkong, he had learned Western governmental methods and made many acquaintances among the foreigners. When he was appointed Prime Minister, he naturally thought of bettering the internal as well as the external situation. He compared himself to the famous Chou Kung, the brother of the first sovereign of the Chou Dynasty (1027?–256 B. C.), who has been considered the author of the Rites of Chou and also the one responsible for laying the foundations of that long-lived dynasty. As his most important proposal along lines of Westernization, Jen-kan composed *A New Work for Aid in Administration*. In the words of a British representative in China, this was a pamphlet "advocating intercourse with foreigners on a footing of equality, the introduction of steam vessels, railways, and other western inventions and containing sounder and more enlightened views of Christianity." It seems to have been the intention of Jen-kan to establish normal and even friendly relations with the Western powers and to advocate the adoption of reforms in internal administration. To accomplish his first purpose he planned to enlist the help of his missionary friends and expected through their friendship to reach an understanding with the foreign powers. This accounts for Mr. Bruce's report that "Heung-jin (sic) has sent a copy of his pamphlet to the Protestant missionaries, and has invited them to join him at Soo-chow" and that "Heung-jin has also sent a letter to Mr. Meadows (British consul), addressed jointly to the consuls of the Three Treaty Powers, through Mr. Jenkins, the Interpreter to the American Consulate, who has lately visited Soo-chow on a trading speculation." All his efforts to cultivate better relations, however, came to nought. Both the time and the means were ill-chosen. Missionaries who got to Nanking with hopes of doing Christian work among the Taipings found them "beyond the control of any human adviser," and were appalled by the travesty of Christianity which the rebel religion represented. While grateful for Jen-kan's friendship, they could hardly have been strong spokesmen for the regime upon their return. Even if they had been, the harm done by the Taipings to trade in the Yangtze Valley could not be talked away. By 1860 the attitude of trade-sensitive British who were then concluding the second treaty settlement with the Manchu government was becoming more and more unfriendly, a fact well shown by the reports of Mr. Bruce, the chief British representative in China. Nor was the rebels' care not to give offense to Westerners in the Shanghai area—a concern which the *Kan Wang* could not have avoided strengthening—of any help.

During his first year in Nanking Jen-kan performed several other tasks besides the preparation and presentation of his political program to the *T'ien Wang*. He presided over the Taiping metropolitan examinations. He caused the re-naming of the degree titles. He was also responsible for the modification of the Taiping calendar; the new version stipulated that 366 days would constitute a year and required that the months of every fortieth year all have twenty-eight days. This was a needed correction. The original Taiping calendar had specified that the year consist of 366 days, with 30 days for the even months and 31 for the odd ones—a sufficiently sensible requirement—but had then decreed that the months of every fortieth year all contain 33 days.

The first year he was premier Jen-kan claims to have formulated and written down a plan for Taiping generals to execute in lifting the siege of Nanking. According to his plan the Taipings were to pretend to make an attack on Hangchow and Huchow so as to draw off the forces of the besieging imperialists and enable the rebels left in Nanking to fall upon the remaining besiegers. Jen-kan discussed the plan with Li Hsiu-ch'eng who with others undertook its execution. The stratagem was very well executed and was successful. Deceived by the false move, the Manchu generals, Ho Ch'un and Chang Kuo-liang, as was hoped, dispatched troops to the succor of the regions of Hangchow and Huchow whence their supplies came. As a result, in May 1860 the siege of the capital was lifted. If this successful plan can be ascribed to Hung, it was the only successful piece of military planning he did. All his other military projects ended in failure.

As suggested above, Jen-kan failed to accomplish anything tangible in the field of foreign policy, despite the fact that at his invitation, several Protestant missionaries came to see him and carried on discussions with him. Symbolic of these fruitless efforts to make use of missionary friendships was the arrival in Nanking in October

1860 of the Reverend Issachar J. Roberts, the former teacher of Hsiu-ch'üan and Jen-kan. Seven years before, Roberts in his zeal to further the Gospel had tried to reach Nanking and had been refused permission by the American Commissioner. Now he was welcomed and given a residence near that of the *Kan Wang* but was given to understand that his religious advice was not needed. Instead, the *T'ien Wang* gave him the temporal rank of Minister for Foreign Affairs and appointed him judge of all criminals belonging to the "outside countries," appointments which Roberts repeatedly refused. Western visitors to Nanking all speak of meeting Roberts; he undoubtedly gave the rebels some assistance in their dealings with Westerners. His unhappy position at the time is described by the Rev. J. L. Holmes, a missionary visitor.

> The Rev. Issachar Roberts . . . remains there still; but he entertains doubts . . . as to whether his duty requires him to continue in, or leave, that sphere of labour. His missionary teachings are not received as he would desire, and he has no inclination for the temporal honours and employment which the Tien Wang wishes to confer on him. He is justly offended at having had to kneel before the Tien Wang on the only occasion on which he was admitted to an audience, and disappointed at finding that the "eighteen churches" that he was assured would be opened at Nanking prove only to be rebel designations for so many of their public offices.

Finally a quarrel occurred with Jen-kan that ended their friendship and resulted in Roberts' leaving Nanking precipitately. Jen-kan attacked Roberts' servant in his presence and beat him so severely that Roberts thought he had been killed. The accusation of murder and Roberts' completely disillusioned appraisal of the Taipings, written Jan. 22, 1862, two days after his departure, were circulated among Westerners. There were no further visits of missionaries after this. After Roberts' departure not only was it impossible to obtain help from missionary friends but other foreigners, hearing the details, began to criticize the Taipings. It had been the Taiping policy not to irritate Westerners, a policy that had had a certain amount of success. Now the growing interest of the Taipings in the regions of Soochow and Shanghai became increasingly incompatible with the trade interests of foreigners in the treaty ports of Shanghai, Hangchow, and Ningpo. The foreigners now saw that peaceful conditions throughout the hinterland were essential to the unimpeded flow of trade. Local trade ceased when the rebels were in the vicinity, whether or not the Taipings were polite to Westerners. Then, in 1862 the rebels came to the point of attempting to capture Shanghai; this antagonized the treaty powers beyond any chance of reconciliation. By the first part of 1862 Great Britain, the leading treaty power, had determined to support the Manchu government, with whom it had concluded the second treaty settlement, and to help it suppress the Rebellion.

As Premier, Hung Jen-kan was unhappily also required to command troops outside Nanking. A troop commander without previous military experience, he almost always fared badly. Before the fall of Anking in 1861 the Taipings had made great efforts to reinforce their forces within the city. Jen-kan himself led an army to Anking, but the Taiping forces were defeated, Anking was captured by the Imperials, and the province of Anhui was taken. This failure inflicted a very severe blow upon the rebels and put them in a precarious position. The year 1862 saw Jen-kan again rushing help to Taiping generals and again undergoing defeat. Besides being inexperienced in it, the *Kan Wang* hated war, and tried on his excursions to make it as little terrible as possible. It is not ironic that Jen-kan nevertheless wrote four pieces of advice for the fighting commanders on the essentials of conducting wars!

After 1862 the situation became steadily worse for the Taipings. The imperialist forces under Tseng Kuo-fan, after having recovered the areas along the Yangtze, established tight siege lines around the Taiping capital as they began the second and final investment of the city. Meanwhile, two other able imperialist generals, Li Hung-chang and Tso Tsung-t'ang, were successful in their campaigns in Kiangsu and Chekiang. The days of the Taiping kingdom were numbered. In 1863 Jen-kan was ordered by special command to look after the *T'ien Wang's* son. By this time he had already determined to stay with the Taiping cause to the end despite his premonition that the Rebellion was doomed. In a conversation with Forrest in 1861 he hinted that if the Manchu government showed mercy to the rebels, the Taiping leaders would hardly be able to keep their armies together. As a man of loyalty he ignored his likely fate and belittled death.

The final siege of Nanking lasted from May 1862 to July 19, 1864. The rebel capital finally fell to forces under the command of Tseng Kuo-ch'üan, the younger brother of Tseng Kuo-fan. More than a month before the final capitulation Hung Hsiu-ch'üan committed suicide, most probably after a fortnight's illness, leaving the throne to his half-grown son Hung Fu (Nov. 1849—Nov. 18, 1864), supported by Jen-kan and Li Hsiu-ch'eng. On the fall of the capital, taking advantage of the confusion and chaos, Jen-kan succeeded in escaping. Though able to reach a point 500 miles southwest of Nanking, he was nevertheless taken by the Imperials at Kuang-ch'ang, Kiangsi on October 9, 1864. Sixteen days later the young Hung Fu was also captured. On November 23 after having penned a statement for his captors Jen-kan was put to death.

✵ 4 ✵

Li Hsiu-ch'eng: Taiping Hero

STEPHEN UHALLEY, JR.

The Taiping Revolution bequeathed to the Chinese people a rich legacy of revolutionary heroes, some of whom seem to have been individuals possessed of truly exceptional qualities. But among the Taiping leaders none compares in all-around appeal with Li Hsiu-ch'eng, commonly referred to as the Chung Wang or Loyal Prince. This Taiping military leader enjoyed for many years a deserved reputation for self-sacrificing courage, for outstanding military prowess, and for the humanity and justice of his administration over conquered areas.

Recently, however, Li Hsiu-ch'eng has been subjected to considerable and complicated re-evaluation at the hands of a variety of scholarly and political writers. The issue has succeeded in becoming sufficiently confused so that it is no longer an easy task to give even a brief, relatively simple and straightforward account of his life. One of the main reasons for this is that before one can proceed with an evaluation of Li, a decision must be made between two fundamentally opposed assumptions which govern the interpretation of most of the available historical evidence.

One of these assumptions holds that Li Hsiu-ch'eng wrote his autobiography with the intent to deceive his captor, Tseng Kuo-fan, the chief of the Ch'ing generals arrayed against the Taipings. This is the theory advanced by the most prominent Taiping scholar living in Communist China today, Lo Erh-kang, the Director of the Taiping Historical Museum in Nanking. The other assumption is

This is an original article, published here for the first time.

that Li's autobiography is not an exercise in deception, but a simple narration of the author's experience with the revolutionary movement replete with some admittedly uncharacteristically compromising comments. The difference between these two positions is considerable, because the implications of a number of Li's comments made in the autobiography differ greatly, depending on which assumption is followed. Making this fundamental choice of assumption all the more important is the fact that Li's autobiography is the single greatest source of information on his career.

Other factors intrude to further complicate contemporary discussions of Li Hsiu-ch'eng. For one thing, there are several extant versions of Li's all-important autobiography. Unfortunately, few of the recent discussants of Li's activities have bothered to determine whether they were using the authentic version. This genuine original document had been discovered only recently in Taiwan where it was published in 1962, thus being made available for the first time after almost a hundred years had passed since it was written. Consequently, only a handful of scholars have consulted the authentic version, while most of those who have been making loud and authoritative assertions concerning Li Hsiu-ch'eng have not. Most of the latter do not seem to be aware that there is a crucial need to make the distinction between the newly discovered original and the previously utilized versions. The need is crucial because the unauthentic versions have obviously been tampered with by Li's captors, as any quick comparison readily discloses.

Further complicating matters is the fact that the scholars and political writers who have recently been concerned about Li Hsiu-ch'eng do not fall into two neat categories, which might have easily resolved the issue. In other words, it is not simply a matter of scholars who have used the authentic version of the autobiography being opposed to those who have not. It would be tempting, for example, to contrast the respective positions of the Chinese Communists' official line in the recent controversy over Li Hsiu-ch'eng with that of Lo Erh-kang. The probability is good that Lo, the author of the deception theory, who therefore maintains that Li Hsiu-ch'eng is clearly a hero, has consulted the authentic version.

On the other hand, the writers representing the official Chinese Communist line hold that Li is not a hero but a traitor. As might be expected, this line was being promoted in order to serve a particular contemporary political purpose rather than to clarify an historical question seriously. Significantly, it would appear that the Communists, in making their case, invariably cite an unauthentic version of the key text. Now this would seem to settle the case, almost *ipso facto*, in favor of Lo Erh-kang, with his superior scholarship. But, complicating matters no end is the conclusion of Jen Yu-wen, the leading Taiping scholar, who resides in Hong Kong, which disagrees with Lo Erh-kang's theory, although not to the extent that Li Hsiu-ch'eng is held to be a traitor. Jen has made use of the authentic autobiography more thoroughly than anyone else. Some Western scholars have independently taken a position akin to Jen's in this matter, although it is not clear that they have themselves used the authoritative text.

This introduction into the complications and uncertainties surrounding the Loyal Prince's autobiography is by no means designed to deter the reader from perusing the record of so fascinating a historic personality. It is hoped, however, that the reader will have been alerted to expect differences of opinion in biographical interpretations of him. The brief account that follows can under present circumstances be at best but a tentative interpretation, however carefully reasoned. The salient features of Li's interesting life are presented, but the overall interpretation is subject to modification by future scholarship.

Li Hsiu-ch'eng was the son of a poor peasant in the hard mountainous farming area of Tenghsien, Kwangsi. An uncle taught him to read, but apparently his concentrated studies were limited to only two or three years of his boyhood, for by the age of ten he had already begun contributing to the livelihood of his poor family. The bitter, grinding poverty that he and his family continued to experience for the next sixteen or seventeen years made him receptive, like so many other peasants, to the attractions of Hung Hsiu-ch'üan's revolutionary doctrines. In 1850 Hung began the Taiping Revolution in Kwangsi, and Li joined one of the chiefs, Wei Ch'ang-hui, in a nearby village. Li's statement that poverty was the only reason for joining may well have been true. But his assertion that he continued to study the Confucian Classics and histories during the march to Nanking could have been one of the first efforts in his autobiography to deceive Tseng Kuo-fan, his captor fourteen years later. It does not seem likely that Li, as a common soldier throughout this first long, hectic campaign, would have seriously read such prohibited works, especially when the revolutionary élan must have been so great. It would not have been the kind of behavior that recommended him for the rapid promotions he received after Nanking was taken in March 1853. Soon after this achievement, Li was made a battalion commander. By the end of the year he served as an officer of Shih Ta-k'ai, the Assistant King, in Anhwei province. In 1854, while serving under Hu I-kuang, the Minister of State, he distinguished himself in an important battle in Anhwei for which he was promoted to Twentieth Commander of the Taiping forces. He had won recognition from the powerful Eastern King, Yang Hsiu-ch'ing.

But this was only the beginning of Li's rapid rise. His real opportunity came as a result of the violent internal upheaval of 1856 in Nanking in which the Eastern King, the Northern King, Wei Ch'ang-hui, and many of their supporters were killed. This crisis also led to the departure from Nanking of Shih Ta-k'ai, after which he was to pursue an apparently independent operation in the interior at the head of a large body of troops. This situation produced a leadership vacuum in the military which was soon filled, in particular by two promising young leaders, Ch'en Yü-ch'eng, the erstwhile Eighteenth Commander, and Li Hsiu-ch'eng, whose brilliance, lately recognized by the deposed Eastern King, was not overlooked. Both men operated for a time under the apparently loose authority of a Commanding General, Meng Te-en, also known as the Tsan Wang. One indication of this meteoric rise by Li Hsiu-ch'eng to a position of considerable military power is the fact that a Ch'ing government intelligence report of 1855 (only the previous year) listed seventy-four prominent Taiping military leaders, among whom Li's name is not to be found.

Li Hsiu-ch'eng's qualifications for his suddenly won power were soon tested. The Taiping's military position in 1856 was perilous. Ch'ing forces had reasserted control over the Yangtze River and at the end of the year the Wuhan cities had been recovered. To meet this threat Li and Ch'en Yü-ch'eng held a conference at Tsungyang, near Anking, to map out their strategy. Li also enlarged his contacts with the rebellious Nien forces. To do this he worked through the southern Nien leader, Li Chao-shou, with whom he had already imaginatively and independently co-operated in another operation in the previous year. Through Li Chao-shou, Li Hsiu-ch'eng made contact with the chief Nien leader, Chang Lo-hsing, whose forces were claimed to comprise a million men. With the alliance that ensued between the Taipings and the Nien, Li Hsiu-ch'eng not only extricated himself from a difficult situation at the city of Tungcheng, in Anhwei, where he had been surrounded by Ch'ing forces and outnumbered by ten thousand men to three thousand, but he also secured the province of Anhwei for some time to come. The Nien proved to be unreliable allies, but they did serve an urgent purpose which, of course, was all important for the Taipings at the time. In November 1858 Li Chao-shou opportunistically capitulated to the Ch'ing side, bringing with him the cities in his charge. Although Li Hsiu-ch'eng at the time wrote to the traitor imploring him to return to the Taipings, Li's later reflection that the defector's troops had been a disorderly lot and were constantly troubling the people probably carried with it the realization that the Taipings were better off without such allies, after they had served their expedient purpose.

By the end of 1857 and in early 1958, further Ch'ing offensives pressed the Taipings, particularly threatening Nanking with a reorganized Imperialist force commanded by Ho-ch'un and Chang Kuo-liang, and Anhwei with renewed assaults by a strong Hunan army under Li Hsu-pin, who was accompanied by one of Tseng Kuo-fan's brothers. To meet this combined threat Li Hsiu-ch'eng called for a second conference at Tsungyang. The strategy agreed upon at this meeting proved equal to the task. First, a combined Taiping force under Li Hsiu-ch'eng defeated the Imperialist army near Pukow, thus breaking the northern half of the siege against Nanking.

Then the Taipings completely annihilated the Hunan army through a joint effort by Ch'en Yü-ch'eng and Li Hsiu-ch'eng. Li Hsu-pin and Tseng Kuo-fan's brother were both killed. Following this important victory of November 15, 1858, Ch'en Yu-ch'eng remained in the vicinity of Anking, while Li Hsiu-ch'eng returned to the Nanking area, where he continued to figure prominently in Taiping political as well as military affairs.

Li Hsiu-ch'eng had already tried to use his influence in Nanking as beneficially as he could, for although he was primarily a military leader, he had good judgment and practical sense as an administrator, qualities which may have been scarce in the confused Taiping administration between 1856 and 1859. He once memorialized Hung Hsiu-ch'üan advocating several reforms, including the selection of more talented officials, the enactment of laws to bring relief to the people, the renovation of court discipline, the enforcement of proper rewards and punishments, the treatment of people with compassion, and the reduction of taxes. He also counseled making greater use of the Assistant King, Shih Ta-k'ai. Li Hsiu-ch'eng received a temporary demotion for such outspoken effrontery, but he was soon reinstated. By the time the siege of 1858 was laid upon Nanking, Li Hsiu-ch'eng was even being entrusted with the general direction of civil affairs, although he was, of course, personally preoccupied with the military problem. Even so, he did restore additional order to the administration of the capital. Before leaving Nanking for military reasons, he placed his own man, Lin Shao-chang, who was later made the Chang Wang, in the strategic position of assisting Meng Te-en, so that the latter's influence would be kept within bounds. Following the resolution of the serious military crisis of 1858, Li Hsiu-ch'eng was suddenly given the lofty rank of Chung Wang, or Loyal Prince, a promotion that clearly indicated the high estimation in which he was held by Hung Hsiu-ch'üan.

The Taipings soon followed up the victory over the Imperialist army north of Nanking with a clever strategy that destroyed the remainder of the siege forces still entrenched to the south of the capital. It was a plan apparently worked out by Li Hsiu-ch'eng in conjunction with Hung Jen-kan, the able new Prime Minister of the

Taiping government and a distant cousin of Hung Hsiu-ch'üan, who had returned to Nanking from the coast in 1859. With an impressive feint Li dispatched a force that succeeded in occupying Hangchow from March 19 to 23, 1860. The unwitting Imperialists rushed to the relief of that important city, seriously weakening their great camp south of Nanking. Li Hsiu-ch'eng's force, in a lightning move, doubled back from Hangchow and in coordination with an attack from the north by Ch'en Yü-ch'eng's troops, which had suddenly rushed in from Anking, the trap was sprung. The Imperialist army was crushed; its commanders, Ho-ch'un and Chang Kuo-liang, were killed.

The Taipings now devised a master strategy whereby they would first secure further territory in the lower Yangtze basin and on the coast, which would provide increased tax revenues and soldiers, and also enable them to receive supplies from foreigners. This would be left to Li Hsiu-ch'eng. After this was accomplished, Li would then proceed along the south bank of the Yangtze River, where at a designated point he would join with Ch'en Yü-ch'eng's army, and the combined force would then proceed to secure the upper Yangtze area as far as Wuhan.

Li Hsiu-ch'eng took Changchow on May 24 and Soochow on June 2, 1860. His policy toward the subjugated areas was characteristic of the man. He cautioned his troops to avoid alienating the population, specifically enjoining them not to kill either the inhabitants or their livestock, or to destroy property. Offenders were summarily executed. The disciplined Taiping army soon restored order, and their occupation contrasted sharply with that of the Imperialists. Li's good reputation spread rapidly throughout the heavily populated and well-endowed lower Yangtze region. Receptivity to the Taipings on the part of the population mounted. Li Hsiu-ch'eng was encouraged to proceed and take Shanghai by many Chinese and foreigners alike. A number of missionaries from Shanghai visited both Li Hsiu-ch'eng and Hung Jen-kan at Soochow. The meetings were invariably friendly.

It appears that had the powers not intervened at this point, the Taipings would have taken Shanghai, and subsequent Chinese history might have been altogether different. It is clear from the record that the Taipings tried to establish direct communications with Western diplomats in Shanghai, but in each case they were ignored by the latter. Both Li Hsiu-ch'eng and Hung Jen-kan wrote to the ministers and consuls residing at the treaty port, but their letters went unanswered. Nevertheless, Li Hsiu-ch'eng persisted in his efforts to reach some kind of accord with the powers through direct negotiation. The Taiping policy toward foreigners was, after all, quite respectable so that there could be no reason why the Western diplomats could not at least talk to them about the important unsettled question of Shanghai. When one foreigner was killed by Taipings in the environs of Shanghai, Li Hsiu-ch'eng had the soldier who was responsible executed and an apology was sent to the city. Li Hsiu-ch'eng established his headquarters at Zikawei, about six miles southwest of Shanghai, and quickly overcame the Imperialist outposts. On his approach to the walls of Shanghai his troops were suddenly fired upon by British and French soldiers. After several efforts to make contact, during which Li was wounded by shrapnel in his face, he decided to withdraw. Of utmost significance for understanding this engagement is the fact that although the Taipings sustained hundreds of casualties they did not return fire toward the foreigners, so that not a single British or French soldier was in jeopardy. Li's letter to the Western diplomats registered acute disappointment at this unfortunate reception, yet with surprising restraint and civility explained that he preferred to withdraw rather than provoke further misunderstandings with the foreigners. Unfortunately, however, the powers had already decided to abandon their long-compromised policy of neutrality in the Chinese civil war. Still, Li Hsiu-ch'eng and the Taipings hoped for a thaw in the foreigners' attitude, and while they were to predicate future policy considerations on this hope, it was to prove tragically forlorn in the end.

Another setback for the Taiping cause is generally believed to be Li Hsiu-ch'eng's failure to follow through with the major strategic plan agreed on earlier. Li was supposed to have met Ch'en Yü-ch'eng at the Yangtze River and with him move against Wuhan. As it turned out, Li arrived at the rendezvous three months late, in June 1861. By this time, Ch'en, leaving a subordinate at that place, had gone on to accomplish some of the mission on his own. As for Li, he found that the Yangtze was at high water and that communications were extremely difficult. We cannot be completely sure of his motives or reasoning at this point, but he must have felt that Ch'en would be able to finish the job in the west successfully on his own. Li was already late and the crossing of the river would have been dangerous. At the same time, the opportunity arose to expand his army with veterans from Shih Ta-k'ai's army who expressed their desire to join him. Consequently, Li swung into Kiangsi where he incorporated these men into his units, then moved back into Chekiang. Here Li Hsiu-ch'eng's vastly enlarged army enjoyed considerable success. By the end of December 1861 his forces controlled Hangchow and the port city of Ningpo. We can reasonably hypothesize that Li Hsiu-ch'eng was again trying to persuade Westerners of the desirability of treating with the Taipings. This time the practical experience of such a working relationship might speak louder and more convincingly than futile efforts to discuss such an eventuality. Thus the Taipings tried to prove at Ningpo that they were capable of responsible government where foreign interests were at stake, and that commerce with them could thrive profitably for the foreigners. And behind this specific, presumed Taiping objective were the again-demonstrated commendable domestic policies of Li Hsiuch'eng. In all of his victories Li showed consideration for his enemies. Government officials who were killed in action were buried with proper ceremony and those captured were accorded due respect. An appeal was made to officials of the Ch'ing to help govern in the new dispensation. Li provided coffins to refugees and supplied the needy with rice and interest-free loans until they could again support themselves.

Unfortunately, the hardline policy of Great Britain and France did not give the experiment at Ningpo a chance. Propagandist and inaccurate reporting distorted what the Taipings had accomplished at Ningpo and elsewhere. Allied with a pirate fleet, the British drove the Taipings from that important port city in May 1862 and handed it back to the Imperialists. And when Li Hsiu-ch'eng, after scrupulously respecting an agreement not to come within thirty miles of Shanghai for the period of one year, once again approached the environs of the city when the year ran out, his troops were suddenly attacked by British and French troops. Henceforth the powers gave determined, direct assistance to the Imperialists in the suppression of the Taipings. The Taiping policy of conciliation toward foreigners, and all of Li Hsiu-ch'eng's fine efforts and hopeful expectations, had been of no avail. Now, in the east, the Taipings could expect to fight both the Imperialists and the foreigners either in their employ or allied with them. The Taipings would fight, giving an heroic account of themselves and winning several signal victories for more than two years to come, succumbing in the end only to superior firepower, not will.

In the west, things also had gone disastrously for the Taipings. Ch'en Yü-ch'eng should have continued on his own to take Wuhan when it became apparent that Li Hsiu-ch'eng could not join him. One of the reasons Ch'en did not complete this mission, very interestingly, is because of foreign interference in his all-important strategy. A British official, Harry Parkes, dissuaded him from his intended course because of possible conflict with British interests. The abortive campaign led eventually to the fall of Anking itself on September 5, 1861, generally considered the key turning point of the war. The very capable Ch'en Yü-ch'eng, the Ying Wang, was pursued and finally killed in May 1862; Li Hsiu-ch'eng lost his best general.

Li Hsiu-ch'eng, at this time, was making progress on the Eastern front despite the fearful odds of combined Imperialist and foreign forces pitted against him, a combination which also enjoyed the mobility afforded by foreign naval transport. On May 21, 1862, Li Hsiu-ch'eng defeated both Li Hung-chang's army and Townsend Ward's so-called "Ever Victorious Army" at Taitsang. He quickly retook the cities of Chiating and Chingpu in the following three weeks, and subjected Sungchiang to an extended siege. Unfortunately, the Taiping capital, Nanking, was being closely pressed again by another brother of Tseng Kuo-fan, Tseng Kuo-ch'üan. Hung

Hsiu-ch'üan sent urgent messages to Li Hsiu-ch'eng urgently asking him to relieve the siege. In late August 1862 just as Sungchiang was about to fall, Li Hsiu-ch'eng returned from the area about Shanghai to Nanking. This crucial move, which dramatically illustrates Li's loyalty, tends to disprove the interpretation that he had been carving out for himself an independent kingdom. And this estimate is reinforced by our knowledge that Li Hsiu-ch'eng for long was prevented by the T'ien Wang from responding to the pleas of his generals holding Soochow and Hangchow, who were pressed by Li Hung-chang and Tso Tsung-t'ang respectively. When permission was finally granted to Li Hsiu-ch'eng to go to the relief of Soochow it was already too late. His initial assault on the siege was unsuccessful, and while he was preparing to attack from another direction, the eight Taiping leaders in Soochow surrendered to Li Hung-chang on December 5, 1863. The story of Li Hung-chang's perfidious treatment of these prisoners is well known; his execution of them, after having said he would not, stands in remarkable contrast to the erstwhile Taiping policy toward captured Imperialist officers.

Li Hsiu-ch'eng's response to Hung's appeal to relieve Nanking in August 1862 had had only negative success. He attacked Tseng Kuo-ch'üan's position incessantly for forty-six days after October 24, 1862, but was unable to remove Tseng. However, Li's assaults kept the pressure off Nanking. Afterwards Li made forays north of the Yangtze into Anhwei almost as far as Hupeh. But Li realized the gravity of the entire situation and the inconclusiveness of this kind of operation. He appealed to Hung to abandon Nanking and to move the seat of Taiping government to another region. Relocated in the Northwest, for example, the Taipings would be able to find a more strategically defensible capital and would be less vulnerable to attacks by foreign military units. Hung refused to follow this advice and Nanking was clearly foredoomed. Once again, however, we can see that Li Hsiu-ch'eng was not so wedded to an independent power base of his own that he would not abandon it to go elsewhere with the Taiping regime itself. And that Li did not leave the area on his own when his advice went unheeded, but stayed with the cause to the end, remains as mute testimony to his steadfast loyalty.

In fact, the remaining months of Li Hsiu-ch'eng's career could hardly have been more of a demonstration of faithfulness, of selfless comradeship, and of benevolent concern for his people. By March 31, 1864, Hangchow had fallen, and Nanking was the sole remaining principal city of the Taipings. It was under close siege, blockaded tightly with foreign help, and subjected to savage attacks. The prospects for the Taipings were at low ebb. In June 1864 Hung Hsiu-ch'üan died, and his personal supplies of rice were distributed by Li to the starving poor of the city, and his money to his soldiers. On July 19, 1864, Nanking finally fell. What followed must go down as one of the greatest bloodbaths in history. In addition to the hundreds of Taipings who took their own lives, thousands more were mercilessly killed by Tseng's troops. Most of the buildings erected by the Taipings were destroyed, as was most of anything that might in any way testify to the very existence of the proud revolutionary movement.

In the midst of this holocaust, Li Hsiu-ch'eng, taking with him Hung Fu, the son of and successor to Hung Hsiu-ch'üan, the Heavenly King, and several hundred others, escaped out of the city. Li gave his own best war horse to the young Heavenly King in perhaps a crowning gesture of loyalty and concern. Tragically, however, the horse which was left for himself was a poor one, and was unable to travel swiftly or far. Before daybreak, Li was forced to hide in the ruins of a temple atop a hill called Fangshan near Nanking. There he rested as best he could, relieving himself of his burden of jewels and silver, which were the best kind of negotiable securities that might be useful in his flight. Suddenly he noticed several villagers approaching, and leaving his possessions, he ran off a short distance. The peasants gave chase and caught him, but when they discovered that he was the beloved Chung Wang, they knelt before him. They hid Li for two days, but unfortunately his personal treasure, which had been discovered by another group of local folk, became the subject of a quarrel that came to the attention of one of Tseng Kuo-ch'uan's generals. This led to Li's capture on July 22, 1864.

While being held captive in Nanking, Li Hsiu-ch'eng was interrogated by Tseng Kuo-fan and ordered to put his answers in writing. From July 30 to August 7, 1864, Li wrote his famous autobiography, which included the story of the entire Taiping movement, as well as his own role in it. This is an eloquent and amazing document, however controversial it may be. It attests to the formidable multi-faceted talent of Li, who without appreciable formal education, and while under considerable duress, was able to write about 4,500 words per day. Even more intriguing is the possibility that, as he wrote, the quick-witted Li may have been devising a clever stratagem that would turn the tables on his captors. There is considerable plausibility to this interpretation. It is consistent with Li's character. On the other hand, the alternative, that the evidences of treacherous and flattering commentary in his autobiography and of the alleged pleading for his own life points to an eleventh hour cowardice and treachery to the Taiping cause on his part, is not consistent with what we know of the man.

Li Hsiu-ch'eng knew that personally he was in a desperate, almost hopeless position. However, he may have had a far different estimate of the over-all situation. He knew that even though Nanking was lost, and with it some 10,000 men, the Taipings still possessed an army in the field numbering between 200,000 and 300,000 men under the command of several capable generals including Li Shih-hsien in Kiangsi, Huang Wen-chin in Kuangteh and Huchow, and Ch'en Te-ts'ai at Macheng in Hupeh. The army was located on both sides of the Yangtze River and in a favorable position for im-plementing an earlier made plan for withdrawing to the Northwest, where it might maintain itself as a continuing threat to the Ch'ing dynasty. He had long considered Nanking to be dispensable. Very importantly the young Heavenly King was alive—Li had seen to this himself—and constituted the rallying point for the Taipings. But Li realized that the fall of Nanking had shaken the revolution-aries. Time was required in order to give them a chance to regroup for the move to the Northwest, and to regain confidence that the cause was not lost.

Although circumstances severely limited the chances for helping his comrades, Li Hsiu-ch'eng was determined to use whatever means were available, however restricted these might be, in order to buy time for the Taipings. He knew that in being a prisoner of Tseng's, and in being interrogated by him, Li himself was in a position to learn what the Ch'ing forces knew and what they needed to know. He also had the opportunity to observe Tseng Kuo-fan, and to determine his apprehensions and desires. Tseng's troops were in poor condition and mutinous. The prospect of facing the large Taiping army, whether in large units or as disorganized fragments spread over the countryside, was not a pleasant one. Tseng greatly desired a quick and complete victory. Only a total victory could ensure a successful pacification program afterwards.

Li Hsiu-ch'eng sized up this situation and made his clever ploy. He proposed to Tseng Kuo-fan a deceptively attractive plan whereby the entire Taiping army might be disbanded quickly and effortlessly. The plan consisted of ten measures to be undertaken by Tseng. These included pardoning Taiping soldiers and granting permits for them to return home safely, ceasing the killing of people in and around Nanking (so that the news of Tseng's "leniency" would soon persuade others that resistance was no longer necessary), and promulgating a general amnesty throughout the country. Li suggested the technical means whereby this all might be accomplished, and emphasized the need to utilize kindness rather than slaughter in order to pacify the country. Along with the plan Li included in his writings many comments designed purposely to lull Tseng. Aside from many references to shortcomings of the Taipings, and the flattery of Tseng, Li managed to convey the impression that the Taiping army was in disarray and in full flight, which Li knew to be untrue. Likewise, Li indicated that the young Heavenly King was dead, although he knew better. The purpose was to protect the young Heavenly King and to convey the impression that there was no urgent need to pursue the Taipings, who did need some respite. The Taipings would not have lost control of the stratagem, Li reasoned, because Tseng lacked both the necessary military strength and the personal ability to carry it out. As it turned out, the deception was partially successful. Judging from his subsequent moves, it is clear that Tseng was deceived as to the young T'ien

Wang's death, thus allowing him to escape, and Tseng was equally misled regarding the condition of the Taiping force in the south so that his measures against it were badly timed.

It is evident that Li Hsiu-ch'eng was not begging for his own life, as the Communist line currently holds. His plan had been a selfless one. Giving Li the most credit, it was a clever scheme, designed to help perpetuate the Taiping Revolution. At the very least, as Jen Yu-wen believes, it was intended for the benefit of the people as a whole, and to save his own relatives. As for himself, Li Hsiu-ch'eng was prepared to die. Tseng Kuo-fan, finished with his captive and unaware that he had been deceived, had Li Hsiu-ch'eng executed at midnight on August 7, 1864. Tseng sought to efface Li's heroic image by making extensive revisions in the autobiography. He even planted the word "surrender" into the text, perhaps to make Li appear to be less of a hero for ostensibly desiring to surrender, a theme readily and ironically echoed by Party historians today. It does not seem likely, however, that ephemeral political requirements will for long submerge a more appropriate memory of Li Hsiu-ch'eng, who certainly remains one of China's outstanding revolutionary heroes.

BIBLIOGRAPHICAL NOTE: Among the works which the reader might consult in looking deeper into this intriguing biography, the following, representative of different points of view, are especially recommended: Jen Yu-wen, *T'ai-p'ing t'ien-kuo ch'üan-shih* (Complete History of the Taiping Heavenly Kingdom), 3 vols. (Hong Kong, 1962). *Li Hsiu-ch'eng ch'in-kung show-chi* (Li Hsiu-ch'eng's Personal Deposition in His Own Handwriting) (Taipei, 1962); an English translation, abridged and otherwise revised version of this authentic document is: W. T. Lay (tr.), *The Autobiography of the Chung-wang* (Shanghai, 1895). Lo Erh-kang, "Chung-wang Li Hsiu-ch'eng k'u-jou huan-ping-chi k'ao" ("An Examination of the Loyal Prince Li Hsiu-ch'eng's Plan of Self-Sacrifice To Delay the Enemy"), *Li-shih yen-chiu*, No. 4 (1964), pp. 21–80. Franz Michael, *The Taiping Rebellion* (University of Washington Press, 1966—). Teng Ssu-yü, "Li Hsiu-ch'eng," *Eminent Chinese of the Ch'ing*

Period (1644–1912), ed. Arthur W. Hummel (U.S. Government Printing Office, 1943–44), I, 459–63. Stephen Uhalley, Jr., "The Controversy over Li Hsiu-ch'eng: An Ill-timed Centenary," *The Journal of Asian Studies*, XXV, No. 2 (February 1966), pp. 305–17.

❖ II ❖

THE REPUBLICAN REVOLUTION

EDITOR'S INTRODUCTION

The Republican Revolution is known as the "Revolution of 1911," a term generally used by historians to refer not only to the Wuchang Revolution of 1911 but also to a series of revolutionary events that took place between 1894 and 1912. It may even be argued that it ended with the death of Yüan Shih-k'ai and Huang Hsing in 1916, the year in which the so-called "first phase" of the revolution really came to an end. For the failure of the Republic did not come to a logical end until Yüan's attempt to become emperor in 1915. The "second revolution" of 1913 was merely a continuation of the war of 1911. The only difference was that in 1911 Yüan was fighting an unpopular war for an alien regime against the revolutionaries without the support of foreign powers, while in 1913 he fought for his own power with funds supplied by imperialist foreign governments. The "counter-revolution" of 1913 was a prelude to the monarchical movement, although the enthronement was postponed and finally canceled.

Yüan's death in 1916 provided a way out of an extremely difficult

Part of these introductory remarks were presented in a lecture delivered by the editor at the Oriental Institute of the Czechoslovak Academy of Sciences, Prague, June 1970.

situation. It was followed by a ten-year struggle for power among warlords ending in 1927 when China was nominally united under Chiang Kai-shek. Within the revolutionary party, no leader could "rank with" Sun Yat-sen after the death of Huang Hsing. Henceforth, in military affairs Sun had to depend on regional military leaders of lesser stature. The vacancy of Huang's military leadership in the revolutionary party was not filled until the founding of the Whampoa Military Academy and the emergence of Chiang Kai-shek in the 1920's.

Causes of the Revolution

The era in which the Chinese Republican Revolution took place was also an age of upheaval in other parts of the world. In the decade after 1910 the great monarchies of Europe tore themselves to pieces. The Wuchang Revolution of October 10, 1911 led to the overthrow of the alien Manchu dynasty which had lasted 268 years and to the establishment of the Republic of China in place of a monarchical system that had existed in China for more than two thousand years. It was the culmination of many decades of growing discontent among the people, and was caused in part by the decay of Manchu rule, foreign aggression, and the interplay of internal and external forces.

Internally, there were wars, rebellions, slaughters, economic dislocation, and famines in the country at one time or another: The Taiping Rebellion in the Yangtze valley (1850–64), the Nien uprisings in north China (1851–68), the Moslem revolt in the Southwest (1855–73), and in the Northwest (1862–73). In addition, the unrest of the peasantry, the rise of the bourgeois class, the intellectual ferment, and the shift of power from Manchus to Chinese in the government after the Taiping Rebellion hastened the downfall of the alien regime.

Externally, China was repeatedly invaded during the seven decades between 1840 and 1910. Twice the capital, Peking, was occupied by foreign armies. China fought and lost five wars: the Opium War against the British invaders (1840–42), a war against the joint forces of Britain and France (1857–60), the undeclared Franco-Chinese War (1884–85), the Sino-Japanese War (1894–95), and the invasion of China by the expeditionary forces of eight powers in 1900. As a result, China paid heavy indemnities, opened more than nineteen ports to foreign trade, permitted foreign ships to navigate upon her rivers, recognized the most-favored nation clause, and signed agreements which led to the loss of her tariff autonomy and to the exemption of foreigners from Chinese legal jurisdiction. China legalized opium trade and recognized the right of missionaries to preach Christianity and to own property anywhere in the interior. Foreign armies obtained the privilege of stationing in a number of areas within the country. Hong Kong, Kowloon, Taiwan, the Pescadores and other territories were ceded. All the territory on the left or northern bank of the Amur River, and the territory between the Ussuri and the sea, where Vladivostok was founded, were ceded to Russia. Port Arthur and Dairen in the Liaotung Peninsula, Kiaochow Bay and Weihaiwei in Shantung province, New Territory in Kowloon, and Kwangchow Bay in south China were leased out for twenty-five to ninety-nine years, along with railway, mining, and other concessions. Not only was China divided into a number of spheres of influence by foreign powers, she also lost what control, direct or indirect, *de facto* or *de jure*, she had exercised over a number of dependent vassal states in the Empire, including Vietnam, Laos, Cambodia, Burma, Sikkim, the Ryukyu Islands, and Korea.

Political Goal of the Revolution

Contrary to the views held by some historians both in China and abroad, the ultimate political goal of the Republican Revolution was never merely the overthrow of the Manchu dynasty. The real aim was to save China from internal crises and foreign domination. The overthrow of alien rule was the means to an end, since it was believed that as long as the Manchus were in power, there was little hope for China. This becomes perfectly clear if, instead of accepting the erstwhile statements that came after the failure of the Republic, we read contemporary revolutionary documents and statements of revolutionary leaders.

The Revolutionary Movement

The initial stage of the Republican revolutionary movement was marked by the founding of the Honolulu Hsing Chung Hui (Revive China Society) in 1894. This was followed by two abortive armed revolts in 1895 and 1900. The second period, between 1901 and 1905, consisted of greatly accelerated anti-Manchu movements that occurred both in China and abroad. The movement in this second period had no unified organization and no single dominant figure. It was not until the formation of the T'ung Meng Hui (United League) in 1905, under the dual leadership of Sun Yat-sen (1866–1925) and Huang Hsing (1874–1916), that a truly unified revolutionary organization emerged. It was to play the leading role in the overthrow of the Manchu dynasty and the establishment of the Republic of China in 1912.

The dual leadership of Sun and Huang offers a key to the understanding of the revolutionary movement in the decade after 1905. In many ways the two were ideal collaborators. Sun enjoyed seniority both in age and in the revolutionary movement. He had firsthand knowledge of the Western world, then much admired by young Chinese revolutionaries. He was a Western-educated Cantonese with connections abroad and great ability, actual or potential, for raising funds. Huang, as a Hunanese of the literati class, belonged to the elite of Chinese society. He had closer contacts with Chinese intellectuals and military circles than did Sun, and was a leader among Japanese-educated Chinese students who formed a new literati which supplied many leaders for the emerging revolutionary organization.

Aside from the impact of the West, foreign aggression, and the incompetence and self-delusion of the Manchu rulers, the overthrow of the Manchu dynasty was affected by the interplay of three forces:

the revolutionary movement led by the T'ung Meng Hui, the Constitutionalists (particularly those members of the provincial assemblies who joined the revolutionaries *after* the Wuchang revolution), and the defection of Yüan Shih-k'ai from the central government.

The revolutionary movement relied mainly on three groups: students, overseas Chinese, and the New Army. Secret society members played a significant part in the early stage of the movement, but their role was a minor one in the final stage of the revolution. Many writings, both in Chinese and English, have at times exaggerated the importance of secret society members in the overthrow of the Manchu dynasty.

It is true that many of the soldiers who took part in the Wuchang revolution were perhaps secret society members. But they were soldiers turned rebels. They were not under the command of the secret societies; nor did they act in their capacity as members of these societies. The scholars (e.g. Professor Mary C. Wright) who quote Mao Tse-tung and Chu Teh out of context to prove the importance of the secret society members overlook the differentiation of role and confuse the contributions of the secret society members at the beginning of the revolutionary movement with their minor role after 1910. Besides, Chu and Mao are hardly authorities on the subject.

Furthermore, to argue that rebel soldiers were secret society members, and therefore, that secret society members played a leading role in the revolution, may lead to a similar "logical" but absurd conclusion with regard to their contributions in the Communist movement: Many poor peasants and unemployed who joined the Red Army were secret society members; therefore, credit should be given to them rather than to the Communist Party and the Army for the final Communist victory.

The revolution succeeded mainly through the efforts of the Chinese. Some scholars claim that American financing, training, and equipment were indispensable to the Chinese Revolution of 1911. Nothing can be further from the truth. Funds raised abroad from overseas Chinese communities were crucial during the revolutionary movement, but they came mainly from Southeast Asia, not from the United States.

The revolutionary movement was, for the most part, instigated from abroad. Having no separate army of its own, the revolutionary party used as its troops the army of the Manchu government. This was not a unique situation in history, for other revolutionaries had used government troops to overthrow their governments. On the whole, there was little fighting, except in Hankow, Hanyang, and Nanking. The provincial authorities fled as soon as rebels started to take action in provincial cities. The Constitutionalists, who at first favored a constitutional monarchical government, joined the revolution voluntarily or as a matter of expediency. However, they were not necessarily opportunists. It should be stressed that, although they contributed a great deal to the final collapse of the Manchu dynasty, they were merely responding to a situation created by the revolutionaries.

Unlike the experience of the Communist leaders whose victory came at the end of a civil war that lasted over twenty years, the revolutionary leaders of 1911 faced the overwhelming problems of a "liberated" China almost overnight. The Communist leaders had the advantage of military, political, and administrative experience in the Communist movement, whereas the top leaders of the Republican Revolution had no similar experience whatsoever. The T'ung Meng Hui had never established a significant power base in the North; and even in the South their success was not based on solid grounds. Yüan Shih-k'ai, therefore, played a very important role in the downfall of the Manchu dynasty. But it would be a mistake to classify him in the category of revolutionary leader.

Yüan Shih-k'ai

It is well known that the main source of Yüan's strength was his New Army and the confidence of foreign powers in him as the "strong man." Despite financial problems and his difficulties with the high command in the Manchu military, which placed Chinese graduates of the Japanese Imperial Military College into the Peiyang Army, and the unreliability of certain generals in the north, Yüan still had under his command the best division troops in the entire country.

Historical interpretations vary according to the era in which they are written. It is, however, difficult for an objective "bourgeois scholar" to understand how serious American scholars of the 1960's still interpret the Revolution of 1911 in a light favorable to Yüan Shih-k'ai, but at the same time are *unnecessarily* overly critical of the revolutionary leaders who aspired to the establishment of a democratic system. Is this "revisionist" view a reaction to the Kuomintang line, or the return of the "traditional" Western view that has always favored counter-revolution rather than revolution in colonial and semi-colonial countries? It was, after all, the illegal "reorganization loan" of £25,000,000 given by foreign powers that contributed to Yüan's victory over the revolutionaries in 1913, a victory which *The New York Times* considered "desirable for the peace of the world." The very man who was going to destroy the Republic was praised by the contemporary London *Times* as "the only man who can prevent the Chinese Republic from falling to pieces." If the London *Times* did not know better then, historians should have ample evidence now to judge Yüan's character and motivation.

Judging by Yüan's life story, one would hesitate to say much of anything in his favor. Putting aside the controversy over whether he had betrayed the reformers in the "Hundred Days' Reform" of 1898, there is sufficient evidence to show that he had defected from the Manchu Court only after he had been assured of the presidency of the Republic. One may question whether he instigated the Peking mutiny of 1912, but the fact remains that he declined to leave Peking for Nanking on the grounds of the mutiny. One may argue that he was forced by circumstances to align himself with the revolution, rather than that he wanted to betray the Manchu government that he served. However, what force other than his own personal ambition compelled him to become an emperor? Indeed, Yüan's aspiration to the throne from the very day he resumed power in

Peking is suggested in a dispatch, dated November 14, 1911, and marked "very confidential," in which British Minister Jordan informed the British Foreign Office of his conversation with a son of Yüan Shih-k'ai who arrived in Peking only the day before, anxious to anticipate British reactions to some of Yüan's intentions. Young Yüan intimated that "A republic would be only a transitional stage, and that his father might be acclaimed Emperor."

T'ung Meng Hui

The students who played a leading role in the revolutionary movement were not all missionary school students. Western historians who usually had no contacts with non-English-speaking students were inclined to overemphasize the importance of those who could converse with them in English. It is true that a handful of Chinese leaders and diplomats with whom the Westerners were more familiar were of Christian family background and of missionary school education in China or abroad. Their education provided them with a better knowledge of Western history and literature than that of their own country.

The students, especially "returned students" from Japan, provided the leadership of the T'ung Meng Hui, which, though not as tightly disciplined and well organized as some of the subsequent parties in China, represented nevertheless the mainstream of the revolutionary movement. Some American scholars confused the mainstream of the revolutionary movement with that of China's national life. Few revolutionary movements of the world are within the mainstream of national life; they are always the activities of a small dedicated group.

It would be impossible to explain the leadership of the provisional government in Nanking without seeing the T'ung Meng Hui as the mainstream of the revolutionary movement. I believe my book *Huang Hsing and the Chinese Revolution*, contrary to the Kuomintang line, was the first scholarly writing in English that gave due credit to the local revolutionaries and organizations in Hupeh for their contributions to the Wuchang revolution. It should be pointed out once again, however, that the great majority of these local revolutionaries were soldiers who provided neither national nor regional leadership after the outbreak of the Wuchang revolution; even in Wuhan the leadership was provided by the T'ung Meng Hui leaders or by Li Yüan-hung, who was forced to assume leadership at gun point. Furthermore, the Literary Society's claim that it had 3000 members in Wuhan is statistically questionable. This figure, like so many Chinese statistics, cannot be verified with certainty. On the other hand, there were 963 members of the T'ung Meng Hui in the first two years of its existence. An authentic T'ung Meng Hui record shows not only the names of these members, but also the dates when they joined the organization and the names of those who introduced them. No intelligent student would ever compare the membership of these two organizations without taking into consideration the qualitative difference and the over-all picture. To deny that the T'ung Meng was the mainstream of the revolutionary movement, on the bases of questionable statistics and a short period of local developments, is manifestly wrong.[1]

Loss of perspective is perhaps partly due to the exclusive identification of Sun Yat-sen with T'ung Meng Hui leadership. If students had paid more attention to the Hunanese faction of the T'ung Meng Hui, they would have seen the significant relationship between the Central China Bureau of the T'ung Meng Hui and the local revolutionaries in Hupeh. They would not have so conveniently overlooked the fact that developments of the local revolutionary organizations in Hupeh can be traced to their connections with Huang Hsing's early revolutionary activities, and that the local Hupeh revolutionists repeatedly postponed their revolts in order to wait for Huang's arrival.

Western Scholarship

Historians remote from the actors and the scene sometimes present

[1] For different, and what I consider erroneous, facts and interpretations of several crucial points on the Revolution of 1911, see Mary C. Wright, "Introduction," *China in Revolution: The First Phase 1900–1913* (Yale University Press, 1968), p. 46.

a superficial picture of history and make specious arguments. If they are further influenced by a party line or a cultural gap, intelligent interpretation becomes more difficult. In the United States, studies on leadership of the 1911 Revolution reflected some significant progress in the 1960's. It began with the publication of an article in 1960, "Sun Yat-sen, Yang Ch'ü-yün, and the Early Revolutionary Movement in China," which is included in this section. The article reveals for the first time in an English scholarly journal the important role of Yang Ch'ü-yün and his group in the "first revolutionary attempt of Sun Yat-sen." It also points out that for sixteen years after the first abortive revolt in 1895, Sun Yat-sen never set foot on the China mainland until two and a half months after the Wuchang revolution in 1911, with the exception of an overnight stay on the Kwangsi-Vietnam border in 1907.

Furthermore, it was not until the publication of my own book, *Huang Hsing and the Chinese Revolution,* in 1961 that the massive Chinese documents and other data pertaining to the revolution were examined for the first time in English. Until then Huang's role in the Revolution of 1911 was almost completely neglected in Western literature dealing with the overthrow of the Manchu dynasty;[2] Sun Yat-sen alone was identified with the founding of

---

[2] There are a few exceptions. As early as 1914 Huang Hsing had been called the "real leader" of the revolution in John J. A. Mullowney's *A Revelation of the Chinese Revolution*; "the George Washington of China" by Paul Myron (pseud. Paul Linebarger) in *Our Chinese Chances Through European War* (1915); and the "Trotsky of China" by T'ang Leang-li in *The Inner History of the Chinese Revolution* (1930). Furthermore, in Linebarger's book *Sun Yat-sen and the Chinese Republic* (1925), a chapter entitled "Sun and Hwang" was devoted to the dual leadership of Sun and Huang.

It is interesting to note, however, that in the late 1960's some Western historians still unconsciously followed the Kuomintang line of crediting Sun Yat-sen for accomplishments that Sun does not deserve. For example, Donald G. Gillin in his *Warlord Yen Hsi-shan in Shansi Province 1911–1949* (Princeton University Press, 1967, p. 13) gives credit to Sun Yat-sen for recruiting Yen Hsi-shan to join the T'ung Meng Hui and for organizing some of Yen's fellow students into a Blood and Iron Society in Tokyo. These tasks were performed, in fact, by Huang Hsing, whose name was not even mentioned once in the book. An original T'ung Meng Hui record shows unmistakably that it was Huang who recruited Yen to join the T'ung Meng Hui.

the Republic.[3] In 1968, Harold Z. Schiffrin's "The Enigma of Sun Yat-sen" was published.[4] It is the best study of Sun Yat-sen now available. In the same year, his excellent book, *Sun Yat-sen and the Origins of the Chinese Revolution,* was published by the University of California Press.

The contributions of these writings can only be appreciated against the background of ignorance. The dramatic description of Sun Yat-sen's activities "in the interior of China" by James Cantlie and C. Sheridan Jones in their book *Sun Yat-sen and the Awakening of China* (London, 1912) was nothing but fiction. J. O. Bland, a long-time resident of China and a noted British "China-watcher" at the beginning of this century, named Sun Yat-sen, T'ang Shao-i, and Li Yüan-hung as the "three men who made the revolution" of 1911.[5] At that time China was an "open society." Foreigners enjoyed all kinds of privileges including the convenience of gathering news and intelligence. In reviewing Bland's book, *Recent Events and Present Policies of China,* in 1913, a good-natured Chinese writer was so irritated by Bland's misinformation and misinterpretation of Chinese politics that he could not help but quip: "If Meng can be Mao then Bland can be Blind!"

In 1931, Yale University Press published Henry B. Restarick's book, *Sun Yat-sen: Liberator of China.* An entire chapter was devoted to the "Unlucky Plan of Revolt in 1904," in which Sun Yat-sen was found at the secret headquarters in Canton personally directing the plot. But the whole chapter was nothing but fiction. It is more than ironical that the book is prefaced by the author with the following remark: "All recent books on China mention Sun Yat-sen; but statements about his early years, as a rule, are singularly inaccurate and misleading."

[3] Of course, it is not uncommon in world history that one leader received more credit than those who became obscure. Hung Ta-ch'üan in the Taiping Rebellion, Huang Hsing in the Republican Revolution, Chu Teh in the Communist movement, and Trotsky in the Russian Revolution are good examples.

[4] Wright, *op. cit.* pp. 443–74.

[5] Li was forced by the rebels to lead the revolution *after* it had broken out, or face execution on the spot. T'ang was sent by Yüan Shih-k'ai to negotiate for peace with the revolutionaries.

Because of ignorance and the prejudice of Western observers toward the Revolution of 1911, any studies on the subject based exclusively on contemporary Western sources should be used with great caution.

The Leaders

The article on Huang Hsing, written by two Communist historians and translated for this volume, merits attention partly because it is the major study on the subject in the twenty years of Communist China. The authors interpret the Revolution of 1911 from Communist viewpoints, and curiously enough accept the Kuomintang line on several important, debatable points, especially when Sun Yat-sen is involved. However, their criticisms of Huang Hsing are not always justified. For example, Huang was even criticized for showing too much interest in developing mines, railways, modern banking systems, and other private enterprises. But this criticism does suggest that Kuomintang historians are wrong in repeatedly claiming that Sun Yat-sen alone emphasized such economic projects.

Other articles in this section deal with Tsou Jung (1885–1905) and Ch'en T'ien-hua (1875–1905), whose anti-Manchu writings held a prominent place in the Republican Revolution. Tsou was probably the first to coin the term, "The Republic of China" (Chung-hua min-kuo). His tract, Ko-ming chün (The Revolutionary Army), offered a constructive post-revolutionary program, and it appeared two years before the publication of Sun Yat-sen's own formative ideas on the Three People's Principles. Part I of the article is a biographical sketch, and Part II contains a full translation of his pamphlet.

Among Huang Hsing's close followers and friends from Hunan province, Ch'en T'ien-hua (1875–1905) and Sung Chiao-jen (1882–1913) possessed the greatest literary talents.[6] They were members of Huang's Society for the Revival of China (Hua Hsing Hui) before

[6] Others may include Chang Shih-chao (1881–) and Yang Shou-jen. Chang, however, never joined the T'ung Meng Hui, but worked for Huang as a secretary and friend. Chang later served as a defense lawyer for Ch'en Tu-hsiu after the latter was arrested by the Kuomintang in 1933. He has lived long enough to serve another Hunanese, Mao Tse-tung, after 1949.

joining the T'ung Meng Hui. The dominant ideology of Huang's revolutionary organization was nationalism. However, the Society for the Revival of China left practically no documentary records. To a certain extent, the writings of Ch'en T'ien-hua and Yang Shou-jen (1872–1911) reflected the "party line." [7] Professor Ernest P. Young's article in this section ably presents Ch'en T'ien-hua's "thoughts and problems."

After Ch'en T'ien-hua's death in 1905, Sung Chiao-jen became the best writer of the Hunan group in the revolutionary organization, T'ung Meng Hui. His assassination in 1913 at the age of thirty-one terminated the embryonic period of the democratic system and led to military rule in China in the subsequent fifteen years. The article, "A Chinese Democrat," sketches his life and may also be used as a case study of military usurpation as well as a study of the relations between democrats and the military in developing countries.

Hu Han-min (1879–1936) and Wang Ching-wei (1883–1944) were two devoted followers of Sun Yat-sen. Their relationship to Sun was similar to that of Sung Chiao-jen to Huang Hsing. Like Sun Yat-sen, both Hu and Wang were from Kwangtung province, and both were contenders for the Kuomintang leadership after Sun's death in 1925. Both were consistent opponents of Chiang Kai-shek after the 1920's, but both also lacked the military power necessary for the struggle. Hu was governor of Kwangtung after the success of the 1911 Revolution, and President of the Legislative Yüan between 1928 and 1931. He never reached the status of a national leader, but was a major figure in regional politics. His interpretations of the Kuomintang dogma were never given official recognition by the party. Professor Melville T. Kennedy's article ably deals with his career and thought.

[7] In a pamphlet entitled *The New Hunan* (Hsin Hu-nan) written in 1903, Yang Shou-jen stressed the importance of violent revolution and a "spirit of destruction." But his advocacy of anarchism, assassination, and terror did not represent Huang Hsing's revolutionary strategy. Born of an official family and a holder of the *Chü-jen* degree, Yang Shou-jen (also known as Yang Tu-sheng or Yang Yu-lin) committed suicide in England after the failure of the Canton revolution of 1911. He bequeathed all his savings to Huang for revolutionary purposes. It was Yang's brother whose daughter married Mao Tse-tung in 1920.

After the success of the Wuchang Revolution, Chang Ping-lin, who was the leader of the Restoration Society (Kuang Fu Hui) faction in the T'ung Meng Hui and also editor of the revolutionary journal *Min-pao,* remarked that if the President of China were to be chosen on the basis of personal contributions to the revolution then Huang Hsing should be chosen; but if ability were the criterion, then Sung Chiao-jen; and if virtue were the deciding factor, then Wang Ching-wei would have to be selected. The career of Wang Ching-wei, analyzed in Professor Howard Boorman's article in this section, was highlighted by his attempt to assassinate the Manchu regent in 1910, his leadership of the Kuomintang left and his struggle for power with Chiang Kai-shek in the 1920's, and finally by his position as head of a Japanese-sponsored government in Nanking in the 1940's.

All the leaders whose political profiles are presented in this section grew up in a period of political corruption and national crisis in China. It was a period when provincial sentiment was strong, and personal politics dominant. But unlike some of the subsequent Kuomintang officials and politicians, none of these leaders accumulated personal wealth while they were in power. Their integrity has never been questioned.

Politics is the art of the possible. Criticisms of the shortcomings of the Chinese revolutionary leaders should be balanced by recognition of their positive achievements. After all, only a few years before the outbreak of the Wuchang Revolution they were young students. Their agitation and struggle finally led to the overthrow of the Manchu dynasty and the ending of the immemorial monarchical system of China. To that extent, at least, the Revolution of 1911 was a success.

Failure of Democracy in China

Besides the overthrow of the Manchu dynasty, the leaders of the Revolution of 1911 were interested in democracy and the modernization of China, two goals that have yet to be realized. "Anti-imperialism" did not become an explicit slogan until after 1919. The failure of democracy in the early years of the Republic has often been explained in terms of the tradition and apathy of the masses. However, that tradition alone cannot explain the failure of democracy in China; nor can it be attributed to the gap between the elites and the masses. The politically conscious elements are frequently a small minority in any system. It is unfair to compare the politics of Republican China in 1912–13 with that of Western democracies of today. Comparison is meaningful only in similar stages of evolution and development. There was a time when the Western states were facing problems similar to those of China in the early years of the Republic. One may even argue that the performance of China's elites in 1912–13 was not worse, perhaps actually better, than that of their counterparts at the initial stage of democracy in the West.

A democratic system needs time to develop and mature. Sun Yat-sen was the Provisional President for six weeks. Huang Hsing was in power for six months, including the time he served as the Resident-General of Nanking. All in all they had a year and a half before Yüan Shih-k'ai provoked them into undertaking the unsuccessful "second revolution" in 1913. What would have happened to American democracy if, after the American Revolution, the President of the United States had not been George Washington but a Yüan Shih-k'ai who was not content merely to be President for life, but wished to be emperor and to establish military rule with the support of foreign "democracies"?

China's problems in the early years of the Republic, indeed the problems of some emerging nations today, may be similar to those of France in the sixteenth or the eighteenth century. In terms of literacy, suffrage, communication, transportation, political participation—and all other elements that make democracy work—one should compare the China of 1912–13 with the United States of 1776 or the France of 1789. The Chinese revolutionary leaders who believed in modern democracy were not supported by Western democracies. The governments of Western democracies instead supported Yüan Shih-k'ai, the "strong man" who turned out to be responsible for destroying the embryonic democratic system by military force. Is this the way "to make the world safe for democracy"?

❦ 5 ❦

Sun Yat-sen, Yang Ch'ü-yün, and the Early Revolutionary Movement in China

CHÜN-TU HSÜEH

Sun Yat-sen is well known as the founder of the Hsing Chung Hui (Revive China Society), but few realize that Yang Ch'ü-yün was the first chairman of that revolutionary organization, retaining the position for nearly five years, and that Yang also played a significant role in what is now known as the "first revolutionary attempt of Sun Yat-sen." According to a veteran revolutionary, although Sun planned to overthrow the alien Manchu dynasty in 1895, he was not opposed to a monarchical institution if the new emperor were to be Chinese. Yang, on the other hand, insisted on the republican form of government.[1] This article is a study of the interplay of their leadership and the Chinese revolutionary movement from 1895 to 1900.

Yang Ch'ü-yün, known as Yeung Ku Wan in his time, was born on December 16, 1861 in Hong Kong. His father was a school teacher and government interpreter. Yang's grandfather, a native of Fukien

Reprinted with permission from *The Journal of Asian Studies* (USA), Vol. XIX, No. 3 (May 1960), pp. 307–18. Some significant changes in the text and footnotes have been made.

[1] Liu Ch'eng-yü, "Hsien tsung-li chiu te lu" (My Reminiscences of Sun Yat-sen), *Kuo-shih kuan kuan-k'an* (Publications of the National Historical Bureau), Vol. I, No. 1 (Nanking, 1946), pp. 48–49. Liu claimed that Sun Yat-sen personally revealed the story to him one day in the former's newspaper office in San Francisco. No specific date was given by Liu, but it was probably in 1910.

province, left China and settled in Penang, Malaya, where Yang's father was born. His father, however, returned to Fukien at about sixteen and then settled in Hong Kong. At fourteen Yang Ch'ü-yün was apprenticed to the Hong Kong Naval Dockyard, but this apprenticeship was cut short because of an accident which resulted in the amputation of three fingers from his right hand. Subsequently, he studied at an English school and, after graduation, taught at a local high school, St. Joseph College. He later became chief shipping clerk at the China Merchants' Steam Navigation Company. In the spring of 1895, when he cooperated with Sun Yat-sen to form the Hsing Chung Hui, he was an assistant manager at David Sassoon, Sons & Co., a British shipping company in Hong Kong.[2]

By March 14, 1892, Yang had founded an organization called the Chinese Patriotic Mutual Improvement Association (Fu-jen wen-she, or Fu Jen Literary Society). The aims of this association were: "(1) To purify the character to the highest possible degree; (2) to prohibit indulgence in the vices of this world; (3) to set an example for future young Chinese; (4) to improve in all possible ways Chinese and foreign knowledge from both a civil and a military point of view; (5) to obtain a good knowledge of Western science, and learning; [and] (6) to learn how to be and act as a patriot, and how to wipe out the unjust wrongs our country has suffered. [The motto was] *Ducit Amor Patriæ* [Be Whole-heartedly Patriotic]."[3]

Among the seven founding members of the Chinese Patriotic

[2] For a biographical sketch of Yang Ch'ü-yün, see *Yang Ch'ü-yün lüeh-shih* (Hong Kong, 1927) by an unknown author; also Feng Tzu-yu, *Ko-ming i-shih* (Fragments of the History of the Revolution), I (Changsha, 1939), 6–8, and V (Shanghai, 1947), 8–15; and Ch'en Shao-pai, *Hsing-chung-hui ko-ming shih-yao* (A Brief Revolutionary History of the Hsing Chung Hui) (reprint; Taipei, 1956), p. 55. When a Chinese or Japanese author has two or more works cited for the second time, a shortened form of the English translation of the title will be given.

[3] The quotation and the English name of the organization are taken from an original record which Tse Tsan Tai's son kindly allowed me to see in Hong Kong when I called on him on December 29, 1963. Tse Tsan Tai, in *The Chinese Republic: Secret History of the Revolution* (Hong Kong, 1924), p. 8, gives March 13, 1892, as the founding date of the association without listing its aims. His book first appeared in serial form in the columns of the Hong Kong *South China Morning Post* of November 1924.

Mutual Improvement Association was Tse Tsan Tai (Hsieh Tsuan-t'ai), who was born in Sydney, Australia, on May 16, 1872, six years after his parents (natives of Kwangtung province) had immigrated there. Tse received his elementary education at the Grafton High School. At seven, he was baptized (in his later years, Tse called himself a "Christian" and "also a staunch supporter of Confucius and his teachings"). At fifteen, he returned to Hong Kong with his mother, two younger brothers, and three sisters and completed his education at Queen's College (high school). He then worked for the Hong Kong government as a clerk with the Department of Public Works for ten years. Six other members whose names can be traced were either shipping clerks or employees of shipping companies.[4] Their organization has been characterized as both "revolutionary headquarters" and a "social club." It was probably in the nature of a study group for "new learning" and social activities.[5]

When the Chinese Patriotic Mutual Improvement Association was founded, Sun Yat-sen was in the last three months of his medical studies in Hong Kong. During the previous year he had met Yang Ch'ü-yün. Both found a common interest in their respective progressive outlooks, though they did not immediately establish close relations. Sun was born into a peasant's family in today's Chungshan district, Kwangtung province, on November 12, 1866.[6] His father

[4] Tse, op. cit. pp. 6–8; and Chesney Duncan, Tse Tsan Tai (London, 1917), p. 1. A photograph of Yang (seated front-row center) with Sun Yat-sen (standing behind) and Japanese friends was reproduced in Wu Hsiang-hsiang, Sun Yat-sen hsien-sheng (Taipei, 1965).

[5] For an analysis of the Fu-jen wen-she, see Wang Hsing-jui, "Ch'ing-chi Fu-jen wen-she yü ko-ming yün-tung ti kuan-hsi" (The Fu Jen Literary Society and the Revolutionary Movement of the Ch'ing Period), Shih-hsüeh tsa-chih (Historical Magazine), Vol. I, No. I (Chungking, Dec. 5, 1945), pp. 35–45.

[6] In his autobiographical sketch written for Herbert A. Giles in 1896 in London, Sun Yat-sen stated that he had been born on November 22, 1866. After a thorough investigation by the Kuomintang authorities many years later, this was proved to be an error. See Tsou Lu, Chung-kuo kuo-min-tang shih-kao (Draft History of the Kuomintang) (3rd ed.; Chungking, 1944), IV, 1194. For a thorough discussion of the subject, see Huang Chi-lu's article in the Chuan-chi wen-hsüeh (Biographical Literature), Vol. IX, No. 2 (August 1967), pp. 6–13. Conclusive evidence came to light with the discovery of the

had been a tailer near Macao at one time.[7] In 1879, Sun left his native village for Hawaii, where his elder brother Sun Mei had a general store. After attending an English missionary school there for several years, he returned to China in 1883. Two years later he was converted to Christianity.[8] In 1892, after five years of uninterrupted medical studies in Hong Kong, he was graduated from the College of Medicine for Chinese.[9] After practicing briefly in Macao and Canton, he went to Shanghai in the spring of 1894. In the summer of that year, he set out with his boyhood friend, Lu Hao-tung, for Tientsin in an attempt to present his reform ideas to the Chihli Governor-General Li Hung-chang.[10] The gist of the program presented to Li was set forth in four balanced lines of four ideographs each: full development of man's abilities; full exploitation of the earth's resources; full use of material instruments; and unhampered flow of

original fortune-teller's forecast of Sun Yat-sen's life. The forecast was requested by Sun's mother, and was found among her belongings. It was generally believed by ignorant people in old times that one's life was determined by one's date and hour of birth. Sun's mother also "gave" her son to the village temple god as a "godson" in order to insure protection of his life. For the story and a facsimile reproduction of the forecast, see the *Ming Pao Monthly* (Hong Kong), No. 23 (November 1967), pp. 86–87.

[7] A private unpublished manuscript by Sun Yat-sen's son-in-law, shown to me by Sun's granddaughter, Venus Victoria Tai.

[8] In 1895, Byron Brenan, British Consul-General in Canton, described Sun Yat-sen as "a person of some intelligence. . . . He professed to be a Christian, but the missionaries with whom he had to do doubted his sincerity." Brenan to Foreign Office, November 18, 1895, *FO 17/1249,* quoted in Mary Man-Yue Chan Sun, *British Policy and the Chinese Revolutionary Movement 1895–1912* (unpublished Ph.D. dissertation, University of London, 1968), p. 52.

[9] Committee for the Compilation of Materials on the Party History of the Central Executive Committee of the Kuomintang (chief editor: Lo Chia-lun; rev. by Huang Chi-lu), ed., *Kuo-fu nien-p'u* (Chronology of Sun Yat-sen's Life: Enlarged Edition) (Taipei, 1969), I, 1–53; hereafter cited as Kuomintang, *Chronology of Sun.*

[10] Kuomintang, *Chronology of Sun,* I, 54–57; also Feng, *Fragments,* III (Chungking, 1945), 28; cf. Lyon Sharman, *Sun Yat-sen: His Life and Its Meaning* (New York: John Day, 1934), p. 32; and Marius B. Jansen, *The Japanese and Sun Yat-sen* (Harvard University Press, 1954), p. 61. Both Sharman and Jansen date Sun Yat-sen's trip to North China in an attempt to see Li Hung-chang as having occurred in 1893 instead of 1894.

commerce.[11] He failed to secure an audience, but instead managed to obtain from Li's aide an official endorsement to raise funds abroad for the purpose of establishing an agricultural association.[12] In the fall of 1894, he went to Honolulu where he founded the Hsing Chung Hui. November 24, 1894, the date on which members of the organization began to pay dues, has officially been considered the founding date of the Hsing Chung Hui.[13]

The chairman and other officers of the organization were chosen from the local Chinese community. An original record shows that from November 24, 1894 to September 2, 1895, one hundred and twelve Chinese—businessmen, traders, cooks, clerks, tailors, laborers, farmers, and local government employees—joined the organization. Practically all of them were of Kwangtung origin, the great majority being from Sun's native district. According to the record, the total amount of funds raised during the period was US$1,388 including the "shares" subscribed to by a few "natives" (probably meaning Hawaiians). Sun took one hundred dollars with him when he returned to Hong Kong while US$1,040 (equivalent to HK$2,000 at that time) was later sent to him. His elder brother's "shares" amounted to two hundred dollars. If Sun's brother, Sun Mei, had contributed more than this amount, as is generally supposed, it is

[11] For the text of Sun Yat-sen's letter to Li Hung-chang, see Sun Yat-sen, *Kuo-fu ch'üan-chi* (Collected Works), ed. Committee for the Compilation of Materials on the Party History of the Central Executive Committee of the Kuomintang (revised ed.; Taipei, 1957), V, 1–12. According to Ch'en, *op. cit.* pp. 7–8, the letter was edited first by Ch'en Shao-pai in Canton and then by Wang T'ao (1828–1897) in Shanghai. It was subsequently published in the Shanghai *Wan-kuo kung-pao* (Chinese Globe Magazine) of October 1894. There is no record that Sun had ever mentioned it in later years (Kuomintang, *Chronology of Sun,* I, 58). It was discovered shortly after his death by a Chinese historian in 1925.

[12] Tsou, *Draft History,* I, 26.

[13] Kuomintang, *Chronology of Sun,* I, 62, n. 15. Among the Kuomintang historians, Tsou Lu was almost the only one who insisted that the Hsing Chung Hui was founded in Macao in 1892. His version has been adopted by some American and Japanese historians, but his source was based solely on the unauthorized and incorrect Chinese translation of Sun Yat-sen's *Kidnapped in London.* See Chün-tu Hsüeh, "An Early Chinese Revolutionary Organization: Controversy Concerning Its Founding," *Chinese Culture,* Vol. VI, No. 2 (March 1965), pp. 19–27.

difficult to understand why it was not recorded, since all the contributions appear to have been business investments.[14]

In January 1895, Sun Yat-sen returned to Hong Kong[15] and shortly afterward cooperated with Yang Ch'ü-yün to form the Hong Kong Hsing Chung Hui.[16] Several members of the Chinese Patriotic Mutual Improvement Association joined the new organization. They established their headquarters at 13 Staunton Street under the cover of the Kuen Hang Club. Of the forty-nine members whose names can be documented, ten were intellectuals, seven government functionaries, eight merchants, three laborers, fourteen secret society members, and seven with occupations unknown.[17] Yang was then 35 years old; Sun, 28; and Tse Tsan Tai, 25. Among Sun's close friends who were active in the organization were two of his schoolmates, Cheng Shih-liang and Ch'en Shao-pai—both of Kwangtung province. Cheng was a graduate of a German missionary school in Canton. Having studied briefly at the Canton Hospital School where he met Sun Yat-sen, Cheng returned to his native village in eastern Kwangtung and opened a pharmacy. He was a member of the Triads, a secret society, and was responsible for the recruiting of Triad members. Ch'en briefly attended the College of Medicine for Chinese. He was probably Sun Yat-sen's closest comrade throughout the Hsing Chung Hui period, but, after 1906, he sank into oblivion.[18]

[14] Committee for the Compilation of Materials on the Party History of the Central Executive Committee of the Kuomintang (chief editor: Lo Chia-lun), ed., *Ko-ming wen-hsien* (Documents of the Revolution), III (Taiwan, 1953), 16–18; hereafter cited as Kuomintang, *Documents*.

[15] Kuomintang, *Chronology of Sun*, I, 62.

[16] Feng Tzu-yu and practically all the Kuomintang publications in the past have given "February 21, 1895" as the founding date of the Hsing Chung Hui in Hong Kong (for example, Feng, *Fragments*, V, 10; and Kuomintang, *Chronology of Sun*, I, 64). Tse Tsan Tai, in his book previously cited, gives no specific date except "in the spring of 1895," and records the "13th of March 1895" as the date of his "first meeting with Sun Yat-sen and others" (pp. 4 and 9). It may be mentioned that in reference to the early Hsing Chung Hui data, the Kuomintang historians often relied on the writings of Feng Tzu-yu who, in turn, relied on Tse's book which was written in English.

[17] Wu, *op. cit.* p. 105. Wu, however, does not list the names of the forty-nine members, and he may have included many who were merely sympathizers.

[18] For their biographical sketches, see Feng, *Fragments*, I, 5 and 37–38; also Ch'en Te-yün, ed., *Ch'en Shao-pai hsien-sheng ai-ssu lu* (An Obituary Record of Ch'en Shao-pai) (Canton, 1934?).

The regulations of the Hong Kong Hsing Chung Hui were sub-stantially the same as, though more elaborate than, those of the Honolulu branch. The avowed aim of both sets of regulations, known as "manifestos," was not to overthrow the Manchu dynasty, but to strengthen China by organizing progressive elements at home and abroad. However, no specific programs were laid down to save China from the "danger of immediate partition" by foreign powers. The Honolulu Hsing Chung Hui regulations consisted of nine articles. The membership fee was five dollars, but voluntary contributions were welcome. No new member was admitted without references from one member of standing. Meetings were held every Thursday evening and were presided over by the chairman or the vice-chairman, who were elected by the members. Among the thirteen other officers were two secretaries and one treasurer—the rest ro-tated routine administrative positions. Decisions were made by majority vote.

The Hong Kong Hsing Chung Hui regulations contained ten articles. Its head office was to be established in China, but branches could be established elsewhere if the minimum membership require-ment of fifteen was met. The branch office was not to be used for gambling or social purposes. In addition to the five-dollar membership fee, members were invited to buy ten-dollar shares with the prospect of increasing their investment to one hundred dollars. New members were admitted upon the recommendation of two members in good standing. Officers, elected once a year, included the chairman, vice-chairman, Chinese secretary, English secretary, treasurer, and ten directors of the board. Decisions were made only after consultation among five members and ten directors. The regulations set forth the following program: the establishment of newspapers to teach the masses and schools to educate the talented, the development of industry for improving the livelihood of the people. Anything that might help China's prosperity was to be promoted. What form of government China should have was not indicated.[19] Although Sun

[19] For the texts of the two regulations of the Hsing Chung Hui, see Kuomin-tang, *Documents*, III, 2–6. Sharman, *op. cit.* p. 36, describes the regulations of the Hong Kong Hsing Chung Hui as if they were the regulations of the

Yat-sen, at this time, worked for the overthrow of the alien Manchu regime, he would not oppose the monarchical system if the emperor were to be Chinese. Yang Ch'ü-yün, on the other hand, insisted on the republican form of government.[20]

The original members in Honolulu and Hong Kong allegedly dedicated themselves under oath to the "overthrow of the Manchu dynasty, the restoration of China, and the establishment of a republican government." [21] But this fact has never been documented. The practice of taking such an oath developed gradually and historians have probably given it retroactive effect. It was unlikely to have taken place in Honolulu at the time when the Hsing Chung Hui was founded, for the aim of Sun's trip there was to raise funds for an agricultural association. Many joined the organization without any idea of Sun's plan to overthrow the Manchu regime. Though Sun may have taken a few people into his confidence, and the initial members may have sworn allegiance to the organization on an open Bible, it is inconceivable that they knowingly took an oath dedicating themselves to revolution.

The background, education, interests, and Western contacts of Yang Ch'ü-yün, Sun Yat-sen, and their friends, were strikingly similar. Hence, their joining hands to "revive China" was not an accident. They were not born into the scholar-official-gentry class; nor did they receive the traditional education of the Chinese literati. Instead, they gained new ideas from foreign schooling and from contacts with foreigners. During their travels they contrasted the state of their own country under Manchu rule with the greater material prosperity and the more efficient administration of colonial governments. Yang, Sun, and Tse also had ties with overseas Chinese families in Malaya, Honolulu, and Australia respectively.

Honolulu branch. Some Chinese publications also fail to distinguish between the two.

[20] Liu, *loc. cit.*

[21] For example, Feng Tzu-yu, *Chung-kuo ko-ming yün-tung er-shih-liu nien tsu-chih shih* ('Twenty-six Years' Organizational History of the Revolutionary Movement) (Shanghai, 1948), p. 16; and Ch'en Hsi-ch'i, *T'ung-meng-hui ch'eng-li ch'ien ti Sun Chung-shan* (Sun Yat-sen Prior to the Founding of the T'ung Meng Hui) (Canton, 1957), p. 33.

The discontent of the populace with their alien rulers had been growing in China. The internal conditions of the country at the end of that century had many of the phenomena which were characteristic of those at the end of every dynasty in the history of China: famines, peasant unrest, rebellions, incompetent rulers, and corruption in the government. After the Opium War of 1840–42, China was repeatedly humiliated by foreign powers. By far the greatest humiliation was her defeat in the war against Japan in 1894–95, which was a shock to the whole nation. Under these circumstances Yang, Sun, and their friends attempted to overthrow the Ch'ing dynasty.

At a meeting on March 16, 1895, a month before the Sino-Japanese Treaty of Peace was signed at Shimonoseki, the rebels decided to capture Canton on October 26, which was the ninth day of the ninth lunar month of that year.[22] It was on that date every year that the Chinese would go to the countryside to offer sacrifices before the tombs of their ancestors. Many Hong Kong residents usually returned to Canton for that occasion. Hence it was a good cover under which to send men to Canton. Sun Yat-sen directed the plot in Canton while Yang Ch'ü-yün raised funds, purchased arms, and recruited men in Hong Kong. Huang Yung-shang, one of Yang's friends, was said to have contributed HK$8,000 for the cause by selling a house.[23] By August 27, the plans for capturing Canton were completed and orders were given to close the Kuen Hang Club. Two days later, the revolutionaries and their sympathizers—among them Ho Kai (Ho Ch'i), a Chinese barrister-at-law and a member of the Hong Kong Legislative Council, Thomas H. Reid of the *China Mail,* and Chesney Duncan of the *Hongkong Telegraph*—met at a hotel to outline the policy of the revolutionists. Reid agreed to work for the sympathy and support of the British Government and the people of England. Later, he and a man named T. Cowen drafted a proclamation to the foreign powers for the revolutionaries.

[22] Tse, *op. cit.* p. 10; and Ch'en Shao-pai, *op. cit.* pp. 9–10. Many Western sources have given September 9, 1895 as the date of Sun Yat-sen's first failure. For example, Sharman, *op. cit.* p. 39; Stephen Chen and Robert Payne, *Sun Yat-sen* (New York: John Day, 1946), p. 32; and "Saggitarius" (pseud.), *The Strange Apotheosis of Sun Yat-sen* (London: Heath Cranton, 1939), p. 15.
[23] Tsou, *Draft History,* IV, 1229.

While the revolt was being prepared, an election was held among the revolutionaries in Hong Kong (October 10) to select the "President of the Provisional Government" in the event that the revolution would succeed.[24] The struggle for the "presidency" between Yang Ch'ü-yün and Sun Yat-sen was keen. Members of the Chinese Patriotic Mutual Improvement Association supported Yang while Cheng Shih-liang and Ch'en Shao-pai sided with Sun. The fight for leadership was so intense that, for a moment, the two groups were on the verge of a split which would have jeopardized the whole endeavor. According to Ch'en, Sun Yat-sen was elected but was forced to resign in favor of Yang Ch'ü-yün. The defeat was a "great blow" to Sun,[25] and "it always rankled in his breast." [26]

The fight for the "presidency" proved to be unnecessary. At the last moment, the revolt, which was scheduled for October 26, was postponed for two days because preparations in Hong Kong were not completed in time. On the 27th, the plot was discovered by the Canton authorities, and three of the rebels were arrested. Sun Yat-sen sent a warning to Hong Kong, but it failed to reach Yang Ch'ü-yün in time to stop the men sent to Canton. On the 28th, forty-five rebels were arrested upon their arrival in Canton, and 205 revolvers and 80 odd boxes of ammunition were confiscated.[27] Sun escaped to Hong

---

[24] Tse, *op. cit.* p. 9.

[25] Ch'en Shao-pai, *op. cit.* pp. 10–11.

[26] Tse, *op. cit.* p. 9. Up to this time the chairmanship of the Hsing Chung Hui was apparently open. Two dubious sources, however, give different versions. In *Yang Ch'ü-yün lüeh-shih* (previously cited), pp. 8–9, it is stated that on September 30, 1895 Huang Yung-shang resigned from the chairmanship in favor of Yang Ch'ü-yün. It is also so stated in "Shun-te Yu-lieh hsien-sheng pa-shih k'ai-i jung-shou cheng-wen ch'i-shih" (An Announcement for Contribution of Articles in Commemoration of the Eighty-first Birthday of Yu Lieh) (Hong Kong, 1935), p. 4, but with a different date: "Feb. 21, 1895." (Yu Lieh may also be pronounced as Wang Lieh).

[27] Memorial of Kwantung Governor T'an to the Throne reporting the attempted revolt of Oct. 26, 1895; reprinted in Feng Tzu-yu, *Chung-hua min-kuo k'ai-kuo chien ko-ming shih* (Revolutionary History Prior to the Founding of the Republic of China), I (Shanghai, 1928), 27–29. Both the scale and scope of the attempted revolt have been exaggerated in subsequent accounts. Several thousand rebels are said to have been mobilized: the number was multiplied after each telling; e.g. Ch'en Hsi-ch'i, *T'ung-meng-hui*, p. 35 (otherwise a careful study). For Sun Yat-sen's own account written about a

Kong; from there he fled to Japan with a price of $1,000 (Chinese silver dollars) on his head. Except for an overnight stay on a Kwangsi mountain on the border of French Indo-China in early December 1907, Sun did not return to the Chinese mainland until after the successful Wuchang Revolution sixteen years later. However, many fantastic and imaginative accounts of Sun Yat-sen's adventures in the interior of China after 1895 have been written in the West. For example, an entire chapter of Bishop Henry B. Restarick's book, *Sun Yat-sen: Liberator of China* (Yale University Press, 1931), is devoted to the "Unlucky Plan of Revolt in 1904," in which Sun Yat-sen was found at the secret headquarters in Canton personally directing the plot with a certain Chang Chau.[28]

With the same price on his head, Yang Ch'ü-yün left Hong Kong for Saigon on November 13, 1895. He then proceeded to Singapore, Madras, Colombo, and South Africa, where he founded a Hsing Chung Hui branch in Johannesburg. In the summer of 1897, he decided to return to the Far East, and arrived in Yokohama on March 21, 1898, an unpleasant surprise to Sun Yat-sen.[29]

After returning from his first trip to the United States, England, and Canada in August 1896, Sun Yat-sen lived in Japan. Through Miyazaki Torazō, a Japanese interested in Chinese affairs, he gained some Japanese support, which was crucial both to his livelihood and to his cause at that time.[30] Although Yang retained nominal chairmanship of the Hsing Chung Hui, his position in the organization

---

year after the event, see his *Kidnapped in London* (London, 1897), pp. 20–27. It is significant that at that time Sun did not claim to be the leader of the revolution.

[28] Restarick claimed to have obtained the information from Chang himself, who was "a public notary of the Territory of Hawaii"! Sharman, *op. cit.* p. 102, also gives (rather skeptically perhaps) a full page to Restarick's "vivid narrative" of this revolt, and has the date "corrected" as having occurred in 1906.

[29] Tse, *op. cit.* pp. 10, 12, and 13; and Ch'en, *op. cit.* p. 35.

[30] For an autobiographical sketch of Miyazaki Torazō and the story of his acquaintance with Sun Yat-sen, see his *San jū san nen no yume* (The Thirty-three Years' Dream) (Tokyo, 1926), pp. 117–183; also Jansen, *op. cit.* pp. 54–58 and 64–68. The latest edition of Miyazaki's book, which was first published in 1902, was published with annotations by his son and Eto Shinkichi by the Toyo Bunko in 1967.

after 1895 declined. Sun's position, on the other hand, was enhanced by Japanese support and by the publicity he gained from the famous kidnapping episode in London in 1896 [31] (where he first made contact with Russian revolutionaries).[32] It was at about this time that Sun Yat-sen was involved in the Philippine revolt against the United States. Sun negotiated on behalf of the Philippine agent Mariano Ponce for the purchase and transport of arms in Japan for the Philippine independent movement under the leadership of Emilio Aguinaldo. It was from the transaction commissions that Sun Yat-sen was able to finance Ch'en Shao-pai in the establishment of the *China Journal (Chung-kuo jih-pao)* in Hong Kong at the end of 1899.[33]

Unlike Sun Yat-sen, who became a professional revolutionary after 1895, Yang Ch'ü-yün was now a middle-aged man with a family to support. In Yokohama, he had to make his living by teaching English. In January 1900, he returned to Hong Kong and resigned from the chairmanship of the Hsing Chung Hui in favor of Sun Yat-sen.

[31] Sun Yat-sen was lured into the Chinese legation in London on October 11, 1896, but was released twelve days later. His *Kidnapped in London* was written after the episode. For a source book on the event, see Lo Chia-lun, *Chung-shan hsien-sheng Lun-tun pei-nan shih-liao k'ao-ting* (A Critical Study of the Official Documents Concerning Dr. Sun Yat-sen's *Kidnapped in London*) (Shanghai, 1930).

[32] Letter of Sun Yat-sen to F. Volkhovzky, dated March 15, 1897. Volkhovzky was then exiled in England. He asked Sun to comment on an article about France and Russia in China for his magazine. "In respond to your request," Sun replied, "I must confess to say that I cannot write anything in perfect English without a friend's help. The one who help [sic] me in my literal works happen [sic] to be absent in town in the last few days." The original letter may be found in the Volkhovzky Collection of the Hoover Institution, Stanford University.

[33] Hirayama's remarks in the Second Round Table Conference which was held by Sun Yat-sen's Japanese friends in Tokyo, February 5, 1930. The records of the five conferences were published in Ch'en Ku-t'ing, *Kuo-fu yü Jih-pen yu-jen* (Sun Yat-sen and His Japanese Friends) (Taipei, 1965), pp. 121–54. Apparently, Ch'en Shao-pai did not know Sun Yat-sen's source of funds, and assumed that it was from Japanese sources. It may be added that the circulation of the newspaper, the *China Journal*, reached 2100 by 1903. At that time the population of Hong Kong was 307,050. See *Hongkong Year Book,* 1903, and Hongkong Government, *Historical and Statistical Abstract of the Colony of Hongkong 1841–1930.*

Tse Tsan Tai was surprised to learn from him that Sun had demanded his resignation. Yang explained the resignation:

> We were dangerously near being split up into two parties some time ago. Dr. Sun Yat-sen informed me one day that the "Ko Lao Whui" party [Ko Lao Hui, or Society of the Elders and Brothers] of the Yangtze provinces had appointed him "President," and hinted that as there could not be two Presidents, it would be obligatory for me to work independently if I would not recognize him in his new position. I confessed to Sun Yat-sen that I was quite pleased to resign my position, and advised him not to encourage separation. I also informed him that I was always willing to sacrifice my life, let alone my position, for the good of the cause.[34]

Yang's decision was the result of Sun's scheming. Sun had tried to gain undisputed leadership of the Hsing Chung Hui by establishing a new organization called the Hsing Han Hui (Revive Han Society) which took in several leaders of the Triads and the Society of the Elders and Brothers.[35] In November 1899, these leaders were brought to Hong Kong to confer with Ch'en Shao-pai and Miyazaki Torazō. They then took an unusual step which gave formal recognition to Sun's leadership in the revolutionary movement: a chairman's seal was made, and Miyazaki brought it to Yokohama and presented it to Sun.[36] The new party, however, gained little recognition and its name was soon dropped. Since Yang Ch'ü-yün did not challenge Sun's leadership, no purpose was served by this new organization. Furthermore, the leaders of the Society of the Elders and Brothers forsook the revolutionary movement and joined the reformers' camp.

Although Sun Yat-sen gained undisputed leadership within the Hsing Chung Hui, he was confronted with competition from other

[34] Tse, *op. cit.* pp. 16–17.

[35] In his autobiography, Sun Yat-sen called the event the "merger of secret societies in the Yangtze Valley, Kwangtung, Kwangsi, and Fukien provinces into the Hsing Chung Hui." (Sun, *Collected Works*, I, 36). This was criticized by a Communist historian as "far-fetched." See Yung Meng-yüan, ed., *Chung-kuo chin-tai-shih tzu-liao hsüan-chi* (Selected Source Materials of Modern History of China) (Peking, 1954), p. 542.

[36] Kuomintang, *Chronology of Sun*, I, 117; Miyazaki, *op. cit.* p. 183. Tse, *op. cit.* p. 17 ff., mistakenly identifies the new organization as the T'ung Meng Hui, which did not come into existence until 1905.

reform groups. Before 1898 a reform movement under the leadership of K'ang Yu-wei directed its appeal to the scholar-official-gentry class in China. After the coup d'état of September 21, 1898, which resulted in K'ang's exile from China and Emperor Kuang-hsü's loss of power, it solicited the support of overseas Chinese, who always had great respect for the scholar-officials from home, and who were easily won over by prominent reformers. For example, Feng Tzu-yu's father, chairman of the Yokohama Hsing Chung Hui, became the manager of a newspaper edited by Liang Ch'i-ch'ao, a leading reformer.

When K'ang Yu-wei was exiled to Japan in November 1898, Sun Yat-sen wished to call on him to express his sympathy, but the reform leader refused to see him. Their mutual Japanese friends tried in vain to have the two groups co-operate,[37] but selfishness and jealousy made co-operation difficult. From the end of 1898 to early 1899, K'ang Yu-wei corresponded with Tse Tsan Tai, who remained in Hong Kong. After K'ang left Japan, Liang Ch'i-ch'ao took up the correspondence. While both sides realized the importance of co-operation, no agreement was reached. Liang met with Yang Ch'ü-yün in Yokohama and the meeting was described by Yang in a letter to Tse, dated June 6, 1899:

> He [Liang Ch'i-ch'ao] advised me to try my best to go on with the work of our party and he will try his best to go on with the work of his party. He does not like to cooperate with us yet. Hong's [K'ang's] party is too proud and jealous of our Chinese-English scholars. They don't like to have the same rank as us; they always aspire to governing us or want us all to submit to them.[38]

Throughout the summer and the fall of 1899, Liang Ch'i-ch'ao held several meetings with Sun Yat-sen in Japan, and at one time the two were said to have come close to an agreement. From the letters written to Sun during this period, it is clear that Liang himself was quite willing to work with the revolutionaries, but his strong sense of loyalty to his former teacher, K'ang, if nothing else, held him back. On January 11, 1900, ten days after his arrival in Honolulu for the

---

[37] For a personal account of the relations between the revolutionaries and the reformers, see Ch'en Shao-pai, *op. cit.* pp. 23–26, 32–34, 36–39, and 41–44.

[38] Tse, *op. cit.* p. 15.

establishment of the Protect-the-Emperor Society, he wrote to Sun:

> There are things that I may be obliged to do here merely for the sake of expediency. But you must forgive me and try to understand my difficult situation. In short, since we have become friends and agreed to cooperate, there should be no disunity between us in the future on world [Chinese] affairs. I have been constantly thinking about this matter day and night. If you will kindly give me time, I trust that I shall find a good method of reconciliation [between the two groups].[39]

While the revolutionaries attacked the reformers for organizing the Protect-the-Emperor Society, the final split occurred after their respective military actions failed in the late summer and early fall of 1900.

The year 1900 was a year of upheaval in China. While the Boxers were active in the North, three governors-general of southern provinces ignored the imperial decree of June 21, 1900 which declared war against the foreign powers. During this time of unrest, the Hsing Chung Hui leaders attempted to use the influence of Sir Henry A. Blake, Governor of Hong Kong, to persuade Li Hung-chang, Governor-General of Kwangtung and Kwangsi, to declare his independence from the Empire. If Li agreed to the plan, they would then support him. The scheme was initiated by Ho Kai, who had been in sympathy with the attempted revolt of 1895. Ch'en then notified Sun Yat-sen, who readily agreed. Ho drafted a letter in English[40] which was signed by Sun Yat-sen, Yang Ch'ü-yün, and seven others members of the Hsing Chung Hui. The name of the organization, however, was not mentioned.[41]

Heretofore, only the Chinese version of this letter was available

---

[39] Feng, *History Prior,* I, 47. Three letters of Liang Ch'i-ch'ao to Sun Yat-sen written during this period are reprinted in facsimile in Feng's book, I, 44–47. Unless otherwise mentioned, all translations in this article have been made by the present author. For further discussion of the subject, see Chang P'eng-yüan, *Liang Ch'i-ch'ao yü Ch'ing-chi ko-ming* (Liang Ch'i-ch'ao and the Revolution in the Ch'ing Period) (Taipei, 1964).

[40] Feng, *Fragments,* IV, 92.

[41] For an excellent account of the episode based on British sources, see Harold Z. Schiffrin, *Sun Yat-sen and the Origins of the Chinese Revolution* (Berkeley: University of California Press, 1968), pp. 198–213.

to Chinese and Western historians. The Chinese version was apparently an abridged translation from an English document given to me by Tse Tsan Tai's son in Hong Kong in 1963. The original English text consists of two parts: "Proclamation" and "Scheme of Reform." The "Proclamation" was addressed "To all whom it may concern." While it attacked corruption and the weakness of "usurping Manchu rulers" for the loss of territories, failure to maintain law and order, "no progress in public works," "nor works for preventing floods, fires, pestilence, nor development of the country's resources by railroads, mines, harbours," it did not explicitly suggest that the regime should be overthrown. It stated instead:

> We the People of China, with the strongest feelings of peace and goodwill, cannot but resolve to get rid of all the corrupt and demoralized officials and govern the country righteously to the best of our ability . . . in doing so we cannot avoid for a time causing alarm to the foreigners having interests in China, so that they may think it necessary to interfere . . . but we hereby pledge ourselves to take the utmost care of all foreign interests, and to refrain from unwarranted acts towards anybody, Chinese or Foreign . . . for the present, a Provisional Government, formed by the patriotic Chinese who at great risk have voluntarily come forward in their country's cause, shall manage the affairs of the country in accordance with this Proclamation.

The "Proclamation" listed eight resolutions, including equal rights under "impartial and uniform laws" made by the "people's representatives, to be elected according to a system to be hereafter proclaimed," the opening of the country to foreigners "of any country that is open to Chinese, for residence, trade, industry, instruction, or any other peaceful purpose, and attention to the "education of the people and the care of children, and therefore also of women." The "Scheme of Reform" included the following programs:

1. To remove the capital to "a central position" such as Nanking, Hankow, or "some other place where international affairs can be conveniently looked after and to which the different provinces can gain an easy access."

2. To establish a constitutional central government "presided over by a Ruler President of great respect and popularity," and assisted

by a "Grand Council composed of a certain number of representatives from different provinces"; to set up a "temporary Advisory Board composed of the Foreign Ministers resident at the Capital"; to establish self-governing provincial governments "presided over by a Governor appointed by the Central Government and assisted by a Provincial Council composed of a certain number of representatives from the various districts of the province"; and to form a "temporary Advisory Board" by foreign consul-generals in the province. Furthermore, all local government officials should be natives of the province.

3. "To accord equal privileges and rights to all within the Empire," such as the development of railways, mining, inland navigation, industries, and trades.

4. To increase the salaries of all officials "in order to enable them to live honestly and discharge their duties to the state faithfully."

5. To reform civil and criminal law by adopting the European and American systems, including trial by jury and abolition of cruel methods of execution and torture for evidence.

6. To replace the contemporary systems of education and examination by special training and examination in literature, law, politics, etc.

Li Hung-chang's reaction to the letter cannot be ascertained, though his aide, Liu Hsüeh-hsün, was reportedly enthusiastic. When in the middle of July it became known that Li was already on his way to take up a new post as Governor-General of Chihli, the revolutionaries and their Japanese sympathizers intensified their preparations for revolt. Shortly before it took place, Sun Yat-sen sent Hirayama Shū, a Japanese adventurer interested in Chinese affairs, to deliver a letter to Liu. In this letter, written under a Japanese pseudonym in September at Taipei, Sun outlined the organization of the revolutionary government. While it was a letter of expediency, it nevertheless reflected Sun Yat-sen's political outlook at the time. It stated:

> I am sending my confidant, Mr. Hirayama, to see you. He will convey my wishes in requesting you to organize a provisional government in order to manage national affairs. A pentarchy form of government will be good enough for the time being. Whether the

head of the government will be called President or Emperor will be your decision, but I will definitely let you have the post. The other three members of the pentarchy will be in charge of the Interior, Finance, and Foreign Affairs [Ministries]. The choice of personnel will be yours.

I should like to suggest, however, that Yang Ch'ü-yün be in charge of Finance, Li Chi-t'ang, of Foreign Affairs . . . and Sheng Hsüan-huai, of the Interior. I myself shall take care of Military Affairs. I shall try to capture some territories first; then you may come. Also if it is desirable to have envoys abroad as soon as possible —I can find qualified persons for such tasks. For example, Ho [Kai] and Yung [Wing] are very well suited for top diplomatic positions. . . .

The most important thing at the moment is to have a large amount of money. . . . I hope that you, Yang, and Li, together with other comrades, will be able to raise one million *yüan* for me immediately. Give the money to Hirayama, and he will bring it to me. . . .

I had intended at first to have Governor-General Li [Hung-chang] head the new government. Since he has accepted the new appointment for peace negotiations, I am afraid that he would not acquiesce in our request. . . . So I will definitely let you have the post. This decision has been made known to the [revolutionary] army, and it will be announced to the public when the appropriate time comes. . . .[42]

Nothing came of this letter. The Waichow revolt broke out on October 8, 1900, on Chinese territory bordering British-leased Kowloon opposite Hong Kong. Military plans had been mapped out by Sun Yat-sen, Yang Ch'ü-yün, and their Japanese friends, and were carried out under the command of Cheng Shih-liang. Although Yang intended to participate in the revolt in the interior, Sun persuaded

[42] The letter is reprinted in Feng, *Fragments*, IV, 98–100. Interestingly enough it cannot be found in any of Sun Yat-sen's *Collected Works* compiled by the Kuomintang. Two persons mentioned in the letter require a word of explanation. Li Chi-t'ang was a son of a wealthy Chinese merchant in Hong Kong. Induced to join the Hsing Chung Hui by Yang Ch'ü-yün, he generously contributed funds for the cause. Yung Wing, the "first Chinese student in the United States," had met Tse Tsan Tai and Yang Ch'ü-yün in Hong Kong early in April 1900. He was on his way to the United States again. They exchanged views on the political situation of China, and Tse wrote to Sun suggesting that the latter meet Yung upon his arrival in Japan. Tse, *op. cit.* p. 18. It is not clear how Sheng Hsüan-huai came into the picture.

him to stay in Hong Kong to rally support among local merchants.[43] The troops that were counted on for this revolution were the armed patriotic bandits in today's Paoan district, Kwangtung province. Some of them were, of course, members of the Triads; but the secret society played only a secondary role.[44] The objective was to capture the coastal areas of Waichow, eastern Kwangtung, then to advance in the direction of Fukien in order to receive military supplies from Taiwan, where Sun Yat-sen was trying to obtain help from the Japanese authorities. But aid did not come, and two weeks later, after a few successful skirmishes, Cheng Shih-liang disbanded his troops. Thus ended the "second revolutionary attempt" of Sun Yat-sen. Cheng died in Hong Kong less than a year after this campaign.

One of the by-products of the Waichow revolt was the enhancement of Sun Yat-sen's prestige in China; for his name was now mentioned along with that of K'ang Yu-wei, the respectable "tutor of the emperor." Official memorials linked the action of the revolutionaries with the attempted armed revolt of the reformers in 1900 though there was no coordination between them.[45] During the early stage of fighting, a Kwangtung official sent an emissary to Yang Ch'ü-yün to bribe the rebels by offering them official positions. Considering it an opportunity for legitimate expansion of the revolutionary forces, Yang readily agreed. He wrote a letter to Sun Yat-sen advising him to accept the offer.[46] Whatever doubts Sun might have expressed with regard to this suggestion, the revolt was so brief that the question did not receive serious consideration. However, Yang became the main target of the Canton agents, especially after the attempted assassination of Te Shou, Governor of Kwangtung.

[43] Letter of Sun Yat-sen to Hirayama Shū, dated July 24 [1900]. Sun, *Collected Works*, V, 20.

[44] Ch'en Shao-pai, *op. cit.* pp. 46–47.

[45] The Hong Kong *China Mail* of October 24, 1900 published a letter written by K'ang Yu-wei, disclaiming any connections with the Waichow revolt.

[46] Ch'en Shao-pai, *op. cit.* pp. 48–49. Official Kuomintang historians have sometimes hinted that Yang "betrayed" the revolution because of this alleged compromise. See Teng Mu-han, "Sun hsien-sheng tsu-shu shih-i" (Notes on Sun Yat-sen's Reminiscences), *Chien-kuo yüeh-k'an*, Vol. I, No. 4 (Aug. 1929), pp. 82–83. The accusation was not justified under the circumstances. It may be noted that later in Japan Sun Yat-sen raised some funds for the Yang family. See letter of Sun to Tse, Feb. 13, 1901.

The attempt on the governor's life on October 28, 1900 was originally part of the Waichow revolt. The aim was to create disturbances in the provincial capital while military action was being taken on the coastal areas of the province. The bomb went off, but the governor was unhurt. Shih Chien-ju, who was responsible for the plot, confessed after his capture that it was through Yang's introduction and influence that he had joined the Hsing Chung Hui. Consequently, Yang was warned by his friends to leave, but although Hong Kong was near Canton, he did not flee. At about six o'clock on the afternoon of January 10, 1901, when Yang was tutoring students in his home at 52 Gage Street, four assassins entered and fired on him in the presence of his wife and the students. He died the next morning, survived by his wife, one son and two daughters.[47]

Years later, Ch'en Shao-pai stated his impression of Yang in these words:

> Yang was a man of great ambition; dignified, healthy, and energetic. In social gatherings, he always unconsciously took the seat of honor. But he was cordial, pleasant, and a good talker. After joining the Hsing Chung Hui, he carried on propaganda work wherever he went; and he could expound very well on the history and theory of revolution in daily conversation. Being educated in English schools, he had little Chinese education, and he later studied Chinese diligently. He was always seen with a book in his hands.[48]

In summing up Yang's career, it should be noted that, although he successfully fought against Sun Yat-sen's leadership in the revolutionary attempt of 1895, his influence in the Hsing Chung Hui waned shortly after that time. But the claim of the Kuomintang historians that the early revolutionary movement was financed solely by Sun's friends and relatives in Hawaii is inaccurate.

As a revolutionary party, the organization of the Hsing Chung Hui

---

[47] Tse, *op. cit.* p. 20; Ch'en Shao-pai, *op. cit.* pp. 52–54; Feng, *Fragments*, V, 13–14, and 32–33. The Hong Kong *China Mail* of October 4, 15, and 18, 1900, carried the news of the Waichow revolt. It reported the assassination of Yang on January 11, 12, and 14, 1901. The Shanghai *Kuo-min jih-jih-pao* (The China National Gazette), No. 2 (August 9, 1903), p. 27, reported the trial of the case on April 24–25, 1903. Only one of the four assassins was apprehended, and he was sentenced to death by hanging.

[48] Ch'en Shao-pai, *op. cit.* p. 55.

left much to be desired. Judging by its regulations, it could hardly be called a secret revolutionary organization. The regulations were seldom observed; and there is little indication that meetings were held according to the prescribed procedures. Nevertheless, as the first political society in modern China, the Hsing Chung Hui has great significance. And in that society it was the members, not the organizational rules, that counted. After 1895, Sun Yat-sen was identified with the party; wherever he went, the place became, in fact if not in name, the Hsing Chung Hui headquarters.

The years between 1895 and 1900 constituted a significant period in the Chinese revolutionary movement. It was the beginning of the end, a single spark that eventually burned down the Manchu house. After 1900, the turning point in the Chinese attitude toward the Manchu throne, a spontaneous revolutionary movement developed at home and abroad. But in those five years almost all the active revolutionaries were of Kwangtung origin (although Yang Ch'ü-yün's family came from Fukien, he was brought up in Hong Kong, so he might well be considered a Cantonese). Their operational bases were overseas Chinese communities, and their activities in China were confined to Kwangtung province alone. Their supporters were recruited from the lower stratum of Chinese society. Sun Yat-sen emerged as the undisputed leader, but he was unable to organize another armed revolt until after the formation of the T'ung Meng Hui (United League), a unified revolutionary organization founded in 1905 under the leadership of Sun and Huang Hsing. Except for Sun Yat-sen, not a single Hsing Chung Hui member played a leading role in the subsequent revolutionary movement.

❊ 6 ❊

Huang Hsing: Co-founder
of the Republic of China

CHIN CH'UNG-CHI AND HU SHENG-WU

Translated by Chün-tu Hsüeh

The modern Chinese bourgeoisie, petty bourgeoisie, and intelligentsia sprang from a semi-colonial and semi-feudal society. From the beginning, they were under heavy imperialist and feudal pressure and were aware of the danger of a national crisis. Yet they were unable to find their own future, which seemed to offer few prospects. Therefore, many of them, naturally stirred by national sentiments, were hostile to the imperialist powers and their running dogs. They became anti-imperialistic and patriotic. Some of them, making use of their knowledge of modern science and politics, took a further step forward, and participated in the national and democratic revolution, playing a significant role in the revolutionary struggle. Since the education they received was a bourgeois education, the family they were born into a feudal family, and the force they depended upon and represented the Chinese national bourgeoisie, which was very weak, they were, therefore, brought up with these inherent weaknesses in their political attitude. They distrusted and were

Translated from the *Li-shih yen-chiu* (Historical Research), No. 3 of 1962 (Peking, March 1962), pp. 11–26. The original Chinese title of this article is "Lun Huang Hsing" (On Huang Hsing). Since most of the forty-nine footnotes of the article were not full citations of the sources, they have been deleted. The footnotes in the English translation are supplied by the translator. Whenever feasible and necessary, the translator has put the original footnotes into the text to indicate the sources used by the authors.

123

sometimes frightened by the masses. At other times, their faith in the revolution was shaken, and, very often, they could not persist to the end.

The attitude of Huang Hsing before and after the Revolution of 1911 reflected that of the bourgeoisie, petty bourgeoisie, and intelligentsia of the time. He represented both the patriotic and anti-monarchial sentiment of the Chinese intelligentsia and their tendency to waver and compromise. Before 1911 he was concerned mainly with revolts; after the establishment of the Republic, compromise became his main guiding principle. Of course, these were characteristics of the revolutionary leaders of the time; but he also must have had his own individuality in these characteristics. Therefore, an analysis of his work and career before and after the Revolution of 1911 is an important step to the understanding of the political characteristics of the modern Chinese bourgeoisie, petty bourgeoisie, and intelligentsia of the revolution.

I

Huang Hsing (1874–1916) began his political career at the beginning of the twentieth century. At that time, Chinese national independence and existence were seriously threatened while the Chinese people, under the heavy pressure of the imperialists and their running dogs, experienced great poverty and suffering. Turn to the first page of twentieth-century Chinese history and one will see the occupation of Peking and northern Chihli by eight arrogant foreign powers, the curfew in Peking, the carving of districts for control, and the establishment of the so-called "provisional government" of Tientsin. Raids, massacres, and looting by the foreign armies were frequent in various areas of northern Chihli, and it was not until the signing of the Boxer Protocol in September 1901 that these came to an end. But with the conclusion of the Protocol, foreign capitalist investment began. Railways and coal mines fell into foreign hands. Foreign economic control began to extend inland, and a scramble for the spoils began in Manchuria, Tibet, and the Yangtze valley. There were even open discussions in newspapers whether China should be divided or a policy of "administrative integrity" should be adopted. This

serious situation inevitably had a great impact on the Chinese patriots. They announced in a journal [published by Chekiang students
in Japan]: "The foreigners are all vampires, sucking other peoples'
blood in the morning, taking their fat in the evening; until they are
about to die, then, they will take over their countries. This is exactly
what is going to happen to China." [In another magazine, published
by Kiangsu students in Japan it was pointed out]: "The patriots of
our country, in view of the fact that our nation may soon be conquered and our generation enslaved, have cried to warn our fellow
countrymen; but we present the bare facts to you: our nation had
already been conquered and our people enslaved."

Under such extremely serious circumstances, the Manchu government was not only unable to protect the national interests, but on
the contrary was following a policy of surrender, selling out China's
sovereignty. Internally, its rule was increasingly ruthless, suppressing
and squeezing the mass of people and restraining all patriotic activities. Naturally, it aroused the resentment and indignation of the
people.

Henceforth, the intelligentsia, spurred on by political circumstances, looked to the West for the nation's salvation and gravitated
toward the path of an anti-Manchu revolution. The intelligentsia,
who came from the gentry class and received the feudal Confucian
education, now began to feel the menace of racial extinction. On the
other hand, because of the gradual breakdown of the society and
economy based on feudalism, which posed a threat to their economic
life, they tried to seek a way out. Hence, their grievances were channeled into the stream of bourgeois revolution. Huang Hsing was one
of this group.

Huang Hsing's original name was Huang Chen, and his courtesy
name Chin-wu. He was born in Shanhua [now Changsha], Hunan.
His father, Huang Hsiao-ts'un, who died when his son was young,
had been a well-known scholar in Hunan. Huang Hsing also received
a great deal of feudal [classical] education. He held a *Hsiu-ts'ai*
degree. In 1898, he studied at the Academy of Hunan and Hupeh
in Wuchang, an institute directed by Liang Ting-fen [1859–1919],
where he continued receiving a systematic feudal education.

Even in his teens, Huang had never been a submissive youngster from the viewpoint of the ruling class. Han-Chinese pride had a deep influence on his ideology. [According to Li Shu-ch'eng], Huang's ancestors in the early Ch'ing period had written that the Huangs should never work for the Ch'ing government. Huang Hsing was deeply influenced by the famous Confucian scholar of the late Ming dynasty, Wang Fu-chih [1619–92]. He once made a remark, when he was very young, that a gentleman living among barbarians should aim high and far. While he was studying at the Academy of Hunan and Hupeh, he told one of his fellow students, Pai Yu-huan [Pai Ch'u-hsiang], "We do not study in order to serve the Manchus. Our purpose is to use our knowledge in the recovery of the rights for the Han-Chinese in the future." This indicated the seed of rebellion that germinated in his ideology.

At that time, Wuhan was a relatively advanced economic area in China. It was also an important center of communication, a place where news and Western ideas were easily accessible. During his studies at the Academy of Hunan and Hupeh, Huang was greatly disturbed by the occupation of the capital by foreign powers and understood that the national crisis was very serious. Meanwhile, he began to read Rousseau's *Social Contract* and other writings, and he came into contact with bourgeois political ideas. He had become more progressive, but he had yet to find a clear and firm political direction. Although he had shown some revolutionary tendencies in his speeches and writings, he had not taken part in revolutionary activities.

Early in 1902, Huang Hsing was sent to Japan by Chang Chiht'ung [1837–1909], Governor-General of Hunan and Hupeh, on "an observation tour of Japanese education." Many Chinese students, after arriving in other countries, began to comprehend better the seriousness of the increasing imperialist aggression in East Asia and realize more the criticalness of the situation in China. The modernization of Japan after the Meiji Restoration provided them with a stimulus in urging a self-strengthening movement in their own country against disintegration. They maintained that to make the country strong and independent in a world where only the fittest could survive, every person should have the right of citizenship. And in order to cultivate good citizenship qualifications one must have citizenship education. They, therefore, particularly emphasized "a war of knowledge," that is, the study and propagation of the Western bourgeois democratic culture. It was believed [in the words of a magazine published by Hupeh students in Japan] that "to talk of arms race and commercial competition without knowing the importance of knowledge, could not possibly be successful. It would be similar to a person who tries to drain the water without knowing from where the water comes. Besides, we are students, and we have the duty of introducing modern culture into China."

Huang Hsing was clearly affected by these ideas when he first arrived in Japan. He studied at the Kōbun Institute and took lessons in military strategy from Japanese officers. Every morning he would practice shooting and riding. He took part in the publication of the *Translations by Hunan Students Abroad* and the *Hupeh Students' Circle,* edited by Hunan and Hupeh students in Japan respectively. He translated from Japanese into Chinese the work of Yamada Kunihiko—"On School's Administrative Law"—which was published in issues No. 2 and No. 3 of the *Translations from Hunan Students Abroad.* These activities could not yet be considered revolutionary. Viewing the situation in perspective, the activities of these patriotic youths could not have stopped with this. With a growing national crisis, many students strongly felt that to study and propagate Western culture alone would not save their country, as water from a distant well could not help a nearby fire. It was under such circumstances that the propaganda of the bourgeois revolutionary democrats, headed by Sun Yat-sen, began to make itself felt among the Chinese students in Japan. As Li Shu-ch'eng, who went to Japan with Huang Hsing and who was a fellow student of Huang in the Kōbun Institute, recalled:

> At that time, Liang Ch'i-ch'iao was publishing the *Hsin-wen ts'ung-pao,* advocating a constitutional monarchy. Many Chinese students in Japan were attracted by his views, and some students from the Kōbun Institute also respected him. Later we came into contact with Chi I-hui, Liu Ch'eng-yü, and Ch'eng Chia-ch'eng,

who were the first few students sent by the provincial government of Hupeh, and who had met Mr. Sun Yat-sen and heard his revolutionary ideas during Sun's stay in Japan. They recommended to us some famous works, such as *The Record of the Massacre in the City of Chiating, A Diary of the Ten Days' Massacre in Yang-chow,* and other books written by the Confucian scholars of the late Ming and early Ch'ing periods, Huang Tsung-hsi [1610–95], Ku Yen-wu [1613–82], and Wang Fu-chih [1619–92]. These books enkindled our national feeling. The humiliations China suffered between the Opium War and the Boxer uprising, the intensification of the foreign aggressions in China, and the possibility of our country being conquered and our nation made extinct were largely due to the Manchu government: its corruption, incompetence, and suppression of Chinese nationalism. We felt that the existence of the Manchu government was an obstacle to the restoration of the nation. In order to save the country, the Manchu government had to be overthrown first. We now agreed that the revolutionary ideas of Mr. Sun [Yat-sen] were right after all. When the question whether the "constitutional reforms" or the "revolution" should be the means to save China was brought up in the evenings in the classroom in the Kōbun Institute, at first there were some heated arguments, but gradually the advocates of revolution gained a majority. Among the students, Mr. Huang K'o-ch'iang [Huang Hsing] had always been quiet and reserved. He [was one of those who] carefully thought out a problem and firmly stuck to the decision once it was reached. . . .

One evening he was having a very heated argument with a group of students. Too excited to speak, he smashed a tea-pot on the ground, expressing the view that he was determined to work for the revolution and that nothing could change his mind.

The remonstration against the Russians in 1903 marked a turning point in the development of the revolutionary ideology of the Chinese students in Japan. In 1900 the Russians occupied Manchuria, and in April 1903, when the Russian army was scheduled to withdraw, Russia did not carry out the second evacuation as promised. The Chinese students in Japan reacted strongly because they saw it as the initial "slicing of the Chinese melon" and the beginning of the foreign conquest of China. Ch'en T'ien-hua said in the *Alarm To Arouse the Age:*

You should not question whether the "slicing of the Chinese melon" is true, but whether the occupation of Manchuria by the Russians is real or not. If the occupation is a fact, then the "slicing of the Chinese melon" will certainly come true. Now, the Germans have taken Kiaochow; the Russians, the English, and the French immediately follow her and occupy a port for themselves. Now the Russians have occupied Manchuria. Into how many areas which would be equivalent to the size of Manchuria can China be divided? I am afraid there will not be enough land to satisfy all of them in the future. If you still ask whether the occupation of Manchuria is true or not, you are only showing your own ignorance.

This passage truly reflected the sentiments and common concern of the patriotic Chinese intellectuals of the time. "Hearing the news," [according to one obituary record] "Mr. Huang [Hsing] was so upset that he vomited more than a peck of blood. Chang [Ping-lin] and Sung [Chiao-jen] called for the doctor, but Huang did not recover until ten days later. He then declared, 'The disintegration of the nation has now reached its apex; only a revolution can save it from falling.'"[1]

Huang Hsing then joined the "Student Volunteer Army" and took part in the activities of the Association for Universal Military Education, organized by the radical Chinese students in Japan. Shortly afterward, the association sent him back to Hunan to organize a revolt.

"All national oppression calls forth the resistance of the broad masses of the people; and the resistance of a nationally oppressed population always leads to national revolt."[2] Increased aggression of and exploitation by the imperialist powers left a great impact on the masses of the suppressed country, including the majority of the patriotic literati. This impact resulted in their awakening to the struggle against the imperialists. This was a logical development of history. The early development of Huang Hsing's political ideas

[1] "Vomit more than a peck of blood," or "vomit several pecks (*tou*) of blood" should not be taken literally. It was a common and favorite expression of classical Chinese writers to describe someone who was extremely upset.

[2] V. I. Lenin, *Collected Works,* Vol. XXIII (Moscow: Progress Publishers, 1964), p. 61.

clearly illustrated this point. Although he had been under the influence of a feudal [traditional] education and was mildly and vaguely
affected by bourgeois political ideas, he was theoretically inadequate
for revolution. But he quickly went over to the ideals of the bourgeois
revolution when faced with a serious national crisis. Many revolutionary youths at that time, although divided in their ideas and
methods of pursuing revolution, eventually chose the road to revolution because of the same decisive factor, that is, a serious national
crisis. Generally speaking, their revolutionary activities were a protest against imperialist aggression, motivated by the maintenance of
national independence and survival. Undoubtedly, it was a progressive step for those who awoke from slumber to oppose national suppression and fight for national independence.

In the summer of 1903, Huang Hsing returned to China and
arrived in Hupeh by way of Shanghai. He spoke at the Academy of
Hunan and Hupeh and won a number of followers by his talks
on the Manchu's racial discrimination and the need for governmental reforms, and also by his discourse against the conservatives.
Chang Chih-t'ung, Governor-General of Hunan and Hupeh, was
infuriated and asked Liang Ting-fen, Mayor of Wuchang and President of the Academy, to have Huang punished. Liang announced
Huang's expulsion; the latter, however, remained [in Wuchang] for
eight days. Before he boarded a ship for Hunan, he had distributed
over four thousand copies of Tsou Jung's *The Revolutionary Army*
and Ch'en T'ien-hua's *Sudden Realization* among the military and
in academic circles. Huang Hsing's behavior reflected the vigorous
anti-Manchu patriotic sentiment of the revolutionary youths of the
time.

Upon arriving in Hunan, Huang taught at two schools, Ming-te
and Hsiu-yeh. Meanwhile, he went on with his revolutionary activities with Chang Chi [1882–1947], Chou Chen-lin, and Hu Yüan-
t'an. On his thirtieth birthday [according to the lunar calendar],
which happened to be on November 4 of that year, he met with
Chang Chi, Chou Chen-lin, Ch'en T'ien-hua, and Sung Chiao-jen.
They decided to establish the Hua Hsing Hui (Society for the
Revival of China) with Huang Hsing as the chairman. On Feb-

ruary 15, 1904, the revolutionary society was formally established. As soon as the Hua Hsing Hui was formed, an armed revolt was vigorously planned. Under the direction of Huang Hsing, two more associations were established: one was the Society Against the Common Enemy (T'ung Ch'ou Hui), which was primarily intended to recruit members from the Society of Elders and Brothers and other secret societies; the other was the Han Society (Huang Han Hui) for subversion in the army. The scope, contact, and scale of this projected revolt were quite extensive, and more than 100,000 members of the Society of Elders and Brothers allegedly took part in the attempted revolt, which was stronger than the one attempted by the Self-Independent Army [organized by T'ang Ts'ai-ch'ang] in 1900. The revolt was scheduled to take place simultaneously in five cities—Changsha, Yuehchou, Changteh, Hengchou, and Paching—on the Empress Dowager's birthday in the fall of 1904. Unfortunately, the plot was discovered. The Hunan governor was shocked and ordered the arrest of Huang Hsing, who had to escape in disguise.

Bourgeois democratic revolutionary parties, such as the Hsing Chung Hui and Hua Hsing Hui, from the beginning and even before they gained any strength in organization and power, had adopted the armed revolt as the main form of struggle. This is a praiseworthy point deserving notice. It was not chosen accidentally, but rather out of the necessity of national survival. First of all, the conflict, involving the imperialists, with their running dogs, the Manchu government, and the masses of the Chinese people, was particularly acute while the nation's survival was in great danger. In desperation, the revolutionaries had no other choice but to rely on armed revolt in order to save the country from the national crisis in the quickest way possible. Secondly, China had been a semi-colonial and semi-feudal nation; the people enjoyed no democratic rights whatsoever.

The Manchu government stubbornly resisted any fundamental change; it tried its best to block any road to national liberation. Even the remonstrance against the Russian occupation of Man-churia in 1903, which was clearly a patriotic movement, was severely suppressed. Since moderation produced no results, the revolutionaries had no alternative but to take up arms against the government. Furthermore, China had a rich tradition of people's revolution. Volumes of Chinese history, particularly modern Chinese history, were filled with stories of armed revolts of the masses against the rulers. Secret societies, armies, and masses of the Chinese people were potential revolutionaries. All of these encouraged the revolutionary intelligentsia of the time. Taking up arms became important means in the revolutionary movement. Thus, Huang Hsing decided on a revolution; and his decision was perfectly correct.

After the insurrection in Changsha failed, Huang Hsing still traveled back and forth between Hunan and Shanghai to organize another revolt. Soon after, he went to Tokyo where, in Chang Shih-chao's residence, he was introduced by Yang Tu to Sun Yat-sen,[3] who had just arrived from Europe. At that time Sun was enthusiastically advocating the amalgamation of Hsing Chung Hui, Hua Hsing Hui, Kuang Fu Hui, and other revolutionary parties in order to centralize and unify the revolutionary movement. However, regionalism was strong among the revolutionaries because of a retrogressive Chinese economy. Some of the members of the Hua Hsing Hui, such as Liu K'uei-i, opposed the amalgamation and wanted a separate "Hunan party." This was a great obstacle to the formation of a united revolutionary organization. Huang Hsing differed from them in his political point of view, which was national rather than regional. [According to Huang's biography written by Liu K'uei-i,] Huang had pointed out at the time when the Hua Hsing Hui was organized:

> It will not be difficult to capture Hunan province as a revolutionary base. However, if the other provinces fail to respond to our initiative, then it will be difficult to conquer the North and to overthrow the Manchu regime; the resources of one province can-

[3] Although subscribed to widely, this is a questionable fact. I believe that Sun Yat-sen and Huang Hsing were introduced by Miyazaki Torazō (Tōten). For an account of their first meeting, see Miyazaki Tōten, *Shina kakumei gundan* (Episodes of the Chinese Revolutionary Army) (Tokyo, 1912), pp. 115–16. For a discussion of the subject, see my research note in the *Chung-yang jih-pao* (Central Daily News) (Taipei), July 9, 1967.

not fight the rest of the nation. I hope, therefore, that our comrades will seek cooperation from the people of other provinces whenever possible, so that when the time comes, concerted action can be taken.

He therefore agreed to join the unified revolutionary organization, T'ung Meng Hui (The United League), as suggested by Sun Yat-sen. His co-operation was very important in the establishment of this new organization.

As soon as the T'ung Meng Hui was formed, Huang Hsing was elected to a position second in command and became the most important leader next to Sun Yat-sen in the organization. Why did he become such an important leader in the revolutionary party? First, although Sun Yat-sen's Hsing Chung Hui was the first revolutionary organization of the Chinese bourgeois democratic group, the Hsing Chung Hui consisted mostly of overseas Chinese and was therefore weak in its connection with Chinese society. When the T'ung Meng Hui was established, many Chinese students in Japan joined it, thereby strengthening the relations between the bourgeois democratic group and Chinese society. Of all the students studying in Japan, those who came from Hunan and Hupeh were the most numerous. Huang Hsing was a Hunanese. He had studied in the Academy of Hunan and Hupeh, and he was held in great esteem among the students of these two provinces. Thus, he naturally represented this important segment of the T'ung Meng Hui and became its important leader. Secondly, although his revolt in Hunan in 1904 failed, it was the first revolt ever organized by a Chinese bourgeois revolutionary democratic group in the interior of China. The rebellion was wider in scope than either the 1895 revolutionary attempt in Canton or the Waichow revolt in 1900. Consequently, it had a great effect in China, and Huang's prestige was greatly enhanced. Lastly, it was his personality and ability. He was intelligent and courageous.

> [According to Liu K'uei-i,] Huang took boxing lessons in the Wu school from Li Yung-ch'iu of Liuyang county when he was young, and he could lift 3,000 catties single-handedly. . . .[4]

[4] An expression of the Chinese classical writer which should not be taken literally; 100 catties = 133 1/3 pounds.

His prose had the style of the writings of Su Tung-p'o and his calligraphy was excellent in the Northern Wei style. He was one of the favorite students of Liang Ting-fen, President of the Academy of Hunan and Hupeh. . . .

According to the regulations of a military athletic society in Tokyo, a silver medal would be awarded to those who could hit the center of the target six times consecutively. Huang Hsing went there for practice and never missed a shot. As a result, his desk was loaded with medals.

Huang was simple, honest, forgiving, and sincere. Many old revolutionarists often praised his character warmly, saying that he was a "reliable and upright person," "a patriot, rather reserved but practical in his study and work and truthful to his friends." Some say that he was "valiant, natural and firm" and "was loved and admired whole-heartedly by many of his fellow revolutionaries."

After the formation of the T'ung Meng Hui, Huang's prestige continued to increase both within and outside of the party. He was ranked with Sun Yat-sen and their names were often linked together by the title "Sun-Huang." During this period, Huang showed two things that deserve our attention.

First, he was the military leader of the repeated armed revolts of the T'ung Meng Hui. From the beginning, he had devoted himself to preparing and organizing armed insurrections. He was personally in charge of recruiting party members from among the Chinese students in Japanese military schools. Many military students who later became prominent military figures in China—Li Lieh-chün, [Yen Hsi-shan,] Ch'eng Ch'ien, Li Ken-yüan, T'ang Chi-yao, Lo P'ei-chin, Chang Feng-hui, Yin Ch'ang-heng, Chao Heng-t'i, Liu Ts'un-hou, K'ung Keng, and Wang Hsiao-chen—were recruited by him. He kept their membership oaths. He also organized a tightly disciplined, secret "league of men of spirit" (Chang-fu t'uan) with a number of reliable military students. Thus he established a close friendship with the revolutionaries in the army. Once disguised as a Chang Shou-cheng, he infiltrated into Kuo Jen-chang's army in Kweilin, Kwangsi, and recruited army officer Ch'ao Sheng and other revolutionaries into the T'ung Meng Hui. The leaders of the Ping-Liu-Li revolts of 1906 in the border regions of Hunan and Kiangsi

—Kung Ch'un-t'ai, Chiang Shou-tan, Hsiao K'o-ch'ang, Li Chin-ch'i, and Wang Sheng—were former followers of Ma Fu-i, leader of the secret Society of Elders and Brothers who had worked with Huang Hsing. In 1907 and 1908, Huang personally directed the four insurrections at Chinchow-Lienchow-Fangcheng, Chengnan-kuan, Chinchow-Lienchow-Shangszu, and Hokow on the borders of Kwangtung, Kwangsi, and Yunnan. In all these insurrections, he had fought courageously and very daringly at the front with his men.

After these unsuccessful revolts, Sun Yat-sen could not remain in the border areas of China; therefore he went to Europe, entrusting the revolutionary work to Huang Hsing and Hu Han-min. However, they had to suspend their military operations temporarily because of repeated failures, meager financial resources, and no suitable revolutionary base. This was T'ung Meng Hui's most difficult period. But Huang Hsing was not discouraged. On April 27, 1911, he led the sensational Canton revolt.[5] The T'ung Meng Hui had pooled all its resources for this revolution and mobilized all its power. Huang was the chief of staff and acting commander of the uprising. He established his cell at No. 5 Eastern Camp near the office of the Governor-General in Canton. It may be said that he was right in the lion's den. He worked at the heart of the enemy line, day and night, under the threat of being discovered. Just before the uprising he wrote, "I am leaving today for the battlefield. I am determined to lead my men to wipe out the enemy. These could be my last words." He then led the Dare-To-Die Corps in a heroic attack on the Governor-General's office. He was wounded and lost his first two fingers. The uprising failed, but it left a great impact on the country. It strengthened the revolutionary spirit of the masses and led to the subsequent success of the Wuchang Revolution and the independence of the various provinces. Huang Hsing was now famous, and his revolutionary prestige was great in China. His name became inseparable from the series of armed

[5] Subsequently known as the "March 29th Revolution," because it took place on the twenty-ninth day of the third month according to the lunar calendar.

revolts of which he had been the leader. In these armed struggles he showed a truly heroic and fearless spirit; his prestige among the revolutionaries was well deserved.

During this period a second aspect of Huang Hsing's activities that deserves attention was that, in the interests of the cause, he worked for the preservation of T'ung Meng Hui unity and helped maintain Sun Yat-sen's leadership, despite the efforts of a number of the comrades trying to split the revolutionary party. In 1907, pointing to the failure of the Chaochow and Waichow revolts as excuses, Chang Ping-lin and T'ao Ch'eng-chang incited Chang Chi, Sung Chiao-jen, T'an Jen-feng, and Pai Yu-huan to call a meeting to impeach Sun Yat-sen and to replace him with Huang Hsing. Huang, however, firmly refused. In a letter to these comrades, Huang said: "Sun Yat-sen is a most renowned and honored person. If you want the revolution to be a success, there should be no misunderstanding among us and you should give him hearty support." With this, the dispute ended. In the same year, the Society for Common Advancement (Kung Chin Hui) was established in Tokyo. Fearing a split within the revolutionary party, he questioned Chiao Ta-feng [founder of the Society], "Why another association?" Eventually, in 1908, Chang Ping-lin and T'ao Ch'eng-chang broke away from the T'ung Meng Hui and re-established the Restoration Society (Kuang Fu Hui). T'ao Ch'eng-chang, Li Hsieh-ho, and six other comrades circulated a pamphlet entitled, "The Crime of Sun Yat-sen." Huang Hsing not only never re-established the Hua Hsing Hui, he even condemned its anti-Sun activities. In 1909, T'ao Ch'eng-chang returned to Tokyo and tried again to win Huang's support, but Huang was still unmoved. Instead, he sent a letter to Li Hsieh-ho, defending Sun Yat-sen. Huang actually had some differences with Sun Yat-sen as indicated in Sung Chiao-jen's *Diary* and Chang Ping-lin's *Autographical Chronology*. It is, therefore, commendable that Huang would, for the sake of revolution, unselfishly stand for the unity of the T'ung Meng Hui and support Sun Yat-sen's leadership when some of its leading members were engaged in splitting the revolutionary movement.

However, Huang Hsing had his weaknesses like the other bourgeoisie, petty bourgeoisie, and intelligentsia in this period. It was under serious national crisis and stirred by patriotism that the intelligentsia at that time began to join the anti-Manchu revolutionary struggle. They were inexperienced in politics and tended to compromise. They were afraid to advocate anti-imperialist slogans and had illusions about imperialist countries. Many were tied to the feudal society in a thousand and one ways. They were unable to criticize the traditional ideas that greatly influenced them. Their target of attack was the Manchu government; the "anti-Manchu" slogans played an important role in the revolutionary activities.

[As Li Shu-ch'eng recently wrote:] "Most members did not fully understand Sun's policy of establishing the republic and redistributing the land. They thought that these things should not worry them at the moment; these were things that would be taken care of after the revolution." Though they were determined to have a revolution, they were weak in spirit and tended to compromise. Their political knowledge and ideology were behind their revolutionary activities. Huang Hsing shared some of these common characteristics of the bourgeois and petty bourgeois intelligentsia. Traditional Han-nationalism played an important role in his revolutionary activities, as indicated clearly in some of his poems in this period. Here are some examples:[6]

> I've not destroyed our foe, restoring Han;
> Thou hast thy life destroyed for th' native land.

> Hundred thousands of weapons with lightning shine
> Sweep the native land.
> They strike down the enemy like the descending sun
> Or brush him away like floating smoke.
> Burning fire covers the sacred land,
> While blood overflows the Yellow River.
> Fast runs the enemy as a flock of foxes,
> Or as if he were swept away by the Western wind.

> Seizure of Wuhan should be the first determined rise,
> Capture of the sacred land shall win the highest prize.

[6] Translated by Dr. F. T. Cheng, former Chinese ambassador to the Court of St. James's, for Chün-tu Hsüeh.

In 1912, after the establishment of the Republic of China, Huang Hsing, looking back at the revolution with complacency, said,

> In this revolution we had been united, appealed to by our fathers and encouraged by our elder brothers. One followed when the other fell. We have avenged the wrongs of the past nine generations and the five races will enjoy the bliss we gained for them. It meant loyalty to the Republic and filial piety to our ancestors.

When Huang Hsing studied at the Academy of Hunan and Hupeh and later in Japan, he began to accept bourgeois political ideas and set his goal for the establishment of a bourgeois democratic republic. However, while accepting bourgeois ideas, he failed to examine his subconscious feudal [traditional] beliefs. Instead, he reconciled the two. When he expounded his ideas on the rights of the people (min-chüan) at the Ming-te School in Hunan after his return from Japan, students who did not understand the concept of "people's rights" asked him to explain the term. His answer was: "Have you ever read the works of Mencius? Mencius said, 'The people are the most important element in the nation; the spirits of the land and grain are the next; the sovereign is the lightest.' This is what I mean by people's rights." Later, he remarked clearly as follows:

> Loyalty and filial piety when applied to a person would produce morality, but when applied to a country would produce peace and order. Though the West may be different from us in their laws and customs, they have not discarded these two essences of the nation. . . . Therefore, the theories of political and social revolution aimed at the reform of the existing political institutions; they were not meant to be contrary to the fundamental principle of loyalty and filial piety.

Although Huang objected to the tyranny of the feudal-monarchical autocratic order, he did not intend to overthrow the existing social order completely. After achieving what he considered the main object of his political struggle—the overthrow of the Manchu dynasty and the establishment of the republic—he lost his desire for further political development.

As a rule, bourgeois revolutionaries were contemptuous of the masses; they were even afraid of them. They often indulged in individualistic heroism. At the same time, their isolation from the masses and resulting weakness led to pessimism and despondency. This can be seen from Huang Hsing's political activities.

In the T'ung Meng Hui period, several armed revolts under his leadership were merely the military adventures of a few persons in his own revolutionary party, sometimes with the assistance of the secret societies. Therefore, these revolts failed repeatedly and seemingly inevitably. After the defeat of the "Canton Revolution of March 29th" 1911, Huang became despondent. [In a moment of despair and anguish,] he thought that nothing more could be done by the T'ung Meng Hui.[7] He felt that hereafter all he could do was to fulfill what he considered his bounden duty—assassinate personally so as to revenge the dead [those who died in the Canton revolution]. Later, when he heard the news of the rapid development of the revolutionary movement in the New Army of Wuchang, he was prepared to go there and take over the leadership again. In a letter to three comrades, he said:

> Representatives from Hunan and Hupeh were here yesterday with their news of the army sympathetic to the revolution and capable of doing so. . . .
> As I see it, the situation in the Yangtze Valley today is similar to the situation of a person who has mounted a tiger and who can do nothing but go on riding. Even without our help and guidance, they will take the initiative to revolt which might become uncontrollable and lead to chaos. The situation might be irremediable later. It is better for us therefore to take advantage of the situation and take a chance on winning. Besides, it would be far less costly than to start from scratch as in the past.

With regard to the Wuhan situation, the things uppermost in his mind were "to take advantage of the situation" and that it would be "far less costly." Meanwhile, he feared that the masses might rise independently and bring about an "uncontrollable," "irremediable," and chaotic situation. One can see clearly from these phrases the attitude of the bourgeois revolutionary toward the mass of the people.

[7] The authors apparently overemphasized here the significance of a fleeting thought of a man in great despair after defeat.

These two basic flaws of the bourgeois revolutionaries in the Revolution of 1911—their lack of a definite and complete anti-imperialist, anti-feudal political program and the absence of arousing the masses and of a firm reliance on them—were clearly reflected in Huang Hsing in the revolutionary period. Here we can also see the signs of Huang Hsing's retrogression after the establishment of the Republic.

However, during the revolutionary period, the most urgent political question was whether there should be a revolution, or whether the Manchu government, which was the running dog of the imperialists, should be overthrown. During this historical stage, Huang Hsing stood firmly for revolution and struggled courageously. He was undoubtedly a dominant figure. Therefore, in assessing his role in the revolution, we should first of all look at these aspects and place him in the position he deserves. Huang Hsing did show some of the positive, progressive, and revolutionary characteristics of the bourgeois and petty bourgeois intelligentsia of the time.

II

In October 1911 the Wuchang Revolution broke out, followed by the independence of various provinces. In the short span of a few months, the Manchu government was overthrown, and the feudal monarchical system which had existed in China for more than two thousand years came to an end. The Republic of China was established. It was a great victory.

However, the bourgeois revolutionary party was rapidly transformed after the victory. The slogan for the Wuchang Revolution and provincial independence was the "anti-Manchu revolution." In the negotiation between the South and the North, the only demand of the South was the abdication of the Manchu government. The revolution was to be considered successful when the Manchu emperor abdicated. Later, the general view was that the Republic of China was established when Yüan declared his support for the republican form of government, and when he was elected to the presidency. Some people who were content with these gains refused to go on with the revolution. What they hoped for was peace and order so that industry could be developed. Others, dreaming of parliamentary politics, devoted their energy to legitimate bourgeois political activities and thought that, as long as they could maintain a majority in the National Assembly, all political problems could be solved. The traditional feudal ideology, which had never been fully analyzed or questioned, once again began to influence the ideas and actions of the revolutionists, who proposed that bygones be bygones and past hostility forgotten. The revolutionists now joined hands with both the Constitutionalists and even Yüan Shih-k'ai, who became the symbol of feudal authority. Yüan, however, played two-faced tricks. He threatened them with military superiority on the one hand and fooled them with dreams of "peace" and "unification" on the other. This furthered the confusion and disintegration of the revolutionary party.

Differences within the revolutionary camp were reflected in the inner circle of the leadership. Chang Ping-lin, who had always been a splitter, openly broke away and organized a new party with Constitutionalist Chang Ch'ien,[8] in opposition to Sun Yat-sen. Wang Ching-wei had virtually gone to the side of Yüan Shih-k'ai, and the group under Sung Chiao-jen and others was seriously and actively advocating so-called parliamentary politics. A change could also be noted in Huang Hsing himself. Despite his contributions after the Wuchang Revolution, which will be dealt with later, he began to show the negative side of his political thought; his passion for the revolution diminished and compromise became a dominant feature of his political ideals.

The basic cause for the changes in Huang Hsing's ideology was the compromising and wavering nature of the bourgeois revolutionaries, which emerged with the success of the revolution. In analyzing this attitude, the social structure and class relations of the period must be considered. But in this regard, Huang Hsing had his own personal characteristics and particularities.

First, the success of the Wuchang Revolution, the collapse of the

[8] For the career of Chang Ch'ien, see Samuel C. Chu, *Reformer in Modern China: Chang Ch'ien, 1853–1926* (New York: Columbia University Press, 1965).

Manchu rule, and the establishment of the Provisional Government of the Republic of China meant to Huang Hsing the fulfillment of the political aims he had persistently pursued for many years. After achieving these goals he lost his aim and direction in the continuation of the revolution.[9] To him, the urgent problem was the unification and the consolidation of the new Republic, so that "the Republic may live for thousands of years" and he might "reap the benefit of a Republican citizen." In a circular telegram he stated, "The real peace and happiness that we had longed for more than ten years have come true. It would be delightful to be able to spend one's leisure time in the countryside." On his thirty-ninth birthday [Chinese reckoning] in 1912, he wrote the following poem:[10]

> At thirty-nine I know what will be wrong at forty.
> Though the song of "Rising Wind" is good I rather homeward go.
> Alas! Tremendous noble works have flowed away like water.
> Therefore I love the more my orchard and the downward sun.
> At night the fish and dragons all keep silent and relax.
> On my native hill all beasts and birds retire without a noise.
> Standing erect alone and thoughtless I'm in a perfect mood.
> Only a gentle breeze at times would touch my plainest clothes.

After Yüan Shih-k'ai became Provisional President of the Republic, Huang still held these views:

> The new laws of our country should aim at the protection of the people and be supervised by the National Assembly. Thereafter, there would be no misunderstanding between the government and the people; taking the other countries as a model and with the construction of railways as the primary policy for the national salvation, we would soon catch up with the foreigners. Will our country then not be prosperous and industries developed?

On another occasion, he wrote: "I wish our people not to be brave

[9] This is a cliché used by Chinese historians to criticize all the revolutionary leaders other than Sun Yat-sen. But if the "unification and consolidation of the new Republic" after 1911 was not a correct direction but an erroneous policy, should Huang Hsing have launched "The Republican Cultural Revolution" of the Maoist style in order to "go on with the revolution"?

[10] Translation by Ambassador F. T. Cheng. "Rising Wind" or "Tempest Song" was composed by the Han dynasty's first emperor, who wished to return home to retire after the founding of the dynasty.

in internal struggles but courageous externally in competing with other powers. Would it then not be a most delightful achievement?" While all this time Yüan Shih-k'ai was scheming and preparing for war, Huang Hsing was totally unprepared and indulged himself in the illusion of a great triumph.

Secondly, under such circumstances Huang Hsing's ideas and activities were influenced and motivated by the traditional feudal ideology that he had never fully analyzed. He even proposed "tightening up discipline" to Yüan Shih-k'ai. Part of the proposal reads as follows:

> Now that the Republic has been established, all the state affairs await to be done. The first thing in politics is a rectification of names, and discipline is the primary need for governing a nation. Our country is the oldest nation in the civilized world, and filial piety, obedience, loyalty, trustworthiness, propriety, righteousness, integrity, and sense of shame are the essence of governing a nation and the spirit of the rule of law. . . . Recently the meaning of a Republic has often been misunderstood by students. Their extreme views have often obscured the truth. If unchecked, rebellion against parents would be considered freedom, and violation of law would be considered equality. Hence, the national order and the five human relationships would be out of control; without the family, there would be no country to speak of. Therefore, I beg of you to issue orders to all the schools and teachers of the nation, explaining to them the meaning of this, so as to prevent the spread of subversive ideology, which might lead the people onto the wrong path. If this tendency is unchecked, law and order would be disrupted, justice would be destroyed, people would be motivated only by selfishness, and material gains and the country would be on the verge of disintegration. The catastrophe would be more serious than the disaster of the flood and the cruelty of the cannibal as described by Mencius. All that I have been working for these years is to safeguard our country. I cannot help but be greatly disturbed by witnessing the coming of the calamity. I beseech you, therefore, to accept my suggestion and carry it out.

In a letter to the Shanghai Society for Promoting Traditional Ethics, he stressed this view again:

> I have heard of what you mentioned in your letter about some people, who, in the name of freedom, have violated the law, and in

the name of equality, have gone against their elder brothers and their parents. This is an unprecedented change unexpected by those of us who first advocated the revolution and the republican form of government. I have formerly requested the President to issue an order to all schools and teachers stressing the importance of discipline and ethics, because I realized this deterioration would greatly affect the future of the republic, and I tried to stop it. I am glad to learn that you gentlemen have established the Society for Promoting Traditional Ethics for the purpose of investigating the traditional law of proper conduct and of reforming the undesirable customs. You fully understand civic responsibility. What you have done is what we had long hoped for since the establishment of the Republic.

Huang Hsing was now clearly an upholder of the traditional ideals and values. What he had hoped for was the development of a capitalistic order; but in this aspect he was influenced by the traditional ideals and customs, which made it difficult for him to distinguish friends from enemies.

Thirdly, after the Revolution of 1911, there was a sudden change in the social status of some bourgeois revolutionaries. Huang Hsing, for example, became the "great hero of the Republic." He found himself in a position to encourage private enterprise. In the later period of the Nanking Provisional Government he requested the government to set aside $300,000 in the annual budget for the Association for the Reclamation of Waste Land, organized by a group of people and sponsored by him. In the proposal applying for the fund he wrote: "After the establishment of the Republic, all the enterprises have to be reconstituted; especially urgent is the work of reclamation." After the dissolution of the Provisional Government at Nanking, he planned to establish the National Bank of China, publish a railway magazine, invest in the China Steam Navigation Company, the Hunan Mining Company, and the Fukuo Mining Company. In his meeting with Yüan Shih-k'ai in Peking, he expressed an interest in devoting himself to the "development and promotion of national industries and resources." He was successively appointed as the Director-General of the Canton-Hankow Railways. By now his interest had clearly shifted to the development of private enterprise. This clearly reflected the desire of the upper strata of the national bourgeoisie, who hoped for "peace" and "order," to develop private enterprise and industry. It resulted in the diminishing of the revolutionary spirit.

Fourthly, because of the distrust of the masses and the gulf between the bourgeois revolutionaries and the people, Huang Hsing often felt his power inadequate. He feared the military threats of Yüan Shih-k'ai. He believed that Yüan was deceitful, scheming, and audacious and that, if his ambitions were satisfied, he would not be faithful to the Manchu government any longer: otherwise, like Tseng Kuo-fan in his suppression of the Taiping rebels, he would put down the revolution for the Manchu court. [As Li Shu-ch'eng recalled,] Huang believed that "so long as Yüan was willing to overthrow the Manchus and return the unliberated part of the country to the Han race, it would be wise to offer him the presidency for a few years in return for the end of the war and peace to the people. Otherwise, Yüan would be our enemy, and, unless we could defeat him we might even lose what we had conquered, not to mention the unification of the whole country."

These negative developments in Huang's ideology made him commit a series of grave political mistakes. At the time of the peace negotiation between the South and the North and after the Nanking Provisional Government was established, the crucial problem in the struggle between the revolutionaries and the counter-revolutionaries was whether the revolutionaries were willing to forfeit their acquired political power and place it in the hands of the counter-revolutionaries. In this basic question, Huang was in favor of compromising with Yüan. During his Wuhan campaign Huang sent a wire to Yüan Shih-k'ai, saying that, if Yüan could overthrow the Manchu court, "not only would the people in Hunan and Hupeh honor you as Napoleon and Washington, but I am sure that the authorities of the other provinces would all be willing to follow your orders." Later in Nanking, Sun Yat-sen, playing on the people's revolutionary sentiment, wanted to continue the war in order to clear away every obstacle and establish a new nation on a new basis,[11] but Huang and others insisted on compromising with Yüan. Of course, Huang Hsing alone should not be blamed for this policy; nevertheless, because of his position and influence at that time, he should be held responsible to a certain extent.

After seizing power, Yüan Shih-k'ai had to stabilize the crumbled old order and decrease the military power of the revolutionaries in the South in order to consolidate his own position. He was waiting for the right time to curb the revolutionary strength. At this moment Huang Hsing proposed a "tightening up discipline," emphasizing "law," "ordinance," "customs," and "order," which were objectively favorable to Yüan's position. Huang was, in fact, giving help to Sung Chiao-jen in the latter's endeavor to organize the T'ung Meng Hui into the Kuomintang by absorbing a large number of old politicians and officials into the party in an attempt to win the coming election. When the clash between the new and the old order became more intense [Huang Hsing] insisted on compromise. He believed that recruiting more intellectuals and talented persons was a matter of first importance. He was, therefore, admired by most of the leaders and members of the other political parties. He favored keeping contact with Yüan Shih-k'ai. To show his sincerity and trust, he accepted an invitation to meet Yüan in Peking in the fall of 1912. While in Peking, Huang Hsing invited everyone to join the Kuomintang, including Yang Tu, Fan Yüan-lien, and all the high-ranking members of the Democratic Party. Later he even invited all the cabinet members to join the Kuomintang and asked Yüan to be the head of the party, believing that by party politics the government could obtain support and political stability could be achieved. In fact, except for Yüan Shih-k'ai, Chou Hsüeh-hsi, Fan Yüan-lien, and the Army and Navy ministers, all the cabinet members applied for Kuomintang membership, including Premier Ch'ao Ping-chün, Yüan's secret police chief. After he left Peking, Huang praised Yüan Shih-k'ai, believing that Yüan was the only

[11] This is another false statement that cannot be supported by evidence. As early as November 12, 1911, Sun Yat-sen had cabled from Paris on his way home that "Mr. Li [Yüan-hung] should of course be elected president. It would also be appropriate if Li would give up the post in favor of Yüan [Shih-k'ai] as reported."

person suitable for the presidency.[12] But Huang's more serious mistake was the disbandment of the revolutionary army in the South. [As Chou Chen-lin writes:]

> Taking the lack of funds for the support of the increasing southern army and the hope for a peaceful order and a unification of the nation as an excuse, Yüan Shih-k'ai asked the South for a general demilitarization. Mr. Huang Hsing agreed to the proposal and ordered the Southern army to disband. He was of the opinion that since political power was handed over to Yüan, peaceful reconstruction should be the next logical step. Many revolutionary comrades at first were unwilling to do so, but Mr. Huang insisted. He believed that even for the purpose of training a better army, demobilization of superfluous troops was necessary first. The comrades of various provinces realized the financial difficulty of supporting the army, and they did not want to increase the burden on the people. As a result, they finally followed Huang's orders.

Of course, financial difficulty was the objective reason for disbanding the Southern army, because Yüan Shih-k'ai withheld financial support from the hundreds of thousands in the army in Nanking, who had to live on porridge. Some of them even mutinied. However, the reason mainly responsible for the South's disarming was subjective. As a result of this mistaken conception, armies were disbanded in various Southern provinces. In Hunan, the entire army was disbanded by T'an Yen-k'ai. In Nanking, hundreds of thousands of revolutionary troops were completely disbanded, with the exception of the Eighth Division. The armies from Kiangsu, Chekiang, and Kwangtung were sent back to their native provinces. In spite of the fact that Huang Hsing intended to establish a peace-

[12] It should be mentioned that Sun Yat-sen went to meet Yüan Shih-k'ai first, and then urged Huang Hsing to come to Peking as soon as possible. Sun's favorable impression of Yüan is indicated in a speech he delivered before the Shanghai Bureau of the Kuomintang on October 5, 1912: "Some people in the South still distrust him [Yüan Shih-k'ai], but I definitely believe in his sincerity. . . . In order to govern the Republic, one must have the combination of new ideas, old experience, and old-fashioned method. And President Yüan is just the right man." In February 1913, Sun told the Japanese press that the "Presidency cannot but fall on Mr. Yüan Shih-k'ai." According to a letter written by Yüan Shih-k'ai to Governor Po Wen-wei in 1913, both Sun Yat-sen and Huang Hsing had invited him to join the Kuomintang during their visits to Peking in 1912.

ful order based on a parliamentary system and to develop national enterprises, the result was just the opposite. Instead, an old order was established with authority in the hands of Yüan Shih-k'ai. Even though Huang Hsing showed his sincerity by disbanding his troops in order to gain Yüan's concessions, the result was just the opposite. Disarming the South served only to strengthen Yüan's position and to enhance his ambition. It greatly weakened the strength of the revolutionary party itself. The revolutionists were willing to lay down their arms because they had already laid down their spiritual weapons. Consequently, when Yüan Shih-k'ai suddenly launched his attack they found themselves in chaos.

In March 1913, Yüan Shih-k'ai was instrumental in the assassination of Sung Chiao-jen. His anti-revolutionary face was fully exposed. Many Kuomintang members in the South were infuriated and proposed a military expedition. At first Huang was opposed to such an action on the grounds that the Republic had not fully recovered from its initial chaos, that evidence of Yüan's ambition to become an emperor was not yet obvious, and that the revolutionary army had been disbanded and had to be reorganized before they were ready for war. He suggested the military expedition be postponed and the issue settled by legal means. He argued that with sufficient evidence after the opening of the National Assembly, the issue could then be effectively settled by a special tribunal. In a report dated May 27, 1913, journalist Huang Yüan-yung stated that "the most agitated was Sun Yat-sen" and that "[the view of] Huang [toward the issue] had changed a little but Sun remained unchanged." Naturally it was the objective situation that accounted for Huang Hsing's behavior. The strength of the Southern revolutionists was really weak because of their isolation from the masses and because they had disbanded the revolutionary army. But Huang Hsing's attitude at this time was completely negative, and it would, therefore, be very difficult to defend him. When Yüan sent his army to the South and war appeared inevitable, Huang still asserted that nothing much could be done, for the people were apathetic. He continued to suggest strengthening the Kuomintang members' influence in the National Assembly and making use of the assembly for legal struggle. Subsequently he took command in Nanking; but seeing the situation hopeless, he left Nanking at the end of July.[13] Even the officers of the Eighth Division, who had been loyal to him, became dissatisfied with his leadership. Furthermore, [according to Chang Lu-ts'un,]

> It was this incident that created the top leadership problem. Sun Yat-sen's leadership was tremendously challenged as a result of making use of Ts'en Ch'un-hsüan as the generalissimo of the provisional government in the struggle against Yüan Shih-k'ai. The rationale was that since Ts'en of the South and Yüan of the North had been prominent officials of the Manchu government, the former's influence might be of great help to the revolution and a blow to the treachery and conspiracy of Yüan. Obviously, this proposal could not have been passed without Huang Hsing's support. This was the main reason for the split of Sun and Huang. It led to the split of the party leadership.

If this were true, then Huang Hsing indeed made a mistake.[14] With Ts'en Ch'un-hsüan as the generalissimo, the political distinction between the old and the new was confused. In the following year (1914), Sun Yat-sen reorganized the Kuomintang into the Chinese Revolutionary Party to prepare for military actions against Yüan Shih-k'ai. Believing that the failure of the revolution was due to the disobedience of party members, Sun Yat-sen this time demanded a personal loyalty oath, fingerprints, and absolute obedience to him as conditions for the admission of new members. Huang Hsing refused to join the party and left for the United States. Though he never openly criticized Sun Yat-sen, it was clear that there was a split between "Sun and Huang." Organizational line should follow the political line. In the past, Huang had been vigorous in the revolutionary struggle. For the revolutionary cause, he had always supported party unity and Sun Yat-sen's leadership

---

[13] Huang left Nanking at the end of August, not July, 1913.

[14] Much of this episode is still shrouded in mystery, but one thing is clear. According to the memoirs (*Hsüeh-sheng nien-lu*, Vol. I, p. 7) of a participant (General Li Ken-yüan), Sun Yat-sen took part in Huang Hsing's conference with Ts'en Ch'un-hsüan.

and prestige. Now, with the deterioration of his revolutionary ideology, he followed the path of the organizational split.[15]

Yüan Shih-k'ai proclaimed himself emperor in 1915. All the people in China and all the overseas Chinese thought that Sun, Huang,
and others would take this opportunity to rise up against Yüan.
The comrades who remained in China repeatedly wired or wrote
to Huang Hsing asking for his return. He answered that, although
he wished for a third revolution, it could not be done without army
support and the army could not be won overnight. It took time
and he was afraid that he was too far away. Although he did engage
in some anti-Yüan propaganda work, he never returned to China
to participate in the armed struggles against Yüan Shih-k'ai.

After the collapse of the monarchical scheme and the death of
Yüan Shih-k'ai [in 1916], Li Yüan-hung succeeded as the president.
The power was in the hands of the Peiyang warlord, Tuan Ch'i-jui.
Huang Hsing had just returned from the United States and advocated "democracy" and "reform." He declared: "It is the great fortune that we witness the Republic re-established again. The handful of political culprits should be punished by law. From now on,
reconstruction should replace destruction. Even though we are not
in power, we should see that it will be achieved." Shortly afterward
an old ailment, a stomach ulcer, recurred and Huang died of stomach
hemorrhage.

It should be pointed out that Huang Hsing had clearly contributed a great deal even after the Wuchang Revolution of 1911.
Shortly after the outbreak of the Wuchang Revolution, he commanded the revolutionary army against great odds at the front at
Wuhan for a month. Later, he was elected acting generalissimo.
When he was about to take his post in Nanking, he heard that Sun
Yat-sen was returning from abroad. Consequently, he delayed his
trip to Nanking. He explained [as Li Shu-ch'eng recalled]: "If I
take up the post before Sun's arrival in Shanghai, it might make
him unhappy and it might result in some misunderstanding among
our comrades. . . . In order to work for the unity, one must not
be concerned too much for one's own position."

[15] The authors do not discuss whether Sun Yat-sen's demands, which
amounted to one-man rule in the party, were unreasonable.

When the provisional government was established, [some comrades suggested that] Huang should take up the premiership. However, Sun Yat-sen insisted on the adoption of the presidential system, and appointed him Minister of War and concurrently Chief of the General Staff. At no time did Huang show any ambition for personal power. For this he should be admired and praised. Even at the time when he had illusions about Yüan Shih-k'ai, he still had doubts and suspicions about him, and refused the title "General of the Army" and other honors conferred by Yüan. In the "Second Revolution," he fought against Yüan in Nanking. Although he refused to join the Chinese Revolutionary Party and left for the United States, and in fact split with Sun Yat-sen, he still had great respect for Sun and never mentioned their differences. Later, he organized the anti-Yüan propaganda campaigns among the overseas Chinese in America and raised some funds for the Yunnan and Kweichow armies that revolted against Yüan. He also wired the Peking diplomatic corps expressing his wholehearted objection to Yüan's monarchical scheme. While these facts should be acknowledged, they did not change his basic compromising tendency at that time.

It was the traditional feudal society that gave birth to the modern Chinese bourgeoisie, petty bourgeoisie, and intelligentsia. Among them was a group of people whose original social status and education were closely connected with feudalism and who kept at a distance from the working class in the lower strata. Not until they were stirred by national crisis and motivated by personal ideas and necessity did they participate in the revolution. But they did not demand, nor did they aspire to a thoroughly democratic revolution. On the contrary, to a certain extent they were frightened that the masses would rise up and make the situation "irremediable" and "chaotic." Such a viewpoint could not sustain the revolutionary spirit for long. After the overthrow of the Manchu dynasty and the establishment of the Republic, their social status was changed and their aims fulfilled. Hence, few of them wished to continue the work of the revolution. What they hoped for was a unification of the country and a stable order, which would preserve their newly-won political power and give them freedom for developing private enterprise. They might have wished to introduce some more reforms to resolve conflicts of interests and contradictions between them and the reactionaries, but they wanted these reforms to be obtained by peaceful means and not by revolutionary measures. Once under the threat and treachery of the seemingly powerful anti-revolutionary forces, they again showed cowardice and wishful thinking. This, in turn, enhanced their inclination to compromise. When pressed too hard by anti-revolutionary forces, and once again stirred by revolutionary sentiment, they engaged in the struggle again. But, on the whole, compromise was their guiding principle. A great number of these people existed in the modern Chinese bourgeoisie, petty bourgeoisie, and intelligentsia. They represented the interests and demands of the upper and middle national bourgeoisie. In this compromising and wavering attitude of bourgeoisie and intelligentsia, we can find the basic cause for the changes of Huang Hsing's political attitude after the Revolution of 1911.

Thus, in Huang Hsing we find a clear reflection of the anti-monarchical, patriotic sentiment and the wavering and compromising attitude of the modern Chinese bourgeoisie, petty bourgeoisie, and intelligentsia. A careful study of these two aspects would be a fruitful lesson for all of us.[16]

[16] For an analysis and a refutation of the Kuomintang line and some of the Chinese Communist views contained in this article, see Chün-tu Hsüeh's article, "Chi-nien Huang kung K'o-ch'iang ping-lun Hsin-hai ko-ming" (In Commemoration of Huang Hsing and a Discourse on the Revolution of 1911), *Cheng-chih p'ing-lun* (The Political Review), Vol. XVII, No. 3 (Taipei, October 10, 1966); *Hui-liu* (Con Currence), No. 1 (New York, January 1967); and also reprinted in *Ming Pao Monthly*, No. 22 (Hong Kong, October 1967). For a summary of Huang Hsing's political views expressed in his numerous speeches published in the Shanghai *Min-li pao* in the first two years of the young Republic, 1912–13, see Chün-tu Hsüeh, "The Life and Political Thought of Huang Hsing, Co-Founder of the Republic of China," *The Australian Journal of Politics and History* (April 1967), pp. 21–33. For an attempt to analyze Huang's political thought in a systematic and theoretical framework, see Jen Cho-hsuan's article in *Cheng-chih p'ing lun*, Vol. XVII, No. 3 (October 10, 1966). In 1969, *Huang K'o-ch'iang hsien-sheng ch'üan-chi* (Collected Works of Huang Hsing) was published by the Committee for the Compilation of the Party History of the Central Committee of the Kuomintang. It contains no significant new material different from that found in the sources used in Chün-tu Hsüeh, *Huang Hsing and the Chinese Revolution* (Stanford University Press, 1961; rev. printing, 1968).

✳ 7 ✳

The Life and Writings
of Tsou Jung

CHÜN-TU HSÜEH AND GERALDINE R. SCHIFF

I

Tsou Jung (1885–1905) was one of the most famous pamphleteers of the Chinese Republican Revolution. Born in Chungking, Szechwan, in the year of the Sino-French War and the annexation of Annam by France, Tsou was the oldest of five sons born to the second wife of his father.[1] The first wife had also borne a son and a daughter. Tsou's mother died when he was very young, and he was raised by a severe stepmother. His father, Tzu-fang, a self-made man and a shrewd businessman, was very strict with his children. Coming from a poor family, the father had established a well-to-do but frugally-run household by the time he had reached middle age. He was conscious of the contempt in which Chinese society held the merchant and encouraged his sons to study so that they might become government officials.

For more than forty years after the Opium War, China, under

This article, including the translations in Part II, is published for the first time. It is an extensive, revised version of a manuscript originally written by Geraldine R. Schiff in 1958.

The Revolutionary Army: A Chinese Nationalist Tract of 1903, introduced and translated with notes by John Lust (The Hague: Mouton, 1968), was published too late to use for the purpose of comparison in this study. It is noted, however, that in Lust's bibliography, Chün-tu Hsüeh's book on Huang Hsing is listed under "Chün" instead of "Hsüeh," and his first and middle names "Chün-tu" become "Tu-hsüeh."

[1] Tu Ch'eng-hsiang, *Tsou Jung chuan* (2nd ed., Taipei: Pamirs Book Company, 1953), p. 6. Most of the information on Tsou Jung's life in Part I of this article is based on Tu's biography.

153

alien Manchu rule which had begun in 1644, repeatedly experienced national humiliations and serious internal disturbances. After the signing of the Treaty of Shimonoseki in 1895 following the Sino-Japanese War, new ideas flowed more rapidly up the Yangtze River along with foreign goods from Shanghai. There had been some American, British, and Japanese businessmen in Chungking before the war, but they now came in greater numbers. It is, of course, impossible to ascertain how much of an influence they could have had on a child ten years old.

Tsou's ability to comprehend and his memory were said to be well beyond that of other children. Undoubtedly, he was a bright child, but as a student he did not prove easy to handle. The schools in Chungking were of the old style; the curriculum consisted largely of studying and memorizing the characters of the Classics. The boy was intelligent and for his age passably well trained in the Classics.

As he grew older, the youth did not trouble to mask his disdain for his previous education. He also showed contempt for the civil service examination, refused to learn the "eight-legged essay" to pass the official examinations, and ceased to concentrate on the Classics. Gradually he began to reject his past mode of life; physical punishment was of no avail. He was treated as an "unfilial son," but his stubborn nature could not be swayed.

The boy may have been aware of the Sino-Japanese War of 1894–95 and the Treaty of Shimonoseki at the time they took place, but it was probably not until some years later that they came to have any meaning for him. The abortive revolutionary attempt made by Sun Yat-sen in 1895 could hardly have been known to him. When the *coup d'état* occurred in 1898, ending the Hundred Days of Reform, and the Empress Dowager made the emperor a political prisoner, Tsou was thirteen. Among the "Six Martyrs" executed by the Court was T'an Ssu-t'ung, who, believing that blood had to be shed before China could be liberated, offered his own to set an example. T'an touched the youth of his time, a martyr who had sacrificed himself, disdaining flight when escape was possible, in order to arouse his countrymen. This event was deeply engraved in Tsou's memory. T'an was a hero. Tsou kept a picture of him and read his book,

Jen-hsüeh (A Study of Benevolence). Out of his great admiration for T'an Ssu-t'ung, Tsou Jung later composed a poem of praise:

> The glorious Mr. T'an is dead,
> And the Hunanese intellectual spirit diminished.
> I hope there will be others,
> Who will follow in his footsteps.

The year 1898 was a very evenful one for Tsou Jung and the Chinese intellectuals. Characteristically, Tsou Jung became more and more critical of the Manchus and of the traditional way, tending to shock his associates in discussions of current events. He did not venerate old age—only intelligence won his respect. Periodicals in particular caught his interest and he read voraciously. In 1900 Tsou was expelled from the Academy for Classical Studies because the teachers were taken aback by his candid opinions and by his ideas, which seemed strange to them. In addition, the families who had formerly considered him as a matrimonial prospect for their daughters now changed their minds. By 1901 Tsou began to feel he had outgrown Chungking and he wanted to go to Japan to absorb more of the "new learning" and to take part in the activities.

In the fall of 1901, at the age of sixteen, Tsou Jung went to Shanghai where he enrolled in a language school (Kuang fang-yen Kuan) to study Japanese. After studying a short time at this school, which was affiliated with the Kiangnan Arsenal of the government, Tsou became disillusioned. According to a schoolmate, he composed the following poem before leaving the school:

> Who will avenge our country?
> The past is far too sad.
> Few are not slaves, my tears fall endlessly
> For China's history I have read.

In the spring of 1902, Tsou Jung left for Tokyo and matriculated at a language school, where he hoped to improve his Japanese and study preliminary science courses in preparation for entrance into an established school. Since the 1898 coup, Japan had become a refuge for Chinese reformers and, for a few years after 1902, the center of the Chinese revolutionary movement abroad. Tsou's academic aspirations were hardly realized when he was caught up in the whirl of revolutionary activity absorbing the Chinese students in Japan. It was an atmosphere he relished.

Chinese student enrollment in Japan had risen to more than 500 by February 1902 and reached 1400 in 1904. Various student magazines were established on the basis of provincial origins, translating and promoting Western political thought. Numerous organizations were said to "spring up like bamboo shoots after a spring rain." One such organization which caught Tsou Jung's fancy was the Young Men's Association, founded by Chang Chi and others in the winter of 1902, advocating nationalism and violence. While in Tokyo, Tsou absorbed all he could, storing his experiences for future reference.

In April 1902 the Russian government had agreed to withdraw from Manchuria the troops sent there after the Boxer Uprising in 1900. A year later the Chinese students in Japan were aroused by the new Russian demands concerning the withdrawal of troops and by rumors of a secret pact with the Manchus. They planned a student volunteer corps to fight the Russians. Tsou was very active and early in May 1903, when the "student army" was disbanded by the Japanese government, the more radical students founded the Association for Universal Military Education with the secret aim of overthrowing the Manchu dynasty. Tsou left Tokyo for Shanghai about this time. He had identified himself with the revolutionary cause, but followed no one person.[2]

In Shangahi, which ranked with Tokyo as an anti-Manchu center for radical literati, Tsou Jung soon became a "sworn brother" of Chang Chi (1882–1947), Chang Shih-chao (1881–), and Chang Ping-lin (1868–1936),[3] all of whom had been in Japan and got along extremely well despite age differences.

[2] Tu, *op. cit.* p. 27, states that "Tsou had established relations with the revolutionary forces under the leadership of Sun Yat-sen." However, no evidence to date bears out any such relationship.

[3] Chang Chi and Chang Shih-chao later joined the revolutionary organization, Hua Hsing Hui (Society for the Revival of China), founded by Huang Hsing. For Chang Shih-chao's reminiscences of this period under discussion, see Committee for Historical Source Materials of the National Committee

Chang Ping-lin was a noted scholar teaching at the Patriotic School. Chang Shih-chao was the chief editorial writer of the *Su-pao* (Kiangsu Journal), a newspaper published in the Shanghai International Settlement by Ch'en Fan, a former district magistrate who had been removed from office in 1898 over a missionary incident. Ch'en Fan was one of the eight Hunanese who, with Huang Hsing, had founded in 1902 in Tokyo the Hunan Translation Society, which published a student magazine, *Yu-hsüeh i-pien* (Translations by Hunan Students Abroad). Subsequently, the *Su-pao* became the general distributor for that magazine in China. In the spring of 1903, the *Su-pao* regularly published radical speeches of teachers and students of the Patriotic School, a progressive academy founded to accommodate students who had left other schools because of strikes. The newspaper gave financial aid to the school. In turn, the teachers, among them Chang Ping-lin and Wu Chih-hui, contributed editorials to the newspaper. Under the editorship of Chang Shih-chao, beginning on May 27, the journal published several violent anti-Manchu articles in the next five weeks. These articles touched off the sensational *Su-pao* case, which resulted in the imprisonment of Chang Ping-lin and Tsou Jung, and the suppression of the paper.

While in Japan, Tsou had drafted a tract of some 20,000 words. It was published under the title *Ko-ming chün* (The Revolutionary Army) in Shanghai with the preface dated April 1903 and an introduction by Chang Ping-lin. It was probably the most violent and outspoken attack on the Manchus ever written by a Chinese. Favorable reviews of the work appeared in the *Su-pao*. The journal also published Chang Ping-lin's refutation of the arguments of the prominent, exiled reformer, K'ang Yu-wei, who maintained that only a constitutional monarchy could save China whereas revolution would only bring partition and disaster to the country. In his famous open letter which was well received by the literati, Chang referred to the Kuang-hsü emperor by name and described him as a *"hsiao-ch'ou* [little clown] who cannot distinguish the weeds from the wheat."

The Manchu government had already been, for some time, greatly

of the People's Political Consultative Conference, ed., *Hsin-hai ko-ming hui-i lu* (Reminiscences of the 1911 Revolution), I and II (Peking, 1961–62).

concerned with nationalist activities in the International Settlement of Shanghai, which was not under Chinese jurisdiction.[4] It now took vigorous steps to suppress the newspaper. The publisher and other personnel of the *Su-pao* as well as some faculty members of the Patriotic School, including Ts'ai Yüan-p'ei and Wu Chih-hui, fled from Shanghai. On June 29, Chang Ping-lin, who refused to flee, was arrested with others by the authorities of the International Settlement at the request of the Chinese government. The charges were discussing the "abolition of the Imperial prerogative and other forbidden questions." Tsou Jung, who could have gotten away, surrendered himself two days later, having received a note from Chang Ping-lin suggesting that he not run away. The two had intended to make martyrs of themselves; Tsou also wanted to care for the older man.

The journal was banned and the school dissolved. This sensational case was brought to the Mixed Court hearing on July 15. It was prolonged while the prisoners were held in custody. Early in December, Tsou received a sentence of two years and Chang three. The intense effort of the Manchu government to extradite the prisoners failed because of the political nature of the case.[5] Three of the

---

[4] The Municipal Council in Shanghai claimed in effect what amounted to exclusive police powers in the International Settlement, except for any police powers that the foreign consuls might wish to reserve for their own nations. The Chinese officials could not make arrests in the Settlement on warrants issued by the Chinese authorities outside or even by the Chinese magistrate on the Mixed Court, except after notifying the municipal police. The Municipal Council insisted that before any Chinese resident was arrested by the municipal police and handed over to authorities outside the Settlement, there should be a preliminary inquiry by the Mixed Court to see if there was a "good *prima facie* case" against the person concerned. *Report of the Hon. Mr. Justice Feetham, C. M. G. to the Shanghai Municipal Council*, I, Part II, 101. A. M. Kotenev, *Shanghai: Its Mixed Court and Council* (Shanghai: North China Daily News and Herald, 1925).

[5] Chung-kuo shih-hsüeh hui (Chinese Historical Association), ed., *Hsin-hai ko-ming* (The Revolution of 1911), (Shanghai, 1957), I, 331–500 contains twelve items relating to Tsou Jung and to the *Su-pao* case. Several articles with valuable information, including one by Chang Shih-chao, were published here for the first time. Chang also discusses some of the factual errors of the case in the Committee for Historical Source Materials of the National Committee of the People's Political Consultative Conference, ed.,

prisoners were acquitted and discharged; one was indicted in connection with another plot.[6]

Tsou Jung appeared to have been restless during the time he was held in custody. He was so disturbed emotionally that he could not gather his thoughts nor find any inspiration to write.[7] After receiving sentence on December 7, 1903, he and Chang Ping-lin were moved to the Western prison from the municipal police station. At the prison they could see no friends and were obliged to work long hours sewing uniforms. They were harshly treated by Indian prison guards and suffered from hunger and cold. Chang was allegedly beaten by the guards on many occasions. Sometimes he would go on hunger strikes in protest. However, he was a matured person capable of enduring the hardships. He possessed an inner strength. Tsou Jung, on the other hand, was only eighteen years old; he suffered more physically and mentally. He could not absorb the Buddhist teachings which Chang had tried to impart to him in the months of the trial before they were sent to the Western prison, teachings which Chang hoped might ease Tsou's sufferings. Unable to conquer his bitterness, the younger man became the victim of his own tortured thoughts. Hard work, cold, hunger, illness, melancholy, frustration —all wore him down. He became ill and for forty days he remained so, until April 3, 1905, when he died at the age of twenty. In less than three months he would have completed his prison term and gained freedom.[8]

---

op. cit. I (Peking, 1961), 247–48 and 275–78. For the international legal and political aspects of the case, with emphasis on the clash between the Peking government and the powers, see J. Lust, "The Su-pao Case: An Episode in the Early Chinese Nationalist Movement," *Bulletin for the School of Oriental and African Studies*, University of London, Vol. XXVII, Part 2, 1964, pp. 408–29. Also Y. C. Wang, "The *Su-pao* Case: A Study of Foreign Pressure, Intellectual Fermentation, and Dynastic Decline," *Monumenta Serica*, Vol. XXIV (1965), pp. 84–129.

[6] *The Times* (London), December 8, 1903.

[7] Letter of Tsou Jung in reply to Liu Ya-tzu, written shortly before sentence was passed. This appears to be the only writing left by Tsou after his arrest.

[8] Chang Ping-lin's biographical sketch and writings on Tsou Jung in Tsou Lu, ed., *Chung-kuo Kuo-min-tang tang-shih kao* (Draft History of the Kuomintang) (3rd ed., Chungking: Commercial Press, 1944), IV, 124–44; and Chung-kuo shih-hsüeh hui, *op. cit.* I, 365–66. Also Chang Ping-lin's own chronological biography, *T'ai-yen hsien-sheng tzu-ting nien-p'u* (Hong

The nation was suspicious about the real cause of his death, and it was rumored that the prison doctors had received bribes to poison him. More than forty Chinese students held a meeting in Tokyo, and a committee of investigation headed by Huang Hsing was set up. Chang Chi was sent back to Shanghai to investigate the matter. But the rumor proved to be unfounded.[9]

Tsou Jung did not live to see the establishment of the revolutionary alliance of 1905 or the Wuchang Revolution which occurred only six years after his death. In 1912 the Nanking Provisional Government conferred upon him the posthumous title of "Great General" and his name was entered into the Temple of Loyalty. The military government of Szechwan province had his "soul" escorted back to his home district. In the winter of 1922, Chang Ping-lin discovered his real place of burial and in April 1924, with Chang Chi, Chang Shih-chao, and twenty others, conducted a public worship there. An epitaph was written by Chang Ping-lin. On March 29, 1941, at the Eighth Plenary Session of the Fifth Central Executive Committee of the Kuomintang, it was decided that a memorial should be erected in commemoration of Tsou Jung. Exactly two years later, on the First Youth Memorial Day, the ground-breaking ceremony for the memorial took place, presided over by Chang Chi.

The year 1903 was a turbulent one characterized by anti-Manchu propaganda in China, and reached its climax with the *Su-pao* case. Yet it is interesting to note that the central figures of the case were not on the staff of the journal. Chang Chi and Chang Shih-chao managed to publish the *Kuo-min jih-jih-pao* (China National Gazette) after the *Su-pao* had been suppressed but the tone was now more moderate.[10]

Kong, 1965) (1st pub. Shanghai, 1928), p. 10. Chang Ping-lin was released from prison in the summer of 1906. He was immediately escorted by T'ung Meng Hui members to Tokyo, where he assumed the editorship of the *Min-pao*.

[9] Sun Chiao-jen, *Wo-chih li-shih* (Diary), April 20, 1905. Tu, *op. cit.* p. 48, states that Chang Chi was sent by the T'ung Meng Hui, but this revolutionary alliance was not established until August 1905.

[10] *Kuo-min jih-jih-pao*, Nos. 2 (August 8, 1903), 6 (August 12, 1903), 11 (September 26, 1903) contain translations of comments from the foreign press on the *Su-pao* case.

Tsou's booklet, even more popular after the lawsuit, became a best seller, and numerous editions were printed. Many revolutionaries used it to provoke anti-Manchu feeling. To avoid censorship, the book companies changed the title to a less subversive one. Copies sometimes had to be smuggled from one place to another to escape confiscation. Of all the popular anti-Manchu works for the general public emanating from the Republican revolutionary movement, Tsou's *Ko-ming chün* shared the foremost place with Ch'en T'ienhua's *Men-hui-t'ou* (Sudden Realization), *Ching-shih-chung* (Alarm To Arouse the Age), and *Shih-tzu-hou* (Lion's Roar).

An extreme nationalist, Tsou implored his fellow Chinese to join in the overthrow of the "barbarous Peking government," the expulsion of all the Manchus, and the killing of the Manchu emperor in order to do away with the monarchial system forever. He urged loyalty not to an individual but to the nation. Tsou advocated the establishment of the Republic of China, freedoms of speech, thought, and the press, and the right to revolt. The future republic, he felt, should model itself after the United States. He was worried about the dissolution of China and the extinction of the Han race. But he had the foresight to anticipate the potential greatness of China as a world power. He attributed her weakness to alien misrule; otherwise, "such countries as England, Russia, Germany, and France—countries which have partitioned and invaded our territory—would have feared our power." Believing that the Manchus had to be deposed before it would be possible to oppose foreign aggression, he was convinced that for China in his day, there had to be a revolution.

Tsou pointed out the difference in treatment received by Chinese abroad compared with that received by foreigners in China and posed a question which was obvious to every Chinese at the time: "Do you not see that if a foreign missionary is killed, the Chinese government has to concede territory or give compensation? If a single foreigner is insulted, it would require an imperial decree of inquiry and appeasement, but our fellow countrymen abroad suffered humiliations which the foreigners would not have their animals suffer—and the Manchu government, as if blind and deaf, pays no attention." He was anti-imperialist rather than anti-foreign. In fact, he had an almost blind faith in Western political philosophies and practices, declaring that the "profound philosophy of Rousseau and the other philosophers are the medicine which can restore the dying soul of China." While he attached great importance to education, he was very critical of the traditional schooling of the literati of the period. But he was sympathetic to the sufferings of the peasants and soldiers and spoke out in favor of the interests of the bourgeoisie.

Tsou was very young; his ideas were still in the formative stage. His knowledge of the world appears at times to have been quite superficial. The text of *The Revolutionary Army* is not free of factual errors. However, it did capture the revolutionary sentiments of the age. Written in a simple and direct style, it fired the imagination of the revolutionary youth of the period and evoked a strong patriotic response. The presentation was dramatic and forceful. Tsou Jung was so disturbed by the state of affairs of his country that his work invariably moved its readers. It rang of sincerity, and even today it remains a dynamic reminder of the past. His ability to paraphrase thoughts of an age and translate them into succinct expressions that caught the imagination made him an outstanding propagandist. It has been said that his tract was a "synthesis of the modern political ideas of the West known to China since the Opium War." [11] It represents the first systematic, popular, written expression in China of Western democratic concepts of government. Furthermore, it offers a constructive post-revolutionary program, the first document of the Republican revolutionary movement that outlined the fundamental principles upon which the future republic should be founded. It appeared two years before Sun Yat-sen, whom Tsou had never met, set down in writing his ideas on democracy.

II *

Preface

I was born in Szechwan province and lived there for sixteen years.

[11] Tu, *op. cit.* p. 51.

* This portion is a full translation of Tsou Jung's pamphlet, *Ko-ming chün* (The Revolutionary Army), omitting Chang Ping-lin's "Foreword." The translation is based on the text in Volume VII of *Man-i hua-hsia shih-mo chi*

In 1901, I traveled down the Yangtze River to Shanghai. In 1902, I went abroad where I remained for one year. I collected the sayings of famous people, which lay buried in my mind, and put my stray thoughts in order so as to recount them to my fellow countrymen in the same manner as in a civilized country where there is freedom of speech, of thought, and of the press. However, the Chinese are slaves, and slaves have no freedom or ideas. I humbly intend to show my gratitude toward my 400,000,000 fellow countrymen, my parents, friends, and my brothers and sisters, who all love me. I do not care whether people condemn me as a rebel or believe my intentions are good. If Rousseau, Washington, and Whitman were still alive, they might laugh and say: "You know, young man, you have brought our doctrines to the East." I believe that if Cheng Ch'eng-kung[1] and Chang Huang-yen[2] were alive, they would smile broadly and say: "Now we have a successor. We can die with our eyes closed." [3] When this literary piece gains recognition, a revolutionary floodtide will result in the world. I have finished my statement, but my mind is not yet at rest.

> Third month, 260 years after the Manchu conquest of China [*ca.* April 1903]. Tsou Jung, a little foot soldier in the Revolutionary Army[4]

(Records of the Barbarous Manchus' Treacherous Conquest of China) (Shanghai: New China Library, 1912), compiled by Yang Tun-i. All footnotes were added by the translators.

[1] Cheng Ch'eng-kung (Koxinga) was a rebel who at the beginning of the Ch'ing dynasty carried on coastal raids against the Manchus from his base on Formosa.

[2] Chang Huang-yen, a native of Chekiang province, was a scholar and writer who served under the last emperor of the Ming dynasty and supported the Prince of Lu as successor to the throne. He was captured while fighting against the Manchus and died as a martyr. Staff of the Commercial Press, ed., *Chung-kuo jen-ming ta-tz'u-tien* (Chinese Biographical Dictionary) (Shanghai: Commercial Press, 1921), p. 960.

[3] This Chinese expression is loosely equivalent to "rest in peace."

[4] Tsou identified himself with the humble foot soldier who led the horse of the leader of the army and, of course, went first into battle.

Introduction

The autocracy of the last few thousand years must be swept away, the slavery of thousands of years abolished. The 5,000,000 barbarian Manchus adorned in their furs, lances, and horns must be destroyed,[5] and the great shame they have inflicted in their 260 years of cruel and harsh treatment expunged, that the Chinese mainland may be purified. All of the Yellow Emperor's[6] descendants can rise to the status of a Washington, rejuvenate themselves, successfully emerge from the 18 stages of hell and ascend to 33 heavenly halls,[7] for their ultimate and resolute aspiration is revolution. Revolution is great!

I had to skirt the Great Wall for 10,000 *li*, ascend the Kunlun Mountains, swim the Yangtze River, and go upstream on the Yellow River. I raised the flag of independence and struck the bell of freedom, crying out to heaven and earth enough to burst my lungs, to make my voice heard to my fellow countrymen. Alas, for our China today, there must be a revolution!

If our present-day China desires to break the fetters of the Manchus, there must be a revolution! If China wishes to take her place among the great powers, exist in the new world of the twentieth century, attain world-wide recognition, and be respected in her own right in the world, there must be a revolution! Among my fellow countrymen, old, middle-aged, and young, men and women, is there any one who does not speak of revolution? My compatriots burn with fervor to live daily a life of revolution. Now in a loud voice I cry out to proclaim to the world the meaning of revolution.

Revolution! The natural evolution of universal law is revolution. The universal principle of the world is revolution. It is a question of a struggle for survival. This is the essential meaning of this transition period. Revolution is in harmony with the natural order of things and fulfills man's needs.

[5] By such descriptive terms the author wished to reinforce the image of the Manchus as uncivilized.

[6] Yellow Emperor (Huang Ti) was a legendary progenitor of the Chinese.

[7] The image relates to a Buddhist concept.

Revolution will force us to abandon our corrupt ways and guide us to natural goodness. It will deliver us from barbarism to civilization and redeem us from the status of slaves to that of free men. One man has one idea; ten men have ten; and a million men represent a million different thoughts. Although everyone has ideas, still, all of these ideas are basically the same—whether they concern a man's home, his food, or his work tools. Through discretion we can determine whether or not a thing is good, whether or not it is noble—all this is intuitive. When we think deeply about it, invariably we choose what is good; we can also determine what is good and what is beautiful or either of the two. We tend to preserve what is beautiful and good and to discard what is not. This is something each of us can distinguish and from this principle evolves the essence of revolution.

Whatever is said below will still refer to this basic conception. If we were to make an extensive survey of religion, ethics, political science, or even of trifling matters, from the past to the present, [we would find that] all of our current ideas were sifted down to us through the process of past revolutions. This is the way. Thus, revolution is as ordinary as this.

However, there is also something extraordinary about it. We have heard of the English Revolution of 1688, the American Revolution of 1775 [sic], the French Revolution of 1870—all of these were revolutions which came in response to the cries of the people.[8] They banished corruption and brought forth natural virtue, transported the people from barbarism to civilization, and raised them from slaves to free men. Individuals were sacrificed for the benefit of the whole country and the nobility were sacrificed for the common people, that the blessings of liberty might be enjoyed equally by every-

[8] Tsou Jung refers to the "Glorious Revolution" of 1688, when the English chose William of Orange as king, and Parliament gained virtual control of government. In 1870 France fell under Napoleon II in the Franco-Prussian War. Napoleon III was forced to surrender after the battle of Sedan; in Paris the regime was overthrown and a newly proclaimed "Government of National Defense" established. It fell within five months, but the National Assembly elected Adolphe Thiers "Head of the Executive Power." Thus, France became and remained a republic.

one. The impact and spread of these revolutionary ideas came together as streams which converge to form a sea of ideas.

What a wondrous thing this is—revolution! Revolution, what a precious thing! Even when I hear about it I cannot help but thirst for it. Therefore, I searched back through the 5000 years history of our country and surveyed our more than 200,000,000 square *li* of land; I questioned others and examined myself in order to find an example in our history to compare with those of England, France, and the United States. Alas, I could not find one! I have given much thought to the reason why I am unable to discover such an example. Over and over I have thought about it and have come to lament the corrupt influence of the autocrats, dictators, and plunderers of past dynasties as the cause.

After the First Emperor of the Ch'in dynasty unified China, he oppressed the nation, subjugated the people to the point of slavery, and set up autocratic institutions. Through the use of contrived portents the emperors of China tried to deceive the people, claiming they themselves ruled by the sanction of heaven. They wanted to keep the national domain as their private property and retain the throne for their descendants in succeeding generations. The more they coveted the throne, the more they showed the people how enviable a position it was. This is why, since the Ch'in, so many usurpations have occurred. Even Shih Le,[9] Genghis Khan, and other nomads and barbarians were able to seize the throne and rule China. Unfortunately, as a result of these revolutions, massacres and arson as well as freedom and equality emerged.

It grieves me that our fellow countrymen have gone through these numerous barbarian revolutions[10] without achieving an eminent place among the other peoples of the world. I also regret that our countrymen are so readily led by any kind of ruler. Yet, I am glad that my people have now come in contact with enlightened political systems and are able to learn of civilized revolutions. It is fortunate, indeed,

[9] Shih Le established himself as head of the Late Chao in the early 4th century. He had been a general of the state of Chao and came from the Chieh people. Cho Hung-sou, *Chung-kuo li-shih nien-piao ho-tse* (A Chronological History of China) (Peking: China Printing House, 1931), pp. 26–27.

[10] The author refers to dynastic changes.

that we can now read translations of Rousseau's *Social Contract,* Montesquieu's *Spirit of Laws,* John Stuart Mill's *On Liberty,* French revolutionary history, and the United States "Declaration of Independence." Is that not to my countrymen's advantage?

The profound philosophies of Rousseau and other thinkers are the medicine which can restore the dying soul of China and which the ailing body of the Chinese nation needs to return it to health. These are the fundamental principles upon which French and American civilizations were developed. My country is now sick and dying; is she not in want of a good strong tonic to infuse her with new life? If so, I should like to wave the flag of Rousseau and other philosophers over our country.

Besides these philosophies, we have Washington and later Napoleon to set examples of revolution for us. Ah, revolution, revolution! If you have it you will survive, but if you don't you will die. Don't retrogress; don't be neutral; don't hesitate; now is the time! This is why I advocate revolution, so that my fellow countrymen may encourage one another to achieve revolution. If there is anyone who does not want revolution, then he will have to wait hundreds of years until the female Christian messiah who advocated equality and emancipation for the colored people comes to advocate equality and emancipation for the enslaved Chinese.[11]

Cause of Revolution

Revolution, revolution—why should my 400,000,000 fellow countrymen want a revolution? First let me speak of injustice. In China it is exhibited in its most unfair and lamentable form through the maladministration of the ambitious, tribal, rapacious Manchus. And yet we are the ones who beg for money and power and, cringing with servile humility, kneel thrice and kowtow nine times, so that we may submerge ourselves in pleasure-seeking, unaware of our shame, not even knowing enough to become conscious of it. Alas, my fellow countrymen have no personal, national, or racial character; they are without any sense of independence.

[11] It is not clear to whom Tsou Jung was referring.

Today's reformers and patriots often tell the public that if China does not hurry to reform she will follow in the footsteps of India, Poland, and Egypt. The tragic drama of India and Poland will be played in China. What I, Tsou Jung, have to say is: What nonsense! What nonsense! How can we be so obsequious and blind as to say such a thing? How can we be so mad as to say such a thing? How can we be so oblivious to the fact that in the past 300 years, under the heels of the Manchus, we have already been reduced to the status of India and Poland? And yet the reformers talk as if it were something that might happen in the future.

But still you ask, why? Let me explain. To the Manchus we Chinese are as the Poles and the Indians. Moreover, to Britain, France, Russia, and the United States, the Manchus are as the Poles and Indians. Yet I would rather be conquered directly, like the people of these dead nations, than be a slave to slaves. England, France, and the other nations could conquer us, as they have a civilization higher than ours; I do not understand why my compatriots prefer to be the slaves of barbarians instead of the slaves of civilized people. Alas! The Ch'ung-chen emperor of the Ming dynasty died for his country.[12] He preferred to let the bandits cut his corpse to bits rather than have them injure his people. The day the best troops of the Eight Banners of the thieving Manchus entered Shanhaikuan[13] and set up their dynasty at Peking was the memorial day of the Manchu conquest of China.

In this world the general rule is that the minority obey the majority, and the foolish obey the wise. The Manchu population was only 5,000,000, which is less than that of one district of one prefecture. Most members of the royal family were illiterate officials and incompetent generals. For the last 300 years there may have been one or

[12] Ch'ung-chen was the reign title of Chu Yu-chien (1611–1644), the last emperor of the Ming dynasty. His reign lasted from 1628 to 1644. He hanged himself when the Manchus were about to seize Peking. Arthur W. Hummel, ed., *Eminent Chinese of the Ch'ing Period* (Washington, D. C.: U. S. Government Printing Office, 1943–44), I, 191.

[13] Located in the extreme northeastern part of Hopeh province, Shanhaikuan is a strategic pass which connects Manchuria with North China.

two outstanding figures, but this was because they absorbed Chinese civilization.

The government of a nation should be run by the people. If they cannot control their administrative bureaus and departments, or participate in an executive capacity, the nation is not a sovereign nation nor are the people of that nation an independent people. This is a universal law, a universal truth.

Suppose we were touring Washington, Paris, and London and asked the people in the street, "Who controls the government, your fellow countrymen or an alien race?" They would answer, "Our fellow countrymen. No alien people may govern our nation." And again if you asked them, "Can your people take part in politics?" They would answer, "A nation consists of people and I am one of the people. The nation's affairs are my affairs; therefore, I should participate." But if they turned around and asked the same questions of our people, the answers would be just the opposite.

May I tell you, my compatriots, about the Manchu policy in relation to us? The Manchus are the smallest minority in the eighteen provinces of China. Those who work for the government are only a small fraction, and yet they are so powerful that they more than equal all the officials in the eighteen provinces of China. Let us take a look at the quotas for Chinese and Manchu officials in Peking.

In the positions of Grand Secretary, Minister, and Vice Minister, the Manchus and Chinese are equal in number. Besides these positions, in the office of the Grand Secretariat there are six Manchu and four Chinese Grand Secretaries, six Manchu and Mongolian and two Chinese Readers, and twelve Manchu and two Chinese Assistant Readers, ninety-four Manchu and Mongolian and thirty Chinese Secretaries. In the office of the Six Boards or Ministries, for the positions of Department Directors, Assistant Department Directors, and Second-Class Secretaries, the Manchu quotas are 400, about thirty of whom are on the Board of Civil Affairs, a hundred on the Board of Revenue, about thirty on the Board of Rites, about forty on the Board of War, about seventy on the Board of Punishments, about eighty on the Board of Public Works, and not one Chinese Assistant

Department Director or Second-Class Secretary on all the others. There are only 162 Chinese in the equivalent ranks of Department Director, Assistant Department Director, and Second-Class Secretary of Ministry.[14]

Every quarterly official directory lists only how many Chinese hold the positions of Department Director, Assistant Department Director, and Second-Class Secretary of Ministry, without mentioning how many vacancies there were for the Manchus—as if the Manchus are trying to hide something from the nation. The quotas for the Manchu officials in the Six Ministries are three times more than that for the Chinese (excluding the lower clerks). The vacancies in the provincial prefectures are generally filled by officials from the Six Ministries. No wonder there are so many Manchus in the provincial departments. As for the Office of Mongolian and Tibetan Affairs, from the Minister on down, all the positions are taken up by the Manchus. Not a single Chinese works in this Office (as if the Office of Mongolian and Tibetan Affairs could only be run by the Manchus. How strange!) Besides this, in the offices of the Chancellors of the National [Hanlin] Academy, Imperial Clan Court, Censorate, Transmission Office, Court of Judicature and Revision, Court of Sacrificial Worship, Court of the Imperial Stud [Stable], Banqueting Court, Court of State Ceremonial, Imperial Academy, Imperial Equipage Department, there are countless positions for which Manchu quotas are greater than Chinese. There is no sense of equality at all.[15]

[14] Translation of the official titles is based on H. S. Brunnert and V. V. Hagelstrom, *Present-Day Political Organization of China,* translated from the Russian by A. Beltchenko and E. E. Moran (Shanghai: Kelly and Walsh, 1912). For a translation of the terminology of the Six Boards, see E-tu Zen Sun, *Ch'ing Administrative Terms* (Harvard University Press, 1961).

[15] After the Manchu conquest, approximately a "fifty-fifty" division of posts between Manchus and Chinese was maintained at the capital until the Taiping Rebellion. John K. Fairbank and Ssu-yü Teng, *The Ch'ing Administration* (Harvard University Press, 1960), p. 69; see also Victor Purcell, *The Boxer Uprising* (London: Cambridge University Press, 1963), pp. 11–12.

Until 1729 the Grand Secretariat (Nei-ko) had been the main organ of government; then the important military organization and state affairs were managed by a new body called the Grand Council (Chün-chi-ch'u). From the time the Grand Council was established to the end of the Ch'ing dynasty, there were altogether 145 Grand Councilors, of whom 72 were Manchus, 64

Furthermore, the prospects for official careers in government are vastly different for Manchus and Chinese. Often cases have arisen whereby a Manchu and a Chinese have held identical positions in given years in the same office, yet the Chinese is unable to obtain a promotion for several decades, while the Manchu may become a Vice Minister and then a Minister and then a Grand Secretary within a short period of time. If you were to say that the Manchus are more talented than the Chinese because they are specially endowed, coming from Manchuria, just as [the founder of] the Han dynasty was endowed by the P'ei district [in Kiangsu] and [the founder of] the Ming dynasty by the Hao district [in Anhwei], it would be rather odd that this has been so for the last several hundred years.[16] The talents of the nation are sacrificed to such an extent for a single ruling race! If it were not for the fact that the Chinese contribution was so great during the four reigns of the Chia-ch'ing [1796–1820], Tao-kuang [1821–1850], Hsien-feng [1851–1861], and T'ung-chih [1862–1874] emperors, there would have been

---

were Chinese, 6 were Mongols, and 3 were Chinese bannermen. The Mongols and Chinese bannermen held only a small number of these posts and disappeared entirely after the Taiping Rebellion. In the Yung-cheng and Ch'ien-lung periods, from 1723 to 1796, the Manchus on the average accounted for 56 per cent of the personnel and the Chinese for 37 per cent. But in the Chia-ch'ing and Hsien-feng periods, from 1796 to 1862, the Manchus made up 38 per cent and the Chinese 53 per cent. This was probably due to the full operation of the examination system which gave the Chinese the opportunity to rise in accordance with their abilities. After the Taiping Rebellion, from 1862 to 1908, the Manchus made up 52 per cent of the total and the Chinese 47 per cent. This was probably due to the fact that the Manchus wanted to increase their power in the central government to counterbalance the increase of Chinese power in the provincial governments. See Alfred Kuo-liang Ho, "The Grand Council in the Ch'ing Dynasty," *Far Eastern Quarterly* (Feb. 1952), p. 175.

On April 17, 1899 the British Chargé d'Affaires in Peking wrote in a dispatch to Lord Salisbury that the tendency to replace Chinese with Manchus in important political posts of the empire was increasing. *Accounts and Papers* (1900), CV, p. 237. H. O. Bax-Ironside to Foreign Office. Of the 62 governors-general, governors, treasurers, and judges of the 18 provinces and Sinkiang, 24 (reported Bax-Ironside) were Manchus, whereas before the 1898 *coup d' état,* only 13 were Manchus. Cited by Purcell, *op. cit.* p. 12.

[16] The P'ei and Hao districts were the places of origin, respectively, of the founders of the Han and Ming dynasties.

little possibility of the Manchus not filling all the provincial openings for governors and governors-general. Since the Taiping Rebellion, had it not been for the Chinese getting into the government through such means as recommendations, contributions in war, and the buying of office, few Chinese would indeed have attained any kind of political career. As for the civil service examination, although 70 to 80 per cent of the candidates who passed the examination are Chinese, it is still difficult for them to gain appointments.

The civil service examination was only a means for managing the Chinese intellectuals so that they would support the government and not harbor any secret schemes. Furthermore, the Manchu government has also provided many proctor positions in various provinces and teaching positions in districts. These are merely designed for extraneous people so that they may perform useless jobs. Even then, should there be one among thousands who fortunately may have obtained promotion to such a position as Grand Secretary, Minister, or Vice Minister, generally he would be an old man without youthful spirit and ambition, receiving a few benefits from the hands of the Manchus! According to regulation and practice, no Chinese can achieve a ministerial position without being in Hanlin first. But the Manchu, regardless of his origin, can obtain civil and military positions as high as Chancellor and General. This is very significant. There is nothing more unfair to the Chinese than this! It is, perhaps, inevitable because this is the way the Manchus treat a conquered alien race.

So far we have talked about only the system of official appointments. As for the various provinces, if the provinces are rich and of strategic importance, then Manchu generals are appointed to rule them and the Chinese have no chance at these positions. In cities such as Nanking, Chengtu, Sian, Foochow, Hangchow, and Chenchiang [Chinkiang], the Eight Banners are stationed and live in a separate inner city. For over the last 200 years the Chinese have been Chinese and the Manchus have been Manchus—there has been no social exchange. This is obviously the intention of the Manchus, that the inferior race should not mix with the superior race!

Furthermore, let us explore the meaning of the two words, "station" and "guard." Are they [the Manchus] not constantly afraid that the Chinese might rebel and thus should be watched as if they were bandits and thieves; otherwise, why do they "station" and what do they protect or "guard" against?

Any Manchu, who can claim the slightest achievement can obtain the rank of duke as easily as picking grass. On the other hand, great Chinese slaves such as Tseng Kuo-fan, Tso Tsung-t'ang, and Li Hung-chang, who slaughtered several millions of our fellow countrymen and offered the southeastern half of China to the Manchus, have ranks no higher than marquis.

If we read the imperial edicts from one emperor to the next [of the Ch'ing dynasty], we will find that if one or two high Manchu officials had good reputations they were overpraised, revealing that they belonged to the inner circle. As for the Chinese, even though there were people as able and wise as Yang Ming-shih, Li Fu, and Tang Ping,[17] who were obedient slaves, they were still often condemned and humiliated by the Court. In addition, cases of abuses to the Chinese are so numerous that they cannot be enumerated.

My fellow countrymen, can we not see through those so-called Eight Banner members of the Manchu clan, with their red and yellow sashes, and the sons of the Beileh?[18] As soon as they reach manhood they are automatically provided with regular salaries. It is not necessary for them to earn any kind of living to support their families. They do not have to read books and ask for guidance to increase their knowledge. From young master (*shao-yeh*), they become old master (*lao-yeh*), from great master (*ta-lao-yeh*), they move on to mandarin-of-rank (*ta-jen*) and on to the Grand Secretary (*chung-t'ang*) with a red hat and peacock's plumes.[19] Thus they try to climb from a low perch to the high rank of Vice Minister and Minister—as if these were heavenly decreed duties. On the other hand, looking at the Chinese, could you ever imagine such a thing!

[17] Three scholars and high officials of the early Ch'ing period.

[18] Red sashes were for the *chüeh-lo,* Manchus not directly descended from the imperial line. Yellow sashes were for the *tsung-shih,* Manchus directly descended from the emperor, a high designation. "Beileh" is a Manchu title bestowed on the sons of the imperial Manchu princes.

[19] "Red hat" and the "flowered collar" are symbols of rank signifying high position.

Chinese people are customarily classified into scholars, farmers, artisans, and merchants. The scholars are at the head of these four groups and are called "literati." When I look at the Americans and Europeans, there is no one who cannot read. In other words, there is no one who is not a literate person. But we Chinese have a special classification of "scholar," or "literati." Therefore, I shall address myself to them.

The Chinese scholars, or literati, are people without vitality. Why? The ordinary people are ignorant because they do not study, but the scholars are stupid and become more so because they do not study what they should. And furthermore, they are restricted, humiliated, made obfuscate, ensnared, and corrupted until they become nothing but empty shells, whipped and forced to obey.

How are they restricted? They are restricted by having to learn to write in the style of the "eight-legged essay" for the examination paper, which takes years and years, leaving no time to learn about current events.

How are they humiliated? They are humiliated by having to take the district, provincial, and metropolitan examinations. (While taking the examination for admission to the Hanlin Academy, they have no seats. They are treated as cows and horses.) Their behavior is like that of beggars. No longer do they know that in this world there is such a thing as human dignity.

Why are their minds obfuscated? They are made obfuscate by the honors gained from the examinations and the positions in government. They are worried about whether they will pass or fail. There is no longer any sense of righteousness or of daring to risk one's life for a worthy cause.

How are they ensnared? They are ensnared by country schools set up by aged scholars and by stone tablets regulating the scholars' lives. They are kept quiet and ignorant so that they dare not criticize politics or write books.

How are they made corrupt? They are corrupted by power and influence which make them hesitant and spineless about doing the right or heroic thing.

The trials of guilt by association began with the reign of Shun-chih [the first emperor of the Ch'ing dynasty], when Chu Kuo-chih, Governor of Kiangsu, arrested more than 100 candidates for the provincial degree in a tax case.[20] The literary inquisition began in the reign of Ch'ien-lung, "a Perfect Old Man" who would put anyone to death because of a word or utterance of seditious libel. This terrified all the officials, and none of the educated in the country dared to say anything. All protests were silenced, wild outbursts unknown.

They are literati in name, but in fact they are worth less than dead men.

The three works *P'ei-wen yün-fu* (Phrase Dictionary According to Subject), *Yüan-chein lai-han* (Phrase Dictionary for Rhyming), and *K'ang-hsi tz'u-tien* (K'ang-hsi Dictionary) are considered by the educated to be true classics. At the time of the K'ang-hsi and Ch'ien-lung emperors the Chinese still maintained a hostile attitude toward the Manchus. The government, therefore, recruited all the famous scholars of the country to edit these three works in order to distract the Chinese from revolutionary ideas and revenge. (Emperor K'ang-hsi proclaimed the Festival of the Ages several times and ordered that all the officials write poems and be served drinks, for the same purpose—to draw the people into his own camp.) My goodness! As I arrive at this point in my writing I cannot help but throw away my pen and exclaim: "The vigorous Northerners and heroes of the nation all follow one another into the trap." Such clever tricks indeed! I must admit that the Manchus are clever in their way of suppressing, ordering, and winning over the Chinese.

[20] Chu Kuo-chih was responsible for what was known as the "Taxation case of Kiangnan" in which 13,800 names of Kiangsu residents were posted for default in payment of taxes, which were actually surcharges. As a consequence, officials were dismissed or downgraded and students punished or deprived of opportunities to advance. Hummel, *op. cit.* I, 165. Cruel measures were employed; eleven student leaders were arrested to await trial. In Chinkiang and other places in Kiangsu, one hundred men were imprisoned on false charges. After the trial began in Nanking, eleven more people from Soochow were arrested, and on August 7, 1661, eighteen were beheaded for treason, the property of eight confiscated and their families exiled to Manchuria. The people of Kiangsu resented bitterly the execution of the "scholars of Soochow." In 1673, Chu Kuo-chih (then Governor of Yunnan since 1671) was killed in a rebellion in his province. *Ibid.* II, 902.

There are schools of Chinese scholarship called the Han Learning, the Sung Learning, the Essayists, and the Bohemian intellectuals. The scholars of the Han Learning give all their attention to paragraphs, sentences, and explanatory notes and have become slaves to the Six Classics, without any creative thought.[21] They would not dare to venture beyond this limited vista. The so-called Sung scholars daily cling to the five masters, the *Chin-szu lu* (Collection of Latest Reflections), and the like.[22] They speak of metaphysics in order to grasp fame and become high officials in the government. As for the Essayists, they style themselves after the T'ung-ch'eng School [23] and the Yang-hu School [24] and write lyrical compositions.[25] The so-called famous literary men achieve success by the following method: one lump of good nature, second-class ability, three-catty capacity for wine, four seasons of clothes, five-scale musical harmony, six ranks of officialdom, seven-word poetic system, eight-

[21] The Six Classics includes the Classic of Music as well as the *Shu-ching* (Book of History), *I-ching* (Book of Changes), *Shih-ching* (Book of Odes), *Ch'un-ch'iu* (Spring and Autumn Annals), and *Li-chi* (Book of Rites).

[22] Compiled by Chu Hsi in collaboration with Lü Tso-ch'ien, the *Chin-szu lu* was completed in the 1170's. For an English translation of the book, see Wing-tsit Chan, trans., *Reflections on Things at Hand* (New York: Columbia University Press, 1966).

[23] The T'ung-ch'eng School was located in Anhwei province. Fang Pao (1668–1749) was the designated founder. He was esteemed as the master of the *ku-wen* style, and the school was established after his death to honor him. The real founder of the school was Yao Nai (1732–1815), who had compiled an anthology in 1773. In the preface he stated that the work should be used by students to discover the "purpose and mode of expression of deeper works," so that they might more easily compose in the *pa ku* (examination) style. His followers believed the anthology held the formula to the teachings of the sages and thus to the examination and the rewards on passing it. Hummel, *op. cit.* I, 235–36. Tseng Kuo-fan helped to spread the fame of the T'ung-ch'eng School and that of Yao Nai. *Ibid.* II, 901.

[24] The Yang-hu School was founded by Chang Hui-yen (1761–1802) and Yün Ching (1757–1817). They were considered founders of the school of *ku-wen* prose writers. The school was named after the district from which they came. *Ibid.* I, 42 and II, 959.

[25] The text reads: "They sang great purple and red kinds of songs." These adjectives are thought to relate to lyrical style and arrangement of form, lyrical songs without concrete meaning.

sided social life, nine paths to the sophisticated life, ten skills of social intercourse.[26]

To restrain and control these four kinds of people—the Han and Sung scholars, the Essayists, and the Bohemian intellectuals who are so busy making fools of themselves—the Manchus, afraid that they might get an idea to revolt, made up special examinations in order to keep them all occupied. In recent years there have been people who are supposedly versed in "contemporary affairs." They pick up one or two phrases from newspapers and imitate two or three ideas from the Western political systems in order to gain admittance to the special examination on political affairs and thus become slaves of the Manchus.[27] Moreover, there are the righteous people who are always talking about nationalism and their aims of destroying the status quo—not that their words are not moving, but what is the use of merely being moved? How lamentable! These are debased circumstances for my fellow countrymen. If one examines the reasons for these phenomena, I dare say that half of them are self-made and half are created by the Manchus. I will repeat that is the reason, even if there is a knife at my back and a gun pointed at me.

The degrading circumstances of the literati of our country have been described as follows: "At the examinations they were given tables to write on, but no ink. Patriotic persons were treated as prisoners. When entertained, they were fed inferior food and looked down upon as dogs and horses. They were allowed to keep only a few of their beautiful robes. At meals served in the examination hall, mere eggs were cooked as if they were ducklings. Once the successful candidates entered the ranks of officials, they no longer took politics seriously. So, in name they were given honorary positions, but in reality they were humiliated; their policies were not carried out. They studied the Classics diligently until their hair

[26] The ten items are a play on words using the number of the phrase as part of the idea.

[27] At the end of the Ch'ing dynasty, the Manchu government created this special field on political affairs to meet the changing times and needs.

turned white. Eventually, when they passed the examination and obtained an office, they expressed thanks to their ancestors' tombs which had brought them luck and were grateful for the favor of their teachers and the examination officials.[28] By then, already in the prime of life, they were more concerned with security for the future. If they were not corrupt, how could they possibly support their families and maintain their family names without taking advantage of their positions to wield power over the village people, taking bribes during lawsuits, and swinging their weight around before the villagers? This is the picture of the activities of the Chinese literati.

One may think that these things do not happen today, but they do. Sometimes you hear that so-and-so entered a school, and so-and-so passed the provincial examination, and that so-and-so bought an office. Society raises a hullabaloo to make a fortune in the government. The lives of the officials are like those of the homosexuals in Peking and the prostitutes in Shanghai. I do not particularly want to be overly critical of my fellow countrymen, but the bad influence of educated persons on society cannot be forgiven, and it is for this reason that I have been so critical.

Now, if we travel to the countryside, we will see men deeply tanned, their feet and hands covered with clay, diligently working in the fields without rest. They are the peasants, our fellow countrymen. These people, these peasants, have been exploited by the landlords and even more so by officials sent by the Manchus. One official may try to seize a man's land. Another tries to suck the people's blood by imposing such notorious bonds as *Chao hsin p'iao* and through special assessments for indemnity payments. For one ounce of silver in tax the peasant must pay five or six times more in the form of numerous surcharges such as *huo-hao, ch'ien-chia,* and *k'u-p'ing.* Consequently, he can hardly pay unless he pawns his wife and children.

---

[28] The Chinese believed that if one buried one's ancestors in the right place at the right time, good luck throughout life would be one's reward. "Wind and water" was the geomantic system used to determine sites for graves, houses, and other buildings.

And yet, the government still talks of light taxes or imperial benevolence. I just do not understand what is meant by reduction of taxes or lightening of taxes. To say that this is imperial benevolence is to say a robber is saving the people when actually he intends to kill them. Under the bandit Manchus' rule the peasants dare not make a move. Isn't the Manchu policy very clever in suppressing the Chinese!

Alas! Alas! Yet I would say that the Manchus are very clever at suppressing the Chinese, even if there were a knife at my back and a gun pointed at my chest.

Have you not seen the Chinese indentured servants in Cuba or the Chinese workers persecuted abroad? Are they not our fellow countrymen, these so-called workers? At first they were refused by America and then by Australia and Hawaii. They had to endure hunger and cold, dying without a place of burial. They are the citizens of the great Middle Kingdom and yet whose fault is it when they are in such a state?

I hear that workers in foreign countries have the right to participate in the politics of their nation, to advocate freedom, to organize labor unions, to have legal protection from industry, to call meetings and make speeches, and to publish newspapers advocating socialism. If we then asked whether we Chinese had any of these rights, the answer would be "No." Do you not see that if a foreign missionary is killed, the Chinese government has to concede territory or give compensation? If a single foreigner is insulted, it would require an imperial decree of inquiry and appeasement; but our fellow countrymen abroad have suffered humiliations which the foreigners would not have their animals suffer—and the Manchu government, as if blind and deaf, pays no attention. Both foreigners and Chinese are human beings. Theirs heads are round and their feet square,[29] but one is venerated and the other humbled. What shame! Even if a knife were at my back and a gun pointed at my chest, still I would have to say that the Manchus are abusing us.

I also hear that wealthy businessmen of foreign countries are legislators with political power, but in China business is considered

[29] The whole expression is "round skull, square feet," which means man.

a very low occupation, looked down upon by the people. Chinese merchants cannot be ranked with the scholar-official class. But when it is necessary to pay war expenses and indemnities as a result of missionary cases, or pay for the pleasures of the emperors or for the support of government officials, the money is obtained from the merchants. Contributions are imposed, merchandise is taxed, and maritime duties are charged, all in the name of patriotism. Or they are lured by the conferment of empty titles or appointments. Ostensibly, these are voluntary contributions but, actually, they are extortions for the support of the Manchu Court or the building of the Summer Palace. And yet I do not see my compatriots arguing about this with the government. Alas! Alas! Even if a knife were at my back or a gun directed at my chest, I would still say the Manchus are pounding at our flesh and drawing our very marrow.

As for the Chinese soldiers, there are things about which I do not have the heart to speak. Each month they are paid three dollars, but 3 per cent is deducted. They are equipped with obsolete weapons, sent into the front lines, and ordered to fight. Thus, either they are all killed or they have to surrender with all their supplies to the enemy. What can be their fate then? If they are killed by the enemy, it is claimed that that is what they deserved. Compensation or ceremonies in praise of the dead are only matters of formality. The wives and children weep, but no one takes the trouble to inquire about them.

If the soldiers are fortunate enough to survive the war, they are sent back to their villages wounded, without jobs. Or they may wander, thousands of miles away, and become beggars. They cannot go home even if they want to. Meanwhile, it is stipulated that all wandering soldiers are to be executed. We have never heard of such cruelty applying to the Eight Banners. What did my countrymen do that they must suffer this kind of cruelty? The Manchus want to kill them one way or another. They will not stop until the soldiers are all exterminated. Good grief! Even if a knife were thrust at my back or a gun barrel directed at my chest, I would still say that the Manchus are exterminating the Chinese.

In a civilized nation if one is killed by accident, the newspapers will carry the news several times or several score of times. In criminal cases, unless the suspect confesses or there is conclusive proof, no judgment can be made, and at the time of the trial no torture can be used. Why? Because they respect human rights.

I look at my fellow countrymen, many of whom have died at the hands of the Manchus under different pretexts. Deaths occur because harsh laws and severe physical punishments are numerous. The cruel punishments applied in China are shameful and lamentable. Many Chinese, therefore, become naturalized citizens of foreign countries in order to secure protection. In the International Settlement there is always a Mixed Court, as though to protect themselves from the tigers and wolves.

The Manchu official authorities sometimes rely on legal loopholes without giving much attention to the true facts. At the present time there is no law which says that if someone violates a law the clan should be eliminated. And yet, why is this sometimes the case with all relatives, close and distant? There is no law prescribing physical punishment. Why then are some defendants whipped to death? There is no law which ordains torture to force a confession. Why then are some made to confess their crimes through whipping? As for the situation in the jails and the cruelty of the wardens, these defy description. Even hell could not be as bad!

And yet the Manchus say that during the busy season of the harvest there should be no lawsuit brought and punishment should be reduced for the welfare of the people. What a hypocritical gesture! Alas! Alas! Even if a knife were held at my back or a gun thrust at my chest, still I would say that the Manchus are butchering us. As for the cruelty and corruption of the government officials, all the languages in the world cannot describe it.

The Summer Palace of the Ch'ien-lung emperor is now burned to ashes and cannot be traced. In our contemporary large buildings and the new Summer Palace, each brick is made with the blood of the Chinese people for the pleasures of one Empress Dowager. The autocratic emperor of the Ch'in dynasty built the A-fang Palace and has been condemned by Chinese historians; people ever since have considered him notorious. Yet can it be compared with any of the

summer palaces of the Manchu dynasty? Still, our fellow countrymen dare not criticize the extreme autocracy of the Manchu government.

Now if you want to establish schools, the government will say
there is no money. If you want to send students abroad, the government will say there is no money. For whatever will benefit the
Chinese, the government says there is no money. But for no reason
at all the government rebuilt and then visited their imperial ancestors' tomb. For that they have money. For no reason at all they
had a birthday party for the Empress Dowager. For that they have
money. My fellow countrymen, just think about that!

"Gain the goodwill of other nations through a proper evaluation
of China's own strength." Are these not the high-sounding words
the imperial edicts proclaim? China is the land of the Chinese
people. The Manchus cede the territory of our compatriots and rob
our fellow countrymen of property for the security and pleasure of
one family with its 5,000,000 slaves [Manchus]. This is the reason
for ceding Taiwan and Kiaochow.[30] It is this which stirs me! These
are curious things. My fellow countrymen, please give them your
attention. My compatriots, mark my words.

When I read *Yang-chou shih-jih chi* (A Diary of the Ten Days'
Massacre in Yangchow)[31] and *Chia-ting t'u-ch'eng chi* (The Record
of the Massacre in the City of Chiating), before I finished I could
not help weeping. Let me tell my fellow countrymen about the ten
days in Yangchow and the three massacres at Chiating.[32] Are they
not typical examples in which Manchus killed Chinese in districts
and prefectures?

The records of these two books are merely a few examples. The
arson and plundering of the army, the shaving of heads, the murder

[30] Taiwan was ceded to Japan in 1895 by the Treaty of Shimonoseki, and
Kiaochow (Chiaochou) was leased to Germany in 1898.

[31] *Yang-chou shih-jih chi* was an eye-witness account by Wang Hsiu-ch'u.
The massacre occurred in May 1645 when the Manchus plundered and
slaughtered for ten days (May 20–29) in Yangchow after capturing the city.
Hummel, *op. cit.* II, 652. Yangchow, in northern Kiangsu, is located north
of the Yangtze River and on the Grand Canal, about fifteen miles north of
Chinkiang.

[32] Chiating is in Kiangsu province.

and vandalism wherever the Manchu army went must have been ten times worse than what actually happened in these two cities. We know what happened in Yangchow and Chiating, but there must be hundreds and thousands of unknown Yangchow's and Chiating's. When I think of it my heart is stirred and I am melancholy. I cannot help but tell my fellow countrymen.

According to *A Diary of the Ten Days' Massacre in Yangchow*: "On the second day [of the month] the officials of the prefectures and the districts had already been appointed. They sent out a proclamation to calm the people." Furthermore, "the corpses in various monasteries and shrines were ordered burned. Many women were hidden in the monasteries and shrines; many died of terror and starvation." According to one record, 800,000 corpses were burned in eight days, excluding those who committed suicide by drowning themselves in the river, jumping into wells, or hanging themselves indoors.

I can tell my fellow countrymen still more. When the bandit Manchus entered the pass of the Great Wall, did they not kill our ancestors? Were the victims not the uncles and brothers of our ancestors? Those who were raped—were they not the wives and daughters of our ancestors? In the *Diary* it is written: "A soldier has been noted as having said, 'When we invaded Korea we harassed females by the tens of thousands, but none of them lost their chastity. Why did this shameful thing happen in the great land of China?'" On reading this account, you can see the extent of the instances of rape.

The *Book of Rites* (Li-chi) says: "The injustice done to your father and brother must be avenged." This is common sense, known to a little child. Therefore, if a son cannot avenge the injustice done to his father and brothers, he will entrust the task to his own son, and his own son will entrust the task to his grandson and then to his great-grandson. Therefore, the injustice done to our great-great-grandfathers was the injustice done to our own fathers and brothers. Not only do we not avenge the injustice done to our own fathers and brothers, but we even work for our enemies. Thus, although we speak about fidelity every day, I really do not know what kind of fidelity we are talking about. If our great-great-grandfathers had physical sensibility after death, I am sure they could not rest in peace.

There is no one who does not respect Confucius as a great sage. Everyone knows that the Confucian temple at Chufu is in the territory of a civilized state;[33] it is worshiped by all people, just as the Jerusalem of Jesus Christ is. But the bandit Manchus leased Kiaochow to Germany, allowing the Germans to insult the land of Yao, Shun, Yu, Wen, T'ang, Wu, and the Duke of Chou.[34] As a result, the undesecrated native village of Confucius was besmirched and 400,000,000 Chinese became barbarians. Whose fault is that? In the struggle between the Catholics and Protestants within the sphere of Christianity, the blood of several million people was willingly shed. What about the Chinese?

The obedient slaves often use posthumous titles to show respect for the emperors, and respectfully call Sheng-tsu, the Benevolent, and Kao-tsung, the Pure.[35] These were the so-called benevolent emperors and great rulers of the past. But when we read *Nan Hsün Lu* (The Record of the Imperial Inspection Tour of the South), all the accounts in this book deal with nothing but rape, robbery, and the activities of rascals that prevailed in China. (The Ch'ien-lung emperor wanted to eat wasps, so they were sent all the way from Kalgen in three days. From this we can see the luxurious life the emperor led.)

Alas! They have drained the vitality of the population in several provinces in order to give pleasure to the K'ang-hsi emperor or the Ch'ien-lung emperor. The activities of these two bandit chiefs were

[33] Chufu is located in Shantung province.

[34] Yao, Shun and Yu were rulers in the mythical period; Yu was called the founder of the Hsia dynasty, supposedly the first dynasty of China. T'ang was the founder of the Shang dynasty. Wen and Wu were emperors of the Chou dynasty.

[35] Sheng-tsu, whose temple-name was Hsüan-yeh (1654–1722) was the second emperor of the Ch'ing dynasty. He is better known by his reign title of K'ang-hsi (1661–1772). Kao-tsung was the temple-name of Hung-li (1771–1799), who was the fourth emperor of the Ch'ing dynasty and is best known by his reign title of Ch'ien-lung (1736–1796). Hummel, *op. cit.,* I, 327, 369, and 415; and II, 648.

worse than those of Emperor Yang of the Sui dynasty and Emperor Wu of the Ming dynasty. I have read a romantic history of Emperor Yang of the Sui dynasty, and I wish someone had written another history of the southern tours of the K'ang-hsi and Ch'ien-lung emperors in order to expose their bestial activities so that their reigns of terror would be known throughout the nation. Someone has compared the Ch'ien-lung emperor with Louis XIV. I cannot help but think this is a very apt comparison.

When the slave-owner sells a slave he asks him whether or not he is willing to be sold. The Manchus are now giving away our territory without asking us, and we endure this. My fellow countrymen do not analyze it, assess it, weigh it; rather they obey and let it go. So it was with Taiwan, Hong Kong, Dairen, Port Arthur, Kiaochow, and Kwangchouwan. We have never heard of the Imperial Gazettes informing the country either before or after territory has been ceded.

Whether our countrymen admit they are slaves or not, I have no way of knowing, but this is what the Manchu minister, Jung Lu, said: "It is better to give away to foreign friends than to give in to domestic slaves."

Horses and cows are kept by shepherds. Why are they kept by people? Because people are the most intelligent animals of all. In this world people control horses and cows, but our fellow countrymen now under Manchu rule are as horses and cows, ruled by shepherds. Our countrymen may not admit that they are horses and cows, but they are treated as such.

How can I make such a statement? Here is the evidence. Nowadays in every district and prefecture if there is an official bulletin asking for taxes and contributions it always uses such phrases as: "Since we have been nourished and fed by the Court for the last few hundred years, we must do our best to serve." This kind of bulletin is put at every crossroad and anyone who can read knows about it. To speak of nourishing and feeding is to imply the feeding of cows and horses. Fellow countrymen, we live by our toil while the Manchus rob us of our property and take over our lands. The Manchus do not consider themselves bandits, yet they treat us like horses and cows. My fellow countrymen, are you or are you not resigned to this situation?

The Manchus have also said: "For 200 years the Chinese people have been eating here and living here through our generosity and benevolence which have permeated down to the bone marrow." But China, which is the China of the Chinese people, does not belong to the bandit Manchus. Therefore, whose food they eat and whose land they live off are clearly without question. When the Manchus made that statement did they or did they not mean it? Let me tell you, my fellow countrymen. The bandit Manchus entered the pass of the Great Wall 260 years ago. They have lived off the food of our fellow countrymen, lived off our land, and benefited from the great generosity of our compatriots to such an extent that they could not repay us with the minutest particle of gratitude, even if they drank our urine or licked our ordure. It is therefore ridiculous for the Manchus to say such a thing.

Beyond Shanhaikuan is a piece of land called Manchuria (Heilungkiang, Kirin, and Mukden). Is this not the land of origin of the bandit Manchus? These are pasture lands and therefore the thieving Manchus should have done their best to preserve them. And yet, now they bow down and surrender these lands to Russia. How can you expect them to protect others when they cannot even protect themselves? How can you expect them to love the property of others when they do not even love their own property?

With a queue and dressed in Manchu costume, sauntering along the streets of London, a Chinese is called by the passerby "PIG TAIL" or "SAVAGE." Why? Good grief! The dignity of the Chinese officials has been wiped out, and the dignified manner and dress of the T'ang dynasty have been lost without leaving a trace.

When I touch my dress and my own hair, I feel sad. When I see the officials in their spring attire, my heart aches. When I see mourning clothes, I feel very depressed, and when I see the guards of the officials with their red and blue clothing, my heart contracts. The queue, the Manchu costume, the official dress—are they Chinese costumes or the wretched clothes of the bandit Manchus from the time of their sheepherding days? Let me advise my compatriots to take account of it.

After the thieving Manchus entered the pass, an imperial order for head-shaving was proclaimed, the gist of which was:

> The head-shaving system has not been a matter of great emergency. I have thought a great deal about it. Therefore, I have left it to each one to decide for himself at his convenience, and I will wait until peace and order are restored to the nation, then enforce it. But emperors are just like fathers and the people are just like children. Fathers and sons are one; no distinction should ever be made. If uniformity is not practiced throughout the nation, then the people will become the people of another country. Therefore, after the proclamation of this order, within ten days in the capital, and also within ten days of the arrival of this order in the province of Chihli and other provinces, all should have their heads shaved. No clemency will be shown to those who dare argue or who try to retain their hair.

What a shame! This was a milestone for us Chinese in our transition into slaves, horses, and cows, in our abandonment of the costumes of the Han and T'ang dynasties, and in our relinquishment of the skin and hair inherited from our parents. My fellow countrymen, my compatriots, I wish you would read the above order every day.

For the sake of money a prostitute will sleep with any man, but to the Chinese, who are the obedient slaves of the bandit Manchus, the subjects and concubines of the thieving Manchus, you never see offered much money. Even though some achieve high positions as governors and ministers, they obtain money only from our fellow countrymen, while the bandit Manchus have not given away one hair. Alas! Why are my fellow countrymen not even comparable to prostitutes?

What today we call "court," "government," "emperor," are no more than what we used to call "eastern barbarians," "southern barbarians," "western barbarians," "northern barbarians," Hsiung-nu, and Tartars. These tribal peoples who used to live outside of Shanhaikuan are not of the same race as the descendants of the Yellow

Emperor. Their territories are dirty, their people are hairy, their hearts are the hearts of animals, and their customs are the customs of barbarians. Their language is not the same as ours, nor are their dialects and their costumes. But they took advantage of the Chinese rebellion to enter China Proper, gain control of northern China, and drive on until they ruled the Chinese people. As a result they gained all the benefits when there were benefits to be gained, while the Chinese suffered disaster when there were calamities.

When the Taiping Rebellion broke out, the Manchu government used Chinese to fight Chinese. The mountains were full of corpses and the sea was full of blood. But the Manchus were protected. In the Sino-Japanese War of 1894, Chinese were used to fight the Japanese. Indemnities of 200,000,00 taels were paid to the Japanese, and a province was ceded, but the Manchus were protected. In the Boxer uprising, Chinese were used to fight the foreigners. Blood was shed in the capital, but the Manchus were protected. Therefore, if today the nation becomes stronger, it is for the sake of the Manchus and not the Chinese. If the country becomes richer, it is also for the sake of the Manchus and not the Chinese. The bandit Manchu, Kang I, used to say: "If the Chinese become stronger, the Manchus will be ruined." [36] The Manchus have known this for a long time. I hope my fellow countrymen will come to realize this.

Since the Manchus have been treating us this way and our people have been suffering because of it, our compatriots should have been aware of this situation and known what choice to make. When a dog or a sheep eats a bone, it still is able to realize when the bone is too big for its throat, but our fellow countrymen who have been suffering such ill treatment do not seem to have any feeling about it. They are like stone horses or bronze camels. The bandit Manchus have treated us worse than this. What I really want to say cannot be described in mere words. I want to take an oath and swear before the people:

If anyone raises the sore question of the ill treatment of the Chi-

[36] Kang I (d. 1900) was an Associate Grand Secretary who led the movement at Court sponsoring the Boxer uprising. Hummel, op cit. I, 407 and II, 863.

nese people by the Manchus, I can reveal all the sources and give a detailed explanation before the whole world. I wish that my body were as numerous as the sands, so that I would have countless tongues to utter infinite sounds and tell my fellow countrymen how the bandit Manchus rule us, butcher us, rape us, trap us, and persecute us. Let me repeat: I wish my body were as numerous as the sands so that like a host of actors I could depict to my compatriots how the bandit Manchus rule us, butcher us, rape us, trap us, and persecute us.

China has all that is needed to become a great power. We have 2,000,000 square *li* of territory, 400,000,000 intelligent people, 5000 years of history, and the good government of "Two Emperors" and "Three Kings." [37] The climate is mild, the people intelligent, and the resources vast. We have what other countries do not have. If we had not suffered the misrule of the bandits Nurhachi, Huang T'ai-chi,[38] and Fu-lin who trampled us underfoot, if we had been emancipated years ago from Manchu rule, I am sure such countries as England, Russia, Germany, and France—countries which have partitioned and invaded our territory—would have feared our power. India, Poland, Turkey, and Egypt would not have been conquered by England and Russia, but by China. This would have been logical, but such is not the case. Instead, we have become the slaves of the earth and have descended to the same level as the Indians and the African Negroes. How shameful and humiliating!

"The conquest of the six kingdoms was by the six kingdoms themselves and not by the Ch'in; and the overthrow of the Ch'in was by the Ch'in itself and not by the nation." [39] Did the Manchus conquer us or did we allow ourselves to be conquered? It has been said that what is past is past, but something can be done for the

[37] The Two Emperors were Yao and Shun, and the Three Kings were Yu of Hsia, T'ang of Shang, and Wen of the Chou dynasty.

[38] Huang-t'ai-chi was the name by which Abahai (1592–1643) was known in official accounts. He was the eighth son of Nurhachi and had two reign titles: T'ien-ts'ung (1627–36) and Ch'ung-te (1636–44). Hummel, *op. cit.* I, 1.

[39] The statement is quoted from the writing of Su Tung-p'o (1036–1101). The six kingdoms period lasted from 333–221 B.C., when the seventh kingdom gained ascendancy, marking the end of the Chou and the establishment of the Ch'in dynasty.

future. The China of yesterday may be considered dead, but today's China can be considered as born anew. From now on should we revitalize China or shall we continue to be slaves for generations to come? The affairs of the nation will retrogress if they do not progress; the nation will be conquered if it does not prosper. Hesitation midway cannot possibly be accepted in this world. My fellow countrymen ought to make a quick decision.

Today our fellow countrymen are suppressed internally by the Manchus and persecuted by foreign powers from the outside. Foreign invasions and domestic crises could dissolve our nation within ten years and make our race extinct within a hundred years. Is that not possible?

However, it has been said that in order to oppose foreign aggression, domestic enemies must be eliminated first. If this is so, then the Manchus, who are the public enemies of our countrymen, should be wiped out. If we, the slaves of the past 260 years, can be emancipated, then the slavery of the last few decades imposed by the foreign powers will automatically be taken care of.

Let me make a pact with my fellow countrymen. We must avenge the injustice done to us in the past nine generations. We must prepare to fight a ten-year bloody war, sharpen our knives, hold high our flag, and expend the greatest possible energy to expel the bandit Manchus who insult and humiliate us. We must restore our inherent rights, regain the freedom with which we were born, and obtain the advantages of equality among men. We must indeed! Shall the Chinese revolt? Shall we revolt? The French did three times and in the United States the revolution took seven years. Thus, China is bound to have a revolution whether we revolt or not. "In a civilized nation we cannot endure conquest by barbarians; together with the heroes of the nation we will restore your country." [40] Do my fellow countrymen have such ambitions?

Revolution and Education

There are barbarous revolutions and there are civilized revolutions.

---

[40] This is a well known saying attributed to one of the generals of the Taiping Rebellion, Shih Ta-k'ai.

A barbarous revolution is one which has only destruction, without reconstruction. It unleashes a period of terror in order to intensify chaos and disorder among the people in the nation, as exemplified in the Boxer uprising of 1900 and the activities of Garibaldi.

The civilized revolution is a revolution which has not only destruction, but also reconstruction, destruction for the sake of reconstruction, to obtain equality and freedom for the people and all the rights of independence and self-government for their benefit.

Revolution is the natural duty of the people, the roots of which lie within the people. It is originated by the people; it is not the private property of one or two persons. Now let us ask—why do we revolt? It must be because there is a demon who obstructs or blocks the natural rights of our people. Therefore, we must wipe it out so as to restore our inherent right. Thus, revolution is a device for getting rid of misfortune in order to achieve happiness. The act of eradicating disaster to gain happiness should be held in great esteem by my fellow countrymen. Such a civilized revolution should be held sacred and in the highest regard by my fellow countrymen.

In order to achieve extensive reconstruction, it is necessary to have destruction first. In order to have destruction, it is necessary to have construction first. This is a truism which has been valid from time immemorial. The revolution which we want to effect today is a revolution of destruction for the sake of reconstruction. Indeed, in order to have destruction, it is necessary to have construction first. What Mazzini, a founder of Italy, says is right: "Revolution and education should go hand in hand." Therefore, I tell my fellow countrymen there must be revolution and education—in other words, before revolution, education is necessary, and after revolution, education is also needed.

Today China is a nation without education. I am loath to describe all the shameful and abhorrent aspects of our society. What I can write for the epitaph is this: "The five senses, the four limbs, and the personality are all incomplete."

I heard that before the revolution, education in France was equal to that of her neighbors and before the American revolution, American education was equal to that of the British. These are the histories of the rising powers, never dreamed of in China. I heard that when India was conquered, it was a country without education, as is China. When Palestine was conquered, it was a country without education, as is China. This is the history of the countries which have been conquered, and we of China are not the only ones with this symptom.

Furthermore, the independence of the thirteen states, the confederation of Germany, the unity of Italy—if we were to read the history of these revolutions, they would raise our people's morale. In these histories we would see the people declaring war against the monarchy, overthrowing the government of the mother country, killing the aristocracy, advocating freedom, struggling for self-government, preparing for national defense from within, and opposing foreign aggression from outside. It often happened that during times of war and disaster, when a nation was in a state of chaos, great institutions from the Parliament and the Constitution down to the local system of government were established, and reconstruction was carried out by the leaders of the revolution, the founders of the nation, men who were willing to shed blood. Their morality, knowledge, and academic training reflected great superiority. I worship and admire them. When I analyze the situation, I find that the reason for their greatness lies in education.

Leaders like Washington and Napoleon are the great heroes of the world, but if there had been only one Washington and one Napoleon without the hundreds of millions of unknown Washingtons and Napoleons, then what could Washington and Napoleon have accomplished? How much more could those who are better than Washington and Napoleon accomplish? There are known heroes and there are unknown heroes. Washington and Napoleon are among those who rose to pre-eminence, representing many, many unknown Washingtons and Napoleons. In China today a single Washington or a single Napoleon cannot achieve much.

We must prepare the way for many, many unknown Washingtons and Napoleons. I have seen many patriots who considered themselves to be Washingtons or Napoleons. Whether their ability was greater than that of Washington or Napoleon, I do not know. I respect them as heroes. As for the numerous unknown heroes, they are lost amid the masses. A respects B, and B respects C.[41] But, I cannot find a leader. Let me elaborate on this point and hope my fellow countrymen agree with what I shall say in the following paragraphs:

1. China is the China of the Chinese. The territory of China is the heritage of our ancestor, Huang Ti. From generation to generation without interruption we were born here, brought up here, and lived here. And we must preserve this continuity. If there is an alien and lowly race which grasps our China rapaciously, which tramples over all the rights of the Han people, my fellow countrymen must expel them even at the expense of sacrificing our lives in order to restore our rights.

2. Everyone should know the meaning of equality and freedom. When one is born, he is free, that is, each one is equal to the other. Also, there is no such thing as king or subject, as in the time of Yao, Shun, Yu, and Chi.[42] These are the people who served and worked for our fellow countrymen. Therefore, our countrymen considered them as their representatives and respected them as their emperors, but actually they were only leaders and, in fact, everyone was equal. But the people of later generations did not understand the meaning of this and allowed numerous dictators, bandits, and despots to come into possession of all that belonged to everybody. Consequently, it became the private property of one family in one household, who called themselves emperor or kings and established inequality without freedom. Even such people as Genghis Khan and the Shun-chih emperor, coming from pastoral, lowly races, led the ruling class of China, enough of an insult to make our ancestor Yellow Emperor turn over in his grave. Thus, my compatriots, today we must expel the entire alien race and kill all the autocratic emperors in order to restore our natural rights, that my fellow countrymen may enjoy freedom and liberty.

[41] Tsou Jung means that each one respects the other, but no one steps forward to lead. All the people have potential, but none realize their potential.
[42] In the earliest legendary time of Chinese history, succession to the throne was not by the same family, but through the ability of the successor.

3. It is necessary to possess political and legal concepts. Government is the general organization for the performance of tasks for the nation. It is not owned by one or two persons. Like a machine, it requires a tabulator key if every part is to function properly. If one part is damaged, then the whole machine cannot operate. The people hold the same relationship to politics. But, if the people have no political ideas, then the nation is lost. India and Poland are examples of this. In any conquered country this is the case. The law exists to keep within bounds the behavior of our fellow countrymen so that they will not commit any wrongs. Some people say that barbarians have no freedom. Why? Because they have no law. If I can kill other people, then other people can also kill me. Therefore, none of us has freedom. Why did the autonomy of the Teutonic people surpass that of other people? Because they had legal concepts.

From the above three statements may be derived four courses of action:

1. To cultivate the kind of spirit which completely maintains our dignity and independence.

2. To cultivate the kind of spirit which risks going forward through fire and water and delights in a willingness to die.

3. To cultivate the kind of public virtue which expresses mutual love, altruism, self-respect, and the fulfillment of duty.

4. To cultivate and upgrade the character of our people, who will practice self-discipline so as to enjoy individual and collective liberty.

Differentiation of Races a Prerequisite to Revolution

The world has white and yellow races. This is a state of nature which enables men of ability and intelligence to compete with each other in the process of evolution. It is a stage at which people can compete on the basis of their intelligence so that the fittest may survive. The love of people for their own race is due to the need for consolidation against outside forces. Therefore, in the beginning a clan unified to oppose other clans; then a village unified to oppose other villages, a tribe unified to oppose other tribes, and finally a nation unified to oppose other nations. This is an axiom which is true of races throughout the world and is also one of the principal reasons for the development of human history. We are of the yellow race; we are the Chinese Han race of the yellow race. Let me give you an account of the unification and the role of various races in East Asian history so that my fellow countrymen can understand.

There are two kinds of yellow races in Asia—one is the Chinese race and the other is the Siberian.

The Chinese race spread through China Proper and Tibet and later into part of India. It is divided into three groups:

1. The Han race: The Han race is the most outstanding race in East Asian history—that is the race of my fellow countrymen. It resided in China Proper, first in the bend of the Yellow River and then it spread out. Our Han race has been the centripetal force of Asian civilization.[43] The Koreans and Japanese are also descendants and emigrants of the Han people.

2. The Tibetan race: From Tibet the Tibetans spread to Kashmir, Nepal, and Burma. This is the race that was made up of the Ti-ch'iang in the Shang and Chou dynasties, the Yüeh-chih of the Ch'in and Han dynasties, the T'u-fan of the T'ang dynasty, and the Hsi-hsia of the Southern Sung dynasty. All these people belong to this race.

3. The Indo-Chinese race: This race spread from southwestern China (Yunnan and Kweichow provinces) to such nations as Annam and Siam. In ancient times this race apparently once occupied China Proper, but was gradually expelled by the Han race. The Miao and the Ching-man peoples of the pre-Chou dynasty and the Nan-chao of the T'ang belong to this race.

The Siberian race spread from northeastern Asia to northern Asia and is divided into three racial groupings:

4. The Mongol race: The Mongol race originally populated the eastern side of Lake Baikal in Siberia, and later migrated southward.

---

[43] To show that China has been the focal point and the fountainhead of Asian civilization, Tsou Jung uses the image of the *mu-chin,* a wooden bell clapper for calling people together. "Centripetal force" was used in the translation.

From Inner and Outer Mongolia it spread to the north of the T'ien Shan range. The Yüan dynasty was founded by this race which almost united Europe and Asia. The Moghul Empire of India also originated from this race.

5. The Tungusic race: From northern Korea through Manchuria it spread over the Heilungkiang area. The Tung-hu of the Ch'in and Han and the Hsien-pi after the Han dynasty, the Mo-ko of the Sui and T'ang dynasties, the Ch'i-tan at the end of the T'ang dynasty, and the Nu-chen of the Sung dynasty, all belong to this race. The Manchus who now rule China are also from this race.

6. The Turkic race: The Turkic race originally populated Inner and Outer Mongolia, and later migrated westward. Today this race occupies the area south of the T'ien Shan range, in Central Asia. The pre-Chou races of the Hsün-yu, and Hsien-yün, Hsiung-nu, Jou-jan, of the Southern and Northern dynasties, the T'u-chüeh of the Sui dynasty, and the Hui-ko of the T'ang dynasty are all part of this race. The Turkish people of present-day eastern Europe were also founded by this racial group.

A chart can be drawn outlining them at present:

YELLOW RACE

CHINESE RACE		SIBERIAN RACE	
Han (Chinese)	Koreans Siamese Japanese Tibetans Other East Asians	Mongol Race: Mongols Manchus (so-called emperors of today) Siberians (Tartars of ancient times) Other northern and central Asians	Turkic Race: Turks Hungarians Other peoples of the yellow race

From what we have said, our Han race originated northwest of the Yellow River, but spread to other areas due to many difficulties and hardships. At the time of the Ch'in and Han dynasties it had already extended through the whole of China, with China Proper as the region in which the people lived, until today when the population has grown to 400,000,000—representing the largest single race on earth, with which there is no comparison. More than 10,000,000 people from this race migrated beyond the Great Wall to places like Tibet and the Chinghai area. Part of the race further migrated into the territory of Japan and up to the Russian territory at the left bend of the Heilungkiang River in the north. People moved southward, entering Annam, Cochin-China, Siam, Burma, and the Malay Peninsula. They went further to the Pacific Ocean, invading Bolivia, the United States of America, Canada, Peru, Paraguay, the South Seas, the Philippines, Java, Brunei, Australia, and Europe—no fewer than three or four million people.

Those who had no capital worked very hard to outdo the people of other countries by sheer toil. Those who had capital of several hundred thousand or a million dollars were able to compete with the wealthy merchants of Europe and America in the market. This proves the Han race's capacity for expansion. To say that the Han race should be respected as the masters of the twentieth century cannot be said to be too far-fetched.

Ah! Our Han race, isn't that the race which can make our motherland strong? Isn't that the independent race on the Asian mainland? Is it not the great race of a great people? Alas! The Han race, although made up of so many, have become merely the slaves of another race. Although the territory of the Han people is extensive, it exists only for the residents of another race. The Han race are nothing but the loyal and submissive subjects of the Manchus. Furthermore, the Han race have become the slaves of the European and American countries through the agency of the Manchus. I would rather see the Han race completely killed or eliminated than see them live under the trousers of the Manchus. In this peaceful world, I would rather have the Han people completely killed off or exterminated than see them become traitors like Hung Ch'eng-ch'ou,[44] interpretors, translators, or compradors under all the people of the world. I lament the plight of the Han race and wish to awaken the Han race to ethnic consciousness.

If you were to accost a man and say to him that his father is not his real father and his real father is someone else, he would become unmistakably angry, then take it upon himself to make inquiries until he found out the real story. In a family of fathers and sons, husbands and wives, and brothers living peacefully at home, if suddenly a robber entered and seized all the property and made slaves of all the members of the household, every member of the family would fight to the death for their property. If a man who is told that he has two fathers does not get angry, and if his property is stolen and he puts up no fight, then this is not a man but a corpse. And I am amazed that my countrymen as a whole would sustain things which one individual would not tolerate, things which one family would not tolerate. It is lamentable indeed!

After the Manchus entered the [Shanhaikuan] pass, the people began to call themselves the loyal subjects of the Ch'ing dynasty. When the Allied Expeditionary Forces captured Peking the people called themselves the loyal subjects of such and such a country. The people of Hong Kong erected a monument to Victoria on which it is written that her virtue is unsurpassed in heaven and on earth. In order to praise the accomplishments of the Meiji emperor, the Formosan people said that his virtues were all embracing and his manner benevolent. Those who were formerly the loyal subjects of the Chin, Yüan, Liao, and Ch'ing dynasties have gone; now there are those who have become the loyal subjects of Britain, France, Russia, and America. The reason for this is that the people have no ethnocentric or national ideas; thus, they can do things humiliat-

[44] Hung Ch'eng-ch'ou (1593–1665) of the Ming dynasty was made Governor-General of northeastern Chihli and Liaotung in 1639. In 1642 he surrendered to the Manchus when the city of Sungshan fell and became one of the most useful tools in the Manchu conquest of China. He served the Ch'ing government as Grand Secretary and in other high offices. Hummel, *op. cit.* I, 358–60.

ing to our ancestors, the men becoming robbers and the women prostitutes.[45]

Allow me to address my fellow countrymen. The nine divisions of China administered by the reputed founder of the Hsia dynasty and today's eighteen provinces—are they not the places where the Han people, my fellow countrymen, were born and brought up? Doesn't the renown of our Han people lie in their being descendants of the Yellow Emperor? Isn't there a marked distinction between China and the barbarians in the east, south, west, and the north? There is no intermarriage between the Manchus and our people. We could, therefore, still maintain our purity as the Yellow Emperor's descendants. People are devoted to their own family, but toward other families of different races the feeling is different. How can my fellow countrymen tolerate insults without any feeling at all? The Irish were ruled by the British, but because they are of a different race, they fought repeatedly with the British until they finally obtained the right of self-government.

There is an old Chinese saying: "Not being of my own race, his heart must be different." It is also said, "If he is a wolf, then he has the heart of a wolf." I wish my fellow countrymen would give some thought to these sayings.

Do my compatriots have the ambition to jump into the vast ocean? Would the ocean water cleanse them of their humiliation, which has insulted their ancestors, and of the depredation which has made men robbers and women prostitutes?

Abolition of our Subservient Nature a Prerequisite to Revolution

Some are human beings while others are slaves. Human beings are strong; slaves are conquered creatures. Human beings are independent; slaves are obedient. Under the Yellow flag of China [the flag of the Manchus] there exists a kind of people who are not really

[45] The statement is a figurative way of showing that the people have fallen into base ways and have become demoralized. The Chinese way of expressing this idea has been retained.

people and a species of slaves who are not really slaves, but a mixture of both. If you want to call them people, you may. I would go so far as to say that none of them are, because all 400,000,000 have the faces of slaves and concubines. Do you call such as they, people? You are insulting this beautiful term. So, you can only say that they are slaves. And I applaud this and say that the Chinese are slaves, which is the only label for them.

The Indians became slaves of Great Britain, not because the British wanted to enslave them, but because the Indians were willing to be slaves. The Annamese were enslaved by the French, not because the French enslaved them, but because the Annamese were willing to be slaves. We Chinese are slaves of the Manchus, the Europeans, and the Americans, not because the Manchus, the Europeans, and the Americans wanted to enslave us, but because we are willing to be slaves. Why are people willing to be slaves? Let me explain.

Slaves are the opposite of people; it is a humiliating term. People have self-governing ability and an independent nature; they have the right to participate in politics and the freedom to enjoy favorable opportunities. Whatever their occupations, they are flawless. But, slaves have neither self-governing ability nor the incentive for independence. Whatever they do, whether they drink, eat, mingle in society, choose their clothes, or select a place of residence, slaves always have to follow the orders of their master. As for their inherent rights and the good fortune they should enjoy, this is also in the hands of the master. They wear the clothes of the master and eat the food of the master, speak and do the bidding of the master. They do not think independently. They manifest no behavior except to obey. They do not laugh, only flatter. Having no occupation, they work only for others. They exhibit no behavior except to serve. When they are summoned, they dare not refuse to come. Dismissed, they dare not stay. Ordered to live, they dare not die, and ordered to die, they dare not live. One look from the master, one smile from the master, is a rare treasure or heaven itself. This is something in which they take pride before their friends. But if they arouse anger in the master they then bow their heads, their knees bending in timidity and fear. It may reach such extremes that even if they are beaten and trampled under foot, they dare not show the slightest resentment or harbor the wish to improve themselves.

That which other people would consider a great humiliation and which could not be tolerated for an instant, they accept without an angry look or inner resentment. They are so content that they do not even know they are human beings. In fact, they are not even looked upon as human beings by others. They are a different breed of men, disdained as an inferior race. Wives are ashamed to have them as husbands, fathers are ashamed to have them as sons, and younger brothers are ashamed to have them as older brothers. They are strictly outside the realm of human beings. This is the manifest nature of the slaves of the whole world, and the whole world looks down upon them. Ah, my Chinese fellow countrymen, your distinction lies in being slaves! The father teaches the son, the older brother encourages the younger brother, and the wife persuades the husband to practice all the maneuvers and methods of servitude from day to day. Alas, how fortunate to be slaves; how unfortunate to be slaves!

The pleasure the Chinese take in being slaves did not begin as of today. It has been said that "people" lived in China prior to the Ch'in and Han dynasties, but since the Ch'in and Han there have been no "people." I am of the opinion that under an autocratic political system all people are nothing but slaves. For the last few thousand years all the great statesmen, high officials, great teachers, and Confucian scholars have been teaching succeeding generations two important ethical principles: one is loyalty, and the other is filial piety. It was further interpreted to mean loyalty to the emperor and filial piety to one's parents. I do not understand what is meant by loyalty to one's emperor. In countries like France and the United States there are no kings to whom one pledges loyalty. Can you say that the people of these countries are not human beings? I have seen that, although the people of these countries have no kings to whom to pledge loyalty, still they fulfill their duties and obligations as citizens without a day's interruption. Loyalty and filial piety, of course, are virtues of human beings and it is all right to speak of loyalty to one's own country, but this is not the same as loyalty to one's emperor. Everyone has parents; without them there is no life. Without a nation there is no life. Therefore, it is inevitable for one to feel this way toward one's parents and one's country, but not toward one family or the running dogs of a family who pose as the state.

The Chinese have no history. The so-called Chinese history of twenty-four dynasties is nothing but a history of slaves. From the end of the Han dynasty until today more than 1700 years have passed, for 358 years of which China was subject to the rule of an alien race. For 759 years the territory north of the Yellow River had been under the rule of alien races. Alas! How can the descendants of the Yellow Emperor bear to see their dear fellow countrymen, and the territory which they inherited, ruled by another race? Why have there been so many instances when people have welcomed an alien army? Wearing festive apparel they welcomed the troops with food and drink. They were so proud to serve the aliens who ruled their own people. "Two emperors [of the Northern Sung] had to serve in prison dress [the table of the Tartars]. The ninth brother [of the Chang family] rode on a white horse and crossed the Yangtze River [to help the Mongol conquer the Southern Sung]." Loyalty to the emperor, loyalty to the emperor indeed! This is how men like Chang Hung-fan[46] and Hung Ch'eng-ch'ou became notorious. This is the reason why the Chinese are slaves.

Tseng Kuo-fan, Tso Tsung-t'ang, and Li Hung-chang were the loyal officers of the Ch'ing emperors. They were even named posthumously as Wen-cheng (cultured and upright), Wen-hsiang (cultured and helpful), and Wen-chung (cultured and loyal), respectively. These were the three so-called heroes of the restoration of the Ch'ing dynasty, admired by the prominent citizens of the time and envied by ordinary people as well as by those who passed the civil service examinations. And yet I have heard that Bismarck, Chancellor of Germany, once sarcastically remarked to Li Hung-chang: "We Europeans take pride in conquering alien races, but we have not heard of people taking pride in butchering their own fellow coun-

---

[46] Chang Hung-fan was instrumental in bringing the Mongols into China and helped them to conquer the Sung. Cho Hung-mou, *op. cit.* p. 927.

trymen." What a shame! I wish I could bring Tseng and Tso to life again just to hear this. I wish also that I could infuse life into those who followed Tseng and Tso, from high officials down to the officials of no importance, just to hear these words. These three persons—Tseng, Tso, and Li—considered themselves educated compared with former sages, and yet they were willing to butcher their fellow countrymen, contrary to justice and righteousness, to be loyal slaves to the Manchus. We need not discuss the others. I cannot compare them with anyone. They cannot even be compared with Li Tzu-ch'eng[47] and Chang Hsien-chung.[48] Li and Chang repeatedly slaughtered fellow countrymen to accelerate the Manchu conquest of China, but they were uneducated, pressured by the corrupt government of the Ming dynasty. Therefore, I can forgive them. But Tseng, Tso, and Li were clearly [educated] Chinese. They butchered their compatriots and asked the Manchus to rule China so that they might obtain honor and position for their children and wives. Them I cannot forgive.

It has been said that the British assisted the Manchus in suppressing the Taiping Heavenly Kingdom and in the conquest of the Han race. He that loves the tree loves the branch. Tseng, Tso, and Li are representatives of the slave-like Chinese. Tseng's, Tso's, and Li's may go, but other Tseng's, Tso's, and Li's will come.

Submission, contentment, obedience, office-seeking, fortune-seeking—all these are textbooks, teaching the Chinese how to be slaves. Take anyone in the country; there is no one who is not a slave. More than 2000 years ago they were all slaves, and 2000 years later they remain enslaved.

[47] Li Tzu-ch'eng (1605?–1645), a leader of the peasant uprisings at the end of the Ming dynasty, captured Peking in April 1644, but was defeated subsequently by the combined forces of the Ming general, Wu San-kuei, and the Manchus. Hummel, *op. cit.* I, 491–93.

[48] Chang Hsien-chung (1606–1647) was a rebel leader in the final years of Ming rule. He declared himself "King of the Great Western Kingdom" with his capital at Chengtu, Szechwan. He was notorious for cruelty and slaughter. Hummel, *op. cit.* I, 37–38. For details, see James B. Parsons, "The Culmination of a Chinese Peasant Rebellion: Chang Hsien-chung in Szechwan, 1644–46," *Journal of Asian Studies,* Vol. XVI, No. 3 (May 1957), pp. 387–400.

My fellow countrymen, you will find no trace of the Annamese people represented in the National Assembly of France; you will find no footsteps of the Indians leading to the British Parliament; there is no Formosan represented in the Japanese Diet. Yet Indians, even though they are slaves, still have the opportunity as policemen to wear red turbans on their heads and the pleasure of arresting Chinese in the streets of Shanghai and Hong Kong. May I ask my fellow countrymen, have you ever tried to find any place on earth where you could act as policemen over a foreign people and enjoy the privilege? Were not one piece of bread and one dish of taro characteristics of the former life of the Negro slaves in Africa? My compatriots, please give it some thought.

Let me first say something which may awaken you. I wish my compatriots would try their best to force themselves to put down their basic servile nature and advance themselves as the people of China. The slaves of pre-revolutionary France eventually achieved revolution and the slaves of the United States prior to independence were eventually able to throw off British control—for no reason other than that they recognized themselves as free men. Therefore, as I have said, servile nature must be abolished before revolution can begin; otherwise, we will be overpowered by the laws of evolution and the principle of the survival of the fittest. If any power tries to seize our territory, then my fellow countrymen may become the slaves of slaves. From the slaves of slaves they will become monkeys, from monkeys to wild pigs, and then oysters, and there will be a wasteland and finally a desert without human beings.

There is a song written by a contemporary writer entitled "It Is Good To Be a Slave."

> It is good to be a slave. It is good to be a slave. Do not worry about domestic politics or foreign affairs. Let us sleep under our coverlets. An old saying advises us: "An official should be loyal; a son should be filial." Everything should be in order. The Manchus have been the conquerors of China for [more than] two hundred years. I have become accustomed to being a slave. The nation belongs to them. The wealth belongs to them. The foreigners will come soon; they still will need slaves. If the foreigners open mines, I could work there. If they start an import-export firm, I could be a

servant. If they recruit an army, I could be a soldier. If they want an interpreter, I could also serve. In the interior there is a captain who collects taxes and who takes care of the jail—honorable, indeed! The toadying Manchus will become the slaves of the foreigners. Slavery's nature is deeply imbedded in our hearts. Fathers and brothers encourage loyalty and filial piety. Who cares about bloodshed, revolution, freedom, or equality of wealth? Revolts jeopardize one's life. Stubbornness will not allow one to conform. We slaves should not commit such mistakes. We may receive benevolence from the Chin [Tartar], Yüan, and Ch'ing. The names of our masters have been changed quite often. There is not much difference if the dynasty is changed to that of Great Britain, France, or the United States.

It is good to be a slave. It is felicitous to be a slave. The strong men of the world we obey with 30 per cent shrewdness and 70 per cent flattery. There is nothing underhanded in world affairs. The nation is well cared for by capable people. Sitting and watching calmly the change of events, I am carefree, even if the race is conquered and the clan destroyed.

It is difficult to find an understanding man. We can laugh at the young reformers of 1898 who were willing to go through hell and deep water, who made the officials angry, and caused the foreigners consternation, who died and were lost to posterity one after another in order to regain the nation's sovereignty without knowing that they were wrong. It is good to be a slave. It is good to be a slave. Everywhere there is a home for a slave. There is no point in protecting one's race and one's country.

Significance of Revolution and Independence

The British Parliament disobeyed King Charles I because the King extended great privileges to the nobility, endangered the business life of the people, increased taxes arbitrarily, enforced bonds, and collected ship money. The French Revolution was a result of titles given without merit. The difference between the rich and the poor was great. People were not well protected and taxes were levied arbitrarily. These were the reasons for the French patriots' revolt. The Americans struggled for independence because a heavy tea tax and a stamp tax were levied and garrison forces were stationed in America without the consent of the legislature. Consequently, the Americans rose in protest against the British, with the American flag waving at Bunker Hill. I want to reiterate the following over and over again: "The reason for a Chinese revolution in our country today is that as slaves of the Manchus we, the descendants of the Yellow Emperor, have been subject to cruelty and persecution from internal and external sources. We are the slaves of several masters and the slaves of slaves. There is great danger of annihilation of the race."

Since the development of science, the theory of the divinity of the emperor has been toppled. Since the advance of modern civilization, the autocratic system has been overthrown. As people's intelligence and knowledge become more advanced, everyone will be able to enjoy natural rights. The Han people today, in order to throw off the yoke of the Manchus and regain all their lost rights, live among the great powers of the world, and possess the natural rights of freedom and equality, must revolt and then safeguard their independence. I, your humble, uneducated servant, am not qualified to describe the great significance of revolution and independence. With great humility, following the example of the American Revolution, I wish to present to my 400,000,000 Chinese countrymen the following policies for your approval and adoption. Let heaven and earth bear witness:

1. China shall be for the Chinese; our fellow countrymen must realize that China is the China of the Chinese.
2. No alien race shall trespass, not even the slightest, on Chinese rights.
3. All obligations to obey the Manchus shall be abolished.
4. The barbarian Peking government established by the Manchus shall be overthrown.
5. The Manchus living in China shall be expelled or killed in revenge.
6. The Manchu emperor shall be killed in order to do away with the age-old autocratic, monarchial system.
7. All Chinese people and foreign countries hostile to our revolution shall be considered enemies.

8. A central government shall be established as the headquarters of the administration.

9. The country shall be divided into provinces. Each province shall elect one general representative who shall elect a provisional president to represent the nation. One vice president shall be elected as well as representatives from various prefectures and districts.

10. All men and women shall be citizens without regard to sex.

11. All men in the nation shall be obliged to serve in the army.

12. Everyone shall be loyal to the nation.

13. Everyone shall pay taxes.

14. All the people, men and women, shall be equal; there shall be no distinction between the nobility and the commoner.

15. The inalienable rights of the people are given by heaven. The people possess inalienable rights.

16. Life, liberty, and all the other benefits are natural rights.

17. No one shall infringe upon freedom of speech, freedom of thought, or freedom of the press.

18. The people's rights shall be safeguarded, and they should be approved by the public at large. The government shall have the consent of the people and the authority to protect the people's rights.

19. Whenever the government shall interfere with the people's rights, the people shall have the right to revolt against the government in order to secure safety and happiness. Once security and happiness are obtained, then through public discussion the people shall redefine their rights and privileges and establish a new government. This is also the right of the people.

However, after the establishment of the government, if it does not fully meet the expectation of even a minority and the people feel the need to rise up in revolt, then the government will be a very unstable one and this is no way to create a state. Nothing is perfect in the world; the important thing is being peaceful. If the defects of the administration are not really very harmful to the people, then it is better to claim the people's rights by peaceful means than to overthrow the government. However, if the government insists on corrupt ways, then it is not only the right but the obligation of the people to overthrow it and set up a new government to protect their rights. The Chinese people have suffered extreme hardship, and they will not tolerate autocratic government once the independence of revolution is achieved. This is why the political system of the past must be changed.

20. The new nation shall be called "The Republic of China." ("Ch'ing" is the name of a dynasty; "Chih-na" is the name used by the Japanese.)

21. The Republic of China shall be a free and independent nation.

22. This new and independent nation shall have the right to declare war, make peace, and arrange alliances and trade—all the things an independent country is entitled to on an equal footing with the other great powers of the world.

23. Our constitution should be modeled after that of the United States, with the necessary modifications to apply to the situation in China.

24. All self-governing laws shall follow the self-governing laws of the United States.

25. All matters relating to the individual, the whole body of the people, negotiations, the government system, the official system, and all the affairs of the nation shall follow the pattern of the United States.

Conclusion

All my 400,000,000 fellow countrymen, men and women, old and young, please be revolutionary. Take revolution as every man's duty; consider it as necessary as your daily food. Don't despise yourselves. Your land occupies two thirds of Asia. Your fellow countrymen comprise one fifth of all human beings. Your tea can supply millions and millions of people in the world and still there would be a surplus; your coal can supply the world for more than 2000 years without being used up. You have the notoriety of being called the "yellow peril." But you also have the power of a race with political institutions which you can administer; you have armaments which you can utilize, lands which you can protect, inexhaustible resources which you can use for yourselves. You have the perfect conditions for revolution in China.

Please lead your 400,000,000 countrymen for their own sake and for the sake of your homeland in a fight against your age-old public enemies, the Manchus. Then wipe out the foreign devils who have infringed upon your sovereignty. Thus, the shame of the nation will be washed clean; the reputation of your countrymen will be held in esteem; your flag of independence will be hung in the sky, and your bells of freedom will resound throughout the nation. The entire magnitude of your independence will be triumphantly commanded from the center of the nation. Your memorial will be erected over a high mound. Your goddess of freedom will point to the sky with her left hand and to the earth with her right hand and will appear on your behalf. Alas, the sky is blue and the earth is white [pure]. Revolution and independence, like a thunderstorm, will awaken the sleeping lion of several thousand years.

Long live the Chinese revolution and independence!

Long live the Republic of China!

Long live the freedom of 400,000,000 fellow countrymen in the Republic of China!

❈ 8 ❈

Problems of a Late Ch'ing Revolutionary: Ch'en T'ien-hua

ERNEST P. YOUNG

In contemplating revolutions which succeed, it is easy to neglect the enormous difficulties in launching them and the profoundly disturbing decisions which the revolutionaries face in the pursuit of their aims. We are encouraged in this by the plethora of deterministic revolutionaries, who talk as if all were ordained by the forces of history. At the very least, a dogged optimism often seems to characterize revolutionary psychology. The most famous figure of early twentieth-century revolution in China, Sun Yat-sen, was a master at optimism, which was one of his best weapons in converting other Chinese to his views. Perhaps a talent for seeing the cheerful side of things was necessary to sustain him and his followers through so many setbacks.

Ch'en T'ien-hua was by nature at the other extreme. He was a pessimistic revolutionary, who kept the faith only with difficulty. A Hunanese, he joined one segment of the movement in 1903 and became one of the most vigorous and popular revolutionary pamphleteers in the first decade of the century. In 1904 he took part in an ambitious, though abortive, anti-Manchu uprising in Hunan

This article is a revision of the author's "Ch'en T'ien-hua (1875–1905): A Chinese Nationalist," *Papers on China*, Vol. 13, pp. 113–62, published by the Center for East Asian Studies, Harvard University. The revision has involved extensive additions and rewriting and is based partly on materials previously unavailable. The permission of the Center to undertake this revision is gratefully acknowledged.

and bordering provinces. In the summer of 1905 he was among the first in the Hunan revolutionary group in Tokyo to advocate co-operation with Sun Yat-sen. Thus, he was one of the key participants in the founding of the first important supra-provincial revolutionary organization, the T'ung Meng Hui, and he was a principal contributor to the first issue of its organ, the *Min-pao*. But even in the midst of this intense three-year career of anti-Manchu activity, he was burdened with doubts and hesitations. The revolution for which he worked so fervently was fraught with dangers, and early in 1905 he seemed momentarily to retract his commitment. He soon renewed it energetically, but by the end of that year, he had killed himself, not out of supreme revolutionary fervor but rather out of fear that his country was not ready for revolution. Ch'en T'ien-hua's pessimistic streak affords an unusual view of revolutionary psychology in early twentieth-century China. He was not a typical revolutionary, but it was part of his peculiarity that he spoke frankly about matters which troubled not only himself, but also a broad section of the nationalist and revolutionary Chinese of his time.

Revolutionary Baptism

Ch'en T'ien-hua was born in the Hsinhua district of Hunan in 1875. We know little of his family, except that it was not well off, although able to provide him with the beginnings of a traditional education. Probably having undergone several years of domestic tutoring, he attended a village school when he was about fourteen years old, and after a year or two of further hard work obtained the first literary degree (*hsiu-ts'ai*). The decade of the 1890's was a time of great ferment in Hunan, and Ch'en's home district shared in the general spread of Western studies. Ch'en attended a newly founded technical middle school. It was from this school that he proceeded to Japan in 1902 or early 1903, probably on a provincial government scholarship.[1] From these few facts about his early life,

[1] The statements about Ch'en T'ien-hua's early life are based on: *Min-pao* (People's Journal), No. 2 (1906), material taken from the back of a portrait of Ch'en; Ch'en T'ien-hua, "Chou-chün Hsin-shuo shih-lüeh" (A Bio-

one can conclude that when he left China for the first time he carried with him a moderately sound classical education as well as at least an introduction to Western subjects. By his own testimony, he was an adherent of reform rather than of revolution before he went to Japan.[2]

Ch'en's arrival in Tokyo coincided with the beginning of a spectacular increase in the number of Chinese students going to Japan to study the newly fashionable "Western learning." Before 1900 there was only a handful. In 1903 the number reached one thousand, and three years later there were perhaps some eight thousand. At home, national consciousness and discontent with the imperial government, especially with the Manchu ethnic monopoly on the throne and in many top posts, was growing. Among young Chinese in Tokyo, the development was accentuated. Temporarily cut off from ordinary social constraints of family and clan, confronted directly by a vigorous, modernizing, and often offensively patronizing Japan, and granted fairly free expression (at least concerning Chinese affairs), the students quickly responded to revolutionary ideas.

---

graphical Sketch of Chou Hsin-shuo), *Min-pao*, No. 1 (1905), pp. 146–48; Ts'ao Ya-po, *Wu-ch'ang ko-ming chen-shih* (True History of the Wuchang Revolution) (Shanghai, 1930), Vol. I, opposite p. 27; Li Yün-han, "Huang K'o-ch'iang hsien-sheng nien-p'u kao" (Draft Chronological Biography of Huang Hsing), in Wu Hsiang-hsiang, ed., *Chung-kuo hsien-tai-shih ts'ung-k'an* (Selected Writings on Modern Chinese History), Vol. IV (Taipei, 1962), pp. 158–59; Hsü Fo-su, "Tui-yü Ch'en lieh-shih tao-hai chih kan-t'an" (Elegy on Patriot Ch'en's Suicide by Drowning), *Hsin-min ts'ung-pao* (New People's Miscellany), No. 74 (Feb. 8, 1906), p. 63; Tsou Lu, "Ch'en T'ien-hua shih-lüeh" (A Biographical Sketch of Ch'en T'ien-hua), *Ko-ming chih ch'uang-tao yü fa-chan* (The Advocacy and Development of the Revolution) (Taipei, 1963), III, 376–78.

A recent collection of Ch'en T'ien-hua's writings is available in: Committee for the Compilation of Materials on the Party History of the Central Committee of the Kuomintang, ed., *Ko-ming hsien-lieh hsien-chin shih-wen hsüan-chi* (Selected Works of Martyrs and Forerunners of the Revolution) (Taipei, 1965), I, 27–140.

[2] Ts'ao Ya-po, "Ch'en T'ien-hua t'ou-hai" (Ch'en T'ien-hua's Suicide by Drowning), *Ko-ming chih ch'ang-tao yü fa-chan*, III, 372. This article contains Ch'en's "Last Testament," which will henceforth be referred to by this name. The pagination will refer to its printing in *Ko-ming chih ch'ang-tao yü fa-chan*, Vol. III.

As the number of Chinese students in Tokyo increased, they developed various associations, often on the basis of common provincial origin. Ch'en naturally became part of the Hunan group, which was one of the most active. The associations usually sponsored publications; under Huang Hsing's leadership, Ch'en was editor of a Hunanese magazine, *Yu-hsüeh i-pien* (Translations by Hunan Students Abroad), first published in November 1902 and offering Chinese translations of foreign works and original articles.[3] Henceforth, his primary political association was with the radical wing of Hunanese students in Tokyo, which in addition to Huang Hsing included Yang Tu-sheng (Shou-jen), Yang Tu, Liu K'uei-i, and later Sung Chiao-jen. His organizational activity was largely guided by Huang Hsing, and Ch'en in turn became the group's chief literary spokesman, a position he retained until his death.

In the spring of 1903, in the Chinese community in Tokyo feeling over the Russian occupation of Manchuria was at a particularly high pitch. Responding to a Japanese report of secret Russian demands on Peking, an inter-provincial assembly of students gathered on April 29 and agreed to organize a military unit among themselves to be put at the service of their government for use against the Russians. The unit was called the Volunteer Brigade To Resist Russia. Although some of the participants were already revolutionary, many were not, and its organizers gave the Chinese government due notice of their aims by telegram and emissaries. This brigade, soon renamed the Student Army, was originally formed as a gesture of loyalty to China and, by implication, its government.[4] According to Ch'en's later account, most of the particpants turned against the government only when the Ch'ing administration insisted that the Student Army was dangerous and asked the Japanese to suppress it.[5] As he wrote in an open letter at the time, the Ch'ing court seemed more concerned about a handful of Chinese students abroad than hun-

---

[3] Li, *loc. cit.* pp. 158–59.

[4] *Ibid.* pp. 163–65.

[5] Ch'en T'ien-hua, "Shih-tzu-hou" (Roar of the Lion), *Min-pao,* No. 9 (1906), pp. 4–6.

dreds of thousands of crack foreign troops threatening the country.[6] If Ch'en had not already been persuaded of the necessity of revolution by his fellow Hunanese, the suppression of the Student Army did the job. The incident was symbolic of the close association of nationalism with a commitment to revolution, an association that characterized his and subsequent generations in China.

After the Student Army was dissolved by the Japanese police (it had actually been engaged in drill and rifle practice), some of its members, including Ch'en, formed an avowedly revolutionary society. It used as a cover name the Association for Universal Military Education, but its actual organization was secret. Its aims were to nurture a martial spirit, to effect the principle of race or nationalism (min-tsu chu-i), to take vengeance on the Manchus, and to resist the foreign powers.[7] Its methods were to be incitement, uprising, and assassination. Huang Hsing, Liu K'uei-i, and Ch'en T'ien-hua elected to carry the movement to Hunan.[8] Before the end of 1903, Ch'en had returned to China and had written the first of his revolutionary tracts, Meng-hui-t'ou (Sudden Realization).[9]

In this way, Ch'en became involved in the most ambitious revolutionary plot of the period. After some prospecting of revolutionary potential in Hunan and neighboring provinces, Huang Hsing enlisted Ch'en and others in a new, mostly Hunanese organization called the Hua Hsing Hui (Society for the Revival of China). Its purpose was to organize a revolt in various parts of Hunan, and to seek sympathetic backing in other provinces. The date chosen for the uprising was the Empress Dowager's birthday, November 16,

[6] "Ch'en T'ien-hua fu Hu-nan t'ung-hsüeh chu-chün shu" (Ch'en T'ien-hua's Letter in Reply to All His Fellow Students from Hunan), Ko-ming chih ch'ang-tao yü fa-chan, II, 129. This letter originally appeared in the Shanghai Su-pao, June 14, 1903.

[7] Chün-tu Hsüeh, Huang Hsing and the Chinese Revolution (Stanford University Press, 1961), pp. 10–11.

[8] Feng Tzu-yu, Chung-kuo ko-ming yün-tung erh-shih-liu nien tsu-chih shih (Twenty-six Years' Organizational History of the Chinese Revolutionary Movement) (Shanghai, 1948), pp. 67–68. Nagai Kazumi, "Chin Ten-ka no shōgai" (The Life of Ch'en T'ien-hua), Shigaku zasshi (The Journal of Historical Science), Vol. 65, No. 11 (Nov. 1956), pp. 50–51.

[9] Nagai, loc. cit. p. 65, n. 35.

1904, and the initial stroke was to be the assassination, by explosives, of high officials assembled locally for her birthday rites. In addition to the support of the students, both those returned from Japan and those enlisted on the spot (for example, Sung Chiao-jen), Huang Hsing secured the co-operation of traditionally anti-Manchu secret society elements in Hunan. Ch'en T'ien-hua's particular role was to win over military support in Kiangsi province. Others were charged with setting up branches in Hupeh, Szechwan, Anhwei, Chekiang, and Kwangtung.[10] Although much of this organization may have been tenuous, the uprising was planned on a grand scale. As the plot was gathering its final momentum, the government learned of it and suppressed it. But most of the Hua Hsing Hui leaders escaped, after some adventure, first to Shanghai and then back to Japan. Ch'en, so recently a convert to revolution, was deeply disheartened by the failure.

Problems of the Foreign Menace and Revolution

If Ch'en published anything before his conversion to revolution, it is not extant. We first meet him as a revolutionary, and the period of his activity on behalf of the Hua Hsing Hui plot in central China forms a distinct unit in the development of his thought. Of his writings from this period, we have two famous propaganda tracts, *Sudden Realization,* already mentioned, and *Ching-shih-chung* (Alarm To Arouse the Age), which was also widely circulated in the Yangtze region, as well as parts of his novel, *Shih-tzu-hou* (Roar of the Lion), which was published later.[11] In his propaganda tracts, Ch'en was speaking on behalf of the entire Hunanese revolutionary group. In a broader sense, he represented to some degree the revolutionary element among his contemporaries. Indeed, many of his

[10] There are several accounts of this uprising. See especially: Hsüeh, *op. cit.* pp. 13–25; Li, *loc. cit.* pp. 167–85; Nagai, *loc. cit.* pp. 49–51; Tsou, *loc. cit.* pp. 376–77.

[11] On the basis of internal evidence, I have concluded that the preface and first two chapters of the novel were composed before Ch'en's contact with Sun Yat-sen. The novel was printed posthumously in installments in *Min-pao*.

views are still prominent aspects of Chinese radical nationalist psychology.[12]

One's first impression of Ch'en's ideas at this time is that he was preoccupied with Social Darwinism. It would be dangerous to underestimate the familiarity of Chinese students in Tokyo in 1903 with at least popularized forms of recent Western social and political theory. Most of them were able to read the extensive literature of Japanese translations, and in addition there was a proliferation of student journals providing translations into Chinese. Liang Ch'i-ch'ao, whose publications were an introduction to Western thought for so many at this time, wrote an article in 1902 on the prominent Social Darwinian, Benjamin Kidd. With little effort, then, Ch'en was able to become acquainted with the doctrine of social and racial struggle.

In the first chapter of his novel, *Roar of the Lion,* Ch'en introduces an abbreviated version of this doctrine. He subscribes to Darwin's thesis of man's simian ancestry and the eventual evolution of the intelligent human. He anticipates the emergence of a more intelligent and powerful animal, which will supersede man. All this, he says, is perceived through Darwin's revolutionary discovery, the laws of evolution. He goes on to say that T. H. Huxley has pointed out that men, through their intelligence and technical progress, have become more numerous, while animals have become fewer. Struggle in the purely human social sphere assumes the same pattern—the more intelligent and socially cohesive supplant the less fit. In this struggle for existence, people band together in groups for defense against each other. The only effective alliance is with people of the same race. Races, too, are subject to the iron law of selection and face the possibility of extinction.

[12] Ch'en T'ien-hua clearly belongs with that group of radical intellectuals (both reformist and revolutionary) which Professor Schiffrin has characterized as "the mainstream of Chinese nationalism." Harold Schiffrin, "The Rise of Sun Yat-sen: 1894–1905," unpublished conference paper, Portsmouth, New Hampshire, August 1965, pp. 33–54.

For a description of the range of personalities and ideas in this main current, see Harold Z. Schiffrin, *Sun Yat-sen and the Origins of the Chinese Revolution* (Berkeley: University of California Press, 1968), pp. 283–99.

Ch'en applies these ideas in his own way to the races of the world, with particular attention, of course, to the standing of the yellow race. The picture is not happy. The yellow race (China, Japan, Korea, Vietnam, and Southeast Asia) developed the first civilization three or four thousand years ago. But in the last hundred years its population has gone from 800,000,000 to only 500,000,000. The red, brown, and black races have all been suffering the same fate of population decline. Meanwhile, the white race, which owes the original elements of its civilization to China, has in the last two or three hundred years discovered many new principles of learning in the areas of astronomy and geography and in the study of light, sound, and steam. It has produced many inventions such as the telephone and the steamship, none of which are over a hundred years old. And what has been the consequence of "the truly amazing progress of the last few decades"? The white race has grown in power and occupied the lands of all other races, except Japan, China, and Siam. One hundred years ago it had a population of 400,000,000, now it numbers 800,000,000. "Of the five races, only the white race is increasing. The other four are yearly decreasing. Why is this? Because all the countries of the world have been destroyed by the white race." [13]

This obsession with the danger of racial decline was a major theme with Ch'en T'ien-hua in this period and was to reappear just before his death. A qualification concerning his use of the concept of race must be offered, however. From the Boxer uprisings to 1905 the greatest immediate danger to China seemed to Ch'en and many other Chinese to come from Russia in the north or from the West European countries. Japan, although the victor in the Sino-Japanese War a decade before, remained more a worthy example of possible progress than a threat to the existence of China. The division between the white and yellow races, therefore, was easy and natural. But just as the English imperialist, when he spoke of the white race, often meant only the English, so Ch'en tended to narrow his

[13] *Ching-shih-chung*, pp. 129–30. The pagination for this work, as cited here, refers to its printing in *Hsin-hai ko-ming* (The Revolution of 1911) (Shanghai, 1956), II, 112–43.

definition of the yellow race to describe only the Chinese. Or rather his concept of race was an elastic one that could be adapted to meet the nationalistic needs of the moment.

After all, how was he to identify the members of this Chinese society in which he was most interested? What distinguished them from the Manchus, against whom he was rebelling, and from the foreigners, whose incursions he would repulse? They were Chinese, of course, but what did that mean? Certainly not subjects of the emperor. Loyalty to one's ruler, one of the five relationships of Confucianism, was a part of the tradition at which he most vehemently railed. Inheritors of an ancient culture? As an advocate of revolution and (as we shall see) Westernization, he could not so define the Chinese without becoming involved in serious conflicts: there were too many elements of that culture which had to be abolished in order to attain his goals. In any case, as opponents of an anti-Manchu revolution pointed out, the ruling Manchus were as qualified by the cultural definition as any Chinese. Ch'en could not define the Chinese as citizens of a Chinese nation, since in his view it was the very absence in most Chinese of the concept of the nation that hindered progress. This lack of alternative made the acceptance of a definition of the Chinese in racial terms natural. The Chinese, inchoate mass though they were, were all, he declared, the descendants of the Yellow Emperor (mythical progenitor of the Chinese).[14] Actual racial feelings, which could hardly have been absent, intensified the emotional impact of these ideas, but Ch'en had no interest in essential racialism, such as the purity of Chinese blood lines. His pseudo-racial definition certainly excluded the Westerner, but it was vague enough to include or exclude other East Asians as the political program required. This concept of race was a working tool in the service of nationalism.

Ch'en used his definition to make vivid the prospect of national failure. National failure to Ch'en was synonymous with partition of China among the powers. In his writings he described the con-

[14] Ch'en's first work, *Meng-hui-t'ou*, begins with an invocation to Huang Ti (the Yellow Emperor). The pagination for this work, as cited here, refers to its printing in *Hsin-hai ko-ming*, II, 144–70.

sequences in racial terms, the only terms available to him: "We must know that the calamity of partition will not simply be the fall of the country, but will certainly be the extermination of the race." [15] He not only forecast such dire consequences, he also felt that, unless drastic changes took place among the Chinese people, there was small chance of avoiding these consequences:

> A Japanese weekly has said that China will be destroyed in ten years, and in a hundred years the race will be gone. We do not need ten years for the country to be destroyed, and less than a hundred years will do for the sure extermination of our race.[16]

True, such statements were part of his effort to arouse the Chinese populace, but they should not be dismissed as mere propaganda. As we shall see, this undertone of pessimism was to reveal itself in the very desperation of his acts in the last year of his life. After all, from a Social Darwinian outlook, a member of a race which so often seemed to demonstrate its lack of "fitness" had reason to be apprehensive.

The anti-foreign feeling of his early writings must also, I think, be granted an underlying sincerity, despite its obvious propaganda purpose. If nothing else, a kind of frenzied eloquence bespeaks the presence of deep personal feeling:

> What's that, what's that! It's coming, it's coming! What's coming? The foreigner is coming, the foreigner is coming! That's bad, that's bad. It's bad for everybody. Old, young; man, woman; the honored and the despised; rich and poor; official, scholar, merchant, artisan —every kind of person. From now on you will all be cattle and sheep in the foreigner's barnyard, stew in his pot. If he wants to kill you, he will; if he wants to boil you, he will; and you won't be able to do a thing about it. Oh! The day of our death has arrived.[17]

And what is perhaps the most extreme statement of his hostility toward the foreigner:

> People today say that China now is extremely poor and weak and has few guns and cannons, so how can she wage war with foreign

[15] *Ching-shih-chung,* p. 123.
[16] *Ibid.* pp. 124–25.
[17] *Ibid.* p. 112.

countries. I appreciate this point. True, if the foreign countries do not come to cut China up, we certainly should not ourselves provoke them without reason, and so imitate the behavior of the Boxers. But today they give us no quarter: they firmly intend to divide us up no matter what happens. Rather than being partitioned unwittingly, it would be better to kill a few of them to put some price on it. There is a popular saying that a dog cornered against a wall will always turn around and take a few bites. Do you mean to say that we, 400,000,000 of us, are not able to match a dog? If the foreign soldiers don't come, that's that. If they do, I exhort you all to summon up your courage and abandon all fear of them. Scholars: put down your brushes. Farmers: lay down your rakes. Traders: abandon your business. Artisans: put down your tools. Everyone, sharpen your knives, supply yourselves with bullets, swear an oath, and cry out. All press ahead. Kill the foreign devils [*yang-kuei-tzu*]; kill the Christian converts [*erh-mao-tzu*] who have given themselves up to the foreign devils. If the Manchus help the foreigners kill us, then first kill all the Manchus. If those corrupt officials help the foreigners kill us, then first kill all the corrupt officials. "Take in hand your ninety-nine knives, and don't stop until the last enemy has been killed." My dearly beloved compatriots, my dearly beloved compatriots! Forward and kill, forward and kill. Kill, kill, kill. Kill our national enemy who has been with us these several generations [the Manchus]; kill our great newly arrived enemy. Kill those traitors who toady to the foreigner. Kill, kill, kill.[18]

Ch'en added fuel to this emotional fire with stories of Russian brutality in Manchuria, American insults to Chinese students, treatment of Chinese in the treaty ports, missionary privileges—a fine catalogue of horrors.

Yet even in this violent passage, we should note that the spilling of blood is a last resort—a desperate act when all else fails and in no sense a solution. Ch'en was forever being driven by his pessimistic strain to devise last resorts. When he was not imagining the worst—before the dog is driven to the wall—he put great stress on not provoking the foreigner unnecessarily. "It must be realized that we must drive out the foreigners with civilized [methods], and must not do it with primitive [methods]." Refuse to give them land for railroads, do not sell them mines, do not allow them to station

[18] *Ibid.* p. 121.

troops. Yet, while on guard against them, provide protection for their churches, missionaries, and merchants. If war does come, refuse to become their soldiers and refuse them provisions, but do not kill civilians or captured soldiers. The primitive method—gathering a few hundred people to burn a couple of churches and killing a few missionaries and converts, or foreign officials and merchants—does nothing but invite the intervention of foreign soldiers and eventually leads to cession of territory and the payment of an indemnity. Ch'en, no doubt like others of his generation, was tempted by the heroic, perhaps mad, anti-foreignism of the Boxer uprisings. But he had learned too well the lessons of the Boxer episode to advocate seriously a violent response to the overwhelming power of Western imperialism. Despite the blood-curdling talk, he and his colleagues were more than likely to be paralyzed into inaction, even in entirely domestic matters, by a fear of foreign intervention.

The general phenomenon of Western encroachment and absorption of other countries Ch'en calls race imperialism (*min-tsu ti-kuo chu-i*). It has its origin in overpopulation in the West and a search for new land. When non-violent, it is even more insidious and deceiving than when it resorts to open cruelty. It takes the form of depriving you of your sustenance: building railroads which put you at the foreigner's mercy, taking interest on loans, laying hands on raw materials in "false commerce," appropriating all the produce of mines, leaving none for the Chinese. If the Chinese do not submit to this encroachment, all is well. If they do, the foreigner will take over the country; the Chinese will be deprived of all education; and through impoverishment or mutual self-slaughter induced by the foreigner, the race will disappear.

Ch'en, then, was obsessed with the foreign menace, seen in the lurid light of a threat to the survival of China and the Chinese. On the other hand, he did not neglect the domestic situation. During the period he was writing his two tracts and the first part of his novel, he was a member of a revolutionary organization, and was soon actually involved in an extensive plot against the Ch'ing government. His preoccupation with the foreign problem and with the imminence of the danger posed by the foreigners would logically seem to exclude diversionary assaults on the Manchus. Would not revolution, as the eminent reformist publicist Liang Ch'i-ch'ao was beginning to argue, lead to foreign intervention, the very thing Ch'en feared most?

Indeed Ch'en was never able to resolve this conflict between domestic and foreign concerns to his complete satisfaction. Yet in this period he devised an ingenious formula of puppet government to ease the conflict:

> You must realize that after they partition China, without a doubt they will still keep the Manchu government for a long time to oppress the Han.
>
> Reader! You say that today China still belongs to the Manchu government? For some time now it has belonged to the various [foreign] countries. . . . Over the Manchu government are established the governments of the various nations; over each provincial governor are established the governors of the various nations. So, if we think of making any sort of move, the governments of the various nations send an order and have the Manchu government send out telegraphic edicts to the provincial governors, who send notes to local officials, who immediately do away with us with great thoroughness on behalf of the foreign countries. . . .
>
> Consequently, if we wish to oppose the foreigner, all we can do is preach revolution and independence. We cannot preach "Assist the King." Since he does not want assistance, how do you begin assisting him? There are people who say, "China cannot now afford to stir up domestic rebellion herself. It would allow the foreigner to take advantage of us." I, too, thoroughly agree with this. Henceforth if the Manchu government would stand firm and seek good government, would reform, would break down the discrimination between Manchu and Han, would dismiss all the rapacious ministers and employ all the loyal and capable, and would determine to fight to the death against the foreign countries, then I would be very willing to discard my former views and with no thought for my family, property, or life would resist the foreign countries on the side of the government. But alas, they hold fast to the view that "one should entrust the empire to friends [foreigners] and not to slaves [Chinese]." You could talk yourself blue in the face and they would pay no attention.[19]

Thus, by conceiving of the Manchu government as a puppet of

[19] *Ibid.* pp. 125–26; the same formulation occurs in *Meng-hui-t'ou*, p. 151.

foreign powers, the revolutionary nationalist can resist the foreigner by attacking the Ch'ing.

For this correct view of the nature of a semi-colonial country Ch'en has received commendation from Marxist-Leninist writers in China and Japan.[20] Ch'en's view does indeed have a contemporary ring to it. Yet, it remained a tenuous argument for an anti-Manchu revolution. It was with reluctance that he committed himself to revolution, preferring co-operation with the Manchus if only they would co-operate—and the true target was always the hated foreign oppressor. Ch'en in his early writings did not ignore the traditional catalogue of atrocities perpetrated by the Manchus on the Chinese, but he devoted less intensity and much less space to them than to foreign dangers and foreign crimes. In Social Darwinian terms, the Manchus could hardly be regarded as more "fit" than the Chinese and thus were no menace to Chinese survival. In nationalist terms, the Manchu government was to be condemned for not taking energetic steps to stave off the foreign menace, but they were merely a negative obstacle to the fulfillment of national dignity, not a positive threat.

The Problem of Modernization

In 1903 and 1904 Ch'en's immediate program was revolution, but he had no illusion that revolution alone was sufficient, if only because he saw the foreigners standing behind the Manchus, and still standing when the Manchus would fall. Insofar as Ch'en concerned himself at all in his early period with the form of government to be instituted after the revolution, he advocated a republic. But "republic" to him was more a word to evoke a range of characteristics than a concrete political form.

[20] For example, Ch'en Hsü-lu, *Tsou Jung yü Ch'en T'ien-hua ti ssu-hsiang* (The Thought of Tsou Jung and Ch'en T'ien-hua) (Shanghai, 1957); Sun Chih-fang, "Ch'en T'ien-hua ti ai-kuo ssu-hsiang" (The Patriotic Thought of Ch'en T'ien-hua), *Hsin-hai ko-ming wu-shih chou-nien chi-nien lun-wen chi* (Collected Essays in Commemoration of the Fiftieth Anniversary of the Revolution of 1911) (Peking, 1962), II, 375–93; Satoi Hikoshichirō, "Chin Ten-ka no seiji shisō" (Political Thought of Ch'en T'ien-hua), *Tōyō-shi kenkyū* (Studies in Oriental History), Vol. 17, No. 3 (Dec. 1958).

In the preface to his novel, Ch'en describes how he was granted a preview of the future Chinese republic by the mythical Yellow Emperor. The vision was first of a large city, with wide streets of white stone, spotlessly clean, lined with seven-story houses. Electric streetcars were weaving back and forth along the street. Overhead was an iron bridge, well traveled by pedestrians. Beneath the ground ran trains. "I said to myself, 'Where is this?' I imagined even London and Paris were not like this." The fiftieth anniversary of the "restoration" (of Chinese rule) was in progress. Inside an immense assembly hall, above the stage, poems in gas lights celebrated the emancipation from three hundred years of slavery. Above the poems was inscribed, "My military prowess is displayed," a quotation from the Great Declaration in the *Book of History* (Shu-ching). In a bookshop Ch'en read from an *Almanac of the Republic,* which revealed that this paradise had 300,000 schools, 60,000,000 male and female students, a standing army of 2,000,000 and many more in reserve or in training, 700 warships, several dozens of vessels that plied under water or through the air, some 100,000 miles of railroads, 40,000 post offices, steamers and sailing vessels totaling twenty million tons, and a yearly budget of $2,800,000,000.

Two things are notable in this description of the future Chinese utopia, which is a curiously suggestive sketch of what China was to become fifty years after the republican revolution. The image is portrayed in terms of material progress and power. And the vision of the "republic" is devoid of the political framework normally associated with the word.

Ch'en was nòt ignorant of the institutional apparatus underlying the leading republics of his time. In his first tracts he exhorted China to imitate France in reforming its corrupt government. The French, he related, threw off the oppression of the king and the aristocracy and established a republic in which both the president and legislative assembly were elected by the people. Nevertheless, representative institutions were never central to Ch'en's thinking about the future Chinese society. If a republic was the best slogan around which to rally the Chinese people, then it was desirable that China should have a republic. The only essential ingredients of China tomorrow were independence and strength, which for him were inseparable.

Rather than political institutions, the central feature of his plan for China's salvation was expressed in the phrase, "enrich the country and strengthen the military" (*fu-kuo ch'iang-ping*). This concept was traditionally associated with Chinese Legalist views, although it was not the exclusive property of that philosophic school and was frequently referred to in Japan during the Meiji period. Although previous interpretations of the phrase had often reflected attitudes rejected by modern nationalists, especially in the sphere of economics, the slogan seems to have been peculiarly adaptable to their needs. The best explanation of Ch'en's use of the term is his application of it in a program.

The Chinese heretofore looked on people who engaged in industrial arts as inferior, not knowing that the wealth and strength of the foreigners came from such skills. "Now China is very poor and weak. If there is no one to make guns and cannons, how can we wage war with foreign countries? If there is no one to make all sorts of machines, how can we struggle to regain the rights and interests which have been lost in commerce?" In his tracts he urged the rich to use their money in buying guns to oppose the foreigner, in making preparations for provisioning troops, in founding schools and printing books, in establishing lecture societies, physical culture societies, anti-foot-binding societies, and anti-opium societies, and in militia training. He then recommended that, for their own as well as the nation's profit, they invest in business enterprises, in building steamships and railroads and telegraph lines, in manufacturing, and in mining.

Martial spirit was as important, in Ch'en's view, as material strength. He roundly condemned Chinese scorn for the soldier and urged that a military career be accorded both respect and high rewards. On the other hand, the soldier in the past had often been more ready to run than to fight, so he, too, must brace himself for the war of survival against the foreigners.

Although the object in acquiring strength was to resist foreign incursions, the model that Ch'en offered in building national strength was that of the West itself. "We must realize that to resist the foreigner we must first imitate the foreigner's strong points." These strong points were: universal education, public morality (toward one's own race, not toward foreign races), love of one's country, and pursuit of any subject that was of benefit, such as military science, politics, and industrial arts. True Western public morality was expressed for Ch'en in the slogan, "Sacrifice the individual for society and sacrifice the present for the future." He wrote, "I want everyone to chant these words constantly." The West, then, was not just an industrial or military model, but a social and ethical model as well. Ch'en's description of the essence of social organization and attitudes might differ from the way the West appeared to itself. But he was not alone among Chinese, or other victims of Western imperialism, in discerning strength in the racial and national solidarity of Western and (by this time) Japanese societies, as compared with his own.

He said he had no use for the "disgrace of the Han race," those who "only practice a few foreign words and run to the foreigner to become a Christian convert and then claim to be in search of the new party [i.e. Western learning]." The acid test was loyalty to China, which excluded any toadying to the foreigner. Christianity itself was not in conflict with national interests, if the adherent combined his religious beliefs with patriotism, as was apparently done in the West. Confucianism, too, was acceptable only insofar as it presented no obstacle to the love and defense of one's country.

We see here no precious protection of Chinese "essence" ($t'i$) while cautiously admitting "application" ($yung$) from the West, as in Chang Chih-tung's formulation. There was only one standard: benefit to China as a nation. This standard excluded no one who did not exclude himself. Conservatives were welcome, insofar as they were driven to expel the foreigner by their desire to keep sacred the land of their ancestors. The monarchical reformers (his rivals) must change, but Ch'en was certain that gentle argument would make them see the light, that is, that revolution was a necessary first step. Indeed, his tracts in the main were a call for a united front of all segments of Chinese society.

In his first two years as a revolutionary, then, Ch'en was a nationalist dedicated to the concept of "enriching the country and strengthening the military," whose enthusiasm was fired by strong anti-foreignism. His emotional anti-foreignism did not, however, induce him to reject Western ideas or techniques. On the contrary, he made a conscious effort to detect the sources of Western strength in order to recommend them to China for her own self-strengthening. And his acute sense of the imminence of partition allowed no room for trifling provocative attacks on individual foreigners, which would only serve to increase the danger.

Ch'en's ingenious concept of the Manchus as a puppet regime justified his anti-Manchu revolutionary action, but his anti-Manchu stand was much less firm than his opposition to Western "race imperialism." The Manchu government was not included in the united front appeal only because it excluded itself. The Western elements that he felt to be the source of strength—education, social cohesion, patriotism, and technology—were not on the face of it incompatible with a reformed Manchu monarchy. It was not a very great step to the idea that the "republic" could be forgone in order to make the united front more inclusive.

Ch'en's "Retrogression"

When the plans for a massive uprising in Hunan were exposed in late October 1904, the leading participants made their way to Shanghai, where Huang Hsing and others reorganized themselves and turned their attention to agitation in Kiangsu province.[21] In Shanghai there were also local groups of the revolutionary-minded. Ch'en in his novel wrote of the disillusionment of one of his characters, a young student, with the Shanghai patriots, who could be found at any time of day lolling in the parks. He heard a new expression: "pheasant government and parrot patriots." Ch'en's student was told that everyone was eventually softened by the Shanghai atmosphere, and that he had better leave before he too was affected.

[21] Li, *loc. cit.* p. 179.

If this passage records Ch'en's impression of revolutionaries in Shanghai after the Hunan failure, as it seems to, the experience can only have added to his discouragement.

The activity of the Hunanese refugees in Shanghai was soon interrupted by the arrest of thirteen of them, including Huang Hsing, in the latter half of November. The police were actually interested in some other case and did not identify Huang and his cohorts as having been connected with the recently exposed Hunan plot. Huang and his group managed to secure their own release and proceeded to Tokyo, where they arrived in December or January. Ch'en, who apparently had avoided arrest, also went on to Tokyo at this time.

Ch'en's behavior soon after his arrival in Tokyo graphically illustrated the tensions and latent contradictions in his revolutionary pronouncements of the previous two years. He entered into a correspondence with Liang Ch'i-ch'ao, the leading advocate among the Chinese in Japan of a program of constitutional reform under the Manchu monarchy. In the early phase of his revolutionary commitment in 1903, Ch'en had denounced Liang publicly, but now he went to see him twice. Then, in late January 1905, he submitted to the Chinese student association in Tokyo a proposal that all students join in a petition to the government in Peking advocating reform. Ch'en proposed to carry this petition to Peking himself, and he distributed a pamphlet entitled, *A Statement of Views on Demanding Salvation from Destruction,* justifying his plan.

As soon as Ch'en's Hunanese revolutionary associates heard of his actions, they reacted with alarm and proceeded to block him. Huang Hsing, Sung Chiao-jen, and others called meetings of Hunanese students, at the largest of which it was agreed to oppose a petition to Peking. The student societies of other provinces joined in objecting to Ch'en's plan. Since the effectiveness of the proposed petition was contingent upon the signatures of the Chinese students in Tokyo, organized opposition through the provincial societies was fatal to the whole project. Huang and Sung also argued privately with Ch'en and tried to persuade him not to undertake the trip to Peking nor to join forces with Liang Ch'i-ch'ao's Protect-the-Emperor Society.

The Japanese police apparently obstructed Ch'en's plan to go to Peking (perhaps to avoid an open incident embarrassing to relations between the Ch'ing government and Tokyo). And eventually he was persuaded by his revolutionary friends not to join the reformers. So the hopeful petitioner was saved for the revolution.[22]

Ch'en's remarkable, even if temporary, abandonment of the revolution highlights his more basic attitudes toward China's predicament. His vacillation concerning the necessity of revolution was, of course, due in part to external events. The failure of the Hunan uprising and his disappointment in the Shanghai patriots no doubt disposed him toward exploring some other approach. One of his fellow conspirators in the uprising, Hsu Fo-su, did actually enter Liang Ch'i-ch'ao's entourage at this time. Another colleague, Yang Tu-sheng, intellectually very close to Ch'en T'ien-hua, decided after the abortive plot that stabbing directly at the nerve center of Peking would be quicker than uprisings in the provinces, and he proceeded quite successfully to infiltrate into the central government while simultaneously sponsoring attempts at political assassination. Ch'en was not alone in casting about for a better method for saving China. At the same time, his behavior in early 1905 was not inconsistent with the main features of his earlier thought, and indeed seems in part to have arisen naturally from them.

Ch'en, in his *Statement of Views on Demanding Salvation from Destruction,* was frank about his motive in seeking to petition Peking: it was despair. He said the crisis had recently become imminent, and having no satisfactory plan of one's own to meet it, all one could do was to ask the government to rescue the Chinese from destruction.

Here again we see Ch'en searching for last resorts. Previously, he had called upon his compatriots, in the event of China's total

---

[22] This account of Ch'en's apostasy is based on the following: Sung Chiaojen, *Wo chih li-shih* (Hunan, 1920), II, 4–7 (hereafter: Sung, *Diary*); Liang Chi'i-ch'ao, "Shen-lun chung-tsu ko-ming yü cheng-chih ko-ming chih te-shih" (Discussion of the Relative Merits of a Racial and a Political Revolution), *Hsin-min ts'ung-pao,* No. 76 (March 9, 1906); Tsou, *loc. cit.* p. 377; Feng, *Ko-ming i-shih,* II, 130; Nagai, *loc. cit.* pp. 52–59; and Li, *loc. cit.* p. 182.

collapse, at least to go down fighting, to put some price on partition. These were brave words, but no one realized better than Ch'en that the few bites a cornered dog may take are small compensation for the fate that follows capture. If the Hunan plot, with its subsidiaries in neighboring provinces, had succeeded, the repercussions might have led to the formation of a new national government ready to stand firm against the foreigner. Now that the plot had failed, Ch'en turned to the only constituted authority available to him.

Even granting that the Manchus might accept a petition, how could Ch'en justify abandoning the revolutionary solution? The essence of the matter, he argued, was the degree of danger to which the country was exposed. When there was no threat from the outside, then revolution was reasonable; otherwise, there would be no end to oppression by the government. But when "the foreign evil" had already penetrated deeply into China and national military strength was insufficient, then the sheer desperation of the situation demanded that the government be given another chance to show its intention to appoint men of ability and save the country from destruction. The purpose of the petition was to give the government another chance and to make explicit the conditions for student support. The horror with which Ch'en viewed the foreign threat, a horror running throughout the pages of his earlier writing, led him close to the view that in a period of danger, one should rally around the constituted authorities.

It is worth noting that the elastic principle of race had been stretched. The Manchus would be forgiven for being rulers of a different race if they passed the test of patriotism and stood firm against the foreigner. What seems like a retreat from principle was simply the logical application of its true meaning: that is, race was being defined, as it always had been, according to nationalist standards. This effort to include the Manchus on the side of China did not mean submission in awe to the augustness of the Son of Heaven. Ch'en was not reversing his opposition to the principle of loyalty to the ruler as traditionally conceived. The Manchu government, like the Christian and the Confucian, had to pass the patriotic test.

Ch'en's proposed petition was, after all, conditional; it was couched in the form of demands.

The demands themselves seem to belie the self-effacement in his statement of motive:

1. Land is not to be ceded to the foreigner, and every last effort must be made to protect our mineral, railroad, and shipping rights.
2. The people are not to be abandoned to the foreigner, and the foreigner must not be allowed to encroach in any measure on the people's rights of livelihood and production.
3. Sovereignty is not to be turned over to the foreigner, and especially, the granting of the right to station troops in the interior and to employ and administer [Chinese] should be decisively ended.
4. The laws must be reformed.
5. The national policy should be made firm.
6. The localities should be granted the right of autonomy.
7. The people should be allowed the rights of free authorship, speech, and assembly.[23]

Two features in this list should be especially noted. First, in contrast to the domestic items (points 4, 5, 6, and 7), the demands placed upon policy toward the foreigner are specific and exact. It would be going too far to say that Ch'en would have settled for a strong foreign policy and would have let the domestic program pass. He had made clear in his earlier writings that reforms that led to national strength were crucial to national survival, his primary concern. Yet here we see more clearly than before how his interest in "enriching the country" was oriented toward foreign competition and encroachment rather than toward some abstract conception of improved economic well-being.

The importance he attached to his program of civil liberties (point 7) is particularly dubious. He had written earlier of the inadequacy of high principles to meet the present crisis:

[23] My understanding of Ch'en's *Statement of Views* is based on quotation from it in Nagai, *loc. cit.* pp. 52–59; and Hsü, *loc. cit.* pp. 63–78.

I see that recently arrived theories have spread everywhere. [The slogans] "a revolution for popular sovereignty" and "equality and freedom" have become platitudes. . . . After partition is a certainty, these theories will have no one to expound them. The so-called patriotic parties, the returned students—all will be gone without a trace.[24]

The priority is clear: the country's salvation from the hands of the foreigner was to precede political liberalism at home.

The second particularly notable element in Ch'en's list was the demand for local autonomy. It is difficult to reconcile his larger aim of a united front against the West with the divisive character of this demand. That such a totally committed advocate of national power as Ch'en should espouse localism (generally interpreted at this time as provincial self-government) is good evidence of the great currency of ideas tending toward separatism. Perhaps this demand was an attempt to gain support for his program among the students. If this was his intent, it had some success. Sung Chiao-jen singled out this demand for approval, and the same meeting of Hunanese students that condemned Ch'en's plan to petition Peking endorsed independence and self-government for the provinces.

Ch'en's interest in local autonomy—an interest held by so many of his compatriots in Tokyo—was not as strange as it may seem at first glance. Regional loyalties have been a strong force throughout Chinese history. On the other hand, political power in China at this time was still formally centralized. If the government structure was inadequate in its domestic and foreign policies, was not centralization a bankrupt policy, in foreign affairs as well as domestic? An association of the elements of provincialism and fear of foreign partition, even if apparently contradictory, arose naturally from the Chinese scene in the first decade of the twentieth century. Their taste of central power and what it might do were perhaps factors in the opposition of K'ang Yu-wei and Liang Ch'i-ch'ao (after some vacillations in Liang's case) to provincial autonomy as unnationalistic.[25] Ch'en was for a while directly under Liang Ch'i-ch'ao's in-

[24] *Ching-shih-chung*, pp. 137–38.
[25] Joseph R. Levenson, *Liang Ch'i-ch'ao and the Mind of Modern China* (Harvard University Press, 1953), p. 114. On Liang's vacillation and K'ang's

fluence, but he retained the intellectual chemistry in which localism (or more accurately, provincialism) and fear of foreign partition were combined.

For a period in early 1905, Ch'en was ready to lay down his sword if the Ch'ing government would see things his way. The Hunan failure suggested that the road to a successful anti-Manchu revolution was a long one, and Ch'en at this time anticipated that before the goal could be reached, China's partition would have already become an actuality. Revolution of any kind would then be impossible. With a continuing disregard for political forms and with his flexible view of race, Ch'en was ready to work with and through the existing regime. If the Manchus were still puppets of the foreigner—well, let them cut their strings and join the fight.

Yet Ch'en was no ordinary memorialist. In the *Statement of Views* he swore that if the government did not listen, he would revert to his former activity, revolution. The petition, even if sent, would have ended in nothing, of course. One also wonders how long someone of Ch'en's fiery nature would have rested content with Liang Ch'i-ch'ao's gradualism. The conditional nature of the proposed petition suggests that he would not have been content for long. In any case, before a petition was sent, Ch'en had been retrieved for the revolution and for a leading role in the founding of the T'ung Meng Hui.

The Founding of the T'ung Meng Hui

After the collapse of the petition plan, Ch'en worked for a time with Sung Chiao-jen in launching a new journal, *Twentieth-Century China,* but resigned in March when the project lacked money and manuscripts. In the summer of 1905, he was one of the handful of Hunanese with whom Sun Yat-sen negotiated a union of forces. In his autobiography Sun wrote that with the founding of the T'ung Meng Hui in 1905 he felt for the first time that the overthrow of the Manchus would be accomplished within his lifetime.

---

response, see Lo Jung-pang, *K'ang Yu-wei: A Biography and a Symposium* (University of Arizona Press, 1967), p. 278.

On this occasion, at least, his undaunted optimism was justified. Ch'en played a leading role in the inauguration of this inter-provincial revolutionary organization, and Sun's leadership seems to have revived Ch'en's revolutionary enthusiasm.

Already a famous figure, Sun arrived back in Japan on July 19, 1905, from a tour of Chinese communities in Europe and America. After establishing preliminary contact with Huang Hsing, Sun met more broadly with the Hunan group, including Ch'en, to argue for a supra-provincial organization. He made two main points. One was that partition by the foreign powers was not a present danger. The other was that lack of co-ordination among the provinces at the time of revolution could lead to Balkanization of the country. A revolution contaminated by provincial separatism might invite foreign intervention and China's extinction. This calamity could be fore-stalled by a unified revolutionary program. In this fashion, Sun urged the leaders of the Hua Hsing Hui to join with him.[26] As an expert on the West, by virtue of education and travel, Sun's assurance that there was no immediate danger of partition must have been a genuine salve to Ch'en's anxieties. His description of the dangers of provincial autonomy served a double purpose: to point up the inconsistency of this aim with a fear of partition, and to convince the Hunanese of the need for joint revolutionary action.

The events of the next day, July 29, revealed that such argument was needed to convert the Hunan group. Sung Chiao-jen, Ch'en T'ien-hua, and Liu K'uei-i met with Huang Hsing at his home to discuss affiliation with Sun. Huang in his previous consultations with Sun had already agreed to formal affiliation but felt that the Hunanese should maintain a separate organization "in spirit." Liu K'uei-i urged that there be no affiliation at all. Sung Chiao-jen favored further study of the question. Ch'en T'ien-hua had apparently been fully converted the previous day and urged full union with Sun.

The Hunanese made entry into Sun's proposed organization a matter of individual choice, but apparently the important leaders were persuaded to Ch'en's view (organic union). A larger Hunanese

---

[26] For translations of relevant portions of Sung's *Diary*, see Hsüeh, *op. cit.* pp. 40–43.

group joined with Sun and others on July 30 in a preparatory meeting. Ch'en, among others, was selected to draw up a charter.[27] A successful public meeting of welcome for Sun was held on August 13, and the formal founding meeting of the T'ung Meng Hui took place on August 20, 1905. Ch'en, with Ma Chün-wu, was made chief of the secretariat.[28] Thus was born the first Republican revolutionary organization that included representatives from nearly all areas of China.

At the August 20 meeting Huang Hsing suggested that Sung Chiao-jen's *Twentieth-Century China*, whose first issue had appeared the previous spring, be adopted as the party organ. The suggestion was approved, but a change was soon made. The second issue of the magazine included an article critical of Japanese activity in China and precipitated a move on August 27 by the Japanese police to confiscate the issue and ban further publication. In reporting the decision to issue a separate journal, Huang Hsing told Sung that since the T'ung Meng Hui did not want a program of anti-foreignism, all obvious connection with the former paper would be cut.[29] Ch'en T'ien-hua was an editor for the new journal, the *Min-pao*. Some favored Ch'en as publisher, but Chang Chi was given this job because of his special facility in Japanese and consequent ability to deal with Japanese officials.[30]

In the first issue, which appeared in November, Ch'en, under various signatures, wrote seven of the seventeen articles. Barring another rupture such as had occurred earlier that year, Ch'en now

[27] All accounts include Ch'en among the authors, except Sung, *Diary*, which states, "Huang Hsing and seven others." Feng, *Ko-ming i-shih*, II, 147, says Huang Hsing and Ch'en T'ien-hua drew up the oath, and Ma Chün-wu, Ch'en, Sung, and Wang Ching-wei formed the committee to draw up the charter. Ts'ao, *Wu-ch'ang ko-ming chen-shih*, I, 16, says that Ch'en T'ien-hua *alone* wrote the charter and the *Strategy of Revolution*. T'ien T'ung, "T'ung Meng Hui ch'eng-li-hui" (Founding Meeting of the T'ung Meng Hui), *Ko-ming wen-hsien* (Documents of the Revolution) (Taipei, 1953–), II, 143, includes both Huang Hsing and Ch'en T'ien-hua among the authors of the charter.

[28] Feng, *Ko-ming i-shih*, II, 147.

[29] Sung, *Diary*; George T. Yu, *Party Politics in Republican China* (Berkeley. University of California Press, 1966), pp. 47–50.

[30] Hu Han-min's "Autobiography," *Ko-ming wen-hsien*, III, 388.

seemed guaranteed a leading place in the Republican revolutionary movement.

The Problem of Establishing the Republican Society

Ch'en's writings in his last period show a mixture of development and continuity. The advent of Sun Yat-sen and the founding of the T'ung Meng Hui mark in some respects a turning point of emphasis in his thought. He toned down his fears of imminent foreign possession of China. He modified the provincialism of his petition period and even wrote a short article against extreme provincial particularism (in which he made a plea that the Hunanese be forgiven for their special participation in the suppression of the Taiping Rebellion and their subsequent prominence as officials in other provinces). At the same time he could never completely purge himself of his obsession with the foreign danger.

Although Ch'en must be classified as a Republican in his earlier revolutionary phase, we have seen that he conceived of a republic chiefly in terms of technological advance, a large number of schools, and a large army. Now it was Ch'en who contributed to the *Min-pao* the article which attempted to justify the T'ung Meng Hui advocacy of a democratic republic. This article is interesting both for what it tells us of his thought and for its relevance to later developments in Chinese revolutionary history. It begins with a bow to Montesquieu, the threefold division of powers, and a republic according to the American example. What would be better, Ch'en asked, for washing away the accumulated filth and evil of the old government? In the past, one dynasty had always given way to another, each new dynasty based on the selfish interests of a single person or family. Such a system was pernicious, and the people's enthusiasm could not be marshaled merely to establish a new ruling house. The dynastic cycle, he said in effect, must be broken. All the people would participate in establishing a republic, since the interests of all were involved. If the fall of the Manchus was followed by various parties struggling for the throne, the result would be chaos. If it was followed by a republic, peace and equality would ensue. The republic would be a source of social cohesion unmatched in the past and would obviate a period of disturbance after the revolution.

Then Ch'en dealt with the question posed by Liang Ch'i-ch'ao: after twenty dynasties of tyrants and oppressors, could the Chinese suddenly hope for the same prosperity and freedom that more mature nations possessed? Specifically, did the Chinese have the latent capacity to establish a republic? Could this capacity be summoned forth from the commonality in a short period? Once the republic was established, could the people participate fully in the new political structure? Would they fulfill their obligations? Liang at this time doubted the readiness of the Chinese for republicanism and feared that some misguided attempt to establish it would result only in chaos and foreign intervention.

Ch'en's answers were seemingly confident. Of course the Chinese had the capacity to found a republic. Throughout centuries of oppression this capacity had always run beneath the surface, as could now be seen in the increasing response to the slogan of nationalism, or the principle of racial solidarity (*min-tsu chu-i*). And there was reason to think that the people could be brought to a state of readiness quickly. Educational techniques had improved, allowing one to learn in two or three years what previously had taken ten. Moreover, the Chinese were an immensely civilized people who had achieved great things when the Westerners had not yet descended from trees. Overcome with their own self-importance, the Chinese had become soft and corrupt. Fortunately, contact with Europe and America had gradually roused China from her lethargy. Now all was ready: the material for the meal had been put on the kitchen table, Ch'en wrote, and all that was needed was to cook it. Japan became a first-class power in forty years. There was no doubt that China could surpass this record.

With respect to obligations and rights under the republic, Ch'en promised that the ordinary Chinese would perform well as citizens. Once the concept of the nation was understood, then the current indifference to the country's affairs would be replaced by a concern to do one's duty and to enjoy one's public rights. Overseas Chinese, Ch'en felt, already had demonstrated their understanding of nationalism. They struggled with the local authorities, even though, in contrast to the European colonials, they received no protection from their home government; and they sent the profits of their labor back to China. They neither bowed to foreign authority nor forgot their native land. They were true nationalists. They were proof of the potential civic quality of the Chinese.

Although fully assuring his reader of the readiness of the Chinese to assume their obligations (including military ones, given proper support from society), Ch'en neglected to dwell upon the public rights, which he mentioned only in passing. In fact, he pointedly cautioned against confusing the democracy which he advocated with anarchism or *laisser-faire*. What he visualized was freedom, not for the individual, but for the whole society. "If you want to obtain freedom for the whole polity, then there must be interference with the individual." Ch'en's conclusion at this point was consistent with his earlier observation: the essence of social morality in the West, and a source of the West's strength, was the sacrifice of the individual for the society.

He concluded his essay by presenting a formula for attaining democracy:

> We have recognized the principle that the only way to save China is to promote popular sovereignty and adopt democracy. However, the step which will precede this is the adoption of enlightened despotism (*k'ai-ming chuan-chih*), which we consider to be preparation for the people's sovereignty and democracy. The very first step is revolution.

Paradoxically, he quieted fears that a democratic revolution would lead to chaos and foreign intervention with the proposal that its immediate result would not be democracy. Had he failed after all to convince himself of the central proposition of his article, that China should inaugurate a democratic form of government through revolution?

This was not the first occasion upon which the young revolutionary Chinese in Tokyo spoke of the necessity of approaching constitutional

democracy through gradual stages after the revolution.[31] The T'ung
Meng Hui was at this time making the idea a part of its *Strategy of
Revolution* (*Ko-ming fang-lueh*), which called for a period of military
law and political tutelage for some years before the establishment
of a fully constitutional government. Indeed, it is quite possible that
Ch'en had a hand in drafting this document.[32] Probably Ch'en
and the T'ung Meng Hui group shared doubts about the aftermath
of a revolutionary upheaval. Although Ch'en spoke confidently of
the effects of improved educational techniques on China's alertness,
we can speculate that he ultimately did not believe that the mass of
Chinese were ready to manage their own destiny. After all, the
schools were not yet built and the populace was not yet educated.
Further, try as he might to believe, with Sun Yat-sen, that partition
was not an immediate danger, he instinctively searched for safe-
guards against it. Accordingly, Ch'en proposed that, while the people
were being tutored, a central government independent of the people's
will would protect the Chinese from the foreign powers. The T'ung
Meng Hui's program of military and political tutelage may have
arisen from like concerns.

Although Ch'en's republicanism had become more central to his
writing than it was in the days of his propaganda tracts, his interest
in Western political forms was still geared to his first concern—
China's power relative to that of the West. Democracy, or liberalism,
recommended itself on the grounds that it was a feature of the
strongest Western states. But in the process of applying the form
to China, Ch'en and many other Chinese of his time who were
concerned with modernization, whether by revolution or reform,
were ready (and even anxious) to discard the liberal element as soon
as it threatened the chief objective, "wealth and strength." As Benjamin Schwartz has said of Yen Fu, whose annotated translations of
Western social philosophers were a guide to Ch'en's generation, his
"concept of liberalism as a means to the end of state power is mor-

---

[31] Robert A. Scalapino, "Prelude to Marxism: The Chinese Student Movement in Japan, 1900–1910," *Approaches to Modern Chinese History*, Albert
Feuerwerker, *et al.*, eds. (Berkeley: University of California Press, 1967),
p. 211.

[32] Feng, *Ko-ming i-shih*, II, 130; Ts'ao, *Wu-ch'ang ko-ming chen-shih*, I, 16.

tally vulnerable to the demonstration that there are shorter roads to that end." [33] Ch'en, with his pessimism, was as concerned about sure roads as about shorter ones. The result was the same.

Valediction and Suicide: The Triumph of Pessimism

China was not destined to see the flowering of Ch'en's early efforts as a T'ung Meng Hui leader. In early December 1905 a Chinese student strike broke out in Tokyo in response to a series of regulations issued on November 2 by the Japanese Ministry of Education. These regulations were specifically designed to control Chinese students and the schools in which they studied. The strike attained considerable proportions, and soon there was unanimous withdrawal from classes. The Japanese press assumed a critical attitude toward the Chinese students. On December 7 the *Ashai Shimbun* wrote that the strike arose from a misunderstanding of the regulations and from the "dissolute and contemptible" actions of the Chinese students. After preparing his "Last Testament" and a letter to the leaders of the Chinese Student Union, Ch'en on December 8 ended his life by throwing himself into the sea at Ōmori, a suburb of Tokyo. He described his act as a denial of the press description of Chinese students as "dissolute and contemptible" and as an exhortation to his compatriots to manifest opposite qualities: perseverence, respect for the commonweal, and diligence in the study of patriotism.

Ch'en's "Last Testament" is the least polemical of his writings. It was written for a purpose, but the purpose was purely of his own making and was not subordinated to the needs of an organization. It was the considered summing up of his experiences, as well as an explanation of his suicide. It was subsequently printed in the *Min-pao*, along with his photograph, which showed him with his hair to his shoulders in an evocation of the Taiping "long-hair" revolutionaries.

The T'ung Meng Hui advocated a revolution of the Chinese racial majority against the Manchu racial minority, and in its propa-

[33] Benjamin Schwartz, *In Search of Wealth and Power: Yen Fu and the West* (Harvard University Press, 1964), p. 240.

ganda put great emphasis on the urgent need for expelling these "Tatars" and on the wonderful effects which would follow. For Ch'en, revolution against the Manchus had always held second place to his concern about the foreign menace, and in his "Last Testament" he spelled out his position clearly. Although a revolutionary, he did not favor emphasis on the principle of race (*min-tsu chu-i*)—and thereby obliquely criticized Sun Yat-sen—but rather advocated attention to the "political" side. He recalled that he had once hoped for reform on the part of the Manchus and the breaking down of racial feelings, in order to defend against the foreigner. The only reason this was not possible was that the Manchus refused to give up their hatred and suspicion of the Chinese. Ch'en declared he had no hatred for the Manchus and still hoped that, like the Tokugawa in Japan, they would voluntarily step aside without spilling any blood. In fact, the revolution should not be attempted at all without a careful preparation of the population, in which the middle class would be taught the principles of revolution and would in turn spread this knowledge to the lower orders. "If revolution is attempted without the majority's being clear about its principles, then it will probably be incapable of saving China and on the contrary will reduce her to chaos." Ch'en's gradualism is remarkable and merited favorable comment from Liang Ch'i-ch'ao, whose own view was not much different.[34]

In his speech at the August 13 welcoming meeting in Tokyo, Sun Yat-sen, confident that partition was not a present danger, spoke of the West only as a challenge to China's capacity to absorb the new political technology, not as a threat to be resisted. On the other hand, he underlined the necessity of spilling blood for a constitution and a republic. In spite of Sun's temporary influence, Ch'en in the few months before his death could no longer reconcile himself to this emphasis, which was exactly the opposite of his own.

Ch'en's depreciation of the racial principle and a continuing undercurrent of anti-foreignism, although diminished in virulence, saved him from some of the errors of Sun Yat-sen. Japan emerged from her war with Russia as China's most powerful neighbor. Al-

[34] Liang, *loc. cit.* pp. 65–66.

though advocacy of a "people's alliance" with Japan could be found in the pages of the *Min-pao,* and Sun until his death cherished the hope for a Sino-Japanese Pan-Asian condominium, Ch'en urged that racial similarities were no basis for an alliance with Japan. The only basis for any alliance, he said in his "Last Testament," was a community of interests and approximately equal power. If China now allied herself with Japan, she would suffer the fate of Korea (a Japanese protectorate since the previous month). Japanese intentions were no secret: "As for the 'clandestine' plotting of the Japanese, it is a matter of common knowledge. Their books and newspapers urge it without any concealment." Ch'en was also suspicious of foreign loans. He was encouraged by the movement in China for the recovery of the railway and other concessions that had been given to the foreigner, but he worried about the methods, which included foreign loans. This could end in borrowing from one country to pay another and would be no improvement over the old obscurantist policy of the government. His program was first to reform the government, educate the people, organize finances, encourage industry, and cultivate managerial talents. Eventually, when China's rights were recovered, she might absorb foreign capital. Ch'en would never have been able to tolerate Sun's uncritical attitude toward co-operation with Japan or his facile acceptance of foreign financial obligations.

Why did Ch'en see fit to end his life at a time when he was still actively interested in politics and when the revolutionary movement had reached a new level of cohesion? The answer lies at both the personal and political levels. He was described by his contemporaries as a man given to emotional extremes, inclined to embarking on arbitrary courses of action without consulting his fellows, and notably changeable and quick-tempered. Though a special hero among the ordinary Chinese students in Tokyo, and a fiery but honest man in behavior and speech, he was a prickly colleague whose actions were unpredictable. Several of them commented after his suicide that he had always been preoccupied with the subject of his death. As early as 1903 in a public letter written during the aftermath of the collapse of the Student Army, Ch'en expressed a regret that events had not developed in a way that would allow him to sacrifice his life. In early 1905, he had planned to take the student petition to Peking himself, fully expecting to be put to death by the government. Sung Chiao-jen quoted Ch'en as saying at the time: "In fact I have no desire to escape for long my death sentence in this human sphere." Ch'en, who had affirmed his intention never to marry, sought an opportunity for the ultimate sacrifice, and in the end could not wait for the opportunity to be given him but did the deed himself.[35]

Although Ch'en was obsessed with the subject of his death, and his suicide may have had even deeper psychological origins which remain obscure, he was at the same time a functioning political activist and his "Last Testament" was a balanced and eminently sane document. In short, we must pay attention to the reasons he gave for his suicide. The reasons are at first glance surprising ones for an ardent revolutionary. His suicide was not one of protest against authority, whether Japanese or Chinese, but rather one of exhortation to his contemporaries. The purpose of his suicide, he wrote, was to inspire the Chinese students to exemplify the opposite of those qualities attributed to them by the Japanese press (dissoluteness and contemptibility).

At the time, the first popular interpretation of his death was that he was protesting the control regulations of the Japanese Ministry of Education and urging the students to return to China in defiance. Somehow this impression has persisted and still appears in accounts of the T'ung Meng Hui.[36] In his "Last Testament" it is quite plain that he meant no such thing and, by implication, that he would have

[35] The description of Ch'en is based on the following: Hsu, *loc. cit.* pp. 76–77; "Chung-kuo chih hsin-min" (pen name), "Chi Tung-ching hsüeh-chieh kung-fen-shih ping shu yü chih i-chien" (Report on the Affair Involving the Public Indignation of the Student Community in Tokyo and an Account of My View), *Hsin-min ts'ung-pao,* No. 74 (Dec. 26, 1905), p. 13; "Ch'en T'ien-hua fu Hu-nan t'ung-hsüeh chu-chün shu," pp. 129–30; Sung Chiao-jen in an appendix to the "Last Testament," reprinted from the *Min-pao,* in *Ko-ming chih ch'ang-tao yü fa-chan,* III, 369–70.

[36] Sanetō Keishū, *Nippon bunka no Shina e no eikyō* (The Influence of Japanese Culture on China) (Tokyo, 1940), pp. 102–104; Ching Mei-chiu, "Ch'ü-ti liu-hsüeh-sheng yü Ch'en T'ien-hua tzu-sha" (Control of the Students Abroad and Ch'en T'ien-hua's Suicide), *Ko-ming chih ch'ang-tao yü fa-chan,* III, 363; Yu, *op. cit.* pp. 51–52, and Tsou, *loc. cit.* p. 377.

opposed the exodus of some 2,000 students that occurred later in December.

His suicide stemmed not so much from the fact that the Japanese had insulted the Chinese students as from the fear that the insult might be valid. "Do my compatriots realize," began his farewell remarks, "what China is today? China's sovereignty has been lost and her rights thrown away. There is nothing which is not an occasion for pessimism." The only remaining hope, he continued, lay with the increasing number of Chinese students abroad. If these students developed patriotism and worked hard at their studies, in ten to twenty years the crisis would be past. As he looked around him, however, he saw that some were mere opportunists, seeking their own profit. Some were uninterested in studies and morally degenerate. Youth in general misunderstood freedom, disobeyed rules, and abused its elders. If the Chinese students abroad were indeed "dissolute and contemptible," then China had already died. Could a race that was "dissolute and contemptible" survive in the twentieth century? China was threatened, he said, and both her potential and present leaders were not properly devoted to the task of saving her. If no reinvigoration occurred, the Chinese deserved their inevitable fate. He pointed out that the Classics say: "Absorb the weak, and punish the wilfully blind; take their states from the disorderly, and deal summarily with those going to ruin."

The opposite of immorality, with Ch'en, was patriotism. He was not an ethical puritan. His attack on the students' behavior stemmed from his belief that it was a hindrance to a strong society. Such behavior was incompatible with "public morality," the crucial cement holding the Chinese together against overt and covert attack from abroad. Working for the foreigner in China was on the same despicable level as cavorting with prostitutes in Tokyo. To shake his compatriots out of their lethargy and moral decline, he said, he was taking this extreme measure.

Insofar as we can accept Ch'en's own explanation of his suicide, the act was quite consistent with the primary concerns of his earlier writing. He was less a revolutionary than a nationalist. He engaged in revolutionary organizations and plots, but with apparent reluctance. Revolution was merely one possible instrument for bringing into being the strong China that he so desired. His suicide was not dedicated to revolution. It was rather an alternate instrument, seized upon in desperation and dedicated to the larger aim always in the forefront of Ch'en's thought: a powerful and worthy nation. Pessimism and despondency were certainly important factors in his suicide. At the same time, he had hope. He outlined a general plan for progress, pointed out some of the dangers, and hoped (here he was helped by the dignity tradition lent his act) that by a hortative suicide he might inspire others to carry the plan to completion.

Ch'en T'ien-hua and the Chinese Revolution

Ch'en, by his own account, was committed to reform until 1903. In that year, probably in reaction to the Ch'ing government's rejection of the Student Army, he turned to revolution. One conspiratorial failure and a few inflammatory tracts later, he saw no hope for China anywhere but in the Ch'ing government itself. Within eight months he was a leader in the first significant inter-provincial revolutionary organization since the Taiping Rebellion. Less than four months after the founding of this organization, he had become disheartened with the human material upon which genuine progress in China had to be based, and killed himself as a warning and an exhortation.

Yet we have seen how, through these vacillations, from the first revolutionary tract in 1903 through the "Last Testament" at the end of 1905, a consistent view of China and her problems was maintained. Changing circumstances (at least as Ch'en saw them), not changing ideas, carried him from one political solution to another.

His central concern was China as a nation. This nation did not yet exist, as he envisaged it, but he directed his efforts toward founding it. There was one overwhelming threat to the founding of this nation, and that was foreign encroachment, chiefly from the West. Founding the nation and resisting the West were simultaneous processes. For China to be a nation, it had to be worthy of pride. To be worthy of pride, it had to be strong as it faced the world. The process of "enriching the state and strengthening the military" was itself the creation of the nation.

By a simple empirical process, he chose the nations of the West or, more conveniently, Japan as models of the wealthy country and the strong army. Whence came the strength of England, America, France, Germany, or Japan? Ch'en's research was not exhaustive, but his answers are understandable: education, industry, social responsibility, and patriotism. Each of these he urged China to nurture.

The similarities between Ch'en and Sun Yat-sen were profound and important. Both were nationalists and interested in Chinese power. Both were led by this interest into opposing the Manchus, who seemed to be an obstacle. Their differences were perhaps less basic but nonetheless significant, for they resulted in differences of policy. I have enumerated some of them: Ch'en's anti-foreign feeling as opposed to Sun's much greater tolerance of Western and Japanese behavior; Ch'en's sense of crisis, only temporarily mollified by Sun's optimism; Ch'en's eagerness to find a ground of co-operation with the existing government as opposed to Sun's single-track anti-Manchu policy (although Sun's persevering anti-Manchuism up to 1911 was more a close adherence to a single line of political action than a preoccupation with racial distinctions).

Ch'en showed no interest in Sun's principle of the people's livelihood, or socialism (*min-sheng chu-i*). He had never been concerned with the people's welfare as such, but only as it was relevant to national power. It is unlikely that Ch'en ever understood what Sun meant by this slogan. Ch'en's interest in economics did not go beyond saving China's resources from the foreigner and building industry to make China strong.

Many influences played on Ch'en's life and help explain the particular cast of his thought. He came from a province—Hunan—which at one time was marked by its fervent exclusion of Westerners but then turned its energies more aggressively than did other places to the introduction of Western thought. In Tokyo, Ch'en continued the exploration of Western ideas that he had begun in Hunan, and referred in his writing to Social Darwinians, Rousseau, or Montesquieu, as often as to Mencius or Huang Tsung-hsi. But the overwhelming influence on Ch'en was Western imperialism, and his authorities were uniformly forced into the service of Chinese nationalism. All his ideas were responses to the immense fear of forces external to China and to his exasperation with the inadequacy of the internal response to these forces.

Ch'en's most intimate associates were Hunanese revolutionaries, most of whom were to play a major part in the 1911 Revolution and the politics of the early Republic. The fear of the foreign powers, which led Ch'en to hesitate before the actuality of revolution, led his fellow-provincials—and other revolutionary leaders—to moderate the intensity of violence in 1911 and perhaps to abort a more thoroughgoing change at that time. Needless to say, apprehension of further Western and Japanese encroachment on China, though not always borne out in fact, was based on real dangers and direct experience. A Chinese had reason to fear foreigners. Ch'en's deep resentment at the apparent necessity of fearing foreigners occasionally induced in him an almost hysterical outpouring of hate against them. He usually held his resentment in check because of the hopelessness of redress. Hence his profound pessimism, which gnawed at him and eventually drove him to suicide. It was this same quality of resentment that, with the May Fourth Movement after World War I, broke through the restraints of fear, has been fed by continuing foreign hostility in one form or another, and has not yet expended itself.

❋ 9 ❋

A Chinese Democrat:
The Life of Sung Chiao-jen

CHÜN-TU HSÜEH

Of all the revolutionary leaders in the early Republican period of China, Sung Chiao-jen (1882–1913) was probably the most consistent in his political ideas. Lean, intense, and with a brilliant, incisive mind, Sung was among the ablest and most influential Chinese advocates of the Western parliamentary system in the first two years of the Republic. He was sincere and idealistic in his desire to establish a constitutional democracy in China. He campaigned for a "responsible cabinet" system when Yüan Shih-k'ai was the Provisional President in Peking in 1912–13, and earlier argued fervently for the same system when Sun Yat-sen was organizing a provisional government in Nanking at the end of 1911. Sun Yat-sen felt strongly

Reprinted with minor revisions from *Revue du Sud-est Asiatique et de l'Extrême-Orient* (Université Libre de Bruxelles), 1969, No. 1, pp. 115–36. This article was presented at the International Conference on Asian History, Kuala Lumpur, Malaysia, August 5–10, 1968. A different version under the title "Sung Chiao-jen and the Failure of Democracy in China: Prelude to the May Fourth Movement" was presented at the abortive 20th International Congress of Chinese Studies, Prague, Czechoslovakia, August 26–31, 1968. A Korean version appeared in *The Journal of Asiatic Studies* (Korea University), Vol. XII, No. 2 (June 1969).

The article is an extensive, revised version of a paper originally written for the Columbia University's Research Project on Men and Politics in Modern China. Its earlier version appears in *Biographical Dictionary of Republican China*, edited by Howard L. Boorman, Vol. III (Columbia University Press). Published by permission.

about, and in fact insisted on, the presidential system when he was to be the provisional president, but once he stepped down from that office he voiced no objection to the cabinet system, because the "responsible cabinet" system was considered a means of curbing Yüan's power as president.

Sung Chiao-jen, however, was more concerned with governmental systems than with personal factors. He acted on convictions of what he considered best for the young Republic. Although Yüan Shih-k'ai was in power in the North, Sung believed that the capital should be in Peking while Sun Yat-sen insisted on Nanking. Sung advocated a centralized government while Hu Han-min preferred a stronger local government. Sung thought in terms of national interest, not regional or personal interest, or even party interest. Politicians are not usually famous for their consistency. Sung's consistency was particularly rare in a country where politicians were often more concerned with personalities than with fundamental institutions, and where political systems and policies were often changed to suit the needs of political leaders.

As Ts'ai Yüan-p'ei (1868–1940) stated in an introduction written for the posthumous publication of Sung's *Diary*:

> The T'ung Meng Hui was the main revolutionary organization in the Ch'ing period. Although its goals included the establishment of the Republic and equalization of land rights, most of the members aimed primarily at the overthrow of the Manchu dynasty. Few conceived of a program of reconstruction, and fewer were prepared to work for the program. Mr. Sung Chiao-jen was one of the notable exceptions.

Indeed, in the last two years of his life, Sung showed remarkable statesmanship. His great talent as a politician was devoid of opportunism and corruption so common to politicians all over the world. He had little personal fortune when he was assassinated at the age of thirty-one. His violent and untimely death was a serious, if not decisive, blow to the cause of democratic government, and it signified almost at the outset what was to be the fate of this type of government in China for years to come. Politically and personally, Sung

Chiao-jen was close to Huang Hsing. Their relationship was similar to that of Hu Han-min and Wang Ching-wei with Sun Yat-sen. Sung, however, emerged as a national figure in his own right during the first years of the Republic, long before Hu and Wang.

I

Sung Chiao-jen was born on April 5, 1882, at Taoyuan, a place of great scenic beauty in western Hunan province immortalized in the utopian fantasy, "The Spring of the Peach Blossoms," by the famous Six Dynasties poet, T'ao Yuan-ming. Of the Sung family itself not much is known except that it was far from wealthy. Although his father died when Sung was only eleven or twelve years old, he was able to continue his studies while his elder brother supported the family.

Sung was brought up during a turbulent period. At the time of his birth, China had already suffered forty years of foreign aggression and internal revolts. He was thirteen years old when Sun Yat-sen (1866–1925) and Yang Ch'ü-yün (1861–1901) started their first abortive revolt in Canton, and when the reform movement under the leadership of K'ang Yu-wei (1858–1927) and Liang Ch'i-ch'ao (1873–1929) began to gain momentum throughout China, especially in Hunan province. This movement, climaxed by the "Hundred Days' Reform" of 1898 was followed by the *coup d'état* which resulted in the imprisonment of the Kuang-hsü emperor by the Empress Dowager and the execution of six noted reformers, including the Hunanese T'an Ssu-t'ung (1865–1898).

In the spring of 1899 Sung entered the Chang-chiang Academy in Hunan. The catastrophic Boxer uprising occurred the next year. In 1902–3, at the age of twenty, he passed the entrance examination for a middle school, which had been established a short time previously in Wuchang, the capital of Hupeh. In 1903, the continued Russian occupation of Manchuria aroused a wave of anti-Russian and anti-Manchu sentiment among Chinese students in China and Japan; by then Japan had become the center for Chinese students abroad. Under the influence of this growing dissatisfaction with the

Manchu regime, Sung joined the Hua Hsing Hui (Society for the Revival of China), a revolutionary organization founded by Huang Hsing in Changsha, Hunan. In mid-1904, Sung, with some of his schoolmates in Wuchang, formed the Sciences Study Group and served as its secretary. The organization was a cover for recruiting soldiers of the "new army" as well as students in support of Huang Hsing's plan for armed revolt. In the planning of concerted revolts at five centers in Hunan during the official celebration of the Manchu Empress Dowager's birthday in November 1904, Sung was placed in charge of organizing the uprising in Changteh, not far from his native Taoyuan. However, early in November the conspiracy was discovered by the government authorities, and Sung fled first to Shanghai and then to Japan. He was then only twenty-two years old, and the father of a three-year-old boy.

Arriving in Tokyo in mid-December 1904, Sung Chiao-jen studied first at the Kōbun Institute, a school established by the Japanese to meet the needs of Chinese students. Many of its graduates were Hunanese, including Huang Hsing and several other Hua Hsing Hui members. In June 1905 Sung transferred to the College of Law and Government. At the same time he became involved in the anti-Manchu revolutionary movement among the Chinese students in Japan. In June, after several months of preparation, he published the first issue of *Twentieth-Century China,* a magazine devoted to the dissemination of revolutionary ideas, nationalism, and patriotism.

In July, Sun Yat-sen returned to Japan from Europe, and he discussed plans with Huang Hsing for the unification of the various existing anti-Manchu societies into a new revolutionary league. When the T'ung Meng Hui (United League) was formally formed in August, with Sun Yat-sen as the chairman and Huang Hsing as the second in command, Sung became an officer of the judicial department of the newly established unified revolutionary organization. At the suggestion of Huang Hsing, *Twentieth-Century China* was made the organ of the T'ung Meng Hui, but because the second issue of the magazine was confiscated by the Japanese authorities on the grounds of public safety, the revolutionary leaders decided to change the name of the periodical to avoid complications with the Japanese authorities. Renamed *Min-pao* (People's Journal), the magazine soon became an influential and effective revolutionary magazine. Under the pseudonym "Ch'iang-chai," Sung, in addition to short political commentaries on current affairs, contributed articles translated from the Japanese on the Russian Revolution of 1905, the socialist movement, and other subjects. Early in 1906 he toyed with the idea of studying at a military academy—a military career appealed to many patriotic young men of the period as an effective way to save their country. But Sung's friends persuaded him to give up the idea and encouraged him to study political science and law.

In February, Sung began a period of several months' study at Waseda University's classes for foreign students. He enrolled under the name of Sung Lien, and by concealing his true identity was able to obtain government educational stipends from the Chinese Legation in Tokyo. The curriculum included Japanese (eighteen hours a week), history, geography, science, painting, and physical education. In the same month he began to study English, first at the Y.M.C.A. and then at Waseda. Although he devoted his attention primarily to political science, he had long been interested in geography, and, stimulated by the Russo-Japanese War of 1904–5, he studied the geography and history of Korea and Manchuria as well as the current situation. Of particular interest to him were the "mounted bandits" who infested the Korea-Manchuria border areas, whom he viewed as potential allies of the revolutionary party. After consulting Huang Hsing, Sung left for Liaotung in March 1907 with the aim of winning over the "mounted bandits" and establishing a territorial foothold for the revolutionaries in Manchuria. However, the vigilance of imperial troops soon put an end to Sung's activities in that area, and, after the arrest of the friend who had accompanied him on the trip, he returned to Tokyo.

Sung was probably the only important T'ung Meng Hui member who kept a diary that covered the years 1904 through 1907. During these years his diary shows that he studied history, law, political science, and the writings of Wang Yang-ming (1472–1529), the neo-Confucian philosopher of the Ming dynasty. He earned his living by doing translations from Japanese into Chinese, mainly on American and European political systems. Some of these translations were commissioned by publishers or by friends who worked for the Manchu government. In comparison with the current rate of translation work from Chinese into English in the United States, Sung's pay was fabulous indeed, as he could make as much as 1.50 *yen* per thousand words. On one occasion, he was paid ninety *yen* for three weeks' work. At that time the monthly cost of living for a Chinese student for room and board in Tokyo was merely ten *yen*. It was no small wonder that he was once accused by his friend of being extravagant because he had spent five hundred *yen* a year.

Sung was the Chinese tutor to Huang Hsing's thirteen-year-old son, Huang I-ou, when the boy joined his father in Tokyo in February 1907. During these years Sung was often moody, disturbed emotionally, pessimistic—not unusual in young men in their mid-twenties. At times he wanted to write a novel portraying Chinese social conditions. Once he spent two and a half months in a second-class, "spacious and clean" room in a hospital for the treatment of neurasthenia. It cost 1.60 *yen* per day and expenses were paid by Huang Hsing. Often Sung was asked by Huang to act on his behalf when he was away from the T'ung Meng Hui headquarters in Tokyo.

Sung's diary also reveals scant but significant information of contacts between the Chinese revolutionaries and the Russian and Vietnamese revolutionaries in Tokyo. On one occasion, the Vietnamese, then called Annamese, were given lodging at the office of the *Min-pao,* the official organ of the T'ung Meng Hui. They communicated with each other in Chinese. On another occasion, the T'ung Meng Hui members met a Russian revolutionary from Siberia. The Russian spoke French, which was translated into Japanese.

About Sung's family in China, we know very little from his diary, except that his grandmother died in 1905, his sister married in 1906, and his mother missed him and asked for money.

Another result of Sung's interest in the Korea-Manchuria border region was his concern over the Chientao question. Chientao (Kantao or Yenpien) was a sizable area on the Manchuria side of the Tumen River which had been heavily settled by Korean immigrants. In past decades it had become the focus of periodic jurisdictional disputes between the Korean government and the Chinese authorities in Manchuria. After the Russo-Japanese War, Japan strengthened her hold on Korea, and the Korean government began to press claims on the Chientao area, forcing the Chinese government to negotiate. The question was eventually settled by the Chientao Agreement of September 4, 1909, which gave the Korean settlers the right to remain in the area but also reaffirmed China's legal jurisdiction over them. From his studies and the first-hand knowledge of the region acquired during his brief journey in 1907, Sung Chiao-jen prepared a pamphlet in which he vigorously upheld Chinese claims to the area and pointed out that the Korean claims were only a cover for Japanese ambition in Manchuria. The following excerpts from the pamphlet reveal Sung's foresight:

> If Manchuria were completely conquered by the Japanese, the Japanese would gain hegemony, and the balance of power [in East Asia] would be broken. It was obvious that other Powers could not remain indifferent. They would all come to take advantage of the situation. Alas! Although China is big, would there be any living place left for us Chinese then?

The pamphlet was published under his name Sung Lien in Shanghai in August 1908 as the *Chien-tao wen-t'i* (The Kantao Question). A copy of the work was said to have been forwarded to Yüan Shih-k'ai, a former Chinese political resident in Korea (1885–95) who had the vague title of Commissioner of Trade, and who was from 1907 to 1908 Minister of Foreign Affairs in Peking. Sung's study was said to have been useful to the negotiators of the Manchu government on the question, and Sung himself was reported to have received a government offer of employment on the strength of the pamphlet.

Because Sung Chiao-jen remained in Japan from 1904 until 1910, he took no active part in the military uprisings organized by Sun

Yat-sen and Huang Hsing from 1906 to 1908. The repeated failure of these revolts contributed to a decline in the morale of the rank and file of the party in Japan; and certain doubts about the handling of party funds led to a growing dissatisfaction with Sun Yat-sen as the chairman of the T'ung Meng Hui. In the summer of 1907 Sung joined other leading members of the party in Tokyo, including Chang Ping-lin (1868–1936), Chang Chi (1882–1947), and T'an Jen-feng, in an effort to replace Sun Yat-sen with Huang Hsing as the chairman. Although Huang was able to dissuade them from carrying out this move, Sung's relations with Sun Yat-sen, which had never been close, remained distant. Sung was also dissatisfied with the party's military strategy which had been focused upon the provinces on China's southern border. With the exception of the Manchurian venture, the revolutionary military strategy of the party was to capture a border province in south or southwest China; practically all of the T'ung Meng Hui revolts were staged in Kwangtung, Kwangsi, or Yunnan. This was mainly dictated by circumstances: the revolutionaries were working from outside, and the border provinces were more easily infiltrated from British Hong Kong or French Indo-China.

Sung Chiao-jen believed that a major blow against the Manchu regime should take place in an area centrally located; that the area of operation should not be too extensive; that war should be limited to a very short period of time; and that the revolutionaries should make use of the government troops to overthrow the government.[1] This strategy reflected the thinking of many revolutionaries of the time. He favored a quick victory not only to avoid a protracted war but also to prevent the threat of any possible intervention by foreign powers. In 1910 he met other comrades in Tokyo and discussed informally their views on the revolutionary strategy. He proposed three possible modes of action: First, and to his mind the best way, capture Peking so as to command the rest of the nation. This could be done by working secretly with the northern army and with additional support from the "mounted bandits" from Manchuria. Second, start

[1] *Min-li pao* (Shanghai), Sept. 25, 1911.

a revolution along the Yangtze valley and set up a revolutionary government to launch a northern expedition so as to drive out the Manchus. Third, set up secret revolutionary cells and establish bases whenever possible in Manchuria, Yunnan, Kwangtung or Kwangsi province. The consensus was that the first plan was too difficult to carry out, the third plan had been repeatedly tried, but had failed. Furthermore, a prolonged struggle might invite foreign intervention and partition. Consequently, the second plan was considered the desirable one.[2] Efforts were made to formulate plans for reactivating revolutionary activity in central China, which had been dormant since the failure of the Pingsiang-Liuyang-Liling uprisings in 1906. It was thus decided that a Central China Bureau of the T'ung Meng Hui should be established in Shanghai, and T'an Jen-feng was dispatched to Hong Kong to present these views to Huang Hsing, who agreed to the plan if financial support could be found.

II

At the end of 1910, Sung Chiao-jen left Japan for Shanghai, where he became an editor of the *Min-li pao*; under the pseudonym Yü-fu he wrote a number of articles. First published on October 11, 1910, the *Min-li pao* became the most important revolutionary newspaper and remained so until publication was suspended on September 4, 1913. Sung's writings were mainly concerned with the problems of international relations, foreign aggression in China, and attacks on the Manchu government as well as on the Constitutionalists who favored a constitutional monarchy. In simple and clear style, he presented his views with logic. He was perceptive, persuasive, and farsighted. For instance, in an article entitled "The Last Twenty Years of the East Asian Situation," he warned that "Japan had been and continued to be China's chief enemy for the future." [3] Having analyzed the various foreign involvements in China, he concluded that there were two main aggressive blocks in China: one,

[2] *Ibid.* Jan. 20, 1913; also Hsü Hsüeh-erh ed., *Sung Yü-fu* (Shanghai, 1913), Vol. I, Section I, pp. 3–4.
[3] *Min-li pao*, Feb. 8, 1911.

an economic aggression headed by the United States, with Great Britain playing the secondary role; the other, a military aggression headed by Japan, with Russia playing the secondary role. He predicted, with a rhetorical flourish, that the Anglo-Japanese alliance would be terminated within five years; Japan and the United States would go to war in the Pacific within ten years as a result of power struggle in China. He favored a Sino-American alliance in order to check the military aggression of Japan and Russia, provided this alliance would not upset the balance of power upon which stability in China depended. In an article discussing socialism, Sung favored a national socialism, but he questioned the desirability and applicability of adopting what he considered two other kinds of socialism, anarchism or communism, in China. While commenting on Portuguese politics, he expressed his view on revolutionary strategy which on the whole coincided with subsequent developments: avoid protracted warfare—in order to avoid foreign intervention and gain acceptance of foreign powers, the revolution should be quickly won; the site of revolution should be centrally located and should not be too extensive in area; the government army should be converted into revolutionary forces.[4]

In April 1911 when the Canton revolt was imminent, Sung's journalistic activities were temporarily interrupted when he left for Hong Kong in response to a call from Huang Hsing to assist in preparing for the assault on Canton. For a short time he served on Huang's general staff as head of a department dealing with legal matters and drafting orders and regulations. After the failure of the revolt on April 27 (known as the "March 29th Revolution"), Sung returned to Shanghai and resumed his newspaper work on the *Min-li pao*.

In May the proclamation of a railway nationalization policy by the Peking government resulted in a national crisis. Sung urged his fellow countrymen to take advantage of the opportunity by working positively to overthrow the ancient monarchical system of China. On July 31, Sung, with T'an Jen-feng, Ch'en Ch'i-mei (1878–1916),

[4] *Min-li pao*, May 17, July 13, 18, Aug. 24–25 and Sept. 25, 1911.

and twenty-six other comrades, formally established the Central China Bureau of the T'ung Meng Hui and with his associates turned to the task of organizing and co-ordinating revolutionary uprisings in the Yangtze region, centering attention on the cities of Wuchang, Hankow, Nanking, and Shanghai.[5]

The establishment of the Central China Bureau of the T'ung Meng Hui served as an important link following the failure of the Canton revolt in April and before the outbreak of the Wuchang Revolution in October. It shifted the revolutionary center from the border areas to the interior. It may be noted, however, that none of the activists of the Central China Bureau were from Kwangtung province, nor were they close to Sun Yat-sen. Of the twenty-nine persons who attended the meeting which established the Bureau, seven came from Hunan province; seven from Chekiang; five from Fukien; four from Szechwan; three from Kiangsu; two from Anhwei; one from Yunnan. Their initial contributions ranged from one to ten dollars. Yü Yu-jen, publisher of the *Min-li pao*, who did not attend the meeting, was from Shensi. Chü Cheng (1876–1951), who later took part in the Bureau's affairs, was from Hupeh province.

Judging from the mailing address of the twenty-nine people, ten were teachers, five were journalists, four (all from Fukien) worked for the Shanghai customs house, two were in publishing or printing works, and eight, including T'an Jen-feng, a professional revolutionary, were unknown.

Of the five officers of the Central China Bureau, two were from Hunan (T'an and Sung), one was from Chekiang (Ch'en Ch'i-mei), one was from Fukien, with the birthplace of the remaining one (Yang) unknown. Besides Ch'en Ch'i-mei, who had played a relatively insignificant role in the Chinese revolutionary movement up to

[5] Unless otherwise noted, the account of the Central China Bureau of the T'ung Meng Hui is based on *K'ai-kuo wen-cheng* (Documents on the Founding of the Republic), Vol. I (Taipei, 1963), which consists of a number of the Central China Bureau's original documents in facsimile; and *Wu-ch'ang shou-i* (The Wuchang Revolution), which is Volume I of the Second Series of documents published in commemoration of the fiftieth year of the establishment of the Republic of China (Taipei, 1961), pp. 1–36.

that time, the most active officers were T'an and Sung, who were former members of Huang Hsing's revolutionary organization, Hua Hsing Hui. It should also be mentioned that even though the Bureau was established independent of the leadership of both Sun Yat-sen and Huang Hsing, the latter was kept informed of its activities. It is interesting to recall that when the idea of forming the Central China Bureau was first raised, Huang Hsing agreed but Hu Han-min opposed it on the ground that it could create problems within the party leadership.[6]

The Central China Bureau was organized under collective leadership, and its chairmanship was deliberately left open for a future "eligible person." According to one source, this was meant to be Huang Hsing when he was available and it was feasible for him to take up the post.[7] Indeed, when Chü Cheng proposed at an officers' meeting that the Bureau should work under the leadership of a capable chairman, although it was readily agreed, it was decided that the matter should be discussed by a plenary meeting, and that the decision should be postponed until they heard from Huang Hsing. Probably it was Huang's recommendation they sought.

The manifesto of the Central China Bureau was drafted by T'an Jen-feng; its regulations were written by Sung Chiao-jen. The manifesto clearly indicated that the Bureau was intended to be a branch within the framework of the T'ung Meng Hui, and article one of the constitution of the Bureau provided that it was to be organized by those T'ung Meng Hui members who expressly wished to join. The aim of the Bureau was to "overthrow the Manchu government and establish a constitutional democracy" (article three). This was a slightly different aim from that of the T'ung Meng Hui, but the difference was perhaps of less real significance than it seemed on the surface.

In the middle of September, the local revolutionaries in Wuhan

[6] T'an Jen-feng, *Shih-shou p'ai-tz'u hsü-lu* (Reminiscences), reprinted in *Chin-tai shih tzu-liao* (Source Materials on Modern History), No. 10 (August 1956), pp. 26–27.

[7] Ch'en Hsü-lu, "Lun Sung Chiao-jen," *Hsin-hai ko-ming wu-shih chou-nien chi-nien lun-wen chi* (Collected Essays on the Revolution of 1911 in Commemoration of Its 50th Anniversary) (Peking, 1962), I, 363–65.

sent Chü Cheng to Shanghai to purchase arms and also to bring Huang Hsing, Sung Chiao-jen, T'an Jen-feng, and other T'ung Meng Hui leaders to Hankow. Chü arrived at Shanghai on the twenty-fifth of the month. After hearing Chü's report on the revolutionary development in Hupeh, the Central China Bureau agreed to instigate simultaneous uprisings in Shanghai and Nanking. An emissary was sent to Hong Kong to report to Huang Hsing asking him to return to Shanghai and take charge of the forthcoming revolt in Wuhan. Pending Huang Hsing's arrival, Sung and T'an agreed to leave for Hupeh first. But before their departure, Sung learned from other sources of information that Hupeh was not quite ready to revolt. As a result he hesitated to proceed to Wuhan, and decided to wait for Huang Hsing's arrival. T'an was angry, and at the Central China Bureau meeting of October 7 declared that he would proceed to Wuhan because he did not want to disappoint the Hupeh revolutionaries; but he hoped that Sung would follow him as soon as possible.

The record of that meeting reveals that the Central China Bureau was not quite prepared to start a revolution right away, because, in the judgment of its members, "the riots in Szechwan had gradually come to an end, and there was no assurance that the revolution in Nanking and Hunan would succeed." The main task of T'an was to settle the differences among the revolutionaries in Hupeh and to wait for the right moment to start the revolution. He was authorized to decide on the spot, according to his judgment of the developments there, how long he should wait. That the T'ung Meng Hui exercised leadership over the local revolutionaries in Hupeh through the Central China Bureau was clearly indicated in Huang Hsing's letters to the executive officers of the Central China Bureau.

The Wuchang Revolution had broken out on October 10 while T'an was on the way. On October 25, Sung Chiao-jen accompanied Huang Hsing from Shanghai to Wuhan. There, working with other leaders of the newly created Hupeh military government, Sung drafted a provisional constitution for Hupeh province and took an active part in organizing the convention of provincial delegates. The convention assembled at the British Concession at Hankow late in November for the purpose of establishing a provisional Republican government, and shortly afterward moved to the new Republican capital of Nanking. In the meantime Sung had left Wuchang for Shanghai on November 10, where he actively campaigned for the election of Huang Hsing as the generalissimo in order to organize a central provisional government.

III

The Provisional Government of the Republic of China was formally established at Nanking on January 1, 1912, with Sun Yat-sen as the Provisional President and Huang Hsing as Minister of War. Sung was appointed to head the Law Codification Bureau in charge of drafting laws and statutes for the new Republic. From his former study of government and politics in Japan, Sung had concluded that the best way to form a democratic government in China was to create a "responsible cabinet" system answerable to parliament and the premier; the premier, as head of the cabinet, would be the chief executive of the government.

But the Organic Law of the Provisional Government made no provision for a premier or for a cabinet system; furthermore, Sun Yat-sen was vigorously opposed to a "responsible cabinet." A widely circulated rumor at that time was that Sung Chiao-jen wanted to be premier with Huang Hsing as the president. This was untrue. As Sung frankly admitted later, it was not that he did not want to be premier, but that he fully realized that his prestige was not great enough for the premiership at the time. Instead, he favored Huang Hsing and others for the part.[8]

In the middle of February, Sun Yat-sen resigned as Provisional President in favor of Yüan Shih-k'ai on the condition that President Yüan would abide by the provisional constitution then being drafted in Nanking and that he would go to Nanking to take up the post. Sung Chiao-jen was one of the delegates sent to Peking to escort Yüan southward. However, under the pretext of army riots in the north, Yüan refused to go to Nanking. When some leading T'ung

[8] Letter of Sung Chiao-jen to the Peking press in *Min-li pao*, July 12, 1912; also see *Min-li pao*, March 12, 1913.

Meng Hui members suggested at a top-level meeting that Huang Hsing should head an army to the north to "escort" Yüan, Ts'ai Yüan-p'ei, who had just returned with Sung from Peking as a delegate of the unsuccessful escort mission, kept quiet although he fully realized the serious consequences of such an unwise move, which should not have been suggested lightly. Sung Chiao-jen, however, spoke out strongly. He spoke against it, because it meant, in fact, a Northern Expedition. As a result, in front of all the leaders present at the meeting, he was denounced as a traitor to the Nanking government and even physically assaulted by Ma Chün-wu (later the President of the University of Kiangsi)—an incident which fully illustrates how crude and unsophisticated some of the leaders were at that time.

Upon his inauguration as Provisional President in Peking, Yüan, in outward compliance with the constitution, set up a cabinet, but to ensure his control over this body he named his old friend, T'ang Shao-i (1860–1938), premier and his trusted subordinates to head the key ministries of war, navy, and interior. As a gesture of concilia-tion to Nanking, Yüan named four members of the T'ung Meng Hui to head four of the less powerful cabinet ministries. Of these Sung was appointed Minister of Agriculture and Forestry in March 1912. Sung was aware that his position was one of little influence, yet he was eager to participate in the workings of the new cabinet system which he had labored so energetically to establish. It soon became apparent, however, that Yüan had no intention of sharing power with the premier, and his arbitrary appointment of the officials quickly brought him in conflict with the cabinet. T'ang Shao-i, although a long-time associate of Yüan's, resigned as premier in the middle of June; Sung Chiao-jen (and the three other T'ung Meng Hui cabinet ministers) resigned early in July.

In a letter to Sun Wu, which appeared in the *Min-li pao,* July 4, 1912, Sung explained the real reason for his resignation. In May he had submitted a political program to the cabinet for discussion. Having received no response from his colleagues, he was convinced that it would serve no purpose to stay on in the government, and that, until the cabinet consisted of men of the same political outlook, there was little hope that the government would successfully undertake the tremendous tasks facing the young Republic. In his political program, designed to meet the needs of the young Republic, Sung Chiao-jen advocated (1) separation of the civil and military rule; (2) centralization of the government; (3) reduction of the number of troops; (4) reform of the revenue system; (5) establishment of the Central Banks; and (6) issue of national bonds. Under these headings a number of specific policies were suggested.

Sung's experience in the short-lived T'ang Shao-i cabinet only strengthened his conviction that, if parliamentary democracy were to succeed in China, a workable cabinet system would have to be imposed upon Yüan to check his authoritarian tendencies. To support a cabinet that would be both politically effective and yet responsible to the legislature, Sung believed it would be necessary to build a powerful political party within the National Assembly. Even before the transfer of the Provisional Parliament from Nanking to Peking in April 1912, he had urged that the T'ung Meng Hui, whose main revolutionary goal was already accomplished, should be changed from a secret revolutionary organization to an open political party. According to the recollections of Chü Cheng, the reorganization of the party was necessary partly because in the early months of the Republic there were some undesirable persons falsely claiming membership and working only for their own interests. The T'ung Meng Hui had been so loosely organized that it was difficult to separate a true member from a self-seeking one. Unless it was reorganized and all members who had joined the party before the revolution registered, there was no way for the party to control the situation.

The T'ung Meng Hui held its first plenary meeting since 1905 in Nanking at the end of January 1912. Early in March it was formally reorganized into an open political party, with Sun Yat-sen as chairman, and Huang Hsing and Li Yüan-hung as vice chairmen. Li was elected because of his role in the Wuchang Revolution; however, his position in the party was nominal and he, who had been forced onto the side of the revolution, soon departed from the revolutionary camp. Wang Ching-wei and Chang Chi were in charge of the Department of General Affairs; Sung Chiao-jen became the head of the Political Department. The aims of the T'ung Meng Hui were now "to consolidate the Republic and to carry out the Principle of People's Livelihood."

After Sun Yat-sen formally relinquished his post as Provisional President on April 1, the Provisional Parliament subsequently moved from Nanking to Peking. The T'ung Meng Hui headquarters also moved northward at the end of the month. However, "as during most of the revolutionary years," as pointed out by a historian, "it [the headquarters] was only the nominal central organization of the party. Party policies and decisions were made at a Contact Center (chi-kuan-pu) in Shanghai, which was the frequent meeting place of Sun [Yat-sen] and Huang [Hsing], who remained the top leaders of the reorganized T'ung Meng Hui." [9]

In the hope that the T'ung Meng Hui would be returned to the National Assembly as the majority party in the forthcoming elections scheduled for December 1912, Sung Chiao-jen worked for the amalgamation of the T'ung Meng Hui with four smaller political groups also represented in the assembly. An agreement was reached and, on August 13, announced jointly by Sun Yat-sen and Huang Hsing. On August 25 the new party, named the Kuomintang (Nationalist Party), was formally inaugurated at Peking. [10] Both Sun Yat-sen and Huang Hsing were elected to a nine-man board of directors of the party. Sun was chosen by the other directors as the general director and thus remained the titular head of the party. Sung Chiao-jen was elected to the board of directors with the largest votes next to Sun and Huang. The purpose of the Kuomintang was to "strengthen the Republic and achieve democracy."

[9] Shelley H. Cheng, "The Chinese Republican Movement, 1894–1912," Paper No. 17 of the International Conference on Asian History, Hong Kong, August 30–September 5, 1964, p. 6.

[10] This is not to be confused with the Chung-kuo Kuo-min-tang, or the Kuomintang for short, which was the name of the party after 1919, headed first by Sun Yat-sen and later by Chiang Kai-shek. It was the ruling party in China for more than two decades before 1949, and it is still the dominant party in Taiwan. There was, of course, a direct chain of developments between the two Kuomintangs.

As the moving force behind the formation of the Kuomintang, Sung Chiao-jen now emerged as the most influential leader after Sun and Huang. As Hu Han-min stated in his *Autobiography*: "Sung became important because of Huang Hsing's support within the party and prominent politicians' co-operation without." However, in the view of a historian:

> The role of Sung Chiao-jen in the establishment of the Kuomintang has . . . often been exaggerated. In fact, his role in the amalgamation . . . seems to have been much less important than those of Chang Chi [executive secretary for liaison and concurrently head of the T'ung Meng Hui's branch for Chihli province, who took an active part in the negotiations prior to the amalgamation] and Chang Yao-tseng [a politician who also participated in the talks that led to the formation of the Kuomintang], let alone those of Sun [Yat-sen] and Huang [Hsing]. It also appears erroneous to picture Sung Chiao-jen as "the leader of the Kuomintang," for Sun and Huang continued to be the two top leaders of the new party as they had been in the period of the T'ung Meng Hui, and their headquarters in Shanghai was the new party's high command rather than the Head Office in Peking which only discharged routine business and carried out policies and decisions made in Shanghai. Sung Chiao-jen does not even seem to be the most powerful of the officials in the Peking office. . . . [He] could not possibly have run the Head Office, for he soon left for his native Hunan (October 18), where he remained until the next January.[11]

It was undoubtedly true that the headquarters of Sun and Huang in Shanghai was the Kuomintang's high command rather than the head office in Peking. However, the views quoted above seem to have overlooked the fact that while Sun and Huang still enjoyed prestige as the top leaders of the new party, they had become figures behind the scenes in national politics. Meanwhile, Sun Yat-sen's position had actually been weakened; Huang and his followers had emerged as the stronger group. In fact, Sun Yat-sen had only reluctantly agreed to the reorganization of the T'ung Meng Hui into the Kuomintang, and he became inactive in party affairs after he left Peking in mid-September. It is significant that Sun, who had always been looked

[11] Cheng, *op. cit.* pp. 6–7.

up to as a great fund raiser for the party, now turned to Huang Hsing when he was asked by the Kuomintang headquarters in Peking for financial support.[12]

Sung Chiao-jen spent much of the autumn of 1912 in the Yangtze provinces campaigning for the election of party candidates to the new National Assembly. During this time he made a trip to his native town in Hunan to see his mother and wife—the first family reunion since he went away in 1904. After a month in the Changsha and Wuhan areas, Sung Chiao-jen arrived in Shanghai on February 15, where he stayed at Huang Hsing's residence in the French Concession.[13] Sun Yat-sen had left Shanghai for Japan a few days before.

In Shanghai, Huang Hsing and Sung Chiao-jen met with the Kuomintang members elected to the National Assembly to map out strategy and policy for the new political situation. The Kuomintang had scored a clear victory in the National Assembly, over twice as many seats as its nearest rival—269 of the 596 seats in the House of Representatives and 123 of the 274 seats in the Senate. The Kuomintang success at the polls was also a personal triumph for Sung, under whose direction the party's campaign had been conducted, and it was generally expected that Sung himself would assume the premiership of a new party cabinet in Peking.

Sung Chiao-jen's political ideas may be seen from the Kuomintang political program which he drafted at this time. He had intended to bring it to the Peking headquarters for discussion and approval. With regard to the political system, he advocated (1) unitary government; (2) responsible cabinet; (3) provincial governors chosen by election·with a view that eventually they would be appointed by the central government; (4) self-government for the provinces and districts; (5) the premier to be chosen from the majority party in the National Assembly and the cabinet members to be chosen by the premier without the consent of the parliament.

[12] Telegram of Sun Yat-sen to Huang Hsing, dated December 23, 1912, in the Committee for the Compilation of Materials on the Party History of the Central Committee of the Kuomintang, ed., *Kuo-fu ch'üan-chi* (Collected Works of Sun Yat-sen), Vol. II (Taipei, 1965), sec. 9, p. 178.

[13] *Min-li pao,* Jan. 10, and Feb. 16–17, 1913.

As to specific policies, he proposed (1) a number of measures regarding political and military affairs, including (a) establishment of a unified military system, (b) reduction of the number of troops, (c) encouragement of military education, (d) expansion of arsenals, and (e) setting up of a number of military zones in the country, in addition to administrative divisions; (2) proper division of powers between the central and provincial governments; (3) financial reforms, including the establishment of accounting and budget systems, the central bank, unification of treasury, bonds and currency reforms; (4) effective administration by enforcing strict civil service examination and other measures; (5) development of industries; (6) improvement of civic affairs including a census of population, police reforms, and sanitary measures; (7) development of national communication and transportation systems such as the railway, telegraph, post office, and steamship; (8) expansion of education including education of women; (9) establishment of an independent and unified judicial system, improvement of prison conditions, and training of lawyers; and (10) flexible diplomacy.

As an ardent admirer of Western parliamentary systems, Sung Chiao-jen, during the political campaign of late 1912 and early 1913, sought to introduce into China some of the electioneering methods current in Europe and America. In a number of provincial capitals in the Yangtze region he had made campaign speeches attacking the Peking government, its national and international policies. However, he showed remarkable style of statesmanship. Public criticism of the government and its leaders was an innovation in China; and it aroused the bitter animosity of many powerful conservatives, including Yüan Shih-k'ai and his political following. Morever, it became apparent to Yüan that Sung would head the new Kuomintang cabinet in Peking. Yüan was now faced with the prospect of an intense political struggle with a potential new premier who would seek to reduce his own existing powers as president. As the time approached for the meeting of the newly elected National Assembly in April 1913, Sung prepared to leave Shanghai for Peking on the evening of March 20. As he was boarding the train at the Shanghai railway station, he was shot twice in the abdomen by an assassin; two days later and only two weeks before his thirty-first birthday, he died of his wounds.[14]

IV

Immediately after Sung's death, the assassin and his associate were seized by the authorities in Shanghai. In the homes of these men several documents were discovered which implicated Premier Chao Ping-chün and indicated that Yüan himself was aware of the plot. Among these documents was a letter to one of the culprits from the Premier and incriminating telegrams from Hung Shu-tsu, confidential secretary of the cabinet. Yüan, however, was able to keep himself from legal involvement in the case; the others were less fortunate. The assassin died in prison in Shanghai; his associate later escaped from jail and was mysteriously murdered in January 1914 on his way from Peking to Tientsin. Soon after, Chao Ping-chün, who was wanted by the Shanghai courts for questioning in the case, also died suddenly and mysteriously while serving as Yüan's gov-

[14] Wu Hsiang-hsiang's *Sung Chiao-jen* (Taipei, 1964) is the best Chinese study on the subject. He argues (pp. 224–26), however, that if Sung and the Kuomintang leaders merely planned to capture the premiership but were prepared to elect Yüan Shih-k'ai to the presidency, Yüan would not have had Sung assassinated. According to Wu, Huang and Sung were not even prepared to offer the presidency to Yüan Shih-k'ai; instead, they were planning to support the mediocre Li Yüan-hung. Wu lists, what I consider, inconclusive evidence and several implausible reasons, and even includes contemporary rumors to prove that intrigue did exist. This is not only taking exception to the generally accepted view, but is also contrary to the information given by Tsou Lu, who was a Kuomintang member elected to the National Assembly. According to an article, "My Reminiscences of 1913," written by Tsou in the winter of that year, "no decision was made [by the Kuomintang leaders in Shanghai] to support Yüan Shih-k'ai. Nor, on the other hand, was there any plan that he should be challenged. It was generally held that if Yüan would abide by the law, it was all right to elect him to the presidency." Furthermore, Sun Yat-sen also reportedly declared in Japan that "the presidency cannot but fall on Mr. Yüan Shih-k'ai."

Perhaps it would be more reasonable to argue that Yüan might very well have believed the widely circulated rumor that Huang and Sung were trying to elect Li Yüan-hung. Consequently, he was prepared for the worst and acted accordingly. But this is not the same as to say that the Kuomintang leaders did plan to oust Yüan from the government.

ernor in Chihli province in 1914. Both deaths were rumored to have been ordered by Yüan to prevent further disclosures concerning the case. The last suspect, Hung Shu-tsu, fled from Peking to the safety of the foreign concession of Tsingtao, where he remained until after Yüan's death. Returning to Shanghai under an assumed name in 1917, Hung was recognized, apprehended, and taken before the Shanghai Mixed Court. Extradited to Peking, he was sentenced to death for Sung's murder and in 1919 was hanged, thus bringing the Sung case to a close.[15]

The investigation of the assassination pointed to the guilt of Yüan Shih-k'ai and his associates, and it exposed the underlying conflict of political interest between Yüan and the Kuomintang leaders—a conflict which rapidly developed into an open and armed struggle. After Yüan secured an illegal "reorganization loan" from the foreign powers, he was determined, with this financial support, to wipe out the power and influence of the revolutionary leaders. Huang Hsing and others were forced to take up arms against the central government in the "second revolution" of July–September 1913. The Kuomintang, which had already suffered serious blows by the repressive measures of Yüan, soon ceased to be an effective political force until its reorganization under Sun Yat-sen a decade later. The nature of the party was changed from a democratic political party to a single-party system. A revolutionary reform of government based on Western ideas was never realized; party politics of the Western model were not given a chance to work; and, judging by the subsequent events, it may not be an exaggeration to say that with the assassination of Sung Chiao-jen, the first opportunity for establishing a Western-style democracy in China was lost. And yet some Chinese historians and politicians, influenced by the political atmosphere and thinking of the later Kuominting and the Chinese Communist Party after the 1920's have tended to criticize Sung for his outright acceptance of Western po-

[15] Sung Chiao-jen was survived by his mother, his wife, *née* Li, a son and a daughter. In 1917 his son, Sung Chen-lü, and his former secretary, Liu Pai, were responsible for recognizing and capturing Hung Shu-tsu, who was involved in Sung's assassination. Before the 1911 revolution, Sung's elder brother, Sung Chiao-hsin, had been arrested by the Ch'ing authorities because of Sung's revolutionary activities and had died in prison.

litical institutions. But what other political system could the Republicans have advocated as a model in 1912? *

* Unless otherwise noted, the sources for this article are: Chün-tu Hsüeh, *Huang Hsing and the Chinese Revolution* (Stanford University Press, 1961, 1968); and the writings of Sung Chiao-jen. Sung's writings are few and scattered. Historically, the most important was his diary, *Sung Yu-fu jih-chi*, also entitled *Wo chih li-shih* (My History), published posthumously in his native district in Hunan in 1920 and reprinted serially in the *Chien-kuo yüeh-k'an* (Reconstruction Monthly) in Nanking between October 1933 and October 1934, omitting, however, Sun Yat-sen's name from the entries between February 28 and March 2, 1907, which contained adverse comments on him. The diary, covering the period from the autumn of 1904 to the spring of 1907, is one of the major primary sources for the history of the founding and early history of the T'ung Meng Hui. Sung's essay on the Chientao question, *Chien-tao wen-t'i*, published in 1908, was subsequently serialized in the *Ti-hsüeh tsa-chih* (Peking) between 1914 and 1916, and in the *Chien-kuo yüeh-k'an* (Nanking) between July and October 1936. A two-volume collection, entitled *Sung Yu-fu*, was published in Shanghai in 1913, which contained some of Sung's political statements, biographical sketches, writings about him after his death, and reports on the investigation of assassination compiled from the *Min-li pao* and other newspapers. A collection of essays and editorials written by Sung Chiao-jen and Tai Chi-t'ao in 1911–12 was published in Shanghai in 1912 under the title, *Sung Yu-fu Tai T'ien-ch'ou wen-chi ho-k'an*, but, with few exceptions, it is impossible to distinguish the authors of the works therein. Most of the works mentioned above are also available in the "Selected Works of Sung Chiao-jen" in the first of the six-volume *Ko-ming hsien-lieh hsien-chun shih-wen hsüan-chi* (Selected Works of Martyrs and Forerunners of the Revolution), edited by the Committee for the Compilation of Materials on the Party History of the Central Committee of the Kuomintang (Taipei, 1965). The Kuomintang Committee, ed., *Ko-ming wen-hsien* (Documents of the Revolution), Vols. 42/43 (Taipei, 1968), contains primary sources relating to the assassination of Sung Chiao-jen.

❧ 10 ❧

Hu Han-min: His Career
and Thought

MELVILLE T. KENNEDY, JR.

Hu Han-min's career as revolutionist and ideologue is one of the more important in modern Chinese politics because of his singular role in the crucial transition from a dynastic to a nominally republican political structure. While closely identified with revolutionists who seized and used power, he appeared not to be ambitious for power himself. His motivations and capacities were largely typical of his fellow activists, yet he seemed to lack the personal qualities of the natural leader. His ambition fell short of that vital thrust that propels the more self-serving types in any political movement into top posts of control and authority. Yet he fully supported the goals of the revolution. His aspirations for China developed in much the same way as did his colleagues'. Somehow, they knew, China had to break with an age-old political and social tradition that stood in the way of its passage into the modern era. An alien moribund dynasty had to give way to a modern system which could both speak for the people and lead them back to unity and to political strength.

In the decades following the Taiping collapse, reformers labored, despite ambivalent loyalties to tradition on the one hand and opposition to the Manchus on the other, to bring about change. Secret so-

This article is a substantially revised version of the author's paper on this topic, which first appeared in *Papers on China,* Vol. 8 (1954), duplicated for private distribution by the Committee on International and Regional Studies, Harvard University. The permission of the East Asian Research Center of Harvard University to undertake this revision is gratefully acknowledged.

cieties, tied more to parochial than to national interests, sought change through other means. From this mixed political company, the revolutionists emerged with no appropriate weapons for political combat in which power was clearly the prize and in which it could be seized only by means deliberately fashioned to that end. The history of the Republican Revolution is replete with accounts of personal courage and selfless commitment. Uprisings and revolts were undertaken against the most discouraging odds; survivors rallied their small forces to strike again with unflagging spirit. There was never a lack of fearless determination. But in the pre-Republican period when revolutionaries' aspirations were the clearest, when political troops were waiting to be mobilized, no leadership emerged capable of designing successful combat strategies or of galvanizing potential political forces into a truly formidable insurrection that might have realized those aspirations.

We find in Hu Han-min's career some of these idiosyncracies of the Republican movement. He was successful in his classical training and won an advanced degree under the old examination system. As a student, academic administrator, editor, writer, and ideologue, he considered himself and was considered by others as a leading representative of the intelligentsia. After joining the T'ung Meng Hui and committing himself to Sun Yat-sen's leadership, he was unavoidably swept into revolutionary action. But it seems likely that Hu was not an activist by temperament, and became one only under the pressures of circumstance.

Thus one looks to his ideas for a better measure of his revolutionary motive and fervor. But there, too, are the uncertainties, the ambivalences, the strange amalgam of Western and Chinese political and economic ideas that served poorly as an ideology both for him and for the Republican movement. The revolutionists were culture-bound. The 19th century had exposed China to other cultures with their contrasting values and social modes. But, with rare exceptions, the real nature of these contrasts had failed to penetrate. They had aroused alarm and stirred confusion. Many Chinese were deeply worried about the relevance of their tradition. Many were enraged by the disclosure of their national frailty. But few, naturally, were ready to abandon their culture which for ages had been pre-eminent and which, more important, assured them their identity. The effect, however, was that very few Chinese thinkers could take a fresh view of their past and critically assess their contemporary setting. They could find no vantage point outside their vast and enveloping culture from which to take a new reading of the problems, political and otherwise, that beset them.

One result of this circumstance was that, in the dying years of the dynasty, reformers and even some Republican revolutionists found it hard to visualize China in any other guise than that of a monarchy. Because Western powers apparently owed their strength in some mysterious fashion to their constitutions, constitutionalism acquired a strong appeal as a device that should be tried in China in some form—but only as an appendage. The concept that successful constitutions, in fact, only confirm existing political processes, that they are incapable in themselves of creating new ones, was clearly an alien idea.

A mixture of Western political concepts—socialism, democracy, even anarchism—stirred the minds of Chinese revolutionists. But these were ideas cut loose from their Western cultural roots. Separated from a distinctively Western view of human nature and the social order, from Western notions of justice and human freedom, these ideas—however intriguing—tended to be distorted and to lack vitality. The values for which these terms stood bore little or no relation to anything at the core of Chinese political experience.

Hu Han-min and his fellow revolutionaries dedicated their lives to the search for a new workable political order in China. However, two cultural features complicated that search. One was the deep ambivalence these leaders felt toward their social traditions on the one hand and their desire on the other to adopt what was politically new and non-Chinese. The other was their inability to step outside their culture sufficiently to comprehend the essence of non-Chinese political experience. Without such comprehension, they had difficulty assessing adequately the political order they wished to supplant. They had equal difficulty in designing the new order they wished to create. Finally, and for the same reasons, neither their long-range revolutionary strategy nor their short-range tactics ever achieved the clarity or the dynamic thrust they would have required to achieve total success for the Republican revolution.

I

Hu Han-min was a southerner, as were many prominent reformers and revolutionaries. He was born in 1879 in Panyu hsien near Canton in the province of Kwangtung. Both parents came from literate and bureaucratic backgrounds. His grandfather and father had been secretaries to minor officials and his mother was from a scholarly family in the neighboring southern province of Kiangsi. Beginning classical studies as a boy, Hu Han-min showed outstanding talent from the outset. By the time he was fifteen, he was tutoring others— many of them his senior—to help support his orphaned family of brothers and sisters.

Early in his career he was hostile to the alien Manchu dynasty. Insurrectionist sentiment was part of the southern intellectual atmosphere which no alert and curious mind could avoid. The Taiping uprising was only a few decades removed. Secret societies were woven into the social fabric. Local rebellions were increasingly common. Prominent intellectuals wrote eloquent appeals for political and social reform as Western encroachments disclosed more and more the Manchu court's ineptitude in defending China.

In his own reading of Chinese history, Hu Han-min was drawn to the accounts of eminent Ming loyalists who resisted the imposition of Manchu rule. China's hmiliating defeat by Japan in the 1894–95 war deepened Hu's antipathy to the Peking regime as it did for many Chinese. At some point soon after the Sino-Japanese war, he decided to go to Japan to broaden his education in the more modern disciplines.

To earn the necessary funds, he began working for a Canton newspaper in 1896. He also resorted to the traditional device of acquiring a degree through the imperial examination system on behalf of a group of wealthy men who sought the perquisites of a degree but who lacked the learning and talent to gain one on their own. In 1900 he won a *chü-jen* degree in provincial examinations, the second level in the difficult course of advancement through the imperial system.

With money in hand, Hu made his first trip to Japan in early 1902. But he was back in Canton before the end of the year after his first brush with the Chinese embassy in Japan. He turned again briefly to journalism, contesting the editorials of a rival paper that supported the monarchist position of the eminent reformer, K'ang Yu-wei. K'ang was widely known as an advocate of constitutional monarchy for China and as a close advisor to the young Emperor during his abortive reform effort in 1898. Hu's forensic skills won immediate notice and drew charges of revolutionary incitement. As a consequence, he left Canton for Wuchow, in Kwangsi province, to teach and lecture on revolutionary themes. Again the authorities forced him to leave for a second trip to Japan in 1904.

Hu Han-min's close association with Wang Ching-wei dates from this period when both enrolled in the Tokyo Law College and became friends and colleagues in the revolutionary movement. Shortly after Sun Yat-sen organized the T'ung Meng Hui in the autumn of 1905, both Hu and Wang were given responsible posts, Hu Han-min as secretary of the party headquarters. While continuing to study for the Law College degree, which he received in 1906, Hu supported the movement chiefly as an editor and writer for the *Min-pao*, the party organ that first appeared in Toyko in November 1905.

When, in the spring of 1907, Japanese authorities acceded to Peking's demands that Sun Yat-sen be expelled from Japan, Hu Han-min, Wang Ching-wei, and others accompanied him to Hanoi. Thus began a four-year period of intensive but generally ineffective effort to establish a revolutionary base in Southeast Asia that would yield funds, manpower, and broad support for spreading insurrection in south China. Sun Yat-sen relied heavily in this effort on a small group of loyal lieutenants, among whom Hu was always prominent, to develop plans and carry out tactics. At one point Hu was sent to Hong Kong to direct revolts in eastern Kwangtung. Later, in Sun's absence, he shared direction of the Hanoi headquarters with Huang Hsing. In the fall of 1908 Hu Han-min took charge of a new T'ung Meng Hui office in Singapore and, with Wang Ching-wei, published another party paper, the *Restoration Daily* (*Chung-hsing jih-pao*). During this period the revolutionary movement was at low ebb. Scattered uprisings in south China thus far had been totally fruit-less. Local militia had been no match for government troops. No significant footholds in China had been secured. The movement had gained nothing with which to elicit enthusiasm and generous sup-port from overseas Chinese. Moreover, the revolutionists were com-peting with the constitutional monarchists whose ideas and program were generally more congenial to the minds of thoughtful Chinese in Southeast Asia.

Hu Han-min's next assignment in 1909 was to head the branch office in Hong Kong and to reactivate plans for uprisings in Kwang-tung province. Energies centered now on organizing a revolt among dissident troops of the imperialist New Army based at Canton. In furthering this plan Hu had the cooperation of an army officer who had defected to the T'ung Meng Hui. When the preparations for the coup were well under way, Huang Hsing came to Hong Kong to plan and lead the military operation. But once again plans went awry, and the project collapsed.

Over the next two years, 1910–11, events moved more rapidly toward the climax of the Wuchang uprising. In 1910 Hu Han-min returned to Singapore in the hope of raising more funds for further revolutionary efforts. Meanwhile, Sun Yat-sen, back from one of his money-raising trips abroad, convened a meeting of his followers at Penang in November 1910 to consider next steps. Hu was on hand and shared in plans to launch another major revolt at Canton.

From Penang Sun returned to Europe, and Huang Hsing and Hu Han-min began the necessary but difficult task of cultivating support and seeking funds among Chinese communities in South-east Asia. The following spring Hu was back in Hong Kong to join Huang Hsing in final preparations for what was to be known as the "Canton Revolution of March 29." However, when Hu Han-min and his colleagues arrived at Canton, the revolt, which was led by Huang Hsing, had already been thoroughly crushed at heavy cost to the re-volutionists. Nothing was left to them but to return promptly to Hong Kong. But the impact of this episode went far beyond that of earlier attempts in arousing anti-dynastic feeling in China. To this day, the "Seventy-two Martyrs" (albeit not an accurate figure) of Huanghua-kang are revered as the vanguard of the 1911 Revolution.

Repercussions were directly felt in the Wuchang outbreak that followed in October. This proved to be the trigger for the anti-Peking movement that rapidly spread across central and south China. Disaffected provincial officials, gentry whose local interests were being thwarted by inept and seemingly capricious rulings from Peking, business and financial interests hemmed in by old-style bureaucratic controls seized on this anti-dynastic revolt as a signal to secede. Although widely known, Sun Yat-sen's direct influence was little felt among these circles. However, sufficient military strength was mobilized to secure first the Wuhan cities against Peking forces and then the lower Yangtze valley including Shanghai. Political councils in key centers declared their secession from Peking's rule followed by a provisional Republican government under the direction of T'ung Meng Hui leaders. Because Sun Yat-sen was in the United States when the October outbreak occurred and elected to return to China via the slowest route through Europe, the movement was deprived for over two and a half months of the central direction his personal presence might have supplied. Whether, in fact, he could or would have taken charge of the revolution in those early weeks is a moot question.

Hu Han-min was in Hanoi at the time of the Wuchang uprising. In early November he returned to Hong Kong to lead a group of overseas Chinese youth who had volunteered for military service against Peking. Following the capitulation of imperial authorities at Canton, Hu was elected at an open meeting on November 9 as Military Governor (*tutu*) of Kwangtung under the provisional government. He was not present at the meeting and did not arrive at Canton to assume his new duties until November 12.

When Sun Yat-sen passed through Hong Kong en route to Shanghai from the United States and Europe, several of his followers, including Hu, came aboard and urged him to form his new government in the south and consolidate a firm base at Canton before undertaking to extend his control over the mixed and uncertain elements in central China. Sun not only rejected the proposal but persuaded Hu Han-min to accompany him to Shanghai to assist in resolving the tangled issues that had arisen among the insurgents.

Together they arrived at Shanghai on Christmas Day, 1911. Four days later Sun had been elected head of the provisional government and was installed as Provisional President of the new Chinese Republic at Nanking on January 1, 1912. He appointed Hu Han-min as secretary general of the President's office. After participating with Sun in negotiating working relationships at Wuchang, between forces in central and south China, Hu was reconfirmed as Military Governor of Kwangtung and returned to his post at Canton. Meanwhile, Sun Yat-sen had stepped aside, turning over the Provisional Presidency to the powerful military leader at Peking, Yüan Shih-k'ai, whose chief role in the revolution had been to counsel abdication by the moribund Manchu court rather than to attempt fruitless opposition.

Early in 1913 the lines of conflict were already drawn between Yüan Shih-k'ai and the Kuomintang, which had been organized the previous August as successor to the T'ung Meng Hui. After the assassination of Sung Chiao-jen and the conclusion of the "reorganization loan," Yüan removed Hu from the military governorship of Kwangtung. Later that year in the general but abortive uprising of anti-Yüan forces, known as the "second revolution," a number of party leaders including Hu Han-min were forced to escape to Japan.

As Yüan Shih-k'ai's style of control reverted to arbitrary and autocratic rule and even to the trappings of monarchy, Sun Yat-sen organized a major campaign against him. Hu Han-min's role in the effort was mainly to raise funds. He spent most of 1915 in the Philippines soliciting both moral and material support in the Chinese community. Following Yüan's demise in June 1916, Hu, with other party leaders, went to Peking to rally party members in the discouraging aftermath of the Yüan regime, particularly those who had been members of Parliament. The great majority of them who were Kuomintang members had rejected Sun Yat-sen's organization of the party in Tokyo in 1914. When Yüan's successor again dissolved Parliament the following year, Hu joined Sun Yat-sen in his next effort to rescue the constitutional order. Sun convened a southern parliament at Canton including many members from Peking and organized a military government under his leadership. Hu Han-min was appointed Minister of Communications.

However, this effort, in turn, proved to be abortive. A military clique based in the neighboring province of Kwangsi held the reins of real power in the South. When Sun discovered that he could neither control nor subdue this element, he returned to Shanghai taking Hu Han-min and other close followers with him.

Three years later, in May 1921—when conditions in the South were somewhat more propitious—Sun Yat-sen was again in Canton to resume his post in the military government. But as a result of the controversial move made by Ch'en Chiung-ming against him during the following year, Sun was forced to flee to Shanghai again. Hu Han-min had been manning one of the forward tactical headquarters when he learned of Ch'en's attack at Canton and of Sun's successful escape to Shanghai. He rejoined Sun Yat-sen at Shanghai to participate in the next crucial stage of the resurgent revolution. By this time Sun had concluded that until the revolutionary party itself had undergone drastic overhaul and reorganization, it was unfit for the massive undertakings that lay ahead. To this end, he asked a committee in September 1922 to begin a study of reorganization. The committee, in turn, assigned Hu Han-min and Wang Ching-wei the task of formulating a declaration of party reform. Following revision and approval by Sun Yat-sen in December, the statement was completed and adopted as the manifesto on Kuomintang reorganization on January 1, 1923.

Meanwhile, the continuing military struggle in the South continued, directly involving Hu Han-min who bore the title of Military Governor of Kwangtung under an earlier appointment by Sun. By February 1923 forces friendly to Sun gained control of Canton allowing him to return and to reorganize and secure his military government by the spring of 1923. Later that year Hu bore the brunt of attacks against the regime by Canton merchants who felt themselves threatened by a revolutionary order colored, now, by co-operative policies with the Chinese Communists and overt assistance from Russian advisors. This antipathy in the commercial sector was actively encouraged by financial backers in neighboring British Hong Kong.

During 1923 preparations were being made for the first national congress of the newly organized Kuomintang. Continuous consultations were being held with Russian advisors. Because Sun Yat-sen was fully aware by this time that his revolutionary program had little future in China until it could mobilize and train its own military arm, he sent Chiang Kai-shek to Russia in late 1923 to observe military organization under party control. In January 1924 Sun Yat-sen convened some 165 delegates at Canton in the first Congress of the reorganized Kuomintang clearly patterned on the Leninist party structure. Hu Han-min was elected by the Congress to the Central Executive Committee. Somewhat later he was also appointed to the Central Political Council.

In May 1924 the Whampoa Military Academy was established near Canton under the headship of Chiang Kai-shek. Its first undertaking was a crash program of cadet training to strengthen both the Kuomintang and Sun's military government. Hu was appointed a political instructor in this combined curriculum of intensive political and military training.

The Whampoa staff and trainees were very early put to the test when called on in October 1924 to help subdue the rebellious Canton Merchants' Association. Sun Yat-sen had left Canton for his forward position at Shaokuan from which he hoped once again to renew his northern expedition, entrusting Hu Han-min with the administration of Canton headquarters. With their own militia, armed and financed partly by angry anti-Sun elements in the British colony, the Canton merchants threatened to take the law into their own hands. Hu called upon Chiang and the Whampoa contingent plus other loyal units to suppress this military defiance by the Association.

Again, in November 1924 and in early 1925, Hu Han-min had to cope with almost continuous unrest among ambitious southern warlords in Kwangtung, Kwangsi, and Yunnan. After abandoning his plans for a northern campaign in 1924 in favor of talks at Peking with Northern warlords, Sun left with Hu his responsibilities as Grand

Marshal and head of the military government at Canton. Hu invoked these military and political powers first to secure Kwangtung, and then to aid loyal militarists to consolidate power in the key neighboring provinces. Once again, Whampoa forces under Chiang played important roles in wresting power from southern warlords.

Sun's death at Peking in March 1925 signalled the premature and gradual decline of Hu Han-min's political role in the Kuomintang as the party moved toward the center of the political stage in China. In their leader's absence, the party first carried out a decision made the previous year at the time of the reorganization. The party had agreed, then, to replace the military government with a civilian administration. This step had been delayed by the relentless jockeying for power among unsympathetic warlords. But by early summer in 1925 conditions in Kwangtung were secure enough for the KMT to move ahead with plans.

Hu Han-min took the lead in convening the Central Political Council. In several meetings during June it arranged to supplant the KMT military headquarters with a new civilian government, inaugurated on July 1, 1925. The question of who was to succeed Sun Yat-sen was not yet resolved. Several close and loyal followers who had been with Sun from early T'ung Meng Hui days aspired to the post—principally Hu Han-min, Wang Ching-wei, and Liao Chung-k'ai. But manifestly no one could fill Sun's role. None had his authority or could evoke the same kind of loyalty.

The government thus took the form of a committee system under the chairmanship of Wang Ching-wei. A committee of sixteen took charge of political affairs of whom five constituted the Standing Committee including Hu Han-min. Hu was also named Minister of Foreign Affairs. Friction developed between Hu and Wang over these appointments which led in later years to deeper policy differences between them.

As the KMT struggled with problems both inside and outside the party in the wake of Sun Yat-sen's death, it sustained another shock in the assassination of Liao Chung-k'ai, a veteran KMT leader on August 19, 1925. The crime has defied satisfactory explanation over the years. But Hu I-sheng, Hu Han-min's cousin, was implicated in such a way as to cancel Hu Han-min's usefulness in party activities in China for the time being, even though he was totally exonerated. Accordingly, he dropped out of political affairs in China for a year and a half.

In this period he served as a KMT emissary to Russia to observe Soviet party affairs and to study social conditions. He also attended the Third Congress of the Comintern where he submitted an application for admission of the KMT to membership.

During Hu's absence, the KMT was fractured again by internal conflict. Late in 1925 an anti-leftist group of Central Executive Committee members seceded and held their own self-styled CEC session at the temporary resting site for Sun Yat-sen's coffin in the Western Hills near Peking. They charged their former party colleagues with betraying Sun's principles and with selling out to the Russian advisors. They claimed for themselves the mantle of Sun Yat-sen.

Soon after, in January 1926, the Second National Congress of the KMT was convened at Canton. With Hu Han-min still in Europe, Wang Ching-wei and his left-wing associates largely controlled deliberations and major decisions. Wang and his appointees also took most of the party posts. Still, Hu was reelected in absentia to both the CEC and its Standing Committee and to the Central Political Council.

Hu Han-min took no part in the Northern Expedition which, under Chiang's leadership, brought the KMT into the cities of the Yangtze valley in late 1926 and early 1927. Hu returned to China in April 1926 while the campaign was underway, but illness forced him to remain quietly in Shanghai. A year later, in April 1927, Hu joined colleagues in plans to purge Communists from the party following Chiang's break with the Communists in early April.

When Nanking was made the new capital of the southern government, Hu Han-min was again named to high party and government posts: chairman of the Central Party headquarters, chairman of the Central Political Council, and chairman of the National Government. With this authority, he issued orders for the arrest of Borodin, the Russian advisor to the left-wing Wuhan faction, along with some two hundred members of the Communist party in a show-down struggle for unification of the party and for conservative control of the KMT movement. In mid-August 1927 Hu Han-min returned to Shanghai together with Chiang Kai-shek and other conservative leaders after only four months as chairman of the government and embarked on another European tour the following January. While passing through Singapore he narrowly escaped with his life as his party was attacked by alleged Communists aiming to assassinate Hu. They succeeded only in wounding one of his companions.

Thus Hu was once again out of the country at a crucial stage in KMT development, namely, the completion of the Northern Campaign. Chiang co-ordinated the assault which led to Peking's capitulation in June 1928 and then turned to preparations for inaugurating the new five-power Nationalist government at Nanking in the fall.

Hu Han-min returned to Nanking in September in 1928 in time to accept appointment as head of the Legislative Yüan, one of the five major organs of government in Sun Yat-sen's scheme of distributed power in the new Chinese republic. From the inauguration of the Republican Nationalist Government in October until he resigned his government post in February 1931, Hu Han-min found himself more and more overtly opposing policies adopted by Chiang and other KMT leaders. The sharpest conflict centered in the decision taken by the government in 1930 to call a national assembly and promulgate a provisional constitution. Hu resolutely held that this decision violated Sun Yat-sen's guidelines for political development in China. Sun had clearly specified that a period of careful tutelage by the party while the country learned at local levels how to conduct republican government was indispensable to success. Only after an initial era of party dictatorship could the nation be prepared for a constitutional order. To ignore Sun's prescriptions, in Hu Han-min's view, was to court political disaster. When he found he was arguing to no avail, he broke with Chiang Kai-shek and resigned.

Chiang retaliated by restraining Hu Han-min under house arrest near Nanking and thereby triggered a sequence of anti-Chiang moves. Four well-known members of the Central Supervisory Committee of the party issued an angry statement against the illegal treatment of Hu Han-min and called for Chiang's impeachment. Other leading party and military figures supported the statement and took steps near the end of May to set up a secessionist government, once again, at Canton. As this conflict moved toward crisis, the Japanese attack in Manchuria in September 1931 suddenly diverted attention and energies sufficiently to relieve hostilities. The sharpest disagreements were resolved through conferences, Hu Han-min was released, and the movement for a separate government disbanded.

Hu Han-min returned to his native Kwangtung and took up residence at Hong Kong. Separatist sentiment which was still strong in the South took organized form in the so-called Southwest Branch Political Council and the Southwest Executive Headquarters of the KMT, both at Canton, under which the provinces of Kwangtung and Kwangsi maintained virtual autonomy. While Hu was not officially associated with these organs, he maintained interest in them and lent them the prestige of his moral support. Possibly because of his prominence and his continuing unequivocal opposition to Chiang's leadership at Nanking, Hu Han-min's name became linked to the famous November 1933 Fukien revolt. This uprising led by dissident Nationalist—mainly military—figures aimed to weaken Nanking by building a separate People's Government based in Fukien. It survived only a matter of weeks. Hu vigorously and publicly disavowed any connection with the movement.

During Hu Han-min's absence on another European trip in 1935, the Fifth National Congress of the Kuomintang once again elected him to membership on the Central Executive Committee. This action was followed by an earnest invitation from the party in early 1936 to return to Nanking for a warm welcome to the inner circle of political confreres. He said that he would return, but the intention was never realized because he died on May 12, 1936 at Canton. Two months later he was buried with the full honors of a state funeral.

II

When we turn to Hu Han-min's thought, we find few signs of revolutionary flamboyance or of the revolutionist's vision of better things. Hu's main role, in his own view, was to serve as Sun Yat-sen's faithful scribe while he lived and to gather his writings for posterity after Sun's death. Hu's aspirations for China and his views of China's recent history and problems seem to have been largely those of his leader and intellectual mentor. Like Sun, he sought for political order in place of chaos, for modern republicanism in place of Manchu despotism, for an end to militarism, for national prestige among the powerful states of the world. As these changes materialized, they would lighten burdens on the backs of peasant masses. But Hu at no time tried to reach the masses, to organize them, to lead them in seizing these ends by mass violence. Clearly, he had used violence, had helped to plan it, and had led insurrectionary militia. But our picture here is of an intellectual leading selected followers, with probably little taste and even less ability for leading the masses.

Before 1911, the language of the revolution was harsh and sentiments were bitter against an alien and moribund dynasty. But after 1912 and until Hu's death, both the ideas and the sentiments of the revolutionists lost their focus. The main visible object of their attack was gone. And a more diffuse and less visible set of targets took its place. The end of the dynasty had not brought panacea. Yüan Shih-k'ai was abusing his new authority in Peking. Militarism was rampant over large sections of the country. Leaders among the republicans—erstwhile revolutionaries—could not agree on major goals and strategies. Following Sun's death still deeper divisions fractured the movement as new coalitions of left, right, and center emerged reflecting different views of what the Leader intended to do or might have done had he lived.

After 1911–12 Hu Han-min found more opportunities for reflective writing than before. There were periods of intensive political activity when he was carrying out Sun's orders and coping with Kwangtung provincial politics. But there were quieter intervals in Shanghai and elsewhere when he turned to the kind of writing of which, in a less turbulent career, he probably would have done much more. As essayist and journalist, much of his work was either hortatory or polemic, or consisted of journalistic records of events. But his work included, also, extensive analyses and evaluations of Western political thought.

Hu appears not to have been a systematic thinker. Nor did he show much breadth of vision. Possibly some of the rigidity in his personal make-up was reflected in the unimaginative and inflexible qualities of his mind. Still, because he was one of the more articulate followers of Sun in the revolutionary movement, we rely on his writings for insight into some of the philosophy and values of the revolutionaries. It should be pointed out that the following observations are taken principally from Hu's writings after Sun Yat-sen's death in 1925 when, presumably, he was heavily conscious of his responsibility to perpetuate his master's precepts and to demonstrate their validity in the light of competing values.

When the Canton government was reorganized in July 1925, Hu Han-min discussed certain features of its foreign policy. He broadly attacked imperialism and the unequal treaties in phraseology that reappeared in Kuomintang pronouncements over the next two decades. Foreign interests were guilty, he declared, of supporting militarists in China who impeded reconstruction and the building of peace. "The abolition of unequal treaties," Hu said, "will at once cut the vicious roots which have been supporting and nourishing all our evils. . . . Our militarism, deprived of foreign support, will crumble to pieces, thus giving the people the chance of establishing real democracy." In another setting, he attributed the thwarting of Dr. Sun's revolutionary goals of fourteen years (since 1911) to militarism and imperialism which supported and utilized each other.

On dealing with other nations, China should reserve its alliances only for those countries that would treat China as an equal and would oppose imperialism. As for enemies, Hu said, the two requirements for China were to know its enemies and to show no fear. To achieve fearlessness and confidence, China needed to develop economic independence from the outside world—which included Hong Kong.

A persistent theme in Hu's speeches and articles was communism and its relation to China. Soon after Sun's death, Hu Han-min stated publicly and vigorously that China had no inclination toward the communist system. If Russian leaders acknowledged that it would require hundreds of years under communism to perfect their country, China under the Three People's Principles would not be emulating the communist system. Moreover, because the Communists in China had adopted the Kuomintang program—not vice versa—the Chinese government could have no interest in practicing communism. Relations with the Russian state were desirable because Russia looked upon China as an equal.

However, Hu Han-min acknowledged that the National Revolution in China was indebted to Russia, at least for operational guidelines. A address entitled "Impressions of the Russian October Revolution" which Hu made in Russia in early 1926 and which was publicized in China in May 1927 outlined four ways in which the revolutions were related. First, the Russian Revolution and the Third International had spurred the Chinese masses to rise against their oppressors and to overcome the interests of Western imperialists who sought to discourage rebellion. Second, Chinese peasants and workers had learned how to think of themselves and how to co-operate from the Russian experience. Third, they had learned the importance of discipline among themselves and the indispensability of a tighty organized party. Finally, the Chinese had learned how to organize and train a political army, to make the party the head of the army while the army become the arm of the party, and to create an army that served rather than oppressed the people. Clearly, Hu was pointing here to techniques and strategies China had adapted to its needs more than social and political philosophy. Nevertheless, he concluded this speech to the Russians with the customary oratorical flourish: "Russian socialism, *wan-sui* (long live Russian socialism); world liberation of oppressed peoples, *wan-sui;* worldwide cooperation of workers and peasants, *wan-sui;* revolutionary Marxism, *wan-sui;* Leninism, *wan-sui;* Sun Yat-senism, *wan-sui!*"

The deep ambivalence in Sun Yat-sen's attitude toward his Soviet associates generally pervaded the Chinese revolutionary movement. In the early months of the Kuomintang regime at Nanking in the fall of 1928, Hu bitterly charged the Soviet advisors and their Chinese colleagues with trying to wreck the Kuomintang and China for their own petty ends. At the same time he was openly commending the organizational competence of the Communists, advocating the same kind of strong discipline and secrecy for the Kuomintang. As for ideology, Hu Han-min was calling attention to the close similarity between the *min-sheng* (people's livelihood) principle of Dr. Sun's Three Principles and communism. Communism was no more than *min-sheng;* and *min-sheng* was the implementing of communism.

In a long essay on "The Interrelatedness of the Three People's Principles" published in December 1928 Hu Han-min disclosed some of the basic components of his political and social thought together with characteristic theoretical structures holding them in meaningful relationship. He introduced this essay by defining some of his most frequently used terms and concepts. Imperialism, he began, was the target of revolution inasmuch as it comprised three anti-revolutionary forces—militarism, capitalism, and bureaucratism. These were three modern guises of the ancient evil of individualism which had been the scourge of mankind. These were the modern devices by which some men sought to dominate and control other men. Militarism was the most direct means of seizing power. Religion, nationalism, economic advantage were all used to reinforce military exploitation.

Capitalism was another form of power through control of property. Property itself was not evil, but in the hands of capitalists it became a means for dominating other men, for gratifying personal satisfactions, and its use was not available for the welfare of all.

Bureaucratism or "officialism" was another form of the same evil—people's urge for power, authority, and rewards. In conservative quarters in many of the major professions—among lawyers, teachers, preachers, philanthropists, even journalists—these tendencies toward militaristic, capitalistic, bureaucratic domination were generally to be found. Across the face of the world these forces had reinforced and supported each other until their power was well entrenched.

Returning to his concept of imperialism as the crystallization of these three evils, Hu pointed out that imperialism ran through history like a river, with some people always dominating others. Mercantilism had preceded imperialism in pre-industrial Europe. Imperialism developed more fully after the Industrial Revolution, the white man justifying himself, always, in forcibly subduing other races when his enterprise required it.

These anti-revolutionary forces were older than revolutionary forces, in Hu's view. But revolution had been stirring among half the world's population for 300 years. Of the great upheavals—English, American, French, Russian, German, Turkish, and Chinese —the Chinese was, of course, the first in East Asia. Moreover, it surpassed the American, French, and Russian revolutions not only in destroying a monarchist tyranny but in developing adequate ideas and programs for carrying out the Three People's Principles.

Hu Han-min found in Sun's ideas both very great range and diversity. They related meaningfully to most of the main currents of thought then to be found in China, whether those currents originated in China or in the West. In this study, for example, Hu showed that the Three Principles disclosed fresh insights into the prevailing views of international relations, of anarchism and of communism. With regard to inter-state relations, the Three Principles upheld the struggle to deter war, to improve international order, and to oppose capitalism. Further, the Principles supported the view that the world should be free of boundaries of all kinds, class conflicts, and wars. Self-determination should apply to all peoples. World government in some form should be established.

As for Marx and his vision of a communist order, Hu Han-min dismissed him as an unscientific utopian. He had gathered his facts from European history to show with allegedly scientific reliability how history moved forward through successive stages of class struggle. But Hu contended that Marx was in fact subjective in his treatment of history and indulged in utopian prophecy more than in scientific social analysis.

Several of Marx's forecasts about the direction of social change were wrong. He was mistaken about proletarian solidarity across national lines in World War I because, according to Hu Han-min, he misunderstood nationalism. He was mistaken about revolutions in the most advanced capitalist nations. Hu believed the root of Marx's error lay in the latter's wrong, or at least distorted, view of historical materialism and the class struggle. Marx called these the causes of social change and progress. Sun Yat-sen, on the other hand, understood correctly that class struggle was not a cause but a by-product.

The cause of social progress was in reality the search or striving for existence (*ch'iu-sheng*) while the economic factors that preoccupied Marx were of secondary importance.

In any event, the Russian Revolution, Hu pointed out, had strayed from Marxist principles. Moreover, Lenin knew that he was violating them. The New Economic Policy bore little resemblance to communism but achieved its purposes and, in principle, represented a step in the direction of *min-sheng*, Sun's concept of the People's Livelihood.

In his critique of Marxism Hu Han-min emphasized Marx's failure to develop his vision of the millennium which led to division among his followers. Kautsky, for instance, saw the revolution taking one direction; Lenin quite another.

Hu summed up this portion of his study on the Principles' interrelatedness by stating that communism in the last analysis comprised anarchism, Marxism, and the Three People's Principles. More than the creation of Marx's mind, it was a fundamental aspiration of humanity long embedded in human experience but not interpreted into practical human application until Sun Yat-sen devised his Three Principles.

In a final chapter of the essay on "The World of the Three People's Principles" Hu Han-min drew two conclusion from this analysis. First, there were close similarities between the objectives of nationalism, anarchism, and communism on the one hand and that of the Three Principles on the other, namely, a world without divisions or classes in which everyone "had, controlled, and enjoyed" the good things of life. Second, Sun's Principles stated the only really comprehensive goal for the people; that is, that while they could not hold complete political power themselves or fully possess and control the distribution of natural resources, they should have full equality in the opportunity for self-development in all fields. The Three Principles were also superior in showing the practical political and economic means to achieve the goal. Politically, the method was democratic—though not the discredited representative system of the West. Sun advocated direct democracy. On the economic side, the Three Principles called generally for public ownership of land and resources and for public planning in the productive and distributive processes. But here, as elsewhere, Hu Hanmin stressed the principle of relatedness and interdependence between the public agencies and the people in carrying out these processes.

Some years later—in 1933 when he was living in Hong Kong—Hu Han-min again turned to the topic of the relation between Marxism and Sun Yat-senism. He explained that he had translated the last two volumes of Max Beer's five-volume *General History of Socialism and Social Struggles* in 1926 to provide Chinese intellectuals with a more adequate explication of the method of historical materialism than was then available. There was much interest in materialism but only at a superficial level. He also wished to stress the clear contrast between the concepts in Beer's work and Sun Yat-sen's. Sun demonstrated that the central fact in history was man's relentless striving for existence. The class struggle so central to Marxist thought accounted for much strife but was not the heart or core of history. Hu Han-min identified himself with Sun in not totally rejecting Marxist theory. Both Hu Han-min and Sun found some truth among both the materialists and the idealists. Any developed system that is consistent within itself, he noted, lays claim to absolute truth, but from a standpoint outside the systems truth is relative. Lenin himself subscribed to this view realizing that science was continuously adding to knowledge and thus changing the boundaries of truth. Hence materialism was not an absolute. It was often useful in Beer's type of analysis, but it failed to define the force behind social evolution. Not materialism but the struggle for existence supplied that energy. Sun Yat-sen found this to be true at all levels—individuals, families, societies, nations, races were all seeking survival. He refined the concept further by pointing out that the struggle revolved around two major needs, namely, food and defense. From the demand for food stemmed our complex modern economies and production systems. From the need for defense had grown modern political and military systems including modern imperialism. Hu argued that the features of the Marxist models of society were in fact only instruments for men's use in the struggle for food and defense.

Hu Han-min then turned to a consideration of "moral principles and human desires" as they are to be found in Neo-Confucianism, Mo Ti's counsel of simplicity, and in Socrates', Plato's, and Aristotle's reliance on knowledge and the intellect to control desires. He referred also to the Hedonists and Ascetics, to Kant, the Utilitarians, and others in developing the general argument that the realm of "matter" which is so central to the economic determinists is really only secondary to the non-material energies and drives that are fundamental to Sun's concept of striving for life.

In Bertrand Russell's critique of Marx in his *Bolshevism: Practice and Theory,* Hu Han-min found support for his position. Russell, in Hu's interpretation, charged the Marxists with ignoring the influence of nationalism and religion in the shaping of cultures along with formative economic forces. Russell also found the insights of modern psychology relevant to an analysis of social forces. Hu said that he agreed with many of Russell's observations.

Hu Han-min closed his discussion by acknowledging that ten years before he had relied upon the same materialist principles that certain young people were currently using to explain China's past. As he had noted earlier, his purpose in translating Beer's work was to assist social analysts in applying the tools of the materialist school to better effect. While the theory and method of the Three People's Principles were, in his view, correct, other theories could nevertheless enhance one's understanding of the Three Principles themselves.

While these selections represent only a fraction of Hu Han-min's writing, they at least support tentative judgments about the intellectual capacity and style of this leading Republican revolutionist. The first observation is that Hu was manifestly strongly committed to defending and supporting his mentor's position—the thought of Sun Yat-sen—against the ideological claims of the Communists. Briefly put, whatever there was in Marxism that might serve China's interests had already occurred to Sun, had been articulated more effectively, and had been developed in more universalistic philosophic terms. Hu did not argue the case on the strategic or tactical level nor did he assert the merit of republican or democratic values or of communist values. It was simply a self-evident matter of the supremacy of Sun Yat-senism over Marxism in understanding the needs of the Chinese people and prescribing accurately and sympathetically for the meeting of those needs.

The other observation is that the thought of this key ideologue of the revolutionary movement seems to disclose little rigorous intellectual discipline or systematic examination and analysis of ideas. Such essential concepts as *ch'iu-sheng* and materialism, for instance, were given no precise meanings; indeed, Hu appears to have tried neither for concreteness nor precision in this kind of discourse. It had the appearance of erudition in its sweeping references to classical Western thought, and it had appealing stylistic qualities. But it was not tied directly to the hard political facts Hu Han-min knew at first hand as a revolutionist. Possibly this was the indispensable role for an ideologue in the circumstances of the Republican Revolution of 1911 and the National Revolution of the 1920's—to argue persuasively for the correctness of the leader's thought and for his infallibility as a revolutionary strategist while relating the movement in only a general way to major currents of reformist and social thought in other parts of the world.

BIBLIOGRAPHICAL NOTE: Through the kindness of Howard L. Boorman, editor of the *Biographical Dictionary of Republican China,* and the Columbia University Press, I was able to read the entry on Hu Han-min before its publication in the dictionary. Hu Han-min edited a five-volume collection of Sun Yat-sen's writings, *Tsung-li ch'üan-chi* (1930). He also wrote extensively on Sun's political thought in the journal, *San-min-chu-i yüeh-k'an* (Three People's Principles Monthly), which Hu founded in early 1933. His major work on the Three People's Principles was, of course, *San-min-chu-i ti lien-huan hsing* (The Chained Relations of the Three People's Principles) (Shanghai, 1928). In two issues of *Chien-she* (Reconstruction), October and November 1919, Hu Han-min presented a sympathetic two-part treatment of the materialist view of history which Professor Benjamin Schwartz describes as more thorough than anything to be found in the writings of the Marxist intellectuals, Ch'en Tu-hsiu and Li Ta-chao. A collection of his speeches, *Hu Han-min yen-chiang-chi,* was published in Shanghai, 1927. An English collection of his *Selected Documents and Addresses* was published in Canton, in 1925. His personality and character were revealed in his daughter's reminiscences published in the *Chung-yang jih-pao* (Central Daily News), Taipei, February 8, 1969.

❧ 11 ❧

Wang Ching-wei:
A Political Profile

HOWARD L. BOORMAN

Man's addiction to wishful thinking and uninhibited hindsight makes it hardly surprising that the history of any people tends to be a volatile blend of myth and reality. In China the triumph of Mao Tse-tung and the Communists at mid-century has obscured earlier developments, even as the apparent triumph of Chiang Kai-shek and the Nationalists in the nineteen-thirties blurred earlier chapters in the evolution of the Chinese nationalist movement. *Ex post facto,* the accomplished fact masquerades as inevitable conclusion, predestined and foregone. The fiction of inevitability is most clearly shown in Peking's version of modern Chinese history, a never-never land where relationships between economic forces and social classes allegedly define all political alternatives, mold all historical patterns, and preclude the need for independent assessment of causation.[1]

Actually men, as well as ideas, institutions, and accidents, shape history. And in China it is notable that one individual, who a generation ago ranked as one of the most prominent figures of the republican period, is already obscured, his memory shrouded by both Nationalists and Communists with the darkest of drapes, that of "national traitor." The man is Wang Ching-wei. For nearly forty

Reprinted with revisions by the author and permission from the *Political Science Quarterly,* Vol. LXXXIX, No. 4 (December 1964), pp. 504–25.

[1] Ho Kan-chih, *A History of the Modern Chinese Revolution* (Peking, 1959) gives an official version of recent Chinese history from 1919 to 1956.

years, from 1905 until his death in 1944, Wang's energy, magnetism, and vitality served to leave his personal imprint on the political history of twentieth-century China. During the early, secret-society phase of the modern Chinese nationalist movement, he was an eloquent spokesman for Sun Yat-sen's cause and became a national hero when he risked his life in 1910 in a bold attempt to assassinate the Manchu prince regent at Peking. Wang remained close to Sun Yat-sen after the 1911 revolution and was a member of his most intimate political circle when Sun died in 1925. During the decade between 1927 and 1937, Wang steadily feuded with Chiang Kai-shek for top authority in the Kuomintang, the ruling political party in Nationalist China. Following the outbreak of the Sino-Japanese War, Wang left Chungking and, after an attempt on his life at Hanoi in 1939, moved to Japanese-occupied territory. There he ended his career as head of a puppet regime established at Nanking in 1940, apparently believing that he could best serve China's national interests through collaboration rather than resistance.

The golden boy of Chinese nationalism at the time of the anti-Manchu coup of 1911, Wang Ching-wei was a many-sided man: a handsome, perennially youthful,[2] romantic poet in quest of China's quintessential soul, and a self-styled political realist who hoped to ensure China's safety and security by emulating Sun Yat-sen's persistent tendency to look first to Japan for aid in time of need.[3] Wang Ching-wei's claim to realism is dubious, for his public career was a monument to miscalculation, poor timing, and exiguous foresight. It is rather as political romantic that Wang Ching-wei may best be remembered, republican China's classic case of the man who perished more for his follies than for his sins. Twenty years after

[2] Wang's youthful appearance and personal allure were legendary in republican China; even after his death, some elderly female hearts in China and Hong Kong beat faster when his name was mentioned. An excellent photograph of Wang in his prime appears in T'ang Leang-li ed., *Reconstruction in China: A Record of Progress and Achievement in Facts and Figures* (Shanghai, 1935), following p. 12.

[3] The most detailed study of this theme is Marius B. Jansen, *The Japanese and Sun Yat-sen* (Cambridge, Mass., 1954).

his death, it is appropriate to attempt to place Wang within the context of twentieth-century Chinese political history.[4]

I

Born on May 4, 1883, at Canton, bustling hub of China's great southern province of Kwangtung, Wang Ching-wei[5] is customarily viewed by his compatriots as a Cantonese, though in fact his ancestral home was at Shao-hsing in Chekiang, the native province of Chiang Kai-shek. During the Ch'ing period (1644–1912) Chekiang was culturally one of the most cultivated areas in the empire,[6] and Wang's father, Wang Shu, was a native of one of Chekiang's most advanced prefectures. For financial reasons, Wang Shu moved south to Kwangtung to take a post as legal secretary, personally employed by an official of the imperial civil service.[7] The youngest of ten children, Wang Ching-wei received his childhood education in the Chinese classics, studying at home under his father's tutelage. The boy's ethical and aesthetic standards during his formative years were conventionally Chinese, his later reminiscences referring particularly to the philosophy of Wang Yang-ming (1472–1529) and

[4] There is no satisfactory critical biography of Wang Ching-wei in either Chinese or English. T'ang Leang-li, *Wang Ching-wei: A Political Biography* (Peiping, 1931) is an adulatory account by a close associate; Don Bate, *Wang Ching-wei: Puppet or Patriot?* (Chicago, 1941) is a sympathetic but superficial journalistic profile. Professor James R. Shirley of Northern Illinois University has dealt with all except the final period of Wang's career in a dissertation prepared for the department of history at the University of California, Berkeley. For the present, bibliographical guidance to some basic Chinese and Western-language sources is given, respectively, in Eugene Wu, *Leaders of Twentieth-Century China* (Stanford, 1956) and T. L. Yuan, *China in Western Literature* (New Haven, 1958).

[5] Wang's given name was Chao-ming. Ching-wei is actually his *tzu,* or courtesy name, which he adopted in 1905 when he assumed his first public position as editor of the *Min-pao* in Japan.

[6] For discussion of the position of Chekiang during the Ch'ing period, see Ping-ti Ho, *The Ladder of Success in Imperial China: Aspects of Social Mobility, 1368–1911* (New York, 1962), Chap. 6.

[7] A description of the system is given in the section on "Private Secretaries" in T'ung-tsu Ch'ü, *Local Government in China under the Ch'ing* (Cambridge, Mass., 1962), 93–115.

to the poetry of T'ao Ch'ien (365–427) and Lu Yu (1125–1210). Like other sensitive young Chinese growing up in the eighteen-nineties, Wang Ching-wei's reading of Chinese history made him impatient of China's weakness and resentful of the alien dynasty then ruling at Peking.

Penury was a constant dimension to life in the Wang family, since his father was in straitened circumstances and forced to continue working until he was over seventy. "It was a poor and miserable life," Wang later wrote.[8] A rapid series of deaths left the family financial situation especially precarious at this time. Wang's father died when the boy was about fourteen. The mother had passed away a year earlier, and two of his three elder brothers died soon thereafter. Wang was admitted to one of the Canton academies in 1898, working as a tutor at the same time to help support the family. He also continued to study independently with the help of an uncle's well-stocked library and in 1903 was able to pass the Kwangtung provincial examination and to gain a government scholarship for study in Japan the following year. Modernizing Meiji Japan opened new vistas for Wang Ching-wei, even as militarized Showa Japan played an important role in his political life a generation later. In Tokyo he found a congenial group of fellow Cantonese students, including Hu Han-min and others destined to become prominent in the politics of republican China. He learned the Japanese language rapidly, supplemented his government stipend by doing translations, and studied constitutional law and political theory at the Tokyo Law College, obtaining his degree in 1906.

Before graduation, however, he joined the new Chinese patriotic society, the T'ung Meng Hui, formed in Japan in 1905 by Sun Yat-sen, Huang Hsing, and other anti-Manchu activists.[9] Elected chairman of one of the three key councils of the T'ung Meng Hui, Wang, then twenty-two, began his close personal association with

[8] Wang offers a brief description of his childhood in his autobiographical memoir in *Tung-fang tsa-chih* (Eastern Miscellany), XXXI (1934), 1–3.

[9] The most perceptive biography of Sun Yat-sen is still that by Lyon Sharman, *Sun Yat-sen: His Life and Its Meaning* (New York, 1934). On Huang Hsing, see Chün-tu Hsüeh, *Huang Hsing and the Chinese Revolution* (Stanford, 1961).

Sun Yat-sen, seventeen years his senior. In the Chinese student communities of Tokyo and Yokohama, Wang Ching-wei first established his reputation as a brilliant polemicist.[10] In November 1905 the pro-republican group in Japan established the *Min-pao,* its official propaganda organ designed to disseminate Sun Yat-sen's precepts and to promote anti-Manchu sentiment.[11] Its principal political competitor in Japan was another refugee group, led by K'ang Yu-wei and Liang Ch'i-ch'ao, which advocated constitutional monarchy for China. Wang Ching-wei wrote the leading article in the premier issue of *Min-pao* (November 20, 1905), and soon proved himself an eloquent controversialist in a literary duel with Liang Ch'i-ch'ao. Drawing upon theories absorbed at the Law College, Wang waxed in stature as an interpreter of "nationalism," later canonized as the first of Sun Yat-sen's Three People's Principles. Forced to leave Japan in 1907, Sun, accompanied by Hu Han-min and Wang Ching-wei, moved to Southeast Asia to expand the T'ung Meng Hui organization and to enlist political and financial support in the overseas Chinese communities. There Wang continued to demonstrate his talents not only as forceful journalist but also as persuasive public speaker on behalf of a political movement which had as yet won scant success in the effort to rid China of Manchu rule. Wang's oratorical brilliance, a quality for which he remained well known throughout his public career, played an important role in attracting new overseas Chinese support to the T'ung Meng Hui and in establishing new branches, the most important of which were in Singapore and Penang.

[10] A more cynical account by a contemporary who later became a Communist depicts the youthful Wang as a gay deceiver, eloquent and attractive on the surface, but underneath a "spineless man, irresolute, easy to change." See Wu Yü-chang, *The Revolution of 1911* (Peking, 1962), 80. Wu Yü-chang (1878–1966), began his career as intellectual radical during the late years of the imperial period and ended his life in Peking, where he was regarded as a prestigious elder statesman of the Communist party of China.

[11] Peking has rendered a valuable service to Western scholars by reprinting the complete text of the *Min-pao* in four volumes (Peking, 1957). The two articles by Wang Ching-wei referred to here are *Min-tsu te kuo-min* (A Nationalistic People), No. 1, pp. 1–31, and No. 2, pp. 1–23, and *Lun ko-ming chih ch'u-shih* (On the Revolutionary Current), No. 25, pp. 1–19, and No. 26, pp. 1–20.

When Sun Yat-sen left Singapore for Europe in 1909, Wang returned to Japan. There he edited a short-lived clandestine edition of the revived *Min-pao,* ostensibly published in Paris by young Chinese anarchists sympathetic to Sun but actually printed underground in Tokyo. The Chinese revolutionaries in Japan were then greatly influenced by the ideas of Russian anarchists, many of whom had fled to Japan after the failure of the Russian revolution of 1905. Wang Ching-wei's editorial tone in this period was thus distinctly militant. In the February 1, 1910 issue of *Min-pao,* he wrote a fiery discourse, "On the Revolutionary Current," advocating assassination to spark the overthrow of the dynasty. During the 1907–10 period, the T'ung Meng Hui had suffered a series of setbacks. Six revolutionary attempts had been suppressed by the Ch'ing government and had resulted only in the arrest and execution of the leaders. In addition to these failures, the T'ung Meng Hui itself was faced with an internal crisis, as two prominent members, Chang Ping-lin and T'ao Ch'eng-chang, had challenged the authority of Sun Yat-sen's leadership. The prospects of the republican revolutionary cause were hardly bright. It was at this juncture that Wang Ching-wei decided to stimulate the movement by drastic measures. He decided to sacrifice himself for the good of both party and nation. Thus he journeyed incognito to Peking early in 1910 and led an attempt to assassinate the Prince Regent Ts'ai-feng by placing a massive bomb under a bridge over which the prince was scheduled to pass. An error on the part of the conspirators upset the plot and aroused the police, who combed the city and apprehended Wang in April 1910. When interrogated, Wang freely admitted his identity and voiced his hope that this sensational act, if consummated in the imperial capital, would arouse the Chinese people to revolution. The Manchu authorities were struck by Wang's forthright stand and courageous bearing; but, more important, the weak position of the dynasty during its final days led the Prince Regent to attempt to placate the revolutionaries by bestowing benevolence on political criminals. Thus Wang was only imprisoned, though he himself had been prepared for execution and a martyr's death. When released in the wake of the Wuchang revolt in October 1911, Wang found himself a national hero at twenty-eight.[12]

Despite his spectacular start, Wang remained aloof from Chinese politics after the establishment of the republic, possibly influenced by anarchist ideas then found in some emancipated intellectual circles.[13] In 1912 he was an active figure in organizing a Society for the Promotion of Virtue, dedicated to the propositions that basic social reform had to accompany political change and that China, if she were truly to build a new society, had first to create a new morality. That same year he was one of the organizers of the movement to encourage and help Chinese students to go to France for a combined work-and-study program. Wang himself sought new integration in marriage. His bride was Ch'en Pi-chün, daughter of a prosperous overseas Chinese family from Penang and an ardent admirer of the dashing young revolutionary in his T'ung Meng Hui days. Following the marriage, Wang left China on a wedding trip to the Straits Settlements and Europe. He then spent the years of the First World War in France, intermittently involved with the training of Chinese students there but quite uninvolved with political maneuverings at home. His relation to China during this interlude of comparative leisure and detachment was rather at the literary level. Wang was a member of the Southern Society, a group including many former T'ung Meng Hui members and significant as the major society advocating and using traditional literary forms during the early republican period. Although he was a radical nationalist intellectually, Wang's connection with the Southern Society exposed the romantic stratum in his personality. His poetry, collected as the *Shuang-chao-lou shih-chi,* reveals an aspect of the man which

[12] Official Kuomintang accounts of the 1910 assassination attempt may be found in Feng Tzu-yu, *Chung-hua-min-kuo k'ai-kuo ch'ien ko-ming shih* (History of the Revolution Before the Establishment of the Republic) (Shanghai, 1946), II, Chap. 50, 230–55 and Tsou Lu, *Chung-kuo Kuo-min-tang shih-kao* (Draft History of the Kuomintang) (Chungking, 1944), III, Chap. 21, 784–95.

[13] See Robert A. Scalapino and George T. Yu, *The Chinese Anarchist Movement* (Berkeley, 1961).

is sensitive, contemplative, oriented to nature in the classical Chinese manner.[14] Its style and serenity stand in marked contrast to the political tumult which dominated his later career.

Wang returned to China late in 1917 and joined Sun Yat-sen, who was then in Canton leading an organized opposition regime and attempting to rally independent military strength. During the next seven years Wang was a member of the personal entourage serving Sun as he sought new theoretical and organizational formulae to guide the nationalist cause. The patriotic outburst stemming from the May Fourth Movement of 1919, combined with Sun Yat-sen's contacts with Soviet representatives in China after the Bolshevik Revolution, led in 1922–23 to Sun's decision to collaborate with the infant, Comintern-dominated Communist party of China.[15] While he played no direct role in the negotiations leading to the alliance between the Chinese nationalist movement and Soviet communism, Wang occupied a prominent political position at Canton. At the First National Congress of the Kuomintang in January 1924, when the party was reorganized on Leninist lines, he was elected second-ranking member of the Central Executive Committee, following Hu Han-min in the number of votes received.

National unification remained Sun Yat-sen's primary objective, and late in 1924 he made a final journey northward to confer with the men holding power at Peking: Chang Tso-lin, Feng Yü-hsiang, and Tuan Ch'i-jui. Sun's group left Canton in November, with Wang Ching-wei accompanying the party leader and serving as his confidential secretary. From Shanghai Sun proceeded to the north via Japan—a constantly recurring stop on his political peregrinations —while Wang went directly by rail to Tientsin to work out arrangements for the talks. Sun Yat-sen arrived in north China at the end of the year, only to discover that Tuan Ch'i-jui, then the Chief Executive in Peking, had no intention of permitting either Sun or

[14] The volume takes its name from the name of Wang's studio, *Shuang-chao-lou*. A sampling of Wang's poetry in English translation is given in *Poems of Wang Ching-wei* (London, 1938).

[15] See Tse-tsung Chow, *The May Fourth Movement: Intellectual Revolution in Modern China* (Cambridge, Mass., 1960) and Shao-ch'uan Leng and Norman D. Palmer, *Sun Yat-sen and Communism* (New York, 1960).

the Kuomintang to interfere in the operation of the new regime there. Sun's health was then rapidly deteriorating, and in January 1925 he was admitted to the hospital of the Peking Union Medical College with cancer. After two decades of association with Sun Yat-sen, Wang Ching-wei was the most senior and trusted Kuomintang leader then in Peking.[16] Except for Sun's young second wife, Soong Ch'ing-ling, and his son, Sun Fo, probably no individual was closer to the dying man. On February 24, Wang drafted Sun's final political testament, or will, a brief injunction to Sun's followers to carry the national revolution through to completion in accordance with the principles set forth in his major writings. This document Sun signed on March 11, 1925, the day before his death.[17]

II

The demise of Sun Yat-sen, who had become the unchallenged symbol and leader of the Chinese nationalist movement, closed an era in twentieth-century China's political history. Within the Kuomintang that event precipitated a period of competition for personal influence and political authority. After Sun Yat-sen's death in March 1925, it appeared that Wang Ching-wei would succeed to Sun's position as Leader of the Kuomintang, though Hu Han-min and Liao Chung-k'ai were also contenders for the honor. Wang appeared to consolidate his supremacy when he was elected chairman of the new National Government formed at Canton in July 1925. The assassination of Liao Chung-k'ai[18] in August placed him in an even more advantageous position, for Hu Han-min was vicariously involved in that incident and had to resign his post in the party. Thus two of Wang's political rivals were removed from competition.

Chiang Kai-shek, another rival of Wang's, was relatively junior

[16] Hu Han-min had remained in the south as governor of Kwangtung, with full authority at Canton.

[17] A discussion of the circumstances of Sun's death and final will is given in Jerome Ch'en, "The Left Wing Kuomintang—a Definition," *Bulletin of the School of Oriental and African Studies,* University of London, XXV, Part 3 (1962), 557–63.

[18] Liao Chung-k'ai (1878–1925) was also a native of Kwangtung province.

in experience in the Kuomintang, though he held a key military position at Canton. He was head of the newly founded Whampoa Military Academy, and commander of the First Front Army. With this control of military power, Chiang was in an increasingly strong position to rival Wang Ching-wei.

During his period of authority in 1925–26, Wang Ching-wei was regarded as a leader of the left-wing Kuomintang camp which advocated collaboration with the Communists, while Chiang Kai-shek was identified with more conservative interests. On March 20, 1926, in the so-called Chung-shan Incident, Chiang ordered the arrest of Communists under his command. While various interpretations have been placed on that incident, one element was Chiang's desire to erode the position of Wang Ching-wei and his supporters. A resolution of the meeting of the Kuomintang Central Executive Committee after the incident held that "in view of the present situation, the comrades of the left should temporarily retreat." Wang Ching-wei was thus forced to resign and left for France in May 1926.

Internecine personal strife inside the Kuomintang evolved within the larger context of the uneasy alliance between that party and the Chinese Communists, one of the more ambiguous sections of Sun Yat-sen's political legacy. The Nationalist-Communist entente, lasting from 1923 to 1927, marked a complex period, of political interest both because of the mutual antipathy of the partners and because of the effect which that alliance had on the political rise of the Nationalists. After the Nationalist military drive to unify China reached the Yangtze valley in central China, the Kuomintang was sufficiently split on the issue of continued collaboration with the Communists that two separate regimes emerged at the beginning of 1927: a right-wing group centered about Chiang Kai-shek at Nanking, and a left-wing group at Wuhan. As the breach between the two factions widened, the government at Wuhan, anxious to offset the growing military authority of Chiang Kai-shek, who had grown in power and prestige during the military push northward, called for the return of Wang Ching-wei from Europe. Wang, still distrustful of Chiang Kai-shek, arrived at Wuhan in April 1927 to become the dominant figure in the Left Kuomintang group then collaborating with the Communists.[19] Chiang broke the alliance with the Communists by launching a bloody coup at Shanghai in April. At Wuhan, Wang Ching-wei's co-operation with the Russian advisers and the Chinese Communists was also short-lived. In late May of 1927, it became clear to Wang that the Communists intended to follow a radical land policy and to maintain autonomous political positions: both policies which he regarded as contradictory to Sun Yat-sen's policies. Moreover, on July 1, M. N. Roy, the Comintern representative at Wuhan, indiscreetly informed Wang of Moscow's aggressive plans for China and the Chinese Revolution.[20] Wang thus severed relations with the Russian advisers and ordered the expulsion of Communists from both the government and the Kuomintang. From that point onward in his political career, Wang Ching-wei was firmly opposed to the Communists, for he regarded them as the major obstacle to national unification and economic reconstruction in China. For several months, the political stew in the Nationalist camp simmered. While all factions were now agreed on an anti-communist line, the clash of personalities continued. Wang believed that he should hold undisputed leadership over the Kuomintang but found himself increasingly harassed by sharp criticism from political antagonists in the party's right wing. Such criticism was particularly sharp at the time of the Communist-led Canton commune affair in December 1927, and Wang, disturbed at the turn of events, abruptly left Shanghai to return to France.

From 1928 to 1931, whether abroad or in China, Wang headed the "Association for Reorganization of the Kuomintang," a group within the Kuomintang which opposed the growing power of Chiang Kai-shek, and was thus denounced as heretical by Chiang's supporters.[21] Having consolidated power at Nanking in 1928, Chiang

---

[19] Detailed consideration of the "Left Kuomintang" group is given in the previously cited paper by Jerome Ch'en, 557–76.

[20] See Robert C. North and Xenia J. Eudin, *M. N. Roy's Mission to China: the Communist-Kuomintang Split of 1927* (Berkeley and Los Angeles, 1963).

[21] The most useful edition of Wang's writings for the period up to 1929 is *Wang Ching-wei chi* (Collected Works of Wang Ching-wei), 4 vols. (Shanghai, 1929). Many of Wang's political statements of the ensuing period

did exercise increasingly dictatorial power over both the National Government and the Kuomintang. This control was manifest at the Third National Congress of the Kuomintang, which met at Nanking in March 1929. Dominated by Chiang Kai-shek supporters, that congress leveled charges of political deviationism at Wang Ching-wei, who only four years earlier had been the senior Kuomintang leader with Sun Yat-sen at the time of his death, and expelled several of Wang's associates from the party. Wang Ching-wei's opposition to Nanking's authority did, however, evoke response from several military leaders dissatisfied with Chiang Kai-shek's policies, suspicious of his intentions, and jealous of his rising star. Among Chiang's leading rivals were Feng Yü-hsiang and Yen Hsi-shan, who controlled substantial armed strength in north China and had begun a brief but destructive civil war with Nanking. In 1930 Wang Ching-wei joined these men in attempting to establish a rival "national government" at Peiping, a move which failed because of Nanking's success in gaining the support of the Young Marshal, Chang Hsüeh-liang, who controlled Manchuria. Following the collapse of the anti-Chiang coalition at Peiping, Wang again found himself a political refugee, a dissident with a cause but little support. He then moved south where, during the early months of 1931, he became the senior Kuomintang leader active in a new opposition movement at Canton, sparked by Chiang Kai-shek's house arrest of Hu Hanmin at Nanking and sustained by the political ambitions of Kwangtung and Kwangsi military leaders. This Canton movement, though not successful in dislodging Chiang Kai-shek, did nevertheless restore Wang's position and pave the way for his rapprochement with Nanking.

were released in English by the China United Press, Peiping and Shanghai. See, for example, *The Chinese National Revolution: Essays and Documents* (1931) and *China's Problems and Their Solution* (1934); also *China's Own Critics*, a selection of essays by Hu Shih and Lin Yü-t'ang, with commentary by Wang Ching-wei (Peiping, 1931). T'ang Leang-li, *The Inner History of the Chinese Revolution* (New York, 1930), provides a useful contemporary statement, intended for Western consumption, of the Reorganizationist case against Chiang Kai-shek.

These domestic dissensions sapped the energies of the National Government established in 1928 and frustrated its efforts at nation-wide unification. The grave challenge posed by Japanese military aggression in Manchuria beginning in September 1931 forced many of the feuding factions in the Kuomintang to set aside differences in the interests of national self-preservation. Temporary political compromises on the part of all Kuomintang leaders followed, though personal frictions continued into the war years. Wang Ching-wei made his peace with the Nanking authorities, and with the re-organization of the National Government in the winter of 1931–32 was named president of the Executive Yuan, or prime minister. He officially assumed that position on January 28, 1932. That very night, the Japanese garrison at Shanghai launched an undeclared attack against Chinese troops in the area. Wang Ching-wei was not to see peace again in his lifetime.

From February 1932 until November 1935, Wang sustained an uneasy collaboration with Chiang Kai-shek, heading the government at Nanking while Chiang supervised the military operations aimed at extirpating the Communist bases in Kiangsi and elsewhere in the hinterland. Although Nanking's positive accomplishments are now often ignored, it appeared to some independent observers during the early nineteen-thirties that a new nation was emerging in the lower Yangtze valley and attracting the loyalty of many patriotic Chinese. The dimensions of reconstruction and expansion were varied: fiscal and financial reform; development of communications, including civil aviation; rural rehabilitation; the modernization of university education; the revitalization of public morals and morale. From 1932 to 1935, when Wang Ching-wei headed the Executive Yuan at Nanking, his political authority and personal incorruptibility did much to make that the most progressive period in the history of the Nationalist Government. Yet the period was not without personal frustrations. Although Wang was prime minister, Chiang Kai-shek never fully trusted him and ensured that his own relatives by mar-riage, H. H. K'ung and T. V. Soong, held key posts at Nanking to guarantee appropriate checks on Wang. Irritated by this suspicion and surveillance, Wang went on leave in October 1932, visiting Europe for six months, allegedly for medical reasons, while T. V. Soong acted in his place at Nanking.

On his return to China in March 1933, Wang resumed his portfolio as Executive Yuan head and served concurrently as acting foreign minister. Although welcomed at Nanking, Wang became involved in negotiations with the Japanese diplomatic and military authorities regarding the establishment of railway and mail communications between China proper and Manchoukuo, and the legal arrangements defining the Japanese position on the mainland of China. While sincerely attempting to defend China's territorial and administrative integrity, Wang found himself in an increasingly vulnerable political position: the man most closely associated in the public mind with the policy of yielding to Japan, the individual censured by all patriotic groups which advocated positive resistance. The climax came on November 1, 1935, when, at a meeting of the Central Executive Committee of the Kuomintang at Nanking, he was shot and wounded by an assassin who disguised himself as a photographer. Surgery in Shanghai failed to remove all the bullets, and Wang was forced to resign all official posts in December to seek medical care abroad.

When Wang left for Europe in February 1936 after four years as administrative head of the National Government, medical exigencies appeared paramount. Beneath the surface, however, lay a deeper malaise. Wang was being ruined politically by the long, agonizing process of appeasement, for which Chiang Kai-shek was ultimately responsible, during the lean years between the Mukden Incident of 1931 and the Marco Polo Bridge attack in 1937. Throughout this period, the forces of reform, patriotism, liberal opinion, Communist pressure, student sentiment, and national self-respect fed the opposition to Nanking's cautious line. Wang Ching-wei had found himself the civilian leader of a government pursuing an intensely unpopular policy, yet unable to profit from the rising opposition, losing popularity while he shielded Chiang Kai-shek from anti-appeasement criticism. Following the Sian incident of December 1936, a move designed to force Chiang to take a firm stand against

Japan, Wang Ching-wei hastened back to China from Europe. But Chiang continued to hold the high cards; and when war finally broke out in mid-1937, he gained full powers as top commander of the Nationalist war effort. In March 1938, when the Kuomintang held a special wartime congress at Hankow, Chiang's special party position was confirmed when he was elected *tsung-ts'ai* (leader), with Wang Ching-wei his deputy. Wang's personal power was now more nominal than real, and his political associates were excluded from key offices in favor of Chiang Kai-shek's intimates.

III

The motivations underlying Wang Ching-wei's decision to desert the central government and to form a separate regime under Japanese sponsorship remain a subject for conjecture rather than exposition. Attuned to the actualities of political power within China, Wang felt himself to be equally perceptive toward the realities of the Japanese invasion. During the first year of the war, he became discouraged over the eventual outcome and proposed that the National Government negotiate a peaceful settlement with Japan. When the government evacuated to Chungking after the fall of Hankow in October 1938, Wang was increasingly dubious of China's ability to sustain a protracted war against the well-trained military forces and well-mobilized industrial system of Japan. He was further disillusioned by the Chinese "scorched earth" policy after the tragic and accidental burning of Changsha in November of that year. All of these elements strengthened his impulse to seek a peaceful settlement with Japan.[22]

On December 16, 1938, Wang sought an interview with Chiang Kai-shek, during which he made no mention of his private pessimism regarding the military situation. Two days later he flew to Chengtu, the Szechwan provincial capital, for a ceremonial occasion, thence emplaned to Kunming, and on December 21 arrived at Hanoi in French Indochina. The day after Wang's emergence at Hanoi, Prince Konoye, the Japanese premier, issued a statement announcing

[22] For a profile of "The Mysterious Mr. Wang Ching-wei" by an experienced Western reporter, see John Gunther, *Inside Asia* (New York, 1939), 263–66.

that Japan would collaborate with a new Chinese regime in order to readjust Sino-Japanese relations on the basis of a "new order in East Asia." Chungking at once refused the Konoye offer. On December 29, 1938, Wang issued a public declaration of his advocacy of peace in a telegram to the central government at Chungking requesting Chiang Kai-shek to halt armed resistance and to work out a peaceful settlement with Japan. Knowing of Chungking's adamancy, Wang planned to leave for France. Yet his instincts were positive rather than merely defeatist. He had left Chungking in order to be able to take independent action to achieve a peaceful settlement with Japan, and his conversations with Japanese representatives at Hanoi during the spring of 1939 were essentially designed to create a framework for political discussions, not to bring about the downfall of the National Government at Chungking.

A stroke of violence shattered the false calm. In the early morning hours of March 21, 1939, secret agents of Chungking, intent upon sabotaging Wang's plans, entered his residence in Hanoi and fired dozens of shots. Wang was uninjured, but his long-time protégé and confidant, Tseng Chung-ming, was fatally wounded.[23] The mystery of the shooting is still unsolved, but the most prevalent theory is that the gunmen were aiming for Wang Ching-wei but shot Tseng by mistake. Whatever the facts, Wang regarded the murder of his friend as a personal outrage. Infuriated to the point of no return, he spent the last years of his life working actively with his country's major foreign enemy. Proceeding from Hanoi to Shanghai in the spring of 1939, he conferred with Chinese who were active in the north China puppet regime and in the so-called Reformed Government already existing at Nanking to arrange a merger of the various Chinese administrations in Japanese-occupied China. After visiting Tokyo twice, in May and again in October of 1939, Wang worked out a joint statement with the Japanese authorities covering the

[23] Tseng Chung-ming (1896–1939) was a French-educated scholar and government official who had had long-standing personal and professional ties with Wang Ching-wei in the Kuomintang. In addition to literary works and translations, Tseng was also the author of *La Chine qui lutte* (Peking, 1930). Following the Hanoi shooting, Wang wrote an eloquent tribute to his murdered friend, *A la mémoire de M. Tsen Tson-ming* (Hanoi, 1939).

"new relations between China and Japan" which was secretly signed at the end of the year.

Wang's movement suffered a setback in January 1940 when two Kuomintang associates who had been privy to the effort from the beginning defected to Hong Kong with copies of Wang's secret agreement with Japan. The leak failed to deter Wang's preparations, although publication of the terms of the secret agreement created a furor in China.[24] On March 30, 1940, a new "national government" of the Republic of China, patterned on the five-yuan structure of the legitimate central government, was formally established at Nanking with Wang Ching-wei as its ranking official.[25] He immediately issued a general invitation to all civil servants and party officials in Chungking to participate. In April, discussions were initiated for a treaty to govern the new relations between Nanking and Japan. Actually, since Japan's original intention in supporing Wang had been to force Chungking into entering peace negotiations, it delayed granting formal recognition to the Nanking regime until the informal peace feelers to Chungking had apparently failed. Tokyo did not sign a basic treaty with Nanking and accord formal diplomatic recognition to that government until November 30, 1940, almost two years after Wang had first left Chungking, and eight months after his regime had been established. The November 1940 agreement, contrary to what Wang and his followers had hoped, maintained strong Japanese military and economic domination over the occupied areas while granting the Chinese authorities at Nanking only token responsibility for internal administration.[26]

[24] The Chinese Communists, for example, at once denounced Wang's actions. See the internal party directive issued on January 28, 1940, and the statements made at Yenan on February 1, 1940, as the Communists launched a massive propaganda campaign against "the traitor Wang Ching-wei." Mao Tse-tung, *Selected Works,* III, 1939–1941 (New York, 1954), 157–74.

[25] The most detailed account of Wang's wartime regime by a Chinese who himself played a substantial role in the Nanking government is given in Chu Tzu-chia, *Wang cheng-ch'üan te k'ai-ch'ang yü shou-ch'ang* (The Beginning and End of the Drama of the Wang Regime, Hong Kong, Ch'un-ch'iu tsa-chih she, 4 vols., 1959–61). A useful review of this work by Robert H. G. Lee appears in the *Journal of Asian Studies,* XXIII (1963), 126–28.

[26] Text of the 1940 treaty and annexed protocol appears in the *American Journal of International Law,* XXXV (1941), supplement, 125–28.

Wang's pessimism regarding China's prospects for effective resistance against the Axis powers was intensified during 1940 by military developments in the European theater, particularly the fall of
France and the desperate position of England in the face of the
German air assault. Within the context of Chinese politics, Wang
Ching-wei took the position that his government was the legitimate
national government of China; his party was the Kuomintang; his
flag was the Kuomintang flag; and the principles of his government
were the Three People's Principles of Sun Yat-sen.[27] Prior to the
outbreak of war with the United States, the ideology underlying the
Nanking government—a pan-Asian, anti-Western mystique—was not
unattractive to many Chinese. In Tokyo's eyes, the Nanking government and the doctrine of Asian solidarity which lay behind it offered
the greatest potential for securing a settlement of the "China Incident" on terms favorable to Japan.[28]

IV

China during the early nineteen-forties was, like ancient Gaul,
divided into three parts.[29] One section was Nationalist China, the

[27] A collection of Sun Yat-sen's pan-Asian writings were issued at Shanghai
in 1941 under the title, China and Japan: Natural Friends—Unnatural Ene-
mies: A Guide for China's Foreign Policy (Shanghai, 1941), with foreword by
Wang Ching-wei.
[28] A detailed Japanese analysis of the 1937–41 period is given by Usui
Katsumi, "Nit-chū sensō no seijiteki hatten" (Political Development of the
Sino-Japanese War, 1937–41), in the recent Asahi Shimbun series, Taiheiyō
Sensō e no Michi (The Road to the Pacific War), Vol. IV, 1963, especially pp.
200–56. See also Robert J. C. Butow, Tojo and the Coming of the War
(Princeton, 1961); David J. Lu, From the Marco Polo Bridge to Pearl Harbor
(Washington, D. C., 1961); and the two articles by Hilary Conroy in the
Pacific Historical Review, "Government versus 'Patriot': The Background of
Japan's Asiatic Expansion," XX (1951), 31–42, and "Japan's War in China:
An Ideological Somersault," XXI (1952), 367–79. Chalmers A. Johnson describes the establishment of Japanese-sponsored puppet governments in Peas-
ant Nationalism and Communist Power: The Emergence of Revolutionary
China, 1937–1945 (Stanford, 1962), 41–48. A valuable study of the years
after the outbreak of the China war, written from Western sources, is F. C.
Jones, Japan's New Order in East Asia: Its Rise and Fall, 1937–45 (London,
1954).
[29] Paul M. A. Linebarger, The China of Chiang Kai-shek (Boston, 1941),
provides an informed contemporary survey of Chinese politics before the

areas in the west extending from Kansu through Yunnan which were controlled by or nominally loyal to the legitimate central government, located at the wartime capital of Chungking. Another was Communist China, a series of expanding Red enclaves behind and between the ports and railway lines of north, east, and central China which were controlled by or loyal to the Communist insurgent government at Yenan in Shensi province. Still a third division was Japanese-occupied China, a series of semiautonomous regions stretching from the Amur river in northern Manchuria to the Gulf of Tonkin in the south. This third China, the area under Japanese domination, was itself sub-divided into Manchoukuo, the Manchurian regime which had been established in 1932; a north China puppet regime at Peiping; Meng-chiang, the Japanese-controlled government in Inner Mongolia; and Wang Ching-wei's "National Government" at Nanking.

The outbreak of the Pacific war in December 1941 brought little immediate change in the political geography of China. The expansion of conflict did, however, enhance the role of the Nanking regime as an important element in Tokyo's China policy as that policy developed during the war between Japan and the Allied powers. Militarily, the Japanese settled into a holding operation on the mainland, with main efforts and power committed farther south. Yet despite the glittering prizes gained in Southeast Asia during 1942, China still remained of vital economic importance to Japan as a source of coal, iron ore, and other essential raw materials. In late 1942 and early 1943, Japan did make certain moves designed to ease the more glaring inequalities in the original position of the Nanking government. Wang Ching-wei again went to Tokyo, where he had conversations with Tojo and other members of the Japanese government, as well as an audience with the Emperor. As a result of these negotiations, Japan relinquished her concessions in China and the right of extraterritoriality, while the Nanking government on

outbreak of the Pacific war. An invaluable reference tool for studying the occupied areas is Frederick W. Mote, *Japanese-sponsored Governments in China, 1937–1945* (Stanford, 1954), which provides annotated bibliographical guidance to relevant Chinese materials at the Hoover Institution.

January 9, 1943, formally declared war against the United States and Great Britain.

During the summer of 1943, following a visit of Tojo himself to China and Japanese pressure upon the representative of the Vichy regime in Nanking, agreements were signed under which Nanking assumed administrative control over the International Settlement and the French Concession at Shanghai. On August 1, 1943, the Nanking authorities entered into formal possession of these areas, long the heart of Western control in China's major trading and financial metropolis. Following the return to Tokyo of Shigemitsu Mamoru, who had been Japanese ambassador at Nanking, to become foreign minister in 1943, Japan's "New China Policy" took more definite shape. Aimed at achieving a settlement with Chiang Kai-shek, this policy embodied the concept that Japan would modify her earlier ambitions for dominant control of East Asia while at the same time blocking the return of the Western powers to their former position of influence.[30]

Japan's gambit had the corollary effect of conceding to Wang Ching-wei's government at least the outward status of an ally and an equal. When a new treaty of alliance between Nanking and Tokyo was concluded on October 30, 1943, voiding the earlier treaty of November 30, 1940, its preamble expressed the resolve of the two governments to cooperate as equal and independent neighbors in the establishment of Greater East Asia. But the key aspect of Tokyo's China policy was not so much its psychological effect upon the "face" of Wang Ching-wei's government as its potential political effect upon individuals and groups in Chiang Kai-shek's government at Chungking. Through the October 1943 treaty with Wang Ching-wei and through covert dealings with Chungking channeled through the redoubtable General Tai Li,[31] Japan pressed the line that

[30] See the section by F. C. Jones in Jones, Hugh Borton, and B. R. Pearn, *The Far East, 1942–1946* (London, 1955), 13–24.

[31] Tai Li (1895–1946) was head of the Chinese Nationalist military intelligence organization during the Sino-Japanese war. Though his activities were cloaked in secrecy, it was generally believed in China that he wielded enormous power and enjoyed the implicit confidence of Chiang Kai-shek, his

Chiang's true interests lay in severing relations with the United States and Britain and in collaborating with Nanking to liquidate the Chinese Communist movement, then steadily growing in strength in the countryside. During 1944, even as Japan absorbed mounting disaster in the Pacific campaigns and Germany was retreating on the Western Front, growing political frustration at Chungking found outlet in renewed alarm over the threat of Mao Tse-tung. And the idea of joint Chungking-Nanking operations against the Chinese Communists reportedly gained some support from conservative elements in the Kuomintang who viewed the Communists as a greater long-term threat than the Japanese, a fact which complicated United States actions and policies in the China theater during that period.[32]

At Nanking, still in ailing health from the bullet wounds received several years earlier, Wang Ching-wei was again forced to go to

---

fellow provincial from Chekiang. Tai Li worked closely with Captain (later Rear Admiral) Milton E. Miles of the United States Navy in planning the Sino-American Cooperation Organization (SACO), the joint intelligence group established in 1943 and active during the remaining war years. At the same time, Tai Li's personal organization provided one major channel of covert communication between the Chinese authorities at Chungking and those at Nanking. Tai was killed in an airplane crash near Nanking on March 17, 1946.

[32] Of the three competing parts into which China was divided during the war years, the Japanese-occupied areas and their puppet governments remain the most obscure despite the fact that these governments then controlled over half of China's area, population, and resources. The volumes giving the United States view of the China-Burma-India theater prepared by the Office of the Chief of Military History, Department of the Army, take virtually no account of developments in the Japanese-occupied areas: Charles F. Romanus and Riley Sunderland, *Stilwell's Mission to China* (1953), *Stilwell's Command Problems* (1956), and *Time Runs Out in CBI* (1959). Nor do the official papers released by the Department of State contain any detailed data on the covert communications and traffic between "free China" and "occupied China" which continued throughout the war: *Foreign Relations of the United States, 1942, China* (1956); *Foreign Relations of the United States, 1943, China* (1957); *United States Relations with China, with Special Reference to the Period 1944–1949* (1949). The major scholarly study prepared by Tang Tsou, *America's Failure in China, 1941–50* (Chicago, 1963), makes no mention of Wang Ching-wei; nor does the earlier volume by Herbert Feis, *The China Tangle* (Princeton, 1953).

Japan for medical treatment. There, at Nagoya, he passed away on November 10, 1944, at sixty-one, without seeing the unfortunate end of his regime or the fate of his loyal Chinese associates.[33] Never able to undermine the position of the National Government as the internationally recognized wartime ally of the Western powers or to attract any substantial group of men of first-class calibre to desert the legitimate Chinese government, Wang had remained surrounded at Nanking by friends bound to him by ties of personal loyalty. Ch'en Kung-po (1892–1946), a Cantonese who had been close to Wang since 1927, formally succeeded him as head of the Nanking government, but Ch'en lacked the prestige which Wang had formerly enjoyed in Nationalist circles. Another individual prominent as political strategist at Nanking was Chou Fo-hai (1897–1948), who had previously been the most widely read Kuomintang theorist prior to his joining Wang Ching-wei's "peace movement" in 1938. Yet it had been Wang Ching-wei's seniority and reputation for probity which had held the government together. By the end of 1944, when Wang died, Japan's hopes of bringing Chinese resistance to an end had dimmed, and the outcome of the war was no longer seriously in doubt.

For the millions of Chinese remote from the world of high policy and international diplomacy who had no practical alternative but to live under Nanking's administrative control, Wang Ching-wei's regime did provide a measure of Chinese protection against the Japanese from 1940 to 1945. In dealing with the Japanese, Wang attempted to maintain maximum integrity and to preserve maximum rights from a brutal enemy which had permitted the rape of Nanking

[33] Early in 1964 the Hong Kong Chinese semi-monthly magazine, *Ch'un-ch'iu,* published a 5,000-word document purporting to be the "political testament" of Wang Ching-wei. Dated October 1944, the month before Wang's death in Japan, the will is entitled, "My Final State of Mind." While controversial, the document is written in Wang's style, and there would appear to be scant reason for forgery. For the Chinese text and discussion of its authenticity, see *Ch'un-ch'iu,* No. 159 (February 16, 1964) and No. 160 (March 1, 1964).

in December 1937 and was for some years thereafter intent upon maintaining "order" in China through bayonets and military police. There was notably little public remonstrance or violence directed against the puppet authorities when Japan surrendered.

Together with his other principal associates, Wang Ching-wei's widow, Ch'en Pi-chün, was tried for treason following the Japanese defeat. In testimony given at her trial, she stressed Wang's sincerity and patriotism in believing that a peaceful accommodation with Japan was the only realistic method of preserving Chinese national interests.[34] An impetuous and determined woman, Ch'en Pi-chün had been one of the early anti-Manchu conspirators of the pre-1911 period. She had exerted great influence on her ambitious husband during their long married life and had been bitter that his later career in the Kuomintang had not matched its earlier brilliance. Sentenced to life imprisonment in April 1946, she died of illness in the prison hospital at Shanghai in June 1959 at the age of seventy-six.[35] After her cremation, the Chinese Communist authorities permitted the remains to be sent out from Shanghai to be finally disposed of by her surviving children, who lived outside China.

In a period of ethical relativism in his country, Wang Ching-wei never permitted scandal or corruption to taint his personal life. In the realm of politics, however, his career was blemished by the fact that his principal consistency lay in devotion to the personal interests of Wang Ching-wei. Believing himself to be the true heir of Sun Yat-sen, he was resentful of Chiang Kai-shek and his wife (Soong Mei-ling), viewing Chiang as a political parvenu of limited intellectual background and distrusting the *bona fides* of the Chiang-Soong "dynasty." Versatile, sincere by his standards, an eloquent public speaker in a country which favors dramatic virtuosity, Wang Ching-wei was nevertheless a thwarted man. Essentially his frustration stemmed from that fatal flaw which was his political opportun-

[34] See Chu Tzu-chia, IV, 90.

[35] See Chu Tzu-chia, IV, 93. Edgar Snow apparently errs in stating that Mme. Wang Ching-wei was still alive in 1960, teaching a literary class in the Ward Road Jail at Shanghai. See *The Other Side of the River: Red China Today* (New York, 1962), 547.

ism. Wang's ardent patriotism outran his political judgment; his surpassing confidence in his own ability at persuasion convinced him that he could get more out of the Japanese by talking than Chiang Kai-shek could by fighting.

Intelligent enough to be a radical in a period when China's new problems required radical approaches, Wang Ching-wei remained a romantic radical. He was a romantic radical both in the modern European sense and in another particular sense in which the term is pertinent to twentieth-century Chinese politics. Wang possessed virtually all of the qualifications required for political success in republican China except one: control of military power. Lacking that vital element, he relied on personal brilliance and virtuosity rather than on political consistency, theoretical insight, or organizational ability. Throughout his adult career, Wang was pre-eminently the opportunist. He failed to create or adapt any unified body of political doctrine which could rally mass support; and he never succeeded in building an integrated political organization through which words could be transmuted into reality. Attractive as he was to many Chinese, Wang Ching-wei was ultimately a dreamer. He became, as one Western observer has put it, the victim of an *idée fixe*, a man who believed that "if he impersonates government devotedly enough, and with careful enough detail, he will become government." [36]

In a larger sense, the label of romantic may also be applied to the political party in the service of which Wang Ching-wei spent the bulk of his active career. As it developed in China during the nineteen-thirties and forties, the Kuomintang was also characterized by an ambivalent escapism. Internally, its most distinctive characteristic was that its top leaders all employed an organizational strategy which relied principally on the manipulation of personal cliques, a conventional Chinese system appropriate to a period of political stability but not to an era of political disorganization and potential revolution. Externally, the Kuomintang's most distinctive characteristic was its refusal to face facts, to confront and analyze disagreeable social realities, and to plan practical programs to mobilize sufficient popular support to deal effectively with those realities. In the end

[36] Linebarger, 200.

it was the Kuomintang's nemesis, the Chinese Communist party, which—eschewing romantic escapism—evolved and sustained doctrine, organization, and military power sufficiently potent to mount a serious attack upon twentieth-century China's massive social problems.

❊ III ❊

THE COMMUNIST MOVEMENT

EDITOR'S INTRODUCTION

The Communist victory in China in 1949 was one of the most important events in history and in world politics. The strategy of the Chinese Communist Party (CCP) in seizing power consisted of three major elements: a party of iron discipline, an army, and a united front. The Party's power base was a self-supporting territory usually located in interprovincial "border areas." Remarkable skill in guerrilla warfare contributed to the strength of the army. The United Front succeeded in neutralizing and winning over non-Communists, especially the politicians and intellectuals who were dissatisfied with the Kuomintang (KMT) government.

Although the Chinese Communists were often mistakenly regarded by outside observers as agrarian reformers in the 1940's, the Party leadership never regarded itself as anything but orthodox in its doctrine, and considered its prolonged operation from the countryside simply a matter of tactics imposed by circumstances. The Party was founded by students and intellectuals under the guidance of the Communist International (Comintern). In the first decade of the Party's history, the Comintern dominated the CCP. After Mao Tsetung gained undisputed leadership in 1935, the Party exercised a greater degree of independence. The Kremlin policy toward the Chinese Communists became one of passive blessing rather than massive aid, with the exception of Russian assistance in Manchuria after World War II. Until the early 1960's, the Party never openly challenged Soviet leadership. When there was a conflict of interests, Moscow's views always prevailed.

For more than thirty years prior to the "Great Proletarian Cultural Revolution" in 1966–69, the CCP top leadership was characterized by its solidarity, with the exceptions of the defection of Chang Kuo-t'ao in 1938, the purge of Kao Kang and Jao Shu-shih in 1954, and the fall of P'eng Te-huai in 1959. Whatever disagreements the top leaders had among themselves, they were kept well within the inner circle of the Party.

I

The Chinese Communist movement may be divided into four periods. The first period began with the founding of the Chinese Communist Party in 1921 and extended to the CCP-Kuomintang split in 1927. The CCP was officially established at its First National Congress in July 1921. It was attended by 12 delegates representing about 57 members. Many points about this congress, including the dates, are in dispute, although the CCP officially celebrates July 1 as the date on which the Party was founded.

One of the first problems confronting the CCP was its relationship to other political parties, particularly the Kuomintang (Nationalist Party). Since the program of the Communist International was based on Lenin's thesis that national liberation movements in colonial and semi-colonial countries could be led to merge with the mainstream of the international proletarian revolutionary movement, the KMT was considered an effective instrument through which the Party could carry on its revolutionary work. The KMT in the early 1920's, as Professor Nathaniel Peffer put it, was only the vehicle of an idea rather than a political organization. It was little more than an expression of a community of general belief—belief in republicanism and modernism, both without precise definition. It had no fixed membership; the discordant elements associated with it were sometimes in the party, sometimes out of it, and sometimes not quite sure of being in or out. The influence of its leader, Sun Yat-sen, was confined to the city of Canton, and even there his power was precarious. But it was the only progressive political force at that time. Hence, the Chinese Communists followed the instructions of the Communist International and joined the KMT with the intention of manipulating it for their own purposes.

In his desperate struggle for power and in his fight against the warlords in the North, Sun Yat-sen welcomed Russian political and military support. In 1923, he sent a young army officer, Chiang Kai-shek, to Russia, and subsequently reorganized the KMT according to the model of the Communist Party in Russia. The Chinese Communists were admitted to the KMT on an individual basis without having to give up their Communist Party membership.

Sun Yat-sen died in 1925, two years after the KMT-CCP cooperation and two years before their split. He did not seem to have fully understood the nature of the Communist International nor the character of the CCP, which was a political novelty to him. He probably thought its members were no different from the youth who had worked with him in the Republican revolutionary movement. Had he lived longer he might have witnessed the KMT-CCP break and consequently might not have enjoyed the respect subsequently accorded him by the Communists.

In 1926 the Northern Expedition was launched under Chiang Kai-shek's command. His army swept out from Canton to Hankow by the end of the year. In April 1927, after his forces had captured Shanghai, he turned against the Communists. In July the Kuomintang government in Hankow, led by Wang Ching-wei, also split with the Communists. Thus ended the first phase of the Chinese Communist movement.

The second stage of the Chinese Communist movement extended from the 1927 split to the outbreak of the Sino-Japanese War in 1937. While Chiang Kai-shek was establishing a central government in Nanking with nominal jurisdiction over the whole country, the Communists tried to capture Canton, Hankow, Changsha, and other cities by armed revolts. Because they overestimated the strength of the city workers, their policy failed at great cost to Communist lives and strength. By 1930 the mainstream of the movement had shifted from cities to rural areas and the peasants began to play a dominant role in the movement. Mao Tse-tung has been given credit for this shift of policy. Some Western writers have claimed that Mao deviated heretically from Marxism-Leninism because he gave such a prominent role to the peasants within the Chinese Communist movement, and because he concentrated on rural areas. It has also been claimed that Mao's *On New Democracy,* published in 1940, represented a theoretical deviation from Moscow-rooted Marxism-Leninism. However, other writers contend that Mao's peasant policy was really an acceptance on his part of Moscow's directives. They point out, also, that *On New Democracy* contained Lenin's 1905 ideas, which both Lenin and Stalin developed further after 1917. Both interpretations overlook the fact that at the beginning of the armed struggle Mao recruited not only the peasantry but the poor and unemployed in both town and countryside, who were used in rebellions throughout the history of China.

The first real center of Communist authority was established in Kiangsi province, where Mao and about 1000 men joined the bandits in the hills. They exercised political authority, and set up a program of agrarian reform dispossessing the rich landlord, dividing up land, and abolishing usury. In November 1931 the First All-China Congress of Soviets was held in Juichin, Kiangsi, and the Chinese Soviet Republic was formally proclaimed.

From December 1930 to October 1933, Chiang Kai-shek launched several "extermination campaigns" against the Red bases. After several unsuccessful attempts, he engaged a group of German officers as military advisers. They were commanded by General von Seeckt, who had organized the nucleus of the army on which Hitler later built his Wehrmacht. A system of blockhouses and fortified points was constructed to encircle the Communist areas and, after starving out the Communist forces by economic blockades, to destroy them in a blow. This strategy made the Communist guerrilla tactics ineffective. As a result, the Communists abandoned their bases and began their retreat across the country, the historic "Long March."

The "Long March" began in October 1934. The main forces of the Red Army—about 90,000—broke through a weak sector in the circle and headed indirectly toward northwest China. When they finally arrived at northern Shensi one year later, they numbered less than 20,000. They had covered about 6000 miles on foot. Although the Red Army was constantly chased and attacked by central and provincial government forces, none of the local commanders wanted to sacrifice military strength to suppress the Communists because they feared it would weaken their own power positions. The rivalry among the regional commanders and between the warlords and the central government partly accounted for the survival of the Communists not only in the "Long March" but also in the entire history of the Communist armed struggle in China.

During the "Long March" the Communists were out of touch with Moscow. Although Mao Tse-tung was the Chairman of the Chinese Soviet Republic, it was during the "Long March" that he seized real control of the Party at the Tsunyi Conference in January 1935. Between 1927 and 1935 the secretary-general of the Party was replaced five times; thrice the post was taken by Russian-educated Chinese, who were the protégés of the Comintern.

At the end of 1936, Chiang Kai-shek prepared a new "extermination campaign" against the Communists in Shensi, one of the poorest regions in China. Had he succeeded in opening this campaign, the Communists would almost certainly have been either "exterminated" or forced to begin another "Long March," probably across Mongolia to Soviet Russia.

What saved the Communists was the "Sian Incident," which was a turning point in history. Chiang was arrested by his own general, who wished to fight against the Japanese rather than the Communists. After the incident Chiang stopped the civil war. When the Japanese struck again in July 1937, he was obliged to resist Japanese aggression. For the first time in a century China embarked on a course of military defense of its sovereignty on a national rather than a regional basis. As for the Communists, the Red Army was reorganized nominally under the command of the Nationalist Government; and the Soviet Republic was dissolved. But all these changes were in name only; in no way were the Red Army and the Communist-controlled areas under the jurisdiction of the central government.

The Chinese Communist movement entered its third stage at the outbreak of the Sino-Japanese War in 1937. It is unnecessary to go into detail concerning the events of the period. Suffice it to say that the devastation of war which lasted for eight years helped the expansion of the Communist movement in many ways: the Communists operated in areas of power vacuum behind enemy lines; they established a number of Communist bases, particularly in north China, where they put their economic reform into practice. Because their military actions and expansion against the invaders were identified with nationalism and wartime national interests, they received more popular support than otherwise. By the end of the war, they claimed to have expanded their army to 910,000 men.

The relations between the Kuomintang government and the CCP during the war were never friendly, but were moderately polite in the first two years. It is interesting to note that it was the Russian-educated group in the Party leadership that advocated sincere cooperation with the Kuomintang. Mao Tse-tung, however, was determined to make use of the opportunity to expand Communist influence and power. Toward the Communist base and the "border region," Chiang Kai-shek adopted a policy of isolation and containment by using a huge army to blockade the area. Throughout the war Mao and other Communist leaders in Yenan had to struggle for self-sufficiency by initiating a number of production campaigns which were not very much different fundamentally from the methods they have been using since they took over the country. This revolutionary experience of isolation and self-reliance has greatly influenced Mao's thought and behavior.

The Communist movement entered its fourth stage at the end of the war in 1945. The Kuomintang and the Nationalist Government were unable to cope with corruption and the problems resulting from World War II followed by civil war, inflation being the most difficult one. And yet no one would have expected that within four years, the Communists would be able to take over the country. Evidence suggests that it was a surprise to Stalin and to the Chinese Communist leaders.

A number of events relating to the final Communist victory are well known: the Yalta Agreement, the Russian occupation of Manchuria, the American mediation, the peace negotiations between the KMT and the CCP, the failure of the Marshall mission, and the full-scale civil war. On October 1, 1949 the People's Republic of China was established. The National Government fled to Taiwan. It was one of the very few cases in history when a government was overthrown after it had fought a victorious war against foreign aggression.

II

With the exception of Chou En-lai and Liu Shao-ch'i, the political profiles provided in this section are those of leaders who were associated with the early Chinese Communist movement. The first two articles, by Professor C. Y. Chih and Maurice Meisner, deal respectively with the two most important leaders of the early Chinese Communist movement: Ch'en Tu-hsiu and Li Ta-chao, two university professors who became Marxists. Li (1889–1927) was educated in Japan in 1913–16 and was the principal director of the Communist movement in north China until he was executed in 1927. Ch'en Tu-hsiu (1879–1942) was educated in Japan at the turn of the century but he did not join the early revolutionary party of the T'ung Meng Hui, as did many of his fellow students. After the Revolution of 1911, he served as secretary to the governor of his native province of Anhwei. He was a leader of the literary and cultural revolution that culminated in the May Fourth Movement of 1919. From 1921 to 1927 he headed the CCP, and after he was expelled from the Party in 1930 he organized a Trotskyite opposition group. Before he became a Communist he was closely associated with two of Huang Hsing's closest friends and followers, Chang Chi and Chang Shih-chao. In fact, Chang Shih-chao was his defense lawyer after he was arrested by the Kuomintang in 1932.

The selection on Chang Kuo-t'ao (1897—), one of the founders of the Chinese Communist Party, is based on his memoir. Chang was a prominent leader of the Chinese Communist movement until 1938, when he defected to the Kuomintang government as a result of conflict with Mao Tse-tung. In the 1930's he had his own military power and separate bases of operations. His native district was linked more closely with adjacent Hunan province than with the rest of Kiangsi. Consequently, during his university days he was associated with the Hunanese students rather than with the Kiangsi students. Perhaps it may not be too far-fetched to group him with the Hunanese revolutionary leaders in modern China in terms of geographical origin.

The next essay is on Ch'en Kung-po (1892–1946), whose life reflected to some extent the intellectual confusion and political upheaval of twentieth-century China. Of the twelve delegates to the CCP's First National Congress, Ch'en and Chou Fo-hai (1897–1948), a Hunanese, were the two early "drop outs." Both became prominent in Kuomintang politics and ended up traitors to their country by joining a Japanese-sponsored government in Nanking during World War II. Ch'en helped found the Chinese Communist Party, but broke away from it in 1922. In the mid-1920's, he identified himself with the left wing of the Kuomintang. As a leading member of the KMT "reorganization faction" (1928–31), as Minister of Industry in the Nationalist Government (1932–35), and as a leading figure in the Japanese-sponsored government at Nanking (1940–45), Ch'en was closely associated with Wang Ching-wei. Ch'en joined the "peace movement" against his better judgment and he did so mainly because of his loyalty to Wang. This is a good example of personal loyalty in Chinese politics.

In January 1924, only two and a half years after the founding of the Chinese Communist Party, Ch'en Kung-po submitted an essay entitled "The Communist Movement in China" for the degree of Master of Arts in the Faculty of Economics at Columbia University. It is possibly the earliest history of the Chinese Communist movement in existence. It had remained an unnoticed manuscript in the Columbia Library for more than thirty years until Professor C.

Martin Wilbur published it. The article on Ch'en is based on Wilbur's introduction to the book.

A journalist and prolific writer, Ch'ü Ch'iu-pai (1899–1935) was a member of the Central Committee of the Chinese Communist Party from 1923 to 1928. He became Secretary-General of the Party after the KMT-CCP split in 1927, but held the post for less than a year. In September 1930 Ch'ü tried unsuccessfully to put an end to Li Li-san's program of seizing cities to spark a national revolution. In January 1931 he was excluded from the Party's central leading organ because he opposed Li Li-san's policies. Henceforth, he became a prominent figure in the League of Left-Wing Writers, working with Lu Hsün in Shanghai. In 1933 he was the Shanghai area representative to the Second All-China Congress of Soviets, held at the main Communist base in Juichin, Kiangsi. Shortly after, he was named People's Commissar of Education of the Central Soviet Government headed by Mao Tse-tung. When the main forces of the Red Army embarked on the "Long March" in October 1934, he stayed behind. At the end of February 1935 he was arrested by the Nationalist army in a Fukien guerrilla area and on June 18, 1935, he was executed.

In 1955, the twentieth anniversary of Ch'ü's death, his remains were moved to the Cemetery of Revolutionary Heroes on the western outskirts of Peking. During the Cultural Revolution, however, he was severely criticized by Red Guard publications for having capitulated to the Kuomintang and for having written *Superfluous Words*. T. A. Hsia's article on Ch'ü is, in Professor S. H. Chen's words, a study of "a dedicated human being struggling with the dilemmas of an earlier Chinese Communist milieu," and an account of the transformation of a man from a Confucian man of letters into a tender-hearted Communist with a ruthless fanatic passion.

The selection on Mao Tse-tung (1893—) is based on his autobiographical sketch as told to Edgar Snow. The interview was held in the blockaded Red area in northwest China in 1936 at the time when the Chinese Communists were generally known as "bandits." Many writings on Mao and Communist China need to be reexamined and reassessed in the light of the Cultural Revolution. Snow's piece on Mao, however, remains today an authoritative account.

In view of the Cultural Revolution, it is worth recalling Chang Kuo-t'ao's description of Mao's personality in an article entitled "Mao —A New Portrait by an Old Colleague," written for *The New York Times Magazine* (August 2, 1953):

> Influenced on the one hand by Chinese history, politics and society, and on the other by the revolutionary thought of the twentieth century, he [Mao] has a mind in which Chinese monarchial concepts, Marxist-Leninist ideas and dream of glory exist side by side.
>
> . . . he occasionally assumes the airs of a scholar of China's old literary elite even in his walk. At the same time, however, he has the manners and eccentricities of a Chinese country jack. . . .
>
> In the years since he won leadership, Mao has acquired a reputation as a Communist theorist. But there is nothing outstandingly original about his social theory . . . he understands power better than the theory. His power structure is a mixture of the modern police state and an old-style Oriental autocracy. He is a "military first" man.
>
> He is not good on civil administration matters, and he is reluctant to accept responsibility if something goes wrong. . . . Although he knows how to use power in the top leadership, he has little talent for building up a large personal following except as a remote symbol.

It may be mentioned that Mao's "military first" is only one of the many "contradictions" to Confucian ideas of government. In the *Analects* a disciple of Confucius asked about government. The Master said, "The requisites of government are that there be sufficient food, army, and the confidence of the people in their ruler." The disciple then raised a question: "If it cannot be helped, and one of these must be dispensed with, which of the three should be foregone first?" "The army," said the Master. The disciple again asked: "If it cannot be helped, and one of the remaining two must be dispensed with, which of them should be foregone?" Confucius answered: "Part with the food. For death is the inevitable lot of men; but if the people have no faith in their ruler, there is no standing for the state." Historians who interpret Communist China in terms of Confucian China and who claim a "continuity" from Communist China back to traditional China should bear in mind that Mao has reordered the three Confucian requisites of government. Mao would give up the army last.

Chou En-lai (1898—), one of the earliest leaders of the Chinese Communist movement, is an extremely capable man whose career has been untouched by personal scandal. Chang Kuo-t'ao said about him in the above-mentioned article in *The New York Times Magazine*:

> Chou En-lai is everything that Mao is not when it comes to implementing a policy—quick, decisive, careful, thorough and smooth. No matter how multitudinous his tasks are, Chou remembers everything. Furthermore, Chou En-lai is probably closer to Moscow than any other Chinese Communist leader and, in my opinion, is the leading candidate for succession should anything happen to Mao.
>
> So far as I know, there are only two major factions in the party —Mao's and Chou's. But the two men are working together even though they are diametrically opposite in temperament and can never be in really complete harmony. . . .
>
> . . . Fortunately for Mao, Chou En-lai . . . has shown no inclination to compete for power with Mao.

In another article written in the following year for *The New York Times Magazine* (April 25, 1954), Chou was characterized by Chang Kuo-t'ao in Chinese fashion as a "round" man, "who is smooth in his dealings with society, who is good at making friends, who never goes to extremes and who always adapts himself to the existing situation." For half a century Chou has gone through numerous intra-Party struggles, but has always emerged a powerful figure. He has been likened to the lead-lighted, round-bottomed Chinese toy figure, *"pu tao weng"* (the old man who never falls down). His performance in the Cultural Revolution again proved the validity of this characterization, as presented in Professor K. Y. Hsu's article.

Until the Communist victory in 1949, Liu Shao-ch'i was known merely as one of the CCP leaders in the trade-union movement. Although practically unknown to the outside world at that time, he became increasingly important in the Party's center after the mid-1940's. When the People's Republic of China was established in 1949, with Mao Tse-tung as the Chairman of the Central People's Government and Chu Teh as the senior-ranking vice chairman, Liu was the second vice chairman. When the Peking government was reorganized in 1954, Liu became Chairman of the Standing Committee of the National People's Congress. In 1959 he replaced Mao as Chairman of the People's Republic of China. By then he had become Mao's heir-apparent and "closest comrade in arms."

Liu Shao-ch'i was the second-ranking member of the Party until August 1966. Shortly afterward he became "China's Khrushchev," "the top Party person in power taking the capitalist road," and a principal target of the Cultural Revolution. In October 1968, the Enlarged 12th Plenary Session of the Eighth Central Committee of the Party adopted a resolution to expel him from the Party and to dismiss him from all posts both inside and outside the Party.

Liu was never really much of a theorist, although when he was in power and heir-apparent, outside observers occasionally attempted to make him become one. He may be assessed as an organization man, a painstaking and patient Communist who rose to the top echelon of command through hard work and devotion. He won the confidence of Mao to run the Party machine for a quarter of a century. He was important because Mao made him important; but the man who made him could also break him.

Although Liu's influence in the Party was strong because of his long-time leadership, he failed to hold his own once Mao turned against him. He completely misjudged Mao's intention and apparently misunderstood the real aim of the Cultural Revolution at its initial stage. He was caught on the defensive at every turn. The Party machinery, which he had painfully built up through the years, collapsed at one blow and, despite the Red Guard protests, no organized opposition rallied to his defense. The career of Mao's heir-apparent came to an abrupt end at the age of sixty-seven before succession took place. Professor Howard L. Boorman's account of Liu's career is the best one on the subject to date.

III

Almost all of the eight leaders whose profiles are presented in this section came from well-to-do families, some even from the very wealthy class. With the exception of Ch'en Tu-hsiu and Li Ta-chao, they all turned Communist in their twenties. As for their education, Ch'en Kung-po studied at Columbia after he had left the Party, and Mao Tse-tung did not go abroad until 1949. Otherwise all were educated in Japan, France, or Russia.

Paucity of material has prevented the inclusion of articles on military leaders in this section. Three military leaders, however, do merit some mention: Chu Teh, P'eng Te-huai, and Lin Piao.

Chu Teh was born in Szechwan province in 1886 to a peasant family of thirteen brothers and sisters. Between 1909 and 1911, he studied at the Yunnan Military Academy, where he came to know Hunanese military officer Ts'ai O, brigade commander and instructor of the academy in 1911. After graduating from the academy in July 1911, Chu Teh served as a second lieutenant under Ts'ai in Yunnan. When Ts'ai was named governor of Szechwan province in July 1916, he made Chu a brigade commander. The death of Ts'ai in that year was a serious blow to him. Ts'ai was not only his commander, but also his teacher and friend, two relationships which the ancient Chinese culture hallowed as second only to filial piety. After a number of unsuccessful years in the military, Chu Teh sailed for Europe to study in Germany in 1922, where he joined the German branch of the Chinese Communist Party. He returned to China in 1926, took part in the Nanchang revolt in 1927, and in 1928 the Chinese Red Army was formed with him as the military commander and Mao Tse-tung as the Party representative. Subsequently, their names, "Chu-Mao," were often linked together in China. For the next twenty years, Chu Teh remained the top military leader in the Chinese Communist movement.

Next to Chu Teh, the Hunanese P'eng Te-huai (1899?—), who joined forces with Chu and Mao in the Chingkiang Mountains in the winter of 1928, was the most important leader in the Chinese Communist military hierarchy. The chain of command may be seen from the pattern of the Red Army when it was reorganized in August

1937 into the Eighth Route Army with Chu Teh as the Commander-in-Chief, P'eng Te-huai, second in command, and Lin Piao, a division commander. Of all the Communist military leaders, these three men had been closest to Mao Tse-tung.

Shortly after the Communist victory in 1949, Chu Teh relinquished his post as Commander-in-Chief of the People's Liberation Army. In the first decade of the Peking regime, military leadership fell to P'eng as a result of Chu Teh's advanced age. In 1959 P'eng was dismissed from his post as Minister of Defense. During the Cultural Revolution, he was reportedly "dragged out" to parade through the streets. Chu Teh was severely criticized by Red Guard publications, but he was re-elected to the Political Bureau of the Central Committee in the Ninth National Congress of the Party in April 1969. However, he was no longer a member of the Standing Committee of the Political Bureau.

Lin Piao (1908—), of Hupeh province, was graduated from the Whampoa Military Academy where Chiang Kai-shek was the commandant. Lin became the Minister of Defense in 1959. Since Chu Teh had become inactive and P'eng Te-huai disgraced, it was logical that when Mao Tse-tung needed army support for the Cultural Revolution, he would turn to Lin Piao, who gave Mao full support, as did Chu Teh in the past. In addition to being an heir to Chu Teh's role, Lin had been designated as Mao's heir-apparent before the Cultural Revolution came to an end. This new role as a professional military leader was unprecedented in the Party's history.

❦ 12 ❦

Ch'en Tu-hsiu: His Career and
Political Ideas

YÜ-JU CHIH

The extraordinary career of Ch'en Tu-hsiu is of compelling interest for the light it throws on the course of modern Chinese intellectual and political history. This study attempts to trace his career and
present a critical exposition of his political ideas as revealed in his
writings and to establish his position as a revolutionary leader who
contributed to the creation of modern China.

Ch'en was born on October 8 (the twenty-third day of the eighth
Chinese lunar month), 1879, at Huaining (formerly Anching),
Anhwei province, in the lower Yangtze region.[1] Information on the
earliest years of his life is scanty. In 1936, while in a Nanking prison
away from the maelstrom of politics, he started an autobiography of
which he finished only the first two chapters, subsequently published
in a booklet under the title of *Shih-an tzu-chuan* (Autobiography),
Shih-an being his courtesy name. This booklet now serves as the
principal source on his childhood and youth.

Actually, Ch'en tells us very little in his short account. He states
that he does not remember his father, who passed away late in 1879,
soon after Ch'en's birth. From Ch'en's own recollections and from

---

This is an original article, published for the first time.

[1] The date of Ch'en's birth can be found in Ho Chih-yü, ed., "Tu-hsiu chu-
tso nien-piao" ("A Chronological List of the Writings by Ch'en Tu-hsiu"),
in *Tu-hsiu ts'ung-shu ch'i-chung* (Seven Works by Ch'en Tu-hsiu) 1948, p. 1.
Galley proofs of this book are deposited in the Library of Congress, a gift
presented by Dr. Hu Shih on the 150th anniversary of the Library.

other available evidence, it appears that the family led a modest life, and consisted of his mother, paternal grandfather, elder brother Meng-chi, and two elder sisters. He speaks of his mother with great fondness, describing her as capable and generous, but sometimes unduly forbearing, a characteristic which he says he may have inherited and exhibited in his later political conduct. As the Imperial examinations in those days were still the direct path to high social station and honor, his mother naturally wished her two sons to pursue a scholar-official's career. The modern school system was yet unknown, so young Ch'en began the study of Chinese Classics at home, in preparation for the examinations, when he was only six. At first he studied under the tutelage of his grandfather, an opium addict and a very strict teacher who often resorted to corporal punishment. After the death of the old gentleman in 1887, the boy continued his studies under a succession of teachers—satisfied with none—and finally under his good-natured elder brother, who had attained the *hsiu-ts'ai,* or the first academic degree. On the whole, Ch'en spent his childhood industriously, if somewhat wearily, in quiet seclusion. Nothing about him was unusual, not even his aversion to the abstruse Chinese Classics.

In the course of time his progress seemed satisfactory and in 1896, at the age of seventeen, he was urged to take the local examination, the *yüan-shih.* Before attempting the examination it was advisable to take one test at the district level and another at the prefecture level; he appeared in both, but ranked low. The local examination's only requirement was the writing of a "truncated-style" essay on the subject of "Fish and turtles are plentiful for consumption and lumber," an incomplete quotation from the *Book of Mencius.* As Ch'en recalls, he composed an equally nonsensical essay by thoughtlessly piecing together a multitude of recondite words and phrases on birds, animals, and plants he happened to have memorized from Prince Chao-ming's anthology, along with some other preposterous classical expressions from the *K'ang-hsi Dictionary.* Curiously enough, the display of familiarity with some classical works, though in an absurd context, greatly impressed the examiner and the young Ch'en passed the examination with highest distinction and earned the *hsiu-ts'ai* degree. This incident, though trivial, convinced Ch'en of the worthlessness of a time-honored institution.

This conviction was further strengthened by his experience with the regional examination he took during the following year. It was customary for Anhwei and Kiangsu to have a joint examination in Nanking, generally known as the *Kiang-nan hsiang-shih*. On the way to Nanking, the young man was distressed to see the Chinese populace in resigned apathy, astonishingly unaware of the exigencies of the time only two years after the humiliating defeat by Japan. An imposing facade, the examination area and its compound, the mismanagement of the examination staff, the frivolous and bizarre conduct of examinees, and above all, the formidable impracticality of the test itself—all combined to disclose the farce of the Imperial examination system, an institutionalized waste and torture. Indeed, this trip to Nanking greatly broadened the horizons of Ch'en's world, both physically and psychologically. It substantiated abundantly what Liang Ch'i-ch'ao had expounded in the *Shih-wu pao* (Current Affairs), then a progressive journal in Shanghai, and thus attracted Ch'en to the ideals of political reform.

In 1897, Ch'en married a girl from the Kao family of the Hochiu district in Anhwei. In six years she bore him three sons and a daughter. The eldest son, Yen-nien (*b.* 1898), was destined to play an important part in the early Communist movement until his death in 1927. The second child, a girl, was named Yü-ying (*b.* 1900). The third child born a year later, named Ch'iao-nien, also played a fairly active role in Communist activities. The last child, Sung-nien (*b.* 1903) was the only child to outlive his father. Immediately thereafter, Ch'en began his revolutionary life and had to abandon the family life.

The Peking political reform of 1898 aroused great enthusiasm and expectations throughout the country. The sudden and tragic ending of the reform must have been a traumatic experience to all those concerned with the destiny of the nation. Though we have no knowledge of Ch'en's reaction, it certainly must have been distressing to a man dedicated to the reformist cause. National salvation through peaceful, constitutional means now seemed closed for the foreseeable future, and the country had to take recourse to other, more radical ways. The Boxer uprising of 1900 signalized the birth of the new nationalism in China. Burning with true patriotic zeal, a great number of intellectuals, including Ch'en, courageously committed themselves to a national revolution, with the primary objective of overthrowing the Manchu dynasty.

During the decade 1900–1910 Ch'en combined teaching and journalism with his revolutionary activities. As a favorite diversion, he dabbled in creative, rhapsodical writing, for which his early classical grounding stood him in good stead. It might be of interest to note that prior to and during this period he used the name of Ch'en Chung-fu, "chung" denoting his being the second son in the family; he also occasionally used the sobriquet of "Tu-hsiu the Mountaineer" among several other informal names. Shortly after the Revolution of 1911 he adopted the name of Ch'en Tu-hsiu, which stayed with him till the end.

The revolutionary work of Ch'en began in 1901 with the founding of a private library in his native district of Anching as a center for the dissemination of his radical ideas. He further used the center for anti-Manchu speeches. Finally, the local authorities, displeased with his activities, closed the library and even issued orders for his arrest. But he fled to Nanking.

In 1902 Ch'en sailed to Tokyo, Japan, and enrolled at the Kōbun Gakuin, which admitted only Chinese students, and where Huang Hsing and many other Chinese studied in 1902–3. Having completed an accelerated course, Ch'en returned to China toward the end of 1902. His short stay of less than a year in Japan offered him a chance to associate with other Chinese intellectuals who shared his revolutionary fervor. He was one of the twenty or so Chinese students in Tokyo, including Chang Chi and Feng Tzu-yu, who organized a Chinese Youth Association, aimed at upholding the principle of nationalism and destroying the existing political order. It was here that he became friends with Su Man-shu, who was to become a well-known monk and poet. Throughout the years, their friendship acquired an intimate and enduring quality.

The *Kuo-min jih-jih-pao* (The China National Gazette), which made its debut in Shanghai (1903), carried the revolutionary torch of the defunct *Su-pao* (Kiangsu Journal). Chang Shih-chao and Ho Mei-shih were among its prominent chief editors whereas Ch'en, Su, Chang Chi, and Liu Ya-tzu were on its editorial staff. None of Ch'en's writings for the newspaper can now be identified, but they must have been in harmony with the general editorial policy of the paper. During its short existence, this newspaper valiantly advocated the overthrow of the Manchu court and the establishment of a liberal constitutional government.

At this time and in the subsequent fifteen years, Ch'en Tu-hsiu's close and cordial friendship with Su Man-shu and Chang Shih-chao paralleled, in a large measure, his interest in literature. He wrote prefaces to the Chinese novels of these two friends. When Su Man-shu translated Hugo's *Les Misérables* into Chinese, Ch'en polished up the Chinese text for publication in the *Kuo-min jih-jih-pao* (China National Gazette). He also instructed Su in the writing of old-style Chinese poetry. He liked the verse of the Sung period and wrote a number of poems himself, including one in the vernacular on the death of his elder brother. He rated the popular novels *Hung-lou-meng* (The Dream of Red Chamber) and *Shui-hu-chuan* (Water Margin Sketches) more highly than the classical writings of Kuei Yu-kuang, a scholar of the Ming dynasty, certainly a daring opinion in those days. Western novels tending toward romanticism and naturalism drew his admiration, and he especially liked the writings of Zola. His basic attitude toward both Chinese and Western literature seems to have favored a realistic description of society, with the chief objective of liberating the individual from social bondage. His literary efforts appeared, in sentiment if not entirely in style, in keeping with his political conviction.

Early in 1904 he went back to southern Anhwei, where he organized the *Anhwei su-hua-pao* (Anhwei Vernacular Daily), the first to recognize the importance of the vernacular in mass education and agitation. He also taught at the Anhwei Academy in Wuhu, devoted to the fostering of a national revolt and training of a revolutionary cadre. Furthermore, in co-operation with Po Wen-wei, he organized the Warrior Yüeh Association, a quasi-military organization dedicated to the overthrow of Manchu rule. In 1905 Chang Shih-chao asked him to go to Shanghai, where, during a brief stay, they participated together in a secret experiment of making high explosives to carry out assassination schemes.

In the summer of 1906 he and Su Man-shu again sailed to Japan where they mingled with the Chinese revolutionaries. But Ch'en did not join the T'ung Meng Hui (United League), organized a year earlier (1905) in Tokyo under the dual leadership of Sun Yat-sen and Huang Hsing, allegedly because of his disapproval of its narrow nationalistic strain. Actually the T'ung Meng Hui espoused a program broad enough to encompass a wide range of views. Furthermore Ch'en's mingling with the lower Yangtze revolutionaries rather than with the Canton-Chekiang group may have been due to geographical and linguistic reasons. At any rate, he returned to China a few months later.

In the autumn of 1907, Ch'en went back to southern Anhwei, where he zealously reengaged himself in journalistic as well as educational activities. Together with Liu Shih-p'ei and Chang Shih-chao he taught at Wankiang High School at Wuhu. Jointly with several others, he started and edited the *Pai-hua-pao* (Modern Language Daily).

The suggestion of his visit to France for advanced studies during this period bears no evidence. Most probably he continued to live and work in the lower Yangtze area. At the death of his elder brother (1909) he made a trip to Mukden to carry the casket back to their native city of Anching in Anhwei. In 1910, as a gesture of defiance of social conventions, he lived with Miss Kao Chün-man, whom he subsequently married. During the following twenty-odd years, marked periodically with turbulence and bloodshed, she stood by his side through sun and shade until her death, in poverty and loneliness, in the mid-1930's while Ch'en served a prison term at Nanking.

During most of the decade from 1900 to 1910, Ch'en roamed in the lower Yangtze region, working either as a teacher or as a newspaper editor, but always as a revolutionary patriot in rebellion against the Manchu court and institutions. His youthful defiance and restlessness were unmistakably apparent in everything he did. A strong and a rugged individual, he demonstrated qualities of leadership in small groups. This explains why, though a fervent revolutionary, he was not found in the mainstream of the Republican revolutionary movement.

The Revolution of 1911 was at least a nominal success. It brought about the downfall of the Manchu dynasty and ushered in the Republican era. With the establishment of the Republic, political power fell into the demagogic hands of Yüan Shih-k'ai. In May 1912, when Po Wen-wei, once a member of the defunct Warrior Yüeh Society and now a member of the revolutionary T'ung Meng Hui, was made Military Governor of Anhwei province, Ch'en was appointed as the secretary-general to the Military Governor. Concurrently with this position, during the next year he held the deanship in the Anhwei High Academy. In retrospect, he might have come closer to the core of the national revolutionary movement had it lasted longer. But, China was bitterly divided between Yüan's government in Peking and the revolutionary forces in the South. The assassination of Sung Chiao-jen (1913) touched off the anti-Yüan campaign, in which Ch'en took an active role. When the campaign failed, he took refuge in Japan.

The unfolding of Yüan Shih-k'ai's monarchical scheme made the betrayal of the 1911 revolution increasingly clear. The chaotic and generally languishing atmosphere prevailing throughout the country caused great distress to Ch'en. His mood was reflected in his writings in the monthly *Chia-yin tsa-chih* (The Tiger), edited by his old friend Chang Shih-chao. In a letter to the editor, under the name of Ch'en Tu-hsiu, he complained of the rapidly deteriorating condition in China and even anticipated the eventual dismemberment of the country by foreign powers.

In November 1914, after some somber reflection, he wrote an article entitled "Patriotism and Self-awareness" for *The Tiger*. The human mind, he said, was governed by "emotion" and "intellect." From emotion flowed patriotism, and from intellect self-awareness. Ch'en lamented the languid, enfeebled state of the Chinese national mind, which failed to react emotionally or intellectually and there-

fore could not develop a high degree of patriotic spirit or self-awareness. The impending future was certainly a gloomy one. Patriotism,
according to Ch'en, though a product of emotion, ought to be tempered by intellect. In its modern sense, a state was conceived as a
political organization designed to protect the rights of the people
and to promote their welfare. Ch'en contended that patriotism must
be based on a knowledge of the aims of the state. In his view, the
German, Austrian, and Japanese examples illustrated how their
peoples were misled in support of their states during World War I,
considering the aggressive designs of their countries. Furthermore,
loyalty to a country necessitated a knowledge of the actual conditions and an examination of the functioning of the state vis-à-vis
its purpose and assigned duties. Patriotism devoid of a knowledge
of the country's purpose and a deep understanding of her realities
would, in Ch'en's words, be "labor lost" and "perilous." Thus he
castigated nations like Korea and Mexico for their endeavors toward
political independence at the expense of the well-being of their
peoples. Ch'en viewed China's case from the same standpoint.

This article is Ch'en's earliest extant political writing and for this
reason is of considerable importance. Steeped in deep pathos, it
reflects his profound concern over China's hapless situation. It further reveals his impatience with, and even a degree of despair for,
China's uncertain future. To be sure, the article often confuses the
concept of government with that of the state, as evidenced, for
instance, in his denunciation of Germany, Austria, and Japan. Yet
the eloquence and bold rationalism, plainly discernible in this article, portended the voice he was to raise, nearly a year later, in the
Ch'ing-nien tsa-chih (Youth Journal). His resentment against the
Yüan Shih-k'ai government at Peking was all too intense. At the same
time, one should not miss the cosmopolitan strand in this article
which conveys an indifferent attitude toward national sentiment in
the formation of a state, while envisioning a world of social justice
and welfare. This cosmopolitan outlook predisposed him to a
Marxist orientation, which, as we shall see, he espoused in 1920.

The years 1915 through 1920 witnessed Ch'en in the role of a
radical liberal, staging a sort of ethical revolution chiefly through

the instrumentality of the monthly *La Jeunesse* (*Hsin ch'ing-nien*). This journal, initially called the *Ch'ing-nien tsa-chih* (Youth Journal), started publication in Shanghai on September 15, 1915. Its editorial board later (January 1917) moved to Peking when Ch'en, its chief editor, assumed the deanship of Liberal Arts at the National Peking University. As its title indicated, it addressed itself mainly to the young intellectuals. Ch'en, believing that China's current malaise originated primarily in the decadence of her public and private virtue, sought to rejuvenate an old civilization. As a point of departure, in the lead article of the journal, "A Call to Youth," Ch'en urged China's younger generation to take up the worthy responsibility history had thrust upon them. After exalting youth with such epithets as "springtime," "morning sunshine," and "new body cells," he proposed six rules of conduct for the young men of China:

    a. independence, not servility
    b. progress, not conservatism
    c. adventure, not retirement
    d. cosmopolitanism, not isolation
    e. realism, not abstraction
    f. scientism, not subjectivism

Infused with an unmistakable affirmation of life, this message is the starting point, as well as the cornerstone, of an ethical revolution unprecedented in modern Chinese intellectual history. In essence, it calls for full independence, development, and fulfillment of individual personality, and thus for an unequivocal and unreserved Westernization in ethical thinking.

Behind this appeal are at least four underlying tenets: a belief in man's rationality which warrants individuality as well as unlimited progress of mankind, the principle of Social Darwinism which not only affirms life but regards it as a relentless struggle for existence through the inexorable process of natural selection, the principle of utilitarianism conducive to human happiness, and an abiding faith in "scientism." A glance at these fundamental principles reveals that they represent a potpourri of political and social ideas produced in Europe in the eighteenth and nineteenth centuries. These ideas, disparate and of various forms and shades, emerged at different times under different circumstances and can therefore hardly be blended into a coherent system. Indeed, many of them may contradict one another either essentially or in certain details. Worse still, some may be fraught with tendencies dangerous to others if not properly channeled or curbed. For instance, does or does not human intellect militate against the Darwinian concept of survival of the fittest? If tension exists between the two, how can it be resolved? If carried to its logical extreme, would not Social Darwinism lead to aggression and war, to disorder, destruction, and utter chaos? Precisely what governs the relationships between the individual and society, either in terms of happiness or something else? Furthermore, although scientism is of indispensable value in empirical studies, would it finally render religion completely useless in practical life, and would metaphysics finally become a meaningless intellectual pursuit? All these questions, among others, seem inherent in the body of Western ideas which Ch'en transplanted to China, but remained unanswered.

Ch'en may never have fully realized these implications and complexities. Even if he did, he did not care much about them. In reading his writings of this period, one gets the impression that he was not attempting to build a system of his own thought (political, social, or ethical) because he paid no attention to intellectual subtleties, perhaps as a result of his lack of scholarly penetration. The immediate and overriding consideration was to find effective measures to drag a nation out of the state of torpidity and backwardness, and to enable her existence in a complex world. He now found that the adoption of the modern Western civilization would effectively help China's metamorphosis into a modern nation. This ardent and rather uncritical attitude toward the West caused some misgivings to one of his readers. In reply to this questioning reader, Ch'en stated, "The vast distance between the West and the East makes it impossible for us to see their shadow, even with redoubled effort in our pace. So there is really no cause for concern in lauding the

West." Ch'en thought it premature for China to fear the possible baneful effects of Westernization.

Ch'en's almost infinite fascination with the West called for a total break with China's past. He viewed the Chinese ethical legacy as being embodied mainly in Confucianism, which he attacked relentlessly and with devastating eloquence. As the Confucian ethics manifested in the creed of propriety involved the three cardinal bonds between prince and minister, father and son, and husband and wife, the Confucian society was bound to be a hierarchical one, binding all individuals in a nexus of social relationships and obligations. Thus Confucianism was deplored for impairing a full development of individual personality, for undermining the principle of equality, and, above all, for weakening the social fabric of the nation.

Confucianism was berated not only on principle, but also on utilitarian grounds. In the West the principle of individualism dominated both economic and moral life. Yet, the Confucian creed forbade a minister to hold any opinion differing from his prince's, a son to deviate from his father's views, or a wife from her husband's. Similarly, it disapproved of a minister serving two princes in succession, a widow remarrying, a man sitting alongside a woman, or even a man having a conversation with his sister-in-law. If a son stayed in deep mourning for three years upon his father's death in conformity with the Confucian rituals, how could he be expected to perform his official duties efficiently? As long as the Confucian code forbade a person to hand things to someone of the opposite sex directly, how could it be possible for people to lead useful and sensible lives? All the Confucian codes and rites, Ch'en was convinced, had long become antiquarian absurdities, unfeasible in modern society and, if allowed to exist, detrimental to social progress.

While Confucianism was the main target of his onslaught, Ch'en did not mince words in criticizing the other lesser beliefs, especially the *Yin-yang* school on account of its alleged quasi-scientific claims and pretensions. Indeed, the entire gamut of traditional Chinese values were indicted. To Ch'en, all had gone wrong in China. Accordingly, he took upon himself the task of a historical catharsis in which he attempted to call forth a new national *élan,* combative and indomitable, strong enough to wash away, once and for all, the traditional vestiges in order to make room for a new morality, patterned on the modern West.

The publication of *La Jeunesse* was an immediate, astonishing success. As one writer put it, it had "the effect of a literary bomb-shell." It won audiences far and near, including the young and still unknown Mao Tse-tung who always read it avidly. Previously known only in the lower Yangtze area as a patriotic rebel, Ch'en suddenly became an articulate spokesman of nationwide renown. Now in his late thirties, he was reaching the peak of intellectual maturity. The force he generated in the ethical revolt culminated in the celebrated May Fourth Movement of 1919, which inaugurated a new culture with far-reaching significance for modern China.

The two important catchwords in the May Fourth, or New Culture, Movement were "democracy" and "science." Democracy constituted the political ideal of Ch'en at this phase of his career. In promoting democracy, he exhorted the Chinese people to take, first and foremost, a keener interest in public affairs than in the past and, furthermore, to discern a steady trend of political change in modern times from autocratic to liberal rule, from government by a single man to government by the entire body of citizens. Democracy seemed to mean two things to him: constitutionalism, by which he espoused rule by law instead of by man, and republicanism. He waged an unflinching fight against Yüan Shih-k'ai and his monarchical schemes until Yüan's death in June 1916. Chang Hsün's efforts to put P'u Yi back on the throne also evoked his implacable fury. In his opinion, a democratic or republican government differed categorically from a monarchy because the former was based on the principle of human equality and the latter on that of human inequality; there existed no possibility of reconciliation between these two forms of government. The monarchical rule was morally wrong, as it necessarily involved a hierarchical order which would do violence to the independence and equality of individuals. "Republicanism," he declared, "is the paragon in politics."

Thus Ch'en's political thought at this stage was a corollary of his views in the realm of ethics. Just as in ethical thinking he stood for independence and full development of the individual personality, his basic political position was that the people, as masters of the state, should run their ·own political affairs and control their political destiny. It was no wonder, therefore, that early in 1917 when K'ang Yu-wei came out with a reaffirmation of his conviction in constitutional monarchy, Ch'en disagreed emphatically and rejected it totally. It might be argued that a monarch's benevolent rule could bring about peace and harmony, at least temporarily, whereas republicanism would more likely give rise to turmoil and disorder. Here, Ch'en insisted, was a matter of principle, on which a fateful decision had to be made. To him, republicanism was the only desirable and ethically sound political doctrine and system which would ensure genuine peace and justice. He said that he would rather accept disorder under a republican government than monarchical benevolence. It was a government "by the people" that he wanted, as distinguished from, or in addition to, a government "for the people."

It should be emphasized, however, that in advocating government by the people, Ch'en sought to promote a political movement of the citizenry in which the entire body of citizens would take part, forming a massive wave to assert their sovereign authority in an attempt to wipe away all political evils. Among all the existing political evils, he resented most bitterly the regional militarists, describing their mocking of law and order as a basic cause for the pervading imbroglio. He did not like political parties, per se, because in his opinion they had divisive effects on the body politic. Of course, it is one thing to dislike party bickering, and quite another to reject the party system as a constitutional principle. Ch'en left little or no doubt that he considered "a political movement of the citizenry" preferable to party politics. In his eyes, the two differed from each other not only in scope but possibly also in character. A political movement by the entire citizen body would produce what might be close to a "national consensus," in which a solid democracy would be rooted, whereas the party system tended to provide merely fragments of public opinion detrimental to national cohesiveness.

Here he obviously underestimated, or simply failed to see, the constructive function of the party as a vehicle in a constitutional democracy. This lack of perception stemmed perhaps from an irrepressible desire for nationwide unity, a matter which weighed heavily on his mind. As a result, his call for a political movement by the entire citizenry appeared crude and only vaguely defined.

Ch'en's belief in republicanism in the political field can be matched by the ardor of his faith in science. Relating the two, he had no hesitation in saying that "Republicanism in politics and science in academics are the two priceless treasures of modern civilization." To him science constituted the core of academic pursuits and was to be treasured for its materialistic and utilitarian values; it helped dispel doubts and solve all the enigmas of the physical world. Ch'en, in the spirit of Comte and Spencer, looked upon science as the powerful instrument in the study of human society. He therefore denigrated all attempts made for the upholding of the Chinese cultural heritage. He discredited Confucianism, an example of idolatry par excellence, and religion which could not withstand empirical investigation.

Had Ch'en wished to formulate only the social laws on the findings of natural sciences, there should have been no disagreement. Clearly, he wanted more; in fact, he urged mankind to move along the path of the natural sciences and pattern all its legal and moral codes on the laws of physical phenomena. He even envisaged a day when man-made laws would coincide with the laws of nature, and thereby merge the cosmological life with the human.

His optimism in this regard is excessive, for a gap seems to exist between nature and society, two entirely different entities to which different methods of thinking apply. Nature is a particular order of elements connected by the principle of causality. Society, a normative order of human behavior, is characterized by what might be called "the principle of imputation," according to which a punishment is "imputed" to a crime without a cause-and-effect relationship. This dualism tends to set a limit to the usefulness of science in investigating human society.

Ch'en's commitment to science, nonetheless, seemed irrevocable.

In ascribing importance to it, he went so far as to declare that science, and science alone, could furnish a sure, although perhaps slow, way to cultivate a genuine new faith. This presaged indeed a new faith—a faith he was to find in Marxism by 1920.

In addition to promoting the credo of democracy and science, Ch'en's ethical revolt made itself felt in the fields of education, language and literature, and the arts. It encompassed practically all major facets of life and ushered in a vigorous new culture. All the views in it may sound like banalities today but were, under the existing adverse circumstances, of such an appallingly radical nature that it must have taken keen insight and exceptional courage to propound them. And in instituting the New Culture Movement, Ch'en, always standing on the frontline of the revolt, proved outstandingly instrumental.

While *La Jeunesse* was illuminating the intellectual scene, Ch'en's interest in practical politics grew and became almost ungovernable. In 1917 he joined a political group in Peking and mingled with politicians. In December of 1918 he, with a friend, Li Ta-chao, published and edited the *Mei-chou p'ing-lun* (Weekly Review), for the chief purpose of voicing his opinions on current political problems.

The year 1919 was eventful both for modern China and for Ch'en personally. This was the year of the May Fourth Movement and its attendant repercussions and consequences of historic magnitude. For Ch'en, the year brought abrupt, appalling reverses. Earlier in the spring, pressure from the ultra-conservative circles in Peking had made him relinquish his position at the National University of Peking. Then came the May Fourth student demonstrations over the Shantung question. When the Peking government tried by ruthless means to suppress the genuine patriotic outburst, Ch'en was outraged and said, "World civilization originates from two places: the science laboratory and the prison." Ironically, on a hot day in mid-June, while distributing protest leaflets against Peking officialdom, he was arrested and imprisoned for eighty-three days. His confinement interrupted the publication of *La Jeunesse* and the *Weekly Review*; the former reappeared in November, but the latter was less fortunate, and stopped for good in August after only thirty-six issues.

Ch'en's reverses drastically changed his perception of the West, whose civilization and democratic system had for years enthralled him. As late as at the end of 1918, he was exalted over the triumphant conclusion of World War I, hailing it as a victory of justice over might. He also called President Wilson a "good man" of integrity and righteousness. But now, in early 1919, the position taken by the Western powers on the Shantung settlement and other problems infuriated him. The Allied nations, bound by the Secret Agreement of London (1915), disregarded completely the noble principles embodied in President Wilson's Fourteen Points. In utter dismay, he exclaimed, "Ah! The world today remains one of pirates. Justice still has to yield to military force!" The moral fiber of Western democracy appeared feeble and unmistakably faulty. This must have been an extremely painful realization; yet it was a harsh fact.

It was also in 1919 that he was seriously concerned about the economic problems of the people. For instance, he regarded the question of "crying of the poor people" as one of vital urgency. The democratic ideal, then, was not limited by him to the political sphere but broadened so as to encompass socio-economic aspects. This view was subsequently reinforced by John Dewey's visit to China. But the American philosopher's pragmatic approach to social and political problems required a gradual build-up of the entire community, as exemplified in the town government in colonial New England. Ch'en, a man of limited patience and rather impetuous temperament, was intent on fast sweeping changes in the national political landscape rather than slow systematic grass-roots work.

In contrast to the hypocrisy of the Western powers, Soviet Russia, shortly after its establishment, offered to annul all unequal treaties with China. And on July 25, 1919, in a direct appeal to the Chinese people, the Soviets further renounced all the Czarist conquests in China, and thus presented themselves as a force of goodwill, peace, and justice. The contrast between the images of the West and of the Soviets was too striking. More importantly, the success of the Soviet revolution served as an example for the underprivileged

Asian nations. The impact upon China was tremendous and, against the general backdrop of persistent Western alienation, it steadily assumed a catalytic function, inducing many Chinese intellectuals to make an assiduous study not only of the Soviet system but also of the Marxist thought that lay behind it.

Marxism came to China late; it spread and aroused wide attention only after the Soviet revolution. The *Communist Manifesto,* the touchstone of Marxism, appeared in Chinese only in 1908, when the translation of its first section was printed in Tokyo's Chinese periodical, *T'ien-yi pao* (T'ien-yi News). A greater part of the document appeared in 1919 in the *Weekly Review;* it was first translated into Chinese in its entirety in April 1920, by Ch'en Wang-tao. Ch'en Tu-hsiu himself was drawn to Marxism primarily because of the scientific puissance it claimed to possess, a claim which was entirely in accord with his own general rational cosmopolitan outlook. Furthermore, pending the realization of the supreme, genuine democracy which would necessitate a foundation no less than a "total consensus," it appeared that democracy could be constructed at varying levels. Since the proletariat formed the overwhelming majority of the people and could be equated with the masses, a government by the proletariat would be a far superior and more logical political system than the bourgeois democracy, as practiced in the West. The yardstick of numerical proportion would differentiate the genuinely democratic from the undemocratic, the more democratic from the less democratic. It seems, therefore, that Ch'en seized upon Marxism as a science and favored the Marxist dictatorship of the proletariat as a political system over the Western democracy but, in all likelihood, a vicarious one approaching a genuine and complete democracy. Moreover, in 1920 Ch'en expressed a strong desire for a collective endeavor which, though not monumental in scope, would long live in people's memory. It would seem that Ch'en's imprisonment had given him a realization of human transience.

Put together, the events stated above—the changed perception of the West, the impact of the Soviet revolution, and, most important, the acceptance of Marxism as a scientifically grounded blueprint for a genuine democracy—made Ch'en, in his passionate desire to assume a memorable task, turn irrevocably toward a Marxist revolution in China. Because of the changed political attitude in the North, which he could no longer bear, Ch'en left Peking for Shanghai in early 1920. Subsequently, with the assistance of Voitinsky, a Comintern agent who arrived in Shanghai in May, Ch'en organized a small local Communist group, which finally, in September of the same year, became the forerunner of the nationwide Communist Party.

In its First National Congress held secretly in Shanghai in July 1921, the twelve participating delegates representing fifty-seven members in the country proclaimed the founding of the Chinese Communist Party. Mao Tse-tung, Tung Pi-wu, Chang Kuo-t'ao, Chou Fo-hai, and Ch'en Kung-po were among the delegates. Ch'en Tu-hsiu, then the Commissioner of Education in the Kwangtung provincial government under the militarist governor Ch'en Chiung-ming, found himself unable to come to the conference; but his intellectual prominence and his towering stature in the embryonic Chinese Marxist movement easily won him the Chairmanship of the newborn Party, a title changed to Secretary-General in the following year.

Ch'en headed the Party from July 1921 to 1927, when he was deposed as a result of the Party's disastrous defeat at the hands of the Kuomintang. This period is often designated in official Chinese Communist literature as the era of "the first civil revolutionary war." At first the Party's program was rather moderate, and its emphasis was on the education and training of party members as well as on labor agitations. At its Second National Congress, in June–July 1922, the Party decided to affiliate itself with the Comintern and to submit to its discipline. The Comintern's involvement with China at this time concerned two cardinal points: the united front policy and the agrarian question. Consequently, it was these two policies which governed the Chinese Communist Party's relationship with the Kuomintang; it was also these two policies which confronted Ch'en with the authority in Moscow.

The united front policy refers to the forming of an alliance the

Party sought with the Kuomintang in carrying out their common task of national revolution. It was a Leninist tactic which derived its legitimacy from the Bolshevik leader and also reflected his dynamic realism. Here Lenin extended Marxism and applied it to a new historical situation, to colonial and semi-colonial areas where a national liberation movement was in ferment. At its second congress, convened in the summer of 1920, the Comintern adopted the "Theses on the National and Colonial Question," whereby it not only asked all Communist parties to lend support by action to revolutionary liberation movements in their respective countries, but deemed it permissible for a proletarian party to establish temporary alliance with a bourgeois-democratic party while maintaining its own independence. Accordingly, the first Comintern directive to the Chinese Communist Party, issued on January 12, 1923, urged "co-ordinated action" with the Kuomintang.

But the alliance between the Chinese Communists and the Kuomintang proved quite difficult to achieve and precarious to maintain. It was perhaps natural to expect Sun Yat-sen to collaborate with the Chinese Communist Party as a logical concomitant of his Russian orientation. However, both before and after the conclusion of the alliance, grave misgivings were expressed around Sun, who took pains to dispel them. Though wanting to place the Chinese Communists in the current of the revolution, he nevertheless insisted that they join the membership of the Kuomintang and work under his guidance.

Ch'en and a number of other leaders initially opposed such an alliance. But in the summer of 1922, Maring, another Comintern agent, proposed the idea of close co-operation, and told Communist members that they should join the Kuomintang while preserving their Party as a separate entity. Ch'en objected to it for fear that it would confuse Party organization and put a curb on independent policy. The authority of the Comintern dignitary prevailed in the end. In February 1923, however, the tragedy of the Peking-Hankow Railway strike revealed fully how weak the Chinese proletariat actually was and thus substantiated the wisdom of Moscow.

When the first united front in the history of the Chinese Communist Party was officially approved at the first Kuomintang national congress, convened in January 1924 at Canton, it admitted individual Communist members to the Kuomintang ranks. It was, of course, a Marxist anomaly in alliance, nevertheless the only form of alliance acceptable to Sun Yat-sen. There was a technical difference between an alliance of two equal partners and the one just concluded. In fact, this difference meant very little, considering the then extremely small membership of the young party. Clearly, by forging such an alliance, the Chinese Communist Party made a tremendous gain as it now emerged into the open from underground, with a leverage by which it could more effectively reach the masses both inside and outside the Kuomintang.

As China was and still is a vast agricultural country, no revolution can be completely successful without solving her acute agrarian problems. Keenly aware of this necessity, the Executive Committee of the Comintern repeatedly pointed out that the peasant problem constituted the main thrust of the entire policy of the Chinese Communist Party. In a directive in May 1923, it made clear that the national revolution in China would necessarily be followed by an agrarian revolution of the peasantry. Subsequently, both its "Theses on the Peasant Question" passed in April 1925 and its "Theses on the China Question" adopted in February–March 1926 reaffirmed this directive. But it was not until the convocation of its seventh enlarged plenum in November–December 1926 that the Executive Committee of the Comintern sought a drastic turn in its Chinese agrarian policy. Stalin appeared and made a lengthy speech at the plenum, lending portentous importance to the meeting. The resolution included the formation of peasant committees as the basis of the people's government and of the people's army in the rural districts and the nationalization of land by successive stages. Furthermore, it called for the disarming of the local militia then in existence and the arming of the poor and middle peasants. All these drastic steps went far beyond the political, social, and economic program envisaged by its Kuomintang ally.

Thus, there was severe tension between the Comintern's united front policy and its advocacy of agrarian revolution, with one tending to jeopardize the other. Ostensibly, however, the united front policy was designed as a temporary measure which would gradually but steadily give way to the agrarian revolution. Such a transition would require subtle, masterful tactical skill. As a matter of fact, under the direction of Borodin, Stalin's double-edged scheme scored a considerable victory in making this transition. By 1925–26, the Chinese Communist Party had greatly increased its membership, had spread its influence to alarming proportions in the rural areas, and, above all, had succeeded in having its members occupy key positions in leading Kuomintang organs.

It must be pointed out that the alliance had always been treated with skepticism by many in the Kuomintang and, as time went on, met mounting opposition. After Sun Yat-sen died, in March 1925, continuing co-operation became impossible. First, in the summer of 1925, Tai Chi-t'ao voiced strong anti-Communist pronouncements, charging the Chinese Communists with parasitic existence. Additional momentum was gained when a group of Kuomintang leaders met in November–December of that year, alongside Sun Yat-sen's coffin in the Western Hills near Peking, and publicly announced their intention of parting company with the Chinese Communist Party. In the meantime, Sun Yat-sen's death left the top Kuomintang ranks in disarray. The assassination of Liao Chung-k'ai, an eminent Kuomintang leader, indicated the degree to which political intrigue was gripping Canton, then the revolutionary base. Assiduously Borodin wooed Wang Ching-wei, as the new political leader in the Kuomintang, and established a magnificent rapport. Between the anti-Communist Western Hills group and Wang Ching-wei, Chiang Kai-shek, Commandant of the Whampoa Military Academy and a high-ranking military officer, maintained a public stance of neutrality in regard to the alliance problem, although his trip to Russia late in 1923 had convinced him of the insincerity of Moscow's attitude toward the Chinese national revolution. As a whole, therefore, the situation in South China in general and at Canton in particular seemed ominous from the second half of 1925 through early 1926.

Finally, after at least several weeks of brooding in anxiety, Chiang decided to assert his will in order to fight a way out of the aggravating situation. On March 20, 1926, over the gunboat *Chung-shan* incident, he struck a devastating blow to the Communist members, in spite of the political authority of Wang Ching-wei. Henceforward, his prestige as well as his power began to rise spectacularly. Soon, in June 1926, the Northern Expedition set out under his command. In April 1927, shortly after the revolutionary forces had reached the Yangtze valley, he took the most decisive action of killing many Communists in Shanghai and annulled the double membership of all Communists in the Kuomintang ranks. The ensuing split between the Nanking government under Chiang and the Wuhan regime under Wang Ching-wei stemmed more from personal animosity than from basic differences in political belief. Stalin wanted the Chinese Communists to continue working with the Wuhan group in the Kuomintang. When, in July of that year, Wang Ching-wei found out for himself the duplicity in the Moscow plan, the united front policy came to a disastrous end.

Thereupon, at an emergency conference on August 7, 1927, Ch'en was removed from leadership of the Party because of his failure to fulfill the desired role.

In retrospect, Stalin's design with respect to China did not fail in 1927 because it adopted and adhered to the united front policy. Nor did it commit a tactical blunder in executing the agrarian policy under the shield of partnership. Intent upon viewing the development of historical forces in the dialectical framework, Moscow tended to underrate human factors as contingencies which might contribute significantly to shaping the history of man. As a result, the rapid rise of Chiang Kai-shek was quite unexpected and his attack caught the Communists by surprise. The chief mistake Stalin made lay in failing to make preparations for all eventualities in the alliance.

Ch'en knew that it would be impossible to extricate himself totally from responsibility for the debacle. Writing, in December 1929, in an effort to clarify his previous position, he contended that he had always opposed the alliance from its inception and had led the Party to defeat largely by carrying out all Comintern instructions faithfully. This self-defense, unfortunately, cannot be entirely vindicated. It is futile to speculate on the course China's political struggle might have taken had there been no alliance. Suffice it to say that without exposing itself the young Party could never expect to advance to victory, although it might well have averted the disaster of 1927. From 1921 to 1924 Ch'en managed Party affairs fairly well; but from 1925 on the political rivalry was intensified, and the basically intellectual Ch'en proved no equal to a task which called for high resolve and a superlative degree of political aptitude and resiliency. While Borodin meandered between the Scylla of the united front policy and the Charybdis of the agrarian policy, resulting in turns and twists in the Comintern directives, the Chinese Communist leader often became irritated. He was unable to come to grips with the real issues and failed in inducing a change of policy based on conviction. Thus under his leadership the Party drifted in a perilous political storm, with no sense of direction or purpose until it met with its fate in 1927.

Curiously enough, Ch'en's own political belief would have led the Party farther from attaining victory; particularly if we consider his articles in the *Hsiang-tao chou-pao* (The Guide Weekly), in which he espoused a "dual revolution" theory, with the bourgeois-democratic revolution and the socialist revolution clearly demarcated. In his view the current Chinese national revolution was basically bourgeois in nature; therefore he counted upon the Chinese bourgeoisie to take the lead in it and expected an ultimate victory for them. On the other hand, the Chinese proletariat, weak both in numbers and in morale, was expected to play merely a supervisory role at that time. The proletarian socialist revolution, which would eventually occur and succeed the bourgeois-democratic revolution, was considered desirable as well as inevitable only when justified by the progress of industrial development. The whole historical process would march on inexorably, with no phase to be skipped. This evolutionary position, taken as a whole, represents a rigid, one-sided interpretation of Karl Marx's view of history. Translated into revolutionary moves, it appears akin to the Russian Menshevik stand as exemplified in Plekhanov; but it is quite at variance with Lenin's dynamic formula of revolution, which envisages the proletariat playing a leading part in both the bourgeois-democratic and the socialist revolution in a backward area. The idea of the "revolutionary bourgeoisie" in the bourgeois-democratic revolution found its way into the declaration of the Third National Congress of the Party, issued in June 1923. Ch'en has been discredited for the insertion of the idea although the theme of that document was soon obscured by the onrush of the rivalry during 1925–27.

The low estimate Ch'en entertained of the peasantry in regard to its revolutionary capabilities might, in particular, have hindered a speedy Communist victory. It was his belief that a peasant movement would be needed and possible only after the national revolution was completely accomplished, domestic industry well developed, and, in consequence, a rural proletariat had emerged with wide capitalization of agriculture. This view, of course, records the orthodox Marxist image of the peasantry, based chiefly on the rural conditions in nineteenth-century Europe; but it fails to take cognizance of Lenin's switch on Marxism in elevating the role of the peasantry to one of partner-in-arms to the proletariat. From the doctrinal point of view at least, Ch'en could not have anticipated the agrarian revolution to be launched in China in the mid-1920's. He has thus been blamed for a party resolution he drafted in September 1926, according to which a limit was to be set to the rising peasant movement. It is a moot point, however, whether he did it from his own belief or simply in compliance with a Comintern directive, for only a month later, in October 1926, Moscow sent a telegram ordering the Chinese Communists to keep the peasant movement in check. Later, when challenged, Stalin admitted that the telegram was a mistake. It is indeed dubious that, with Borodin holding supreme power over the Party, Ch'en ever had much of a chance to apply his own opinion of the peasantry to practical politics. Also deserving mention in this connection is the fact that in the winter months of 1926–27, when he directed a peasant movement in Hunan, Mao Tse-tung by and large acted in accord with the dominant Comintern line on the agrarian revolution but in defiance of the Chinese Communist leadership under Borodin and Ch'en. From all this it becomes clear that, during the years 1921–27, in spite of being the leader of the Party, Ch'en exerted on the Chinese Communist movement an influence which seemed hardly more than tangential.

The year 1927 marked a critical turning point in Ch'en's public career as well as in his personal life. It was the year which witnessed not only his fall from Party leadership but also the tragic loss of two of his sons in the cause of communism. The oldest, Yen-nien, reputedly a capable person and at that time secretary of the Party's Kiangsu-Chekiang regional committee, was arrested in Shanghai in June and later executed. His second son, Ch'iao-nien, died shortly afterward. Following the personal failure and the loss of his sons Ch'en lived in relative seclusion, devoting himself to soul-searching reflection. From time to time, however, he wrote short comments, mostly on current events, for the Party organ *Pu-erh-sai-wei-k'o* (Bolshevik) in a characteristically forceful, incisive style. Although now merely a member, because of his seniority he still commanded some prestige and was occasionally consulted on certain Party matters. But the new Party policy of armed uprisings suffered one defeat after another and disenchanted him increasingly.

In mid-1929 Ch'en clashed with the central leadership over the Chinese Eastern Railway incident in Manchuria. In the Sino-Russian dispute the official Chinese Communist Party position was to support the Soviet Union with a view to promoting the cause of world proletarian revolution. Ch'en, however, felt this policy was too doctrinaire for the broad masses in China and therefore proposed a slogan of "opposing the damage-the-country policy of the Kuomintang government." The new Party leadership then maintained that Ch'en's proposal erred in lacking "class content." As the arguments grew bitter, Ch'en finally went so far as to blame the Party for repeatedly following the opportunist line as practiced during 1925–27 and, consequently, for committing the blunder of "putschism" instead of staging a retreat in the face of the rising bourgeois forces. When putschism ran into obstacles, he further asserted that the Party had resorted to "commandism" in the organization, and had disregarded the democratic principles laid down by Lenin.

It should be pointed out that by 1929 Ch'en definitely saw an absence of revolutionary surge and during this period supported peaceful democratic slogans such as "convene a national assembly" as guidelines in Party work. He believed that by the adoption of these measures the masses could work openly and shake the very foundation of Kuomintang power and bring about a new revolutionary tide. His opposition to the official Party line drew him close to the Trotskyite view, which occupied an analogous position in relation to the Stalin government. Thus he shared the sentiments of the small numbers of Chinese Communists with Trotskyite leanings who had returned to China from Russia early in 1929 and had worked on the journal *Wo-men ti-hua* (Our Words).

Ch'en's broadside assault on the central leadership resulted in a curious request from the party. On October 6, he was asked to undertake editorial work and his first assignment was to write an article denouncing Oppositionist views and activities. Ch'en declined this request. Thereupon the Party adopted some stern and uncompromising measures on organization and discipline, forbidding the formation and existence of inside factions and specifically ordering the former Party leader to work under the current Party line. When Ch'en refused, the central leadership on November 15, 1929, expelled him from the Party. On February 8, 1930, the Comintern wired Ch'en and asked him to come to Moscow to take part in an investigation of his expulsion. Refusing to do so, the former Chinese Communist leader replied that his expulsion from the Party was not merely a personal problem but one which involved a wide range of vital political questions. This refusal blasted the slightest chances of a compromise.

Thereafter, for nearly three years, Ch'en labored under the banner of Leftist Opposition. One after the other, he edited *Wu-ch'an-che* (Le Prolétaire) and *Huo-hua* (Iskra), recalling Lenin's early namesake journals and thus leaning on his undisputed authority. The Leftist Opposition insisted that the 1925–27 Chinese revolution had already ended in failure and accordingly urged preparations for the next revolution. *Ad interim* it demanded a revolutionary democratic struggle involving such open, non-violent measures as "con--ening a national assembly." It claimed, in essence, adherence to a revolution in breath rather than in depth; but, to its opponents, it was "liquidationist." As far as Ch'en was concerned, this concrete program was quite in tune with his basic belief of "dual revolution" theory as applied to the period of bourgeois revolution.

While Ch'en's feud with the central leadership continued undiminished, the government authorities suddenly arrested him in Shanghai (October 15, 1932) and put him on trial on charges of sedition. To defend himself he acquired the services of three lawyers, including Chang Shih-chao, an old friend with whom he had worked closely on the *China National Gazette*. In addition, he wrote a stoic defense of his position and persuasively presented his views. Nevertheless, in July 1934, the court found him guilty and sentenced him to eight years' imprisonment in Nanking.

Some vital political problems, such as the national assembly versus the Soviets, occupied his mind in the prison. It was here that he attempted his autobiography. Prison solitude drew him to the research of ancient Chinese phonology and related subjects, an academic interest traceable to pre-*La Jeunesse* days. In 1928, he prepared a draft for the romanization of modern Chinese. From 1932 on his research findings appeared intermittently in the form of articles in magazines.

At the time of the Sino-Japanese War (1937) the National Government, amid the clamor for unity to meet a national crisis, permitted itself to co-operate with the Chinese Communist Party and as a result decided to release a number of political prisoners; Ch'en was one of them. In September he moved to Wuhan, up the Yangtze River. When war threatened the safety of that city in the spring of 1938, he moved farther up the river and settled in Chiangchin, across from the wartime capital Chungking, in Szechwan province. The imprisonment severed all his political ties with the outside world; after regaining personal freedom, he never associated with any political group but, rather, led a quiet life, supported either by a famed publishing firm through advance payments or by a salary from the National University of Peking, then in Kunming. He died in Chiangchin on May 27, 1942, five years after his release.

During the last five years Ch'en expressed his political views in regard to the war against Japan and supported it unreservedly. Admittedly it was a "national" war and Ch'en considered it profoundly important for modern China's historical mission. He thought that politically the war would advance the democratizing process started in 1911, as it would necessitate a solidification of all political parties and peoples; economically, it would accelerate the capitalist economy, which he believed must precede the socialist economy in historical development. Therefore, he urged the rich and the talented to contribute to the war efforts their money and their talents.

When Hitler's invasion of Poland in September 1939 touched off a global conflagration, the Sino-Japanese War became a phase of the Second World War. And this broadened Ch'en's parochial vision of the Sino-Japanese conflict. In a few essays and a number of letters to his friends Ch'en made a positive pronouncement which crowned "six or seven years" of deep, untrammeled thinking and a lifelong fight. This pronouncement was a call for "mass democracy" or "proletarian democracy."

In Ch'en's opinion, human history is meaningful in being a record of democratic struggle, an annal of continuing democratization. Seeing World War II as a mortal battle between democracy and dictatorship, he placed himself squarely on the side of the Allies. Western democracy, he said, was a product of the struggle against the political tyranny of approximately seven hundred years and should be treasured for all the fine attributes it had earned. Ch'en even blamed Lenin and Trotsky for failing to appreciate the beneficial aspects of Western democracy. But, in spite of its basic validity, he considered the Western political system a limited, bourgeois democracy because of its narrow social base. And yet he found no trace of democratic principles in any dictatorship, be it Hitlerian or proletarian. Hitlerian dictatorship, of course, was anathema to Ch'en. The proletarian dictatorship merited credit inasmuch as it was built on the broadest social foundation; but, its dictatorial nature would inevitably entail cruelty, deceit, and a corrupt bureaucracy, as in the case of the Stalin regime. So, neither the Western democratic system nor the proletarian dictatorship received Ch'en's approval. What he envisioned was a proletarian democracy which, by synthesizing "proletarian" dictatorship and bourgeois "democracy," would represent a marked advance over both systems. It would possess the same democratic content as Western democracy and also have the broadest mass social base. It may be called "mass democracy," obviously with a Marxist stamping; nevertheless, a democracy. Freedom of organizing parties opposing the government in power was regarded by Ch'en as the most significant attribute of a democracy. Ch'en had come a long way to grasp the quintessence of a democratic system.

Ch'en furnished no specific answer to the question of how and when the proletarian democracy would be achieved, though his Marxist orientation made him preclude the developing of capitalism into a mass society—in the Tocquevillian sense. He favored a full flowering of capitalism in the belief that, unless capitalism ran its course and lost its potency, mass or proletarian democracy would be entirely inconceivable. It is logical for him to say then, as he actually did, that mass democracy was "not as yet in sight." The notion of historical evolution dominated his mind. But by advocating a mass-based democracy, he pointed to a noble idealism toward which he prodded humanity to move.

The cause of democracy, with varying import, constitutes the key to Ch'en's political thought. To promote this ideal, he devoted his full talents and extraordinary energy to a life marked by dazzling personal triumphs and bitter defeats and disappointments. His crusading spirit, impregnated with gusto and pugnacity, always placed him at the forefront of intellectual and political battles. On the one hand, by illuminating politics with intellectual vigor, he magnified the tradition of such eminent Chinese public polemists as Liang Ch'i-ch'ao. On the other hand, his patriarchal stature in the nascent Chinese Marxist movement, his orthodox Marxist stance of advocating a "dual revolution" doctrine, his low estimation of the peasantry, his oft-expressed nationalistic sentiments despite his generally cosmopolitan outlook, and even his ultimate estrangement from the party—all pose him as a parallel to Plekhanov in modern Russia. A man of lofty ideals and humanistic tendencies—though inept in political action—he stands as an intrepid warrior who made a supreme effort to destroy the traditional values and structure of Chinese society in anticipation of a new political order.

BIBLIOGRAPHICAL NOTE: Of the general literature on Ch'en Tu-hsiu's life and political thought, Ho Chih-yü, "Tu-hsiu chu-tso nien-piao" ("A Chronological List of Writings by Ch'en Tu-hsiu") in *Tu-hsiu ts'ung-shu ch'i-chung* (Seven Works by Ch'en Tu-hsiu) merits mention for the valuable personal data which can hardly be obtained elsewhere, such as Ch'en's birth date and the years of birth and death for his immediate family members. Ho's bibliographical work should be reliable on the whole since Ch'en, before his death, had entrusted him with the job of keeping, collating, and collecting all his manuscripts with a view to possible publication. Also useful as a bibliographical guide, although by no means complete, is Kimura Yasuko, "Chin Dokushu Shūhitsu Katsudō Nempu" ("A Chronological List of Writings by Ch'en Tu-hsiu"), in *Ihō* (Gazette), No. 2 (April 1963), Modern China Research Institute, Toyo Bunko, Tokyo. Ch'en Tung-hsiao (ed.), *Ch'en Tu-hsiu p'ing-lun* (Essays on Ch'en Tu-hsiu) (Peiping, 1933) collected a number of informative and analytical essays written by various writers immediately after Ch'en Tu-hsiu's arrest in 1932; some of these essays, while they are wide-ranging in views and occasionally inaccurate in fact, shed light on Ch'en's life and political thought. Further, two theses on Ch'en Tu-hsiu may be consulted: Julia Lien-ying How, "The Development of Ch'en Tu-hsiu's Thought, 1915–1938" (M.A. Thesis, Columbia University, 1949) and Chih Yü-Ju, "The Political Thought of Ch'en Tu-hsiu" (Ph.D. Dissertation, Indiana University, 1965).

Information on Ch'en's pre-*Hsin ch'ing-nien* days is still scanty. The *Shih-an tzu-chuan* (Autobiography), which he started in 1936 while in a Nanking prison, covers only the first eighteen years of his life. The Committee for Historical Source Materials of the National Committee of the People's Political Consultative Conference (ed.), *Hsin hai ko-ming hui-i lu* (Reminiscences of the 1911 Revolution), 4 vols. (Peking, 1961–62) touches upon the activities of Ch'en against the Manchu government. His literary activities of this period are recorded in Liu Ya-tzu (ed.), *Man-shu ch'üan-chi* (Complete Works of Su Man-shu), 5 vols. (Shanghai, 1928) and in Liu Wu-chi, *Man-shu ta-shih chi-nien chi* (Works of Su Man-shu: A Memorial Volume) (Chungking, 1943). The *Chia-yin tsa-chih* (The Tiger) published a number of literary works written by Ch'en during those years.

For Ch'en's political, ethical, and social beliefs as a liberal and as a staunch proponent of the New Culture Movement, see his writings in the first seven volumes of the *Hsin ch'ing-nien* reprint, 14 vols. (Tokyo: Daian, 1962), which many consider his *magnum opus*. In addition, his writings in the *Mei-chou p'ing-lun* (Weekly Review) reflect many of his opinions on current political issues.

During 1920–27, Ch'en led the nascent Chinese Communist movement. His views on the basic nature of the Chinese revolution are contained in Hsing ch'ing-nien she (ed.), *Chung-kuo ko-ming wen-t'i lun-wen chi* (Essays on the Chinese Revolution) (n.p., 1927). The *Hsiang-tao chou-pao* (Guide Weekly), reprint, 5 vols. (Tokyo: Daian, 1963), the main organ of the Chinese Communist Party during those years, published many of Ch'en's articles and his incisive comments on national as well as international affairs. Also of importance are the last volumes of the *Hsin ch'ing-nien,* which embraced the communist cause from 1920 on. For important directives of the Comintern to the Chinese Communist Party, see the *International Press Correspondence*; the first two volumes of Jane Degras (ed.), the *Communist International, 1919–1943,* 3 vols. (London: Oxford University Press, 1956–65); and Xenia J. Eudin and Robert C. North (eds.), *Soviet Russia and the East: 1920–27* (Stanford University Press, 1957). Major pronouncements of the Chinese Communist Party may be found in Ch'en Kung-po, *The Communist Movement in China,* ed. C. Martin Wilber (New York: Octagon Books Inc., 1966); Hu Hua (ed.), *Chung-kuo hsin-min-chu chu-yi ko-ming shih ts'an-k'ao tzu-liao* (Materials on the History of the New Democratic Revolution in China) (Shanghai, 1951); Robert C. North and Xenia J. Eudin, *M. N. Roy's Mission to China* (Berkeley: University of California Press, 1963); and, of course, the *Hsiang-tao chou-pao*. Among the many interpretations of the defeat of the Chinese Communist movement in 1927, particularly concerning Ch'en's role in it, Chang Kuo-t'ao's memoir, "Wo-ti hui-i," published serially in the *Ming-pao yüeh-k'an* (Ming Pao Monthly) (Hong Kong), Vol. I, No. 3 (March, 1966–), deserves special attention for the excellent insights furnished by this series of articles.

As leader of opposition to the new Chinese Communist leadership, Ch'en propounded his views on the Chinese revolution in "Kao ch'üan-tang t'ung-chih shu" ("A Letter to All Party Members"), December 10, 1929, and in Ch'en Tu-hsiu et al., "Wo-men ti cheng-chih yi-chien shu" ("A Statement of Our Political Views"), dated December 15, 1929. Also indispensable are the *Wu-ch'an-che* (Le Prolétaire) and the *Huo-hua* (*Iskra*) which carried many articles expressing his political convictions.

Finally, Ch'en's reflections on the future of humanity as well as on current national and world politics during the last five years of his life can be found in *Ch'en Tu-hsiu tsui-hou tui-yü min-chu cheng-chih ti chien-chieh* (Ch'en Tu-hsiu's Final Views on Democracy) (Hong Kong, 1950).

Li Ta-chao and the Intellectual Prerequisites for the Maoist Strategy of Revolution

MAURICE MEISNER

Half a decade before the organization of the Chinese Communist Party, the two young intellectuals who were to be the co-founders of that party debated the problem of the role of the intellectual in Chinese political life. The polemic between Ch'en Tu-hsiu (1879–1942) and Li Ta-chao' (1888–1927) appeared on the pages of a rather obscure periodical, *Chia-yin tsa-chih* (The Tiger), read mostly by Chinese students and political exiles in Tokyo. The debate of 1915 was a brief and rather minor episode in the intellectual history of modern China. It was little noticed at the time and has not been much celebrated since. Yet the issues raised (and the way they were treated) were to foreshadow important developments in the years that followed, particularly the different ways in which Marxist theory would be interpreted and employed in the modern Chinese historical environment.

The sense of despair which pervaded much of the Chinese intellectual world in 1915 was reflected in Ch'en Tu-hsiu's major contribution to the debate, an essay entitled "Patriotism and Self-Consciousness." It was with both fear and a feeling of impotence that Chinese intellectuals looked upon the impending monarchial institutionalization of the tyranny of Yüan Shih-k'ai and the Yüan regime's capitulation to the aggressive demands of Japanese imperialism. Political oppression and regression within China was

This is an original article, published for the first time.

coupled with the threat of foreign conquest from without—and yet Chinese society seemed moribund and inert. It was this ominous situation that led Ch'en to the anguished conclusion that China was not really a nation at all, for China lacked the "self-consciousness" that was prerequisite for true nationhood. How was China to acquire "self-consciousness"? Certainly not through "patriotism," for in the Chinese situation there could be no true patriots. Indeed, Ch'en argued, "patriotism" was a barrier to the development of "self-consciousness" for it promoted blind loyalty to the existing state and old traditions. What China required was knowledge and men who were capable of thinking clearly about specific problems rather than emotionally inspired patriots. Only after the development of "self-consciousness" through knowledge could patriotism become a progressive force in Chinese life.[1]

The import of Ch'en's argument was that the intellectual should not dissipate his energies in the corrupt quagmire of Chinese politics because of a false sense of national loyalty. Rather, he first should gain knowledge of particular social problems; above all, he should study and learn. He thus should withdraw from political life and devote himself to educational activities and moral reform until social and political conditions offered real opportunities for fruitful political participation.

Li Ta-chao's reply to Ch'en's "Patriotism and Self-Consciousness" was an essay entitled "Pessimism and Self-Consciousness." By substituting "pessimism" for "patriotism," he suggested that the former rather than the latter was the real barrier to the achievement of self-consciousness. Indeed, Li was bitterly (if implicitly) critical of Ch'en himself for having contributed to the "fog of pessimism" that had engulfed the Chinese intelligentsia. For it was pessimism and despair, Li argued, that inhibited the emergence of a "self-conscious" intelligentsia prepared to act to rescue China from its desperate situation. A "pessimistic and deterministic" outlook he wrote, "weakens the spirit of struggle," thus preventing men from "exerting efforts to move forward . . . to change the situation to suit our will."

[1] Ch'en Tu-hsiu, "Ai-kuo-hsin yü tzu-chüeh-hsin" (Patriotism and Self-Consciousness), *Chia-yin tsa-chih*, Vol. I, No. 4, pp. 1–6.

Patriotism, moreover, was not an obstacle in the acquisition of knowledge but rather an essential pre-condition for "self-conscious" action, a necessary means to inspire men to reconstruct the nation on new foundations: "The meaning of self-consciousness lies in the spirit of changing the nation and in seeking to make the country lovable and loving it." A nation is "a creation of men," Li argued, and the intellectuals were duty-bound "to change the nation" in accordance with their will and their consciousness. And this could not be accomplished unless intellectuals were willing to participate actively in politics. Nor could it be accomplished "without the patriotism of the people." [2]

Li Ta-chao and Ch'en Tu-hsiu shared many of the same intellectual assumptions and social and political ideals. Although Ch'en was perhaps a good deal harsher in his condemnation of the Chinese past, both had rejected traditional values and both looked to similar Western sources for new ideas and ideals. The intellectual orientations and political hopes which were to draw them together were more important than the issues which separated them. In 1917 Li was to join Ch'en as an editor of *Hsin ch'ing-nien* (La Jeunesse), the foremost radical organ of China's newly-emergent modern intelligentsia. In 1918 Ch'en was to bring Li to Peking University where they (and their student followers) were to do so much to mold the intellectual environment that gave rise to that most crucial of turning points in modern Chinese history—the May Fourth Movement of 1919. And both, eventually, were to turn to Marxism to bring about the regeneration of a new "young China."

Yet Li and Ch'en were to be very different kinds of Marxists in the 1920's and their differences as Marxists were not unrelated to the different intellectual and emotional predispositions apparent in their debate on "self-consciousness" in 1915. Whereas Ch'en (in 1915) saw self-consciousness as essentially a process of education and evolution and the gaining of knowledge about specific problems, Li took self-consciousness to mean a process in which purposeful men actively

---

[2] Li Ta-chao, "Yen-shih-hsin yü tzu-chüeh-hsin" (Pessimism and Self-Consciousness) *Li Ta-chao hsüan-chi* (Selected Writings of Li Ta-chao) (Peking, 1958), pp. 28–32 (hereafter referred to as *Hsüan-chi*).

engage in changing their political and social surroundings. Whereas Ch'en had no use for patriotism (and, indeed, characteristically distrusted all overt manifestations of nationalism), Li extolled the virtues and political uses of patriotism. It was thus not inconsistent for Ch'en later to interpret Marxism in a generally orthodox and deterministic fashion and to be drawn to the genuinely internationalistic content of original Marxist theory. Nor is it surprising that Li's Marxism was to be governed by his politically activistic and deeply nationalistic impulses. His voluntarist assumption that men were free to mold historical reality was to result in an interpretation of Marxism that did much to mitigate the deterministic implications of the theory and allow him to abandon Marxian orthodoxies entirely when they conflicted with concrete opportunities for revolutionary action. And Li was to receive the internationalist message of Marxism as a promise for the fulfillment—and not a demand for the abandonment—of Chinese nationalist aspirations.

That Li Ta-chao took it upon himself (in 1915 and at other times) to admonish his fellow intellectuals for having fallen victims to pessimism and despair is no less relevant for understanding his political mentality (both before and after his conversion to Marxism) than were his strongly voluntaristic and nationalistic predispositions. The issue of "pessimism" or "optimism" is not as trivial a matter as it might at first sight seem. For men must be able to hope before they can act; they must have not only ideals but a sense of hope that their ideals can be realized through their own actions. In politics, optimism (or the lack of it) is a matter of very considerable significance.

Perhaps more than anything else, it was Li Ta-chao's ardently optimistic world view and his inexhaustible sense of hope for the future of China that determined his political orientations. Although the themes were to be repeated and elaborated upon in many different ways throughout the remainder of his life, Li's highly optimistic faith in the future was never better expressed than in the essay in which he established his reputation as a leading member of China's new intelligentsia. In "Spring" (Ch'ing-ch'un), written early in 1916—and published later that year in La Jeunesse—Li presented a transcendental philosophy of historical development based upon an eternally self-renewing "tide of Reality" in accordance with which history proceeded in a dialectical fashion through inevitable processes of life, death, and rebirth. Employing the metaphors of the life cycle in the world of nature—in which death is but the inevitable prelude to rebirth—Li confidently predicted the inevitable historical rebirth of a "young China" from within the "corpse" of old China. It was the youth of China—those who could capture the eternal spirit of "Spring" and those who embodied "the spirit that moves mountains"—who were to be the seeds of this rebirth: "Our young people must pledge themselves to show the world not whether old China is going to live or die but that we are busily paving the way for the resurgence of a young China. . . . Whether or not we can stand up in the world depends not on the survival of old China but on its resurrection as young China; for life is a cycle of death and birth and our problem is not one of national survival but of being born again and recovering the springtime of our nation." [3]

The idea of the inevitable rebirth of a young China from within the very womb of the dying civilization was to become a dominant theme among the new generation of young intellectuals who so suddenly were to burst into political prominence with the May Fourth Incident of 1919 and who were to transform the course of modern Chinese history. Indeed, this notion was to become a deeply rooted emotional belief which molded much of both the form and content of the later Chinese Communist mentality.

Li Ta-chao's faith in the inevitability of the rebirth of China promised not only hope for the future. It was combined with a demand for action in the present. The youth could truly become the seeds of rebirth only if they "grasped the present," for, as Li wrote, "the present is the springtime of our youth (and) with this eternal Spring we are capable of everything and should have no worries or fears." Thus Li Ta-chao's inexhaustible sense of optimism for the future supported his constant injunctions for political activism in

[3] Li Ta-chao, "Ch'ing-ch'un" (Spring), *Hsin ch'ing-nien*, Vol. II, No. 1 (September 1, 1916), pp. 1–12. For an excellent English translation of a part of this poetic essay see *Chinese Literature* (May 1959), pp. 11–18.

the present. His nationalist faith in the inevitable regeneration of a "young China" was inextricably linked to his voluntarist belief that the actions of dedicated young men was all that was needed to bring about that regeneration. An optimistic faith in the future supported a demand to mold the future, and in order to mold the future it was necessary to "grasp the present."

The Pre-Marxian Phase

Of what is known of the early life of Li Ta-chao—and of his times—there is nothing that might have predisposed him to an optimistic world view, much less to that very special kind of messianic optimistic hope that Marxism was to offer. One can only repeat the platitude that men respond differently to similar situations, and that, for some men, an optimistic faith in the future serves to compensate for personal unhappiness and social despair.

Li's childhood was a particularly tragic one. The son of a nineteen-year-old farmer, Li was born in a village in Hopeh province on October 6, 1888. His father died before his only child's second birthday, and only a few months later his mother also was dead, leaving the young orphan to live with his grandparents. Although Li was later to describe his childhood in the most somber fashion, it would appear that he was relatively well treated by his grandparents. His grandfather, a petty rural merchant turned village landlord, provided for the education of his young ward. At the age of four, Li began to attend a private village school where he received a rudimentary classical education. The grandfather also provided for his marriage; at the age of eleven Li was married to a young girl with bound feet, the daughter of a neighboring peasant.

When Li's grandfather died, he left a portion of his modest estate to his grandson. This enabled Li to leave his village home in 1905 to enroll in the Yung-p'ing prefectural middle school, where he was first introduced to the "new learning" of the West. In 1907 Li went to the treaty port of Tientsin to pursue Western studies at the Peiyang College of Law and Political Science, an institution based on modern Japanese educational patterns. In Tientsin, in the years 1907–1913, Li majored in political economy and studied Japanese and English. It was there that he also began his political career.

For the man who shortly was to gain fame as the first important Chinese intellectual to declare his support for the Bolshevik Revolution and to become the pioneer of Marxism in China and the co-founder of the Chinese Communist Party, Li Ta-chao's early political orientations were formed in a rather conservative mold. Although Li expressed his admiration for Sun Yat-sen and especially for the martyred Sung Chiao-jen—and although he had a brief flirtation with Chiang K'ang-hu's mildly reformist "Socialist Party"—his early political ties were with much less radical groups and people. In Tientsin, for example, he played a leading role in the organization of the Peiyang Legal and Political Study Society, a group closely associated with, and financially supported by, Yüan Shih-k'ai and other northern warlords. He managed the Society's magazine, *Yen-chih tsa-chih* (Statesman), and wrote articles expressing the hope that Yüan Shih-k'ai would bring order out of political chaos and thus save China from the internal danger of opportunistic "party politicians" and the external threat of "the evil foreigners."

Li's support of the Yüan regime was shortlived; by early 1913 he came to the conclusion that Yüan had betrayed "the will of the people." Yet this led him not to the revolutionary nationalists of Sun Yat-sen, but to an uneasy association with a newly formed group of rather conservative constitutionalists loosely organized as the Progressive Party (Chinputang). Li was perhaps attracted less by the political philosophy of the Progressive Party than by the financial patronage of one of its principal founders, the well-known constitutional monarchist T'ang Hua-lung. It was T'ang's support that enabled Li to complete his last two years of college in Tientsin and to enroll at Waseda University in Tokyo in the autumn of 1913.

During the nearly three years Li Ta-chao spent in Japan he read the writings of a wide variety of Western philosophers and political theorists. There is no need here to trace Li's intellectual development during this period except to note that, although Li was introduced to the Marxist writings in Japan (early in 1916), he apparently was not sufficiently impressed with what he read to study Marx seriously until after he announced his support for the Bolshevik Revolution more than two years later. In 1916 he was much more influenced by the writings of Henri Bergson, Ralph Waldo Emerson, and Saint Simon and the Japanese utopian socialist "New Village" movement.

Nor, for the purposes of the present essay, is there any need to describe Li's political activities in Japan. Suffice it to note that while Li worked closely with the followers of Sun Yat-sen in the Chinese student movement in Japan, he retained his ties with the more conservative Progressive Party through his patron T'ang Hua-lung. When the latter requested him to return to China in April of 1916 to participate in the movement against Yüan Shih-k'ai's faltering regime, Li hurriedly left Tokyo to serve as personal secretary to T'ang, first in Shanghai and then in Peking. Shortly thereafter, he became editor of the Peking *Ch'en-chung pao* (The Morning Bell), a newspaper sponsored by the Progressive Party.

Li's political career in the Progressive Party was to be a brief one. He was soon to discover that his Populist conception of parliamentary democracy, which he defined as "wei-min chu-i" (lit., "only people-ism"), was to prove incompatible with the opportunistic political maneuverings of T'ang Hua-lung and Liang Ch'i-ch'ao. His political break with T'ang and Liang came in late October 1916. When the latter refused to permit Li to publish an editorial critical of their attempt to form an alliance with the government of Tuan Ch'i-jui, the leader of the powerful Peiyang warlord clique, Li resigned as editor of *The Morning Bell* and terminated his association with T'ang. His ideological break came during the course of the next year when he reluctantly arrived at the conclusion that China could be saved not by parliamentary government but only through revolution.[4]

But what kind of revolution? The revolution in cultural and moral values advocated by Ch'en Tu-hsiu and the members of the New Youth group—with whom Li became closely identified in late 1917

[4] See, for example, Li's article "Pao-li yü cheng-chih" (Violence and Politics), *T'ai-p'ing yang* (Pacific Ocean), Vol. I, No. 7 (October 15, 1917), pp. 1–12.

and early 1918 [5]—seemed to Li a wholly inadequate response to the desperate plight of China; his temperament and his philosophy demanded direct political action in the here and now. Nor did Li any longer share Ch'en's faith in Western-style democracy or his hope that an Allied victory in the World War would somehow bring to China democracy and self-determination. It was the Russian October Revolution that provided Li with an answer to the question of the kind of revolution which would bring about the rebirth of a "young China." While Ch'en and the "new intelligentsia" were still looking to the Western democracies, Li began to look to the Bolshevik Revolution as the model for China to follow and for a program for immediate political action.

The Reception of Bolshevism

It was in July of 1918 that Li first publicly announced his support of Bolshevism, in an article entitled "A Comparison of the French and Russian Revolutions." Just as the French Revolution of 1789 heralded the progressive historical tendencies of the nineteenth century, he wrote, the Russian Revolution of 1917 foreshadowed the historic tendencies of the twentieth century. But whereas the French Revolution was a nationalistic revolution with "a social revolutionary flavor," the Russian Revolution was a socialist revolution with "a world revolutionary color" and one that expressed the fundamental aspirations of all humanity. Whereas the impact of the French Revolution had by-passed China, the Russian Revolution seemed to Li to be of truly universal significance. It heralded the creation of a new world civilization which would unite East and West and to which China could make a distinctive contribution. By accepting the internationalist message of the October Revolution, China would preserve her national identity and at the same time join the universal forces of progress. China could thus accept the advanced material

[5] A frequent contributor to *Hsin ch'ing-nien,* Li formally became a member of its six-man editorial board in January, 1918. A month later, he was appointed chief librarian of Peking University and, concurrently, professor of economics. In 1920 he became professor of history.

civilization of the West without surrendering the essence of her own nationhood and still become part of "the new tide" of a new world based upon the principles of "freedom and humanism." [6]

The notion of China finding national fulfillment through the "internationalism" of a new world order was one of the two major themes in Li Ta-chao's initial response to the Bolshevik Revolution. The other was the notion of the advantages of economic and social backwardness. Li attributed the dynamism of the Russian Revolution to the "surplus energy for development" that had accumulated through the ages because of Russia's "comparative slowness in the evolution of civilization." [7] For Li, Russia's leap from backwardness into the very forefront of world progress seemed to confirm all the philosophic assumptions of his pre-Marxian view of dialectical historical development and his conception of a resurgent "young China" suddenly breaking out from the dead shell of the past. The spectacle of the most backward of European nations dramatically appearing as the advanced guard of modern civilization in defiant challenge of the imperialist Western world was not only emotionally satisfying to Li as a nationalist but also intellectually satisfying to him as a dialectician who viewed all phenomena as inevitably producing their opposites. For Li, the rebirth of backward Russia was merely the prelude to an even more dramatic rebirth of backward China. This belief that China's backwardness offered immense advantages for both the tempo and content of her future development, and the notion that all the evils of old China were about to be transformed into their opposites, were ideas soon to be of the greatest appeal to growing numbers of Chinese intellectuals.

Yet more was involved in Li Ta-chao's response to Bolshevism than the nationalistic appeal of the promise to transform rapidly a backward society. Also very much present was a chiliastic expectation that the world stood on the brink of a gigantic historical transformation that would soon produce a more just and more ethical world order. This chiliastic feeling was most forcefully expressed (and

[6] "Fa-o ko-ming chih pi-chiao-kuan" (A Comparison of the French and Russian Revolutions), *Hsüan-chi,* pp. 101–4.
[7] *Ibid.* pp. 102–3.

communicated) in Li's highly influential article "The Victory of Bolshevism," [8] published in the November 1918 issue of *La Jeunesse*. Drawn more to the ideas and revolutionary imagery of Trotsky than of Lenin, Li described Bolshevism as a single and irresistible global wave of revolution that was in the process of "combining the whole of mankind into one great mass." "In the course of such a world mass movement," he declared, "all those dregs of history . . . such as emperors, nobles, warlords, bureaucrats, militarists and capitalists, will certainly be destroyed as though struck by a thunderbolt." "From now on," he proclaimed, "every place in the world will see the victorious flag of Bolshevism and hear the triumphal song of Bolshevism. The bell of humanitarianism is sounding. The dawn of freedom has arrived!"

The global tide of revolution that Li perceived in the Russian Revolution, and so confidently anticipated, proved slow in reaching Chinese shores. Among the members of the new intelligentsia in 1918 and early 1919, Li stood virtually alone as a Chinese advocate of Bolshevism. It was not until the profound disillusionment with the Western democracies provoked by the betrayal of Chinese interests at the Versailles Peace Conference—and the turbulent political activism of the May Fourth Movement of 1919—that Ch'en Tu-hsiu and other members of the hitherto "pro-Western" democratic intelligentsia also began to look to the Bolshevik model.

In the meantime, Li's radicalism began to attract the interest of growing numbers of young student activists at Peking University. By the end of 1918 Li's office in the Peking University library already had become known as the "Red Chamber," the meeting place for a variety of newly-organized radical student groups that were to play a central role in the May Fourth Movement and in the organization of the first Chinese Communist groups in 1920. To the office of the librarian of Peking University came increasing numbers of students in search of intellectual and political guidance. Their names were still unknown in the Chinese intellectual and political world, but many of them were to become the most prominent leaders of the Chinese Communist Party.

[8] "Bolshevism ti sheng-li," *Hsin ch'ing-nien*, Vol. V, No. 5, pp. 442–48.

Li's chiliastic interpretation of the universalistic historic significance of the Bolshevik Revolution offered great hope for the future but provided little guidance about what to do in the Chinese present. Li's conversion to what he accepted as the universally valid principles of the Russian Revolution immediately posed two crucial problems. The first one was the problem of what to do with Marxist theory, for the acceptance of the principles of the Russian Revolution demanded a commitment to the Marxist-Leninist doctrines upon which that revolution was based. Like later Chinese converts to communism in a land which lacked a Marxian social-democratic tradition, Li had committed himself to the task of carrying out a Marxist revolution long before he had seriously begun to consider Marxist theory. He was thus faced not only with the problem of studying Marxism but also with the much more difficult problem of adapting Marxism to the specific needs of revolution in the Chinese historical environment.

The second problem was to determine (and to undertake) the practical political activities necessary to bring about that "rebirth" of China which the "universal tide" of Bolshevism seemed to promise. For Li was never one who believed that "history" made itself; both before and after his conversion to communism he was convinced that it was the actions and consciousness of men that made history.

The two problems were not unrelated. Before Marxist theory could be effectively employed in Chinese politics, it not only had to provide for its Chinese converts a plausible explanation of the Chinese historical situation in which they found themselves but also it had to serve as a guide to meaningful forms of practical political activity to transform that situation. The problem of achieving some degree of correspondence between theory and political practice was demanded both by the premises of Marxist doctrine and by the emotional and intellectual needs of those who accepted Marx's dictum not only to understand the world but also to change it. It was necessary, in short, to interpret Marxist theory so that it could be applied to the task of organizing a revolutionary political movement in the Chinese environment.

Li began to study Marxist theory in the latter months of 1918. The intellectual results of his labors will be discussed briefly in the following section. Here it might be noted that the initial political product was the formation (in late 1918) of the Marxist Research Society (Ma-k'e-shih chu-i yen-chiu-hui), the first group in China organized specifically for the purpose of the study and promotion of Marxist theory. Many of the future luminaries of the Chinese Communist Party were introduced to Marxism through the secret evening discussions sponsored by the society in the sanctuary of Li's office in the university library. Among them was the young "non-student" Mao Tse-tung, who served as library assistant to Li in the fall and winter of 1918–19. "Under Li Ta-chao, as assistant librarian at Peking National University," Mao later reported in his autobiography, "I had rapidly developed towards Marxism." [9]

While Li was studying and propagating Marxism in the bleak winter of 1918–19, he became concerned with a problem for which he was soon to provide a very non-Marxist solution. The problem was the isolation and political impotence of the radical intellectuals in Chinese society and their separation from the seemingly inert masses of the people. And the solution he offered was a call for young Chinese intellectuals to emulate the Russian Populist "go to the people" movement of the 1870's. In a series of articles published in February of 1919 in the Peking *Ch'en-pao*, Li urged the youthful intelligentsia to leave the corrupting life of the cities and "go to the villages" in order to enlighten and liberate the peasant masses and to join with them in the purity of rural life. By merging with the peasant masses, the intellectuals were to find their social and political salvation, and the peasantry was to find its road to salvation through the "principles of humanism and socialism" which the young intellectuals were to bring to the village. Foreshadowing Mao Tse-tung's famous "Hunan Report" by almost a decade, Li Ta-chao was already convinced by early 1919 that the Chinese revolution should and would be a peasant revolution: "Our China is a rural nation

[9] Edgar Snow, *Red Star Over China* (New York: Random House, 1938), p. 140. In addition to Mao, Li's early student disciples included Teng Chung-hsia, Ch'ü Ch'iu-pai, Chang Kuo-t'ao, Lo Chang-lung, Ho Meng-hsiung, and the future Trotskyist, Liu Jen-ch'ing.

and most of the laboring class is made up of peasants. If they are not liberated, then our whole nation will not be liberated." [10]

Although the themes of "Youth and the Villages" bear rather remarkable intellectual affinities with early Russian Populist thought, it is highly unlikely that Li was influenced directly by the writings of the Russian *narodniki*. It would seem, rather, that Li's knowledge of the Russian "go to the people" movement was gained from secondary historical sources as he undertook to study the history of the Russian revolutionary movement as a result of impact of the Bolshevik Revolution. It was not the writings of Herzen and Chernyshevskii that inspired Li (for there is no evidence that he read them), but rather it was the romantic example of a heroic revolutionary effort of the past that captured his imagination and seemed to him to fit the needs of the Chinese situation. Yet the essentially Populist views which Li so passionately expressed in the early months of 1919 were not to disappear in China as they had in Russia. Populist assumptions were to influence profoundly Li's interpretation of Marxist theory in the years that followed and were to re-emerge explicitly in the peasant-based revolutionary strategy that Li was to advocate in 1925–26. Unlike Russia, where Populism was overtaken by Marxism and suppressed by Leninism, in China the Populist strand which Li introduced survived to become very much a part of the Maoist-Marxist outlook and a distinctive element in Maoist revolutionary strategy.

The problem of the gap between the tiny radical intelligentsia and the masses of Chinese society—the problem which preoccupied Li Ta-chao in early 1919 and for which he originally offered a Populist "solution"—was soon to be resolved by the dramatic events that began on May 4, 1919. The demonstration of university students which took place in Peking on that fateful day marked the beginning of a violent wave of nationalism and anti-imperialism which soon engulfed much of urban Chinese society and radically transformed the character of Chinese political life. The student activists were joined not only by many of their university professors

[10] "Ch'ing-nien yü nung-ts'un" (Youth and the Villages), *Hsüan-chi*, pp. 146–50.

but by urban workers and portions of the newly emergent Chinese bourgeoisie. Modern Chinese nationalism had become a mass movement and Chinese society, which had for so long seemed inert, suddenly was seething with intellectual and political ferment.

It was on the basis of this ferment that the organizational foundations of the Chinese Communist Party was established. It was the political activism of the May Fourth Movement and the powerful sense of nationalistic mission and political hope to which it gave rise which attracted Ch'en Tu-hsiu and many other future leaders of the Chinese Communist movement to the messianic promises that the Bolshevik Revolution offered and drew them together with Li Ta-chao as the first advocates of Marxism in China. Disillusioned as they had become with the Western "democracies," they now viewed Marxist theory as the most advanced product of modern Western thought (thus reaffirming their rejection of traditional Chinese values) but a theory which condemned the West in its contemporary capitalist and imperialist form. As perceived in the context of the Bolshevik Revolution, Marxism thus not only served to satisfy profoundly anti-Western nationalistic resentments but also promised a program for concrete political action in the course of which a new and modern China would emerge and fully participate in a universal process of revolutionary transformation.

The activities of Li Ta-chao and Ch'en Tu-hsiu, along with their student disciples and Comintern advisors, in organizing China's first Communist groups in 1920 and formally establishing the Chinese Communist Party in 1921 have been described many times (even though in different fashions) and the story need not be retold here. Nor is it necessary for the purposes of the present essay to discuss Li Ta-chao's role as leader of the Communist Party in North China in the 1920's. For, however important Li was as a Communist political leader, he was to prove much more historically important as a Chinese interpreter of Marxist theory. Indeed it was Li's "domestication" of Marxism-Leninism in the early 1920's which established the intellectual and ideological prerequisites for the later Maoist strategy of revolution and it is this subject that now deserves our attention.

The Reinterpretation of Marxism

It is generally assumed that Marxism came to China in its Leninist form. Even though it is usually conceded that "Leninism" did not necessarily provide a ready-made program for revolution, it has become something of a truism that it was Lenin's revision of original Marxism which made Marxism seem relevant to those concerned with the problem of carrying out a socialist revolution in economically backward China.

Of course, there can be no doubt about the enormous appeal of the Leninist theory of imperialism (to nationalist intellectuals of non-Communist as well as Communist persuasions), nor is there any reason to doubt that Lenin's rather ambiguous writings on the revolutionary role of the peasantry and his principles of party organization were matters that eventually were to prove of very considerable significance in the history of Chinese communism. But there are good reasons to question whether specifically Leninist writings played a decisive role in the introduction and early adaptation of Marxism in China. For one thing, there is little evidence that the early Chinese converts to communism read very much of Lenin. Moreover, that which they did read tended to be the least "Leninist" of Lenin's writings. For example, State and Revolution, which essentially is an expression of the revolutionary utopianism of original Marxism, was by far the most widely read and most influential of the rather few works of Lenin actually read by the early Chinese Marxists.[11]

Secondly, even had they been more familiar with his writings, it is highly unlikely that the early Chinese Communists would have been able to appreciate what is specifically "Leninist" in Lenin. For one of the most characteristic features of these writings is that Lenin failed

---

[11] State and Revolution was first translated into Chinese in 1921. Except for selections from Lenin's writings on "national self-determinism" and contemporary post-1917 political developments, State and Revolution was the first of Lenin's major theoretical works to appear in Chinese. See "Liehning chu-tso i-pen nien-piao" in Chang Ching-lu, Chung-kuo hsien-tai ch'u-pan shih-liao (Materials on the History of Modern Chinese Publications) (Shanghai and Peking: Chung-hua, 1954–56), III, 452–66.

to draw Marxist theoretical conclusions from the new elements of revolutionary strategy that he advocated and practiced. The implications of Leninist revolutionary practice for Marxist theory are never made explicit in Lenin—indeed, they are deliberately obscured by the constant invocation of standard Marxist formulas—and these theoretical implications hardly could have been recognized by those so unfamiliar with the Marxist tradition as were the early Chinese converts to Bolshevism. Even in its Leninist form, in short, the Marxist doctrine inherited by the Chinese Communists upheld all of the fundamental theoretical formulations of Marx.

The problem was that whereas the Russian Revolution brought the chiliastic hope for an immediate revolutionary transformation, the Marxist doctrine that followed brought the disheartening message that Chinese society lacked the material and socio-economic prerequisites for the realization of the Marxist socialist program. The Chinese converts to communism were inspired by the messianic expectations of the Bolshevik Revolution, but along with these expectations they inherited the Marxist theory of class struggle and the fundamental Marxist principle that the socialist revolution was to be the work of the urban proletariat. They also inherited the materialist conception of history, with all of its deterministic formulas on the relationships between "being" and "consciousness" and between economic and political forces, as well as the entire Marxist scheme of the historically necessary stages of social development. Above all, they inherited the Marxian paradox that man, the maker of history, is also the object through which the objective, determining forces of history express themselves.

These were problems which neither the writings of Lenin nor the Bolshevik Revolution had "solved" for the new Chinese converts to communism. With the introduction and spread of Marxist ideas in China they became Chinese problems which had to be confronted in the context of the specifically Chinese environment. It was to these problems that Li Ta-chao addressed himself in the early 1920's in his attempt to refashion Marxism into a doctrine that would meet the demand for immediate revolutionary action in the contemporary Chinese historical situation. And it was largely on the basis of his

readings of the works of Marx and Engels that Li attempted to adapt
Marxism to Chinese needs, as he perceived those needs. In doing so,
Li Ta-chao was to make fundamental departures from Leninism as
well as from original Marxist theory, and these departures were to
become the underlying intellectual and ideological presuppositions of
the doctrine which later came to be known as "Maoism."

Much of Li Ta-chao's writings on Marxism can be seen as an effort
to mitigate the deterministic implications of Marxist theory by attempting to reconcile (for the purposes of revolutionary action in
China) the dilemma of combining a doctrine of historical inevitability
with a belief that the consciousness of men and their practical political activities are the decisive factors in the historic process. Here his
treatment of the materialist conception of history is of particular interest for understanding something about the nature of the Chinese
"domestication" of Marxism.

In his first serious encounter with Marxism in 1919 Li had expressed grave reservations about what he regarded to be the deterministic and fatalistic implications of Marx's theory of history and he
quite candidly criticized historical materialism for failing to give
sufficient weight to "ethical" and "spiritual" factors.[12] Although he
soon was to announce his unconditional acceptance of the "objective
laws" of historical development that the materialist conception of history set forth—and, indeed, wrote lengthy treatises arguing that
human consciousness was no more than a reflection of material reality[13]—he was never content to leave the future of China in the im-
personal (and uncertain) hands of the economic laws of history. Nor
was he prepared to abandon his voluntarist faith in the abilities of
purposeful men to change objective social reality in accordance with
their will and consciousness. While formally accepting the Marxist
proposition that the ideas and ethical principles of men are essentially

[12] Li Ta-chao, "Wo-ti Ma-k'o-ssu-chu-i kuan" (My Marxist Views), Part I,
Hsin ch'ing-nien, Vol. VI, No. 5 (May 1, 1919), p. 536.
[13] See, for example, "Wu-chih pien-tung yü tao-te pien-tung" (Material
Change and Ethical Change) Hsüan-chi, pp. 256–73. And "Yu ching-chi
shang chieh-shih Chung-kuo chin-tai ssu-hsiang pien-tung ti yüan-yin" (An
Economic Explanation of the Causes of the Changes in Modern Chinese
Thought), Hsin ch'ing-nien, Vol. VII, No. 2 (January 1, 1920).

the reflections of their material-social existence, Li continued to attribute an independent and historically creative role to the powers of the human conscience. And he attempted to reconcile the deterministic formulas of Marx with his own voluntaristic and activistic world view by interpreting the materialist conception of history as a call to revolutionary action rather than a pre-ordained scheme of historical development. He argued that whereas all "pre-Marxian" views of history tend to paralyze "the moral powers of the individual," the materialist conception of history has a "completely different effect on the human spirit" in that it interprets historical change as the result of man's own efforts, thus providing men with a "self-consciousness of their own powers," a feeling of "great hope and courage," and a recognition of their own creative potentialities to transform society.[14]

In his writings on historical materialism, Li drew upon those elements in Marxist historical theory that tended to support, or could be interpreted to support, these voluntaristic predispositions. He emphasized the Marxian promise of radical revolutionary breaks with the past and the utopian social goals toward which, according to Marxist theory, the historic process was inevitably moving—the chiliastic promise of man's leap from his "pre-history" to a "truly human history." He constantly stressed the original Marxian view that man is the producer as much as the product of his history and he was drawn especially to the original Marxian belief that "man makes history." Above all, he emphasized the Marxian notion of "self-consciousness" and its role in the historic process. But he was not prepared to deal seriously with the problem of how the existing level of productive forces condition the manner in which "man makes history," nor was he disposed to bother with the question of the socio-economic prerequisites which Marx had posited for the emergence of that "self-consciousness" which would enable men to create the socialist utopia of the future.

[14] Li Ta-chao, "Wei-wu shih-kuan tsai hsien-tai shih-hsüeh shang-ti chia-chih" (The Value of the Materialist Conception of History in Contemporary Historical Study) (December, 1920), *Hsüan-chi*, pp. 334–40. See also Li's book *Shih-hsüeh yao-lun* (The Essentials of Historical Study) Shanghai: Shang-wu yin-shu kuan, 1924).

To be sure, Li repeatedly reaffirmed all the "objective laws" of historical development set forth by Marx and declared that socialism would be the inevitable result of the workings of these laws. But he perceived these laws not as objective forces to which the activities of men had to conform, but rather as expressions of conscious human activity. And the evidence for the existence of the "laws of history" were to be sought less in objective historical reality than in the consciousness and actions of men.

While there is no reason to doubt Li's belief in the inevitability of socialism (for he always was convinced in the imminent advent of the millennium), he never really acquired a specifically Marxian confidence in the objective, determining forces of history. His voluntarist belief that men could shape historical reality in accordance with their will remained largely unrestrained by the more deterministic Marxist formulas which bound men to history. His chiliastic acceptance of the Marxist vision of the future remained largely undisciplined by the Marxian conception of the necessary stages of social development. His faith in the "inevitability" of socialism ultimately resided in his faith in the spirit, will, and consciousness of men.

Thus for Li the value of the materialist conception of history lay not so much in its claim to be a scientific analysis of the laws governing objective historical processes than in what he perceived to be a historical world view which would give rise to the necessary psychological preconditions for revolutionary political action. Its real value was that it would provide men with the sense of hope and the "spiritual energy" which would inspire them to shape history rather than to be bound by history. He embraced the Marxist theory of history less for what it said than for what it promised.

Li Ta-chao's emphasis on the factors of "will" and "consciousness" and his extreme voluntarist approach to history and the making of revolution were also reflected in his treatment of the Marxist theory of class struggle and in his radical reinterpretation of the Marxist view of the relationship between economic and political forces. In Marxist theory the development of classes and their struggles are functions of the development of the material forces of production, and class consciousness is seen as the expression of the particular objective socio-economic positions of particular classes. For Marx, the class struggle that would lead to socialist revolution presupposed the existence of capitalist relations of production and the consequent emergence of a "proletarian class consciousness" among the actual proletariat. "The existence of revolutionary ideas in a particular age," Marx wrote, "presupposes the existence of a revolutionary class." [15]

Li Ta-chao perceived the road to socialism in a very different fashion. First, he attributed a latent socialist class consciousness to virtually all men, an innate "spirit" of "mutual cooperation" common to all humanity since time immemorial and one which would emerge in the course of revolutionary struggle.[16] While he ardently advocated the necessity and desirability of class struggle, he perceived this struggle as one which was at least as dependent on the powers of the human spirit as upon the forces of production. Indeed, he went so far as to argue that "the power of the human conscience is completely spontaneous." [17] Therefore, the emergence of a revolutionary socialist consciousness (and a revolutionary socialist movement) need not be dependent upon any particular level of socio-economic development; in the Chinese situation this meant that one might look for (and find) signs of proletarian consciousness even if it proved difficult to locate the actual Chinese proletariat.

Secondly, the search for an immediate Chinese road to socialist revolution was facilitated by Li's tendency to view the class struggle not as a process taking place within individual countries (in which case social classes would have to be defined on the basis of specific, existing economic and historical situations) but rather in terms of a single, final world struggle between the reactionary forces of international capitalism and the Bolshevik forces of international regeneration. In this dramatic and climactic world class struggle, China, according to Li, had a unique role to play as a uniquely "proletarian nation." Unlike the Western nations where the proletariat was op-

[15] Karl Marx, *The German Ideology* (New York: International Publishers, 1939), p. 40.

[16] See, for example, "Chieh-chi ching-cheng yü hu-chu" (Class Struggle and Mutual Aid), *Hsüan-chi*, pp. 222–25.

[17] "Wu-chih pien-tung yü tao-te pien-tung," *op. cit.*

pressed by individual national capitalis classes, in China all the people suffered under the yoke of world capitalism. Indeed, the impingement of foreign imperialism on Chinese economy and society were so all-pervasive that "the whole country gradually has been transformed into part of the world proletariat." [18]

While the details of Li's "proletarian nation" theory need not concern us here, the conclusion derived from the theory might be briefly noted: if China stood in a "proletarian" position in the international capitalist economy, then China was entitled to a proletarian world view and thus was both economically and ideologically qualified to participate in the world proletarian revolution. According to Li's concept of the class struggle, in short, China as a nation was transformed into the revolutionary class that in Marxist theory was the prerequisite for the existence of revolutionary ideas. Whereas Marx had looked to the proletariat itself as the bearers of socialist consciousness, and whereas Lenin had found the carriers of this consciousness to be the revolutionary intelligentsia who would impose it on the amorphous proletarian mass movement, Li Ta-chao attributed a socialist class consciousness to the Chinese nation as a whole (by virtue of China's "proletarian" status in the international economy) and also saw it as an almost innate characteristic of the human spirit.

Given these perspectives, it is hardly surprising that Li was not disposed to allow Marxist theoretical considerations on the relationship between economic and political forces to inhibit efforts to promote a socialist revolution in China. Like Trotsky, he contended that it was not simply internal socio-economic factors but international political tendencies that made possible the realization of a socialist revolution in China; indeed, he quite explicitly argued that in the Chinese situation a high level of industrial development was to be the product of the socialist reorganization of society rather than its precondition.[19] For Li it was not China's economic maturity but the Chinese political situation—the political consciousness of the

[18] "Yu ching-chi shang chieh-shih Chung-kuo chin-tai ssu-hsiang pien-tung ti yüan-yin," *op. cit.* pp. 50–51.
[19] Li Ta-chao, "Chung-kuo ti she-hui-chu-i yu shih-chieh ti tzu-pen chu-i" (Chinese Socialism and World Capitalism), *Hsüan-chi,* pp. 356–57.

Chinese people and the practical activities of men—that eventually would determine whether the Marxist program would be realized in China.

The highly nationalistic implications of Li's notion of China as a "proletarian nation," his impulse to identify the Chinese nation with the international proletarian movement, and his extreme, revolutionary voluntaristic interpretation of Marxist theory were not unrelated to the nationalistic and chiliastic manner in which he first received the message of the Bolshevik Revolution in 1918. From originally perceiving Bolshevism as the signal for the long-awaited rebirth of the Chinese nation it was but a short ideological step to interpret this process of national rebirth in terms of the world revolutionary struggle for universal historical redemption. If China lacked a developed urban proletariat to carry out the proletarian class struggle, then Marxist theory was to be bent so that the whole nation could be looked upon as an integral part of the worldwide forces of international proletarian revolution. If the economic preconditions for socialism were lacking in China, then the socialist reordering of Chinese society was all the more necessary—and all the more urgent —to achieve these very preconditions. In Li Ta-chao's activistic and chiliastic world view, Marxist theory was not to restrain but was to be used to encourage the revolutionary action necessary to consummate this final, grand alliance between the Chinese nation and the world revolution.

It is this ideological blending of a voluntaristic revolutionary Marxism and a militant Chinese nationalism that explains, in large measure, why Li Ta-chao was the first Chinese Communist to enthusiastically support the Comintern-proposed alliance between the Chinese Communist Party and the Kuomintang in the early 1920's—and why he was the first to abandon it. For if international capitalism rather than Chinese capitalism was the main enemy, then the revolutionary struggle was not to be confined to the actual Chinese proletariat but included virtually all social classes, since all Chinese suffered from imperialist oppression. Indeed, the whole idea of a "national revolution," a revolutionary united front of all the people against foreign imperialism, was fully in accord with Li's view of China's place in the international economy and his conception of the relationship between the "proletarian" Chinese nation and the world revolution.

But in supporting the alliance with the Kuomintang—and in playing a most prominent role in it[20]—Li interpreted the purposes and nature of the "national revolution" in a very different manner than the way it was conceived in Moscow and conveyed to other leaders of the Chinese Communist Party. For Li the national revolution was not simply a discrete and definable stage in a predetermined, universalistic scheme of social and political development, nor was the alliance with the Kuomintang simply a tactical maneuver to serve immediate revolutionary ends, much less Russian national ends. Rather, he viewed the "national revolution" as basically "proletarian" in character because he was convinced that it logically reflected the elemental forces of the Chinese nation in revolt against the capitalist-imperialist world order. It was also "permanent" in character for it was part of a continuous revolutionary process leading directly to socialism and intimately related to the world revolution. For Li the world revolution was imminent and China as a nation had a very special and an especially creative role to play in this process of universal transformation.[21] This identification of the Chinese national revolution with the world proletarian revolution seemed only natural in view of his nationalist-populist predisposition to treat "the people" as a single entity and his attribution of a "proletarian" consciousness to the Chinese nation as a whole. Li's radical interpretation of the "national revolution" and the Communist alliance with the Kuomintang had the great virtue of satisfying both his Chinese nationalist impulses and his revolutionary Marxist commitments.

Li Ta-chao was soon to discover that he had attributed to the alliance with the Kuomintang aims more radical than the alliance

---

[20] Li was the only Communist on the five-member presidium of the Kuomintang central executive committee during the period of the Kuomintang-Communist alliance.

[21] For Li's argument that the anti-imperialist revolutionary movement in China might be the decisive factor in determining the success of the entire world revolutionary struggle, see his article "Ma-k'o-ssu ti Chung-kuo min-tsu ko-ming kuan" (Marx's Views on the Chinese National Revolution), *Hsüan-chi*, pp. 545–55.

proved able to bear. This became apparent in north China earlier than elsewhere; by late 1925 the rise of the highly conservative and virulently anti-Communist Western Hills faction in the Peking Kuomintang organization had largely vitiated the policy of collaboration in the northern provinces. In responding to this situation, Li was to prove that he was not simply a Chinese nationalist in Marxist guise. Revolutionary Marxist goals (as he understood them) were no less important than Chinese nationalist goals; indeed, the two were inseparable. Although Li had been the most ardent Chinese Communist advocate of the policy of collaboration with the Kuomintang, he became the first to actually renounce that policy and he did so by advocating armed peasant revolution—a new political strategy that was neither in accord with the terms of the Kuomintang-Communist alliance nor with prevailing Comintern and official Chinese Communist Party policies. Confronted with the *de facto* breakdown of the alliance with the Kuomintang in Peking and the lack of any significant urban proletarian support, Li in 1925–26 (as he did in 1919) once again began to look to the countryside and the revolutionary potentialities of the peasantry.

In his last writings on the peasantry,[22] Li was clearly drawn to the spontaneous revolutionary energies of the peasantry, energies that he described as "a gigantic force" which "roars like the expanse of the ocean." But he also emphasized the role of the Communist revolutionary intelligentsia in providing the knowledge and organizational leadership which would transform local loyalties into national loyalties, transform embryonic forms of class consciousness into true revolutionary consciousness, and direct the elemental revolutionary energies of the peasantry into the proper political channels. Here we find that characteristically Populist combination of a passionate faith in the spontaneous revolutionary energies of the people and the equally passionate conviction that the revolutionary intelligentsia must bring

---

[22] See "T'u-ti yü nung-min" (Land and the Peasants), originally published in the Peking Communist periodical *Cheng-chih sheng-huo* (Political Life) between December 30, 1925 and February 3, 1926 (in *Hsüan-chi*, pp. 523–36) and "Lu, Yü, Shan teng-sheng ti Hung-ch'iang-hui" (The Red Spear Societies of Shantung, Honan, and Shensi), also published in *Cheng-chih sheng-huo*, probably in the spring of 1926 (in *Hsüan-chi*, pp. 564–70).

enlightenment and leadership to the mass movement. But if the Communists were to lead the peasant movement, they were to do so in the villages and not from the cities. And in doing so, they were to be unencumbered by inherited Marxist-Leninist formulas and urban political considerations. Since the Chinese proletariat was too fragile to bear the burden of revolution and the united front with the Kuomintang had proved too undependable a revolutionary instrument, the rising tide of agrarian revolution was more than sufficient to overcome such deficiencies. In the great masses of the Chinese peasantry, Li Ta-chao found not only a great revolutionary force but also a class that embodied the elemental energies of the Chinese nation and the carrier of her national traditions.

Li Ta-chao's last important political action—the identification of the liberation of China with the liberation of the peasantry and the advocacy of armed peasant revolt as the appropriate strategy for the Chinese revolution—was the logical culmination of the voluntarist, nationalist, and Populist predispositions which had influenced decisively his whole interpretation of Marxist theory—and it was also a prophetic pointer to the future. When the alliance with the Kuomintang began to break apart and when the peasants in north China spontaneously began to rise in revolt (often under the banner of such traditional-type secret societies as the Red Spears), it was not difficult to perceive in the peasantry that latent proletarian revolutionary consciousness that he had previously attributed to the nation as a whole. The peasants of China, after all, constituted the overwhelming majority of the Chinese population, as Li never failed to point out. And if Li's call for armed class struggle between Chinese peasants and their Chinese class oppressors was not fully consistent with his view that China was a "proletarian nation" exploited by international capitalism, this class struggle, nevertheless, was to be undertaken by the vast majority of the nation. The "nation" and the "people" could be redefined to exclude those relatively few Chinese oppressors who could be dismissed as politically or economically dependent on foreign imperialism, and the revolutionary potentialities of the peasantry could be utilized to carry out the "national revolu-.

tion" and thus consummate China's alliance with the forces of world proletarian revolution.

Li Ta-chao was arrested on April 6, 1927 when military police acting under the direction of the Manchurian warlord Chang Tso-lin entered the Russian embassy compound in Peking where Li had taken refuge during the preceding year of political repression. He was still in his thirty-ninth year when he was executed by strangulation later that month. Li Ta-chao has since been honored in Chinese Communist writings as the most heroic of Communist revolutionary martyrs.

His friend Ch'en Tu-hsiu, with whom Li had shared the historic task of founding the Communist movement in China, managed to escape the executioner's rope in 1927 but he was not to escape either the calumnies of his former Communist comrades who survived the bloodbaths of 1927 or (later) the prisons of the Kuomintang. Ch'en became the Comintern scapegoat for the disasters which almost destroyed the Chinese Communist Party in 1927. Accused (among other things) of "right-wing opportunism," he was dismissed from his post as Secretary-General of the Party in that year and in 1929 excommunicated entirely for the heresy of "Trotskyism." In Chinese Communist literature he appears as both an ideological heretic and a political renegade.

In the Chinese Communist glorification of Li Ta-chao and the vilification of Ch'en Tu-hsiu, one senses more than the usual political need to find heroes and heretics. For Ch'en represented and expressed the more internationalistic and Western-oriented Marxist tendencies which were to perish in the modern Chinese historical environment. He felt a need to be identified with the Chinese urban proletariat, both because of Marxist-Leninist theoretical consideration and because this was the only progressive class in Chinese society (however embryonic) that had been forged in the image of the modern West. Li Ta-chao, on the other hand, felt not this need but rather a need to be identified with the elemental forces of the Chinese nation, and especially the peasant masses, for he was the forerunner of those revolutionary voluntaristic, Populist, and nationalistic impulses which since have governed the Maoist version of Marxism-Leninism. These were the tendencies and impulses which made Li willing to abandon the Western-influenced cities and the proletariat to look to the Chinese countryside for the true sources of national rebirth and revolutionary regeneration. And it was this combination of nationalism, Populism, and a voluntaristic interpretation of Marxism, which Li pioneered and Mao Tse-tung inherited, which became the intellectual and ideological foundation for the development of the Maoist strategy of peasant revolution that eventually was to lead the Chinese Communists to victory.

❖ 14 ❖

The Early Life of Mao Tse-tung

EDGAR SNOW

Childhood

I was born in the village of Shao Shan, in Hsiang T'an Hsien, Hunan province, in 1893. My father's name was Mao Jen-sheng, and my mother's maiden name was Wen Ch'i-mei.

My father was a poor peasant and while still young was obliged to join the army because of heavy debts. He was a soldier for many years. Later on he returned to the village where I was born, and by saving carefully and gathering together a little money through small trading and other enterprise he managed to buy back his land.

As middle peasants then my family owned fifteen *mou* of land. On this they could raise sixty *tan*[1] of rice a year. The five members of the family consumed a total of thirty-five *tan*—that is, about seven each—which left an annual surplus of twenty-five *tan*. Using this surplus, my father accumulated a little capital and in time purchased seven more *mou,* which gave the family the status of "rich" peasants. We could then raise eighty-four *tan* of rice a year.

When I was ten years of age and the family owned only fifteen *mou* of land, the five members of the family consisted of my father, mother, grandfather, younger brother and myself. After we had acquired the additional seven *mou,* my grandfather died, but there

This autobiography was told to Edgar Snow by Mao Tse-tung. Reprinted by permission of Grove Press, Inc., from Edgar Snow, *Red Star Over China* (New York: Random House, 1938), pp. 113–39 (New York: Grove Press, 1961; pp. 123–56). Copyright © 1938, 1944 by Random House, Inc.

[1] One *tan* is a *picul,* or 133⅓ lb.

came another younger brother. However, we still had a surplus of forty-nine *tan* of rice each year, and on this my father steadily prospered.

At the time my father was a middle peasant he began to deal in grain transport and selling, by which he made a little money. After he became a "rich" peasant, he devoted most of his time to that business. He hired a full-time farm labourer, and put his children to work on the farm, as well as his wife. I began to work at farming tasks when I was six years old. My father had no shop for his business. He simply purchased grain from the poor farmers and then transported it to the city merchants, where he got a higher price. In the winter, when the rice was being ground, he hired an extra labourer to work on the farm, so that at that time there were seven mouths to feed. My family ate frugally, but had enough always.

I began studying in a local primary school when I was eight and remained there until I was thirteen years old. In the early morning and at night I worked on the farm. During the day I read the Confucian Analects and the Four Classics. My Chinese teacher belonged to the stern-treatment school. He was harsh and severe, frequently beating his students. Because of this I ran away from the school when I was ten. I was afraid to return home, for fear of receiving a beating there, and set out in the general direction of the city, which I believed to be in a valley somewhere. I wandered for three days before I was finally found by my family. Then I learned that I had circled round and round in my travels, and in all my walking had got only about eight *li* from my home.

After my return to the family, however, to my surprise, conditions somewhat improved. My father was slightly more considerate and the teacher was more inclined to moderation. The result of my act of protest impressed me very much. It was a successful "strike."

My father wanted me to begin keeping the family books as soon as I had learned a few characters. He wanted me to learn to use the abacus. As my father insisted upon this I began to work at those accounts at night. He was a severe taskmaster. He hated to see me idle, and if there were no books to be kept he put me to work at farm tasks. He was a hot-tempered man and frequently beat both me and my brothers. He gave us no money whatever, and the most meagre food. On the 15th of every month he made a concession to his labourers and gave them eggs with their rice, but never meat. To me he gave neither eggs nor meat.

My mother was a kind woman, generous and sympathetic, and ever ready to share what she had. She pitied the poor and often gave them rice when they came to ask for it during famines. But she could not do so when my father was present. He disapproved of charity. We had many quarrels in my home over this question.

There were two "parties" in the family. One was my father, the Ruling Power. The Opposition was made up of myself, my mother, my brother and sometimes even the labourer. In the "United Front" of the Opposition, however, there was a difference of opinion. My mother advocated a policy of indirect attack. She criticized any overt display of emotion and attempts at open rebellion against the Ruling Power. She said it was not the Chinese way.

But when I was thirteen I discovered a powerful argument of my own for debating with my father on his own ground, by quoting the Classics. My father's favourite accusations against me were of unfilial conduct and laziness. I quoted, in exchange, passages from the Classics saying that the elder must be kind and affectionate. Against his charge that I was lazy, I used the rebuttal that older people should do more work than younger, that my father was over three times as old as myself, and therefore should do more work. And I declared that when I was his age I would be much more energetic.

The old man continued to "amass wealth," or what was considered to be a great fortune in that little village. He did not buy more land himself, but he bought many mortgages on other people's land. His capital grew to $2,000 or $3,000.

My dissatisfaction increased. The dialectical struggle in our family was constantly developing.[2] One incident I especially remember. When I was about thirteen my father invited many guests to his home, and while they were present a dispute arose between the two

[2] Mao used all these political terms humorously in his explanations, laughing as he recalled such incidents.

of us. My father denounced me before the whole group, calling me lazy and useless. This infuriated me. I cursed him and left the house. My mother ran after me and tried to persuade me to return. My father also pursued me, cursing at the same time that he demanded me to come back. I reached the edge of a pond and threatened to jump in if he came any nearer. In this situation demands and counter-demands were presented for cessation of the civil war. My father insisted that I apologize and k'ou-t'ou as a sign of submission. I agreed to give a one-knee k'ou-t'ou if he would promise not to beat me. Thus the war ended, and from it I learned that when I defended my rights by open rebellion my father relented, but when I remained meek and submissive he only cursed and beat me the more.

Reflecting on this, I think that in the end the strictness of my father defeated him. I learned to hate him, and we created a real United Front against him. At the same time it probably benefited me. It made me most diligent in my work; it made me keep my books carefully, so that he should have no basis for criticizing me.

My father had had two years of schooling and he could read enough to keep books. My mother was wholly illiterate. Both were from peasant families. I was the family "scholar." I knew the Classics, but disliked them. What I enjoyed were the romances of Old China, and especially stories of rebellions. I read the *Yo Fei Chuan* (*Chin Chung Chuan*), *Shui Hu Chuan, Fan T'ang, San Kuo,* and *Hsi Yu Chi,* while still very young, and despite the vigilance of my old teacher, who hated these outlawed books and called them wicked. I used to read them in school, covering them up with a Classic when the teacher walked past. So also did most of my schoolmates. We learned many of the stories almost by heart, and discussed and re-discussed them many times. We knew more of them than the old men of the village, who also loved them and used to exchange stories with us. I believe that perhaps I was much influenced by such books, read at an impressionable age.

I finally left the primary school when I was thirteen and began to work long hours on the farm, helping the hired labourer, doing the full labour of a man during the day and at night keeping books for my father. Nevertheless, I succeeded in continuing my reading, devouring everything I could find except the Classics. This annoyed my father, who wanted me to master the Classics, especially after he was defeated in a lawsuit due to an apt Classical quotation used by his adversary in the Chinese court. I used to cover up the window of my room late at night so that my father would not see the light. In this way I read a book called *Words of Warning* (*Shen Shih Wei-yen*), which I liked very much. The authors, a number of old reformist scholars, thought that the weakness of China lay in her lack of Western appliances—railways, telephones, telegraphs and steamships—and wanted to have them introduced into the country. My father considered such books a waste of time. He wanted me to read something practical like the Classics, which could help him in winning lawsuits.

I continued to read the old romances and tales of Chinese literature. It occurred to me one day that there was one thing peculiar about these stories, and that was the absence of peasants who tilled the land. All the characters were warriors, officials or scholars; there was never a peasant hero. I wondered about this for two years, and then I analyzed the content of the stories. I found that they all glorified men of arms, rulers of the people, who did not have to work the land, because they owned and controlled it and evidently made the peasants work it for them.

My father, Mao Jen-sheng, was in his early days, and in middle age, a sceptic, but my mother devoutly worshipped Buddha. She gave her children religious instruction, and we were all saddened that our father was an unbeliever. When I was nine years old I seriously discussed the problem of my father's lack of piety with my mother. We made many attempts then and later on to convert him, but without success. He only cursed us, and, overwhelmed by his attacks, we withdrew to devise new plans. But he would have nothing to do with the gods.

My reading gradually began to influence me, however; I myself became more and more sceptical. My mother became concerned about me, and scolded me for my indifference to the requirements of the faith, but my father made no comment. Then one day he went out on the road to collect some money, and on his way he met a tiger. The tiger was surprised at the encounter and fled at once, but my father was even more astonished and afterwards reflected a good deal on his miraculous escape. He began to wonder if he had not offended the gods. From then on he showed more respect to Buddhism and burned incense now and then. Yet, when my own backsliding grew worse, the old man did not interfere. He only prayed to the gods when he was in difficulties.

Words of Warning stimulated in me a desire to resume my studies. I had also become disgusted with my labour on the farm. My father naturally opposed this. We quarrelled about it, and finally I ran away from home. I went to the home of an unemployed law student, and there I studied for half a year. After that I studied more of the Classics under an old Chinese scholar, and also read many contemporary articles and a few books.

At this time an incident occurred in Hunan which influenced my whole life. Outside the little Chinese school where I was studying, we students noticed many bean merchants, coming back from Changsha. We asked them why they were all leaving. They told us about a big uprising in the city.

There had been a severe famine that year, and in Changsha thousands were without food. The starving sent a delegation to the civil governor, to beg for relief, but he replied to them haughtily, "Why haven't you food? There is plenty in the city. I always have enough." When the people were told the governor's reply, they became very angry. They held mass meetings and organized a demonstration. They attacked the Manchu yamen, cut down the flagpole, the symbol of office, and drove out the governor. Following this, the Commissioner of Internal Affairs, a man named Chang, came out on his horse and told the people that the Government would take measures to help them. Chang was evidently sincere in his promise, but the Emperor disliked him and accused him of having intimate connections with "the mob." He was removed. A new governor arrived, and at once ordered the arrest of the leaders of the uprising. Many of them were beheaded and their heads displayed on poles as a warning to future "rebels."

This incident was discussed in my school for many days. It made a deep impression on me. Most of the other students sympathized with the "insurrectionists," but only from an observer's point of view. They did not understand that it had any relation to their own lives. They were merely interested in it as an exciting incident. I never forgot it. I felt that there with the rebels were ordinary people like my own family and I deeply resented the injustice of the treatment given to them.

Not long afterward, in Shao Shan, there was a conflict between members of the Ke Lao Hui, a secret society, and a local landlord. He sued them in court, and as he was a powerful landlord he easily bought a decision favourable to himself. The Ke Lao Hui members were defeated. But, instead of submitting, they rebelled against the landlord and the Government and withdrew to a local mountain called Liu Shan, where they built a stronghold. Troops were sent against them and the landlord spread a story that they had sacrificed a child when they raised the banner of revolt. The leader of the rebels was called P'ang the Millstone-maker. They were finally suppressed and P'ang was forced to flee. He was eventually captured and beheaded. In the eyes of the students, however, he was a hero, for all sympathized with the revolt.

Next year, when the new rice was not yet harvested and the winter rice was exhausted, there was a food shortage in our district. The poor demanded help from the rich farmers and they began a movement called "Eat Rice Without Charge." My father was a rice merchant and was exporting much grain to the city from our district, despite the shortage. One of his consignments was seized by the poor villagers and his wrath was boundless. I did not sympathize with him. At the same time I thought the villagers' method was wrong also.

Another influence on me at this time was the presence in a local primary school of a "radical" teacher. He was "radical" because he was opposed to Buddhism, and wanted to get rid of the gods. He urged people to convert their temples into schools. He was a widely discussed personality. I admired him and agreed with his views.

These incidents, occurring close together, made lasting impressions on my young mind, already rebellious. In this period also I began to have a certain amount of political consciousness, especially after I read a pamphlet telling of the dismemberment of China. I remember even now that this pamphlet opened with the sentence: "Alas, China will be subjugated!" It told of Japan's occupation of Korea and Formosa, of the loss of suzerainty in Indo-China, Burma and elsewhere. After I read this I felt depressed about the future of my country and began to realize that it was the duty of all the people to help save it.

My father had decided to apprentice me to a rice shop in Hsiang T'an, with which he had connections. I was not opposed to it at first, thinking it might be interesting. But about this time I heard of an unusual new school and made up my mind to go there, despite my father's opposition. This school was in Hsiang Hsiang *hsien* (county), where my mother's family lived. A cousin of mine was a student there and he told me of the new school and of the changing conditions in "modern education." There was less emphasis on the Classics, and more was taught of the "new knowledge" of the West. The educational methods, also, were quite "radical."

I went to the school with my cousin and registered. I claimed to be a Hsiang Hsiang man, because I understood that the school was open only to natives of Hsiang Hsiang. Later on I took my true status as a Hsiang T'an native when I discovered that the place was open to all. I paid 1,400 coppers here for five months' board, lodging, and all materials necessary for study. My father finally agreed to let me enter, after friends had argued to him that this "advanced" education would increase my earning powers. This was the first time I had been as far away from home as fifty *li*. I was sixteen years old.

In the new school I could study natural science and new subjects of Western learning. Another notable thing was that one of the teachers was a returned student from Japan, and he wore a false queue. It was quite easy to tell that his queue was false. Everyone laughed at him and called him the "False Foreign Devil."

I had never before seen so many children together. Most of them were sons of landlords, wearing expensive clothes; very few peasants could afford to send their children to such a school. I was more poorly dressed than the others. I owned only one decent coat-and-trousers suit. Gowns were not worn by students, but only by the teachers, and none but "foreign devils" wore foreign clothes. Many of the richer students despised me because usually I was wearing my ragged coat and trousers. However, among them I had friends, and two especially were my good comrades. One of those is now a writer, living in Soviet Russia.

I was also disliked because I was not a native of Hsiang Hsiang. It was very important to be a native of Hsiang Hsiang and also important to be from a certain district of Hsiang Hsiang. There was an upper, lower and middle district, and lower and upper were continually fighting, purely on a regional basis. Neither could become reconciled to the existence of the other. I took a neutral position in this war, because I was not a native at all. Consequently all three factions despised me. I felt spiritually very depressed.

I made good progress at this school. The teachers liked me, especially those who taught the Classics, because I wrote good essays in the Classical manner. But my mind was not on the Classics. I was reading two books sent to me by my cousin, telling of the Reform movement of K'ang Yu-wei. One was called the *Journal of the New People* (*Hsin Min Ts'ung Pao*), and was edited by Liang Ch'i-ch'ao. I read and re-read these until I knew them by heart. I worshipped K'ang Yu-wei and Liang Ch'i-ch'ao, and was very grateful to my cousin, whom I then thought very progressive, but who later became a counter-revolutionary, a member of the gentry, and joined the reactionaries in the period of the Great Revolution of 1925–1927.

Many of the students disliked the "False Foreign Devil" because of his inhuman queue, but I liked hearing him talk about Japan. He taught music and English. One of his songs was Japanese and was called "The Battle on the Yellow Sea." I still remember some charming words from it:

> The sparrow sings,
> The nightingale dances,
> And the green fields are lovely in the spring.
> The pomegranate flowers crimson,

> The willows are green-leaved,
> And there is a new picture.

At that time I knew and felt the beauty of Japan, and felt something of her pride and might, in this song of her victory over Russia.[3] I did not think there was also a barbarous Japan—the Japan we know today.

This is all I learned from the "False Foreign Devil."

I recall also that at this time I first heard that the Emperor and Tzu Hsi, the Empress Dowager, were both dead, although the new Emperor, Hsüan T'ung [the late P'u Yi], had already been ruling for two years. I was not yet an anti-monarchist; indeed, I considered the Emperor as well as most officials to be honest, good and clever men. They only needed the help of K'ang Yu-wei's reforms. I was fascinated by accounts of the rulers of ancient China: Yao, Shun, Ch'in Shih Huang-ti, and Han Wu-ti, and read many books about them. I also learned something of foreign history at this time, and of geography. I had first heard of America in an article which told of the American Revolution and contained a sentence like this: "After eight years of difficult war, Washington won victory and built up his nation." In a book called *Great Heroes of the World*, I read also of Napoleon, Catherine of Russia, Peter the Great, Wellington, Gladstone, Rousseau, Montesquieu and Lincoln.

Days in Changsha

. . . I began to long to go to Changsha, the great city, the capital of the province, which was 120 *li* from my home. It was said that this city was very big, contained many, many people, numerous schools, and the yamen of the governor. It was a magnificent place altogether! I wanted very much to go there at this time, and enter the middle school for Hsiang Hsiang people. That winter I asked one of my teachers in the higher primary school to introduce me there. The teacher agreed, and I walked to Changsha, exceedingly excited, half-

---

[3] The poem evidently referred to the spring festival and tremendous rejoicing in Japan following the Treaty of Portsmouth and the end of the Russo-Japanese War.

fearing that I would be refused entrance, hardly daring to hope that I could actually become a student in this great school. To my astonishment, I was admitted without difficulty. But political events were moving rapidly and I was to remain there only half a year.

In Changsha I read my first newspaper, the *People's Strength* (*Min Li Pao*), a nationalist revolutionary journal which told of the Canton Uprising against the Manchu dynasty and the death of the Seventy-two Heroes, under the leadership of a Hunanese, Wang [Huang] Hsing. I was most impressed with this story and found the *Min Li Pao* full of stimulating material. It was edited by Yü Yu-jen, who later became a famous leader of the Kuomintang. I learned also of Sun Yat-sen at this time, and of the program of the T'ung Meng Hui. The country was on the eve of the First Revolution. I was agitated so much that I wrote an article, which I posted on the school wall. It was my first expression of a political opinion, and it was somewhat muddled. I had not yet given up my admiration of K'ang Yu-wei and Liang Ch'i-ch'ao. I did not clearly understand the differences between them. Therefore in my article I advocated that Sun Yat-sen must be called back from Japan to become President of a new Government, that K'ang Yu-wei be made Premier, and Liang Ch'i-ch'ao Minister of Foreign Affairs!

The anti-foreign capital movement began in connection with the building of the Szechwan-Hankow railway and a popular demand for a parliament became widespread. In reply to it the Emperor decreed merely that an Advisory Council be created. The students in my school became more and more agitated. They demonstrated their anti-Manchu sentiments by a rebellion against the pigtail. One friend and I clipped off our pigtails, but others, who had promised to do so, afterward failed to keep their word. My friend and I therefore assaulted them in secret and forcibly removed their queues, a total of more than ten falling victim to our shears. Thus in a short space of time I had progressed from ridiculing the False Foreign Devil's imitation queue to demanding the general abolition of queues. How a political idea can change a point of view!

I got into a dispute with a friend in a law school over the pigtail episode, and we each advanced opposing theories on the subject. The law student held that the body, skin, hair and nails are heritages from one's parents and must not be destroyed, quoting the Classics to clinch his argument. But I myself and the anti-pigtailers developed a counter-theory, on an anti-Manchu political basis, and thoroughly silenced him.

After the Wuhan Uprising occurred, led by Li Yuan-hung, martial law was declared in Hunan. The political scene rapidly altered. One day a revolutionary appeared in the middle school and made a stirring speech, with the permission of the principal. Seven or eight students arose in the assembly and supported him with vigorous denunciation of the Manchus, and calls for action to establish the Republic. Everyone listened with complete attention. Not a sound was heard as the orator of the revolution, one of the officials of Li Yuan-hung, spoke before the excited students.

Four or five days after hearing this speech, I determined to join the revolutionary army of Li Yuan-hung. I decided to go to Hankow with several other friends, and we collected some money from our classmates. Having heard that the streets of Hankow were very wet, and that it was necessary to wear rain-shoes, I went to borrow some from a friend in the army, who was quartered outside the city. I was stopped by the garrison guards. The place had become very active, the soldiers had for the first time been furnished with bullets, and they were pouring into the streets.

Rebels were approaching the city along the Canton-Hankow railway, and fighting had begun. A big battle occurred outside the city walls of Changsha. There was at the same time an insurrection within the city, and the gates were stormed and taken by Chinese labourers. Through one of them I re-entered the city. Then I stood on a high place and watched the battle, until at last I saw the Han[4] flag raised over the yamen. It was a white banner with the character Han in it. I returned to my school, to find it under military guard.

On the following day, a tutuh[5] government was organized. Two prominent members of the Ke Lao Hui were made tutuh and vice-tutuh. These were Chao Ta-feng and Chen T'so-hsing, respectively.

[4] Han, i.e., Chinese.
[5] A tutuh was a military governor.

The new government was established in the former buildings of the Provincial Advisory Council, chief of which was T'an Yen-k'ai, who was dismissed. The Council itself was abolished. Among the Manchu documents found by the revolutionaries were some copies of a petition begging for the opening of parliament. The original had been written in blood by Hsu Teh-lih, who is now Commissioner of Education in the Soviet Government. Hsu had cut off the end of his finger, as a demonstration of sincerity and determination, and his petition began, "Begging that parliament be opened, I bid farewell [to the provincial delegates to Peking] by cutting my finger."

The new *tutuh* and vice-*tutuh* did not last long. They were not bad men, and had some revolutionary intentions, but they were poor and represented the interests of the oppressed. The landlords and merchants were dissatisfied with them. Not many days later, when I went to call on a friend, I saw their corpses lying in the street. T'an Yen-k'ai had organized a revolt against them, as representative of the Hunan landlords and militarists.

Many students were now joining the army. A student army had been organized and among these students was T'ang Sheng-chih.[6] I did not like the student army; I considered the basis of it too confused. I decided to join the regular army instead, and help complete the revolution. The Ch'ing Emperor had not yet abdicated, and there was a period of struggle.

My salary was seven dollars a month—which is more than I get in the Red Army now, however—and of this I spent two dollars a month on food. I also had to buy water. The soldiers had to carry water in from outside the city, but I, being a student, could not condescend to carrying, and bought it from the water-pedlars. The rest of my wages were spent on newspapers, of which I became an avid reader. Among journals then dealing with the revolution was the *Hsiang Kiang Daily News (Hsiang Kiang Erh Pao)*. Socialism was discussed in it, and in these columns I first learned the term. I also discussed Socialism, really social-reformism, with other students

---

[6] T'ang Sheng-chih later became commander of the Nationalist armies of the Wuhan Government of Wang Ching-wei, in 1927. He betrayed both Wang and the Reds and began the "peasant massacre" of Hunan.

and soldiers. I read some pamphlets written by Kiang [Chiang] K'ang-hu about Socialism and its principles. I wrote enthusiastically to several of my classmates on this subject, but only one of them responded in agreement.

There was a Hunan miner in my squad, and an ironsmith, whom I liked very much. The rest were mediocre, and one was a rascal. I persuaded two more students to join the army, and became on friendly terms with the platoon commander and most of the soldiers. I could write, I knew something about books, and they respected my "Great Learning." I could help by writing letters for them or in other such ways.

The outcome of the revolution was not yet decided. The Ch'ing had not wholly given up the power, and there was a struggle within the Kuomintang concerning the leadership. It was said in Hunan that further war was inevitable. Several armies were organized against the Manchus and against Yuan Shih-k'ai. Among these was the Hunan army. But just as the Hunanese were preparing to move into action, Sun Yat-sen and Yuan Shih-k'ai came to an agreement, the scheduled war was called off, North and South were "unified," and the Nanking Government was dissolved. Thinking the revolution was over, I resigned from the army and decided to return to my books. I had been a soldier for half a year.

I began to read advertisements in the papers. Many schools were then being opened and used this medium to attract new students. I had no special standard for judging schools; I did not know exactly what I wanted to do. An advertisement for a police school caught my eye and I registered for entrance to it. Before I was examined, however, I read an advertisement of a soap-making "school." No tuition was required, board was furnished and a small salary was promised. It was an attractive and inspiring advertisement. It told of the great social benefits of soap-making, how it would enrich the country and enrich the people. I changed my mind about the police school and decided to become a soap-maker. I paid my dollar registration fee here also.

Meanwhile, a friend of mine had become a law student and he

urged me to enter his school. I also read an alluring advertisement of this law school, which promised many wonderful things. It promised to teach students all about law in three years and guaranteed that at the end of this period they would instantly become mandarins. My friend kept praising the school to me, until finally I wrote to my family, repeated all the promises of the advertisement, and asked them to send me tuition money. I painted a bright picture for them of my future as a jurist and mandarin. Then I paid a dollar to register in the law school and waited to hear from my parents.

Fate again intervened in the form of an advertisement for a commercial school. Another friend counselled me that the country was in economic war, and that what was most needed were economists who could build up the nation's economy. His argument prevailed and I spent another dollar to register in this commercial middle school. I actually enrolled there and was accepted. Meanwhile, however, I continued to read advertisements, and one day I read one describing the charms of a higher commercial public school. It was operated by the Government, it offered a wide curriculum, and I heard that its instructors were very able men. I decided it would be better to become a commercial expert there, paid my dollar and registered, then wrote to my father of my decision. He was pleased. My father readily appreciated the advantages of commercial cleverness. I entered this school and remained—for one month.

The trouble with my new school, I discovered, was that most of the courses were taught in English, and, in common with other students, I knew little English; indeed, scarcely more than the alphabet. An additional handicap was that the school provided no English teacher. Disgusted with this situation, I withdrew from the institution at the end of the month and continued my perusal of the advertisements.

My scholastic adventure was in the First Provincial Middle School. I registered for a dollar, took the entrance examination, and passed at the head of the list of candidates. It was a big school, with many students, and its graduates were numerous. A Chinese teacher there helped me very much; he was attracted to me because of my literary tendency. This teacher loaned me a book called the *Chronicles with Imperial Commentaries (Yü P'i T'ung Chien)*, which contained imperial edicts and critiques by Ch'ien Lung.

About this time a Government magazine exploded in Changsha. There was a huge fire, and we students found it very interesting. Tons of bullets and shells exploded, and gunpowder made an intense blaze. It was better than fire-crackers. About a month later T'an Yen-k'ai was driven out by Yuan Shih-k'ai, who now had control of the political machinery of the Republic. T'ang Hsiang-ming replaced T'an Yen-k'ai and he set about making arrangements for Yuan's enthronement.

I did not like the First Middle School. Its curriculum was limited and its regulations were objectionable. After reading *Chronicles with Imperial Commentaries,* I had also come to the conclusion that it would be better for me to read and study alone. After six months I left the school, and arranged a schedule of education of my own, which consisted of reading every day in the Hunan Provincial Library. I was very regular and conscientious about it, and the half-year I spent in this way I consider to have been extremely valuable to me. I went to the library in the morning when it opened. At noon I paused only long enough to buy and consume two rice cakes, which were my daily lunch. I stayed in the library every day reading until it closed.

During this period of self-education I read many books, studied world geography and world history. There for the first time I saw and studied with great interest a map of the world. I read Adam Smith's *The Wealth of Nations,* and Darwin's *Origin of Species,* and a book on ethics by John Stuart Mill. I read the works of Rousseau, Spencer's *Logic,* and a book on law written by Montesquieu. I mixed poetry and romances, and the tales of ancient Greece, with serious study of history and geography of Russia, America, England, France and other countries.

I was then living in a guild house for natives of Hsiang Hsiang district. Many soldiers were there also—"retired" or disbanded men from the district, who had no work to do and little money. Students and soldiers were always quarrelling in the guild house, and one night this hostility between them broke out in physical violence. The soldiers attacked and tried to kill the students. I escaped by fleeing to the toilet, where I hid until the fight was over.

I had no money then, my family refusing to support me unless I entered school, and since I could no longer live in the guild house I began looking for a new place to lodge. Meanwhile, I had been thinking seriously of my "career" and had about decided that I was best suited for teaching. I had begun reading advertisements again. An attractive announcement of the Hunan Normal School now came to my attention, and I read with interest of its advantages: no tuition required, and cheap board and cheap lodging. Two of my friends were also urging me to enter. They wanted my help in preparing entrance essays. I wrote of my intention to my family and received their consent. I composed essays for my two friends, and wrote one of my own. All were accepted—in reality, therefore, I was accepted three times. I did not then think my act of substituting for my friends an immoral one; it was merely a matter of friendship.

I was a student in the Normal School for five years, and managed to resist the appeals of all future advertising. Finally I actually got my degree. Incidents in my life here, in the Hunan Provincial First Normal School, were many, and during this period my political ideas began to take shape. Here also I acquired my first experiences in social action.

There were many regulations in the new school and I agreed with very few of them. For one thing, I was opposed to the required courses in natural science. I wanted to specialize in social sciences. Natural sciences did not especially interest me, and I did not study them, so I got poor marks in most of these courses. Most of all I hated a compulsory course in still-life drawing. I thought it extremely stupid. I used to think of the simplest subjects possible to draw, finish up quickly and leave the class. I remember once drawing a picture of the "half-sun, half-rock," [7] which I represented by a straight line with a semi-circle over it. Another time during an examination in drawing I contented myself with making an oval. I called it an egg. I got 40 in drawing, and failed. Fortunately my marks in

[7] The reference is to a line in a famous poem by Li T'ai-po.

social sciences were all excellent, and they balanced my poor grades in these other classes.

A Chinese teacher here, whom the students nicknamed "Yuan the Big Beard," ridiculed my writing and called it the work of a journalist. He despised Liang Ch'i-ch'ao, who had been my model, and considered him half-literate. I was obliged to alter my style. I studied the writings of Han Yü, and mastered the old Classical phraseology. Thanks to Yuan the Big Beard, therefore, I can today still turn out a passable Classical essay if required.

The teacher who made the strongest impression on me was Yang Chen-ch'i, a returned student from England, with whose life I was later to become intimately related. He taught ethics, he was an idealist, and a man of high moral character. He believed in his ethics very strongly and tried to imbue his students with the desire to become just, moral, virtuous men, useful in society. Under his influence, I read a book on ethics translated by Ts'ai Yuan-p'ei and was inspired to write an essay which I entitled "The Energy of the Mind." I was then an idealist and my essay was highly praised by Professor Yang Chen-ch'i, from his idealist viewpoint. He gave me a mark of 100 for it.

A teacher named T'ang used to give me old copies of the *People's Paper* (*Min Pao*), and I read them with keen interest. I learned from them about the activities and programme of the T'ung Meng Hui. One day I read a copy of the *Min Pao* containing a story about two Chinese students who were travelling across China and had reached Tatsienlu, on the edge of Tibet. This inspired me very much. I wanted to follow their example; but I had no money, and thought I should first try out travelling in Hunan.

The next summer I set out across the province by foot, and journeyed through five counties. I was accompanied by a student named Hsiao Yü. We walked through these five counties without using a single copper. The peasants fed us and gave us a place to sleep; wherever we went we were kindly treated and welcomed. This fellow, Hsiao Yü, with whom I travelled, later became a Kuomintang official in Nanking, under Yi Pei-chi, who was then president of Hunan Normal College. Yi Pei-chi became a high official at Nanking and got Hsiao Yü appointed to the office of custodian of the Peking Palace Museum. Hsiao sold some of the most valuable treasures in the museum and absconded with the funds in 1934.

Feeling expansive and the need for a few intimate companions, I one day inserted an advertisement in a Changsha paper, inviting young men interested in patriotic work to make a contact with me. I specified youths who were hardened and determined, and ready to make sacrifices for their country. To this advertisement I received three and one-half replies. One was from Liu Chiang-lung, who later was to join the Communist Party and afterwards to betray it. Two others were from young men who later were to become ultra-reactionaries. The "half" reply came from a noncommittal youth named Li Li-san. Li listened to all I had to say, and then went away without making any definite proposals himself, and our friendship never developed.

But gradually I did build up a group of students around myself, and the nucleus was formed of what later was to become a society that was to have a widespread influence on the affairs and destiny of China. It was a serious-minded little group of men and they had no time to discuss trivialities. Everything they did or said must have a purpose. They had no time for love or "romance" and considered the times too critical and the need for knowledge too urgent to discuss women or personal matters. I was not interested in women. My parents had married me when I was fourteen to a girl of twenty, but I had never lived with her—and never subsequently did. I did not consider her my wife and at this time gave little thought to her. Quite aside from the discussions of feminine charm, which usually play an important rôle in the lives of young men of this age, my companions even rejected talk of ordinary matters of daily life. I remember once being in the house of a youth who began to talk to me about buying some meat, and in my presence called in his servant and discussed the matter with him, then ordering him to buy a piece. I was annoyed and did not see this fellow again. My friends and I preferred to talk only of large matters—the nature of men, of human society, of China, the world, and the universe!

We also became ardent physical culturists. In the winter holidays we tramped through the fields, up and down mountains, along city walls, and across the streams and rivers. If it rained we took off our shirts and called it a rain bath. When the sun was hot we also doffed shirts and called it a sun bath. In the spring winds we shouted that this was a new sport called "wind bathing." We slept in the open when frost was already falling and even in November swam in the cold rivers. All this went on under the title of "body-training." Perhaps it helped much to build the physique which I was to need so badly later on in my many marches back and forth across South China, and on the Long March from Kiangsi to the North-west.

I built up a wide correspondence with many students and friends in other towns and cities. Gradually I began to realize the necessity for a more closely knit organization. In 1917, with some other friends, I helped to found the Hsin Min Hsüeh Hui ("New People's Study Society"). It had from seventy to eighty members, and of these many were later to become famous names in Chinese Communism, and in the history of the Chinese Revolution. Among the better-known Communists who were in the Hsin Min Hsüeh Hui were: Lo Man, now secretary of the Party Organization Committee; Hsia Hsi, now in the Second Front Red Army; Ho Hsien-hon, who became high judge of the Supreme Court in the Central Soviet regions and was later killed by Chiang Kai-shek; Kuo Liang, a famous labour-organizer, killed by General Ho Chien in 1930; Hsiao Chu-chang, a writer now in Soviet Russia; Ts'ai Ho-sheng, a member of the Central Committee of the Communist Party, killed by Chiang Kai-shek in 1927; Yeh Li-yün, who became a member of the Central Committee, and later "betrayed" to the Kuomintang, and became a capitalist trade-union organizer; and Hsiao Chen, a prominent Party leader, one of the six signers of the original agreement for the formation of the Party, but who died not long ago from illness. The majority of the members of the Hsin Min Hsüeh Hui were killed in the counter-revolution of 1927.

Another society that was formed about that time, and resembled the Hsin Min Hsüeh Hui, was the "Social Welfare Society" of Hupeh. Many of its members also later became Communists. Among them was Wen Teh-ying, its leader, who was killed during the counter-revolution by Chiang Kai-shek. Lin Piao, now president of the Red Army Academy, was a member. So was Chang Hao, now in charge of work among White troops. In Peiping there was a society called Fu Hsieh, some of whose members later became Reds. Elsewhere in China, notably in Shanghai, Hangchow, Hankow and Tientsin, radical societies were organized by the militant youth then beginning to assert an influence on Chinese politics.

Most of these societies were organized more or less under the influence of *New Youth* (*Hsin Ch'ing Nien*), the famous magazine of the Literary Renaissance, edited by Ch'en Tu-hsiu. I began to read this magazine while I was a student in the normal college and admired the articles of Hu Shih and Ch'en Tu-hsiu very much. They became for a while my models, replacing Liang Ch'i-ch'ao and Kang Yu-wei, whom I had already discarded.

At this time my mind was a curious mixture of ideas of liberalism, democratic reformism, and Utopian Socialism. I had somewhat vague passions about "nineteenth-century democracy," Utopianism and old-fashioned liberalism, and I was definitely anti-militarist and anti-imperialist.

I had entered the normal college in 1912. I was graduated in 1918.

Prelude to Revolution

. . . During my years in normal school in Changsha I had spent, altogether, only $160—including my numerous registration fees! Of this amount I must have used a third for newspapers, because regular subscriptions cost me about a dollar a month, and I often bought books and journals on the news-stands. My father cursed me for this extravagance. He called it wasted money on wasted paper. But I had acquired the newspaper-reading habit, and from 1911 to 1927, when I climbed up Chingkanshan, I never stopped reading the daily papers of Peiping, Shanghai and Hunan.

In my last year in school my mother died, and more than ever I lost interest in returning home. I decided, that summer, to go to Peiping—then Peking. Many students from Hunan were planning trips to France, to study under the "work and learn" scheme, which

France used to recruit young Chinese in her cause during the World War. Before leaving China these students planned to study French in Peiping. I helped organize the movement, and in the groups who went abroad were many students from the Hunan Normal School, most of whom were later to become famous radicals. Hsu Teh-lih was influenced by the movement also, and when he was over forty he left his professorship at Hunan Normal College and went to France. He did not become a Communist, however, till 1927.

I accompanied some of the Hunanese students to Peking. However, although I had helped organize the movement, and it had the support of the Hsin Min Hsüeh Hui, I did not want to go to Europe. I felt that I did not know enough about my own country, and that my time could be more profitably spent in China. Those students who had decided to go to France studied French then from Li Shih-ts'un, who is now president of the Chung-fa (Sino-French) University, but I did not. I had other plans.

Peiping seemed very expensive to me. I had reached the capital by borrowing from friends, and when I arrived I had to look for work at once. Yang Chen-ch'i, my former ethics teacher at the normal school, had become a professor at Peking National University. I appealed to him for help in finding a job, and he introduced me to the university librarian. This was Li Ta-chao, who later became a founder of the Communist Party of China, and was afterwards executed by Chang Tso-lin. Li Ta-chao gave me work, as assistant librarian, for which I was paid the generous sum of $8 a month.*

My office was so low that people avoided me. One of my tasks was to register the names of people who came to read newspapers, but to most of them I didn't exist as a human being. Among those who came to read I recognized the names of famous leaders of the renaissance movement, men like Fu Ssu-nien, Lo Chia-lun, and others, in whom I was intensely interested. I tried to begin conversations with them on political and cultural subjects, but they were very busy men. They had no time to listen to an assistant librarian speaking southern dialect.

* Mao was probably a library assistant rather than an assistant librarian.—Ed.

But I wasn't discouraged. I joined the Society of Philosophy, and the Journalism Society, in order to be able to attend classes in the university. In the Journalism Society I met fellow-students like Chen Kung-po, who is now a high official at Nanking; T'an P'ing-shan, who later became a Communist and still later a member of the so-called "Third Party"; and Shao P'iao-p'ing. Shao, especially, helped me very much. He was a lecturer in the Journalism Society, a liberal, and a man of fervent idealism and fine character. He was killed by Chang Tso-lin in 1926.

While I was working in the library I also met Chang Kuo-t'ao, now vice-chairman of the Soviet Government; K'ang P'ei-ch'en, who later joined the Ku Klux Klan in California [!!!—E. S.]; and Tuan Hsi-p'en, now Vice-Minister of Education in Nanking. And here also I met and fell in love with Yang K'ai-hui. She was the daughter of my former ethics teacher, Yang Chen-ch'i, who had made a great impression on me in my youth, and who afterwards was a genuine friend in Peking.

My interest in politics continued to increase, and my mind turned more and more radical. I have told you of the background for this. But just now I was still confused, looking for a road, as we say. I read some pamphlets on anarchy, and was much influenced by them. With a student named Chu Hsun-pei, who used to visit me, I often discussed anarchism and its possibilities in China. At that time I favoured many of its proposals.

My own living conditions in Peking were quite miserable, and in contrast the beauty of the old capital was a vivid and living compensation. I stayed in a place called "Three-Eyes Well" (San Yen-ching), in a little room which held seven other people. When we were all packed fast on the *k'ang* there was scarcely room enough for any of us to breathe. I used to have to warn people on each side of me when I wanted to turn over. But in the parks and the old palace grounds I saw the early northern spring, I saw the white plum blossoms flower while the ice still held solid over the North Sea. I saw the willows over Pei Hai with the ice crystals hanging from them and remembered the description of the scene by the T'ang poet Chen

Chang, who wrote about Pei Hai's winter-jewelled trees, looking "like ten thousand peach-trees blossoming." The innumerable trees of Peking aroused my wonder and admiration.

Early in 1919 I went to Shanghai, with the students bound for France. I had a ticket only to Tientsin, and I did not know how I was to get any farther. But, as the Chinese proverb says, "Heaven will not delay a traveller," and a fortunate loan of $10 from a fellow student, who had got some money from the Compte School in Peiping, enabled me to buy a ticket as far as P'u-k'ou. *En route* to Nanking I stopped at Ch'u Fou and visited Confucius' grave. I saw the small stream where Confucius' disciples bathed their feet and the little town where the sage lived as a child. He is supposed to have planted a famous tree near the historic temple dedicated to him, and I saw that. I also stopped by the river where Yen Hui, one of Confucius' famous disciples, had once lived, and I saw the birthplace of Mencius. On this trip I climbed T'ai Shan, the sacred mountain of Shantung, where General Feng Yü-hsiang retired and wrote his patriotic scrolls.

But when I reached P'u-k'ou I was again without a copper, and without a ticket. Nobody had any money to lend me; I did not know how I was to get out of town. But the worst of the tragedy happened when a thief stole my only pair of shoes! Ai-ya! What was I to do? But again, "Heaven will not delay a traveller," and I had a very good piece of luck. Outside the railway station I met an old friend from Hunan, and he proved to be my "good angel." He lent me money for a pair of shoes, and enough to buy a ticket to Shanghai. Thus I safely completed my journey—keeping an eye on my new shoes. At Shanghai I found that a good sum had been raised to help send the students to France, and an allowance had been provided to help me return to Hunan. I saw my friends off on the steamer and then set off for Changsha.

High marks of my first trip to the North, as I remember it, were these excursions:

I walked on the ice of the Gulf of Pei Hai. I walked round the lake of T'ung T'ing, and I circled the wall of Paotingfu. I walked round the wall of Hsuchou, famous in the *Three Kingdoms* (*San Kuo*), and round Nanking's wall, also famous in history. Finally, I climbed T'ai Shan and visited Confucius' grave. These seemed to me then achievements worth adding to my adventures and walking tours in Hunan.

When I returned to Changsha I took a more direct rôle in politics. After the May Fourth Movement I had devoted most of my time to student political activities, and I was editor of the *Hsiang Chiang Review,* the Hunan students' paper, which had a great influence on the student movement in South China. In Changsha I helped found the Wen-hua Shu Hui (Cultural Book Society), an association for study of modern cultural and political tendencies. This society, and more especially the Hsin Min Hsüeh Hui, were violently opposed to Chang Ching-yao, then *tuchun* of Hunan, and a vicious character. We led a general student strike against Chang, demanding his removal, and sent delegations to Peiping and the South-west, where Sun Yat-sen was then active, to agitate against him. In retaliation to the students' opposition, Chang Ching-yao suppressed the *Hsiang Chiang Review.*

After this I went to Peking, to represent the Hsin Min Hsüeh Hui, and organize an anti-militarist movement there. The Hsi Min Hsüeh Hui broadened its fight against Chang Ching-yao into a general anti-militarist agitation, and I became head of a news-agency, to promote this work. In Hunan the movement was rewarded with some success. Chang Ching-yao was overthrown by T'an Yen-k'ai, and a new régime was established in Changsha. About this time the Hsin Min Hsüeh Hui began to divide into two groups, a Right and Left wing—the Left wing insisting on a programme of far-reaching social and economic and political changes.

I went to Shanghai for the second time in 1919. There once more I saw Ch'en Tu-hsiu. I had first met him in Peking, when I was at Peking National University, and he had influenced me perhaps more than any one else. I also met Hu Shih at that time, having called on him to try to win his support for the Hunanese students' struggle. In Shanghai I discussed with Ch'en Tu-hsiu our plans for a League for Reconstruction of Hunan. Then I returned to Changsha, and began to organize it. I took a place as a teacher there, meanwhile continuing my activity in the Hsin Min Hsüeh Hui. The society had a programme then for the "independence" of Hunan, meaning, really, autonomy. Disgusted with the Northern Government, and believing that Hunan could modernize more rapidly if freed from connections with Peking, our group agitated for separation. I was then a strong supporter of America's Monroe Doctrine and the Open Door.

T'an Yen-k'ai was driven out of Hunan by a militarist called Chao Heng-t'i, who utilized the "Hunan independence" movement for his own ends. He pretended to support it, advocating the idea of a United Autonomous States of China, but as soon as he got power he suppressed the democratic movement with great energy. Our group had demanded equal rights for men and women, and representative government, and in general approval of a platform for a bourgeois democracy. We openly advocated these reforms in our paper, the *New Hunan*. We led an attack on the provincial parliament, the majority of whose members were landlords and gentry appointed by the militarists. This struggle ended in our pulling down the scrolls and banners, which were full of nonsensical and extravagant phrases.

The attack on the parliament was considered a big incident in Hunan, and frightened the rulers. However, when Chao Heng-t'i seized control he betrayed all the ideas he had supported, and especially he violently suppressed all demands for democracy. Our society therefore turned the struggle against him. I remember an episode in 1920, when the Hsin Min Hsüeh Hui organized a demonstration to celebrate the third anniversary of the Russian October Revolution. It was suppressed by the police. Some of the demonstrators had attempted to raise the Red Flag at that meeting, but were prohibited from doing so by the police. They then pointed out that, according to Article 12 of the (then) Constitution, the people had the right to assemble, organize, and speak, but the police were not impressed. They replied that they were not there to be taught the Constitution, but to carry out the orders of the governor, Chao Heng-t'i. From this time on I became more and more convinced that only mass political power, secured through mass action, could guarantee the realization of dynamic reforms.

In the winter of 1920, I organized workers politically, for the first time, and began to be guided in this by the influence of Marxist theory and the history of the Russian Revolution. During my second visit to Peking I had read much about the events in Russia, and had eagerly sought out what little Communist literature was then available in Chinese. Three books especially deeply carved my mind, and build up in me a faith in Marxism, from which, once I had accepted it as the correct interpretation of history, I did not afterwards waver. These books were *The Communist Manifesto,* translated by Chen Wang-tao, and the first Marxist book ever published in Chinese; *Class Struggle,* by Kautsky; and a *History of Socialism,* by Kirkupp. By the summer of 1920 I had become, in theory and to some extent in action, a Marxist, and from this time on I considered myself a Marxist. In the same year I married Yang K'ai-hui.

❦ 15 ❦

Chang Kuo-t'ao and
the Chinese Communist Movement

CHÜN-TU HSÜEH

I

Chang Kuo-t'ao, one of the founders of the Chinese Communist Party, was born to a family of the gentry class in 1897, near Shangsu town, in Pinghsiang county, Kiangsi province.[1] Shangsu, a coal-mining town, was twenty-seven miles from the Pinghsiang county seat and seven miles from the border of the Liling and Liuyang counties in Hunan province. It was a mountainous crossroad of the Hunan-Kiangsi-Hupeh border area which was characterized by incessant fighting among bandits and miners. Partly because of the geographical location, it served as an important base for members of secret societies. In 1906, at the age of nine and while a student at a small

This article, written especially for this book, is based mainly on Chang Kuo-t'ao's memoir, "Wo-ti hui-i," which was published serially in a Chinese magazine *Ming Pao Monthly* (Hong Kong), Nos. 3–48 (March 1966–December 1969). Other sources are indicated in footnotes. No attempt was made to compare his accounts with those of others, but readers who care to do so will note the differences of some crucial points on the subject.

[1] Chang's grandfather lived with all other branches of the family. Four of the six branches, including his grandfather, passed civil examinations and the remaining two bought government offices. Each of the six families owned land that produced some 500 to 1000 *tan* of rice. Ironically, Chang's grandfather, who died at the age of eighty-nine, was publicly tried by the peasants' association during the Communist movement, and his aunt was once kidnapped by the guerrillas. Chang's father, who also passed the provincial examination, later studied in a law school in Chekiang and died in 1930.

private school, Chang witnessed a revolt against the Manchus organized by a secret society called the Hung Chiang Hui and known
as the "Ping-Liu-Li" uprising in Kuomintang history (Pinghsiang of
Kiangsi, Liuyang and Liling of Hunan). The leader of this revolt,
Kung Chun-t'ai, was a follower of Ma Fu-i, who had aided a revolt organized by Huang Hsing in Changsha in 1904. It was Chang's first
revolutionary experience—not as a participant, but merely as an eye-
witness.

In the spring of 1908, Chang began to study at the Pinghsiang
County School, a school founded after the traditional examination
system was abolished in 1905. In the new transitional educational
system, Chang learned not only about Confucius, but also about
Napoleon, Washington, Newton, Watt, and Rousseau. The local
conservative populace strongly resented foreign manufactured goods
and the building of railways—it believed the railroad would not
run unless it was worshiped by the sacrifice of a child each day by
throwing him into the stack of the locomotive. On the other hand,
the enlightened school teachers and students strongly attacked what
were considered the four main evils of China at that time: foot binding, opium, superstition, and bureaucracy. Chang, who was considered a well-behaved student in the school, was belittled by his
fellow students when he put a white cloth around his pigtail to
commemorate the deaths of the Kuang-hsü emperor and the Empress Dowager in November 1908.

The students' anti-Manchu feelings were reflected by one incident
in 1909 when twenty-nine students in the school cut off their pigtails to demonstrate against the regulations. Whenever they could
smuggle in revolutionary publications from Changsha or Shanghai,
they were eagerly passed around. In 1910 and 1911, many of the
young students secretly joined the new army, in contrast to the traditional concept that a good man would not become a soldier. Chang
was too young, since he was only thirteen or fourteen years old.

After the outbreak of the Wuchang Revolution in October 1911,
Chang's father came to the school to take him home. Young Chang
cut off his pigtails to show his determination to break with Manchu

rule even though the older generations were sitting on the fence. In the spring of 1912 he resumed his studies at his former school, now renamed Pinghsiang Middle School.[2]

As a student, Chang helped Kuomintang members during the "second revolution" against Yüan Shih-k'ai in 1913. In February 1914 he argued with the resident of a student hall, who wanted to expel him for insulting the teachers. Instead of apologizing for his behavior in order to remain in school, he transferred to Hsin-yüan School in the provincial capital, Nanchang. Here he began to study English and science, which opened the gate of modern knowledge to him. Chang read Yen Fu's translation of Darwin's writings while preparing to enter the university to study natural sciences.

At this time Chang began to read the newspapers regularly and became quite concerned with the state of affairs in China. During World War I, anti-Japanese feeling among the Chinese people ran high because Japan attempted to dominate China by presenting "Twenty-one Demands." Chang became a "fanatic patriot" and his interest in politics far surpassed his interest in science.

In July 1916, he visited his father, who was then the magistrate of Hsiangshan county, Chekiang province. Then he went to Shanghai and associated with a number of revolutionaries who had fought against Yüan Shih-k'ai. Chang had a glimpse of the romantic adventure and idealistic life of the revolutionaries, who lived for a cause and shared its excitement and danger.

In October Chang traveled from Shanghai to Peking for the first time. At that time Peking University was headed by Ts'ai Yüan-p'ei. The faculty members of the university were of sharply diverse schools of thought, and the university student body contained many individualistic students who set their own rules in their academic and pri-

---

[2] Chang Kuo-t'ao recalled in his memoir that at the end of 1912 "a revolutionary great man, Huang Hsing, came to Pinghsiang after he had visited his hometown in Hunan. Huang believed that he had historical relations with the area because of the 1906 uprisings and took advantage of the home journey to come for a visit. The school gave a welcome party for him, and the prominent local people came to meet him. . . . Huang had an impressive appearance . . . but I could not remember what he said, partly because I could not quite understand his Hunanese accent."

vate life. Chang enrolled as a science student in the preparatory class for the university.

Intellectual turmoil was evident at the university when Ch'en Tu-hsiu, editor of *La Jeunesse,* which began publication in the autumn of 1915, became the Dean of the College of Arts. Chang, like many other students, supported a new movement which advocated science and democracy. The campus was also racked by movements advocating socialism and anarchy. This was an age of conflict between old and new ideas, and under this influence Chang dissolved his engagement to a girl which had been arranged by his grandfather. In the middle of this patriotic and cultural movement, Chang co-operated with other students in organizing the People's Magazine Society, which published *People's Magazine Monthly* in January 1919. Only four issues were published; it ceased publication after the May Fourth Movement in which many members of this society were very active.

In the spring of 1919, Chang's father came to see him in Peking. By this time Chang had become an active radical. Naturally, his father did not approve of it, but otherwise the two got on well. When the father left for the south by train, Chang saw him off at the station. He suggested subtly to his father that, for the sake of the latter's own position in the old society, it would be better for the father to sever father-son relations in order to avoid any consequences as a result of his activities. The father kept his silence, feeling sad, and it was in this atmosphere that they parted.

With Teng Chung-hsia and others, Chang organized the People's Education Society which advocated social reforms by means of mass education. His active role in the May Fourth Movement led to his arrest by the police early in June 1919. Later he was one of several student representatives from Peking to attend the National Student Association meeting in Shanghai. Returning to school in Peking in October 1919, Chang joined an organization formed by Teng Chung-hsia. Most of the members of this organization were Hunanese and it supported the anarchist "new village" idea which advocated mutual help, mutual work, and mutual life. December of 1919 found Chang in the capacity of student representative fleeing to Shanghai to avoid police arrest. In January 1920 Chang met Sun Yat-sen for the first time. He also met a number of ranking members of the Kuomintang and made contacts with labor unions. In March he became Secretary General of the Executive Council of the National Labor Union, whose Chairman of the Board of Directors was Ts'ao Ya-po, a revolutionary veteran who helped Huang Hsing escape after the abortive Changsha revolt of 1904.

II

Before the May Fourth Movement Chang Kuo-t'ao was a purely fanatical patriot, but after its failure he turned to Marxism in the hope of finding a way to save China from internal and external crises. The Russian declaration renouncing former rights in China made a great impression on Chinese intellectuals. Under the leadership of Professor Li Ta-chao, Marxist study groups became active in Peking University. Early in May 1920 Chang returned to Peking. About this time the Far Eastern Bureau of the Communist International at Irkutsk sent agent Gregory Voitinsky to Peking. Disguised as a newspaper man, Voitinsky was assisted by Yang Ming-chai, who had joined the Communist Party in Russia. Through a Russian language instructor at Peking University, Voitinsky met Li Ta-chao, and through Li, Voitinsky met Ch'en Tu-hsiu in Shanghai.

In mid-July of 1920 Chang visited Ch'en Tu-hsiu as his house guest in Shanghai. Although Ch'en was a leader of the New Culture Movement, his magazine articles were not favorable to the Russians until early 1919. It was late in 1919, when Ch'en fled from Peking, that he began to accept Marxism as the political ideology which would save China. Before Chang arrived in Shanghai, preliminary steps for the establishment of the Shanghai Communist group had been taken. The Shanghai Communist group held preliminary meetings in May and June 1920 and was formally established in August, shortly after Chang Kuo-t'ao had left Shanghai for Peking. The Shanghai group, which was established after Ch'en Tu-hsiu had met Voitinsky, included Ch'en Tu-hsiu, Li Ta, Li Han-chün, and Shao Li-tzu.

At the end of August, Chang returned to Peking and reported to

Li Ta-chao on developments in Shanghai. Subsequently, the Peking Communist group was organized, and in mid-September held its first meeting in Li Ta-chao's office with nine attending. Li contributed eighty dollars from his monthly salary for the expenses. He also proposed the organization of a Marxist study group. Five of the nine attending were anarchist students from Peking University who later in November withdrew from the organization because they opposed the idea of the dictatorship of the proletariat.[3] Several members of the Socialist Youth Corps which had also been established in September were invited to join the Peking Communist Youth Group. By late November the Peking branch of the Communist Party was formally established, and hereafter Chang Kuo-t'ao took an active part in the labor movement. His initiative led to working with the laborers on the Peking and Hankow railways.

Between 1920 and 1921 a number of Communist groups were established in Shanghai, Peking, Changsha, Shantung, Wuhan, Chungking, and Canton. The students were the core of the Communist groups. The Shanghai group established a foreign language school to train students who wished to study in Russia. In the winter of 1920 Liu Shao-ch'i was among the first students sent by the school to Russia for study.

The fact that Communist groups were organized in such provinces as Hunan and Shantung was not an accident. These areas were constantly troubled by civil war and internal strifes. The youth of Shantung were very sensitive to the Japanese aggression in the area. In Wuhan, which was a crossroads of civil war, and where the people desperately wanted peace and order, educated youth sought radical solutions for the political situation. Hunan province, which had produced a number of outstanding historical figures in modern times, was also plagued by civil war and strife. The Hunanese people were characterized by a stubborn, persistent nature. Between 1920 and 1921, many politicians who were opposed to the Peking government came to Hunan province and advocated a program of federated autonomous provinces. In order to avoid war, a number of leftist

[3] One of these students was Huang Ling-shuang, who attended the Congress of the Toilers of the East in Russia in 1922.

youths including Mao Tse-tung, who initiated the Communist group in Changsha, also supported this program. In May 1921 Chang Kuo-t'ao and Liu Jen-ching, serving as representatives of the Peking group, arrived in Shanghai for the formation of the Chinese Communist Party. In July 1921 the First National Congress of the Chinese Communist Party was held. It started on July 1 in Shanghai, but because of police interruption the Congress ended on a boat in South Lake, Chiahsing, on or about July 10.[4] Originally there were thirteen delegates, but one, Ho Shu-heng, was considered unqualified and sent back to Hunan on the eve of the Congress under some pretext. The remaining twelve delegates represented fifty-nine members. At this time the Socialist Youth League had about 350 members.

In the conduct of its business the First National Congress did not formally request to join the Communist International. (This matter was decided upon at the Second National Congress.) Near the end of the meeting members of the Communist International were invited to give speeches, but Maring, the Comintern agent, only suggested suspending the meeting in order to avoid police arrests.

Chou Fo-hai, who returned to Shanghai from Japan to attend the meeting, recalled:

> Having received a letter from my comrades in Shanghai, I was aware that a national congress was to be held sometime in July. It happened to be during the summer vacation, and I therefore returned to Shanghai. The Party had really developed very rapidly. Not only had organizations been established at the places where we had planned last year—Shanghai, Hankow, Changsha, Peking, and Canton—but there was also a branch at Tsinan. At that time Ch'en Chiung-ming was in charge of political affairs in Kwangtung. Prior to the *coup d'état*, he invited [Ch'en] Tu-hsiu to serve as Educational Commissioner. Consequently, he (Ch'en Tu-hsiu) was unable to take charge of the Congress [in Shanghai] personally. The representative from Kwangtung was [Ch'en] Kung-po. Chang

---

[4] The Chinese Communist Party celebrates July 1 as the date on which the party was founded in 1921 at its First National Congress. There is much uncertainty, however, as to when the Congress actually was held. For an excellent discussion of this point, see C. Martin Wilbur's Introduction to *The Communist Movement in China* by Ch'en Kung-po (New York: East Asian Institute, Columbia University, 1960), pp. 15–21.

Kuo-t'ao and Liu Jen-ching represented Peking, while Mao Tse-tung and an elderly man by the name of Ho [Shu-heng] represented Changsha. From Hankow there were Ch'en T'an-ch'iu and Pao Hui-seng, and from Shanghai, Li Ta and Li Han-chün. I do not remember who was the representative from Tsinan. Although Ting Mo-ts'un, who was also in Shanghai, was not a representative, he was actually an active member of Communist Youth Corps. I was supposed to represent Chinese students in Japan. In reality, with the exception of Sze Ts'un-t'ung, no other Chinese was engaged in Communist activities at Kagoshima. I was therefore in fact representing Sze and myself. The Third International sent Maring to act as its highest representative. Three or four of us, including Mao Tse-tung, lived upstairs at the Po-wen Girls' School near Pei-na Road. At that time the students were away for the summer vacation; therefore we rented the place to live. There was no bed; we slept on the floor. The meals were, of course, provided by outside cooks. A meeting was held every night at the home of Li Han-chün on Pei-na Road. Maring and Voitinsky also attended. Maring was an experienced revolutionary; for on the fourth evening he said, "We have been holding meetings for several nights and we must have drawn the attention of the police. We must move to another place tomorrow evening." We felt, however, that the following evening would be the last meeting anyway, that it was quite difficult to find another place, and that perhaps there was no risk after all. Consequently, we decided to hold the meeting at the same place. On that afternoon, I suddenly got diarrhea and due to the severe pain in my stomach I was unable to go out. I slept on the floor by myself and dozed into slumber while thinking about the steps we should take regarding our work. Sometime at mid-night, I suddenly awoke and saw Mao Tse-tung entering the room looking suspiciously. He asked me softly: "Nothing happened here?" I was shocked and found out that something had happened.

It happened that when they were holding a meeting a stranger suddenly came into the room. There was no one to stop him from coming upstairs as there was no guard at the door and Han-chün was living with his townfolks. Upon entering the room, the man took one look and said, "Excuse me, I have come to the wrong place." Then he left at once. Maring immediately sensed that something was wrong. He said, "Let's disperse quickly; he must be a police agent." The meeting was immediately adjourned. Kung-po, however, remained to chat casually with Han-Chün. Within fifteen minutes, French detectives, Indo-Chinese policemen, and Chinese agents all surrounded the house and rushed upstairs. The detectives asked them why they were holding a meeting. They (Kung-po and Han-chün) answered that they were all Peking University students and that they were holding a meeting to discuss plans for the publication of a magazine and some books. The policemen then inquired why there were two foreigners. They said that the two foreigners were Peking University professors who were invited to come to give advice. One of the Chinese policemen pointed at Kung-po and asked: "Are you not a Japanese?" After a long explanation he was proved to be a Cantonese. When the police found that all the books on Han-chün's bookshelf were on the subject of socialism, he lectured and scolded him on why one should not read these books. After some questioning, they left. Fortunately, the police did not search their clothes. Hidden in their pockets were a draft outline of the Communist Party program. If found [the two men] were bound to be arrested. Mao Tse-tung at first thought that the Po-wen Girls' School must have been discovered [by the police] too, and he was afraid to enter it. After watching suspiciously for some time, he then returned. I only learned all about this later.

Having heard Mao Tse-tung's report, I felt that falling short of success by one step was such a pity. I discussed it with him and held that we should definitely continue our meeting on the following day—perhaps not within the Shanghai Concession. Suddenly I remembered that Mrs. Li Ta was from Chiahsing. Why not hold a meeting at Chiahsing? Consequently, in spite of my indisposition, I went to see Li, who was then living at Ch'en Tu-hsiu's home on Yuyang Lane. It was then decided that Mrs. Li was to take the early train to Chiahsing the next morning and hire a boat to be waiting for us. We were to take the next train and then sail on South Lake. That same evening we separately notified everybody concerned. On the following day we headed in groups of two or three for the North Station to board the train. I carried my sick-bug along. Upon arriving at Chiahsing, Mrs. Li was already at the terminal waiting to take us on the boat. The local people thought that we were tourists at South Lake and paid no attention to us. When we had sailed the boat to the middle of the lake a rain storm suddenly came up. We convened the meeting anyway and passed the Party's program and Organizational Constitution.

Ch'en Tu-hsiu was elected [in absentia] as the chairman of the Party; and I, vice-chairman. Chang Kuo-t'ao was head of the Organization Department, and Li Ta was head of the Propaganda Department. During the period before Ch'en arrived in Shanghai, I was to act for him. Thus, inside the small lonely boat floating on the lake in the midst of mist and rain the Chinese Communist Party was born.[5]

In addition to administering and supervising the organizational work of the Party, Chang Kuo-t'ao was also appointed to the three-man Central Committee of the Party. From the Comintern representatives he requested for the Party a monthly budget of slightly more than $1000 (Chinese dollars), which was readily approved.[6]

In August 1921 Ch'en Tu-hsiu, having resigned as Educational Commissioner, returned to Shanghai from Canton to become Secretary of the Central Committee of the Party. Immediately he became entangled in a number of conflicts within the Party. On a number of occasions he refused to see the Comintern agent, Maring, partly because the latter had sent Chang T'ai-lei to Japan without consulting him. Annoyed by Ch'en's attitude and ignorant of social relations in Chinese society, Maring at one time even suggested that Chang

[5] *Ku-chin pan-yüeh k'an* (Past and Present Semi-Monthly), No. 19 (Nanking, April 1943); also quoted in Shen Yün-lung, *Chung-kuo kung-ch'an tang chih lai-yüan* (The Origin of the Chinese Communist Party), (Taipei, 1959), pp. 10–12. Chou Fo-hai's reminiscences of the Chinese Communist movement, sometimes with slight variations, may also be found in the following works: *Shih-tai wen-hsüan* (Literature of the Time), Vol. I, No. 8/9 (Shanghai, November 20, 1939); *Ku-chin pan-yüeh k'an*, No. 2 (April 1942), No. 3 (May 1942), Nos. 9 and 12; and *Wan-i chi* (My Past) (Nanking: Ku-chin ch'u-pan she, 1943).

[6] Cf. Chou Fo-hai's 1927 reminiscences in "T'ao-ch'u-liao ch'ih-tu Wuhan" (Escape from Wuhan, the Red Capital): "Expenses? Of course, it goes without saying that the money was exchanged from rubles. Every month I was given 80 dollars for living expenses. In addition, I had an expense account. In the middle of September [1921], Ch'en Tu-hsiu returned to Shanghai, quarrelled with Maring, and refused to see him. This was due to Maring's criticism that the Third International had spent more than 200,000 dollars in China in one year, but the result was poor: the Chinese comrades did not work hard enough. Ch'en Tu-hsiu was of the opinion that the Chinese never used that much money: most likely that was spent by the Comintern agents for their own comfort. . . . Of course, I did not know how much was actually spent, because I was in Japan. But during the time when I was the acting chairman [of the Party], I spent 12,000 dollars in two months. This did not include the expenses for the Secretariat of the Labor Union Federation organized by Chang Kuo-t'ao, who received funds directly without going through me."

Kuo-t'ao desert Ch'en Tu-hsiu so as to take over the Party leadership.
In October Chang Kuo-t'ao was preparing to make his first trip to
the Soviet Union to attend the Congress of the Toilers of the East,
scheduled to be held at Irkutsk. Later it was changed to Moscow in
January 1922, with the closing session in Leningrad. Following
Ch'en Tu-hsiu's instruction, Chang Kuo-t'ao contacted a Russian who
was living among the white Russians in Shanghai; the latter gave him
a store's card marked with a needle hole as a secret identification that
could not easily be detected and which would introduce him to the
owner of a barber shop in Manchuli who would escort him across the
border to Siberia.

III

It was an exciting trip for Chang Kuo-t'ao, but, at that time, the
miserable conditions in Russia puzzled the idealistic 24-year-old
youth. One problem was to find a competent interpreter, for no one
in the Comintern could handle the Chinese language. Among the
overseas Chinese there were a few Bolsheviks, but they could only
speak "broken Russian." Chang's old schoolmate, Ch'ü Ch'iu-pai, had
been in Moscow for more than a year. Ch'ü's Russian was not fluent,
but adequate; however, he had tuberculosis and had to remain in the
hospital most of that time. Liu Shao-ch'i, P'eng Shu-chih, and six
other Chinese students were studying in Russia, but their Russian
was quite poor.

While in Russia, Chang Kuo-t'ao was received by Lenin at the
Kremlin. The Russian leader impressed him as comparable to "a
school teacher in rural China." When asked for instructions on the
Chinese revolution by another Chinese delegate who was present at
the meeting, Lenin replied quite candidly through his English interpreter that he knew very little about the situation in China, and
therefore declined to offer any suggestions. He raised the question
whether the Chinese Communist Party (CCP) could co-operate with
the Kuomintang (KMT). He inquired about the Korean Communist movement and was answered by Korean representative
Kim Kyu-sik, who spoke better English than the Chinese representatives. Lenin listened so intently during their conversation that Chang

thought either Lenin had difficulty hearing or that the Oriental's English was terribly poor. The content of their conversation was quite simple, but the meeting lasted for more than two hours because translation took up much of the time.

Chang returned to Shanghai in March 1922, and in May he directed a meeting at Canton sponsored by the China Trade Union Secretariat, which established the All-China Federation of Labor. In July he attended the Second National Congress of the Chinese Communist Party, which was held in Shanghai. The Congress was attended by nine delegates (and several unofficial delegates), representing the total Party membership of 123. In August, a special meeting of the Party center was held at West Lake to discuss relations with the Kuomintang.[7] Although Chang favored some sort of united front with the Kuomintang, he opposed a proposal that the CCP members join the KMT, because the Party identity and political purpose might be lost. After Maring invoked the authority of the Comintern, the Chinese Communist leaders reluctantly adopted the Comintern decision to have Communists join the KMT. Shortly afterward, Maring was recalled by the Comintern, perhaps because of his high-handed manner. Ch'en Tu-hsiu, however, conditioned his acceptance of the Comintern orders on Sun Yat-sen's withdrawal of the personal loyalty oath and finger-printing as requirements for joining the Kuomintang.[8] Shortly after Sun Yat-sen escaped to Shanghai from Canton, he agreed to the request. In September Chang Kuo-t'ao joined the Kuomintang. He was introduced by Chang Chi, who officiated at the introductory ceremony for a number of Communist leaders and who at that time strongly supported KMT-CCP co-operation and alliance with Soviet Russia.

The famous Sun-Joffe joint manifesto of January 1923 was announced without prior consultation with the Chinese Communist leaders, who considered the statement that "the communistic order, or even the Soviet system, cannot actually be introduced into China,"

[7] Besides Chang Kuo-t'ao, the meeting was attended by Ch'en Tu-hsiu, Li Ta-chao, Maring, Ts'ai Ho-sen, Chang T'ai-lei, and Kao Shang-te.

[8] For the background and discussion of Sun Yat-sen's demand for a personal loyalty oath and finger-printing, see Chün-tu Hsüeh, *Huang Hsing and the Chinese Revolution* (Stanford University Press, 1968), pp. 166–69.

as belittling the task of the Chinese Communist Party, but accepted it as "diplomatic language" on the part of the Soviet diplomat. After the "February 7 Incident," in which railway workers and Communist organizers were killed by warlord Wu P'ei-fu's troops, Chang Kuo-t'ao went to Moscow to report and discuss problems of the labor movement with the Comintern.

In June 1923 the Third National Congress of the Chinese Communist Party was held in Canton. It was attended by seventeen delegates who had voting power (and other official delegates) representing some 400 members. Chang Kuo-t'ao continued to resist the Comintern policy of creating a Communist bloc within the Kuomintang. He stressed the importance of the independence of the workers' movement. He did not oppose CCP-KMT co-operation in principle. He merely wished to maintain and develop the labor movement independently of the Kuomintang, although within the general framework of the CCP-KMT co-operation. As a result, he failed to be elected to the five-man Central Committee.[9] Ch'en Tu-hsiu, the chairman of the CCP, shared Maring's views that the Chinese working class was weak, that the Kuomintang should be recognized as the center of the revolutionary movement, and that all the Communist members should join the Kuomintang on an individual basis. It was at this congress that the role of peasants became the subject of discussion for the first time in Party history. It was brought up by Mao Tse-tung, who stressed the importance of the peasants in the revolutionary movement. He was not aware of the peasant movement led by P'eng P'ai in eastern Kwangtung at that time.

Early in September 1923 Chang Kuo-t'ao returned to Peking to organize a National Railway Workers Union. At the end of the month, Borodin arrived in Peking on his way to Canton to become Sun Yat-sen's political adviser. Early in November, Voitinsky, who replaced Maring as the Comintern representative, arrived in Peking on his way to Shanghai. He told Chang that the Comintern did not approve of Maring's attitude deprecating the CCP as an independent force, and that the Comintern's advocacy of co-operation with the

[9] Ch'en Tu-hsiu, Li Ta-chao, Ts'ai Ho-sen, Mao Tse-tung, and Ch'ü Ch'iu-pai comprised this committee.

KMT did not mean that the CCP should be absorbed by the Kuomintang.

The First National Congress of the reorganized Kuomintang was held in Canton in January 1924. Chang Kuo-t'ao attended the meeting as one of the delegates from Peking, but he was inactive and said very little. Nevertheless, he was elected an alternate member of the Central Executive Committee of the Kuomintang. However, he assumed no official position in the Nationalist Government in Canton. In fact, on January 23, before the KMT First National Congress came to an end, he left for Peking to continue the task of organizing the National Railway Workers' Union. Among the Communists who attended and spoke out most at the KMT First Congress were Mao Tse-tung and Li Li-san.

It was in January 1924 that Chang married Yang Tzu-lieh, who had joined the CCP in Wuhan in 1921 and who was then working as a proofreader for a magazine.

In the middle of May 1924, Chang Kuo-t'ao went to Shanghai for an enlarged CCP Central Committee meeting, which was attended by some ten persons including three members of the Central Committee—Ch'en Tu-hsiu, Ts'ai Ho-sen, and Ch'ü Ch'iu-pai. The main topic of the meeting was CCP-KMT co-operation. Friction and tension had taken place between the two parties. The Chinese Communist Party, under the leadership of Ch'en Tu-hsiu, now came around to Chang's earlier view that the Party should pay more attention to its own development and the expansion of the labor movement.

Chang and his wife were arrested by Peking police on May 21, 1924, on suspicion of the attempted assassination of Wellington Koo, then Minister of Foreign Affairs of the Peking Government. They were imprisoned until Feng Yü-hsiang staged his coup and occupied the capital in October.

Shortly after Chang regained freedom, Sun Yat-sen accepted an invitation of northern warlords to come to Peking. The Peking Committee of the CCP headed by Chao Shih-yen was opposed to Sun's move on the ground that Sun was compromising himself with the warlords. Chang, however, supported Sun's position. His view, which was also favored by the Comintern, eventually prevailed. On March 8, 1925, four days before Sun Yat-sen died in Peking, Chang left Peking for Shanghai. He had been re-elected to the Central Committee at the Fourth National Congress of the Party in January 1925.

Arriving in Shanghai on March 16, the Changs shared a house with Liu Shao-ch'i and his bride; the house served as the headquarters as well as the office of the Labor Movement Committee of the Central Committee. By this time Party membership had increased to about one thousand. There was not yet a political bureau, but one of the regular weekly meetings, attended by four Central Committee members[10] and the Comintern representative, Voitinsky, was similar to a political bureau meeting because it discussed mostly policy problems. There was another regular weekly meeting attended by more than nine persons including several Central Committee members; it dealt with routine business and was similar to the Work Conference of the Party Central Committee.

The Party had greatly expanded, and it was much better organized than before. It now paid a great deal of attention to the united front policy of uniting with the KMT left, winning the support of the KMT middle, and opposing the KMT right. There was a difference of opinion between the CCP and Borodin, who, after the death of Sun Yat-sen, concentrated on building up the Whampoa Military Academy as the force for the "revolutionary dictatorship." Borodin believed that the KMT had only two factions: the left and the right, but that there was no middle. On the other hand, Voitinsky, who was the liaison between the CCP and the Comintern, always worked well with the CCP.

At this time Ch'en Tu-hsiu was very much concerned with the CCP's leadership and power; he disliked unnecessary Russian interference. The Peking and Canton Committees of the Party tended to act on their own. The Canton Committee often followed the directives of Borodin, who received instructions directly from Stalin; but his directives were often in conflict with those of the CCP center in Shanghai. Of the Kuomintang leaders, Borodin did not trust Hu

[10] Ch'en Tu-hsiu, Chang Kuo-t'ao, Ts'ai Ho-sen, and Ch'ü Ch'iu-pai.

Han-min, but preferred to support Wang Ching-wei; he also preferred to support Chiang Kai-shek, while the Russian military adviser General Galen favored Chiang's superior, Hsü Ch'ung-chih.

In Shanghai, Ch'en Tu-hsiu was the Secretary of the Party and, concurrently, Director of the Party's Organization Department. He and Voitinsky determined matters of finance. The money came mainly from the Comintern, and it was not submitted for discussion at the Central Committee meetings. Although P'eng Shu-chih was the Director of the Propaganda Department, the editorial policy of the *Guide Weekly,* edited by Ts'ai Ho-sen and Ch'ü Ch'iu-pai, was determined directly by the Party center without being subject to the jurisdiction of the Propaganda Department. Chang Kuo-t'ao was in charge of the Labor Movement Committee, and he was concurrently Director of the Military Department of the Central Committee, which was established after the "May 30th Incident" in which police in the International Settlement at Shanghai fired on Chinese. Chang was active in the anti-imperialist agitation that followed the incident.

Chang Kuo-t'ao was sent to Canton for the Second National Congress of the Kuomintang, which was held in January 1926. A sharp division within the Kuomintang had developed in Canton as a result of the assassination of Liao Chunk-k'ai, a leading figure of the Kuomintang left. As soon as he arrived in Canton, Chang conferred with Borodin. The CCP center in Shanghai believed that the Canton Committee had deviated too much to the left. Borodin, on the other hand, did not agree with the rightist gestures in Shanghai, which were designed to win the Kuomintang middle. He believed that the CCP, without making any compromise, should unite with the KMT left to fight against the KMT irght, while forcing the KMT middle in line with the CCP's position.

Chang Kuo-t'ao returned to Shanghai at the end of January 1926, only to go to Canton once again in April as a result of the "March 20th Incident," which occurred during Borodin's temporary absence from China. Chiang Kai-shek staged a coup against the Communists, although he had no intention of splitting with the Communists. His meeting with Chang Kuo-t'ao, therefore, was cordial. Both expressed their wish for continued co-operation. At the end of April, Borodin returned from Russia. He blamed the CCP center for the "March 20th Incident" on the ground that the CCP's compromise with the KMT middle encouraged the KMT rightists against the Communists. Although Chang believed that the incident was partly due to the Canton Committee's aggressive leftist activities, he and the Party center in Shanghai accepted the judgment for the sake of Comintern prestige. Concerning the increasingly difficult KMT-CCP relations, Chang suggested arming peasants and workers in order to counter Chiang Kai-shek's power. This was rejected by Borodin as an inopportune time. Following Comintern instructions, the CCP decided to remain within the Kuomintang.

The CCP membership had increased to about 30,000 by the time the Enlarged Central Committee meeting convened in Shanghai in the middle of July. The Communist leaders in Shanghai underestimated the ability of the Nationalist armies of the Northern Expedition against warlords. In August, Chang relinquished his post as chief of the Labor Movement Committee to Li Li-san in order to devote himself completely to the task of helping the Northern Expedition as Director of the Military Department of the Central Committee. Chang's title, however, was more impressive than real, for the Department at that time had only two young staff members, whose main task was to collect military intelligence through newspaper clippings.

After the initial success of the Northern Expedition, Chang Kuo-t'ao moved to Hankow in September. Shortly afterward, Chou En-lai came from Canton and replaced him as the Director of the Military Department. Under Chou's leadership, the CCP began to have effective military work and laid the foundation for subsequent armed revolts.

In October, Chang moved to Wuchang after its occupation by the Nationalist troops. In November, he became Secretary of the Hupeh Committee of the Party, in addition to being a representative of the Central Committee in the area. In December, Borodin arrived in Wuhan, followed by the left-Kuomintang leaders and the newly established Nationalist Government. The anti-Chiang Kai-shek movement then began. Borodin, who had harbored anti-Chiang feelings after the "March 20th Incident" now took definite steps to oppose Chiang's leadership by winning over T'ang Sheng-chih, a Hunanese general.

In February 1927, Voitinsky came to Wuhan from Shanghai. He maintained that Borodin's premature split within the revolutionary camp was unwise, but his trip to Nanchang to see Chiang Kai-shek accomplished nothing. In March, Chiang began anti-Communist activities by executing a Communist labor leader in Kiangsi; this was followed in mid-April by a large-scale execution of Communists in Shanghai and Nanking. Although the Comintern had instructed the CCP to hide the arms of the workers, who could not possibly resist regular armies in military confrontations, the Party center was not alert enough to heed the warning. The consequence was a disaster to the Party.

The central organs of the Communist Party moved to Wuhan in April because of the difficulty of operating underground in Shanghai. The CCP's inability to control the extreme leftist activities of the peasant movement, particularly in Hunan province, greatly affected its relations with the Wuhan government of the KMT left.

If the CCP wished to maintain co-operation with the KMT in Wuhan, the peasant movement had to be curbed, partly because many KMT leaders were of the gentry class and many army officers were landlords. The peasant movement was most extreme in Hunan. This is illustrated by the case of Li Li-san's father, who escaped to Wuhan to join his son after being branded as a "village boss and bad gentry" in his native Liling county, Hunan province. Later he returned home with a letter written by his celebrated son, guaranteeing that the old man would not oppose the peasant association. The letter appeared to have been forwarded to the Liling Peasants' Association by the Hunan Committee of the Party, but it did not save the man from execution. Li Li-san took it very hard, but said nothing.

The Party held its Fifth National Congress on April 27, 1927. It was attended by eighty delegates, representing nearly 60,000 members. A Political Bureau was formally set up with seven members.[11]

[11] Ch'en Tu-hsiu, Chang Kuo-t'ao, Ch'ü Ch'iu-pai, T'an Ping-shan, Ts'ai Ho-sen, Li Li-san, and Chou En-lai.

The decision-making organ, however, was not efficiently run. The Political Bureau meeting, chaired by Ch'en Tu-hsiu and held at Borodin's residence, became a round-table conference. The working style of Ch'en Tu-hsiu had been changed from "head of the family" to "democratic." Often he did not even have a prepared agenda. The meeting usually began with a lengthy talk by M. N. Roy, a member of the Executive Committee of the Comintern who had arrived in Wuhan two months earlier. Roy's remarks were usually followed by Borodin's refutation. Then Ch'en, Ch'ü, Voitinsky, and others joined in the arguments, most of which were theoretical rather than practical. Resolutions were made only at the conclusion of the meeting after several hours of discussion had exhausted everyone.

The Party was wavering between the different views of Borodin and Roy. Roy advocated "intensive revolution, Wuhan consolidation line, and land revolution," while Borodin advocated "extensive united front, the Northwest line, and correction of extreme worker and peasant movement." Theoretically, Roy was right, but Borodin was more realistic. Meanwhile, the leaders neglected to prepare for the eventual KMT-CCP split. In July, the Kuomintang left carried out a violent purge of the Communists in Wuhan. The KMT-CCP coalition came to an end.

While the split had been imminent, the Comintern policy still clung to the illusion that although the CCP participation in the Nationalist Government had come to an end, the CCP members should remain in the Kuomintang. The motivation was to avoid complete dissolution of Russian influence in China. Ch'en Tu-hsiu and other leaders, however, believed that the CCP should not only withdraw from the government, but also from the KMT; it was impossible to hang on any longer. On July 15, 1927, Ch'en resigned from his post as Secretary-General of the Party and lived in great secrecy. He could not be reached directly and even Chang Kuo-t'ao could reach him only through a contact. Under the circumstances, Chang and Chou En-lai moved the Political Bureau to Wuchang and took up the responsibility of managing Party affairs. One of their most urgent tasks at that time was to send their comrades away in safety. Chou did the job so well that he earned great respect from his comrades, and his importance in the Party may date from this time.

On July 20, 1927, Chou En-lai, who was then the head of the Military Department of the Central Committee, left for Nanchang to take charge of the preparations for armed revolt there. He organized the Front Committee with himself as the Secretary. Realizing that Nanchang could not be defended, he planned to move the Communist forces to Chaochow and Swatow in eastern coastal Kwangtung in order to gain peasant support and supplies from Moscow. This important decision was made without consulting Moscow.

On July 21, Ch'ü Ch'iu-pai, who had secretly accompanied Borodin to Lushan the week before, returned to Wuhan. In his secret hideout in the French Concession at Hankow, he informed Chang Kuo-t'ao that a new Comintern representative, Lominadze, would arrive within a couple of days. He also suggested that Ch'en Tu-hsiu be selected as the chief scapegoat for the CCP defeat in order to save the Comintern's "face" and to maintain the prestige of the CCP leadership. He also revealed that this suggestion was a result of his discussions with Borodin in Lushan.

Two days later Lominadze arrived in Hankow. He told Chang that the CCP had not followed Comintern directives and that the Comintern had decided to reorganize the CCP center. Chang Kuo-t'ao was angered by the unjustified criticisms from this Comintern representative, who was merely twenty-nine years old. As to the Nanchang revolt, Lominadze was at a loss as to what to do. He reported to the Comintern and asked for instructions. When the instructions came, the Chinese Communist leaders were disappointed that Moscow forbade Soviet advisers' participation in the revolt and that the rebels should not expect any financial support from abroad. Moscow was of the opinion that if there was no chance of success the Chinese Communists should not attempt to revolt; instead they should withdraw their comrades in the armies and dispatch them to various regions among the peasants. Consequently, Lominadze asked Chang to go to Nanchang to inform the comrades there of the Comintern instruction. Reluctantly Chang accepted the mission. He was not happy with the Comintern guidance, but he felt helpless under Soviet control.

Having stopped over at Kiukiang for two days on the way, Chang arrived at Nanchang on the morning of July 30. He immediately consulted with his comrades there. Chou En-lai threatened to resign if the revolt was canceled. Yeh T'ing, whose army was one of the main forces counted upon for the revolt, was of the opinion that it might be a good idea to postpone the revolt and return with the left Kuomintang general, Chang Fa-k'uei, to Kwangtung. Most of the responsible comrades, however, believed that the preparation of the revolt had reached the point of no return. As a result Chang Kuo-t'ao reluctantly agreed to go ahead with the revolt plan.

The Nanchang revolt of August 1, 1927, was the first of the Chinese Communist armed revolts, although it was carried out under the name of the Kuomintang Revolutionary Committee, and many leaders of the KMT left were listed as members of the committee without their knowledge. The CCP had no troops of its own, but the Northern Expedition forces of the Kuomintang included a number of Communist officers who held important commands. The total strength of the rebels, including the forces of Yeh T'ing, Ho Lung, and civilian personnel of the Revolutionary Committee, totaled 25,000 men, with some 13,000 rifles. Chu Teh, commander of the Ninth Army, had only about 1000 men. He became the Chief of Public Security in Nanchang after the capture of the city. By August 5, however, all the Communist troops were forced to withdraw from Nanchang to eastern Kwangtung.[12] As a result of mass desertions on the way, the Ninth Army had only one hundred men by the time it arrived at Juichin, Kiangsi. Consequently, the Ninth Army was abolished. It may be mentioned in passing that it was after the battle of Huichang and while en route to Kwangtung at the end of August that Ho Lung joined the Communist Party. The ceremony was performed by Chang Kuo-t'ao in Juichin. Ho, a Hunanese bandit turned

[12] For an English translation of several accounts of the Nanchang revolt and "Southern Expedition," August 1–October 1, 1927, written within a few weeks of the events by Chang Kuo-t'ao and other participants, see C. Martin Wilbur, "The Ashes of Defeat," *The China Quarterly*, No. 18 (April–June 1968), pp. 3–54.

revolutionary, was very tense during the ceremony. When it was over he was pleasantly surprised that the procedure was much simpler than that of joining the bandits or the secret societies.

IV

Shortly after Chang Kuo-t'ao and the Communist forces arrived at Swatow at the end of September 1927, Chang T'ai-lei, newly elected Political Bureau member and the Party Secretary of the Kwangtung Committee, secretly arrived from Hong Kong. He revealed that the Party center had moved back to Shanghai with Ch'ü Ch'iu-pai as the Secretary. After the Emergency Conference of August 7, which had been held in great haste, all those who had taken part in the Nanchang revolt lost their leading positions in the Party. Chang Kuo-t'ao and Chou En-lai were demoted to alternate members of the Political Bureau.[13] The reorganized Political Bureau consisted of seven members, four of whom were workers.[14] Chang T'ai-lei also relayed the Party's instruction that hereafter the Party should no longer act in the name of the Kuomintang, the Revolutionary Committee should be replaced by the Soviets, and the army should move to another eastern Kwangtung area around Haifeng and Lufeng, so as to organize a peasant-worker army. In the midst of defeat early in October, this decision was announced to the rebels by Chou En-lai in his capacity as Secretary of the Front Committee. Thus the alliance of the CCP with the KMT formally came to an end.

As a result of successive defeats, all of Ho Lung's forces were disarmed by the enemy. Yen T'ing's remnants escaped to join the organized peasants in Haifeng and Lufeng. The only main forces that had not been completely wiped out were those of Chu Teh, which had remained in an isolated area. He did not join the "south-

[13] T'an P'ing-shan and Li Li-san also lost their Political Bureau membership. Chou En-lai, however was more fortunate. When he arrived in Shanghai, he immediately expressed full support for the new Party leadership, accepted the Comintern line, and opposed opportunism. He was not only re-elected to the Political Bureau, but became still more important.

[14] The new seven Political Bureau members were: Ch'ü Ch'iu-pai, Su Chao-cheng, Li Wei-han, Chang T'ai-lei, Hsiang Ying, Hsiang Chung-fa, and Lu Fu-t'an. It was after Su Chao-cheng's death that Ch'ü Ch'iu-pai formally became the Secretary General of the Party.

ern expedition," and managed to recruit another army of 1000 men. With these troops he eventually joined hands with Mao Tse-tung in the Chingkang Mountains to found the Red Army.[15]

On October 5, 1927, Chang Kuo-t'ao and Li Li-san sailed separately to Hong Kong by fishing boat, thence to Shanghai. Chang was criticized for not enforcing the Comintern directive which discouraged the Nanchang revolt. The Party center, under the leadership of Ch'ü Ch'iu-pai, arranged to have Chang and Li settled in a comfortable house off Chungking Road in the International Settlement. But Ch'ü avoided seeing them, and the other Political Bureau members who did come to see them refrained from discussing Party policy with them. Chang was not allowed to participate in the Enlarged Conference of the Central Committee of November 14. The conference resolution which criticized him was based on a report by Chang T'ai-lai, who followed Lominadze's order to make unjustified accusations. Chang Kuo-t'ao considered Ch'ü Ch'iu-pai's "putschism" (blind actionism) to be wrong and dangerous, but the Party would not consider any of Chang's suggestions until he admitted his errors and accepted the resolutions and policies decided at the Emergency Conference of August 7 and at the Enlarged Conference of November 14. During this period of eight months, the only work Chang did for the Party was to help Chou En-lai reassign comrades who escaped to Shanghai from Chaochow and Swatow. But after two mornings of this he did not feel like working any more. The failure of the three-day Canton revolt in December strengthened Chang's conviction of the erroneous line of Ch'ü Ch'iu-pai. In February 1928, Chang saw Ch'ü Ch'iu-pai. He threatened and angered Ch'ü by saying that unless the latter changed the policy which necessarily

[15] For an English translation of a Communist report on the history and condition of the Chu-Mao Red Army, dated September 1, 1929, and published in issue No. 1 of the *Chung-yang chün-shih t'ung-hsün* (Central Military Correspondence), January 15, 1930, see Chün-tu Hsüeh and Robert C. North, "The Founding of the Chinese Red Army," *Contemporary China*, Vol. VI (Hong Kong University Press, 1968), pp. 59–83. The report was issued in the name of "Tung-li," who cannot be identified. The authoritative nature of the report suggests that it was probably written by Mao Tse-tung himself.

sacrificed comrades' lives, he might consider organizing a real worker and peasant party.

Meanwhile, two incidents had taken place that prompted Chang to find a safer place to live. The first was the attempted suicide of Ho Pao-chen, wife of Liu Shao-ch'i. The Lius arrived in Shanghai from Wuhan shortly before the Canton insurrection. They were assigned to stay with Chang Kuo-t'ao. In the middle of December, the wife of Chang T'ai-lei, who had died in the Canton insurrection, also came to Shanghai and stayed at the same place. Partly because of unjustified jealousy over her husband's attempts to comfort the widow, and partly because of her loss of faith in the future, Mrs. Liu attempted suicide within the first few days of 1928. Running a great risk of exposing himself, Liu Shao-ch'i rushed her to a hospital. Although she was saved, Chang Kuo-t'ao felt that his house was no longer safe. By this time his wife had joined him. They decided to move out. He was not to see Liu Shao-ch'i again until 1937. Shortly after they found a place for themselves, however, the Changs had to move again as a result of the defection of Ho Chih-hua, former wife of Chu Teh.[16] After the second move, they lost complete contact with the Party center. The only person who occasionally visited them was Hsiang Ying, the new Party Secretary of the Shanghai Committee. During this time, Chang renewed contact with Ch'en Tu-hsiu, who had returned to Shanghai to live in secrecy. Ch'en,

---

[16] Ho Chih-hua, ex-wife of Chu Teh, was then married to Ho Chia-hsing, a returned student from Russia in charge of the Communists who escaped to Shanghai. In March 1928, she voluntarily became an informer. One day she walked to the police headquarters of the International Settlement and proposed that she would submit a list of the names and addresses of some 350 Communists in Shanghai if the police would give her a passport, US $50,000, and a promise not to reveal the source of their information. In order to prove the accuracy of her information and thus induce the police to make a deal with her, she revealed the address of Lo Chüeh, Party Secretary of the Shanghai Committee. Ho's betrayal threatened the whole Party apparatus. The Party center usually could learn half an hour in advance of any imminent arrests of its members. But in this case Lo was picked up without warning. Before the full list was submitted to the police, however, the Party moved swiftly. It recovered the list, and Ho's husband was assassinated. She survived the serious injury and subsequently returned to her home town in Szechwan.

who opposed Ch'ü Ch'iu-pai's policy, was interested in Chang's suggestion of organizing a worker and peasant party independent of
the Comintern. But the plan never materialized because of financial
difficulties.

In the middle of May, Chang was informed by the Party center
that he, along with Ch'en Tu-hsiu, Ts'ai Ho-sen, Teng Chung-hsia,
and Lo Chang-lung, was invited by the Comintern to attend the
Sixth National Congress of the Chinese Communist Party, which
was to be held in Moscow. These invitations were issued in the
hope of unifying the CCP, as the Comintern had also become critical of Ch'ü Ch'iu-pai's "putschism." Chang accepted the invitation,
but Ch'en declined the offer. Ch'en believed that the Sixth Congress
might be able to correct putschism; but he felt that the Comintern
had decided to sacrifice him, that the resolution of the Emergency
Conference of August 7 was too critical of him, and that, even if he
went to Moscow, the verdict against him would not be reversed.
However, he would continue writing articles for Party publications;
he would not defend himself and he would not attack others. If the
Sixth Congress turned out to be a success, he would not oppose the
CCP or the Comintern. Should the Comintern want him to come
to Moscow in the future, he might favorably consider it. But no invitation was extended to him again, and he soon became leader of
the Opposition.

V

At the end of May 1928, Chang left Shanghai for Russia via Manchuria. When he arrived in Moscow, he was escorted to the suburb
where the Sixth National Congress of the Chinese Communist Party
was to be held under Comintern guidance at the end of June. The
meeting was attended by more than thirty delegates. Soviet leader
Bukharin confirmed that the Comintern did send a telegram to stop
the Nanchang revolt, although he also admitted that, as military
action against the Kuomintang, the revolt was basically correct.
Bukharin did not often come to the meeting, but Pavel Mif, President
of Sun Yat-sen University in Moscow, attended every meeting. He
put pressure on Chang Kuo-t'ao to co-operate with Ch'ü Ch'iu-pai.

Based on Bukharin's report, the political resolution of the Sixth Congress declared that the "present stage of the Chinese Revolution" was "bourgeois-democratic." Therefore, the "two major tasks of the revolution" were "the overthrow of imperialism and agrarian revolution." The resolution further declared that these two tasks did not yet exceed the scope of the capitalist mode of production—but they could "only be accomplished by overthrowing, through the revolutionary method of armed insurrection, the rule of the imperialists and that of the landlord-warlord-bourgeois KMT and by setting up a democratic dictatorship of workers' and peasants' Soviets under the leadership of the proletariat." This formula later became the blueprint of Mao Tse-tung's "New Democracy."

The Sixth Congress elected a new Central Committee. Although Chang Kuo-t'ao was severely criticized for his "rightist opportunism," he was elected to its new Political Bureau.[17] He remained in Moscow as the CCP representative to the Comintern. The Sixth Congress of the CCP, under Bukharin's influence, condemned Ch'ü Ch'iu-pai's putschism. Ch'ü maintained, however, that Bukharin's view did not represent that of Stalin. Li Li-san told Chang Kuo-t'ao that under the circumstances the CCP should not follow Bukharin's rightist line. Instead it would be better to take a leftist policy. Thus, influenced by the intra-party struggle of the Communist Party of the Soviet Union (CPSU), the Sixth Congress did not in fact completely correct putschism. This accounted for the subsequent development of the Li Li-san line.

Chang Kuo-t'ao stayed in Russia from June 1928 through January 1931. He attended the Sixth World Congress of the Comintern and was elected an alternate member of its Presidium and alternate secretary of its Secretariat (Ch'ü Ch'iu-pai was elected to both organs as a full member). Early in November 1928, Chang was asked to see Stalin. It was their first meeting. During their three-hour interview, in which Ch'ü served as interpreter, Stalin first

[17] The new Political Bureau consisted of the following members: Hsiang Chung-fa (Secretary), Ch'ü Ch'iu-pai, Chang Kuo-t'ao, Chou En-lai, Ts'ai Ho-sen, Li Li-san, and Hsiang Ying. Ch'ü and Chang were the CCP representatives to the Comintern. Li was to be in charge of organization; Ts'ai, propaganda; Chou, the military; and Hsiang, labor.

showed great concern for their living conditions in Moscow; then he raised two questions. The first was whether persons like Madame Sun Yat-sen would betray their Communist friends. Would such persons inform the police if they saw a Communist in the street? The second question was whether Ch'en Tu-hsiu was capable of obtaining financial support to publish a newspaper. He was pleased with Chang's negative answers to both questions, because it meant that the Chinese Communists still had allies and fellow-travelers in China, and that Ch'en Tu-hsiu could not undertake effective organized opposition. Anticipating Ch'en's opposition after the Sixth Congress of the CCP, Stalin dropped him from the new Central Committee.

During his sojourn in Russia, Chang Kuo-t'ao repeatedly clashed with Pavel Mif, the President of Sun Yat-sen University, on problems involving the Chinese students. Mif did not want the Chinese delegation[18] to interfere with university affairs, but he often had to seek its assistance when he could not handle the Chinese students in the university. With the exception of a handful of students, notably the "28 Bolsheviks" headed by Ch'en Shao-yü, most of the 1000 Chinese students in the university opposed Mif's administration. The members of the Chinese delegation did not see eye to eye on a number of issues, but they were all opposed to Mif's leadership and high-handed manner in dealing with Chinese students. In the 1929 purge initiated by Stalin, many Chinese students in Sun Yat-sen University were expelled as Trotskyites. Although Chang was not involved, his wife, who had joined him in Moscow at the end of 1928 and attended Sun Yat-sen University as a special student, as well as Yang Chih-hua, wife of Ch'ü Ch'iu-pai, were punished by being sent to work in factories.

During the summer of 1929, Chang saw Borodin quite often. It

[18] The Chinese delegation consisted of Ch'ü Ch'iu-pai, Chang Kuo-t'ao, Teng Chung-hsia, Yu Fei, and Wang Jo-fei. The first two were the CCP representatives to the Comintern. Teng and Yu were representatives to the Profintern (Communist Trade Union International), and Wang was the representative to the Krestintern (Peasant International).

was through Borodin's mediation that Ch'ü Ch'iu-pai ceased attacking Chang and a cordial relationship between the two Chinese Communist leaders was somewhat restored. In the fall of that year Chang voluntarily gave up all but 20 rubles of his high monthly salary of 250 rubles in order to become a special student at the Lenin Institute, a higher Party school of some three hundred students recommended by the Communist parties of various countries.

The anti-rightist campaign in the CPSU and Comintern policies unintentionally encouraged the Li Li-san line in China. In the middle of November 1929, Ch'en Tu-hsiu was expelled from the CCP. In December, Ch'en openly supported Trotsky. Although the Comintern approved the expulsion of Ch'en Tu-hsiu, it sent two agents to correct Li Li-san's tendency toward adventurism. In April 1930 Chou En-lai was summoned by Moscow to influence Li Li-san. Chou was even invited to speak at the 16th Congress of the CPSU and was the first Chinese Communist to receive this honor. But when he returned to China, he made no attempt to correct Li Li-san's adventurism.

When Li mapped out a plan to attack Changsha, he requested the Comintern to take co-ordinating actions by ordering the Soviet Red Army to attack Manchuria and the Mongolian army to invade Peiping and Tientsin. The Comintern was stunned by the request. It decided to send Chang Kuo-t'ao back to China to strengthen the Comintern line. In the middle of October Chang agreed to return to China. At the end of the month, Li Li-san arrived in Moscow and admitted all his errors.

VI

Chang Kuo-t'ao and his wife arrived in Shanghai via Manchuria about ten days after the Fourth Plenum of the CCP Central Committee had convened in Shanghai in January 1931. The Fourth Plenum formally abandoned the Li Li-san line and, under the guidance of Mif, reorganized the Party center. The Comintern representative's protégés, who were students returned from Russia, took over the leadership. The most objectionable issue to the "senior cadre faction" headed by Ho Meng-hsiung was the election of Ch'en Shao-yü to the Political Bureau. At that time Ch'en was not even a Central Committee member.[19]

Chang Kuo-t'ao was confronted with unexpected incidents and intra-Party struggles when he arrived in Shanghai. Only a few days before, his old friend, Ho Meng-hsiung, former Party Secretary of Shanghai, and several others were arrested by the police when they secretly met to discuss opposition to the new leadership of the returned students. Lo Chang-lung, Chairman of the All-China Federation of Labor, went so far as to accuse Ch'en Shao-yü of the betrayal that led to the arrests. Chang believed that had he returned to China sooner the Party schism might have been avoided.

In order to soothe the feeling and opposition of the "senior cadres," Chou En-lai suggested the establishment of a standing committee of the Political Bureau, which was approved without much debate. The reason given, however, was to facilitate secret meetings. The Standing Committee of the Political Bureau consisted of Hsiang Chung-fa, Chang Kuo-t'ao, and Chou En-lai. Hsiang, who had become the nominal Secretary of the Party since the Sixth Congress, never exercised effective leadership.

At the same time there were many defections and revolts among the rank and file of the Party.[20] In spite of his dissatisfaction with Mif and of an unpleasant meeting with Mif's successor, Chang did his best to unify the Party. After his brief trip to Tientsin in

[19] Other "returned students" and protégés of Mif received the following posts: Chang Wen-t'ien, Ch'in Pang-hsien, and Yang Shang-k'un, took over propaganda, secretaryship of the Communist Youth Corps, and labor, respectively. But Chao Yün (K'ang Sheng), of the "senior cadre faction," was in charge of organization.

[20] One of the most notable but least known cases was the defection of Huang Ching-hun. A graduate of the Whampoa Military Academy and an important cadre who had worked under his best friend Chou En-lai, Huang was so discouraged by Party affairs at that time that he decided to defect to the Kuomintang. He wrote a letter to his former school commandant, Chiang Kai-shek. Chou En-lai tried his best to dissuade him, but it was in vain. For the sake of Party security and discipline, Chou immediately managed to have him killed before reporting to the Party center. Chang Kuo-t'ao was never told how Chou discovered the letter and how Huang was executed.

February 1931, the Party's North China Bureau renewed its confidence in and support for the central leadership.

Early in 1931 the Chinese Red Army made great strides in Kiangsi province and in the Hupeh-Honan border area. These military victories greatly inspired the Party center's hope in the future of the Chinese Soviets. Of all the Soviet areas and Communist forces, only three had sizable military power. The forces of Mao Tse-tung, Chu Teh, and P'eng Te-huai had 15,000 rifles in Kiangsi; the Fourth Red Army had about 10,000 rifles in the Hupeh-Honan-Anhwei border area; and Ho Lung's forces had 7000 rifles.

With these military forces a number of Soviets were established on the county level and below in border areas. But these Soviets were more in the nature of guerrilla bases than governments. These political regimes managed to survive because of military power. There is great truth in the saying that in China political power grew out of the barrel of a gun. But the Chinese Soviet movement as well as the land reforms did not have much appeal.

Although the guerrillas repeatedly asked the Party center in Shanghai for material assistance, especially arms, medical supplies, radio and other communication equipment, binoculars, compasses, and even watches, Li Li-san did not seem to have forwarded the requests to the Comintern representatives. Mif always stressed the importance of self-reliance in the guerrilla areas. In fact, at times the silver and gold which had been shipped to Shanghai by the guerrillas became a major source of income for the Party center there.

In order to strengthen the Party's leadership over the Red Army and the Soviet areas, and because of the increasing difficulty of the underground work of the Party center in Shanghai, the Chinese Communist Party decided to move its central apparatus to the Soviet areas. Chang Kuo-t'ao chose to go to the Hupeh-Honan-Anhwei border region, as the Secretary of the Hupeh-Honan-Anhwei Branch of the Party's Political Bureau and Chairman of the Military Council. He left Shanghai on April 1, 1931, and after eight days of secret journey, he arrived at his destination. Thus began his guerrilla life for the next five years.

In November 1931, the first All-China Congress of Soviets met at Juichin, Kiangsi.[21] Mao Tse-tung was elected Chairman of the Central Soviet Republic, with Hsiang Ying and Chang Kuo-t'ao (elected in absentia) as Vice Chairmen.

In 1932, as a result of Chiang Kai-shek's military pressure, Chang Kuo-t'ao led the Fourth Front Army, which was commanded by Hsü Hsiang-ch'ien, on a westward retreat to northern Szechwan. There, as before in the Hupeh-Honan-Anhwei region, Chang developed his own power base. However, in 1935 provincial military pressure forced him to retreat. When his army had a rendezvous with Mao Tse-tung's First Front Army during the "Long March" in the summer, Chang came into open conflict with Mao on military strategy and basic political issues. Among the basic issues was whether the Soviet should be the form of the Chinese Communist government. Chang was of the opinion that the policy was fundamentally wrong, but Mao disagreed.

These disputes led to Chang's demand for reorganization of the Party center. Chang pointed out that of the seven Political Bureau members elected by the Sixth National Congress of the Party in 1928, only two (Chang and Chou En-lai) remained in their posts in 1935. Ch'en Shao-yü was elected to the Political Bureau at the Fourth Plenum of the Central Committee in 1931; Chang Wen-t'ien, Ch'in Pang-hsien, and Wang Chia-hsiang were elected to the Political Bureau by the Fifth Plenum in 1934; and Mao Tse-tung, at the Tsunyi Conference in January 1935. Since then Mao had in fact taken over leadership, but his election was legally questionable. Since the Political Bureau had no authority to elect its own members, Chang suggested convening an enlarged Central Committee meeting to elect the new leadership. Mao was absolutely opposed to this re-

---

[21] Hereafter, the rest of the article is mainly based on Chang Kuo-t'ao's biographical sketch written by his wife, Yang Tzu-lieh, for the *Ming Pao Monthly* (March 1966), and Chang's Introduction (published in the *Tsu Kuo*, i.e., *The China Monthly,* July 1, 1968), to *Collected Works of Liu Shao-ch'i* (Hong Kong: Union Research Institute, 1968), because the last part of Chang's own memoirs had not yet been published at the time of writing. Yang's *Memoirs* were published as a series in the *Chan-wang* (Look Fortnightly), Hong Kong, beginning with issue No. 158 (September 1, 1968).

quest and denounced Chang's attempt to use military pressure to reorganize the Party center. As a result, the Party split into two centers: one was led by Mao's Political Bureau and the other by Chang.

In 1936 however, military defeats forced Chang to join Mao in northern Shensi. Conflicts again ensued. In the spring of 1937, struggles against Chang broke into the open. He was blamed politically for adopting a "Right opportunist line," organizationally for setting up a parallel central leadership, and militarily for splitting the Red Army. By then Chang had suffered heavy military losses which undermined his power position. Although he remained a member of the Political Bureau, for several months he did not attend its meetings.

In the bitter intra-Party struggle of these years, two Communist leaders, Chou En-lai and Liu Shao-ch'i, somehow did not get involved. Chou was busy dealing with the Kuomintang and various outside Party affairs and negotiations, while Liu was working in the underground.

In June 1937 Liu arrived at Yenan from Peiping. KMT-CCP relations were in a delicate stage at that time. Liu submitted a long report re-examining the Party's policy of the previous sixteen years. He concluded that the Party had consistently committed the error of "Leftist adventurism" rather than that of "Rightist opportunism." During the first united front period, the CCP was extremely weak, and yet it even attempted to take over the KMT leadership. The subsequent peasant uprisings and the Kiangsi Soviets went even a step further toward Leftist putschism and adventurism. Liu suggested that the Party should not repeat the same errors in future co-operation with the Kuomintang.

The Political Bureau was stunned by the report. If Ch'en Tu-hsiu was considered as having committed Leftist adventurism, Liu Shao-ch'i was more of a Rightist than Chang Kuo-t'ao. But discovering that there was no collaboration between Chang and Liu, and that Liu was not opposed to Mao's leadership, Mao Tse-tung decided to win Liu over to his side in order to prevent a Chang-Liu coalition and to weaken the influence of Chang Wen-t'ien and other "returned students" in the Party. Subsequently, Liu was elected to the Political Bureau.

After the outbreak of the Sino-Japanese War in July 1937, Chang became Acting Chairman of the Shensi-Kansu-Ninghsia Border Government. In April 1938, he left Yenan to represent the Party in the traditional ceremony held in Sian to offer sacrifices to the legendary Yellow Emperor. He took the opportunity to defect to the Nationalist Government in Hankow. Later, he moved to the wartime capital, Chungking, where he remained until the end of the war. He was nominated by the Nationalist Government as a member to the People's Political Council, but took no active role in its activities. At the time of the Communist victory in China in 1949, this founding member of the Chinese Communist Party moved to the British colony of Hong Kong, where he lived simply and quietly. In November 1968, Chang and his wife emigrated to join their son in Toronto, Canada.

❈ 16 ❈

The Variegated Career of Ch'en Kung-po

C. MARTIN WILBUR

A Sketch of Ch'en Kung-po's Early Life

Ch'en's Youth The published facts about Ch'en's early life are scanty except for what he provides in his *Han Feng Chi* [The Cold Wind], a collection of reminiscent articles and literary works written at different dates, which he published in October, 1944. Biographic sources in Chinese, Japanese, and English are full of contradictions and mistakes. For example, most biographic sources give the date of his birth as the sixteenth year of the Kwanghsu era, or as 1890. However, the correct date was probably the 19th of October, 1892.

His ancestral home was Shang-hang in southern Fukien, but his ancestors moved to Ju-yüan in northwestern Kwangtung. The family was Hakka. Kung-po's grandfather moved to Canton, but the family seat remained Ju-yüan. Kung-po's father, Ch'en Chih-mei, was a military officer, who served as a militia chief in Kwangsi, but resigned or was removed from his post in 1895. He was a leader in the anti-Manchu secret society, San Ho Hui. In 1907 he moved from Canton to Ju-yüan, taking Kung-po with him. There he conspired to revolt, but the rebellion collapsed in 1907 and Chih-mei was arrested and imprisoned, remaining in prison until after the Revolution of October 1911, when he was released. He died in September, 1912.

This article is reprinted with footnotes omitted from Ch'en Kung-po, *The Chinese Communist Movement,* edited with an introduction by C. Martin Wilbur (East Asian Institute, Columbia University, 1960), pp. 3–13. By permission of its new publisher, Octagon Books. The title and the footnote of the article are supplied by the present editor.

Kung-po had a happy childhood. He received a classical education but in addition was given traditional military-athletic training and taught to ride a horse. He read Chinese novels as well as history. His schooling was interrupted when he was 15 *sui* to help with his father's secret correspondence, but he managed to get tutoring in English. In 1907 after the discovery of his father's plans for revolt, he was hustled off to Hongkong to escape his father's penalty. There he worked on a revolutionary Chinese newspaper as a proof-reader and occasionally wrote short articles. He returned to Canton in the summer of 1908 but his family was in hard straits: his father in prison, his mother ill, and income practically nil. With the help of a few friends, by keeping pigs, and by taking a piece-work job, Kung-po was able to enroll in a modern school, the Yü Ts'ai Academy where he studied English for three years. He also tutored others in English. It was a very difficult period financially.

After the successful Wuhan revolt of October 1911, Kung-po's father was released from prison, elected as a member of the Provincial Assembly, and appointed a military adviser to the Governor. Kung-po was chosen Chairman of a *hsien* Assembly, and was also a staff officer in a revolutionary army. He was then 20 *sui* and a very cocky young man. Kung-po's father however, ordered him to give up these offices and enroll in a student battalion. He was in the army only a few months, and very much disliked the experience. After the battalion was disbanded, he taught for two and a half years in his former school and then in 1914 entered the Canton Law College. He supported himself as a reporter. He graduated from the Law College in 1917, but feeling dissatisfied with his education he decided to go to Peking to study philosophy. He departed for Peking in the summer.

Study at Peita   Peking National University was an extremely stimulating place for a patriotic Chinese intellectual during the years after Ts'ai Yüan-p'ei became Chancellor in January, 1917, and Ch'en Tu-hsiu became Dean of the Department of Letters. Ts'ai, a revolutionary who combined a classical education with long years of study in Germany and France, brought together a brilliant faculty of independent scholars and intellectual leaders, ranging from conservatives to radicals. Ch'en Tu-hsiu brought with him the popular magazine *Hsin Ch'ing-nien* (The New Youth), having the French title *La Jeunesse,* a monthly journal of opinion, which became a forum for discussion of intellectual, cultural and social reform. Hu Shih's proposals for literary reform and Ch'en Tu-hsiu's espousal of literary revolution appeared in its pages, along with discussions of the position of women in China, of marriage, of modern education, attacks on Confucianism, advocacy of science and democracy, Pragmatism and Marxism, and of the need to create a new, modern Chinese culture. Students in the University were inspired by the critical spirit of some of the faculty members and of *The New Youth*. In January 1919 they founded a student magazine named *Hsin Ch'ao* (The Renaissance). There were many student societies such as an Association of Students to Practice Thrift, a Society for Collecting Folk Ballads, a Journalism Society, a Marxist Study Group.

Kung-po says he was not active in student life; he spent most of his time at his books. His few close friends were mostly from Kwangtung. T'an P'ing-shan was his roommate; T'an's nephew, T'an Chih-t'ang and Ch'ü Sheng-pai, later an anarchist, are among those he mentions in his reminiscences. The two T'ans later were fellow officers with Kung-po in the Kwangtung branch of the Communist Party. Ma Hsü-lun, who was then a teacher at Peita, mentions in his autobiography that Ch'en and T'an P'ing-shan always sat together in his lectures. Mao Tse-tung, in his autobiography, mentions knowing Ch'en as a fellow member of a journalism society. T'an P'ing-shan joined the New Tide Society but Kung-po declined to because, he says, he disliked a person he knew in it.

One of the most exciting events that occurred during Ch'en's student years was the "May 4th Movement," the demonstrations organized by Peking students to oppose the post-war award to Japan of Germany's territorial rights in Shantung. It was an event of utmost psychological and historical importance to the Chinese. The demonstrations began on May 4, 1919, and continued in Peking for more than a month, involving thousands of students, hundreds of whom were arrested. Ch'en devotes several pages of his Master's essay to the demonstrations of May 4th and the subsequent days. "It is very interesting and stirring for me to recall my memories of this period," he wrote five years later. "I was in the midst of the great wave, witnessed the radical movement from beginning to end, the deepening of dissatisfaction among the masses, and the stiffening of resistance. How much in beauty and sorrow this picture resembled the general strike of college students of Russia in the winter of 1898–99!" In his article "I and the Communist Party," written in 1943, he relates that he followed the May 4th procession not as a participant but as a reporter for some Kwangtung papers. He left before the students broke into the homes of two allegedly pro-Japanese officials; he only learned of the attack later while studying in the library. He says the May 4th Movement had little effect upon him.

In his Master's essay, Ch'en follows his account of the May 4th Movement with a descriptive list of some organizations which developed as a result of it and from which future Chinese Communists were drawn. He does not say he was active in any of these organizations, but he identifies himself most clearly with the Renaissance Group. "Now many communists come from that group," says Ch'en, "and the way we think and the results of our thinking have influenced the Communist Party."

Early Career After graduation from Peita in the summer of 1920, Ch'en and his friend T'an P'ing-shan, returned to Canton. They decided to start a newspaper in order to spread the "new culture" to south China, although they had no very clear idea what the "new culture" was. They named the paper *Kwangtung Ch'ün Pao* [Kwangtung Masses]. Kung-po was Editor-in-Chief, P'ing-shan was News Editor and T'an Chih-t'ang was Literary Editor. They had a capital of only 3000 dollars. On the day the first issue was to come out the military authorities in Canton, who were from the neighboring province of Kwangsi, ordered all papers to suspend publication. This was to prevent their giving public support to the Kwangtung general, Ch'en Chiung-ming, who was threatening to take the city. After General Ch'en had taken Canton (October 1920) Kung-po was called upon by his Peking classmate, Ch'ü Sheng-pai, who introduced two proteges of the General, Ch'en Ying-sheng and Ch'en

Ch'iu-lin. General Ch'en was offering to place them on the staff of *Ch'un Pao* and pay a subsidy of $300 per month. The men were accepted to do the detailed work, but Kung-po asserts that he declined the subsidy except as salary for the two men, and insisted the paper would not become the organ of any person. Kung-po and P'ing-shan both held teaching positions and were able to devote only a part of their time to the publication.

Ch'en Kung-po and the Chinese Communist Party

The Beginnings of Communism in Canton In 1920 Ch'en Tu-hsiu, the famous radical professor of Peita with whom Kung-po had studied, was turning towards Communism. He had moved to Shanghai and was in touch with Comintern agents. A Communist group was secretly started in May of 1920. Ch'en Tu-hsiu became interested in establishing a Communist Party in Canton. Two Russian agents came to Canton in the guise of merchants and got in touch with the anarchist, Ch'ü Sheng-pai, then with the *Ch'ün Pao* group. Kung-po says they agreed to the Russian's proposal that their group establish a Communist Party in Kwangtung, starting with a socialist youth corps to publicize socialism in Canton. They agreed because Kwangtung was politically unstable, the Kuomintang was without organization or program, they were distressed at the condition of China, stirred by Lenin's victory in Russia and impressed by Ch'en Tu-hsiu's interest.

They had no difficulty recruiting teachers and students from the colleges in which they taught. An interest in socialism was fashionable even among Kuomintang members. But it was difficult to interest industrial labor. The Party Center advocated that the Youth Corps push into the Mechanics Union, the Seamen's Union and even recruit tradesmen. Late in 1920 Ch'en Tu-hsiu came to Canton on the invitation of General Ch'en Chiung-ming to be Provincial Commissioner of Education. He asked Kung-po to become chief of a publicity office to push forward Communist Party organizational work.

In July of 1921 Ch'en Kung-po went to Shanghai to attend the

First Congress of the Chinese Communist Party, taking his bride with him. Many points about this Congress are in dispute including even the date. . . . Kung-po attended four meetings but missed the final one which was held on a houseboat on a lake near Chia-hsing (Kashing). The Conference made a bad impression on him according to the reminiscences written in 1943; his break with the Party about a year later stemmed, he says, from this sour impression.

The facts about Ch'en Kung-po's role in the Canton Party branch in the following year are in dispute. I shall first present his own account in the article "I and the Communist Party." Ch'en Tu-hsiu left Canton for Shanghai after his election as Secretary of the Chinese Communist Party. The most active members of the Canton branch were T'an P'ing-shan, Secretary, T'an Chih-t'ang, in charge of propaganda, and Ch'en Kung-po, who handled matters of organization. Most of the work, says Kung-po, devolved on him. "Strange to say, the Canton Party did not receive a cent of Russian money, had no fixed location, and paid no salaries." The three friends of the *Ch'ün Pao* contributed from their salaries for the expenses of the Party. Aside from Youth Corps members there were about 20 in the Party itself, about half of them laborers. The principal work was agitating among labor unions. When the Hongkong seamen's strike occurred in January 1922 the Communists were active among the strikers who moved to Canton; they added many seamen to the Party.

Ch'en states he was seriously troubled by the fact that he was responsible for the Kwangtung Communist Party and yet could not respect Communist philosophy, which he regarded as popular propaganda. He could not get adequate materials on Marx and his philosophy nor had Ch'en Tu-hsiu been able to answer many of his questions. He determined, therefore, to go abroad for further study. He decided upon America because of his command of English. Ch'en Tu-hsiu, he says, gave his approval while still in Canton.

The Issue of Collaboration with Sun Yat-sen   After Ch'en Tu-hsiu had left for Shanghai, a representative of the Communist International named "Slevelet," together with Chang Chi, came from Shang-

hai to Kwangtung. He had been expelled from Java for propagandiz-
ing Communism and had now come to China as a representative of
the Third International. Kung-po had a talk with "Slevelet" and
Chang Chi in a Canton restaurant where Chang (one of the
elders of the Kuomintang) raised the question of the amalgamation
of the Kuomintang and the Communist Party. This was not the
question of the Kuomintang taking in the Communists. Ch'en felt
sure the matter had been discussed by the two in advance and they
had reached agreement. The interpreter was Chang T'ai-lei, later
an important Communist leader. They asked Ch'en's opinion and
he disagreed for several reasons. Although "Slevelet" advocated this
amalgamation and planned to discuss it with Sun Yat-sen in Kweilin,
he left the arguing to Chang Chi. The latter argued that the Kuomintang was old and needed the new blood of the Communists, that the
Three Principles of the People and Communism were alike, that the
new economic measures which Lenin had introduced in Russia were
merely the Principle of the People's Livelihood. Ch'en says that
"Slevelet" and Chang went to Kweilin to see Sun but did not see
Ch'en on their way back to Shanghai; he heard that little was accomplished by their trip.

To Support Sun or Ch'en Chiung-ming   During the spring of 1922
Sun Yat-sen and General Ch'en Chiung-ming were at odds. Sun
wished to push his Northern Expedition to unite the country while
General Ch'en—theoretically his subordinate—opposed and obstructed the plan. Sun attempted first to break into Hunan from
Kwangsi. Unsuccessful, he returned to Kwangtung in April 1922 to
deal with General Ch'en and to launch his campaign from Shao-kuan
into Kiangsi. General Ch'en withdrew from Canton to his base in
Huichow [Waichow] on April 20. Just at this time Ch'en Tu-hsiu,
Secretary of the Communist Party, came to Canton to prepare for the
first Congress of Socialist Youth to be held the first week in May
and to inspect Party affairs. According to Ch'en Kung-po's reminiscent account, Tu-hsiu decided to go to Huichow to see General
Ch'en, his former patron, and asked Kung-po to come along. As a
travelling companion, Kung-po took his Kuomintang friend, Ch'en

Ch'iu-lin, who had been placed on the *Ch'ün Pao* by General Ch'en. Kung-po says he was not in the conference between Ch'en Tu-hsiu and Ch'en Chiung-ming; he spent the day seeing the sights of Hui-chow with his friend. On the boat trip back, however, Ch'en Tu-hsiu told him the signs all pointed to a military push by General Ch'en and trouble for Canton.

The day before Ch'en Tu-hsiu was to return to Shanghai he had a private talk with Kung-po, who describes the details. Tu-hsiu said that in the impending struggle for Kwangtung the Communists ought to know whom they would support. From the point-of-view of principle they ought to ally with Sun Yat-sen, but from the viewpoint of power they should support General Ch'en. Kung-po does not know whether Tu-hsiu was merely testing him out, but asserts that he, himself, maintained they should unquestionably support Sun, a truly national figure. Ch'en Tu-hsiu replied that they should wait and see. This account has a bearing upon Kung-po's separation from the Communist Party.

In view of the unsettled conditions, Kung-po started preparation to leave for America to study. He lacked money and had to arrange for the care of his mother. Wang Ching-wei gave him a letter of introduction to the Commissioner of Finance, but just then Ch'en Chiung-ming's "revolt" against Sun Yat-sen occurred on June 16. Sun had to flee to a gunboat and Canton was disturbed by many days of bombardment. Finally, Sun left for Shanghai. Because of the revolt, Kung-po's funds for the American trip were held up.

At this time news from Party Headquarters in Shanghai was extremely scarce so T'an P'ing-shan wanted to go there to learn what was up. Kung-po called a meeting which elected P'ing-shan the delegate of the Kwangtung Communist Party to Shanghai. Kung-po, who was busy with his preparations for study abroad, stayed in Canton to look after Party affairs. After the revolt was over, he remembers seeing in the paper that Sun had appointed many delegates to work on the reorganization of the Kuomintang and that Ch'en Tu-hsiu was one of them. Kung-po also reveals how he helped effect the release of Liao Chung-k'ai, who was held prisoner in General Ch'en Chiung-ming's camp. He reiterates that he did not know General Ch'en but got a confidant of the General to persuade him to release Liao.

Party Headquarters Tries to Discipline Ch'en   At this point Ch'en Kung-po had a distasteful experience which brought on his separation from the Communist Party. His preparations to leave for America were nearly complete when suddenly Chang T'ai-lei arrived in Canton bearing a letter from Ch'en Tu-hsiu and instructions from Party Headquarters. Kung-po was requested to go immediately to Shanghai to answer charges that he was assisting General Ch'en Chiung-ming. Kung-po stoutly denied any connection with General Ch'en. He declined to go to Shanghai because he was waiting for his American visa, nor could he waste his precious travel money on such a trip. Chang T'ai-lei then asked why he did not go to Soviet Russia rather than America to study. Kung-po asserts that he felt outraged at Ch'en Tu-hsiu and his old friend T'an P'ing-shan, both in Shanghai, who knew all about his plan to go to America and about his non-involvement with General Ch'en. He gave Chang T'ai-lei a long letter to Ch'en Tu-hsiu asking whether he remembered their recent conversation about the relative merits of Sun and General Ch'en. He added a postscript for T'an P'ing-shan reminding him of their long friendship and collaboration and asking why T'an had not spoken out about the things he knew so well. Next day Kung-po reported the experience to a meeting of the Kwangtung Party and announced that he would no longer perform his Party duties. The Party members were indignant at Shanghai's action. T'an Chih-t'ang and Liu Erh-sung both spoke out, and the entire group advocated that the Kwangtung Party should be independent. Later T'an Chih-t'ang was removed from the Party rolls because he supported Kung-po (he was readmitted two years later), while Liu Erh-sung received a stern warning and some of the others were also punished.

Kung-po makes a strong point throughout the article "I and the Communist Party" that he did not know General Ch'en, was never employed by him nor worked on his behalf. There are writers who assert the opposite. Ch'en T'an-ch'iu, one of the founding members of the Chinese Communist Party, states in his reminiscences published in 1936 that after General Ch'en's uprising against Sun, Ch'en Kung-po helped the General in his struggle against Sun and after repeated warnings was expelled from the Communist Party. Chang Kuo-t'ao, another Chinese Communist founder, states in his autobiography that before the revolt Ch'en Tu-hsiu was trying to effect a means of cooperation with the Kuomintang. After General Ch'en's revolt, the Central Committee of the Communist Party in Shanghai wrote to T'an P'ing-shan and other responsible members of the Canton branch ordering them to sever all connections with General Ch'en and declare support for Sun. But Ch'en Kung-po and T'an Chih-t'ang continued to work in the newspaper *Ch'ün Pao* and write articles supporting General Ch'en. After the Second CCP Congress (July 1922), the Central Committee again wrote the Canton branch, threatening Kung-po and Chih-t'ang with expulsion if they did not change their attitude and threatening T'an P'ing-shan, the Secretary of the branch, with severe discipline if he continued to tolerate the defiant attitude of the others. Because the Canton comrades did not fully comply, Chang continues, T'an Chih-t'ang was expelled, Kung-po received a scathing warning and withdrew, and T'an P'ing-shan was reprimanded and temporarily relieved of his duties as Secretary.

These accounts were written long after the fact by people who were not in Canton at the time. Several Japanese sources, late and secondary, link Kung-po to General Ch'en. They say that when the General became Governor of Kwangtung, Kung-po became a secretary in his office, and after his fall from power Kung-po left for the United States to study.

It is worth recalling in connection with General Ch'en Chiung-ming's opposition to Sun Yat-sen some facts in the situation that have become obscured by the later cult of idolatry towards Sun. The General had a record as an anti-Manchu revolutionary in his own right and in 1920 had made possible Sun's return to Canton by freeing the city from control of a Kwangsi military group. He also brought Ch'en Tu-hsiu to Canton as Provincial Educational Commissioner; the leader of the Communist Party was indebted to him. Sun and General Ch'en disagreed on Sun's favorite scheme of a military expedition northward to unite China. Many eminent Kuomingtang comrades agreed with the General in his opposition to Sun's attempts. According to Li Chien-nung, "all intellectual circles" urged Sun to resign his presidency, and General Ch'en's action was in accord with the general desire of the people for peace. He mentions Ts'ai Yüan-p'ei as one who wished Sun to give up his plan. The "Brief History of the Chinese Communist Movement," one of the earliest Chinese Communist sources, states frankly that it was evident Sun's northern expedition would fail and that the Communist Party was not sympathetic to Sun though it did not openly support Ch'en Chiung-ming. It says that other groups were also unfavorable to Sun. "The best-educated and the most democratic elements were on Ch'en Chiung-ming's side." It mentions Dr. Hu Shih as one of these. "Many of Sun's friends and followers advised him to give up political life completely in view of his demonstrated inefficiency." As Chang Kuo-t'ao tells the story of the revolt, the advocates of a federation of autonomous provinces, in the southwest, supported General Ch'en and many Kuomintang leaders abandoned Sun. Forty-nine Kuomintang veterans, led by Li Shih-tseng, Ts'ai Yüan-p'ei, Wu Chih-hui and Wang Chung-hui jointly issued a call for Sun to retire. It was a terrible blow to Sun and was probably one of the factors which led him to accept the collaboration of the minuscule Communist Party.

Under these circumstances it would not have been surprising if Ch'en Kung-po had supported the General or if the newspaper *Ch'ün Pao,* with some of its staff in the General's pay, had supported him. But on this matter, which apparently was the issue which precipitated Ch'en's separation from the Communist Party, the limited evidence is simply contradictory.

After Communism

Ch'en Goes to the United States and Studies at Columbia   Early in November 1922, Kung-po sailed for Japan, not even stopping at

Shanghai. In Japan Liao Chung-k'ai requested him to return with him to Canton where Liao offered him the presidency of the Law College. Ch'en, however, declined. On another occasion, he saw Liao in Atami. Liao asked Kung-po what he thought about the cooperation between the Nationalists and the Communists. Ch'en told Liao of his earlier discussion of the matter with "Slevelet" and Chang Chi. Liao then proposed they discuss it with Adolph Joffe, which was the first that Kung-po knew of the Russian envoy's presence in Atami. Joffe told him, says Kung-po, that Soviet Russia had ordered the Chinese Communist Party to enter the Kuomintang in order to complete the Chinese National Revolution. Joffe also told Kung-po in great seriousness that China could only fulfill Sun Yat-sen's Three Principles and certainly could not carry out communism. In answer to Kung-po's query, Joffe expressed doubt that Soviet Russia could put communism into effect in Russia even in sixty years! Liao laughed at Kung-po's doubts and said, "When we build a revolutionary party we want one for the present, not one for a hundred years later. We should energetically put into effect the Three Principles of the People and not discuss the matter further."

Kung-po says he sailed for America on February 12, 1923; he registered at Columbia on February 28, paying his fees March 1.

According to the records of the Registrar of Columbia University, Ch'en Kung-po entered the Graduate School in the spring term of 1923 about a month late. He was then thirty years old, though the birth date (28th August, 1891) he mistakenly gave would have made him thirty-one. He took courses during the spring, summer and fall of 1923, almost entirely in economics, and accumulated well over 30 points during his first year of study. He completed his MA thesis, "The Communist Movement in China," and had it approved by Professor Vladimir Simkovitch on January 31, 1924, delivered two copies on February 6 and received the MA degree on February 22. He took courses for two more semesters, the spring and fall of 1924, but he did not achieve the Ph.D. degree.

After arriving in New York, he learned from his friend, T'an Chih-t'ang, that the Communist Party in Shanghai had determined that Kung-po must undergo Party investigation because of his disobedience of orders to go to Shanghai and to study in Soviet Russia. By then, however, he was already disaffected. However, he decided to make a thorough study of the works of Marx and Engels. He became disillusioned with Marxism but also rejected the economics of Adam Smith and English liberalism, and decided that Sun Yatsen's principle of People's Livelihood would build up and revive China. So he plunged in to study American "practical economics" in order to benefit China. He reports that he had considerable dealings with the American socialist, Scott Nearing. He supported himself teaching in a Chinese school in New York.

He left America in February 1925 without completing the doctorate because, he avers, he could not afford to pay for printing the dissertation. He jokingly calls himself the "One-Quarter Doctor," since he half earned the Columbia doctorate which was worth half as much as the same degree at Harvard, Princeton or Yale! Kwangtung University where he was to teach paid his travel expenses back to Canton and he returned via Europe.

A Sketch of Ch'en Kung-po's Later Career After his return to China in the spring of 1925, Ch'en had an active career in politics, journalism and government, but none of it bears upon his thesis, "The Communist Movement in China." Therefore I shall merely outline the main facts.

Ch'en joined the Kuomintang as a protege of Liao Chung-k'ai, and became Director of the Bureau of Workers and Peasants in the Kwangtung provincial government, a position which put him into close working relations and conflict with Communist organizers particularly in connection with the Hongkong strike. After the assassination of Liao Chung-k'ai in August, 1925, Ch'en became head of the Peasants Department in Central Headquarters of the Kuomintang. He was also for a time acting President of Sun Yatsen University and chief of the Political Training Department of the Military Council. At the second Kuomintang Congress in January, 1926, he was elected to the Central Executive Committee, a mark of his political importance. He was by now closely connected with Wang Ching-wei. During the first stage of the Northern Expedition Ch'en was Director of the Bureau of Political Affairs of the General Headquarters of the National Revolutionary Army directly under Chiang Kai-shek. After the capture of Hankow and Hanyang, he was appointed Commissioner of Foreign Relations in the new Hupeh provincial government, and also Chairman of the Financial Council of the Hupeh government. In Hankow he was active as an agitator against Great Britain. After the capture of Kiangsi he was appointed head of the Political Council of Kiangsi, a position similar to Provisional Governor. In March 1927 he was elected to the 9-man Standing Committee of the Kuomintang Central Executive Committee and head of the Laborers Department of Central Party Headquarters. An important figure in Wuhan governmental affairs on the radical fringe, he supported Wang Ching-wei in the decision of June to break the alliance of the Kuomintang with the Communists.

Thereafter Ch'en's political career was closely related to the fortunes of a Wang Ching-wei. He participated during the summer and fall of 1927 in the effort to reconcile the Wuhan and Nanking factions of the Kuomintang, but when results failed to satisfy Wang, both men withdrew. Ch'en supported Wang in his effort to establish a new National Government in Canton, but the Communist uprising of December 11–14, 1927, put both Wang and Ch'en under a cloud for a time. Ch'en was not allowed to attend the Fourth Plenum of the Second CEC of the Kuomintang held in Nanking in February, 1928, although he was a member of the CEC.

As a Cantonese, a leftist, and a follower of Wang Ching-wei, Ch'en was active in the Reorganization Clique in the Kuomintang which opposed the growing power of Chiang Kai-shek. In May, 1928, he started publishing a weekly magazine in Shanghai, *Ko-ming P'ing-lun* (The Revolutionary Critic), which became the widely read organ of the Clique. The journal was ordered suppressed by the Nanking Government in September 1928. According to a foreign observer, "Students, workers, the younger officers in the army, those who were formerly Communists and are now leaderless, party workers, distressed Government officials who can no longer tolerate confusion—all these classes turn (1928) to Mr.

Chen Kung-po for leadership." In December, 1928 he published a book, *Revolutions in Chinese History*. Ch'en also founded Ta-lu University in Shanghai during 1928, but it was ordered closed by the government in May, 1929. On March 12, 1929, Wang Ching-wei, Ch'en Kung-po, Ku Meng-yü and eleven other prominent members of the Kuomintang issued a manifesto denouncing the Third Congress of the Party, to open on March 15, as illegal. The Congress, in turn, "permanently" dismissed Ch'en from the Kuomintang and warned Wang and other members of his leftist group. Ch'en and Ku Meng-yü were editors of *Min-hsin Chou-k'an* (Heart of the People) which advocated continuing the spirit of Sun's 1924 Reorganization, basing the Party upon peasants, workers, and the petty bourgeoisie.

Wang and Ch'en participated in several revolts against the Nanking Government, the most important being led by the northern generals, Feng Yü-hsiang and Yen Hsi-shan, in the summer of 1930. This anti-Chiang movement failed when the forces of the new Government in Peking were attacked by troops of Chang Hsüeh-liang from Manchuria. Wang and Ch'en withdrew to Canton. The Japanese invasion of Manchuria, beginning on September 18, 1931, helped to bring about a partial reconciliation of various factions of the Nationalist Party. A new Central Executive Committee brought Wang and his followers, including Ch'en, back into its membership, and in a governmental reorganization at the beginning of 1932, Wang became Chairman of the Executive Yuan and Ch'en Minister of Industry.

Ch'en served as a minister in the Nanking Government for nearly four years, resigning late in 1935 after someone attempted to assassinate Wang Ching-wei, though he continued as a member of the KMT Central Executive Committee. He published in 1936 an account of his four years in government, *Ssu Nien Ts'ung Cheng Lu*. During 1936 and 1937, he travelled in Europe, particularly in Italy and Germany, returning to China after the Sino-Japanese war broke out. Although he was a member of the Central Executive Committee of the Kuomintang, Chairman of the Committee's People's Training Department, and a member of the Central Political

Council, he was not given an important role in government. He was appointed Chairman of the National Government's Committee on Cooperative Enterprises. He was also a sort of "whip" for Kuomintang members in the People's Political Council, which held its first session at Hankow in July, 1938.

When Wang Ching-wei left Free China in December, 1938, on the first step of his fateful move towards collaboration with Japan, Ch'en conferred with him in Hanoi. In 1939, Ch'en reputedly tried to dissuade Wang from heading a Japanese-sponsored government, but ultimately followed him into it, becoming President of the Legislative Yuan. In October of 1940, he became Mayor of Shanghai. After Wang's death in Japan on November 10, 1944, Ch'en became President of the Nanking Government. At the end of the war, he went to Japan but was brought back to China for trial, was sentenced to death, and met his fate at Soochow on June 3, 1946.*

* Ch'en Kung-po was survived by his wife, Li Li-chuang, whom he had married in 1921, and a son who was studying engineering in the United States at the time of his father's death. Both subsequently took up residence in the United States.

Most of Ch'en Kung-po's writings are scattered in various magazines and newspapers of the time. Among his other works were *Chung-kuo li-shih-shang ti ko-ming* (Revolutions in Chinese History) (1928), *Ssu-nien ts'ung-cheng lu* (Four Years in Government Service) (1936), and *Han-feng-chi* (The Cold Wind) (1944). The first was one of the earlier Chinese attempts at an economic interpretation of the popular uprisings in Chinese history; the second describes his work as Minister of Industry in the National Government; and the third is a collection of his essays written between 1933 and 1943, containing much information on his life.—Ed.

❊ 17 ❊

Ch'ü Ch'iu-pai's Autobiographical Writings:
The Making and Destruction
of a "Tender-hearted" Communist

T. A. HSIA

I

We do not know much about the inner life of "hard-hearted" Communists, save that they get along well within the limits of the dogma and discipline set by the Party. Some are even in a position to impose them. They have successfully remoulded their personalities, they are perfect adjusters. But the life of a "tender-hearted" Communist, we can imagine, is miserable. He is too weak to become a good revolutionary fighter, though he has to put up a show of toughness. Trying to quit involves too many practical difficulties; moreover, the Party may have still some lingering meaning for him. But to stay on is to suffer frustrations, indignities and hypocrisies. His conscience, which he has somehow kept alive, is no help to deliver him from the dilemma. He is constantly aware of his personal tragic errors as well as the errors of the Party. But he is also beset with solitude. In the air of mutual suspicion that envelops his life, he cannot communicate his true feelings to his comrades; but he has lost contact with the old non-Communist world. As an individual, he is no match for the Party in strength, and he may not be able to offer a system that can take the place of Communism. But with all his weaknesses, he has maintained a little islet of indi-

Reprinted with permission from *The China Quarterly* (London), No. 25 (January–March, 1966), pp. 178–212.

vidualism which refuses to be swallowed up by the dark, turbulent seas roaring all around. As the doubter, the worrier, the silent, intro-spective rebel, he is a much more interesting character than his tough colleague. The very existence of this isolated, troubled soul is a silent protest against the totalitarian movement. Though the "tender-hearted" Communist has appeared as the tormented, meditative hero of many a political novel, he is no mere imaginary character. His existence is illustrated by the examples of the Koestlers, the Spenders, the Djilases and the Ssuma Lus, whose vivid descriptions of their first-hand experiences reveal, as nothing else, the feelings and thoughts of a Communist in bewilderment.

Nothing can induce us to describe Ch'ü Ch'iu-pai (1899–1935) as a disloyal Communist, but what makes him such a fascinating study is that he was a writer and that he wrote at great length about himself. In the bulk of his works written between 1923 and 1934 we hear only the voice of one who spoke for the Party though the voice sometimes also has the ring of personal conviction. But the two books he wrote during his first trip to Soviet Russia (1920–22) are remarkable for an astonishing candour. The books are not mere travelogue or propaganda, but chronicle the author's mental state in poverty-stricken Russia during the critical years when he was chang-ing from a non-Communist into a Communist. The introspective nature of the second book is obvious from the title, A History of the Heart in the Red Capital; the title of the first, A Journey to the Land of Hunger, implies a Confucian ideal transposed. Later, after more than a decade of bitter struggle, he reviewed his life in a prison in Changting, Fukien, and wrote, in addition to a few lyrics, his testament, the Superfluous Words, one of the most intimate records of the soul of a Communist.

Today Ch'ü Ch'iu-pai is honoured as a martyr,[1] and his good name as a worthy leader and comrade, once fallen into disgrace, has been rescued by a resolution of the Central Committee under the

[1] "The remains of Comrade Ch'ü Ch'iu-pai, who was executed by the KMT reactionaries twenty years ago in Changting, Fukien, were interred in the Martyrs' Cemetery at Pa-pao-shan, Peking, on June 18." NCNA, June 18, 1955. Jen-min Jih-pao (People's Daily), June 19, 1955.

direction of Mao Tse-tung.[2] Mao is a man of long memory. He will never forgive the coolness or unkindness shown him by his former "bosses" in the Party, Ch'en Tu-hsiu, Li Li-san, Ch'en Shao-yü or Ch'in Pang-hsien, but his relationship with Ch'ü is known to have been more cordial. A certain degree of friendship or mutual respect might have existed between the two men.[3] It would seem natural for Mao to care for the posthumous reputation of Ch'ü. But Ch'ü's distinguished career should also speak for itself. He will long be remembered for the part he played in the struggles against the "patriarch" of the Party, Ch'en Tu-hsiu in 1927. His policy of riots in 1927 and his conciliatory attitude towards Li Li-san, the author of the famous "tough line of action," in 1930 have been called into question by his comrades, but they reflect no discredit on his eager desire for revolution. His arrest and execution only crowned a long record of struggle marked by the spirit of self-sacrifice. If he was not an unusually clever schemer or able organiser, he was, at least, a quite formidable fighter.

[2] "Comrade Ch'ü Ch'iu-pai, who was supposed to have committed mistakes along the line of conciliation, was a Party leader of prestige and did much useful work (mainly cultural) even after blows were dealt to him, and died a hero's death in June 1935 at the hands of the KMT executioners." Mao Tse-tung, "Resolutions on Some Questions in the History of Our Party," *Selected Works,* Vol. IV (New York: International Publishers, 1956), p. 183. See also the note on p. 340, *ibid.* ". . . he was attacked by the 'Left' doctrinaire-sectarians and excluded from the Party's central leading body."

[3] "Comrade Ch'iu-pai was very respectful towards Comrade Mao Tse-tung. . . . [After only a part of Mao's lengthy] 'Report of an Investigation into the Peasant Movement in Hunan' . . . was published in the *Hsiang Tao (Guide Weekly)*, its editor, P'eng Shu-chih, was not willing to publish the remainder . . . Ch'ü, then in Wuhan, not only published the full text as a book but also wrote a preface to it." Hsiao San, *Chi-nien (Personalities and Reminiscences) Jen-wu yü* (Peking: San Lien Bookstore, 1952), p. 221.

Ch'ü also taught at the Training Centre for the Agrarian Movement, which was under the direction of Mao in Canton. See Wen Chi-tse "Ch'ü Ch'iu-pai t'ung-shih chan-tou te i-sheng" ("Comrade Ch'ü Ch'iu-pai's Battling Life") *Hung ch'i p'iao p'iao (Red Flags Are Flying)* (Peking: Chinese Youth Publications Association, 1957), Vol. 5, p. 93.

In Kiangsi, he was said to be on cordial terms with Mao, though he did not get along well with other Communist leaders. See Hsüeh-hua, "Introduction to the *Superfluous Words*," *I-ching Fortnightly,* Vol. II, No. 25, March 5, 1937.

Ch'ü is also known to have been a man of letters and there is no doubt that he used his pen bravely and diligently in the service of the Party. His name became inseparable from the Leftist Literary Movement in Shanghai. He surely knew how to express himself in lucid Chinese and his mastery of the Russian language was a rare ability among the Communist leaders of his time. Besides his elucidation of Communist theory, especially on literary subjects, he endeavoured to put language to its best use as a weapon for agitation and propaganda. He aimed at a larger audience and advocated a "language for the masses," to be distinguished from the *pai-hua* which he disdained as scarcely more lively than the "dead" *wen-yen* it was supposed to supersede.[4] He went so far as to deplore the poor readability of Lu Hsün's translations.[5] Lu Hsün could only take this criticism gracefully despite the fact that it echoed opinions of "bourgeois" critics like Liang Shih-chiu,[6] since it came from a friend who had the linguistic demands of the masses in view. The useful work Ch'ü did in this field is recognised by the Party. Though not all his critical views are accepted today,[7] Ch'ü's name as a writer will be perpetuated through his literary works (not his political

[4] See the five essays on Literary Revolution and Language Problems, *Ch'ü Ch'iu-pai Wen-chi* (*Collected Works of Ch'ü Ch'iu-pai*) (Peking: Jen-min Wen-hsüeh Ch'u-pan She, 1953), Vol. 2, pp. 593–704.

[5] See his two letters on translation to Lu Hsün, *Collected Works,* Vol. 2, pp. 917–42.

[6] Liang's essay on "Lun Lu Hsün hsien-sheng te ying-i" ("Mr. Lu Hsün's 'Hard Translation'") appeared in the *Hsin Yueh* (*Crescent Moon*), Vol. 2, Nos. 6 and 7 (a combined issue). Lu Hsün's rebuttal, "Lun ying-i yü wen-hsüeh te chieh-chi hsing ("Hard Translation and the Class-nature of Literature"), is found in *Lu Hsün Ch'üan Chi* (*Complete Works of Lu Hsün*) (Peking: Jen-min Wen-hsüeh Ch'u-pan She, 1957), Vol. 4, p. 155.

[7] In 1932 Ch'ü wrote an essay on the "Revolutionary Romantic" ("Ko-ming te lang-t'ou ti-k'e"), which looks disapprovingly at the "romantic elements" contained in a leftist novel *Ti Ch'uan* (*Spring from the Earth*), by Hua Han. This essay is found in an earlier collection, *Luan Tan* (*Vulgar Music*) (Shanghai: 1949), but is excluded from the authorised *Collected Works*. One reason is perhaps that "revolutionary romanticism" is an essential part of the literary policy of the Chinese Communist Party under Mao Tse-tung. Kuo Mo-jo believes that one of Mao's poems, Tieh li hua, is a "typical combination of revolutionary realism with revolutionary romanticism." *Wen I Pao*, No. 7, April 11, 1958.

writings), published in a set of four imposing volumes.[8] Lu Ting-i, Minister of Propaganda of the Chinese Communist Party, said of Ch'ü: "His noble qualities and the meritorious deeds he did in his lifetime will live forever in the hearts of the people; they are immortal." [9]

Before Ch'ü assumed the halo of immortality, he revealed himself, in his two early works, as a character quite different from the hero brandishing his pen against a background of surging masses. His is an altogether more complex and lonesome character. Enthusiasm for revolution is probably there, but that is only one of his many facets. We are able to see him more or less in depth, and he is found to be affectionate, sentimental, meditative, idealistic, capable of absorption into scenes of natural beauty, introspective to the degree of self-pity, and haunted by a sense of loneliness. These are the qualities customarily associated with a poet in the traditional Chinese sense rather than with a revolutionary. But then his revolutionary career had barely begun. There was plenty of time ahead for him to overcome his weaknesses and to hammer such fragile material, which was not only adulterated with all forms of sentimentality but marred by a serious case of tuberculosis, into a first-rate fighter.

The inevitable question is: how successfully did he transform his character? It is hard to believe that the young writer, whose love for his parents, cousins, friends, wild flowers and moonlit nights made such poignant reading, should develop into a revolutionary whose name was equated with terrorism, blind fury and relentlessness, especially after the series of notorious riots staged under his leadership. To make this possible, he must have discarded his tender half since the two sides of his character were irreconcilable. But here an interesting psychological question arises: can a person be entirely cut off from his past? Can his early training be wiped out, his memory suffocated, and his mental habits all reformed? He may accomplish this to a certain degree with the power of his will. But can he control his subconscious mind? Hard work may help. To

[8] *Collected Works of Ch'ü Ch'iu-pai, op. cit.*
[9] *Jen-min Jih-pao (People's Daily)*, June 19, 1955.

drive oneself at a feverish rate so as to exhaust oneself mentally and physically is a proven measure against dangerous thoughts. That was how Ch'ü treated himself most of the time. But now and then leisure was forced upon him, as relapses of his tuberculosis would require a rest cure. Then he was arrested and put into prison. The leisure so hard-earned, together with other circumstances such as his interrogation by Kuomintang officials, softened up his defences against his own past. With the loss of freedom, his mind, paradoxically, was set free. As his thoughts roamed, the urge for self-expression returned. The few poems he wrote then are nostalgic in nature, and in the *Superfluous Words,* he came to understand himself better when he admitted to his "dual personality." Which one is the real Ch'ü Ch'iu-pai, the fighter or the ruminating sentimentalist? Perhaps both, if we believe that even Communists can have split personalities.

II

On January 29, 1899, Ch'ü Ch'iu-pai was born into a family in Changchow, Kiangsu, that had for generations "smelt of the scent of books." His grandfather, a high official under the Manchus, left behind a considerable fortune which, however, was quickly dissipated. After a few comfortable years in early childhood, Ch'iu-pai was soon to experience a poverty which was degenerating from the genteel sort into the abject. His father, who should be held responsible for the decline of the family fortune, must have been one of those decadent young men so often found in the mandarin houses in China in the late nineteenth and early twentieth centuries. To seek employment was thought to be beneath them and anyway they were not good at anything except dabbling in art and indulging in refined idleness. They were intelligent, but weak-willed, full of good intentions but short in spirit for any kind of exertion. The changing times, hurried on by the advent of the republic, caught them unprepared. In the case of Ch'iu-pai's father, who, among all the possible hobbies, chose occult Taoism, he managed to live for years on the family treasures—paintings, calligraphy, art-objects, fine furniture. Among Ch'iu-pai's experiences in his teens were constant visits to the pawnshop. The family land must have been liquidated at the same time, for the family had to find shelter in the "clan temple."

After Ch'ü's shiftless, opium-smoking[10] father had gone to Shantung to accept the position of a schoolteacher which did not promise more than subsistence pay, the burden of raising a family of six children[11] fell upon the shoulders of his mother. The good woman seemed the prototype of the daughter of a mandarin house who, while practising the virtues of patience, meekness and modesty, had much more character than the man she married. She was sensitive, intelligent, narrow-minded and fiercely proud. She had domineering qualities, for she had been trained since girlhood to rule as a daughter-in-law and eventually as a matriarch over a large household. Men could afford to forget about the world in their hobbies, but women had no way of escaping from the day-to-day problems of housekeeping. The burden on Ch'iu-pai's mother turned out to be more than she could cope with. For with all her accomplishments, she shared the fatal weakness of the gentry class: she did not know where to look for a source of income. The best she could do was to live frugally and to haggle energetically so as to get the most out of what little was left of the family collection. But the family inevitably ran into debts.

Regular education for the children was something that a family of high standing like the Ch'üs of Changchow could not afford to neglect even in its reduced circumstances. When Ch'iu-pai was too young to be sent to school, he had learned to recite the famous T'ang poets at his mother's knee. His father taught him to paint and he studied the carving of seal stones from an uncle.[12] Ch'iu-

[10] No other source mentions that Ch'ü's father was an opium smoker, but he himself admitted to this in an interview held in prison in 1935. "Ch'ü Ch'iu-pai fang-wen chi" ("An Interview with Ch'ü Ch'iu-pai") by Li K'ech'ang, *Kuo-wen Chou-pao* (*Kuowen Weekly*), Vol. 12, No. 26, July 8, 1935.

[11] I do not know exactly how many children she had. But Ch'ü noted at the time when he was leaving for Russia, that he and two younger brothers were in Peking, and two other younger brothers and one younger sister were in Hangchow. They had to depend on the relatives only after their mother's death. *A Journey to the Land of Hunger*, p. 8, *Collected* Works, Vol. 1.

[12] Tsao Tsu-hsi, *op. cit.*, p. 3.

pai's school education bore the marks of that period of Chinese history. Lessons in patriotism, public duty, and modernisation filled the curriculum, and even militarism was taught as a way of national salvation. Although he was only twelve, Ch'iu-pai received some sort of military training after the news of the 1911 Wuchang uprising reached his high school.[13] Ch'iu-pai was a bright student in both primary and secondary school. But one year before his graduation from the Changchow High School, when he was sixteen *sui,* he was compelled to quit for financial reasons. Considering the four younger brothers and one younger sister who needed to be fed and educated, he got a job in the neighbouring district of Wusih as a schoolteacher. Thus he not only saved the family the expense of his own education, but he began to support himself. Instead of bringing satisfaction to his mother, however, this became another source of sorrow. She hated herself for not being able to keep in school a son in whom she saw great promise for learning.

Soon after, Ch'ü's grandmother died. The old lady had seen much better days while her husband was alive, but she had become the grumbling, pathetic figure of the family. Her daughter-in-law must have had a hard time in catering to her needs. The expenses incurred by her long illness were also beyond the means of this particular branch of the Ch'ü clan. To get rid of the burden, Ch'iu-pai's mother suggested moving the old lady to Hangchow so that she could be better taken care of by one of Ch'iu-pai's uncles.[14] But the travel proved fatal, and the old woman died after she arrived in Hangchow. The whispers that had been exchanged among the relatives now became audible. Ch'iü-pai's mother was accused of being unwifely, for her husband had to leave home; she was unmotherly, for she would not let her son finish high school; she was undaughterly, for she hastened the death of her invalid mother-in-law by moving her about. These criticisms, in addition to the difficulties with the dunners who became particularly importunate at

[13] Wen Chi-tse, *op. cit.,* p. 80.

[14] The uncle could be the "fourth paternal uncle" on whom Ch'iu-pai's brothers were to depend. He was probably also the uncle who had served as magistrate of certain districts in Chekiang (mentioned in *Interview,* note 10).

the end of the lunar year, drove her to despair. She ended her life by drinking phosphorous heads of red matches watered down with a quaff of tiger-bone wine. On the night of the second day of the first moon, in the year of *i-mao* (February 19, 1915),[15] Ch'iu-pai rushed home from Wusih when he heard the news. He was not too late to witness the dreadful scene.[16]

His mother's suicide was one of the most terrible blows in Ch'iu-pai's life, a trauma which perhaps never healed. As he reflected on the incident in 1920, on the eve of his departure for Russia, he wrote:[17]

> My mother has been driven out of this universe by Poverty; my father is nothing but jetsam cast off by the same force, . . . The large family system . . . was first quivering and shaking, and then it will topple and gradually become lost to sight. I shall take up one phase of this social phenomenon—the dying system of the large family in China, a phase that I have personally witnessed and participated in. I can only see that day after day this system is drawing closer to its end. The best one can say of the system is that under it, everybody lives a dry, static life. On the side of its evils, one can see that because of the conflict of economic interests and the looseness of family ties, especially between husband and wife, the members of such a family—fathers, sons, brothers, sisters-in-law, uncles—while staring blankly at each other under the mask of Confucianism, will stop at nothing to give vent to their jealousy and hatred in secret, to grumble, to murmur, to curse, and to kill with their venomous tongues. The relations between man and man have troubled me as a great puzzle. The meaning of life is absolutely obscure to me. Though I believe I have within me a harmonious chord, no harmonious music can I play.

[15] The date, the second day of the first moon, is agreed upon by Wen Chi-tse, *op. cit.*, p. 81; Tsao Tsu-hsi, *Ch'ü Ch'iu-pai te wen-hsüeh huo-tung (Ch'ü Ch'iu-pai's Literary Activities)* (Shanghai: Hsin Wen-i Ch'u-pan She, 1958), p. 5, and Shang-kuan Ai-ming, *Ch'iu-pai wen-hsüeh (Ch'ü Ch'iu-pai and Literature)* (Nanking: Kiangsu Wen-i Ch'u-pan She, 1959). Shang-kuan Ai-ming said that the day was February 19, 1915, in the solar calendar. But I checked on the calendar, and found it to be February 15. Yang Chih-hua, Ch'ü's widow, does not give a definite date. She only refers to February 1915. "I Ch'iu-pai" ("In Memoriam, Ch'iu-po"), *Red Flags Are Flying*, Vol. 8, p. 26, 1958. The other biographers stress poverty as the cause of the suicide. Yang Chih-hua brings in the interesting factor of the relatives' accusations.

[16] Wen Chi-tse, *op. cit.*, p. 81.

[17] *Journey to the Land of Hunger, Collected Works*, Vol. 1, pp. 13–14.

The family was broken up. After several months spent in mourning, Ch'iu-pai, with the aid of various uncles and cousins, left home and ventured into the world. The small world he left behind was not altogether hateful. It had at least contained something he treasured most dearly, his mother's love. Compared with the cities he was going to visit, Wuchang and Peking, both cultural and revolutionary centres with enough intellectual activities to challenge the growing powers of the young man, his native town had been narrow in its intellectual horizon but not without quiet beauty and an artistic tradition.

Life might have been happy but for poverty, to which indeed he attributed his mother's death, the dissolution of his family, and the jealousy and hatred inside the clan. And poverty was to pursue him even in the big cities. Whatever grudges he bore against his relatives, he was to continue to rely on their help. For the clan system, or the large family system as he called it, was an odd mixture of conventional virtue, genuine humanity and hypocrisy. It served as a sort of social security, so that a bereaved, penniless member of the clan could always get the money to buy a coffin for the deceased, and an orphan would not be left in the world uncared for. The system also provided some schooling which he could not have obtained elsewhere. A child was expected to learn proper manners from his elders, but he was inadvertently exposed to the ugly side of life in the behaviour of those he was taught to revere. Even at a tender age he would have to accept vice and injustice as the facts of life. A sensitive youth, particularly if he had been snubbed by the better-off branches of the clan, could only rouse himself with rebellious thinking in order to avoid the depression he would otherwise have felt from what he saw around him.

Ch'iu-pai emerged from this background a little dazed, without quite understanding the forces that had been working on him. The major political events, the founding of the republic and the fall of Yüan Shih-k'ai, had left him unimpressed. He described himself in retrospect as an escapist,[18] in the sense that he had been wholly absorbed in the world of poetry, classics and inspiration. Now that

[18] *Journey, Collected Work,* Vol. 1, p. 21.

his mother's death had deprived him of his last protection, he had to fend for himself, if not for the younger members of the family, his brothers and sister. His objectives were not high: to go back to school, and if possible, to get a college diploma so as to qualify for better positions than that of headmaster of the obscure school at Wusih. To seek independence in big cities while keeping up the genteel tradition was the aim of many young men of Ch'ü's generation who, in spite of their tastes and inclinations, suddenly found that they could no more live with their families. Ch'iu-pai was then more melancholy than rebellious, intent upon seeking his own fortune rather than denouncing the society that made such adventure necessary. He was to continue to enjoy the help and warmth provided by the clan system. He did not go to nearby Nanking or Shanghai, for there he might have been alone in a strange world. He went to Wuchang in the mid-Yangtze Valley, where his cousin Shun-po was ready with brotherly help, which included, if nothing impressive in terms of money, at least a home and mature advice which the young man would need to advance in the world. Ch'iu-pai would have to depend on him for years to come.

Ch'iu-pai might have turned his attention to the political and social problems in his new environment, but under the influence of another cousin, a Mr. Chou, he devoted more time to the subtle and challenging art of composing classical Chinese poetry. Under the same influence, he discovered a "revived interest" in Buddhism. Such studies necessarily furthered his introverted tendencies, while his juvenile ideas about a "political solution of social problems," he later admitted, had to wither before they had a chance to bud forth.[19] He was even induced into a mystic state of peace.

For a short time Ch'iu-pai attended the Foreign Language College in Hankow. It was perhaps his cousin's transfer to Peking that caused him to make a similar trip there sometime in 1916. He was denied enrolment at the National Peking University because he could not pay the tuition, but the lecture halls of the august institution were open to him, as well as to many other young men who then swarmed to the capital to quench their thirst for learning.

[19] *Ibid.* p. 22.

What impressions Ch'en Tu-hsiu or Li Ta-chao made on him then are not on record, although he later joined the Socialist Studies Group formed under Li's direction.[20] In the summer of 1917, he was admitted into the Russian Language College, a tuition-free training school for foreign service, affiliated with the Ministry of Foreign Affairs. It was clear that Shun-po, himself a government employee,[21] wanted his young cousin to follow in his footsteps in the government service.

Ch'iu-pai was gradually taking in Western ideas, but he persevered in his own plans of study. He worked very hard, with the aid of his Buddhistic studies, towards a personal solution of life's problems which kept baffling him. He might have become a poet and philosopher in his own way, while leading the philistine life of a career diplomat. What changed him was the May Fourth Movement. Indeed, no one has more right to the title of a man born of that movement. From then on he had to revise his views to fit into the Marxist doctrine he came to accept, and revolutionary activity began to take precedence over poetic and religious meditation. He was the best authority on the progress from an aspirant yogi to a would-be commissar in those critical years. In *Journey to the Land of Hunger,* he wrote:[22]

> The three years from my arrival in Peking to the eve of the May Fourth Movement were the most solitary in my life. I had then no friends. The new bureaucracy in the capital, with their "republi-

[20] In 1920, Li Ta-chao started the organisation of Socialist Studies Small Groups (She-hui-chu-i Yen-chiu Hsiao-tsu) at several schools in Peking as well as the Communist Small Group (Kung-ch'an-chu-i hsiao-tsu). The latter was more closely related to the Third International. Wang K'e-feng, *Wu-ssu yün-tung yü chung-kuo kung-ch'an tang chi tan-sheng* (*The May Fourth Movement and the Birth of the Communist Party*) (Nanking: Kiangsu Jen-min Ch'u-pan She), pp. 34–35. According to Wen Chi-tse, Ch'ü joined the Socialist Group, *op. cit.,* p. 85.

[21] According to Cheng Chen-to, Shun-po was a *k'e-yüan* of the Ministry of Foreign Affairs. But Ch'ü himself told the interviewer in prison that Shun-po was an employee of the Ministry of War; *cf.* note 10. "Chi Ch'ü Ch'iu-pai tung-shih tsao-nien te erh-san shih" ("A Few Anecdotes in Comrade Ch'ü Ch'iu-po's Early Life"), *Hsin Kuan-cha* (*New Observer*), No. 12, June 16, 1955.

[22] *Journey, Collected Works,* pp. 22–24.

can" way of living, disturbed me as a source of painful irritation. I became more and more convinced of my misanthropic views of life with the three years' study of philosophy. But a change had come over my mind, since I felt then a positive disgust which took the place of my earlier escapist attitude. My interest in classical studies led me to the ambition to reform such studies through a revival of the "Modern Text School." My attempts at solving life's problems through Buddhism resulted in another ambition: to humanise Buddhism and practise altruism as contained in the idea of Bodhisattvahood (*p'u-sa-hsing*). These were the vain and boastful wishes of a young man, but they epitomised the dualistic view of life evolved in my solitude. I allotted a part of my time to preparing for the discharge of my "worldly" duties—training for a career in which I was supposed to make a livelihood. Another part of my time was used on the "transcendental" level, for I had also to prepare myself diligently for the "service" (*kung-teh*, a Buddhistic term) of saving China by cultural means. I never relaxed in my philosophical studies which added heavily to the load of work at the Russian Language College. That I had to live like an ascetic and to study more than eleven hours a day was only a manifestation of my pursuit of the dual aims. Social intercourse could not have a place in my life. I studied Russian because thereby I could someday eat my own rice; for the rice I then ate was not mine, but my cousin's. My parasitic existence could not fail to stimulate me, now and again, into thinking about social problems, the problem of the relationship between man and man.

A bright path gradually revealed itself out of my studies in Buddhism: I believed that the world was to be saved through the practice of Bodhisattvahood and that everything was impermanent, including the social system. But such a philosophy could not hold long when the May Fourth Movement sucked me in like a whirlpool. My solitude was finally broken. My comrades in the Peking Social Service Club,[23] Ch'ü Shih-ying (an uncle), Cheng Chen-to, Keng Chi-chih and Chang Chao-teh (the last two being my schoolmates at the Russian College), all, like myself, joined the movement with an unbelievable fury.[24] We were all aware of the deep-

[23] She-hui fu-wu hui in the original. But the name should be more correctly Society Promotion Society, a social service branch of the YMCA, Peking. *Wussu Shih-ch'i Ch'i-kan Chie-shao (An Introduction to the Periodicals in the May Fourth Era)* (Peking: Jen-min Ch'u-pan She, 1958), Vol. 1, p. 320.

[24] As to his activities during the May Fourth Movement, he was arrested together with 800 others and imprisoned for three days, Wen Chi-tse, *op. cit.*, p. 84. On the very day of the demonstration, he came home spitting blood, Hsiao San, *op. cit.*, p. 218.

seated maladies of the society where we belonged but yet ignorant of their cure. Feelings alone, however, ran so strong that restlessness could no more be contained. That was, so far as I can see, the real significance of the student movement. There was a demand for change, and that demand came out in an outburst. It had then at least its shocking and rousing effects, for as Prince Kropotkin said, "One riot does more than thousands of books and pamphlets."

The unhappy situation of those eight and nine years after the founding of the Republic had to produce a reaction. Then the ideological revolution as reflected in *La Jeunesse* and the *New Tides* joined forces with the public sentiments in the student movement; and they together raised cataclysmic waves that shook through all China. The patriotic movement had actually a deeper meaning than mere patriotism. The taste of colonialism, in its full bitterness, had never come home to the Chinese until then, even though we had already had the experience of several decades of foreign exploitation behind us. The sharp pain of imperialistic oppression then reached the marrow of our bones and it awakened us from the nightmares of impractical democratic reforms. The issue of German possessions in Shantung which started the national uproar could not be separated from the larger problem. The industrial powers of the modern world are beset with the problems of capitalism which take the form of imperialism in the colonies. It was because of this that the students' movement in China inevitably leaned towards socialism. Our social problems became further complicated with the bankruptcy of the clannish rural economy which took away the basis from the old social structure. The problems of Confucianism, women, labour, and social reform, the literary problems centred on the vernacular, and the philosophical problems related to the view of life all rose up at the same time; they have ever since revolved around the social thinking of new China.

Like many other sensitive youths of that time, Ch'iu-pai did some thinking on his own. His active interest in social problems could be seen from the articles he contributed to *The New Society,* a magazine published, curiously enough, under the sponsorship of the YMCA and edited by Ch'iu-pai and some friends.[25] Among his articles were "The Family of Chinese Intelligentsia," "Time for Reform Is Arrived," "The Labor Problem of China and of the

[25] About the details of the *New Society,* see *Introduction to Periodicals, op. cit.,* p. 320. The titles of Ch'ü's essays are found on p. 326.

World," "The Spoils of Knowledge," "Victims of Social Movement," "On the New Christian Corporate Life in the USA" (to
which he objected), "Society and Evils," "The Society of the Future
and the Countercurrents of Today," "The Pan-Labor Theory of
A. Bebel" (of which he approved) and "Whose Weapon is This—
La grève, le sabotage?" The French words in the last-mentioned
were perhaps meant to show off the author's linguistic ability, but
more likely to cover up the dangerous thoughts contained in "strike"
and "sabotage" which, in Chinese, could easily be recognised by
the police. The magazine had a life of only six months; it was
banned on charges of containing socialist propaganda which might
have been true, but not all its contributors were sympathetic with
Bolshevism. Ch'iu-pai was on the left, while the others like Cheng
Chen-to, the literary-historian-to-be, then a student in the School of
Railway Management, and Ch'iu-pai's uncle, Ch'ü Shih-ying (a
student of philosophy at Hui-wen College who later got his Ph.D.
at Columbia, taught philosophy at Yenching University, and actively supported the Rural Reform Movement under Dr. James
Yen), were for a more mild, idealistic line in their editorial policy
as well as in their sophomoric political programme. But as Ch'iu-pai
did not insist on something which he did not think he really understood,[26] no serious quarrel split the small group. This handful of
young men, while drifting apart, could still see that they agreed
more than they disagreed. The conflicts that alienated Hu Shih
from Ch'en Tu-hsiu, or that tore asunder the Young China Association, leaving only two mutually antagonistic groups of Communists and extreme Nationalists,[27] simply did not happen to them.

[26] "No one at that time understood the meaning of materialistic view of
history." This statement of Ch'ü's is definitely applicable to his small group.
Whether he held the same view of people like Li Ta-chao and Ch'en Tu-hsiu
is doubtful. The quotation is from *Journey, Collected Works*, Vol. 1, p. 24.

[27] The Young China Association was the predecessor of the rightist Young
China Party (Chung-kuo Ch'ing-nien Tang), but its early members included
such eminent Communists as Mao Tse-tung, Li Ta-chao, etc. The struggle inside the Association was one of the most interesting phases of Chinese ideological and political history in the early twenties. For a brief account see *Introduction to Periodicals, op. cit.*, p. 235.

Although he objected to its idealist connotation, Ch'iu-pai accepted the name *Humanité*[28] for their new magazine, replacing the defunct *New Society*. Only one issue came out, to which Ch'iu-pai contributed "Voice of the Heart," a poem that did not attempt to conceal his idealism. Ch'iu-pai was leaving for Russia when the YMCA came up with an apology that it was no longer in a position to continue its financial support. So *Humanité* was forced to cease publication, but the small group of writers launched a more venturesome enterprise, the Literary Research Society, which made history.[29]

III

Ch'ü Ch'iu-pai went to Russia as a correspondent of the *Ch'en Pao* (*Morning News*) of Peking.[30] The offer, which came a few days after the publication of *Humanité*, was tempting. It meant an op-

[28] The first issue of *Humanité* was published on August 15, 1920. See *ibid.* p. 328.

[29] Four of the founders of the Literary Research Society (Wen-hsüeh Yen-chiu Hui) were originally associated with the *Humanité*: Cheng Chen-to, Ch'ü Shih-ying, Keng Chi-chih, and Hsu Ti-shan. The Society was founded in January 1921, when Ch'ü Ch'iu-po was in Russia. Both *Journey to the Land of Hunger* and *History of the Heart* were listed as publications of the Wen-hsüeh Yen-chiu Hui Ts'ung Shu.

[30] Li Ta-chao might be an influence behind the appointment. "The Peking *Ch'en Pao* was formerly known as the *Ch'en Chun Pao* (*The Morning Bell*), an organ of the Progressive Party, headed by the bourgeois reformers Liang Ch'i-ch'ao and T'ang Hua-lung. The same political group became later the Constitution Research Society (Hsien-fa Yen-chiu Hui) or, in its better known name, the Research Clique (Yen-chiu Hsi). At the inception of the *Ch'en Chung Pao* (August 15, 1916), its editor-in-chief was Li Ta-chao, only recently returned from Japan. . . . He was discharged from service, however, after only two months, because of differences in opinion. . . . In September 1918, eight newspapers in Peking were banned on account of their publication of the news about Japan's huge loan to Marshal Tuan Ch'i-jui. Among them were the two papers of the Research Clique: *Ch'en Chung Pao* and the *Kuo Min Kung Pao*. In December of the same year, the *Ch'en Chung Pao* resumed publication under the name of the *Ch'en Pao*. In February 1919, its page 7 (or supplementary page) went through a reorganisation. Li Ta-chao, who had acquired some rudimentary knowledge about Communism, was brought back to work on it. From then on the paper made it clear that it was favouring the new cultural movement." *Introduction to Periodicals, op. cit.*, p. 95.

portunity to travel, to see the socialist revolution at first hand and to earn his independence. The annual pay of $2,000 (Chinese currency) was a considerable jump from the six dollars a month he got as a schoolteacher in Wusih.[31] But he was also warned of the hardships and perils in a land torn by civil war and afflicted with utter destitution. Relatives and friends tried to dissuade him from making the hazardous trip but in vain. He agreed that Russia was a Land of Hunger, but could not they see that the appellation had an allegorical meaning? To seek death by starvation was in the noble tradition of Confucian idealism. He was only doing what was expected of a Confucian superior man; no consideration of material comfort or personal safety should be allowed to interfere with the pursuit of lofty ideals. Soviet Russia was his promised land, the fulfilment of his devout wishes. He reminded them of the essay *On the Land of Hunger* by the eighteenth-century scholar Kuan T'ung:[32]

> The Land of Hunger is located at the extremity of the Cosmos, separated from China by immeasurable distances. Bare is the land where no rice, sorghum, wheat, bean, cow, sheep, chicken, pig, fish, turtle, melon, or fruit ever grows, nothing that nourishes the human being. Those who are desirous of attaining unto it must first rid themselves of appetite, in the same manner as the Taoists who practise breathing exercises and claim that they can thereby live without food. The first stages of the journey are unendurably hard; but if fortitude should urge the traveller on, the destination may be reached within less than ten days. The entrance will take him into an open bright country which looks as if it were a new universe. Then management falls into disuse and thought comes to a stop. There is no occasion for hustle and bustle, no need for paying calls. One becomes completely at ease where one is beyond the reach of the cries of one's children, the vituperation of one's wife and concubines, and all manner of sarcasm, insult, frivolity, and derision that human society inflicts. But in spite of all these benefits, the common people, minding the hardship encountered in the initial stages of the journey, strive with every possible means to

[31] The amount paid by the *Ch'en Pao* was revealed in his interview with Li, Li K'e-ch'ang, *op. cit.* The amount paid by the school in Wusih is given in Shang-kuan Ai-ming, *op. cit.*, p. 3.

[32] *Kuan T'ung: O Hsiang Chi* can be found in many anthologies. My source is *Han Fang Lou Ku Chin Wen Ch'ao*, Vol. 86.

avoid the road that will take them thither. If, as ill luck would
have it, they come within sight of it, they will become regretful
and allow themselves to be dissuaded from proceeding further.
Therefore the land is barred to all but those who go against or
deviate from the ways of the world, or those who choose the paths
of integrity, honour, propriety and righteousness. Nevertheless,
unless they are unshakable in their determination to accept death
for the sake of truth they will turn back even when they have
almost arrived.

Ch'iu-pai replied to his goodhearted friends who tried to dissuade
him from making the trip:[33]

> I shall find in the Soviet Union my Land of Hunger. Let us ignore
> the facts of hunger and coldness, that there one will have nothing
> to eat, nothing to wear, etc. The significant fact is that this is the
> first country that has realised socialist revolution: it is the centre
> of world revolution where the western and eastern cultures meet.
> I shall not be troubled by the means I take to make the trip pos-
> sible. . . . I know I am not qualified for the task assigned me but
> I'll go as a newspaper correspondent. I should not accept the offer
> but I have accepted it. Nor shall I ask excuse for my ambition in
> my attempt to lead our thoughts with my power of persuasion to
> the right path out of the ideological confusions as reflected in the
> Ch'en Pao. I believe there is no private possession of thought, and
> that's why I have made up my mind to go.

When Ch'ü took an early train the next morning for Manchuria,
he was fired with enthusiasm, not unmixed with some pride in the
sacrifices he was ready to make but melancholy, too, at the thought
that he would miss all that was hateful and dear to him in China.
He could feel the emotions that assailed him, but he could not see
the essential conflict in his attitude. To plunge into the revolution
if only to report on it (and his reports were to clear the ideological
confusions produced by the May Fourth Movement in China) and
at the same time to satisfy the reporter's "inner urge"—there was
nothing incompatible so far as he could see then, between the two-
fold purposes of his mission. He was not yet fully aware of the
scope or variety of his "inner demands." We see from his own
statements how he longed for many other things that a revolution-

[33] *Journey, Collected Works,* p. 27.

ary should never tolerate. Even when he was talking about the bright future, about a universe filled with "red light" and a land covered with "red flowers stained in blood," [34] he found it hard to sever his ties with the "Land of Black Sweetness," [35] the old China with its intricate family relationships and aesthetic ideals. He had to resist the tender love he felt for all the persons, places and things he had held dear since childhood. Such human weaknesses must be a part of his "inner demands," but what an impediment they turned out to be to his "urge" for spreading the socialist revolution! When the living conditions in the Land of Hunger became hard to bear, his yearning for the Land of Black Sweetness grew strong. For the two terms represent two different attitudes of life, two sets of values, and he was caught in between. The conflict would continue to torment him throughout his life.

Meanwhile, before he left China, he had a ritual to perform, bidding farewell to his relatives and friends. He spent a night in Tsinan, Shantung, with his father, then Tientsin and back to Peking. The relatives whom he visited all spoke about their uneasy circumstances and unhappy family life. He had to write to obtain extension for the family debts in his native town. (It is surprising that this should have been left to the care of the son, who had barely attained manhood, rather than the father.) His exercises in classical poetry and prose were collected and edited at his father's behest.[36] He wrote to the friends of his childhood as if he would see them no more. "The meaning of my departure from China was tantamount to 'renunciation of the world'" (*ch'u shih*).[37] I did not know when I should come back once I had left, and I do not care about the loss of my life. My letters were written with such an intent, therefore, that they should carry a farewell forever." [38] The premonition would prove to be correct, for when he returned more than two years later, he had already entered a "new life." The

[34] Introduction, *ibid.* p. 5.
[35] Hei T'ien Hsiang connotes "sleep." In the Introduction, *ibid.* pp. 3–5, he characterises the lethargic, comfort-loving Chinese as "sleepers."
[36] I don't know whether the collection has even been published.
[37] Introduction, *Journey, op. cit.,* p. 15.
[38] *Ibid.* p. 16.

affectionate youth who felt so keenly about the saddening effects of
the autumnal wind, the rustling willows and reeds, the withered
grass, and the darkening clouds which accentuated the several scenes
of parting, was to come home a Communist whose revolutionary
duties would forbid him to resume his normal relationships.

One of the friends he visited in Tientsin was Chang T'ai-lei, a
schoolmate in the Changchow High School. Chang would play an
important part in Ch'ü's life. It was he who introduced Ch'ü into
the Communist Party. And it was he who was to die in the Canton
Insurrection in 1927 as victim of Ch'ü's Policy of Riots. In 1920,
Chang was already a member of the Socialist Youth Corps.[39] Ch'ü
must have found something exciting in the radical views of his
chum. The two young men, with two other friends, discussed
"Chinese social life" for a whole night.

The two co-founders of *Humanité,* Cheng Chen-to and Keng Chi-
chih who was to win fame as a translator of Russian literature, presented Ch'ü with a farewell poem typical of the doggerel that passed
under the name of "new poetry" at that time:[40]

The whistle is blowing, once and again, to hurry;
The wheels are rolling, rolling, slowly.

[39] "His original name was Chang T'ai-lai, also Ch'un-mu. He changed it to
Chang T'ai-lei after he joined the revolution." Wang I-chih (Chang's widow):
"In Memoriam, T'ai-lei." *Red Flags Are Flying,* Vol. V, p. 13. Ch'ü gave his
name as Chang T'ai-lai, *ibid.* p. 28.

Chang's activities in 1920 are summarised in *Men and Politics in Modern
China,* Fifty Preliminary Biographies, edited by Howard L. Boorman (New
York: Columbia University, 1960): "By 1920 he had become active in radical politics in Shanghai. In August of that year when Ch'en Tu-hsiu, with
the help of Voitinsky, organised the Chinese Socialist Youth Corps, Chang
became one of its first members. . . . He was in Tientsin in October 1920
when Ch'ü Ch'iu-pai, then not yet committed to Communism, passed through
there on his way to Russia. Chang was then probably assisting Li Ta-chao in
organising in north China a Socialist Youth Corps modelled after the one
which had been set up earlier in Shanghai" (p. 20). About Chang's role in
introducing Ch'ü into the Communist Party. "February 1922. Ch'iu-pai
joined the Communist Party through the recommendation of Comrade Chang
T'ai-lei." Yang Chih-hua, *op. cit.,* p. 27. Ch'ü himself added Chang Kuo-t'ao
in his interview with Li. "The next year (1921), Chang Kuo-t'ao, Chang T'ai-
lei, etc., came to Russia. They introduced me into the Communist Party."
[40] *Journey, Collected Works,* Vol. 1, pp. 28–30.

> You are going . . .
> Going into the Red Light . . .
> The whistle has broken our hearts,
> Our hearts are rolling away with the wheels.

The epistle by his philosophical uncle Ch'ü Shih-ying was also in character. Besides quotations from Tagore and Bergson, two of the most popular thinkers in 1920, it offered some comforting thoughts:[41]

> We are going to part for just a little while,
> But I believe:
> We are still living in the great harmony of the universe.
> Harmony—Oneness. . . .

In the poem that Ch'iu-pai sent back to them are found the significant lines:[42]

> To urge me ahead, the Universal Will;
> To greet me, the Natural Harmony.
>   If it is said,
>   Honey is extracted from flowers,
> And flowers wither after honey is made,
> But turn your head and look . . .
> What flourishing and what splendor!

If Ch'iu-pai had formulated any theory of his own out of his philosophical studies, it was an eclecticism, a cross of Ch'ü Shih-ying's idealism and Chang T'ai-lei's materialism. His earlier "misanthropic views" had given way to optimism. He accepted the inevitability of socialist revolution, but that, to him, was more a stage in spiritual evolution than a necessity conditioned by economic factors. In interpreting historical materialism in a metaphysical framework of Buddhism plus Bergsonianism, he was advancing a heresy in the pure Marxist's eye. He philosophised on several occasions in the two books, but with the dominant concepts of Universal Will and Current of Life, he always seems to favour a dualism, if not downright idealism. This, of course, he had to drop after he joined the Communist Party. But then perhaps metaphysical speculation ceased to be of any interest to him. While still in China, Ch'ü wrote:

[41] *Ibid.* p. 31.
[42] *Ibid.* p. 33.

The Living Force in the universe, or the Third One [besides subjectivity and objectivity] is present everywhere and complete in itself. It is the Prime Mover, which is neither itself moving nor rests stable. The harmony felt in a person's heart and the echoes he finds in his environment are the proofs of the universal truth. As the living force, it does not attach itself to appearances, but it is found in appearances. Thus its reflections can be perceived. It exists in personality and in society; but it also exists in non-personality and in non-society. It seems to be the Third One but it is not the Third One.[43]

The sacredness of labour and paradise is not the product of the pen of the intelligentsia. It is to be found in the progress of the actual life of the proletariat. Spiritual comfort, the harmony between matter and mind—when the "universal motions" reflect upon and stimulate each other—is made possible by nothing but the Inner Strength of the human being. The motive behind the evolution of an individual, a race, or mankind as a whole is the necessity for, or the demands made upon, the Inner Strength to cope with economic life.[44]

In the *Postscript* to the *Journey to the Land of Hunger* (dated October 1921, when he had been nine months in Moscow), Ch'ü still manifested a predilection for Buddhistic concepts and symbols.

Human history throughout the centuries is but a series of visions, one nightmare quickly succeeded by another, which appears in one's consciousness as in the moment when the blood is rushing to the heart. Therefore we cannot have more than faint impressions of them. Social phenomena, with all their endless involvements and myriad reflections, cannot also but leave faint traces, because they are only so many undulations of the heart-wave. Everything in human life rests on Reality, just as so many rivers find their home in the heart-sea. . . . The heart-sea is ever in motion and the heart-wave heaves and rolls in every possible manner. They compose the phantasmagoric world of ours. The closer we are to awakening, the more real, and probably also the more terrible, the dreams appear. Since the heart-sea is all pervasive, so the world is in one dream; but since the heart-waves rise and fall in all grotesque shapes, the starlight they catch glitters with a brilliance that is different from here to there. . . . [Then the author stretches the metaphors and alludes to himself.] So long as the compass points

[43] *Ibid.* p. 11.
[44] *Ibid.* p. 44.

to the right direction I shall some day make a circuit of the universal heart-sea and return to my real Homeland.[45]

In another entry, dated December 24, 1921, only two months before he became a Communist, he wrote:

Unite Ego with Non-Ego and there is likeness. Oppose Ego to Non-Ego and there is the awareness of the uniqueness of personality.

There must be a way to unite the two; and that is Love.

It is nothing censurable for a child to like to play. But if he does not know that there is Mother's bosom for him to return to, then he will become lost in his play. He will experience fear. Our prideful nature, if not improved by Love, will become likewise our curse.[46]

Rhapsodical and obscure musings like these and, more prominently, the "mood pieces" outbalance factual reports in the two books, especially the second one which covers an eventful year (February 1921 to March 1922) spent mainly in Moscow.[47] One wonders whether Ch'ü's heart responded to the social upheavals and human sacrifices with the same force as it responded, say, to the landscape. He never lost his feelings for natural scenery. Lake Baikal, the Urals and the Russian steppes, for instance, with their weird bleakness and their hidden gigantic power braving the rigours of winter, caught his imagination and he left some vivid passages of writing into which he unmistakably put his heart. One would

[45] *Ibid.* pp. 90–91.

[46] *History of the Heart, Collected Works,* Vol. 1, p. 173.

[47] More information, he said, was provided in a third book, *On Russian Revolution,* which I have not had a chance to read. But since Ch'ü described the book as "a social science treatise," containing "observations on history and interpretations of institutions" it could not have been much help to our understanding of his personal life. "Comrade Ch'iu-po wrote another book of studies on Soviet socialism. It was sold to a certain publisher. But under the pressure of the Northern Warlords and then the KMT Government, it never had a chance of getting published. The MS. was destroyed in a fire during the war in Shanghai in 1932." *A Chronological Catalogue of Ch'u Ch'iu-pai's Writings and Translations (Ch'ü Ch'iu-pai chu I-hsi Nien Mu-lu),* compiled by Ting Ching-t'ang and Wen Ts'ao (Shanghai: Jen-min Ch'u-pan She, 1959), p. 99.

The title Ch'ü used was *O-lo-ssu Ko-ming Lun.* Hsiao San said it was "A Revolutionary History of New Russia" ("Hsin O Ko-ming Shih"). The publisher identified was the Commercial Press, *ibid.* p. 98. See also note 3.

expect this kind of vividness in his descriptions of the human scenes of the revolution, but judging from the style, his imagination was not much stirred by what he had gone to such great lengths to see. His books are not enlivened by the portrait of a single memorable character, or a single memorable scene of mass movement which can justify his illusions about the Communist revolution. The flat and perfunctory style only indicates that he was not thrilled or enraptured by what he was seeing, for he could be more effective when he chose to be so. A demonstration in the Red Square is dismissed in two or three lines.

> A vast field, where thousands of Red Army, infantry, cavalry, artillery, the militia units of the labour, the military training units of the Communist Party, workers both men and women, children and youths, paraded in formations. Eulogies from the delegates of various nations. Shouts of cheer.[48]

Lenin was faintly etched in his memory, so far as his reports indicate, as one whose large head made an impressive silhouette and whose tone of voice sounded "determined." [49] The Kremlin, the setting of many interviews and conferences, was noted for its "magnificent, tall walls and splendid old architecture," and also, as he went on in his absent-minded exploration, for its "smooth, shining floor, resplendent columns and sculptures by famous Italian artists." [50] He did not reserve his literary skill for the revolutionary fervour of the ordinary people either. The general impression is that none of them seemed either happy or enthusiastic about what the revolutionists were doing in their name.

But then neither was our author happy. The vast Eurasian country was truly a Land of Hunger. Famine left its terrible scars everywhere, and the New Economic Policy, recently put into effect, could at best elicit some faint shadows of a grim smile out of the ubiquitous gloom. The miserable material conditions turned his attention further inward. It was only by accident that he did not lose his enthusiasm altogether. But his health deteriorated so badly that he became almost

[48] *History of the Heart, op. cit.,* p. 127.
[49] *Ibid.* pp. 128–29.

a human wreck at the time when he was accepted into the ranks of the Communists.

A Journey to the Land of Hunger and the *History of the Heart in the Red Capital* are records of his moods, registered in a language that borrows heavily from the vocabulary of Chinese lyrics and Buddhistic scriptures that made up the author's early studies. He did not write for the proletariat, nor for the semi-educated, but for the class to which he himself belonged: literate readers who had been brought up on classical Chinese but were now readjusting themselves under the impact of Western cultural forces. Their tastes largely determined the manner and matter of the new literature born of the May Fourth Movement.

Self-expression, a main trend in Chinese literature, was further encouraged by Western models and precepts. It has never been sufficiently emphasised what fertile soil Chinese lyricism provided for the transplantation of European romanticism, interpreted as the awakening of the individual soul. The vernacular movement, with its accompanying literary theories, facilitated the gush of sentiments from the literati and resulted in a large number of literary productions notable for eager self-expression. Clamour for fighting, for battles specified or unspecified, and for victory in the battles, a magnified projection of the writer as a hero, a lover, a martyr, or as one who feels and suffers more deeply than the rest of humanity, a stupefied and dislocated psyche which insisted on opening its wounds to the view of the world—such were the literary fashions of the twenties in China and Ch'ü was not far above the fashions.

Today, Ch'ü's two books are dated. They have the special flavour of that period when literature belonged to a small minority, when prose could be indistinguishable from poetry, or vice versa, when the *pai-hua,* while accepted as a vehicle for literary creation, had still to rely on the *wen-yen* for its richness, precision and evocative power. The best parts of Ch'ü's two books are elaborately written, too elaborate, perhaps, for the purpose of journalistic reporting. But Ch'ü's literary talent is unmistakable; he is at his lyrical best when he comes to describe his moods. The tone, the texture and the choice of words are evidently those of a man who does not want to conceal his study of classical Chinese poetry. It is an ironic comment on the cultural scene of China in the early twenties that Ch'ü's eulogy of Soviet Russia, which must be among the earliest of the kind, should be overladen with sighs of personal grief. Since it comes from Ch'ü Ch'iu-pai, this incongruity is especially revealing. We cannot know how much fire he possessed as a person, but his early writings show a sickly pallor.

IV

At about eleven o'clock at night, January 25, 1921, Ch'ü Ch'iu-pai arrived in the Yaroslavsky Vokzal of Moscow. "Under the chilly moon, and amidst the hubbub of the crowds in the railway station, I knew I was in the Land of Hunger. . . . Moscow, situated at the peak of waves of the heart-sea of the European proletariat, was surging with the warm blood of Russia labourers. . . . The child from the Orient was now feeling within him the rise of his inner strength." [51]

If his "inner strength" rose at the end of the long journey which took about two months to complete, it did not sustain him for long. There were no doubt periods, during his stay in Moscow, of concentrated, dispassionate study which produced his third book and the series of informative articles published in the *Ch'en Pao*.[52] There were exciting moments too: his meeting with Lenin, for instance, and what was more important, his reunion with Chang T'ai-lei, but they are summarily dealt with, if not entirely left out, in the *History of the Heart*. The dominant tone of the book is melancholy.

As a visitor with a regular source of income, Ch'iu-pai did not have to share the fate of the famished Soviet masses in the terrible year of 1921. He could buy whatever was sold on the market under the N.E.P. of March that year before he had exhausted the private hoard he had brought with him from China. Then, at the newly established University of the Toilers of the Far East, he obtained a position as an

[51] *Journey, op. cit.*, p. 84.
[52] The *Introduction to Periodicals, op. cit.*, has 14 titles of Ch'ü's correspondence on serious subjects published in the *Ch'en Pao* from June 1921 to November 1922. For the dates of these and other articles, see Ting and Wen, *op. cit.*

interpreter and lecturer which may have paid him handsomely. One of the old-time students reminisces how Ch'ü used to invite them to a rice dinner. They relished it, as a delicious change from the black bread which was their sole sustenance, but they wondered where he got the rice.[53]

Ch'iu-pai's unhappiness was induced by illness, loneliness, and the cheerless aspects of life, as well as nature, in Russia. His was not simply the case of a sensitive, homesick youth, in an unpleasant alien country, for his ideals were embodied in its very unpleasantness. He could quit the unlovely place, but he could not so easily leave his ideals behind. The Bolshevik revolution, still at an experimental stage, had few solid achievements to provide cheer and comfort, while the disconcerting evidence of public discontent or apathy was abundant. The necessity of defending it in writing, to convince himself no less than the readers in China of the truth and goodness of all that was going on, must have caused considerable inner strain. The hard facts of revolution, which had been forced upon his attention ever since he entered Siberia, had sobered the hot-headed youth of the May Fourth Movement. Natural harmony, once a basic tenet of his juvenile metaphysics, was nowhere to be found. Each of the two personalities within him was demanding undivided allegiance but to pay them equal attention was impossible. One was to follow his natural inclination, to satisfy the longing for mildness, tenderness, pretty objects and cosy atmosphere; the other was to pursue what reason taught to be right, to accept unquestioningly the revolution in its wholeness, together with the harshness, ugliness and abnormality that accompanied it. If no compromise could be effected, he had to make a choice. It is remarkable that he joined the Communist Party at a time when his physical strength was at its lowest ebb, when what he needed was apparently more rest, not more struggle. But for him there would be no rest unless he attained peace of mind. By becoming a Communist, he entered a new life. He had been weak and solitary, but now he was to be supported by the organised strength of the Party. He had been divided within himself, but now

[53] Wang Hung-hsün, "Wei-ta te shih-yüeh sheng-li" ("The Baptism of the Great October"), *Red Flags Are Flying*, Vol. 4.

the revolutionary in him could dominate. His sleepless agony during those critical months before he joined the Party was a symptom of this inner struggle.

The first crisis came around August. In a short rhapsody, dated August 5, he wrote:

> A few days ago, the doctor found a lesion in my left lung and advised me to go home. Wasn't it that I again spat blood yesterday? I was laid up for one month in July,[54] and I felt that I had become lifeless, that my soul was wearing away. . . . Oh! return to me my character, return to me the energy I would need for social service! Alas! the wind, the cold, and the thick snow of the North, the black bread and the rotten meat that makes up one's nourishment.
>
> By ten thousand *li* I am separated from home—how can I enjoy tenderness and the affection once more? The manners, the climate, the sky are all so different from those at home. A whiteness that fills up the universe for five long months—the weird, phantom-like drifts of snow—the pressure in the air that almost deprives one of the power of breathing. Ice—snow—storm—how can those compare, as spiritual nourishments, with the scenes of the South of the Yangtze—the bright, colourful spring-time and the autumnal flowers, in rich array, each trying to surpass the other?
>
> But the culture and the fertility of the South is doomed. It will turn into, nay, it has already become, a colony. The British overlords are there. . . .
>
> Rising with obscure thoughts in a delirium, with anxiety and fever, there appear the indistinct shadowy dreams of the South: the golden flowers of the rape, the translucent pond, the peach blossoms. . . .
>
> Alas, the mind is unfixed, the nostalgic dreams are haunting to no purpose. I am gone far in illness, or am I?[55]

Ch'ü wrote a poem "Moon of the East" on the cloudy night of September 16 (the Mid-Autumn Festival in Chinese Calendar). It contains not one cheering note, but suggests unmistakably a disappointment in his "inner demands" symbolised by the hidden moon.

> Wandering over ten thousand *li*, here in this land of hunger and cold,

[54] The Third Congress of the Comintern was held June 22 to July 12, 1921. Georg von Rauch, *A History of Soviet Russia* (New York: Praeger, 1959). Ch'ü wrote a brief report on it on July 6. He may have fallen ill afterwards.

[55] *History of the Heart, op. cit.*, pp. 129–30.

It is said that "Snowfall begins in the eighth moon under the Barbary sky";
Though nothing here but the dreary autumnal touches, the subtle chilliness.
But my "Moon of the East" is hidden, behind the clouds of the Red Capital.

.   .   .   .   .   .

Roundness, the perfect shape, will appear only in dreams,
Memory is hard to bear under the lamp.
My regret is for the thickening cloud,
Which allows not a single beam of hope to penetrate.[56]

Feverish, coughing and spitting blood, Ch'ü felt that he was too ill to work. His growing awareness of his incompetence for newspaper work had compelled him to consider terminating his service with *Ch'en Pao*. Nine days after he composed the poem, he wrote to Yü Sung-hua who had left in May that he was determined to go home. Yü had left because he did not know Russian, but now in Berlin he probably could better discharge his duties as a foreign correspondent. It seemed that of the three correspondents in Moscow Ch'ü alone would end up in ignominious failure. But he was not to admit defeat so soon. He procrastinated for the ostensible reason of difficulties of transportation. The Trans-Siberian Railway still was not running on time and his luggage was greatly increased by the books he had acquired. Then he cancelled the plan altogether and did not leave until some fifteen months later in December 1922.

Ch'ü's hesitation to pack saved for the Chinese Communist Party one of its early leaders. It is hard to conceive how he could have regained his self-confidence if he had departed at that time, out of disgust, if not entirely with Russia, at least with himself. Though it is hard to verify the dates, it might have been when he had sunk to the lowest depths of dejection that the University of the Toilers of the East offered him a job.[57] The Chinese students who were to attend that university had arrived,[58] about 42 in all, the élite of

[56] *Ibid.* pp. 136–38.
[57] Wang Hung-hsün mentions that the university was established in summer and class started in the autumn. By autumn he might mean September.
[58] Ts'ao Tsing-hua, known for his translations from Russian, has an interesting article about his difficulties with the Russian language while attending the

a rising generation, the flower of the revolutionary spirit, but whatever credentials they carried with them, they were handicapped by
their slight acquaintance with the Russian language. They could not
follow lectures in Russian; their reading ability was doubtful. No
good Russian-Chinese dictionary was then available, the one published in Harbin being unreliable. Of the Russian faculty, only one
member, V. S. Kolokolov, spoke Chinese. But in the opinion of
Ch'ü, not even Kolokolov, who was brought up in China and had
a Chinese name, could do a fluent job of interpretation.[59] The language problem might have seriously retarded the training programme
and upset the time-table for world revolution prepared by the Kremlin. To avoid the delay, somebody suggested the names of the two
Chinese correspondents, and so both Ch'ü and Li were hired.

Ch'ü was to teach Russian as well as to prepare a Chinese version
of the courses in indoctrination. The additional work would of course
do his health no good. But its rewards were more than monetary.
He could now live independently of the *Ch'en Pao*. He was brought
into closer contact with Communists, both the veteran Russian and
the fledgling Chinese, and their company might somehow relieve his
loneliness. The homework he did for the indoctrination courses also
imparted a meaning to his life as nothing else could. In struggling
with ideological matters where a mistake in translation might be
viewed as heresy, he was gradually led into the arcana of orthodox
Marxism-Leninism. He was no more an amateur who would compound Marx with Buddha and Bergson. He was receiving strict

University of Toilers. "Tien-ti I Ch'iu-pai" ("Tidbits of My Reminiscences of
Ch'iu-pai"), *Wen I Pao*, No. 11, June 15, 1955.

Liu Shao-ch'i, in a rare reminiscent mood, recalls, in an address to the mass
meeting for Soviet-Chinese Amity, held in Moscow on December 7, 1960,
how he travelled from China to Russia in the spring of 1921, together with
other members of Youth Corps, dozens in number. It took three months for
the train to reach Moscow from Vladivostok. He joined the Communist Party
in the winter of that year. (*People's Daily*, December 9, 1960.) He was probably one of the students.

[59] When Ch'ü first arrived in Moscow, he received help from Kolokolov, official interpreter assigned by the Commissariat for Foreign Affairs. Ch'ü said
that Kolokolov did not translate well, but they became fast friends anyhow.
Journey, op. cit., p. 88.

theoretical training, a necessary preparation for the revolutionary career to come.

But he still had chinks in his armour to mend, monsters to slay and enemies to subdue before the quest for supreme Marxist-Leninist truth could be accomplished. Homesickness, quite unworthy of a revolutionist, was still doing its worst to harass him. For more than six months he had been anxiously expecting a letter from his home. He became ashamed of his weakness. He observed:

> A part of my ego was becoming strange. The "social self" within me was mocking at me and laughing at me from the shadows of darkness.[60]

When in November he finally received a letter from his brother which bore a March postmark, he burst into tears. A phrase meant to be comforting particularly struck him. What did it mean that "everybody at home is well"? Was not his brother sensible enough to see that they had no more home of their own, that their mother had been killed by poverty, "leaving her tender love as her only legacy," that the brothers were scattered, living as parasites, that his own "home" was now this Land of Hunger, that the old gentry class of China was doomed? The questions that had previously troubled him rushed back in the excitement of drinking in the long anticipated letter from "home." But the answer to them, if once vague now became clearer:

> There will be a day, all the gentry class will be proletarianised. Then we shall do whatever we can do. There will be such a day.[61]

On December 12, he was moved to a sanatorium. There, his mind became more restless. He had been comparing himself to Raskolnikov, who always "asked more of life." [62] Now he was haunted by another hero of Russian fiction, Rudin, the ineffectual intellectual. He found that the conflict between heart and head, between romanticism and realism had turned him into what Turgenev called a "superfluous man."

[60] *History of the Heart, op. cit.,* p. 161.
[61] *Ibid.* p. 164.
[62] *Ibid.* p. 166.

Alas! Regret, lamentation, sorrow. . . . I used to regard myself as unusual, but looking back, can I find anything unusual about me? How ridiculous! "What indeed can you do? Why not identify yourself with the masses?" Reason has reached a conclusion, but the force of inertia is too great.[63]

In the antiseptic quietness of the hospital bed, he also had his moments of peace—peace not emerging as a solution to his problems, but rather a faint recapitulation of the days of innocence when the conflict had not yet been so sharply formed. He would imagine himself strolling under the willows along the Nan-wan-tsu, in Peking. In another instant, he was revisiting the country home of his aunt in a village outside the Northern Gate of Changchow, snugly ensconced in the bend of the Bracelet Creek.[64] In January 1922, he translated two poems by Tyutchev, one entitled *A Moment* and the other, the much celebrated *Silentium*.[65] The mystic joy and the sense of "oneness with nature" contained in them might bring relief to a mind more diseased, perhaps, than the body. But as a stretch of agonised introspection would follow a transient mood of lyrical serenity, he had to disown them both.

The source of his restlessness as he repeatedly discovered, was his over-individualised self. What he learned from Turgenev (the danger of not identifying himself with the masses) and from the petty officer of the Red Army (to render service to others in order to forget about himself) would become for him the supreme lesson in life, something more valuable than the treatment of his tuberculosis. Sometime in January he was allowed to leave the sanatorium to attend the Congress of the Toilers of the Far East.[66] He felt a

[63] *Ibid.* p. 171.

[64] *Ibid. Huan-hsi* (*About Bracelet Creek*), see Shang-kuan Ai-ming, *op. cit.*

[65] *History of the Heart, op. cit.*, pp. 175–78.

[66] "After the first session of the Conference in Irkutsk [held in November 1921] its delegates travelled to Moscow and then to Petrograd, where they were joined by new delegates. Their deliberation continued from January 21 to January 27, as the First Congress of Toilers of the Far East." Eudin, X. J., and R. C. North, *Soviet Russia and the East, 1920–1927* (Stanford University Press, 1957), pp. 145–46. Ch'ü apparently did not go to Irkutsk, though he attended the meetings held in Moscow and Petrograd.

Here I have to argue with Wen Chi-tse about Ch'ü's status at that time. Said Wen: "In early February 1922, Comrade Chang T'ai-lei, a founding

momentary exultation at the release from the regimen of the sanatorium. The Congress itself revived his enthusiasm. Upon this he wrote an essay, "Morning Glory," which perhaps is more symptomatic of a hectic brain than of a real sense of joy.

> Look at the Far East, how bright the purple and red flames shine forth as they spin! The blazing clouds, just sprouting, but how roaringly they shoot towards the firmament! How fierce, how dazzling, the wheel of light is spinning! Ah, morning glory, morning glory! [67]

---

member of the Chinese Communist Party, came to Moscow. Through his introduction, Comrade Ch'ü joined the CCP. After that, he together with Chang T'ai-lei and other comrades, was appointed by the Party to attend the Congress of the Peoples of the Far East, in the spring of 1922." Wen, *op. cit.*, p. 90.

This statement is questionable on several points:

(a) Chang T'ai-lei was very active in Russia throughout 1921. It was he who drafted the invitation to the Congress. He conferred with the Far Eastern Secretariat in Irkutsk, and debated with M. N. Roy in the Third Congress of the Comintern; Eudin and North, *op. cit.*, pp. 139–47. Ch'ü must have seen him on the occasion of the Comintern Congress though he was silent on the subject in the *History of the Heart*. What did they talk about then? Did Chang try then to introduce Ch'ü into the Party?

(b) If Ch'ü joined the Party as late as February 1922, then it was after, and not before, he attended the Congress of the Peoples of the Far East, which, according to the Russian sources quoted by Eudin and North, was held in January.

(c) Again, if Ch'ü did not join the Party until February, then he attended the Congress as a "non-Party" delegate (even possibly as an interpreter.) He could not share the official duties with Chang T'ai-lei who was already a member of the CCP. There were fourteen "non-Party" members in the Chinese delegation. Allen S. Whiting, *Soviet Policies in China, 1917–1924* (New York: Columbia University Press, 1953), p. 299.

Hsiao San is likewise confused on these points: "In the spring [which month?] of 1922, the Congress of the Peoples of the Far East was convened in Moscow. Comrade Ch'iu-pai and others, representing revolutionary organisations in China, actively participated. At that time, Lenin showed love and respect towards Comrade Ch'iu-po." *Op. cit.*, p. 98.

Does the following remark made by Ch'ü on December 3, 1921, suggest that he was then no more a fellow-traveller but a member of the Communist Party? "Of course I am only a common foot-soldier, but I am enrolled with the pioneers of the world cultural movement which will not only open a new road for the world but also restore glory to ancient China." *History of the Heart, op. cit.*, p. 166.

[67] *Ibid.* p. 178.

Ch'ü followed the delegates to Petrograd as the meeting place was shifted and there again with a typical absent-mindedness he noted impressions of the meeting:

> The sombre, dim lights filled the hall, but the red light shone forth in every direction. The voice of the Orientals, cheers, shouts, applause, the "Internationale." [68]

After the meeting, he tried to walk two *verst*. Under the arctic night, he found the freezing air unbearably oppressive. He met a woman (probably another delegate), who supported him all the way back to the hotel. Blood again came out with the cough. He was laid up for four or five days, regretting the opportunity he missed to report on the city of Peter. On February 7, senseless, he was carried back to Moscow, and the routine of the sanatorium started again.

Communist sources, with questionable authority, assert that Ch'ü Ch'iu-pai joined the Communist Party in February 1922.[69] From Ch'ü's own accounts, February of that year could possibly have been the climacteric month. For two or three days before he collapsed in a Petrograd hotel, he was actively enjoying the leave of absence granted by the sanatorium. It was probably on one of those days that he took the decisive step. But we have to point out that he spent the remainder of the month in sick bed and that his moods were not altogether improved by his newly won status. One week after he was removed back to Moscow, *i.e.*, on the thirteenth, he wrote "Snow in Russia," a poem which, especially if read side by side with the more famous and more vigorous work on snow by Mao Tse-tung, revealed a soul that was miserably shrinking, groan-

[68] *Ibid.* p. 181.
[69] *Cf.* Yang Chih-hua and Wen Chi-tse. Lu Ting-i, Minister of Propaganda, Chinese Communist Party, reported at Ch'ü's funeral in 1955 that Ch'ü joined the Party in 1922, but no month was given, *People's Daily,* June 19, 1955. Ch'ü's own account is vague. It only says that he joined the Party after his meeting with Chang Kuo-t'ao, Chang T'ai-lei, etc. It might be either 1921 or 1922.

Hsüeh-hua, who published the *Superfluous Words,* offers another date, which is plausible. "In May 1921, Chang T'ai-lei came to Moscow and recommended him to the Communist Party. In September, as Ch'ü was employed by the University of Toilers, he became a regular member of the Party." *I-ching Fortnightly,* Vol. II, No. 25, p. 19, March 5, 1937.

ing and perplexed by the spectacle of a "vast, white dream" that seemed to be the only thing left of the living universe.[70] He was still recuperating in the sanatorium on March 20, the day he wrote the concluding piece of the *History of the Heart*. It was remarkable for a more optimistic tone:[71]

> The world is real; man is living.
> The real world must be made to appear from the dreamlike life. Everything in reality is living; everything that is living is also real. Since activities for the new culture are in the real world, those who work in the real world are also in the midst of life. They are all living.

V

How much our knowledge about the Communist movement in the 20s and the 30s would be enriched if Ch'ü Ch'iu-pai had continued to keep a record of his inmost thoughts after he had joined the Party. But he had to break off the habit. To prattle away the secrets of his revolutionary activities would be tantamount to treacherous betrayal. Even in the *History of the Heart*, he was careful not to say a thing about Chang Kuo-t'ao, Chang T'ai-lei and other Chinese visitors who came to Moscow to confer with the Third International. If he did not successfully get rid of the doubts, worries and longing for the amenities of life, he had to conceal them so as not to jeopardise his position in the Party. That he should sanction the publication of the *History of the Heart*, without expunging the sections that smack more of individualism than of Marxism, is sufficient indication that he did not want his past buried. If that book succeeded in arousing admiration for Soviet Russia, it would nevertheless have a counter-productive effect in promoting the self-centered, maudlin tendencies of new literature in China. In the introduction to the book, dated August 4, 1923, he advanced the heretical opinion that literature should be allowed to serve the individual. "The personality of the author should be somehow brought forth in a literary work." [72]

---

[70] *History of the Heart, op. cit.*, pp. 182–83.
[71] *Ibid.* pp. 194–95.
[72] *Ibid.* p. 97.

Even though he was already a member of the Central Committee of the Chinese Communist Party when he wrote this, it is obvious that his thoughts still needed to be corrected. And they were corrected, to a considerable degree. There is hardly any evidence of the intrusion of the author's personality in the large body of theoretical studies and propaganda he later produced. It should have gratified him to think that of all his bodily and spiritual weaknesses, he conquered at least one: exhibitionism.

In 1933, when he was no more a commanding figure in the Party as a result of intra-party strife, he wrote an essay, curiously indicative of a relapse into the dark moods with which we are familiar. Here again he was writing a chapter, though a brief one, of the history of the heart. It is one of a group of thirteen essays which he wrote while living in close company with Lu Hsün. To hide their authorship, for Ch'ü was on the "wanted list," Lu Hsün allowed them to be published under one or another of his own numerous pseudonyms. Lu Hsün went so far in assuming the responsibility for them that he included them in a collection of his own works. All except one of the thirteen essays by Ch'ü are found today in Lu Hsün's books, and the one exception is entitled "Childhood." There must be something in its weak sentimentality that even a fellow-traveling "fighter" like Lu Hsün would find objectionable. That it should come from the pen of a true Communist is almost inconceivable.

> Those who have not found meaning in their life hold especially dear their youth and childhood. Romantic reminiscences do not arise from a new discovery that childhood is really wonderful, but from a feeling of decline that comes after one has reached middle age. . . . He who sees his life "floating away like a dream" is also the one who has taken much from the world but given back little. Such a man will inevitably feel a death-like fatigue, so much so that he does not have even the strength to take anything more from the world. The sad awareness of age and impotence will weigh on him like lead.
>
> When one cannot move ahead one wants to retrace his footsteps, to recover the ground that has already been travelled. I wish for the return of innocence so that I might regain the joy of learning. How sorrowful the stoppage of growth is!

Bygones will remain bygones, and the future is yet to come. What do I mourn for? I ask myself.[73]

A far more revealing account is of course the *Superfluous Words,* which he wrote in the prison while awaiting death. This was perhaps the best time in his life to say what he liked to say about the Communist Party and himself. All scruples about his personal safety were then gone. The worst punishment he could expect for a bold statement of an unfailing, undying and ever-growing faith in Communism was death, and he was prepared for it.

On the other hand, he could not care less about what his comrades might think of him. The walls of prison had separated them from him and if he chose to do so, he could use personal rather than Party standards in reviewing his past. As it turned out, in the *Superflous Words,* an intimate autobiography, it is not Ch'ü the apologist for Marxism, but Ch'ü the self-analyst, that is speaking. But we must guard against a rash conclusion that he was finally disenchanted. He perhaps remained a Marxist to his death, one who might not find Marxism entirely satisfactory, yet a Marxist nonetheless. He confessed in unequivocal terms to his "dual personality" and we may accept him as such: a revolutionary hypochondriac, a socialist-minded aesthete, a sentimental hater of the old society, a practitioner of Bodhisattvahood trained in Moscow, a Pilgrim in quest of the Land of Hunger who could not stand black bread, or, in a word, a tender-hearted Communist. *Superfluous Words* does not register a new development in his character; it only confirms our impression of him through his two early books. Ch'ü Ch'iu-pai the Secretary of the Party, the theoretician, the leading leftist writer, or Ch'ü Ch'iu-pai the prisoner remained essentially Ch'ü Ch'iu-pai the young man who sighed over the clouded moon in Moscow and uttered a despairing cry at the mysterious, appalling Russian snow.

In *Superfluous Words* Ch'ü repeatedly emphasises his ineptitude and distaste for political work. He said he must classify himself with the "Man of Letters," not the writer or the literary critic in the modern sense, but a shiftless, faint-hearted and self-deceiving non-

[73] *Collected Works,* Vol. 1, pp. 441–42. Concerning the thirteen essays, see *ibid.* p. 456, note.

entity whose only strength, as the Chinese of the old days would say, lies in "singing of the wind and toying with the moon." [74] With the painful seriousness of an egotist who resents being misunderstood, he hammers on this point:

> I think that it is really a "historical misunderstanding" for a man of my disposition, capacity, and cultural training to become a leader of the Chinese Communist Party. I am no better than a "half-baked" man of letters; to this last minute I have never cured myself of my "chronic literary habits." From 1927 on I gradually lost interest in politics until I became completely unconcerned in the past year, the year I spent in Juichin. I did my work only perfunctorily; I did not even care to learn of politics on the national scale. The reason was of course on one side my poor health and lack of energy which resulted in a state of utter exhaustion, and on the other hand, my distaste for the kind of work which was contrary to my temperament and inclination but which took up more than ten years of my life when I served, first as a "political interpreter" and then as a political worker. It has been indeed a misunderstanding, a nightmare.
>
> I have no intention of clearing myself of any responsibility when I make this confession. I will never try to shirk, or for emotional reasons, to excuse or minimise my responsibility in my relations to the Communist Party or the "party-state" of the Kuomintang. I mean only to tell the truth before I die. In a word, I am a common literary man who has ironically borne the title of a leader of a certain political party for so many years. If it is not a "historical misunderstanding," then what is it? [75]

These confessions, if they can be accepted as truly from Ch'ü, will demand a reappraisal of his character and position in history. He would lose the honour due to a revolutionary and martyr. It is not suprising, therefore, that his official biographers in Communist China never use *Superfluous Words* as a source of material. They seldom mention it and apparently prefer to reject it as spurious. Hsiao San wrote in the *Lives of the Martyrs,* a collection of authorised biographies published in 1936:[76]

[74] *Ibid.* No. 27, April 5, 1937, p. 6.
[75] *Ibid.* No. 25, p. 22.
[76] Publisher unknown, p. 185. The book, "published in celebration of the Tenth Anniversary of the Chinese Communist Party," is available in the Far Eastern Library, University of Washington, Seattle.

The patriotic poems composed by Comrade Ch'iu-pai, during his imprisonment and at the time of his execution, together with his will contained in his letters, were all witnessed by newspaper reporters. Comrade Ch'iu-pai obviously wanted to deliver, through the service of the gentlemen of the press, a message to the whole nation, to make a last appeal, as he was himself bidding farewell, for resistance against Japan and national salvation. But under the pressure of reactionary forces, what appeared in the newspapers to pass for Comrade Ch'iu-pai's works after his heroic death, were not in their original form. Some letters and documents are obvious forgeries, published by the enemy for the purpose of damaging Comrade Ch'iu-pai's good name.

Hsiao alludes to the "original form" of Ch'iu-pai's works but it can be presumed that he never saw any of the poems as they were originally written. Yang Chih-hua, Ch'ü's widow, noted in 1958 in Peking:[77]

At the time, Ch'iu-pai wrote a number of poems and a book, *Superfluous Words,* but they were all taken away by the bandits [meaning the KMT].

She neither confirmed nor denied the authenticity of the poems and the book as we know them. The long letter which Ch'ü wrote to her before his death never reached her, though a "thick envelope" was seen by her mother.[78] So the Communists are themselves in the dark regarding what Ch'ü wrote in prison.

Hsiao San may not have seen *Superfluous Words* in any form when he wrote his comment for it was published for the first time in 1937, in the literary fortnightly *I-ching,* as a literary "discovery."[79]

[77] Yang Chih-hua, *op. cit.,* p. 55.

[78] A man called on her mother and displayed the envelope. Yang dared not appear to claim the letter. It might have been a trap set to arrest her. *Ibid.* p. 52.

[79] My evidence is a letter to the editors of the *I-ching,* in which a reader expressed his gratitude for being able to gain access to an important document in modern history, of which he had only heard. "About Ch'ü Ch'iu-pai" ("Kuan-yu Ch'ü Chiu-pai"), by Huang Lu-chen, *I-ching,* Vol. 2, No. 28, April 20, 1937. *Look,* a magazine published in Hong Kong, reprinted the *Superfluous Words* in 1958 (November and December). Nothing is said, however, about the history of the text. Comparing the two, I presume that the *Look* version is only a reprint of the *I-ching* version, unless they are both reprints of an identical MS. The *Superfluous Words* is mentioned as a work by

In 1937, after the Sian Incident and before the outbreak at Lukou-chiao, the KMT and the Communists were working towards a united front and there was little need for the KMT to defame a Communist leader. In reprinting *Superfluous Words*, the *I-ching* (*Vanishing Classics*), had its own reputation to consider. Its editors are known for the service they rendered to the studies of modern Chinese history. Thanks to their efforts, many documents related to the Taiping Rebellion, long unknown or thought to be lost, were rediscovered and published in the pages of the *I-ching*. It was perhaps in the same spirit that they reprinted Ch'ü's *Superfluous Words*. The good faith of the *I-ching*, so it seems to me, is beyond reproof. The only regrettable fact is that we know nothing of the person, using the pen-name Hsüeh-hua, who contributed the transcribed copy. He did not describe the circumstances under which he got hold of the work and even if it was not a hoax, we do not know whether or not the manuscript had been altered.

The one man who definitely saw the original manuscript and even read a part of it was Li K'e-ch'ang, probably one of the disappointing reporters mentioned in Hsiao San's article. From his account of an interview with Ch'ü in the prison, we can deduce the true nature of *Superfluous Words*. We know that it is not in any way critical of the KMT. It does not have a "patriotic" theme as Hsiao San might claim, for in 1935 the Communist kind of "patriotism," understood as an immediate and all-out war against Japan, was not tolerated by the KMT. If the manuscript had contained anything that might be considered subversive, inflammatory, agitating for proletarian revolution, detrimental to Sino-Japanese relations, or otherwise harmful to the KMT régime and the KMT policy, it would have been destroyed by the vigilant warder. Since the prison authorities permitted Li to take it out for a few hours, they must have

---

Ch'ü Ch'iu-pai in *Chung-kuo Wen-hua Chieh Jen-wu Ts'ing-chien* (*Who's Who in Chinese Cultural Circles*) (Peking: 1940), edited by a Japanese. No data are given. Robert S. Elegant, in his *China's Red Masters* (New York: Twayne, 1951), pp. 54–56, quotes a few passages from the *Superfluous Words* without, however, giving due credit or accepting the rest of the "confession."

thought it politically harmless.[80] When Ch'ü said that he had the intention of getting it published so as to get "a couple of hundred dollars for pocket money," [81] he must have been sure that the book stood a chance of passing the censor. He asked Li to read it carefully, "and then you will know better about my life and my recent thoughts and impressions."

Li represents Ch'ü in prison as unruffled, unalarmed, in complete command of his faculties, and spending his time reading, composing classical Chinese poetry, and carving seal-stones. People like Mao Tun[82] might still reject this as "a fanciful fabrication of the "rumour-mongers" and "a malicious aspersion of character." They might still think that their hero had been pining away defiantly in the clutches of the enemy. But this picture of calm in prison has been accepted by one of the official biographers. Wen Chi-tse wrote in 1957:[83]

> The bandits put him in solitary confinement. . . . In his blue-cloth jacket and white-cloth pants, he looked in good spirits. His attitude was leisurely composure. He spent his time partly in writing poems and off-hand essays, and partly in carving seal stones.

When Li entered the cell, at eight o'clock in the morning, June 4, 1935, Ch'ü was bending over the desk, carving a stone. He was obliging enough, talking freely about his life and various other subjects, such as Lu Hsün, Ting Ling and Hu Shih. He agreed to carve a seal for the reporter and present him with a piece of calligraphy. What he wrote down was three poems, recently composed, all very sad. One, beginning "Twenty years' floating and sinking, everything comes to nothing" was probably meant as an elegy for himself. The other two, no less elegiac, centred on his wife from whom he had not heard anything since the June of the preceding

[80] "An Interview with Ch'ü Ch'iu-pai," *Kuo-wen Chou-pao,* Vol. 12, No. 26, July 8, 1935, p. 6.

[81] *Ibid.* p. 5.

[82] Mao Tun, "Chi-nien Ch'iu-pai t'ung-chih, hsüeh-hsi Ch'iu-pai t'ung-chih" ("Commemorate Comrade Ch'iu-pai, Learn from Comrade Ch'iu-pai") *People's Daily,* June 18, 1955. Reprinted in *Hsin-hua Yueh-kan (Hsin Hua Monthly),* July 1955.

[83] Wen Chi-tse, *op. cit.,* p. 105.

year. He wondered, in one of his poems, why his "amorous thoughts were still revolving around the clouded mountains" after he had already attained, as he thought, a sort of nirvana. His wife, who was an underground agent in Shanghai, had tried to accompany him to Kiangsi, but she was ordered to stay behind. So the sentimentalist's dream of matrimonial bliss was shattered by the perversity of politics. Of course, neither husband nor wife had made any complaint. They understood their duty. But in prison, the "thousand-fold nocturnal thoughts" of the poet kept flying to his wife whose whereabouts he did not know but whose safety now mattered more to him than his own.* He had lately composed more than ten poems, all affixed on the wall of the cell. Some of them might be in higher key with a patriotic theme, as Hsiao San so firmly believed, but Li noted only these three delicate, plaintive pieces, all expressive of a lingering love for life in the face of imminent death. They are apparently the works of a man who placed his personal sorrow above the fate of his country.

But the interview is of greater interest than the poems, in as much as it bears more directly upon the "thoughts and impressions" Ch'ü said he had put into *Superfluous Words*. He told Li about the period when he was in charge of the Party after the downfall of Li Li-san.

> I have always believed that I have never rid myself of the habits of a man of letters. So I am not fit for political work. Moreover, my health has been bad and my nerves are extremely weak. Every year in the spring I suffer attacks of haemorrhage in the lungs. I said to the others, "The field is to be plowed by the buffalo, not by a horse. Now you have a horse plowing the field. I am afraid that I can show no results though I might try to use up my energy."

* Ch'ü Ch'iu-pai was married to Wang Chien-hung in Shanghai in 1923, who died shortly thereafter. In 1924, he married Yang Chih-hua, a student at Shanghai University. She had previously been the wife of Shen Chien-nung, the son of Shen Ting-i, one of the founding members of the Party in 1921. The marriage, however, ended in divorce. Yang Chih-hua, also known as Yang Hsiao-hua, was with Ch'ü in Moscow from 1928 to 1930 and in Shanghai during the early 1930's. After Ch'ü's execution she again went to Moscow. In 1937 she was assigned to work in Sinkiang, where she was arrested and imprisoned until 1946. After the Communist takeover in 1949, she held a prominent position in the All-China Federation of Trade Unions, and she became a vice chairman of the Women's Federation in 1957.—Ed.

And they said, "Before we had the buffalo, will the horse please keep on working?" Not long afterwards, the buffalos came. Ch'in Pang-hsien, Ch'en Shao-yü, Chang Wen-t'ien and others came back from Moscow.[84]

The same sentiments are expressed in different metaphors in *Superfluous Words*:

There is a saying in my native town, "to catch a crow and force him to make a nest," which means, of course, that the nest will never be made. That a mediocre man of letters, who may be even described as silly, should bear the burden of the tasks of a political leader, is indeed ridiculous, but it is a fact.[85]

When a jaded, decrepit horse is pulling a cart with a several thousand *chin* load up a steep slope in staggering steps, he cannot move back, but to climb ahead is utterly beyond his power. That was exactly my feeling when I was carrying the burden of a political leader. The fatigue from the work that I wished to stop but could not became a pressure unspeakably heavy to me. Weariness in spirit made me thirst for a "sweet" repose, so much so that my nerves became numb and I ceased to think.[86]

These parts of *Superfluous Words* agree essentially with the interview, the only difference being that the latter, in a casual style, is less intense. What stands out in *Superfluous Words*, but is not found in the interview, is his earnest request that the "historical misunderstanding," the "farce" must be stopped. To the Communists, he said that he had long ceased at heart to be their "comrade." He would rather assign himself to oblivion than continue to occupy a place in history which he did not deserve. He wished that since he had spilled out everything about his unworthiness, he should not be remembered as a martyr after his death. Of his wife, his "only dear one in life," he asked forgiveness, for not even to her had he had the courage

---

[84] *Kuo-wen Chou-pao, op. cit.*, p. 3.

Li Ang has this to say about Ch'ü's incompetence as a Communist leader: "Ch'ü was really a mediocre plotter who, as the saying goes, was not gifted with the talent to command, nor could he win admiration for his virtue." *Hung-se Wu-t'ai* (*The Red Stage*) (Chungking: Sheng-li Ch'u-pan Kung-ssu, 1941), p. 51. "Ch'ü was indeed a blockhead (*fan-t'ung*) or rice-vessel in its fullest sense. He could never carry out any plan as he wished." *Ibid.* p. 133.

[85] *I-ching, op. cit.*, No. 27, p. 9.

[86] *Ibid.* No. 26, March 20, 1937, p. 16.

to reveal his heart. He wished that she would henceforth detest him and forget him so that his soul might rest in peace.

Nothing would disconcert historians in Communist China more than this modest request, so it is only natural that they should dismiss it as a base trick of defamation. But it would be hard for them to reject *Superfluous Words* as a whole. Evidence compels us to believe that even if the work was a forgery, the KMT did not have a hand in it. For there is a conspicuous absence of anything that may be remotely interpreted as a reconciliation with the KMT. A forger in the service of the "reactionary forces" would not miss the opportunity to please his masters. But *Superfluous Words* is an intensely personal document, and its very intensity indicates that the author, whoever he may be, must have had powerful personal feelings about his subject. Besides acknowledging Ch'ü's unfitness for political work, which can be confirmed by the interview, *Superfluous Words* is also rich in penetrating self-analysis which no one but Ch'ü himself or a forger gifted with exceptional intuitive and imaginative powers could produce. Though the work contains a great deal of material which might be used in a political biography of Ch'ü Ch'iu-pai (which I have refrained from using from the same scruples as the "official" biographers), *Superfluous Words* has little to do with politics. It was written by a man to whom politics represents all that is hateful in the world: exhaustion of vitality, moral fatigue, death in the heart, numbness of the senses, eternal lies and destruction of natural affections. As a plaintive assertion of a weak, tired ego, the book is above politics, above class struggle, above any ideology. It is inconceivable that a forger with political motives would produce such a non-political or even anti-political book. I am inclined to accept *Superfluous Words* as a genuine work by Ch'ü Ch'iu-pai, with only due reservations for clerical errors on the part of the transcriber.

Taken as Ch'ü's testament and confession, *Superfluous Words* does not possess much literary or humanistic value. Its strength is in the keen, relentless anatomy of a sickly ego, but its weaknesses are numerous and fatal. Its field of interest is too narrowly restricted, its focus is too constantly on the analysed subject who has nothing but meaningless despair left, and behind all the effusions, which sometimes sound tediously redundant, there is a vacuity, a complete disregard of life's purposes, and a total absence of moral judgment. When the author declared, describing his experience in the period from early 1930 to August or September 1934, "I did not care if the universe would collapse; I did not care if I was a revolutionary or anti-revolutionary; I only wanted to have a rest, a rest, a rest!" [87] we hear the gasp of a dying man. The "sweet repose" he enjoyed in prison was too brief for him to rebuild his strength. Before he had recovered enough to think into the future, to form a new vision of the world, to find a meaning of his past experiences, he had been taken to the execution ground.

It is most likely that Ch'ü did not give up Marxism in the end. This insight could only have come from a man who had lived under the spell of Marxism:

> But to say that I have given up Marxism is not correct. If you want to discuss with me any political problem, I have no approach to it except what I can deduce from my imperfect knowledge of Marxism. These deductions, as a matter of fact, perhaps contain also many elements of opportunism, *i.e.*, viewpoints that are contrary to Marxism-Leninism. Therefore, it has become unnecessary for me to exert myself to think in vain about any problem. There is no possibility to change my way of thinking which, ever since my youth, has been moving towards Marxism. I don't know whither this road, leading to Marxism, but intersected at many points by non-Marxist paths, will eventually take me. The principal fact is that I am tired; I cannot go any farther. I no longer have the energy to think over politics from the viewpoints of social sciences.[88]

There should be no more misunderstanding about Ch'ü's "dual personality" after *Superfluous Words*, and he acted it out up to his last minute. Probably under the influence of liquor, as a true martyr, he sang the "Internationale" [89] in Russian before he went to face the

[87] *Ibid.* No. 27, p. 9.
[88] *Ibid.* No. 26, p. 19.
[89] According to the *Ta Kung Pao*, reprinted in part in *I-ching*, No. 28, p. 43. Ch'ü first heard the Internationale in 1920 when he was joining the local Russians in celebrating the October Revolution in Harbin, *Journey, op. cit.*, p. 52. Later he translated it into Chinese, but it was still the Russian version that he sang at the time of his death.

firing squad. But his final written document is a poem, a composite of four lines by three different poets, a regular literary exercise for the Chinese. He was writing this, according to the *Ta Kung Pao*,[90] when, in the most dramatic possible manner, he received the summons to the execution grounds, on the morning of June 18, 1935. The poem has a little preface:

> On the night of June 17, 1935, I dreamed I was walking on a mountain path. The setting sun was glorious but was sometimes hidden, and a cold stream was moaning nearby. It was like a fairy land. The next morning as I was reading the T'ang poets, I came upon the line, "Setting sun, in ragged ridges, now bright, now dim." So I made a poem impromptu, a composite of these four lines:
>
> Setting sun, in ragged ridges, now bright, now dim;
> Falling leaves and cold stream, in two tunes sing requiem.
> Ten years' solitude was mine to endure,
> Ties all dissolved, my heart clinging to half a hymn.

[90] Reprinted in *I-ching, op. cit.*

Robert C. North, quoting another source, describes the scene differently from the *Ta Kung Pao*: "On that day [January 18, 1935] according to a story then current, he was brought from prison to the place of execution on a stretcher. There he drained a glass of whisky, asked for brush and paper, and wrote down this poem:

> The colourful splurge of the setting sun etches the mountains of Fukien.
> The rustle of the falling leaves and the sound of the running stream show the winter is near.
> These are eternal.
> Ten years I have passed in worldly undertakings, and now I am prepared to join heaven,
> But I leave with desires unfilled."

Moscow and the Chinese Communists (Stanford University Press, 1953), p. 165.

According to the *Ta Kung Pao*, he was writing the poem when he was summoned to the execution ground and he walked "in a leisurely manner" to the place rather than being carried on a stretcher. And the date was June 18, 1935, not January 18.

❧ 18 ❧

Chou En-lai

KAI-YU HSU

Among the earliest leaders of the Chinese Communist movement, Chou En-lai the perpetual compromiser, the tireless persuader, the many-time Party saver, stands unique not only because of his survival in a position of power, but also because he continues to be indispensable to Peking and the Chinese Communist Party.

There is much in Chou's intellectual growth and political experience that has contributed to his position today—a position of strength not in the sense of dictatorial power, but rather in the sense of a quality badly needed in the Communist movement in modern China, or in any revolutionary movement. The Peking regime is held together by three forces—the youth and intelligentsia, the army, and the Party apparatus. Chou's strength lies in his ability to work with all three of them.

It is no accident that Chou can speak persuasively to the students and intellectuals. There was something about the man and his words that put him in direct communication with his audience, a crowd of college students and reporters, on a warm spring afternoon in Chungking in 1941. The assembly was sponsored by a student association, and Chou had just finished analyzing the tragedy surrounding

Part of the material used in this article has been published by the author in "Chou En-lai: The Indispensable Man of Compromise," *New Republic* (April 8, 1967), pp. 21–25; and in Howard L. Boorman, ed., *Biographical Dictionary of Republican China,* Vol. I (Columbia University Press, 1967). Permission for use by the above publishers is gratefully acknowledged by the author.

517

the destruction of the Communist New Fourth Army by the Nationalists. "My fellow schoolmates," he said, with a restrained tremor
in his voice, "this is *our* country. Whatever has happened to cause
that fratricidal tragedy must be forgotten. From now on, we must
look ahead. . . . As for me (here he paused and bent his handsome head as though in pain), the grave of my mother to whom
I owe everything I am and hope to be, is in Japanese-occupied Chekiang. The poplars must have grown quite tall there by now. And
how I wish I could just go back there once to clear the weeds on
her grave—the least a prodigal son who has given his life to revolution and to his country could do for his mother. . . ." There was
audible sniffling in the audience. The speaker had struck a chord in
his listeners on the theme of sentimental patriotism, an emotional
force that had been motivating high school and college students to
abandon their books for rifles.

He could have been referring to the grave of his own short-lived
mother, a sensitive and cultured woman from whom he may have
inherited the kind of classical Chinese finesse which includes a
knack for literature and art. Or he could have been referring to the
grave of his rich aunt, the most affluent among the seven branches
of the Chou clan (Chou's own father was the least successful), who
adopted him and raised him as the first son of her family. His
foster mother, herself an adopted child, was a woman of strong will,
illiterate, wily, but intelligent, who ran her household in Shanghai
with an iron hand. When she raised her voice, which was quite
often, none of the younger generation dared to remain seated or
speak. Only Chou En-lai could pacify her. Once when she learned
that her own son had become interested in a pretty actor, a female
impersonator in the Peking opera tradition, she flew into a rage.
Chou En-lai calmly watched them for a minute, then he interrupted
the matriarch's tirade with a disarming smile to say to his cowering
younger brother, "Of course, you mustn't squander the family fortune
and dissipate yourself over an actor, but," he turned to his foster
mother, "it's all right to learn about opera, it's poetry and music,
isn't it, Mother? The best scholar-statesmen of the past all had to

know these things. . . ." Thus he diverted the matriarch's anger and gently revised her instruction, and the next day he brought home sets of colorful Peking opera costumes for his brother, whom he later inducted into the Communist Party, and got everybody interested in talking about the theater. The matriarch never again said a thing against theater-going.

The need to appease her and shelter the younger generation and servants, and the need to survive in that complicated Chou clan of seven branches with all its tensions and pressures, enabled Chou En-lai to cultivate the art of dealing with people, of making compromises to achieve harmony while never losing sight of one's ultimate objective. He perfected this art in his political life as time and again he subtly modified the ruling voice in order to keep peace and harmony within the Communist Party while working toward the Party's real objective. Today Mao Tse-tung, in his mid-seventies, cannot be more intractable and harder to deal with than that matriarch who died with greater affection and respect for her foster-son, Chou En-lai, than for her own child.

Although his native place was Huaian, Kiangsu province, Chou En-lai was born in 1898 in Shaohsing, Chekiang, where his family belonged to the local gentry and owned a small business. His father died when he was still a child. It was in Mukden, far from an old-fashioned family and its stifling influence, that he received his grade-school education, which made him aware of a world around him that was going through the dramatic throes of rapid change. High School in Tientsin, the first educational institution that experimented with liberal education in China, pushed him further along the road of development of China's new youth—starry-eyed, intensely patriotic, politically puerile, but eager to try everything to realize their twenty-five years of political life, as their civics textbooks urged them to do. He was almost femininely handsome, enough to be cast in a female role in a school play and teased by his rougher Manchurian classmates. His speech was cultivated later than his pen, which excelled that of all his classmates in facility and grace of expression. Even as a high-school boy he was already winning admirers with his words, and among them was the school principal, who later helped him out of jail and watched in awe the growth of the young man's political career.

Then followed a year and a half in Japan where he continued to circulate among the restless Chinese students, reading provocative articles by the socialist professor Hajimi Kawakami, but never formally enrolled in any college. When a former high-school chum in Tientsin wrote him, "Our country is about to cease to be a country; what are you doing with your books there?", having accepted the help of a friend whose wife sold a ring to raise travel funds for him, he packed up and came back to north China to plunge himself into the mad rounds of student demonstrations in 1919. He took over the college paper, wrote inflammatory articles urging student action to protest the government's appeasement policy toward Japan, and marched at the head of the column on the police headquarters to get himself promptly arrested.

In addition to giving expression to his fellow students' emotional patriotism, Chou also in a certain manner provided them with intellectual leadership. Trivial though it may seem, giving arithmetic lessons to his fellow prisoners in 1919 was symbolic of an academic achievement that outdistanced those of his contemporary rebels. Later when he theorized on communism, he perhaps lagged behind the classical poetry-writing Mao, but what he said made sense to professional revolutionaries, unionists, and Red soldiers, and above all, to students and college professors as well. No attempt to pretend profundity, Chou's words can communicate with and convince the proletariat and the intelligentsia at the same time.

It was in the same year, 1941, that the New Fourth Army incident occurred on January 17, and the next day there was much consternation in the nation, with fear of an instant renewal of a full-scale civil war between the CCP and the Kuomintang. As chief CCP delegate in the Kuomintang wartime capital of Chungking, Chou's statement, a difficult one to write in his situation, was an epigram in classical Chinese consisting of only sixteen characters. Its untranslatable literary subtlety and allusions aside, the meaning of the epigram is something like what follows:

Injustice unprecedented in history,
To the south of the River, a lonely leaf *
Up in arms in the same house,
Unfeeling is the beanstalk burning under the pot to cook its own
  beans within.

Within a matter of hours after the release of his epigrammatic statement, at least one-half of the nation had read or heard it, and they
still remember it today.

Chou's influence over the Red Army has an even more colorful
background. There is something about Chou's military career that
suggests the famous propaganda poster of Lenin which shows him
not in shining armor on a white steed, but looming large above the
landscape with one hand pointing in the direction of the anti-revolutionary enemy, while in the shadow of his raised arm strong-
muscled Red soldiers dart under a tidal wave of Red flags. Communist
revolution calls for a breed of politico-military strategists who can
combine Marxist theory with guerrilla warfare or even terrorist action,
and they do not have to go through a military academy before commanding troops. Chou never commanded a regular army in his life,
but he is a founder of the Chinese Red Army, not a fact of mere
historical accident.

Back from France late in 1924, Chou soon got a job from Chiang
Kai-shek to assist in running the political department of the Whampoa Military Academy (China's West Point) in Canton. Before long
the head of the department, a senior Kuomintang man, let the
twenty-six-year-old Chou take over the department to run the way he
pleased. Chou signed up as his deputy Nieh Jung-chen, later vice
premier in the Peking regime, a bright young man whom he had
recruited for the Chinese Communist Party while in France. Together they indoctrinated Chiang Kai-shek's hand-picked cadets with
communism and built up a nucleus of followers among whom was
Lin Piao, the defense minister supporting Mao in the Great Cultural
Revolution of 1966–69.

* Here Chou makes a pun on the name of the New Fourth Army Commander, Yeh T'ing. Yeh (literally means "leaf") was taken prisoner by the
Kuomintang forces.

Chiang Kai-shek himself appreciated the need to give political indoctrination to his soldiers, something he had observed in Russia and wanted to copy for building up his Nationalist revolutionary army to fight the warlords. But he soon felt the threat of communism among his rank and file. His officers began to complain about the interference of the political commissars, most of whom held dual membership in the CCP and the Kuomintang. On March 19, 1926, one of Chiang's gunboats sailed to the Whampoa Academy and the captain telephoned Chiang to request instruction. Having given no order to the vessel to move close to his quarters, the surprised Chiang thought that an earlier rumor about a Communist plot to kidnap him had been confirmed. He moved swiftly, dismissing all Russian advisers and known Communists from his army. Two Russian advisers accompanied Chou En-lai to call on Chiang to protest the action. Chiang did not back down, but was mollified enough to let Chou work out an uneasy truce between the Communist Party and the Kuomintang. Chou knocked heads with the tough-line comrades in Canton and the soft-line comrades in Shanghai, developed a compromise posture for the CCP which he offered to Chiang Kai-shek. Chiang accepted it, believing that the Communists could still be harnessed through Chou to serve the Kuomintang purpose. Thus Chou compromised to make the uneasy truce possible until the bloodbath of 1927 drove him and his comrades underground.

As political tutor to some of the most able soldiers trained by Chiang, and one who later fought under the Red flag, Chou has been able to maintain a substantial following in the Red Army. He went on to distinguish himself as a politico-military strategist, steering his hunted Party from clandestine, terrorist activities into a new phase of open revolt. It was he who directed the first series of Communist armed insurrections in Shanghai and Nanchang in 1927, and the date, August 1, has been observed as Red Army Day ever since. On that day, Nanchang fell into Communist hands. The insurrection was directed by Chou and Chu Teh, with Ho Lung and Yeh T'ing taking an active part.

Chou continued from that day on to head the military affairs department of the CCP's Central Committee. In 1931–34, he ran the

Red Army college in the mountain stronghold of the Kiangsi Soviet, for veterans of years of combat experience, lecturing and writing on guerrilla tactics. In 1934 on the eve of the historic Long March, he had mobilized within twelve months 112,000 Youth Guards, using his student demonstration technique of 1919 to swell the ranks of the Red Army, making that 6000-mile retreat possible. During the Long March, he shared with Mao the final responsibility of charting the map of survival for his steadily dwindling comrades. He alone was responsible for their continued political indoctrination to uphold morale against hunger, disease, local resistance and harassment, while fleeing for their lives over literally impassable terrain with Kuomintang troops in hot pursuit.

He is no combat hero, and there are many brilliant Red generals whose war records outshine his. Nor is he infallible in overall military strategy, about which he and the CCP's Central Committee were proved wrong and Mao right just before the Long March. And yet that peculiar agility of the mind which combines political perception with military acumen never failed to impress even the most seasoned professional soldier, Eastern or Western. Lord Montgomery of Britain, among many others, was so impressed by Chou that he wanted to have him as a long-term house guest. This is where Chou has his political capital with the military—they listen to him.

In manipulating the Party apparatus, Chou, the organization man, has a most impressive record. He was not at the founding meeting of the CCP in 1921 in Shanghai; he was busy recruiting for a Chinese Communist cell in Europe. It may be noted that of the twelve delegates present at the inaugural meeting, two were ousted soon afterward, and most of the rest either defected or sank into oblivion without having done a thing for the advancement of communism. Only Tung Pi-wu (who represented the CCP at the founding of the United Nations in San Francisco) and Mao Tse-tung stayed in the Party. In contrast, the nucleus cultivated by Chou in Paris and Berlin contributed many extremely able Party leaders who either died for the Communist cause during the darkest days in the CCP's history, as did Chao Shih-yen and Ts'ai Ho-sen, or survived to become very prominent after the Communist victory, as did Nieh Jung-chen, Ch'en Yi, Teng Hsiao-p'ing, Li Fu-ch'un, Ts'ai Ch'ang (wife of Li Fu-ch'un), and a host of others.

Back in China at Chiang Kai-shek's Whampoa Military Academy, the military elite cultivated by Chou were also trained to be political operatives, and subsequently each combined his military career with politics. But those he cultivated at Whampoa did not form a clique, and this turned out to be Chou's strength. His real stature in the CCP grew not because he was the leader or a part of any die-hard clique, or because he knocked down other leaders or stayed away from controversy, but rather because he always took the orthodox Party line and stuck to it until the tide was really turning. Then he plunged into the deadlocked controversy to cast his deciding vote.

However complex the CCP intra-party conflicts may have been, a few main lines can be traced. These are: hard revolution versus soft revolution, mobilizing industrial workers first versus cultivating the peasantry first, scattered mobile guerrilla attacks to whittle away the enemy versus building up a substantial Red Army for frontal attack, developing Soviet bases in remote areas and gradually consolidating them versus starting armed revolts in major metropolises to seize national power overnight, national revolution versus world revolution, and more dictatorship versus less dictatorship.

On top of these issues there have been the conflict of personalities and the conflict between the Chinese Communist Party and the Comintern, when neither has been unified or consistent in its approach and policies.

Small wonder that there have been many shifts and oscillations in the Party line. Each shift has involved personal greed for power and honest revision of one's view on the changing realistic situation. The latter seems to have been the case each time Chou En-lai adjusted his position on the Party line.

In 1925–27, the scholarly Marxist Ch'en Tu-hsiu headed the CCP's Central Committee in Shanghai. He favored a softer line while other Communist leaders in Canton favored a tougher one. When the latter suffered repeated setbacks in the abortive insurrections in 1927, Ch'en felt that he was vindicated and urged greater compromise with Chiang Kai-shek. Chou En-lai had tried to hold the three sides together as long as he could—the Shanghai faction and the Canton faction of the CCP and the Kuomintang. After the CCP had lost too many of its leaders and comrades and even he himself had had several brushes with death, Chou went to Moscow in 1928 to seek advice from the Comintern.

Stalin called the Shanghai faction rightist-opportunist and admonished the Canton faction for its "playing with uprisings." He told Chou to go home to build a strong Red Army and carry out land reform in the countryside, but to avoid too much scattered guerrilla activity, as that would deplete the Party before the arrival of a revolutionary high tide.

The Comintern had spoken, and Chou En-lai together with two other top CCP leaders, Hsiang Chung-fa and Li Li-san, returned to China to carry out the Comintern orders. But how? Somebody on the scene had to size up the situation and decide on how to build a substantial Red Army and judge when the revolutionary high tide was rising. Li Li-san, another member of the nucleus Chou En-lai had cultivated in France, was now heading the Party and he had to make the decisions.

"China needs a Lenin and China needs me," said Li Li-san repeatedly in top-secret CCP caucuses. Possessed by the same hunger for action that had driven Lenin to the November 1917 coup in Petrograd, Li pressed for continuous uprisings in eastern and central China. Chou went along with Li, partly because he was outvoted by Li and Hsiang and partly because he shared Li's view that a revolutionary wave was about to sweep the entire world. When one comrade who had been sent to start an uprising in a village reported that there were only seven Communists in that area, Li's assistant replied, "Get each of them to set fire to a house, and there will be seven houses on fire!" Chou raised no objection. The magic of Lenin's experience was too powerful to dispel.

But more and more comrades were lost in death, defection, or dispute, and the situation deteriorated rapidly for the CCP. The revolutionary high tide was still nowhere in sight. In 1930 Chou En-lai again went to Moscow to seek advice. This time the Comintern

called Li Li-san a putschist, blaming him for blindly pushing insurrections without adequate preparation.

Chou returned from Moscow to witness the demise of the putschist
policy and to find the Central Committee packed with the Moscow-
trained Bolsheviks headed by Ch'en Shao-yü, a feat accomplished by
the Comintern representative in China, Mif, who was there to preside
over the meeting of the new Central Committee. To what Stalin
had told Chou En-lai two years before, the Comintern now added
two more points of advice: consolidate the Communist-controlled
bases and organize them into Soviets; declare an anti-imperialist
policy in anticipation of a war with Japan.

Chou's first task was to reunite the badly fragmented Party under
the new Central Committee operating out of Shanghai, which in
those days was a place of daily cold-blooded political assassination and
counter-assassination. To maintain iron discipline over his underground comrades and to prevent defections, Chou directed a Red
terrorist network, the gory extent of which was partially brought to
light in the Ku Shun-chang case. Ku had been Chou's right-hand
man until his arrest by the Kuomintang in the early spring of 1931.
His defection caused the deaths of over 800 Communists, and to
punish him Chou ordered the murder of Ku's family. Chou managed
to keep the clandestine Party machinery working in the Kuomintang-
controlled metropolis, but it was increasingly apparent that a different
location would have to be found soon if the Central Committee was
to function effectively.

Chou's next task was to organize the scattered Communist bases
of doubtful strength into a centralized Soviet. Among the few Communist bases, the Kiangsi Soviet under Mao Tse-tung was the more
firmly established and usable. However, Mao refused to co-operate
with the Central Committee and the disagreement reached its show-
down stage when Mao's troops wiped out a unit of soldiers from
another Soviet base loyal to the Central Committee. As chief of the
Central Committee's military affairs department, Chou reported on
the incident and reprimanded Mao. But by autumn 1931 the table
seemed to have been turned as Chou tried to smooth the way for the
Central Committee to seek protection from Mao.

Once again Chou's quiet persuasion won a victory for Party unity in behalf of the Central Committee. Although this took some time to accomplish, he did succeed. By the end of 1933, Mao had to back down against his will and bow to the Central Committee on military strategy against his better judgment. Mao even temporarily withdrew from the policy-making oligarchy and waited in the mountain hideout of Yütu until the eve of the Long March. The deteriorating situation eventually proved that Mao's hit-and-run guerrilla approach was correct, but it was too late, and the whole Kiangsi Soviet decamped and ran for 6000 miles.

Mao had proven that under the circumstances which existed in China at that time, his way was the only road to Communist survival. Chou took the Central Committee to Mao, and from 1935 on it has remained under Mao's dominance, which would not have been possible if Chou had not cast his lot with Mao.

Chou's record in the CCP shows that he has actually switched lines time and again, but he always did it gracefully without rage or rancor. The only time he came close to an abject admission of error was in January 1931 when he renounced his defense of the Li Li-san line, and this he did with a prefatory note to his famed Shao-shan Report. This kind of line-switching does not leave the impression that he was cunning or playing politics, but rather leads one to accept it as a considered modification of one's position in the light of a realistic situation. Furthermore, he had repeatedly demonstrated a genuine indifference to the Number One position. When Liu Shao-ch'i revised the Party bylaws and emerged as Mao's heir with his popular pamphlets on communism in 1945, Chou graciously yielded the Number Two position to him. When Teng Hsiao-p'ing rose as the CCP's secretary-general in the 1950's, Chou again graciously yielded to him the Number Three position. What really speaks for Chou's strength in the Party hierarchy and apparatus is that after each submission his comrades know that he is still indispensable.

Equally important is Chou's service to the CCP in rallying luke-warm Communists and non-Communists behind the Peking regime. The CCP claims a mammoth membership of some fifty million people

—about the size of the population of France. Only two out of every five are full-fledged members; the rest are young students, workers, and some peasants, belonging to the various youth groups loosely affiliated with but serving as a training ground for the hard core of the CCP. By experience and temperament, Chou remains the best man in the CCP leadership to keep these divergent youth groups together.

For forty years Chou has been making peace among political groups of all shades, always swinging them a bit toward the left, to be sure. Before 1927 he kept the Kuomintang and the CCP together. Between 1936 and 1945 he again tried to keep the Kuomintang and CCP together to fight the Japanese. And after 1945 he sat with the Kuomintang at a negotiation table to buy time for a Communist build-up, while winning with his words the sympathy and support of all the non-Kuomintang groups. In 1949 he organized the delegates of all these non-Kuomintang groups into a People's Political Consultative Conference (PPCC) to set up the Peking regime. The PPCC thus served for Chou and for the CCP as a device to bring together the divergent groups outside the Communist hard core. In principle the PPCC, as a scaffolding, should have been abolished the moment the National People's Congress was convened in 1954. But it did not go out of existence. On the contrary, with its National Committee expanded to 1200 members in 1964, it had grown to proportions sufficient to rival the People's Congress itself. And Chou is in charge of the PPCC. Using its pyramidal chain of control all the way down to the county level, Chou has been able to keep the half-converted and unconverted Chinese in line to serve the cause of national unity. Through the PPCC the non-Communist masses are made to feel that somehow they have a share in the Communist-controlled government.

Since 1949 Chou's main concern has been how to intensify the socialist indoctrination of the entire nation, particularly the youth, and how to reinforce national unity. He knows that Red China cannot afford a paralysis in the Party or a decline in the zeal of the youth toward socialist reconstruction of the country. To avoid such dangers, he and his comrades have used various means to keep the nation awake and alert, including international pressure on communism as in the cases of Korea and Viet Nam.

In 1950 when the new regime sought to involve the students and intellectuals in a socialist reconstruction of the country, Chou triggered off a socialist cultural revolution with his famous speech "On Reforming the Intellectuals," delivered at the workshops of Peking and Tientsin university faculties. The ensuing thought reform movement raged and stormed for six long years until Chou believed that the Party and the regime were sufficiently secure to involve the intellectuals in a new task. His three major reports on the intelligentsia presented to the regime's three highest policy-making bodies in January 1956 set the stage for the Hundred Flowers Movement to unfold three months later, allowing the people to talk and criticize authority. By August 1957 the Hundred Flowers (a hundred different schools of thought) seemed to have bloomed a little too wildly for national unity and brakes were applied with the introduction of an anti-rightist campaign. Two years later Chou again felt the need for some relaxation of tension, which was provided through a campaign to "Remove the Rightist Cap," or to halt the abuse of using the rightist label to condemn just anyone. Between 1959 and 1964, there were four such campaigns coupled with four drives to "Declare Amnesties for War Criminals," all aimed at producing a more relaxed atmosphere. At each of these turning points Chou's words and deeds revised the prevailing application of Communist ideology and re-channeled the fad of action.

As the chief architect of Red China's foreign policy, Premier and Foreign Minister Chou has been representing his country in nearly all the important negotiations abroad and at home since 1949. Even after 1958, when he handed the Foreign Office to Ch'en Yi, who had been his junior associate in Paris in the early 1920's, he continued to lead Peking's delegations in visits of foreign capitals and to speak for the Peking government. It is under his tutelage that Peking has developed its present stature in international affairs.

During the first seventeen years of Communist rule on the mainland, Chou made seven trips to Moscow; the first three resulted in treaties and alliances of political and economic co-operation. Through these agreements Russia relinquished some of her historical interests in China, advanced loans to Peking, and sent technicians to help Communist China in building dams, steel plants, and railroads.

Between his fourth trip (April 1954), which concerned mainly the war in Viet Nam, and his fifth trip (February 1959), strain began to show in the Moscow-Peking axis. Less than complete fulfillment of the generous aid promises, coupled with the anti-Stalin line inaugurated in Moscow in 1955, made it increasingly clear that the conflict of interest between these two countries was not to be easily resolved. In 1958 Moscow hinted at some measure to keep Peking in line; Peking's reaction, not revealed until 1963, was violent. Russian criticism of Peking's handling of the Sino-Indian dispute in June 1959 further aggravated relations. The quarrel at Bucharest in June 1960 precipitated the withdrawal of Russian technicians from China. The final confrontation between Chou and Khrushchev occurred at the 22nd Russian Communist Party Congress in October 1961. Immediately after Khrushchev's downfall, Moscow invited Chou to a round of high-level talks in November 1964, but Chou did not relent. Back in Peking he continued to warn his Chinese comrades not to overlook the danger of Khrushchevism without Khrushchev in person.

But even more earnestly Chou warned against excessive internecine struggle in the Communist camp, lest aid and comfort be extended to their common foes. In his government work reports, summarizing the year's progress, he continued to admonish against ultra-chauvinism as a detriment to world revolution.

Next to his effort in dealing with Moscow, Chou's major contribution to the international stature of Red China has been her spreading influence on the emerging pro-Leftist and neutral forces in the Afro-Asian bloc. Chou's motto has been: win the leadership of this bloc and through it a bargaining position with the West.

Within six months of the establishment of the Peking regime, eight Asian nations extended diplomatic recognition to the People's Republic of China. The Geneva and Bandung Conferences, in 1954 and 1955 respectively, raised Peking's prestige and elevated Chou's personal stature as the champion of underdeveloped nations. Regarding Viet Nam, Chou first conferred with Ho Chi-minh in July 1954, then met with Pham Van Dong, the North Viet Nam Prime Minister, in November 1956 and the spring of 1960, resulting in a joint verbal attack on America and American-supported South Viet Nam.

The six joint statements Chou worked out with Burma between June 1954 and July 1964 established, reiterated, and expanded the now well-known five principles of international behavior centering around mutual aid and peaceful co-existence. Chou's visits to Rangoon were all successful and gala affairs. Until the summer of 1967, Peking and Rangoon had maintained exceedingly friendly relations.

With Indonesia, Chou's diplomatic offensive began at the Bandung Conference in April 1955 when he signed a separate treaty with Sukarno to clarify the problem of dual citizenship of the Chinese settled in that country. But the rising anti-Chinese sentiment and anti-Communist strength in Indonesia made it necessary for Chou to remain conciliatory with Sukarno even after the latter had issued his Number Four anti-Chinese policy statement in May 1959. When more Chinese aid offered to Indonesia failed to produce any friendly response, Chou had to dispatch ships to bring the Chinese back from Indonesia. The uneasy situation worsened after Sukarno's removal from power in 1965.

Another diplomatic setback awaited Chou En-lai when the Sino-Indian border incident flared up in August 1959. After the clash, Chou flew to New Delhi to call on Nehru, but their seven conferences proved fruitless. Neither did the twenty-two memoranda exchanged between Chou and Nehru improve matters. The summer and fall of 1962 saw more border clashes. Communist China ordered a dramatic withdrawal of her troops after a smashing military victory, while getting the Colombo Conference nations to help mediate. But Nehru died a bitter enemy of Chou and every bus driver in Kashmir nursed his resentment against Peking because he believed that the Red Chinese had snatched away his Ladek sheep. Chou's policy seems to be one of "wait-and-see," as he urged his fellow countrymen in the winter of 1964: "If India persists in her refusal to talk to us about the border problem, it doesn't matter. We can wait."

Chou's international junkets to Cambodia, Pakistan, Ceylon, and Nepal were nearly always pleasant and successful. In Cambodia, particularly, he was greeted as an Asian hero, and a large Cambodian plywood plant was promptly named after him as a token of admiration.

In December 1963 and January 1964, Chou toured Africa in an effort to rejuvenate the Bandung Conference spirit. He reiterated the theme that modern Western civilization had been built on the blood and bones of cheap Afro-Asian labor; these laborers should, henceforth, rise to overtake the West. He played on the rising nationalism in those countries, and urged the natives to oppose imperialism in all its new and old forms. And he pledged Red China's support, at the huge Afro-Asian banquet arranged back in Peking on March 24, 1964, by declaring: "Our friendship has been tempered through many an international storm. It is perpetual and indestructible."

Peking's contact with Eastern Europe, though relatively limited, was established by Chou, who in January 1957 visited Budapest and Warsaw. Hungary's Kadar and Poland's Gomulka greeted him warmly because of his sympathy with them in the wake of their anti-Moscow revolts. The Albanians, remembering that Chou had stood by them against Khrushchev in 1961, went wild over the Peking Premier when he arrived there on New Year's Eve in 1963.

Chou visited Ulan Bator in May 1960 and signed a treaty of economic aid which delivered a long-term Chinese loan of 200 million rubles to Outer Mongolia. Toward the Arab nations Chou was also full of friendliness and generosity. He ignored Nasser's criticism of the Communist coup in Tibet and paid another visit to Nasser in the winter of 1963 to reinforce amicable relations. Since Castro's rise in Cuba, Chou has missed not a single opportunity to cite and commend Castro as the model of Latin American revolution. In 1960 alone, he invited no less than fifty Latin American friendship missions to visit Peking.

The attitude of the Chinese Communists toward the United States, at one time not hopelessly hostile, was prejudiced by the

U.S. role in the 1945–48 Communist-Kuomintang negotiations in Chungking and Nanking, then aggravated by Truman's assignment of the U.S. Seventh Fleet to patrol the Taiwan Straits, and still later by the Korean War. Then in April 1954 at Geneva Chou En-lai impressed the Western powers with his moderate approach to international problems, and joined the majority to declare a policy of excluding all foreign troops from the territory of Viet Nam, with the U.S. the only major Western power abstaining. A year later Chou formally proposed at Bandung that there be a Sino-American conversation toward a peaceful settlement. The proposal led to the Warsaw talks at the ambassadorial level which has been, fitfully, going on and on. The major difficulty has remained over the Taiwan issue, with Peking insisting on the withdrawal of U.S. troops from that area before discussing anything else. And on this point Peking and Washington remain deadlocked.

While credit for French diplomatic recognition in January 1964 should not be given to Chou alone, there is no doubt that he knows how to win friends. He never fails to put his full talent to good use whenever there is a visitor from abroad. By impressing his visitors that he can be had as a friend, he has already converted his visitor into a friend.

At the height of the Cultural Revolution commotion in Mainland China, a leader of the Young China Party who had known Chou for many years observed in Hong Kong: "Chou En-lai is the only man the Communist Party has now, and survival or collapse, the Peking regime depends upon him." Indeed, even at the end of 1967 Chou remained the infallible and indispensable premier, the only man elected to the Political Bureau at the Fifth National Congress of the CCP in 1927 who continued to serve as a member of that body after the Seventh National Congress of 1945. In September 1956, the Eighth National Congress of the CCP (and again in the Ninth Party Congress of April 1969) returned him to both the Central Committee and the Politburo. His seniority, his long devotion to communism in China, and his broad experience combined to give him a degree of versatility unrivaled among the top command at Peking.

Significantly Chou produced no unified body of doctrinal writing, but his Shao-shan Report of 1930 in many ways anticipated the subsequent development of the CCP's grand strategy, and a summary of the voluminous reports and statements he has made in behalf of the CCP and the Peking regime would provide an adequate profile of the history of Chinese communism and the development of the Peking regime.

When still a young student deeply involved in the patriotic demonstrations in Tientsin after the May Fourth Movement, Chou met his future wife, Teng Ying-ch'ao. They were married in 1925 in Canton, and from that time on she remained at his side and together they have made a most enviable team of Chinese Communist leaders. She also earned her position on the CCP's Central Committee with her own contributions, including sharing the hardship of the Long March. They have no children, but they appear to be a happy couple in Peking and their marriage has been praised as truly exemplary.

❦ 19 ❦

Liu Shao-ch'i:
The Man and the Iceberg

HOWARD L. BOORMAN

For twenty years since the Communist field armies under Lin Piao, Ch'en Yi, Liu Po-ch'eng, and other Red generals swept to the conquest of the mainland, China-watchers throughout the world have searched for keys to unlock the puzzles of Mao Tse-tung's political system.

One favorite channel of long-distance analysis has been biographical: interpretation of Chinese Communist plans and policies through appraisal of the origins, personalities, and styles of the individuals composing the top command at Peking. Early diagnoses of the 1950's emphasized presumed tensions between a moderate, predominantly nationalistic faction at Peking and a radical, devoutly internationalist clique loyal to Moscow. More recent and more sophisticated—though not necessarily more conclusive—estimates, influenced by methodologies employed in study of Soviet politics, have sought enlightenment through exploration of a cleavage between commissars who stress the primacy of doctrinal factors and political controls, and planners who accord priority to practical matters of construction and production. Analysis, unhappily, has often outstripped data. Indeed, since 1966, events have not infrequently outstripped analysis. The unprecedented turmoil of the Great Proletarian Cultural Revolution

This article is an extensive revision of "Liu Shao-ch'i: A Political Profile," which originally appeared in *The China Quarterly* (London), No. 10 (April–June, 1962). The permission of that journal to reprint certain passages is gratefully acknowledged.

has shattered elite cohesion at Peking, ruptured the organizational structure of the Communist party throughout China, and crumpled the morale of outside scribes responsible for composing the obituary of Chairman Mao or of dissecting the succession crisis in the Forbidden City.

Western mystification with respect to the smoky clouds pervading the corridors of power at Peking has perhaps more justification than any unitary explanation of the origins or ultimate implications of the blaze. Far more has been written than is known about most senior Communists either in or out of power in the Peking Establishment. Many basic biographical details remain elusive; meetings, decisions taken at meetings, and voting patterns remain undocumented; and the revelations of the Red Guards must be treated with discretion, for they present *ex post facto* evidence calculated to prove contemporary points.

The case of Liu Shao-ch'i illustrates the general problem. After twenty years as executive officer of the Chinese Communist Party and *fidus Achates* to Mao Tse-tung, Liu Shao-ch'i suffered nationwide public vilification in China for two years as the principal target of the Cultural Revolution and was finally officially expelled from the Party late in 1968. The historian resurveying the signals and symbols which have surrounded the strange case of Liu Shao-ch'i confronts the fact that the data cast light only on the man as public political figure: leader of the Chinese trade-union movement, Iron Bolshevik, Red Monk of the international Communist movement, Chinese Jew from the Kaifeng area, Mao Tse-tung's closest comrade-in-arms, mastermind of the Chinese Communist doctrinal and organizational apparatus, China's leading revisionist taking the Khrushchev path. Liu Shao-ch'i as human being scarcely emerges in the polemical pyrotechnics. And the iceberg of the Chinese Communist Party in which Liu has spent his entire adult career remains, for the Western observer at least, still largely uncharted, unmeasured, difficult of approach.

From the standpoint of the critical biographer, the major fact regarding the first two decades of Liu Shao-ch'i's life is that so little is known of it. The traits of personality and style, the austere dedication that marked his later lifelong search for order as Communist Party organizer and leader, were shaped during childhood and youth in his native Hunan. Yet so exiguous is the evidence that the record of those formative years may be chronicled at a rate of roughly twenty words per year. He was born in 1899 at Yinshan in Ninghsiang hsien, Hunan, the youngest child in a family that numbered four boys and five daughters. The area was not far away from Mao Tse-tung's native village of Shaoshan in Hsiangtan hsien. And the Liu family, like that of Mao, may be described as moderately well-off peasant stock, small landowners in Hunan but by no means affluent by modern Western standards.

Like his siblings, Liu Shao-ch'i attended primary school in the native village. Family resources were sufficient to permit him to go to Changsha, provincial capital of Hunan, where he was enrolled in 1916 at the First Provincial Normal School. That institution was then a center of liberal sentiment, and many of its graduates became politically active in China in later years. Mao Tse-tung studied there from 1913 until 1918, and Jen Pi-shih and Li Li-san were school contemporaries of Liu Shao-ch'i. Younger than Mao Tse-tung, Liu Shao-ch'i, like Mao, absorbed patriotic and reformist ideas during school days at Changsha. He planned to go to France with a work-study group from Hunan, and in the summer of 1918 he journeyed to north China, where he briefly studied French in preparation for that trip. For unknown reasons, Liu decided not to go to France, however, and he soon returned to Hunan. There he was struck with patriotic fall-out from the exuberant May Fourth Movement of 1919; and during the summer of that year he may have assisted Mao Tse-tung in editing the *Hsiang-chiang p'ing-lun* (Hsiang River Review), a short-lived but influential publication designed to circulate the views of the politically emancipated youth of Hunan.

Communist Party Organizer (1920–35)

In the summer of 1920, Liu Shao-ch'i went to Shanghai to earn funds for further education. There he stumbled into the Socialist Youth League, organized in August 1920 by Gregory Voitinsky, the

Comintern representative in China, and his young Chinese assistant and interpreter Yang Ming-chai. Liu then returned to Hunan, where he was arrested for political radicalism. Released on bail, he again went to Shanghai where he joined a small language class to study Russian in preparation for going to the Soviet Union. At that time, Liu later (1960) attested, "I only knew that Socialism was good, heard about Marx and Lenin and the October Revolution and the Bolshevik party, but I was not clear what Socialism was or how it could be realized."

In the winter of 1920, Liu Shao-ch'i was one of a small group of Chinese youths, including Hsiao Ching-kuang, Jen Pi-shih, and P'eng Shu-chih, recruited by the Comintern to go to Russia. The group traveled via Vladivostok, then still under Japanese occupation following the First World War, and took three months to reach Moscow. After arriving there in the spring of 1921, the group from Shanghai was enrolled at the new Communist University of the Toilers of the East, established under the supervision of the People's Commissariat of Nationalities to train cadres from "eastern nationalities" of the Soviet Union and foreign students from "colonial countries," particularly those of Asia. In 1921–22 the institution was still chaotic in organization and unprepared for Chinese students. There was no systematic course of study; no interpreters were available to render lectures into Chinese. With scant Russian, the Chinese students were able to absorb little from the political lectures, which at best would doubtless have appeared to shed limited light on the contemporary situation in China, then dominated by ineffectual central government, political regionalism, and military conflict. At the same time, drab living conditions prevailing in Moscow did little to diminish the homesickness felt by Liu and his comrades for Chinese life and Chinese food. Despite tedium and austerity, Liu joined the Chinese Communist Party branch in Moscow after its First National Congress which met at Shanghai in July 1921.

As an earnest young Chinese patriot, Liu was struck with the dedication and discipline found in Lenin's Russia. But his initial stay in the Soviet Union could hardly have impressed him with the political subtlety of the Bolsheviks in comprehending China or

Chinese problems. After returning to Shanghai in the spring of 1922, Liu was assigned to work under Chang Kuo-t'ao, then a prominent figure in the Communist group active in labor organization and chairman of the China Trade Union Secretariat. Work as a labor organizer was an approved activity for young Communists in China, and Liu proved himself both energetic and reliable.

After several months of tutelage under Chang Kuo-t'ao at Shanghai, Liu was assigned to the Anyuan coal mines at Pinghsiang on the Kiangsi-Hunan border. The Anyuan colliery was a constituent unit of the Han-yeh-p'ing iron and steel complex, composed of steel works at Hanyang (Han), iron mines at Tayeh (yeh), and the Anyuan coal mines at Pinghsiang (p'ing). As principal fuel source for the Hanyang steel mill, the Anyuan mines were of economic as well as political importance. Li Li-san was then the leading Communist organizer at Anyuan, and Liu Shao-ch'i was his principal assistant. In September 1922 they organized and won a strike among the miners. In February 1923 they led a sympathy strike in protest at the execution by Wu P'ei-fu of railroad workers and Communist organizers on the Peking-Hankow rail line. Li Li-san left for Peking early in the spring of 1923, but Liu Shao-ch'i remained at the Anyuan mines and developed a strong Communist-led organization there.

In the winter of 1923, Liu went to Canton where the political alliance between the Communists and the Kuomintang was being forged. There he entered a propaganda school established by the central headquarters of the Kuomintang and was among the first twelve graduates of that institution. In the spring of 1924 he worked with Teng Chung-hsia in preparing for the convening of the first National Labor Congress. A year later, after the death of Sun Yat-sen, Liu wrote a special eulogy to Sun in the Shanghai *Chung-kuo kung-jen* (China Worker, No. 4, April 1925). When the second National Labor Congress met at Canton in May 1925, Liu attended the meeting as a delegate representing the Han-yeh-p'ing union. He was elected vice chairman of the executive committee of the All-China Federation of Labor. That summer he was at Shanghai, where he helped to organize anti-British agitation after the May 30th Incident, when police in the International Settlement fired on Chinese. In August 1925, as a representative of the Shanghai General Labor Union, he greeted a Russian trade-union delegation visiting Shanghai. In May 1926 he was again at Canton, where he served as secretary general of the third National Labor Congress and delivered major reports on the development and status of the Chinese labor movement.

After the launching of the Northern Expedition from Canton in the summer of 1926, the Communists played an important role in political agitation as the military units of the National Revolutionary Army marched toward the Yangtze. The Communist-led organization which Liu had earlier developed at Anyuan provided a useful base for political action in 1926–27. After the capture of Wuhan, China's industrial heartland 600 miles up the Yangtze from Shanghai, most of the Communist labor organizers gathered there. In October 1926 Liu was named secretary general of the Hupeh Provincial Labor Union.

In January 1927, Liu Shao-ch'i sparked an anti-Western demonstration at Hankow which forced the British to abandon their concession there later that year. In April he spoke at a special meeting honoring the Communist minister of labor in the Wuhan government, Su Chao-cheng, who had arrived from Canton with an international delegation that included Jacques Doriot of France, Earl Browder from the United States, and Tom Mann from England. Only a few days later, Chiang Kai-shek, military commander of the National Revolutionary Army, launched a campaign of terror at Shanghai designed to exterminate Communist influence in the lower Yangtze valley. Despite that threat, the Communists at Wuhan continued to be active for a few weeks longer. In May, Liu Shao-ch'i, Li Li-san, and Su Chao-cheng represented the Chinese labor movement at the Pan-Pacific Labor Conference held at Hankow. Liu also served as secretary general of that conference and presented a major report on the state of the labor movement in China. In the same month he was named secretary general of the All-China Federation of Labor. At the Fifth National Congress of the Chinese Communist

Party, which met at Wuhan in April–May, he was elected for the first time to membership on the Party's Central Committee.

By the summer of 1927, Liu Shao-ch'i had built a record for performance that was solid but not spectacular. After five years of organizing miners and urban industrial workers, he had established himself as a reliable servant of the Chinese Communist Party, though he was hardly a major political figure. At the time he was identified only as one of the young Hunanese Communists of student background, like Li Li-san and Teng Chung-hsia, who had helped to build China's embryonic but potentially significant labor movement.

After the collapse in the summer of 1927 of the first united front alliance between the Communists and the Kuomintang, Liu Shao-ch'i, like the Communist Party he served, faced the elemental problem of survival. Because he worked underground in Nationalist-controlled areas for the next several years, data regarding movements and activities are even more elusive than for the pre-1927 period. At the Sixth National Congress of the Chinese Communist Party, which met in Moscow in the summer of 1928, Liu became director of the workers department in the Party's central apparatus, an empty honor because the Communist-led labor movement in China had then been virtually crushed. In 1929 he was reportedly appointed secretary of the Communist Party organization in Manchuria, where Chang Hsüeh-liang was consolidating political control after the death of his father in the previous year. In 1930, Liu was again in Shanghai, where Chou En-lai was also active in the Communist underground. Liu's mission was doubtless to attempt to renovate the labor organization that had been shattered in 1927; and he organized a strike to protest the Japanese invasion of Manchuria that began in September 1931.

By 1932, however, tight Nationalist police controls had made Shanghai too dangerous for effective Communist activity, and Liu Shao-ch'i moved to the relative security of the main Communist base in Kiangsi. His political position there is unclear, though some reports credit him with membership on the Political Bureau of the Chinese Communist Party after 1932. In the Communist government structure of the period, Liu was a member of the Central Committee of the Central Soviet Government. In practice, his main attention was devoted to political mobilization of workers in the primitive arsenals and workshops that supplied the Communist military forces, then labeled the Chinese Workers' and Peasants' Red Army.

When Nationalist military pressure dislodged the Communists from the Kiangsi base in October 1934, Liu Shao-ch'i accompanied the Communist retreat during at least a part of the Long March. Later he left the Long March units to return to Nationalist-controlled territory, which Communist jargon labeled the "white areas" of China. Late in 1935, he was identified at Peiping in north China, where the Japanese, after their creation of Manchukuo, were attempting to expand political and military controls south of the Great Wall. In Peiping Liu Shao-ch'i used the pseudonym Hu Fu, a term common in ancient China to refer to the garb of northern barbarians. With other Communist political workers in the area, Liu was active in spreading the contemporary programmatic line which called for an end to the Nationalist-Communist civil war and for unified national resistance in China against Japanese imperialism. While Liu Shao-ch'i's precise position at Peiping in the winter of 1935 remains obscure, he did play an important role in organizing the major student demonstrations of December 9, 1935, designed to protest Japanese pressures aimed at the creation of an autonomous region embracing the five provinces of north China.

Communist Party Leader (1936–49)

Between 1936 and 1942 Liu Shao-ch'i served successively as secretary of three regional bureaus of the Central Committee of the Chinese Communist Party: in north China, in the so-called Central Plain area, and in central China. In an *ex post facto* (1945) review of Party history, the Communist Party praised him for the manner in which he had directed underground political work in key areas during those years. Faced with unfavorable odds, Liu shaped a program that was essentially conservative in the sense that it was directed not at immediate breakthroughs, but rather at long-range maximization of

Communist political authority. Despite stringent policy controls and censorship, he attempted to preserve and to develop the Party apparatus, and to rely on "utmost possible exploitation of overt, legitimate means" to extend Communist influence wherever possible.

Liu Shao-ch'i's programs were directly supported by the growing Japanese military threat to China, a threat that enabled him to mobilize Chinese nationalism and to direct it into anti-Kuomintang channels. During 1936–37, for example, when Liu headed the north China bureau of the Communist Party, anti-Japanese feeling ran strong in the major universities, both public and private, of Peiping and Tientsin. The Communist organizational and propaganda apparatus in north China encouraged these flames with a politically impeccable fan: the banner of the so-called "anti-Japanese national salvation movement." Making political capital from frustrations created by the inaction of Chiang Kai-shek in the face of Japanese pressures, and enlisting political support, either active or passive, from patriotic young intellectuals, the Communists were able to expand their authority in north China even while that area was still nominally under Chinese Nationalist control. The underground work directed by Liu Shao-ch'i and other Communists in the north bore fruit after the outbreak of war with Japan in 1937, which led to a significant flow of university students and graduates from the cities to Communist-controlled areas in the interior. Liu Shao-ch'i also played a personal role in creating the situation that led to the first major presentation of the story of Mao Tse-tung and the Chinese Communist movement to the outside world. Many years later, it was confirmed that it had been Liu, as the senior Communist underground in north China in 1936, who had authorized an "invisible ink" letter of introduction with which the American journalist Edgar Snow entered the Communist areas of northern Shensi, a trip that led to Snow's best-selling *Red Star Over China*.

In the spring of 1937 Liu himself went to the Communist wartime capital of Yenan, while the routine work of the north China bureau was transferred to P'eng Chen. In Shensi Liu participated in important party meetings, notably a Political Bureau meeting in August 1937 and the sixth plenum of the sixth Central Committee, held in

October–November 1938. During this period Edgar Snow's wife Nym Wales, who was at Yenan, interviewed Liu, whom she described as the Chinese Communist Party's "leading expert on labor problems." Much of the material supplied by Liu later appeared in the book by Miss Wales, entitled *The Chinese Labor Movement,* published in 1945.

In July 1939 Liu Shao-ch'i delivered an important speech at the Institute of Marxism-Leninism at Yenan. This report, often in English translation entitled *How To Be a Good Communist* (later, and more accurately, *On the Self-Cultivation of Communists*), was the first political statement by Liu to have been preserved and published under his own name. Originally presented as two lectures on July 8, 1939, the Chinese text appeared in three issues (Numbers 82–84) of *Chieh-fang* (Liberation). While the basic theme of Liu's essay appears simple, its political implications were important. Many members of the Chinese Communist Party, he stated, come from non-proletarian-class backgrounds and thus bring with them into the Communist Party remnants of the tainted ideologies of these social classes. They must therefore pass through an extended period of "cultivation and self-cultivation" designed to overcome their backgrounds and to ensure a proper proletarian outlook. "Ideological cultivation" in the Chinese Communist Party, Liu concluded, meant that the individual Party member must, through sustained study of Marxism-Leninism and through direct participation in "revolutionary struggles," train himself to be a model Communist, "honest, pure, and progressive."

At least two elements in Liu's 1939 speech are worthy of note. First, he stressed that being a good Communist is essentially a matter of self-discipline, self-examination, self-criticism, self-cultivation. Indeed the concept of self-cultivation, a concept with distinctly Confucian antecedents in Chinese political and ethical thought, is implicit in the phrase *hsiu-yang* used in the Chinese title of the published essay. Second, Liu argued that being a good Communist is a function of the individual state of mind, not a product of economic or social circumstances. Even though he should come from a bourgeois-class background, an individual may acquire a proletarian political outlook. Thus the basic Marxist concept of the proletariat as a distinct and identifiable socio-economic class was attenuated, and the term in Liu Shao-ch'i's usage was expanded to include all individuals who, through appropriate training, discipline, or practical experience, acquire a proletarian "spirit." If political self-cultivation could create political consciousness, then no Communist organization need lack a proletariat, even if none was present in reality. For a party that was by definition the vanguard of the proletariat, this approach had impressive political potentialities in wartime China where, in the process of expanding Communist power, nationalism was more important than conventional class struggle as defined by Marxist doctrine.

During his tenure as secretary of the central China bureau of the Communist party organization after 1939, Liu worked to spur formation in Kiangsu and Anhwei of guerrilla units for anti-Japanese action. After the so-called South Anhwei incident of January 1941, when the Chinese Nationalists attacked the Communist New Fourth Army, capturing its commander Yeh T'ing and killing his deputy, Liu Shao-ch'i guided reconsolidation of Communist strength in the Yangtze valley. Two weeks after the Nationalist attack, Yenan announced a new chain of Communist command in the area. Ch'en Yi was named acting commander of the New Fourth Army, with Liu Shao-ch'i as political commissar and Teng Tzu-hui as chief of its political department. Liu's appointment confirmed the fact that the Communist top command appreciated the importance of political factors in wartime military operations in the lower Yangtze area. Liu himself enunciated policy guidelines in an important article entitled "Present Conditions and Tasks in Central Kiangsu," in the New Fourth Army journal *Chiang-Huai jih-pao* (Yangtze and Huai River Daily), published at Yencheng, Kiangsu, on March 22, 1941. In this article, Liu stressed Communist-guided mass education as a method of instilling national consciousness in the local populace. Another important statement by Liu, delivered at the Central China Party School in July 1941 on the twentieth anniversary of the founding of the Chinese Communist Party, was entitled *On Inner Party Struggle*. It provided authoritative definition of the role of political "struggle" within the Party organization and gave specific comments on its nature and importance in ensuring maximum political vitality.

By 1942, when the Chinese Communist Party launched a major *cheng-feng* (political rectification) campaign designed to promote better discipline in an organization whose membership had become geographically scattered in operation and increasingly heterogeneous in social background, Liu Shao-ch'i had engaged the attention of Mao Tse-tung as a reliable spokesman on problems of organizational control and as a stern but realistic political moralist in setting standards to be maintained by Party members and cadres. In October 1942 he was recalled from the Communist area in northern Kiangsu to Yenan. Liu traveled northward through Shantung and Hopeh, was temporarily isolated by Japanese offensive action, but then continued through northern Shansi and Suiyuan to the Communist-controlled Shensi-Kansu-Ninghsia border region. When he joined the top command at Yenan in the winter of 1942, Liu represented that element in the Chinese Communist political elite with sustained experience in urban work and labor organization and appeared to buttress and balance the experience of Mao Tse-tung and others gained primarily in China's interior. By 1943 Liu Shao-ch'i was identified as a member of the inner nucleus of the Party power structure, the Secretariat of the Central Committee. Other members at that time were Mao Tse-tung, Chu Teh, Chou En-lai, and Jen Pi-shih. On July 1, 1943, Liu authored the principal article, *Liquidate the Menshevist Ideology Within the Party,* designed to mark the twenty-second anniversary of the Party's founding. He was also identified as a vice chairman of the People's Revolutionary Military Council in northern Shensi.

The position of Liu Shao-ch'i as the Political Bureau member most concerned with problems of organizational tactics was confirmed in the spring of 1945, when he presented a comprehensive report on revision of the Party constitution at the Seventh National Congress of the Chinese Communist Party. In this major statement of May 14, 1945, later usually known under its abridged English title *On the Party,* Liu confirmed the party's reliance on conventional democratic centralism and explicitly placed the Thought of Mao Tse-tung at the heart of the Party's doctrinal structure. At the same time, Liu's statement reiterated the Chinese Communist view that it was political and ideological, not socio-economic factors that shaped the Chinese Communist Party as a "political party of the proletariat" despite the fact that its membership, then over 1.2 million, was overwhelmingly peasant in origin.

By the time of the Japanese surrender in the Second World War, Liu Shao-ch'i, as executive officer of the Chinese Communist movement, was marked as one of the men standing closest to Mao Tse-tung. When Mao flew to Chungking in the autumn of 1945 for discussions with Chiang Kai-shek, Liu acted in Mao's place at Yenan for several months. The Chinese Communist leadership was then preoccupied with the changed strategic situation in China resulting from the removal of Japan as an effective factor in the politics of East Asia and with the political and military requirements for expanding Communist power within China. Its view of the postwar role of the United States in Far Eastern politics was still embryonic. In September 1944, in conversations with American Foreign Service officer John S. Service of the United States Observation Group at Yenan, Liu Shao-ch'i and others had stressed the potential importance of American economic assistance to China's postwar reconstruction. Some months later, in the spring of 1946, Liu articulated the growing political pretensions of the Chinese Communist movement itself. In an interview with American journalist Anna Louise Strong, he stated that Mao Tse-tung had in effect transformed Marxism-Leninism into a new practical creed for application in Asia. Mao's revolutionary doctrines, according to Liu, charted a path to power not only for the Chinese Communists but also for "the billion people who live in the colonial countries of Southeast Asia." This interview was reported by Miss Strong in an article, "The Thought of Mao Tse-tung," which appeared in *Amerasia* in June 1947.

After the breakdown of the United States mediation effort and the eruption of general civil war in China in the later months of 1946, Liu remained with the top command. In March 1947, when a Nationalist military drive under Hu Tsung-nan forced the Communists to evacuate Yenan, the party elite, for reasons of security and flexibility, split itself. Mao Tse-tung, Chou En-lai, and Jen Pi-shih remained in northern Shensi; while Liu Shao-ch'i, Chu Teh, and an alternative working group moved to the Communist-controlled Shansi-Chahar-Hopeh base area carved out by Nieh Jung-chen and others during the Japanese war years. The group headed by Liu was located in 1947 in the Pingshan district of Hopeh province. There, in September 1947, Liu presided over a major conference on agrarian policy which passed a land law designed for application in Communist-held areas. This draft law was promulgated by the Chinese Communist Party in October 1947 and served as a basis for later land reform legislation designed for application on a national basis. The working group headed by Liu remained in southern Hopeh during 1948 and was later joined there by Mao and the central organs of the Party.

Although military operations and domestic political planning were of primary importance during this period, the Chinese Communists did not neglect international issues. After the Tito apostasy in the summer of 1948, when Yugoslavia broke with Moscow, Liu Shao-ch'i, speaking on behalf of the Chinese Party leadership, voiced sharp criticism of Belgrade's position. *On Internationalism and Nationalism*, released on November 1, 1948, the day that units of Lin Piao's Fourth Field Army entered Mukden, scored Yugoslav recalcitrance and condemned Tito not only for a breach of political discipline but also for a fundamental doctrinal error: "bourgeois nationalism." In contradistinction, Liu Shao-ch'i stressed true "proletarian internationalism" interpreted by the Chinese to mean a confederation of national Communist parties allied on an equal and voluntary footing, united in common outlook and in allegiance to the Soviet Union.

Early in 1949, the Chinese Party leaders gathered in southern Hopeh for the second plenum of the seventh Central Committee elected in Shensi four years earlier. This meeting (March 16–23, 1949) was of major significance because it confirmed that the center of gravity of the Communist revolution in China was moving from the rural areas to the cities and emphasized the industrialization of China as a long-range objective. After that meeting, senior political leaders of the Party moved to Peiping, which had come under Communist control several weeks earlier. In September, they convened the Chinese People's Political Consultative Conference with the mission of creating a new national government for China. On October 1, 1949, Mao Tse-tung became Chairman of the Central People's Government of the People's Republic of China. Liu Shao-ch'i became second-ranking vice chairman in the new governmental structure, following Chu Teh, Mao's veteran military associate.

Chinese Communism in Power: Charisma or Cadres?

In the new Communist-dominated structure of authority created at Peking in late 1949, the influence and prestige of Liu Shao-ch'i were based on his senior position in the Communist Party hierarchy. In the nucleus established earlier at the Seventh National Party Congress in 1945, Liu had become the third-ranking member of the Central Committee and a vice chairman of the Political Bureau. Following only Mao Tse-tung and Chu Teh in the power structure, Liu also wielded major executive authority in his position as general secretary of the central Secretariat of the Chinese Communist Party. The Eighth National Party Congress (September 1956) and its second session (May 1958) made changes in the top hierarchy which indicated both continuity and gradual expansion of personnel. For practical purposes, the top decision-making organ of the Party structure then came to be the seven-man standing committee of the Political Bureau, on which Liu ranked second to Mao (other members were Chou En-lai, Chu Teh, Ch'en Yun, Lin Piao, and Teng Hsiao-p'ing). For a decade after 1956, Liu also served as the top-ranking vice chairman of the Central Committee and the Political Bureau. The key post of general secretary of the Central Committee, which Liu had occupied since 1945, was filled after 1955 by Teng Hsiao-p'ing.

Liu Shao-ch'i also held top posts in the Central People's Government and in what the Chinese Communists described as "people's organizations." Named one of the three Communist vice chairmen of the Central People's Government in 1949, Liu held that position for five years. In the governmental reorganization of September 1954 at the inauguration of a new national constitution, he became chairman of the Standing Committee of the National People's Congress, the top organ of government to which all other organs were technically responsible. After an announcement in late 1958 that Mao Tse-tung intended to relinquish governmental responsibilities, Liu Shao-ch'i was elected Chairman of the People's Republic of China in April 1959. At that time, Liu was officially described as Mao's "closest comrade in arms." The move appeared to be designed to elevate Liu Shao-ch'i above possible rivals and thereby to ensure later succession to the decisive position of chairman of the Chinese Communist Party. From 1949 to 1954, Liu headed the Sino-Soviet Friendship Association, a mass organization designed to "further and consolidate fraternal friendship and co-operation between the Chinese and Soviet peoples." In recognition of his earlier role as labor organizer in the 1920's, he was elected honorary chairman of the All-China Federation of Labor at its sixth congress, held at Harbin in August 1949, and was re-elected to that post at its seventh congress in 1953.

During the 1950's the public statements of Liu Shao-ch'i provided a useful guide to Peking's evolving views on a wide spectrum of domestic and international issues. In November 1949, in the opening speech at Peking before the Trade Union Conference of Asian and Australasian Countries, Liu recited the Chinese Communist catechism on foreign relations, posed the People's Republic of China as the model for revolutionary (that is, Communist) movements in "colonial and semi-colonial countries," and struck the vibrant note of nationalistic militancy that characterized Peking's early foreign-policy pronouncements. In the winter of 1949, when Mao Tse-tung journeyed to Moscow for negotiations with Stalin, Liu Shao-ch'i remained in top authority at Peking. In 1950 he reverted to domestic topics. His two major speeches of that year dealt with labor problems and with agricultural policy and provided authoritative statements delineating the relatively moderate policies then followed by the Chinese Communists in these sectors. In July 1951, on the occasion of the Party's thirtieth anniversary, Liu produced a report laced with adulation of the "correct leadership" of Chairman Mao and stressed that it had been Mao and Mao alone who had consistently understood the correct application of Marxism-Leninism in agrarian China.

In October 1952, Liu Shao-ch'i went to Moscow to attend the nineteenth congress of the Communist Party of the Soviet Union, his first publicly confirmed trip to the Russian capital since he had studied there as a Comintern trainee thirty years before. After the congress ended, Liu remained in the Soviet Union for over three months on undisclosed business. The fact that this extended stay took place during the final months of Stalin's lifetime stirred speculation outside China, but the brief report which announced his return to Peking in January 1953 gave no clarification of his mission or of the degree of its success. A month later, he delivered the principal speech marking the third anniversary of the signing of the Sino-Soviet Treaty of Friendship and Alliance, a statement which confirmed that the Chinese Communist leaders at Peking appreciated the practical advantages of being joined in military alliance with a super-power while the war in Korea was still unsettled.

After the death of Stalin in March 1953 and the signing of an armistice agreement in Korea in July, Peking shifted primary attention to political consolidation and to domestic economic development tasks. Communist Party affairs continued to be important, however, and the top command dealt firmly with a short-lived challenge to its authority. Acting in accordance with a Political Bureau resolution of late 1953, the seventh Central Committee held its fourth plenum early in February of 1954. With Mao discreetly absent, Liu Shao-ch'i, in his role as general secretary of the Party, delivered a slashing attack which stressed the need for solidarity and for "collective leadership" under the party chairman. That meeting was a prelude to the disclosures released in the spring of 1955 regarding the activities of Kao Kang and Jao Shu-shih.

In September 1954, Liu Shao-ch'i delivered an authoritative report on the new draft constitution submitted to the National People's Congress and later adopted by that body to serve as the formal framework of state authority in the People's Republic of China. Two years later, in September 1956, Liu presented the key political report to the Eighth National Party Congress of the Chinese Communist

Party, which by then had grown to become the largest Communist Party organization in the world with an estimated membership of 10.7 million. When the fortieth anniversary of the Bolshevik Revolution in 1957 prompted Mao Tse-tung to make a second trip to Moscow, Liu again remained behind as Mao's proxy at Peking. There he highlighted a massive rally in honor of the occasion with a major statement, *The Significance of the October Revolution.* This 1957 speech was a significant indicator of Peking's awareness of the significant changes in world political geography that had stemmed from the Second World War, and direct interest in the so-called "national independence forces," the developing new nations of the Middle East, Africa, and Latin America.

Later in the 1950's Liu Shao-ch'i produced two major political reports at Peking. In May 1958, at the second session of the Eighth National Party Congress, he focused attention on the role of the Communist Party in China's "socialist construction" and outlined a new economic development strategy that involved the mobilization of underemployed rural labor in China on an unprecedented scale. And on October 1, 1959, when Nikita Khrushchev was in China for the tenth anniversary celebrations of the People's Republic of China, Liu Shao-ch'i's special article, *The Victory of Marxism-Leninism in China,* written for the *World Marxist Review,* was released in both Peking and Moscow.

By 1960, the tensions and antagonisms that later mushroomed into the bitter Sino-Soviet conflict were already apparent. One thorny issue in that emerging conflict within the Communist bloc was the problem of the international position and doctrinal authority of Mao Tse-tung. Within China, the official political line already placed Mao in direct line of succession to the classical theorists of the Communist revolutionary movement—Marx, Engels, and Lenin—and projected Mao as principal arbiter of political and military strategy for the emerging nations in their long-range conflict with the Western bourgeois world. This position was hardly appreciated in Moscow, where the Soviet leaders had long regarded their views as paramount and decisive. From the Chinese standpoint, it was notable that Mao Tse-tung did not go to Moscow in late 1960 for the gathering of world Communist leaders after the observance of the forty-third anniversary of the Bolshevik Revolution. Rather it was Liu Shao-ch'i, with Teng Hsiao-p'ing as his deputy, who made the trip at the head of a strong Chinese Communist contingent. Liu's personal role in the Moscow discussions and in the formulation of the final statement issued on December 6, 1960 is unknown. But his presence suggested that Mao Tse-tung then regarded his deputy Liu as competent to negotiate with Khrushchev on his behalf.

Liu Shao-ch'i continued to play an active political role at Peking during the early 1960's. As the second-ranking individual in the Party hierarchy, he made the principal speech at the meeting that marked the fortieth anniversary of the Chinese Communist Party in July 1961, when Party membership had swollen to over 17 million. A year later, on August 1, 1962, the *People's Daily* at Peking devoted six complete pages to a re-issue of Liu's July 1939 speech, *How To Be a Good Communist*. At the same time, a double issue of Peking's principal theoretical journal, *Hung-ch'i* (Red Flag), also carried the full text. In political terms, re-issue of a doctrinal statement of this type appeared to constitute a major accolade, for public sanctification of that order had normally been reserved in Communist China for the texts of Mao Tse-tung. At the time, the re-appearance of *How To Be a Good Communist*, twenty-three years after original publication at Yenan, seemed to confirm the authority of Liu's position as successor to Mao and symbolized the relative consistency that had characterized doctrinal training for Chinese Communist Party members and cadres over an unusually long period. In the 1962 edition, the phraseology of the text had been altered considerably, though the fundamental structure and argumentation remained identical with the 1939 version. There were additions, notably passages bearing on the Sino-Soviet conflict; and there were new quotations taken from the writings of Mao Tse-tung, principally from *On Practice* and *On Contradiction* (both 1937) which had not existed in the earlier text. A new English translation of *How To Be a Good Communist*, designed for international distribution, appeared somewhat later, in February 1964.

In his capacity as chief of state at Peking, Liu Shao-ch'i handled many ceremonial functions and some foreign travel. In 1963, accompanied by foreign minister Ch'en Yi, Liu made his first trip outside the Communist bloc when he paid a state visit to Indonesia and Southeast Asia. In March 1966, again accompanied by Ch'en Yi and a large official party, Liu made a state visit to Pakistan, where he was greeted by President Mohammed Ayub Khan. Liu was welcomed at Rawalpindi and at Lahore; and his public statements laid stress on Chinese friendship for Pakistan, manifest in political backing that Peking had given Pakistan in the inconclusive conflict with India in the autumn of 1965, and in a flow of military equipment to Pakistan from the People's Republic of China.

Beginning in 1966, the upheaval of the Cultural Revolution in China was accompanied by an unprecedented series of public attacks on senior members of the Chinese Communist Party and created a centripetal movement that shattered the relative cohesion of the party elite—a cohesion which, if never complete, had been unique, by Soviet or other standards, in the history of the international Communist movement. As the Cultural Revolution gained momentum during 1966, the position of Liu Shao-ch'i became increasingly difficult. In June his associate of thirty years, P'eng Chen, then a Political Bureau member, vice premier, and mayor of Peking, was vilified, along with other senior Communists who had worked closely with Liu in north China in mobilizing the anti-Japanese student movement of December 1935. At the eleventh meeting of the eighth Central Committee of the Chinese Communist Party, held in August 1966, Lin Piao, minister of defense at Peking, emerged as Mao Tse-tung's new heir apparent; Liu Shao-ch'i was downgraded from second to eighth place in the ranking of top party leaders issued after that meeting. As pressures mounted, Liu was forced to make a self-examination in writing in October 1966 at a work conference of the Central Committee. There Liu allegedly admitted to blunders in political judgment extending back to 1946 and stated that he had made particularly serious errors in the weeks just prior to the Central Committee plenum of August 1966. Although he still appeared with other leaders on several occasions when Mao Tse-tung witnessed massive Red Guard demonstrations at Peking, Liu was no longer in the limelight. By the end of the year the Red Guards demanded that Liu and Communist Party general secretary Teng Hsiao-p'ing be dismissed from their positions.

In 1967 Liu Shao-ch'i was singled out as the leading target of the Cultural Revolution and was denounced as "China's Khrushchev" and as the "No. 1 man in authority taking the capitalist road within the Party." The spring of that year brought mounting public demonstrations against Liu in every city of China, and the press devoted major attention to his political heresies. On July 1, 1967, the forty-sixth anniversary of the founding of the Chinese Communist Party, the journal *Hung-ch'i* (Red Flag) proclaimed the "overthrow" of Liu and of a "handful of party people" associated with him. He was conspicuously absent on October 1 of that year when the Chinese Communists marked their eighteenth year of power with a traditional celebration rally in Peking. Despite the major public attack, Liu Shao-ch'i was never actually identified in official publications, and there was no official announcement of his dismissal as chief of state, a position to which he had been re-elected in 1965 for a new term by the National People's Congress.

Among the notable aspects of the Cultural Revolution in China in the mid-1960's was the admixture of personal and political vilification. Prior to 1960, little had been known in the West of Liu Shao-ch'i's private life. Despite his irregular, danger-ridden, and peripatetic existence over many years, he had reportedly had several wives at various times before and during the war years in China. In the early 1960's he began to appear publicly with the last of these, a chic woman many years younger than Liu. Wang Kuang-mei, a 1943 graduate of Fu-jen University in Peking and a member of a prominent north China family, was then regularly seen at official functions in Peking and accompanied her husband on state visits to Southeast Asia and to Pakistan. Like her husband, Wang Kuang-mei, during the course of the Cultural Revolution, was sternly and extensively condemned for bourgeois tendencies by the Red Guards and other guardians of public morality in China.

The violent attacks of the Cultural Revolution period centered on several sectors of the power structure that had previously been regarded as bases of Liu's position in the hierarchy: party committees, propaganda organs, labor unions, and organized youth groups. While informed opinion regarding the implications of the Cultural Revolution varied considerably, many outside observers felt that the movement reflected the impatience of Mao Tse-tung with the inflated Party structure as an effective apparatus of control and mobilization, and a calculated intention on the part of Mao to rely increasingly on other forms of political organization and motivation to gain long-range objectives. In this view, Liu Shao-ch'i, as the Chinese Communist Party's pre-eminent expert on the theory and practice of organization and as a proponent of strong and orthodox organizational structure, epitomized an approach to political and social revolution which conflicted with the stated aims and slogans of the latter-day reformation movement.

One theme running through the accusations against Liu Shao-ch'i and the men supporting him was the allegation of a negativistic political style. Liu was said to have promoted a doctrine of organizational passivity, an attitude aimed at maintaining centralized organizational discipline at the expense of mass enthusiasm. He allegedly pressed for an orderly approach to social revolution which would stifle mass movements and curb class struggle. In the economic realm, he reportedly stressed the decisive importance of material incentives in encouraging production and criticized the Great Leap Forward and Mao Tse-tung's emphasis on the ideologically-inspired activism which it represented. And, in the international sphere, he was said to have favored caution in promotion of revolutionary insurgency and moderation in China's struggle against "revisionism" in the international Communist movement and against United States "imperialism" in East Asia.

The campaign against Liu Shao-ch'i culminated in a decision taken by the enlarged twelfth plenary session of the Eighth Central Committee in October 1968. That meeting hailed the Cultural Revolution, launched and led by Communist Party Chairman Mao Tse-tung, as a major success and declared that all policies laid down and actions taken under the leadership of Mao and his deputy Lin Piao were correct. The gathering then formally dealt with Liu Shao-ch'i, who was finally identified by name. The statement said that the plenum expressed "deep revolutionary indignation" at the "counter-revolutionary crimes" of Liu Shao-ch'i and unanimously adopted a resolution, based on investigations by a special party group, to expel him from the Chinese Communist Party and to dismiss him from all posts both inside and outside the party "and to continue to settle accounts with him and his accomplices for their crimes in betraying the party and the country."

It would be naive to accept at face value the 1967–68 accusations against Liu Shao-ch'i as reliable indicators of actual policy positions and preferences taken by Liu and the individuals supporting him. Yet the thrust of the accusations does delineate decisive differences between Liu Shao-ch'i and Mao Tse-tung in their approach to the making and implementing of revolutions, differences which had been overshadowed by commonality of goals in years past but had become explicit during the decade following the Great Leap Forward.

Critical assessment of the role played by Liu Shao-ch'i in the Chinese Communist movement is hampered both by inadequate biographical data and by conflicting evidence with respect to key aspects and problems of Party history. Unquestionably Liu played a central role in developing and sustaining political discipline in the Chinese Communist Party, both when it was an insurgent group during the 1940's and after it had assumed governmental responsibilities during the 1950's. At one level, Liu Shao-ch'i has often been cast as what might be defined in the West as the organization man: a patient and painstaking individual who rose to high position through merging personal aspirations with the larger demands of the organization to which he committed his loyalty. Viewed at another level, his career was marked by skill in the art of political indoctrination as well as by success in the science of bureaucratic organization designed to serve a modern single-party dictatorship. Often portrayed as reserved, austere, and colorless, Liu nevertheless either possessed or developed the common touch. He spent most of his active career attempting to influence a wide variety of Chinese who were, at best, indifferent or unsympathetic to him and, at worst, overtly hostile to his precepts and preconceptions.

During the critical decade of the 1940's, Liu Shao-ch'i, as much as any other single Communist leader in China, was responsible for setting the political style of that Party and for defining the social responsibilities of Party members. As political moralist, Liu Shao-ch'i, in stubborn preoccupation with the qualities of the ideal Party member, helped to create and sustain standards for the organizational mechanism that powered the only major Communist-directed social revolution in twentieth-century Asia. To the symbols and myths of the international Communist movement, Liu added imagination, insight, and wide experience with his country and his people. His forte lay in the theory of mass psychology and in the practice of mass organization for Communist purposes in a technologically primitive agrarian land, largely illiterate but immensely proud, attempting the difficult passage toward modernity.

It is commonplace in history and politics that the loser tends to be forgotten. The downfall of Liu Shao-ch'i in the 1966–68 period meant at one level that he had failed in the first requirement of revolutionary political leadership: maintenance of a position of power. Yet his downfall left unresolved many of the issues involved in the Communist revolution in China, notably the relative weights to be accorded, on the one hand, to revolutionary voluntarism, or, on the other, to organizational controls as critical elements in determining the course and velocity of the revolution. Mao Tse-tung's preference for activism is as well known as it is inconclusive. The massive problems of feeding, housing, clothing, modernizing, and inspiriting a fifth of the earth's population are unlikely to be handled by activism and revolutionary enthusiasm alone. Organization, precise planning, orderly operation, recognition of the appeals of material rewards are still required to power modernization. In this context, the impact of Liu Shao-ch'i on the pattern of the Chinese Communist revolution may yet be more significant than his personal career as political leader. The iceberg may outlast the man.

BIBLIOGRAPHICAL NOTE: Basic data on Liu Shao-ch'i are given in Howard L. Boorman (ed.), *Biographical Dictionary of Republican China,* volume II (New York: Columbia University Press, 1968), pp.

405–11, based in large part on an earlier article, "Liu Shao-ch'i: A Political Profile," which appeared in *The China Quarterly*, No. 10, April–June 1962, pp. 1–22. A thorough survey of Western-language materials on Liu is included in an honors thesis by Ralph Keyes, "The Man in the Grey Flannel Tunic," done at Antioch College, June 1967. *Who's Who in Communist China* (Hong Kong: Union Research Institute, 1966) contains an article on Liu (pp. 410–11) which provides detailed, usually reliable, encyclopedia-type data.

Control of much contemporary Chinese-language materials is given by Chün-tu Hsüeh in two bibliographies, *The Chinese Communist Movement, 1921–1937* (1960) and *The Chinese Communist Movement, 1937–1949* (1962), published by the Hoover Institution, Stanford University. *The Red Flag Waves: A Guide to the Hung-ch'i p'iao-p'iao Collection*, by Robert Rinden and Roxane Witke (eds.), University of California, Berkeley, China Research Monograph No. 3, 1968, also provides useful references on Liu and other Chinese Communist leaders.

Although only limited material on Liu Shao-ch'i was available in pre-1949 Western works on the Chinese Communist movement, many books and articles on contemporary China published since that time contain scattered references to him. Notable in this connection are Jean Chesneaux, *Le Mouvement ouvrier chinois de 1919 à 1927* (Paris: Mouton, 1962); Chalmers A. Johnson, *Peasant Nationalism and Communist Power* (Stanford: Stanford University Press, 1962); John Wilson Lewis, *Leadership in Communist China* (Ithaca: Cornell University Press, 1963); Franz Schurmann, *Ideology and Organization in Communist China* (Berkeley and Los Angeles, University of California Press, 1966); and Edgar Snow, *The Other Side of the River: Red China Today* (New York: Random House, 1961). Nym Wales (then Mrs. Edgar Snow), *The Chinese Labor Movement* (New York: John Day, 1945), is useful because it records the only known extensive interview given by Liu Shao-ch'i to a Western writer. Yung Ping Chen, *Chinese Political Thought: Mao Tse-tung and Liu Shao-ch'i* (The Hague: Martinus Nijhoff, 1966), is an uninspired compilation of data. Howard L. Boorman, *"How To Be a Good Communist*: The Political Ethics of Liu Shao-ch'i" (*Asian*

Survey, Vol. III, No. 8, August 1963, pp. 372–83), offers an analysis of some aspects of Liu's thought.

Paradoxically, Liu Shao-ch'i received far more publicity during his post-1966 period of disgrace than he did when he was an active senior figure in the Chinese Communist top command. In May 1967 a Peking Red Guard unit issued a detailed biographical chronology entitled "Down with Liu Shao-ch'i: The Life of Counter-revolutionary Liu Shao-ch'i" (English translation in American Consulate General, Hong Kong, *Current Background* No. 834, August 17, 1967, pp. 1–29). Source of data given there is not identified, but the material was doubtless compiled through "team research" drawing on testimony of individuals who worked with Liu in earlier years. Translations of other portions of the massive public attack on Liu Shao-ch'i during 1967 are scattered in materials, notably issues of *Current Background* and *Survey of China Mainland Magazines,* prepared by the American Consulate General, Hong Kong. Other Red Guard materials are recorded in Chinese in Ming Pao Monthly Editorial Committee and Ting Wan (ed.), *Chung-kung wen-hua ta-ko-ming tzu-liao hui-p'ien* (Source Materials on the Chinese Communist Great Cultural Revolution), Volume 1 (Hong Kong, 1967), pp. 258–67. *Collected Works of Liu Shao-ch'i, 1958–1967* (Union Research Institute, Hong Kong, 1968), with an introduction by Chang Kuo-t'ao, provides a useful English version of seventy-two works by Liu over the past decade, including three "self-examinations" of the Cultural Revolution period.

Much material on Liu Shao-ch'i was also released after 1966 in Japan and in Taiwan, particularly in *Issues and Studies* published by the Institute of Iinternational Relations in Taipei. A detailed chronological biography of Liu appeared in *Fei-ch'ing yen-chiu* (Studies on Chinese Communism), issued by the Institute for the Study of Chinese Communist Problems, Taipei (March 31, 1967), pp. 102–13.

Hans Heinrich Wetzel, *Liu Shao Chi: Le Moine rouge* (Paris: Denoel, 1961), is an ambiguous imaginative work hardly useful for serious study of the career of its subject.

Conversion Table

1 catty = 1⅓ pound

1 *li* = 0.36 mile

1 *mou* = 0.667 hectare = 0.1647 acre

1 *picul* (100 catties) = 133⅓ pounds

1 £ (sterling pound) = US$4.86 (October 1, 1911)

1 *tael* = 1 ounce of silver. (A *tael* is not a minted coin. Its value in foreign trade varies according to the price of silver, which was US$0.54 in 1910, $1.34 in 1920, and $0.38 in 1930).

1 *tan* = 100 catties = 133⅓ pounds

1 (Japanese) *yen* = US$0.84 at par. Its value on June 21, 1938, was 28.86 cents.

1 *yuan*, a currency adopted in 1932, contained three-quarters of an ounce of silver.

Chinese Names

Chan-wang	展望	*Cheng-chih p'ing-lun*	政治評論
Chang Chi	張繼	Cheng, F. T.	鄭天錫
Chang Feng-hui	張鳳翽	Chengnankuan	鎮南關
Chang-fu t'uan	丈夫團	Cheng Shih-liang	鄭士良
Chang Kuo-t'ao	張國燾	Ch'eng Ch'ien	程潛
Chang Ping-lin	章炳麟	Chiang Shou-tan	姜守旦
Chang Shih-chao	章士釗	Chientao	間島
Chang Shou-cheng	張守正	Chih Yü-ju	郅玉汝
Chao Heng-t'i	趙恆惕	Chinchow	欽州
Ch'en Chiung-ming	陳烱明	Chin Ch'ung-chi	金冲及
Ch'en Kung-po	陳公博	*Ching-shih-chung*	警世鐘
Ch'en Shao-pai	陳少白	Chou Chen-lin	周震麟
Ch'en T'ien-hua	陳天華	Chou En-lai	周恩來
Ch'en Tu-hsiu	陳獨秀	Chou Fo-hai	周佛海

Chu Teh	朱德	Kōbun Institute	弘(宏)文學院
Ch'ü Ch'iu-pai	瞿秋白	*Ko-ming chün*	革命軍
Fangcheng	防城	Kung Ch'un-t'ai	龔春台
Fu-jen wen-she	輔仁文社	Kung Keng	孔庚
Ho Chia-hsing	何家興	Jen Cho-hsuan	任卓宜
Ho Chih-hua	賀芝華	Li Chin-ch'i	李金其
Hsia, T. A.	夏濟安	Lienchow	廉州
Hsiao K'o-ch'ang	蕭克昌	Li Hsieh-ho	李爕和
Hsing Chung Hui	興中會	Li Ken-yüan	李根源
Hsiu-yeh	修業	Li Lieh-chün	李烈鈞
Hsu Kai-yu	許芥昱	Li Shu-ch'eng	李書城
Hsüeh Chün-tu	薛君度	Li Ta-chao	李大超
Hu Han-min	胡漢民	Liu Hsiu-ch'eng	李秀成
Hu Sheng-wu	胡繩武	*Li-shih yen-chiu*	歷史研究
Hua Hsing Hui	華興會	Liu Shao-ch'i	劉少奇
Huang Ching-hun	黃馨魂	Liu Ts'un-hou	劉存厚
Huang Hsing (Huang K'o-ch'iang)	黃興 黃克強	Lo P'ei-chin	羅佩金
		Ma Fu-i	馬福益
Huang Te-hua	黃德華	Mao Tse-tung	毛澤東
Hui-liu	匯流	*Men-hui-t'ou*	猛回頭
Hung Hsiu-ch'üan	洪秀全	*Min-li pao*	民立報
Hung Jen-kan	洪仁玕	*Min-pao*	民報
Hung Ta-ch'üan	洪大全	Ming Pao Monthly	明報月刊
Kagoshima	鹿兒島		
Kao Lao Hui	哥老會	Ming-te	明德

Miyazaki Torazō 宮崎寅藏
(Toten)

Pai Yu-huan 白逾恒
(Pai Ch'u-hsiang) 白楚香

Pinghsiang 萍鄉

Shangsu 上栗

Shangszu 上思

Shanhua 善化

Shih-tzu-hou 獅子吼

So Kwan-wai 蘇均煒

Sung Chiao-jen 宋教仁

T'ang Chi-yao 唐繼堯

T'ao Ch'eng-chang 陶成章

Tse Tsan Tai 謝纘泰

Tsou Jung 鄒容

Tung-li 東立

Waichow 惠州

Wang Ching-wei 汪精衞

Wang Hsiao-chen 王孝縝

Wang Sheng 王滕

Yang Ch'ü-yün 楊衢雲

Yang Shou-jen 楊守仁
(Yang Tu-sheng;
Yang Yu-lin) (篤生;毓麟)

Yang Tzu-lieh 楊子烈

Yen Hsi-shan 閻錫山

Yin Ch'ang-heng 尹昌衡

Selected Bibliography

Arendt, Hannah. *On Revolution*. New York: Viking, 1963.

Boorman, Howard L., ed. *Biographical Dictionary of Republican China*. 4 vols. New York: Columbia University Press, 1967—.

Brinton, Crane. *The Anatomy of Revolution*. Englewood Cliffs: Prentice-Hall, 1952.

Chang Kuo-t'ao, "Introduction," *Collected Works of Liu Shao-ch'i*. 3 vols. Hong Kong: Union Research Institute, 1968–1969.

Ch'en, Jerome. *Mao and the Chinese Revolution*. London: Oxford University Press, 1965.

Chung, Hua-min and Arthur C. Miller. *Madame Mao—A Profile of Chiang Ch'ing*. Hong Kong: Union Research Institute, 1968.

Edinger, Lewis. "Political Science and Political Biography," *The Journal of Politics*, Vol. 26, Nos. 2 and 3 (May–August 1964), pp. 423–39, 648–76.

Hook, Sidney. *The Hero in History: A Study in Limitation and Possibility*. New York: Humanities Press, 1943.

Hsu, Kai-yu. *Chou En-lai: China's Gray Eminence*. Garden City: Doubleday, 1968.

Hsüeh, Chün-tu. *Huang Hsing and the Chinese Revolution*. Stanford: Stanford University Press, 1961. Rev. printing, 1968.

―――. "The Cultural Revolution and Leadership Crisis in Communist China," *Political Science Quarterly*, Vol. LXXXII, No. 2 (June 1967), pp. 169–90.

―――. "The Life and Political Thought of Huang Hsing: Co-Founder of the Republic of China," *The Australian Journal of Politics and History*, Vol. XIII, No. 1 (April 1967), pp. 21–33.

Hummel, Arthur, W., ed. *Eminent Chinese of the Ch'ing Period.* 2 vols. Washington, D.C.: U.S. Government Printing Office, 1943–44.

Jansen, Marius. *The Japanese and Sun Yat-sen.* Cambridge: Harvard University Press, 1954.

Johnson, Chalmers. *Revolutionary Change.* Boston: Little, Brown and Company, 1966.

Lewis, John Wilson. *Leadership in Communist China.* Ithaca: Cornell University Press, 1963.

Lifton, Robert Jay. *Revolutionary Immortality.* New York: Vintage, 1968.

Linebarger, Paul. *Sun Yat-sen and the Chinese Republic.* New York: Century, 1925.

Meisner, Maurice. *Li Ta-chao and the Origins of Chinese Marxism.* Cambridge: Harvard University Press, 1967.

Mullowney, John J. *A Revelation of the Chinese Revolution.* New York: Flemming H. Revell, 1914.

North, Robert C. with de Sola Pool, Ithiel. "Kuomintang and Chinese Communist Elites." *World Revolutionary Elites: Studies in Coercive Ideological Movements,* edited by Harold D. Lasswell and Daniel Lerner. (Cambridge: The M.I.T. Press, 1965), pp. 319–455.

Payne, Robert. *Chiang Kai-shek.* New York: Weybright & Talley, 1969.

Rue, John E. *Mao Tse-tung in Opposition.* Stanford: Stanford University Press, 1966.

Schiffrin, Harold Z. *Sun Yat-sen and the Origins of the Chinese Revolution.* Berkeley: University of California Press, 1968.

———. "The Enigma of Sun Yat-sen." *China in Revolution: The First Phase 1900–1913,* edited by Mary C. Wright (New Haven: Yale University Press, 1968), pp. 443–74.

Schram, Stuart. *Mao Tse-tung.* New York: Simon and Schuster, 1966.

Schwartz, Benjamin I. *Chinese Communism and the Rise of Mao.* Cambridge: Harvard University Press, 1951; New York: Harper & Row, 1967.

Sharman, Lyon. *Sun Yat-sen: His Life and Its Meaning.* New York: John Day, 1934.

Smedley, Agnes. *The Great Road: The Life and Times of Chu Teh.* New York: Monthly Review Press, 1956.

Snow, Edgar. *Red Star Over China.* New York: Random House, 1938; Grover Press, 1961.

Wales, Nym (Helen Foster Snow). *Red Dust: Autobiographies of Chinese Communists* (as told to Nym Wales). Stanford: Stanford University Press, 1952.

Editor and Contributors[*]

CHÜN-TU HSÜEH (LL.B., Chaoyang, China; Ph.D., Columbia) is Professor of Government and Politics at the University of Maryland. He was Visiting Professor and Acting Head of the Division of Chinese and East Asian Politics at Otto Suhr Institute of the Free University of Berlin for the summer of 1970, Senior Associate Member of St. Antony's College, Oxford University, for part of Michaelmas Term, 1969, and Research Associate of Political Science at Stanford University in 1959–62. He has taught at Columbia University and the University of Hong Kong. In 1969 he was invited to lecture at the USSR Academy of Sciences, Moscow. He has also lectured at the Oriental Institute of the Czechoslovak Academy of Sciences, Prague (June 1970) and the Center for Afro-Asian Research of the Hungarian Academy of Sciences, Budapest (July 1970).

Dr. Hsüeh is the author of *Huang Hsing and the Chinese Revolution* (Stanford University Press, 1961, 1968), and a two-volume annotated bibliography, *The Chinese Communist Movement* (Hoover Institution, Stanford University, 1960–62). His articles in several leading Chinese newspapers and magazines in China and abroad appeared in a book form with an English title *Selected Writings of a Decade* (Hong Kong: Universal Book Co., 1964).

HOWARD L. BOORMAN is Professor of History and Director of the East Asian Studies Program at Vanderbilt University. General editor of the four-volume *Biographical Dictionary of Republican*

[*] Including authors of reprints.

China (Columbia University Press, 1967—), he has written extensively on recent Chinese history, politics, and personalities.

EUGENE P. BOARDMAN (Ph.D., Harvard) is Professor of History at the University of Wisconsin, Madison. He is the author of *Christian Influence upon the Ideology of the Taiping Rebellion, 1851–1864* (University of Wisconsin Press, 1952).

YÜ-JU CHIH (Ph.D., Indiana) is Professor and Chairman of the Department of East Asian Languages and Literature at Indiana University. He is the editor of *Readings in Modern Chinese History and Social Sciences* (University of Michigan, 1967). He wrote his Ph.D. dissertation on the political thought of Ch'en Tu-hsiu.

T. A. HSIA (1916–65) was Associate Research Linguist at the Center for Chinese Studies, University of California, Berkeley.

KAI-YU HSU (Ph.D., Stanford) is Professor and Chairman of the Department of Foreign Languages at San Francisco State College. His publications include *Twentieth Century Chinese Poetry* (Doubleday, 1963), and *Chou En-lai: China's Gray Eminence* (Doubleday, 1968).

MELVILLE T. KENNEDY, JR. (Ph.D., Harvard) is Professor of Political Science at Bryn Mawr College.

MAURICE MEISNER (Ph.D., Harvard) is Professor of History at the University of Wisconsin, Madison. He is the author of *Li Ta-chao and the Origins of Chinese Marxism* (Harvard University Press, 1967).

FRANZ MICHAEL (J.D., Freiburg, Germany) is Professor of International Affairs and Far Eastern History, and Director of the Institute for Sino-Soviet Studies, George Washington University. He is the author of several books, including *The Origins of Manchu Rule in China* (The John Hopkins University Press, 1942), and *The Taiping Rebellion*, 3 vols. (University of Washington Press, 1966–), and co-author of *The Far East in the Modern World* (Holt, Rinehart and Winston, 1955, 1964).

GERALDINE R. SCHIFF (Certificate, East Asian Institute, Columbia University) wrote her M.A. thesis on Tsou Jung.

EDGAR SNOW is a journalist and author of *Red Star Over China*

(Random House, 1938), and *The Other Side of the River* (Random House, 1961).

KWAN-WAI SO (Ph.D., Wisconsin) is Associate Professor of History at Michigan State University.

STEPHEN UHALLEY, JR. (Ph.D., University of California, Berkeley), Senior Specialist at the East-West Center of the University of Hawaii for 1970–71, is Associate Professor of History at Duke University.

C. MARTIN WILBUR (Ph.D., Columbia) is George Sansom Professor of History at Columbia University. His publications include *Slavery in China During the Former Han Dynasty* (Field Museum Press, 1943; Kraus, 1968), and (with Julie Lien-ying How) *Documents on Communism, Nationalism and Soviet Advisers in China 1918–1927* (Columbia University Press, 1956). His forthcoming book is tentatively entitled *The Rough Road to Power: Revolution in China 1922–1928*.

P. M. YAP (M.D.) is formerly Medical Officer-in-Charge of the government Mental Hospital, Hong Kong. His training included honors in psychology at Cambridge University and psychiatric works at the Institute of Psychiatry, University of London.

ERNEST P. YOUNG (Ph.D., Harvard) is Associate Professor of History at the University of Michigan, Ann Arbor.

Index

DATE DUE

AUG 3 0 2009		
WITHDRAWN		

DEMCO 38-296

Please remember that this is a library book,
and that it belongs only temporarily to each
person who uses it. Be considerate. Do
not write in this, or any, library book.